HD
8083
.I3
D398
1989

Derber, Milton.

Labor in Illinois.

$47.50

DATE			

BAKER & TAYLOR

Labor in Illinois

Labor in Illinois

The Affluent Years, 1945–80

Milton Derber

University of Illinois Press

Urbana and Chicago

This book is printed on acid-free paper.

Library of Congress Catalog-in-Publication Data

Derber, Milton
  Labor in Illinois

  Includes index.

  1. Labor and laboring classes—Illinois.
  2. Collective bargaining—Illinois. 3. Industrial
relations—Illinois. I. Title.
HD8083.I3D398 1989   305.5′62′09773   88–1339
ISBN 0–252–01529–0 (alk. paper)

400 S. STATE ST.   60605

Contents

Acknowledgments   vii

Introduction   1

PART I

The Working People of Illinois

1. The Demographic and Economic Setting   9
2. Incomes and Living Standards   14

PART II

The Organizational Picture

3. Employee Organization   31
4. Unions and Collective Bargaining: Selected Cases   37
   A. The Amalgamated Clothing and
      Textile Workers Union   40
      David Nicolai and Milton Derber
   B. The Chicago Building Trades Council   58
      David Nicolai and Milton Derber
   C. Steelworkers District 31   85
      David Nicolai and Milton Derber
   D. United Auto Workers Local 6   108
      David Nicolai and Milton Derber
   E. Teamsters Local 743   128
      David Nicolai and Milton Derber
   F. Hospital Employees Labor Program   142
      David Nicolai and Milton Derber
   G. American Federation of State, County, and
      Municipal Employees   159

PART III

Labor, Politics, and the Law

5. Electoral Politics   175

6. Legislation   184

7. The Courts   198
   Neil M. Fox and Milton Derber

PART IV

Labor in the Community

8. The Chicago Story   230

9. Rockford   252
   Kraig Kircher and Milton Derber

10. The Quad Cities   271
    Kraig Kircher and Milton Derber

11. Peoria   293
    Curtis A. Scott and Milton Derber

12. Decatur   309
    Janet Snow-Godfrey and Milton Derber

13. East St. Louis   323
    Curtis A. Scott and Milton Derber

14. Community Service and Labor Education   334
    David Nicolai and Milton Derber

PART V

Social Forces

15. The Decline of Labor Radicalism   359
    David Nicolai and Milton Derber

16. Corruption and Organized Crime   371

17. Blacks, Hispanics, and Fair Employment   383
    Christina E. Shalley and Milton Derber

18. More Voice for Working Women   412
    Christina E. Shalley and Milton Derber

19. The Quality of Working Life   430

Conclusions   441

Appendix   456

Index   458

Acknowledgments

This book could not have been produced without the devoted and conscientious work of the following graduate students: David Nicolai, Neil M. Fox, Christina E. Shalley, Kraig Kircher, Michio Fujiwara, Marick Masters, Meredith Miller, Curtis A. Scott, and Janet Snow-Godfrey. Although their research and writing contributions varied in scope and duration, all were important to the completion of the study. I have tried to characterize their respective contributions in the notes for relevant sections.

Four contributors warrant special mention. David Nicolai, a Ph.D. candidate, was responsible for the research and much of the writing on a significant segment of the book—the detailed case studies of chapter 4 on unions and collective bargaining, the discussion of labor and community services in chapter 14, and the analysis of radicalism in retreat in chapter 15. Neil M. Fox, a joint law and labor relations student, was responsible for much of the content of chapter 6 on legislation and chapter 7 on the courts. Christina E. Shalley, a master's and later doctoral candidate, researched and prepared lengthy reports that were the bases of chapters 2, 17, and 18. Kraig Kircher, a Ph.D. candidate, researched and wrote the substance of the community case studies for Rockford and the Quad Cities in chapters 9 and 10.

The evidence used in the book came from numerous sources. Given the comprehensive character of the study, heavy reliance was placed in the first instance on the products of other writers. In some areas, such as job discrimination, these were fortunately numerous and are cited wherever relevant. Most topics, however, had received little or no careful investigation by academicians, journalists, or other observers. In such cases, the research was normally based on newspapers, magazine articles, governmental documents, union and management publications, and a miscellany of archival materials. Supplementing these written sources, a considerable number of informal interviews were conducted either in person or by phone. Citations are given in the text and in notes for each chapter to both the written references and to the interviews.

The list of organizations and individuals to which we are heavily indebted is very long. Deep appreciation is extended to all of them; we regret overlooking any organization or individual.

The following organizational sources were of particular value: the magnificent library of the University of Illinois, including its departmental branches at the Institute of Labor and Industrial Relations (ILIR), the College of Law, and the College of Communications; also on the University of Illinois campus, the Institute of Government and Public Affairs and the Illinois Historical Survey; the Chicago Historical Society with its important archival collection; the Municipal Reference Library of Chicago; the libraries of the *Chicago Tribune* and the *Chicago Sun-Times;* the publication files of the Illinois AFL–CIO, the Amalgamated Clothing Workers, UAW Local 6, and the Chicago and Cook County Building Trades Council; the city libraries of Chicago, Rockford, Moline, Peoria, and Decatur; the Illinois State Archives in Springfield; the Illinois Commission on Human Relations; and the Illinois Commission on the Status of Women. Thanks are also due to the Iowa Labor History Oral Project directed by Roberta Till-Retz, and to the Roosevelt University Oral History Project in Labor and Immigration directed by Elizabeth Balanoff for making available a number of their interviews with union activists.

I am particularly indebted to my long-time colleague, Phillips L. Garman, whose knowledge of Illinois labor was unmatched, and who skillfully and insightfully critiqued virtually the entire manuscript. In addition, I would like to single out the following for their extremely helpful long-term aid: Margaret Chaplan, University of Illinois Institute of Labor and Industrial Relations librarian, who for more than six years was invariably gracious and expertly helpful in tracking down and securing innumerable documentary sources in Champaign-Urbana and throughout the state, and colleagues Ronald Peters, Bernard Karsh, Vernon Talbott, and William Adelman, who wholeheartedly shared with us their years of experience and knowledge about the Illinois labor movement and labor relations. Peters, Karsh, and Talbott, as well as Melvin Rothbaum, Francine Blau, Helen Elkiss, and Charles Craver of the University of Illinois College of Law also reviewed and made valuable suggestions on one or more chapters. Glenn Zipp, director of NLRB Subregion 33, kindly reviewed the section on Peoria, and his comments were of significant help.

To Anice Birge, Nancy O'Connell, and the office staff, Brendon Lenoir, Emma Jean Mahoney, Marian Brinkerhoff, and Mary Schoville who typed and retyped seemingly endless drafts of the materials in the book, our deep appreciation is extended for their friendly spirit of cooperation, their good-natured patience, and their skillful performance.

Finally, we are grateful to the National Endowment for the Humanities through Grant RS-0179-80 and to the Institute of Labor and Industrial Relations for the financial support that enabled the field research to be carried out and the manuscript to be written. Without the needed funds, the services of the research assistants could not have been readily obtained nor their travel expenses covered, office costs provided, nor the time of the project leader made available. Walter Franke, ILIR director, was unfailingly supportive. Neither the NEH nor the ILIR is responsible for the information or the views expressed in this book. Whatever errors of fact or interpretation may be found are entirely attributable to the author.

Introduction

Thirty-five years are a short time in historical perspective, but they represent a significant stage in Illinois labor history. When the 900,000 men and women who served in the armed forces during World War II returned home in 1945, they found a new Illinois economy that had rebounded from ten years of deep depression thanks chiefly to the insatiable appetite of the great military machine created to defeat the Nazis and Japanese. Whereas unemployment in March 1940 was estimated at 600,000 (out of a civilian labor force of 3.355 million or 17.9 percent), in March 1945 it stood at only 24,000 out of 3.293 million or 0.7 percent.[1] In August 1945, at the war's end, public aid recipients numbered 214,712, compared with 1,226,686 at the outset of the war in Europe in 1939.[2]

Nor did the predicted postwar depression materialize. Nonagricultural employment rose to more than 3.1 million contrasted with 2.3 million in March 1940, and remained above 3 million during the rest of the decade, including the relatively mild 1949 recession.[3] Thereafter, until the mid-1970s, the economy continued to grow, although at a decreasing rate, and average annual unemployment remained below 5 percent except for cyclical troughs in 1954, 1958, and 1961.

But it was an uneasy, shifting march to economic well-being for Illinois labor, one strongly influenced by erratic national and international factors. Just as the Great Depression was ended by World War II, so the Korean War gave a sharp economic stimulus to the economy of the fifties, and the Vietnam War helped to stimulate (indeed to overstimulate) the economy of the late sixties. The problem of stagflation in the seventies was in turn intensified by such international forces as world grain shortages and OPEC oil policies.

Underneath these unpredictable international events, less conspicuous but equally powerful domestic forces were helping to reshape the Illinois economy. One of these was the changing demographic patterns resulting from the huge post-World War II baby boom and from the sizable migration into the state first of blacks and later of Hispanics. The baby boom between 1946 and 1964 resulted in an unprecedented expansion in the educational system and indirectly set the stage for the massive collective bargaining movement among teachers that crystallized in the early sixties. It also produced by the middle sixties a large youth population that encountered disproportionate difficulties in finding and retaining employment when they entered the labor market. The war brought numerous women into the labor market, and the tradition against work outside the household for women with young children was shattered, although they were encouraged to go back home at the war's end. By and large, however, young people, women, and minorities either filled the less skilled and lower paid jobs or comprised the bulk of unemployed.

Another powerful force transforming the Illinois economy was the rapid shift in the composition of industry because of changing competitive factors, technological development, and geographic relocation. The once important meatpacking industry disappeared from centers in Chicago and East St. Louis to operate more efficiently near the cattle-raising sites further west. Basic steel, autos, farm equipment, clothing, and electronics faced increasing difficulty in meeting foreign competition. The great railroad hub of Chicago suffered a severe decline of passengers and freight while air transport, buses, and interstate trucking expanded. Manufacturing overall lost ground to the rapidly developing South and West, with their huge defense, space, electronic, and energy programs. At the same time, local and state governments in Illinois expanded their activities on a large scale.

Certain segments of the population fared markedly better than others in achieving economic benefits. The Illinois economy became more affluent but not much more egalitarian. During the postwar period Illinois was strongly unionized, ranking fourth among the states in number of union members and seventh in membership as a percent of nonagricultural employment. Except for those unionized industries such as meatpacking and garments, which suffered from severe out-of-state or foreign competition, union members as a whole improved their economic status. On the other hand, classes of the "working poor," including some unionists and welfare recipients, continued to form a significant segment of the economic scene.

The institution of collective bargaining, with its deep historical roots in the state, maintained a generally strong position in the private sector and spread its influence into the public sector. Teachers, nurses, firefighters, and police, as well as other municipal employees and a majority of state government employees, became covered by collective bargaining agreements. Strikes and other manifestations of industrial conflict were generally moderate in number and character.

Nonetheless, the proportion of nonunion employees remained well over 60 percent. Many of these employees benefited from the economic spillover effects of collective bargaining in the same or allied industries. Others worked in occupations or industries that were in relatively favorable economic positions and preferred or were persuaded by their employers to stay unorganized.

A substantial number of nonunion employees were among the economically disadvantaged.

It was not only a matter of employment and money, although these were crucial to industrial relations. The years after World War II were also a time for labor to win a more equitable status in society. One of the most significant social developments was the movement of blacks to end discrimination in housing and education as well as in employment, for a greater political voice at all levels of government, and for more evenhanded treatment by police and judges. These issues were eventually extended to include women and Hispanics.

Organized labor was to play a divided role in respect to civil rights and racial discrimination. In the political arena, however, it extended its range of interests and expanded its influence. Labor's connection with the Democratic party in both Chicago and the state as a whole was greatly strengthened, while the once close ties to the Republicans deteriorated. Nevertheless, some Republican governors and legislators maintained friendly relations with important branches of organized labor. Because of the growing Democratic linkage, the political fortunes of organized labor fluctuated in a state in which the major political parties were balanced evenly and governmental power shifted frequently from one party to the other.

Paralleling the national trend, radical political ideologies, which had a long history in Illinois going back to Civil War days, steadily lost ground after World War II. Within labor's ranks, ideological conflict occurred for a time in the state CIO, with the "moderates" triumphing over the "leftists" and Communists. During the McCarthy years of the early fifties, Illinois was a targeted area for antiradical pressure, both in industry and in the schools, universities, and governments. Loyalty oath legislation was a major issue of debate. Most of the civil rights struggle in the sixties was likewise conducted outside of industry. During the Vietnam years, most of both organized and unorganized labor supported the war effort, but a minority joined with the antiwar student and radical groups. The riotous events associated with the Democratic convention of 1968 took place in Chicago, and so did the trial of the anti-Vietnam War leaders in 1969 and 1970. The winding down of the war seemed to exhaust the radical movement, and quiet reigned throughout the rest of the seventies.

Whereas labor radicalism waned, corruption in some branches of organized labor did not. If anything, the tremendous growth of pension and health and welfare funds soon after World War II made union control more attractive to organized crime. The Illinois problem, as in the past, centered mainly in Chicago, although corrupt conditions were reported in East St. Louis, Peoria, and elsewhere. According to Peter F. Vaira, the attorney in charge of the Chicago strike force of the U.S. Department of Justice in 1978, "the degree of corruption in the labor movement in Chicago is among the worst in the country."[4] He also observed that "nearly every major local union of three international unions is controlled by the Chicago Crime Syndicate," as well as "other unaffiliated local unions." However, Vaira was careful to add that corruption of this type was confined to a relatively small segment of organized labor, primarily in industries that had long been susceptible to racketeering and crime in many places such as trucking, restaurants, and unskilled construction labor.

A distinction must be drawn between corrupt or racketeering leadership and undemocratic leadership. A number of local unions, especially in the Chicago area, were created by one or a few individuals politically astute enough to maintain organizational control over a long period of time. Some of these local leaders obtained lucrative positions for themselves and their allies without ties to organized crime or the exercise of violence; some were ideologically motivated and were interested primarily in establishing a small power base within organized labor; some were autocrats running the organization like a personal barony while achieving benefits for the rank-and-file members. There were many variations of leadership from genuinely committed unionists to producers of sweetheart agreements.

The question of union democracy and evoked controversy in Illinois (as elsewhere) since before the turn of the century. Local unions tend to be more democratic than their internationals because they are smaller and ordinary members can become directly involved in the decision-making process. In unions comprised of members from a number of enterprises in a variety of locations, such as a large multiemployer local, a joint board, or a district, the opportunity for direct member participation is reduced. Full-time paid officials may gain dominant positions. Nevertheless, the record is replete with strongly contested electoral campaigns.

The quality of working life became one of the more widely discussed themes during the post-World War II era, particularly in the sixties and seventies. Chicago, the home of Studs Terkel, was one of the chief sources of information for his 1962 best-seller, *Working*, which popularized the theme of worker alienation. But Chicago was also the site of a variety of programs to increase job satisfaction and improve working life in both unionized and union-free enterprises and industries. Drugs and theft became prominent features of some workplaces, as did a concern for employee privacy and freedom from sexual harassment.

If life within the workplace changed significantly, so did life outside—in the household and in the community. Thanks to shorter work weeks and to longer paid vacations and holidays, employees enjoyed far more paid leisure time than ever before. The postwar years were also a period of great change in the use of leisure time, chiefly as a result of dramatic technological and social developments. Just as the automobile and the motion picture revolutionized leisure life in the twenties and thirties, so television and jet planes affected the fifties and beyond.

Not only were the means of using leisure time transformed, but its content was also changed because of changes in education, health, and family structure. Despite widespread criticisms of deteriorating public school systems, there was a substantial increase in literacy and general knowledge. The number of blue-collar workers who graduated from high school and the number of their children who graduated from college jumped markedly. The health of workers improved, and life expectancy mounted. On the other hand, the family structure became more fragile as divorce rates skyrocketed and women and adolescents asserted personal autonomy. Institutionalized religion maintained its numbers but declined in influence. The use of drugs spread, together with crime in the streets. All of these social changes affected the lives of Illinois workers after World War II.

Writing history poses organizational problems. Should a period of some thirty-five years be treated as a single unit, or can it be divided into distinctive subunits of time? Another problem is to determine what questions and factors should be discussed over time. Within any period, an infinite number of stories are unfolded. Which stories should be treated as focal, and which of these should be dealt with independently or interwoven with other stories?

The answer to the time unit issue is closely related to the focal questions of the study. As the preceding section has indicated, the central aim of this study is to describe and explain the movement of Illinois labor toward its major goals—improved economic status and an enhanced quality of life in the workplace and in society. Were there any decisive turning points in labor's march toward higher economic status and enhanced quality of working life? Were there any significant environmental or ideological developments that made a pronounced difference in the march?

It is clear that World War II was such a decisive turning point in comparison with the decade of the Great Depression that preceded it and the years of relative affluence that followed. During the next three-and-a-half decades, however, the Illinois labor scene did not change dramatically despite some deviations from the mainstream. There were a number of important events of a local, national, or international nature, such as the passage by Congress of the Taft-Hartley law in 1947, the enactment of fair employment laws in Illinois (1961) and in Washington (1964), the Korean and Vietnam Wars, the Chicago Democratic convention riots of 1968, the end of the twenty-one-year Daley mayoralty in Chicago in 1976, and the era of stagflation (rising prices and rising unemployment) following the OPEC oil boycott in 1973. But overall, it seems appropriate to treat the postwar period as a single unit. Accordingly, the subsequent chapters will be topical in character and cover variable time periods as needed.

NOTES

1. *Financing Unemployment Compensation in Illinois,* pt. 2, table 5 (Urbana: University of Illinois Institute of Labor and Industrial Relations, 1953), p. 82.

2. Theodore C. Pease, *The Story of Illinois* (Chicago: University of Chicago Press, 1965), pp. 247–48.

3. *Financing Unemployment Compensation in Illinois,* pt. 2, table 4, p. 80.

4. Statement of Peter F. Vaira before the Senate Permanent Subcommittee on Investigations of the Committee on Governmental Affairs, April 24, 1978, Washington, D.C.

PART I

The Working People of Illinois

The focus of chapter 1 is on the chief demographic and economic characteristics of Illinois, which is shown to be one of the nation's, and indeed one of the world's, largest and most advanced economic units. Until the severe recession of the mid-seventies, it was also an unusual mirror-image of the entire United States in terms of population, industrial composition, and economic diversification.

The period under review (1945–80) was significantly influenced by the baby boom of the fifties and sixties, as well as by dramatic technological and competitive developments. These were reflected in notable changes in the size, structure, and distribution of the work force. Although overall employment grew substantially, some industries (e.g. mining and railroads) declined, while others (e.g., state and local government, contract construction, and finance, insurance, and real estate) increased. Manufacturing employment in total increased moderately, but subindustries varied immensely from sizable expansion to noteworthy contraction.

Economic growth was the dominant theme until the mid-seventies. Recession epitomized the remaining years of the period and beyond. It is suggested that the process of decline was in large measure the product of forces inherent in the years of affluence. These trends will be examined in the remainder of the volume.

Chapter 2 deals with the incomes and living standards of the Illinois population and work force. It demonstrates the impressive gains achieved in real income by most workers although economic adversity continued to plague a significant, if declining, minority. The growth of overall affluence was reflected not only in income, but also in other quality-of-life measures such as housing, education, leisure activities, and vital statistics.

The terms *labor, working people,* or *workers* mean essentially those persons employed (or who seek employment) in nonmanagement positions for a wage or salary. Because statistics do not always match this definition, the terms *labor, working people,* or *workers* will often be used more loosely and encompass various categories of management as well as the self-employed. Labor with a capital *L* usually refers to organized or unionized workers.

1

The Demographic and Economic Setting

Illinois is a big state; in 1980, it was the fifth most populous in the United States; its population of 11.4 million exceeded the population of some 75 of the 125 nations reported on by the World Bank. Its gross production of $104 billion in 1978 surpassed the gross national product of all but thirteen nations.[1]

Illinois has also been, in many ways, a microcosm of the United States.[2] An examination of comparative data in the 1980 U.S. Census[3] revealed a virtual identity of percentages with respect to major population characteristics: females in population (51.5 percent for Illinois, 51.3 percent for U.S.); blacks in population (14.7 percent and 11.8 percent); foreign born (7.2 percent and 6.2 percent). With respect to education, the comparable percentages were identical—12.5 median school years completed for persons aged 25 years and over, and 66.5 percent of persons aged 25 and over completing four years of high school.

One significant demographic difference was in residence, with 83.3 percent of the Illinois population living in urban communities compared to 73.7 percent for the U.S. The higher urban percentage in Illinois was attributable to the fact that about half of the state's population lived in the Chicago metropolitan area.

The Illinois labor force, like the population as a whole, closely mirrored the national labor force. Percentages of men and women in the labor force, of employment by industry, and of occupation of employed persons rarely differed by more than one or two percentage points. The higher percentage of manufacturing employment in Illinois (25.8 as against 21.1) was perhaps the chief deviation from the national profile.

Like the U.S. as a whole, Illinois boasted a remarkably well-balanced economy. It was a national leader in agriculture, principally in the production of corn and soybeans. Its coal resources were reported to be the largest in the country, although high in sulfur content. It was a wide-ranging center of manufacturing, with particular strength in nonelectrical machinery, electrical machinery, food products, fabricated metals, chemicals, and printing and publishing. It was a national hub for air, rail, bus, and trucking services. It led the nation in nuclear energy for power. It was one of the nation's major exporters of both farm and industrial products. It had a comprehensive educational system (including some fifty community colleges, and three universities, among others, of international rank) and a cultural network that included a world-class symphony orchestra, a major art museum, and two outstanding museums of science and technology. It had the nation's largest medical school, one of its strongest health care systems, three nationally eminent law schools, and three distinguished engineering colleges, and it was a major exporter to other states and abroad of high-level professional talent.

In short, it was an advanced industrial economy. In 1980, Illinois was estimated to have had a per capita personal income of $10,448 compared to $9,494 for the U.S. as a whole, $11,020 for California, $10,242 for New York, $9,352 for Pennsylvania, $9,439 for Texas, and $9,798 for Michigan.[4]

Despite its relative economic development and affluence, however, Illinois, like the entire United States, had deep pockets of poverty, especially in the vast ghetto of South Chicago, in the impoverished industrial area of East St. Louis, and in rural Southern Illinois (27 of the state's 102 counties, sometimes referred to as "the other Illinois"). In 1979, per capita personal income ranged from $10,473 in DuPage County adjoining Cook County to $4,683 in Pulaski County in the deep south. Of the 102 counties, 10 had per capita personal incomes of $8,000 and above, while 8 had per capita personal incomes of $6,000 and below.

Statistics on "income less than the poverty level" in 1979 by county ranged from 2.3 percent of 3,960 families in DuPage County to 22.4 percent of 536 families in Pulaski County. Much more serious than the latter figure, however, was the rise of the percent of poverty-level families in Cook County from 7.6 percent 1969 to 10.8 percent in 1979.

This was the period of the baby boom. Between 1940 and 1950, the population grew, primarily because of the high birthrate after 1945, from 7.9 million to 8.7 million, or by 10.1 percent. It was 10.1 million, or 16 percent higher in 1960, and in 1970, it stood at 11.1 million, or 9.9 percent higher than a decade earlier. From the middle sixties, however, the birth rate declined almost as precipitously as it had risen, and population growth slowed. During the seventies, the population rose only to 11.4 million in 1980, or by 2.7 percent. The rise and fall of the Illinois birthrate paralleled the national trend.

The baby boom dramatically altered the age composition of the population. Between 1950 and 1970, the median age of males fell from 32.4 years to 27.4; that of females, from 32.9 years to 29.6. In the seventies, the decline in the birth rate, combined with an increase in life expectancy, restored the median age to 1950 levels. In part because of a higher birthrate and in part because of migration from other states, the percentage of blacks in the population rose from under 5 percent in 1940 to 14.7 percent in 1980. The median age of blacks in 1980 was 24.3 years, compared to 31.5 years for whites.

Ethnicity (apart from race) also continued to be a significant feature of Illinois life, although the number of foreign-born citizens or those of foreign parentage reportedly declined. For the state as a whole, the percentage of foreign born in 1980 was only 7.2, but 11.5 percent of persons five years and over spoke a language other than English at home. Of growing importance was the Hispanic or Spanish-speaking population which, it was estimated, numbered about 110,000[5] in 1960, 247,000 in 1970, and 619,000 in 1980.

The changes in the population induced important changes in economic life. However, separate economic and technological forces were also influential in affecting the labor force and labor conditions.

Total nonagricultural employment rose from 2.4 million in 1940 to 4.9 million in 1980, or 104.2 percent, but the industrial composition changed appreciably. Mining, for example, declined by 36 percent, and railroads by 69.3 percent (from 1947). On the other hand, government employment rose 243.2 percent; contract construction, 142.1 percent; finance, insurance, and real estate, 116.5 percent; wholesale trade, 87.3 percent; trucking and warehousing, 63.3 percent (from 1947); and manufacturing, 40.9 percent.[6]

It is significant that, except for the 1966–69 period, manufacturing, the largest sector, experienced little or no growth after 1947. In that year employment was 1,268,600, in 1960 it was 1,225,400, in 1970 it was 1,358,600, and in 1980 it was 1,208,200. Within manufacturing, employment in food products fell by 33.1 percent between 1947 and 1980, and in apparel and other textile products by 64.4 percent. In contrast, fabricated metal products rose 11 percent; machinery, except electrical, 17.3 percent; and motor vehicles and parts 31 percent.

The huge increase in government employment—from 283,800 in 1949, to 502,400 in 1965, to 756,400 in December 1980—merits special note. Federal government employment in Illinois hovered around 100,000 during most of the period under study (it peaked at 116,900 in 1970 and was down to 104,200 in 1978). State government employment, however, advanced from 93,300 in 1965 to 140,300 in 1975 and to 144,700 in December 1980. State education (mostly colleges and universities) represented about 30 percent of these figures. The bulk of government employment (60–70 percent) was local, of which education, rising from 154,000 in 1965 to 273,300 in 1978, represented slightly over half. The increase in state and local education was a product of the large number of returning war veterans and of the baby boom that followed.

Whereas the decades of the forties, fifties, and sixties were periods of rapid demographic and economic growth, that of the seventies was characterized by slack or declining conditions in a number of important respects. As noted earlier, population rose by only 2.7 percent in contrast to the rates of 10 percent or more in each of the preceding three decades. Total employment increased by 15 percent between 1970 and 1980, but manufacturing and construction were practically stationary. Within manufacturing, employment was stable or declined in such industries as primary metals, fabricated metals, electrical machinery, and equipment, food products, and textiles. The slack in these areas was made up numerically by relatively large gains in trade, finance, hospitals and health service, education, and nonprofit institutions. But the skill requirements and experience of the two sectors differed markedly.

In the process of the declines, Illinois began to diverge from the national picture. As Ruth A. Birdzell of the University of Illinois Bureau of Economic and Business Research wrote in late 1978, "For many years Illinois has been considered almost a mirror image, on a smaller scale, of the Unites States economy. In the past couple of years, however, there have been some noticeable divergences. . . . With the exception of 1974, increases in nonfarm income in Illinois have lagged behind those in the U.S. throughout the early 1970s . . . Illinois growth rates lagged behind U.S. rates in most of the main sectors—mining, construction, transportation and public utilities, trade, finance-insurance-real estate, and services—and most particularly in manufacturing, the biggest sector of all."[7] By 1980, the *Chicago Tribune* could report that "The Great Lakes states are leading the nation into a free falling recession that could become one of the worst regional downturns since World War II."[8]

In summary, this study deals with a major segment of American political and economic life in a period primarily characterized by growth and affluence. However, it was by no means a "golden age" as its deficiencies and limitations indicated.

NOTES

1. *Illinois Data Book* (Springfield: State of Illinois, Department of Commerce and Community Affairs, 1980); *World Bank Atlas* (Washington: World Bank, 1980).

2. Robert N. Schoeplein with Hugh T. Connelly, *The Illinois Economy: A Microcosm of the United States* (Urbana: University of Illinois Institute of Government and Public Affairs, 1975). A printed summary of this report is Robert N. Schoeplein, *Illinois and the United States: Some Economic Parallels* (Urbana: University of Illinois Institute of Government and Public Affairs, March 1976).

3. The sections for Illinois on "General Social and Economic Characteristics" were of particular value.

4. *Statistical Abstract of the United States, 1986* Table 735 (Washington: Bureau of the Census), p. 440.

5. *Chicago's Spanish-Speaking Population: Selected Statistics* (Chicago: Department of Development and Planning, September 1973), p. 1.

6. These data are derived from U.S. Department of Labor, Bureau of Labor Statistics, *Employment and Earnings: States and Areas, 1939–68*, Bulletin 1370–6, and *Supplement for 1977–81*, Bulletin 1370–16 (Washington: Government Printing Office).

7. "Income Growth Rate Unchanged in 1976," *Illinois Business Review* 35 (November 1978): 1.

8. "Area Economy Leads the Nation—Down," *Chicago Tribune*, July 9, 1980, sec. 6, p. 5.

2

Incomes and Living Standards

It is probably safe to say that, in economic terms, Illinois labor as a whole "never had it so good" as it did in the three decades between 1945 and 1974. The upward trend started with the outbreak of war in Europe in September 1939. It came to an end about 1973–74, when the OPEC oil boycott, a world grain shortage, and sharp health cost increases combined with other factors to produce a serious inflationary movement and high unemployment.

The effect of World War II and the pent-up demand for goods and services on the reconversion period is shown in a study by Richard C. Wilcock.[1] Real per capita income in Illinois rose about 32 percent from 1940 to 1949. In the same period, workers covered by unemployment compensation law improved their annual real wages by about 27 percent.

During the next twenty years, according to the census,[2] the median income of Illinois families rose from $3,627 in 1949 to $10,959 in 1969, or by 202 percent while the consumer price index rose by only 54 percent. Other evidence of improved economic status is found in personal income data, particularly wage and salary payments. Between 1958 and 1974, wage and salary payments rose from $16.6 billion to $47.1 billion, or 184 percent, whereas the national GNP implicit price deflator rose only 76 percent. In contrast, between 1974 and 1979, wage and salary payments rose 51 percent while the implicit price deflator rose 43 percent, indicating comparatively much less change in real terms.[3]

Still another component of advancing worker economic status is employment. In mid-March 1946, Illinois had 2.4 million employees at work. Ten years later, the comparable figure was 2.8 million, or 17 percent higher. By 1966, employment had risen to 3.4 million, or 18 percent above 1956. During the seventies, employment was estimated to have increased from 4.5 million in 1970 to 5 million in 1980, or 11 percent over the decade.[5]

The growth in the employment of women added significantly to family income. In 1950, the labor force participation rate for women was 33.3 percent; in 1960, it was 39.1 percent; by 1980, it was 52.6 percent compared with a male participation rate of 79.6 percent.[6] A substantial increase occurred in the employment of mothers with children under eighteen years of age.

While the general trend was upward, the demand for labor periodically was unable to keep pace with the mounting supply of new young entrants, immigrants, and women; it also varied with cyclical fluctuations. These factors are reflected in the state's average annual unemployment rate, which varied from a low of 2.8 percent in 1966 to a high of 8.3 percent in 1980. However, if 3 or 4 percent unemployment is judged to be an acceptable level, then only a few years posed problems before the recession of 1974–75.

The unemployment rate for different geographical locations was more varied than for the state as a whole. Chicago, for example, ranged from 1.7 percent in May 1953 to 8.3 percent in May 1958, but from 1962 to 1974, it varied only between 2.4 and 4.4 percent. Peoria had a low of 2.4 percent in May 1957 and a high of 9.1 percent in May 1958, but from 1959 through 1974, the rates varied only between 2.4 and 6.2 percent. The St. Louis metropolitan area, including East St. Louis, was the hardest hit urban center. It registered unemployment rates of 6.5 percent or higher in 9 of the 21 years between 1953 and 1974, including a 10.5 percent rate in May 1954, 9.6 percent in May 1958, and 7.4 percent in May 1971. Some rural areas, especially in Southern Illinois, experienced even higher rates of unemployment.[7]

Another factor governing worker economic status was inflation. Except for the immediate postwar reconversion years 1946–48 and the Korean War year of 1951, the Consumer Price Index was remarkably stable (increasing less than 3 percent per year) throughout the fifties and sixties. Starting in 1968, however, inflationary pressures stemming from the Vietnam War became evident. They temporarily abated in 1971–72 as a result of the Nixon economic stabilization program, but spurted ahead in the remainder of the seventies as wage-price controls were relaxed and abandoned, world grain shortages developed, and OPEC quadrupled oil prices. It was then that the phenomenon of stagflation drew national attention.

In addition to unemployment and inflation, the picture of increased worker affluence was further qualified by its unequal distribution. Capitalism is inherently a noneqalitarian economic system because rewards are expected to vary in accordance with market forces and contributions to productivity. In addition, bargaining power, organizational practices, and discriminatory factors, among others, affect income distribution. The consequences of these elements may be illustrated by Table 1, wherein median annual earnings are shown by industry and sex for the two decades between 1950 and 1970.

Table 1 suggests that the interindustry differences existing in 1950 remained basically intact twenty years later, especially for males. The differential between the top and bottom industries for males was roughly 78 percent in both 1950 and 1970. There was a much bigger spread in 1960, but this seems mainly due to special factors affecting farm earnings. Except for professional services and trade, females fared considerably more poorly than males between 1950 and 1970, but had similar interindustry spreads.

Table 1. Median Annual Earnings, Illinois, 1950–70

Industry	1950 M	1950 F	1960 M	1960 F	1970 M	1970 F	% Increase 1950–70 M	% Increase 1950–70 F
Finance	$3,638	$2,061	$6,104	$3,194	$9,703	$4,583	167	122
Transportation	3,319	2,406	5,670	3,762	9,578	5,144	189	113
Government	3,291	2,445	5,650	3,336	9,116	5,442	177	123
Prof. services	3,291	2,021	5,577	3,162	9,073	5,397	176	167
Construction	3,234	2,290	5,482	2,860	8,781	4,642	172	103
Manufacturing	3,223	2,001	5,414	3,640	8,754	4,325	172	116
Trade	3,078	1,632	4,984	2,861	8,163	4,153	165	154
Business services	3,014	2,122	4,813	1,988	7,502	2,954	149	39
Personnel services	2,450	1,087	3,761	1,238	6,277	2,246	156	107
Agriculture	2,045	913	2,546	993	5,491	2,587	169	183

C.P.I. (1967 = 100): 1950 – 72.1; 1960 – 88.7; 1970 – 116.3
Increase 1950 – 1970 – 61.3%.

Source: Bureau of the Census.

Another illustration of income disparity is found in data on occupations and race in standard metropolitan areas of 250,000 or more (Table 2). In this case the income is for families with heads in the experienced civilian labor force as of 1969.

Table 2. Median Annual Income, Illinois, 1969

Occupation	White	Black	Hispanic
Professionals	$14,586	$12,248	$13,650
Managers, except farm	16,484	12,804	13,642
Sales workers	13,954	9,145	11,139
Clerical workers	11,132	8,367	9,030
Craftsmen	12,508	10,491	10,839
Operatives except transport	10,342	8,781	8,520
Transport operatives	11,467	9,811	9,943
Laborers, except farm	9,448	8,871	8,660
Farmers and farm managers	8,420	5,341	——
Farm laborers	5,955	5,088	6,333
Service workers, except private	9,720	7,890	8,273
Private household workers	4,536	3,983	——
Total	12,321	9,177	9,605

Source: *Illinois Economic Abstract*, 1977, Table 5.11.

In a strongly unionized state such as Illinois, one would expect organized labor to fare better economically than nonunion labor. This is shown in Table

3 in which a comparison for selected years is made between average weekly earnings in a set of industries that was well organized and another set that was not well organized.

Table 3. Average Weekly Earnings, Illinois, 1958–78

	1958	1964	1974	1978	% Increase 1958–78
Well-organized					
Mining	$107.43	$133.92	$248.06	$322.26	204
Construction	125.20	159.37	315.89	377.62	202
Blast furnaces, basic					
steel	110.48	37.78	245.77	339.64	207
Apparel	55.31	65.59	111.50	149.13	170
Trucking	115.05	146.41	291.68	401.19	249
Communications	82.43	110.79	207.00	342.01	315
Poorly Organized					
Wholesale trade	97.75	119.25	207.43	261.83	168
Retail trade, except					
eating, drinking					
places	64.43	75.95	118.40	175.27	172
Banks	73.95	84.68	138.65	182.58	147
Laundries	49.33	64.00	117.77	148.60	201
Insurance carriers	86.52	90.17	147.23	184.58	113

Source: U.S. Bureau of Labor Statistics, *Employment and Earnings, States and Areas*, Bulletins 1370–11, 1370–18. The figures for 1958 and 1964 are not strictly comparable to those for 1974 and 1978, but they are in the correct direction.

Finally, there is the phenomenon of the people with incomes below the poverty level, whether holding jobs (the so-called "working poor") or on social security, public aid, or various forms of private dependency. In 1969, for example, 7.7 percent of Illinois families had incomes below the poverty level as then defined ($3,500 according to the Social Security Administration). Of these, a fourth were headed by persons 65 years and over, and 39.1 percent were headed by a female. Some 23.1 percent of all families received public assistance, but 74 percent of families' heads were in the labor force. In 1975, a recession year, the percentage of families below the poverty level was put at 8.3 percent; in 1980, it was 8.4 percent.[8]

Lamentable as this low-income picture was, the significant feature of the period was the reduction in the proportion of people in the poverty category from earlier years. A sample survey of family income in 1949, for example, revealed that 9 percent had annual incomes of less than $1,000, 14 percent less than $1,500 and 19 percent less than $2,000. The poverty line was then generally defined as $2,000 per family. The median income of all families was $3,627.[9]

From 1974 to the end of the decade, the march toward affluence came to a halt largely because of stagflation. The unemployment rate reached 7.1 percent in 1975, gradually declined to 5.5 percent in 1979, and then rose again to 8.3 percent in 1980. Inflation rose to more than 10 percent in 1974 and, after a brief decline to about 5 percent in 1976, leaped to double digits in 1979. Per capita wage and salary payments rose from $10,652 in 1975 to $14,490 in 1979, or by 36 percent, but the C.P.I. (1967 = 100) rose from 161.2 to 217.4, or by 35 percent.[10] As a result of rising taxes and "bracket creep," the average worker had less disposable real income than before. Only the increased participation of women in the labor force and the increase in multiple-worker households helped to preserve living standards for many. An analysis of census data for the seventies in Chicago by the *Chicago Reporter* concluded that "the proportion of residents with incomes below the poverty line rose from 14.5 percent to 19.9 percent. While most areas of the city saw some increase in poverty, it was in the black and Latino communities that poverty worsened the most."[11]

Income is a basic determinant of living standards, and it tends to be highly correlated with the various components that comprise a satisfactory or unsatisfactory standard of life. Nevertheless, an examination of specific components is also necessary for an adequate understanding of trends in the quality of life.

According to the Illinois Commission on Human Relations, the greatest problem of the postwar period was housing, especially in Chicago and other industrial communities that experienced a large influx of blacks between 1940 and 1950.[12] During this decade the white population of the state increased 7.6 percent while the nonwhite (primarily black) population increased 60 percent. However, it was not only a matter of differential population growth. In most white Chicago neighborhoods, for example, formal or informal restrictive covenants prevailed, and a combination of white residents, real estate agents, and mortgage bankers prevented the entrance of blacks regardless of income. Very little new housing was built for the new nonwhite market. The commission estimated in 1953 that more than 700,000 Illinois families (white and black) lived in blighted areas in substandard housing.

With the postwar reconversion, the number of housing units in Illinois increased rapidly and steadily. Census data revealed a total of 2,672,000 units in 1950, 3,276,000 in 1960, 3,703,000 in 1970, and 4,329,000 in 1980. The number of units in the three decades increased by 62 percent, while the population grew by only 31 percent. Home ownership also increased from 40 percent in 1940, to 57 percent in 1960, and to 63 percent in 1980.

Other indicators of housing improvement in Illinois were the number of persons per room and the availability of plumbing facilities. Fifteen percent of all occupied housing units had more than one person per room in 1940, 12 percent in 1950, 9 percent in 1960, 7 percent in 1970, and 5 percent in

1980. In 1940, 37 percent of housing units lacked complete plumbing facilities; in 1950, 32 percent; in 1960, 13 percent; in 1970, 4 percent; and in 1980, 2 percent.

This generally favorable picture was not shared by most blacks, and the gains that were achieved came only after persistent struggle and government intervention. In 1948, for example, the U.S. Supreme Court in *Shelly v. Kramer* ruled that although individuals could choose to abide by restrictive covenants, "governmental support of such covenants is contrary to public policy of the United States and cannot be enforced by State or Federal Courts."[13] The Federal Housing Administration in 1949 announced that its financial aid would no longer be extended to property that had occupancy restricted on the basis of race, creed, or color. Measures of this type were helpful to blacks with decent jobs and incomes, although white resistance to neighborhood integration was often fierce (sometimes violent as in Cicero and Fernwood Park), and progress was slow. In Chicago, large numbers of whites fled to the suburbs, so that although the population of the city declined after 1951–53, that of Cook County and adjoining counties grew rapidly. Gradually, however, well-to-do blacks, supported by black organizations, sympathetic white liberals, and the federal courts managed to break through the barriers in many communities. Hyde Park in the University of Chicago area was a widely publicized example of successful integration. In 1960, according to a *Chicago Reporter* analysis, 12.5 percent of the 854 census tracts in Chicago were racially mixed; in 1970, the ratio was virtually unchanged; but in 1980, it was almost 20 percent. The comparable figures for predominately black tracts were roughly 13 percent, 25 percent, and 33 percent, respectively.[14]

For the vast majority of low-income blacks throughout Illinois—the working poor and those on public welfare—controversy raged over low-cost public housing, slum clearance, and urban redevelopment. It was particularly severe in Chicago, with its massive, rapidly expanding, hemmed-in black population, although similar problems arose in every part of the state, from Rockford in the north, to Peoria in the center, to Cairo and East St. Louis in the south. Two central issues emerged. One was whether public housing projects should be constructed within the black neighborhoods or distributed in segments throughout the city. The other, and related, issue was whether the projects should be integrated.

Almost all of the projects were high-rise, heavily populated structures in predominately black neighborhoods. Some, like the Carbrini-Green project, received adverse media publicity because of gang and crime problems. Integration was notably absent. In 1980, Chicago was still almost as segregated in its housing—both public and private—as it had been at the end of World War II.[15]

The picture of educational achievement in Illinois was very similar to those of income and housing, and indeed a high correlation appears to exist among all three. For the majority white population, including blue-collar workers, educational opportunities expanded substantially. The millions of returning servicemen and women wanted jobs, marriage, families, and houses, and they saw more and better education for themselves and their children as a means to these goals. The impact on higher education was almost instantaneous; in primary and secondary education it followed the baby boom of the fifties and early sixties.

At the college and university level, public institutions in particular responded, although before the war, in 1940, more than two-thirds of college enrollment was in private institutions. Even before the end of the war, the Commission to Survey Higher Educational Facilities in Illinois set up by the General Assembly in 1943, recommended that the junior college system should be expanded throughout the state. In 1945–46, seven public school districts operated junior college programs. Between 1946 and 1949, five more were started, and between 1955 and 1962, an additional seven. These nineteen were ultimately to be expanded to a total of fifty community colleges. Enrollments grew from 22,000 in 1957, to 66,200 in 1965, to 230,000 in 1977. The Chicago junior colleges accounted for two-thirds of Illinois enrollments during the fifties; downstate enrollment did not equal Chicago until 1966 but by the end of the sixties, the former exceeded the latter by a 70:30 ratio. Less than half of the junior college students were interested in going on to baccalaureate degrees. Most students sought initial training or refresher courses for occupational careers in technical and paraprofessional fields.

The Illinois college and university system expanded just as rapidly. Enrollment at the University of Illinois, for example, rose from 10,667 in 1945 to 60,705 in 1980. Because facilities at the Urbana campus could handle only about 16,000 students and applications in March 1946 totalled some 23,000 (mostly returning veterans), the decision was made to open up temporary two-year extension centers at cooperating high schools (31 schools participated). Separate branch campuses were also established temporarily in Galesburg and at the Navy Pier in Chicago. In 1965, the Navy Pier quarters were replaced by the permanent Chicago Circle campus, which rapidly grew to more than 20,000 students. In 1965, university-wide enrollment reached 38,928, and in 1970, it was 55,630.[16]

The state's five teachers colleges or "normal schools"—Southern, Eastern, Western, Northern, and later Illinois State Normal—all sought comprehensive educational status, dropped the word *Teachers* from their names, and became general universities.

In addition to the conventional academic and professional curricula, there was a substantial development in extension courses for adults on both a credit and noncredit basis. During 1959–60, the six universities enrolled 23,000 students in 1,058 courses in 190 cities. Enrollments ranged from 345 at Eastern to 10,000 at the University of Illinois.[17] By 1980, enrollment exceeded 76,000. A wide variety of subjects were offered, including programs, which began in 1946, for organized labor through the Institute of Labor and Industrial Relations at the University of Illinois.

Higher education in Illinois was, of course, not confined to public institutions, although they bore the brunt of the postwar expansion. Such eminent private universities as the University of Chicago and Northwestern University, as well as some fifty other institutions at the four-year level and beyond contributed to an exceptionally rich array of educational opportunities. In 1970, the enrollment of degree-credit students at public and private four-year institutions exceeded 300,000. Illinois became a net exporter of university-trained personnel to other states and foreign countries.

The children of blue-collar and low-income white-collar workers, as well as business and professional people, took advantage of the relatively low cost of public colleges and universities in large numbers. Higher education, at least until the recession of the seventies, was believed to correlate closely with higher incomes and occupational success, particularly in a society rapidly moving from an industrial to a service base. The advance of women was especially impressive. Minorities had more difficulty in overcoming the barriers of discrimination as well as their disadvantaged backgrounds, nevertheless, the percentage of blacks attending college rose significantly.

Primary and secondary education experienced a much more troubling course of development than higher education, initially because of the growth pressures from the baby boom and then because of the minority (especially black) integration problem. Enrollment in full-time public elementary and secondary day schools increased from 1,154,000 in 1949–50 to 2,325,000 in 1969–70, necessitating extensive new buildings and facilities as well as greatly enlarged teaching and support staffs.[18]

A more positive aspect was the record of years of schooling completed. In 1970, according to the Bureau of the Census, 2.5 million Illinois persons had completed high school, 711,000 had completed four years of college or more, and the median for all persons aged 14 and older was 12 years. Males and females had the same median; whites had a median of 12.1 years, blacks 10.7 years, and Hispanics 9.6.

The negative side of the educational picture became a matter of increasing concern, particularly during the seventies—slow progress in racial desegregation, a decline in the results of scholastic aptitude tests, a growth in the use of drugs and alcohol by teen-agers and younger children, an increase in high school dropouts, and intensification of school disciplinary problems. The problems were most serious in Chicago's inner city schools but were widely reported and discussed in suburban and downstate schools as well.

By 1980, only six of some one thousand school districts were reported to be in noncompliance with State Board of Education desegregation guidelines. But this apparent progress was overshadowed by the fact that 82.4 percent of black and 73.1 percent of Hispanic pupils were concentrated in the seven largest school districts of the state, and segregation had actually increased within these school districts. For example, in Chicago, 39 percent of black students attended schools with greater than 98 percent black enrollment in 1963; in 1977, more than 60 percent attended such schools.[19]

From 1969 to 1979, the average SAT verbal scores in the state declined from 489 to 467, and the average of mathematics scores fell from 518 to 511. Between 1974 and 1979, the high school dropout rate increased slightly from 5.8 percent to 6.3 percent but returned to 5.9 percent in 1980. Dropout rates in 1980 were 5.2 percent for white males, 11.2 percent for blacks, and 13.8 percent for Hispanics. The comparable figures for females were 4.1 percent for white females, 8.3 percent for black, and 10.8 percent for Hispanic. An analysis of census data for 1980 by the *Chicago Reporter*[20] concluded that there was a high correlation between income and education and that years of school completed varied directly with the family income level in the case of whites and blacks. The Hispanic situation was somewhat more complicated because of the mixed composition of nationalities of the category.

These statistics combined with problems of poverty, drugs, alcoholism, and discipline marred an educational scene that had the potential of extending educational opportunities and rewards on a scale hitherto unmatched.

Entertainment, the arts, and other uses of leisure represent another important indicator of the standard of living. The years following World War II witnessed an extraordinary proliferation of entertainment pursuits—both of a popular and a fine arts nature. The advent of television was perhaps the single most far-reaching influence on the use of leisure, followed by the jet airplane and computer-controlled communications. But older forms of leisure activity such as sports, reading, concerts, and movies also persisted, and in some cases expanded.

William Kornblum's study of the steelworkers of South Chicago between 1968 and 1970 provides significant insights into some of the leisure behavior of an ethnic working class community.[21] He notes in particular, the unique role of occupational, ethnic, and neighborhood (inter-ethnic groups) taverns.

> In general the taverns are the locus for primary group activity which exits outside the home. In their homes, blue collar families most often associate with relatives and friends of long standing who are free to drop in at almost any time. Invitations to other neighborhood friends are reserved for special occasions in the life cycle, such as marriage, birth, death, or important holidays during the year. Thus the tavern is among the most important of neighborhood institutions where people can form and maintain friendships with others whom they know well but

may not associate with at home. This is especially true of friendships formed at work which may reach across ethnic or territorial divisions in the neighborhood or the larger community.[22]

In addition to the taverns, churches, fraternal benefits societies, and sports teams were still prominent but declining centers of leisure-time activity.

Working-class communities of the type described by Kornblum were becoming less common in the sixties and seventies as a result of the movement of numerous white Chicagoans to the suburbs, the decline of heavy industry, and the geographic dispersal of industrial enterprises. Downstate, except for some black neighborhoods, ethnicity and religion were secondary considerations in determining residence, and leisure was more likely to be influenced by income and education. Age, of course, affected leisure use by all groups as did family size.

A study conducted in 1970–71, by Elizabeth K. Abbas of twenty-five blue-collar and twenty-five professional employees and their spouses at the University of Illinois, Champaign-Urbana, revealed the principal leisure activities of each.[23]

Table 4. Leisure Activities, Blue-Collar and Professional Families

	Blue Collar		Professional	
	Husbands	Wives	Husbands	Wives
Watching TV	72%	56%	20%	36%
Sports participation and exercise	60	48	68	32
Movies, concerts etc.	48	56	48	40
Gardening & yard work	64	12	40	8
Arts, crafts, do-it-yourself	32	72	20	64
Reading	24	28	64	72

Source: Elizabeth K. Abbas, "Leisure Time Attitudes and Activities of 25 Blue Collar and 25 Professional Worker Families," M. S. thesis, University of Illinois, 1974, p. 93.

A somewhat similar study by Joan M. Sampson in 1964 of fifty married couples in the same community but of lower income and education than the Abbas study revealed basically the same picture in terms of average hours per week spent.[24]

Annual vacations were reported by only about half the sample families in the Sampson survey in contrast to almost all of the later Abbas sample, a reflection of the continuing growth in the concept of paid vacations and of the spreading custom of taking vacation away from home.

In a vast metropolitan and tourist center like Chicago, institutionalized entertainment and the arts captured an increasing proportion of leisure time. Professional sports attendance, especially baseball, football, and basketball, was a prominent example. In 1946, 983,403 went to Comiskey Park to see the White Sox play. By 1951, the number had soared to 1,323,234. But even more significant was the upsurge of interest in fine arts and science. The Museum of Science and Industry reported a five-year increase of attendance from 2,547,000 in 1959 to 2,907,000 in 1964; the Field Museum from 1,075,000 to 1,511,000, and the Art Institute from 1,048,000 to 1,627,000.[25]

According to George M. Irwin, chairman of the Illinois Arts Council, before World War II "arts activity was as much a plaything of the few in Illinois as in other parts of the country." The development of popular interest, participation, and support came after 1945. Most of this growth was at the "amateur or 'semi-professional' level, with the fully professional programs largely confined to Chicago and a few university centers." Irwin also observed: "Today, both business and labor leaders at local and national levels are concerned that their employees enjoy opportunities in our increasingly affluent society which brings with it an expanded amount of leisure time."[26] He noted further that although the Illinois Arts Council had the third largest state arts council budget in the country, only about a fourth of the funds in 1965–67 came from state appropriations; the rest came from the National Endowment for the Arts, the U.S. Office of Education, the municipal Chicago Committee on Urban Opportunity, private foundations like the Chicago Community Trust, Quincy Foundation, and Woods Charitable Fund, certain large corporations like Sears, Roebuck and Illinois Bell Telephone, and individuals.

The mounting interest in leisure activities was also reflected in the expansion and elaboration of professional leisure study programs such as that developed by the University of Illinois in 1948. A study by Allen V. Sapora estimated that in 1977 public tax money expended annually in the Illinois leisure services system (primarily parks, playgrounds, and other outdoor recreational facilities) was about $443 million and that the annual payroll of commercial sports in 1975 was at least $132 million. Sapora noted that it was impossible to make a complete or accurate accounting of private and commercial expenditures on leisure activities but, including tourism, more than $6.5 billion was by no means the minimum figure.[27]

Finally, brief consideration of a few vital statistics is necessary. Although not conclusive evidence, infant mortality rates, death rates, and life expectancy rates are generally considered to reflect trends in living standards. Other social indicators—marriage and divorce rates, health and sickness data, and crime statistics—are also relevant, but are excluded in the interest of brevity.

According to the Illinois Department of Public Health, the infant mortality rate (per 1,000 registered live births) declined remarkably from 35.3 in 1940 and 31.6 in 1945 to 15.1 in 1979. Between 1960 and 1979, the infant mortality rate for whites declined from 22.2 to 12.1 while the rate for blacks declined from 39.9 to 26.8—still a long way to go but considerably improved. The death rate (per 1,000 population) declined more gradually—from 11.3 in 1940 and 11.9 in 1945 to 9 in 1979. However this statistic is less meaningful because it fails to take into account the changing age composition of the population. One would expect a younger population (resulting from the post-war baby boom) to have a lower death rate than an older population.

As national data make clear, life expectancy rose significantly during the period, but the causes of death varied significantly.[28] In Illinois, bacterial diseases like pneumonia and influenza were greatly reduced. Heart disease rates peaked about 1945 after a continuous rise from 1920, then stabilized through the fifties and began to decline in the seventies. Cancer deaths, on the other hand, continued to rise as cures of some types were offset by the spread of new forms. The suicide rate declined from a peak in 1930 until the mid-fifties and then stabilized. Motor vehicle fatalities declined until about 1960, and then more or less remained at a plateau. In contrast, homicide rates almost trebled between 1955 and 1979.

A statewide study of public opinion conducted by the University of Illinois in 1978[29] listed the following items as the ten most serious social problems: adequate housing, government-citizen relations, job opportunities, pollution and littering, law enforcement, community planning, recreation services, community services, education, and health services. The ranking of problems differed by geographical location—except for first two. All segments of the state agreed that housing and government-citizen relations were the most serious problems. But for Chicago residents, law enforcement, pollution and littering, education, and business and industry were the next most serious issues, whereas residents in suburban Cook County and the "collar" counties rated transportation, job opportunities, and community planning as next most important, and in the rural downstate areas, the problems of transportation, health services, recreation services, and public safety were high on the problem list. Unfortunately, a comparable survey was not available for the earlier years of the period. However, in rough terms the opinion results appeared to lend support to other available quantitative indicators.

From the standpoint of living standards, the 1945–80 period had witnessed substantial improvements in such areas as economic status, educational opportunities, health, and civil rights. Nonetheless, progress was far from complete as wide disparities continued to exist in economic status and efforts to remedy shortfalls in some programs, like unemployment, public housing, and inner-city education, proved unsuccessful. Moreover, even relative affluence itself stimulated problems: industrial development brought unexpected health and safety hazards; pollution effects on water, air, and land multiplied; and abuse of drugs and alcohol created serious conditions for families of all incomes.

NOTES

I am indebted to Michio Fujiwara and Christina Shalley for the research contained in this chapter.

1. *Financing Unemployment Compensation in Illinois*, pt. 2 (Urbana: University of Illinois Institute of Labor and Industrial Relations, 1953), p. 12.

2. 1950 Census, "Illinois," Table 3, and 1970 Census, "Illinois, General Social and Economic Characteristics," Table 57 (Washington: Government Printing Office).

3. Data derived from Russell E. Smith, "Changes in the Sources of Personal Income, by Industry, 1958–1979," *Illinois Business Review* 38 (May 1981).

4. *Illinois Economic Abstract* Table 4.14 (Urbana: University of Illinois Bureau of Economic and Business Research, 1977).

5. Illinois Bureau of Employment Security, *Women and the Labor Force* (Chicago: State of Illinois, September 1981), p. 19.

6. I.B.E.S., *Women and the Labor Force*, p. 20.

7. See reports on employment and unemployment of the Illinois Bureau of Employment Security, Research and Analysis.

8. The 1969 data came from the U.S. Bureau of the Census, *General Social and Economic Characteristics, 1970, Illinois*, Table 69. The 1975 estimate is from *The Statistical Abstract* (Washington: Government Printing Office, 1980), p. 467; the 1980 figure is from the U.S. Census. The poverty-level figure is from U.S. Bureau of Labor Statistics, North Central Region, *Poverty—The Broad Outline: Chicago*, March 1970, p. 12.

9. U.S. Bureau of the Census, *1950 Census of Population*, pt. 13, *Illinois*, Table 32. For an authoritative discussion of the concept of poverty, see Margaret S. Gordon, ed., *Poverty in America* (San Francisco: Chandler Publishing, 1965), pp. 4–11.

10. The wage and salary data ($49 billion in 1975, $71 billion in 1979) came from Smith, "Changes in the Sources"; the number of wage and salary recipients was estimated at 4.6 million in 1975 and 4.9 million in 1979 from *The Illinois Labor Market Information Review* (Chicago: State of Illinois).

11. "Chicago Became Blacker, Poorer in 1970's: Minorities Bear Brunt of Poverty Increases," *Chicago Reporter*, April 1983, p. 1.

12. Illinois Commission on Human Relations, *Non-White Housing in Illinois*, Chicago, June 1953, Foreword.

13. Illinois Commission on Human Relations, *Non-White Housing*, p. 15.

14. "Chicago Became Blacker, Poorer in 1970's," *Chicago Reporter*, p. 1.

15. Ibid., p. 2.

16. See Illinois Community College Board, *Illinois Junior College Development, 1946–1980*, Springfield, 1980.

17. Data provided by University of Illinois Office of School and College Relations.

18. Commission of Higher Education, State of Illinois, *Annual Report 1960*, Springfield, p. 44.

19. U.S. Department of Health, Education, and Welfare, National Center for Educational Statistics, *Statistics of State School Systems* (Washington: Government Printing Office).

20. "Poverty and Education in Chicago, 1980," *Chicago Reporter,* January 1983.

21. William Kornblum, *Blue Collar Community* (Chicago: University of Chicago Press, 1974).

22. Kornblum, *Blue Collar Community,* pp. 80–81.

23. Elizabeth K. Abbas, "Leisure Time Attitudes and Activities of 25 Blue Collar and 25 Professional Worker Families," M.S. thesis, University of Illinois, 1974, p. 93.

24. Joan M. Sampson, "A Study of Leisure Time Use and Related Expenditures of Husbands and Wives in Fifty Families," M.S. thesis, University of Illinois 1966, p. 19.

25. Mayor's Committee for Economic and Cultural Development, *A Program for the Arts in Chicago* (Chicago: John Price Jones, 1966).

26. Illinois Arts Council, *Survey of the Arts, 1966–67,* pp. 2, 4, Chicago.

27. Allen V. Sapora, *Leisure Services in Hungary and Illinois: A Comparative Study* (Champaign: Stipes Publishing, 1981), pp. 189–97. See also Sapora, "The Economic Impact of Parks and Recreation in Illinois—The Tip of the Iceberg," *Illinois Parks and Recreation,* September-October 1983, pp. 12–16.

28. See *Vital Statistics, Illinois 1961,* "Crude Mortality Rates for Selected Causes of Death, Illinois: 1920–1961," p. 8, and *Vital Statistics, Illinois 1979,* "Death Rates," Table R, p. 1.31 (Springfield: Department of Public Health).

29. *Illinois: Today and Tomorrow,* (Urbana: University of Illinois Institute for Environment Studies, and Institute for Government and Public Affairs, May 24, 1978).

PART II

The Organizational Picture

From the 1880s onward, Illinois had been one of the nation's centers of unionization. In terms of membership it ranked fourth among the states throughout the post-World War II period, and in ratio of membership to non-farm employment it ranked seventh. Labor organization membership reached a historic peak (about 40 percent of nonfarm employment) by the middle of the fifties, although this achievement was soon followed by signs of rigidification and gradual decline. Like the employment picture, the overall membership figures obscured counteracting submovements. Membership in manufacturing, railroad transportation, and coal mining unions decreased, whereas membership in public service, food and commercial trade, health care, and transportation, unions other than rail expanded.

The seven cases described in some detail in Part II are obviously not a scientifically selected sample of all Illinois unions. However they were chosen purposively because they were of major leadership importance in the Illinois labor movement (the Chicago Building Trades Council and District 31 of the Steelworkers); they represented significant aspects of union activity (the "social unionism" of the United Auto Workers); they were prominent examples of successful organization among new unionized categories of workers (women, minorities, and public—Local 743 of the Teamsters, the Hospital Employees Labor Program, and the State, County, and Municipal Employees Union); they were a notable illustration of the destructive impact of domestic and foreign competition (the Amalgamated Clothing Workers).

All but one of the cases was located in Chicago. This was not originally intended, but rather evolved for two reasons as the study proceeded: cost effectiveness, that is, centralizing data collection proved to be more feasible and efficient; and considerable information on local unionism was gathered in the course of the community surveys described in Part 4, without necessitating the accumulated detail of a case study.

Economic and technological factors were clearly important considerations in the rise or decline of labor organizations. In some instances such as meat-packing, they were domestic in origin and became apparent rather early in the period of study. In other cases such as basic steel, the effects of foreign competition did not become visible until the recessions of the seventies. The construction industry was largely subject to cyclical fluctuations; the goods-producing industries were impacted by secular foreign factors. Less explicit reasons but looming significantly in the background were changing demographic forces, the emergence of minority and women's pressure groups seeking greater social equity, the spread of higher education, and changing worker attitudes toward jobs.

3

Employee Organization

The history of Illinois is studded with notable names and dramatic events like the Haymarket affair, the Pullman strike, the Hart Schaffner and Marx agreement, and the Memorial Day Massacre. Unfortunately, statistics on union membership are not highly reliable, and statistics on a state basis are especially weak so that precise measures are not available. One of the first serious efforts to collect state data was made by Leo Troy for the years 1939 and 1953. The Bureau of Labor Statistics began to issue state statistics in 1964 on a biennial basis. The methodology of these two surveys is quite different, and the data therefore are not uniform. Nevertheless, the results seem generally consistent.

Troy's study estimated that union membership in 1939 was 590,700, ranking Illinois third among the states.[1] By 1953, the membership had risen to 1,358,700, placing Illinois in fourth position behind New York, Pennsylvania, and California. The percentage increase was 130 as compared to 148.8 for the entire United States.

When Troy related union organization to nonagricultural employment, he found that Illinois had a penetration ratio of 25.9 percent in 1939 and 39.7 percent in 1953. Illinois ranked eighth among the states in the earlier year, and ninth in the latter. The growth in union membership was largely attributable to a few major unions—the Teamsters (86,700), the Auto Workers (76,100), the Brotherhood of Electrical Workers (72,400), the Steelworkers (67,100), and the Machinists (58,700).

Union growth in relation to employment apparently peaked in the mid-fifties; however, fairly reliable trend data did not become available until 1964 when the BLS began its biennial series (Table 5).

The absolute membership figures in Table 5 are not strictly comparable over the years, and in a number of years they omit or understate the membership of independent unions, employee associations, and local unions. For example, when members of the Illinois Education Association, the Illinois Nurses Association, the Policemen's Benevolent Society, and the Illinois State Employees Association are added to the union members, the total membership in 1970 becomes 1,613,000. The ratio of total union and association membership to employment in 1970 was 37.3 percent.

Table 5. Illinois Union Membership, 1964–80

	National Union Membership (thousands)	Illinois Rank Among States	Percent of Nonagricultural Employment	Illinois Rank Among States
1980	1,487	4	30.4	8
1978	1,590	4	31.5	7
1976	1,451	4	31.8	8
1974	1,584	4	34.9	7
1972	1,526	4	35.4	7
1970	1,548	4	35.8	7
1968	1,538	4	36.0	7
1966	1,465	4	35.9	7
1964	1,394	4	37.9	7

Source: *Directory of National and International Labor Unions in the United States*, 1965 and 1969; *Directory of National Unions and Employee Associations*, 1971, 1973, 1975, and 1979; *Directory of U.S. Labor Organizations*, 1982–83 (Washington: Bureau of Labor Statistics).

Two conclusions may be drawn from these statistics. One is that Illinois remained high among the states throughout the thirty-five-year period. The other conclusion is that after rising through the war years and the first postwar decade, membership was practically stable or in slight decline relative to employment for the next two decades, and then dropped several percent in the last half of the seventies in terms of both absolute membership data and of the membership to nonagricultural employment ratio.

The gross data, however, obscure a number of contrasting developments. Organization declined in several industries chiefly because of declining employment and to some degree because of rising antiunion sentiments. The most notable examples of these industries were in manufacturing, the railroads, and coal mining. These declines were largely offset by employment gains and organizational advances in nonmanufacturing industries, notably transportation (except railroads), trade, health care, and, most of all, public service (federal, state, municipal, and educational). In the absence of membership statistics by industry, the employment data shown in Table 6 are broadly indicative of the general trends.

Organized labor was divided into two major segments from the mid-thirties until the merger of the AFL and the CIO in 1955, but the merger of the state federations in Illinois was not consummated until 1958, and that of the Chicago central bodies not until 1962. At the time of merger, the Illinois State Federation of Labor claimed affiliates with about 850,000 members, and the State CIO Industrial Union Council about 350,000. This total of 1,200,000 was about 34 percent of the 3.5 million employees in the nonagricultural labor force in 1957.

Table 6. Employment (Thousands), 1950–80

	1950	1960	1970	1980
Declining Industries:				
Mining (until the 70s)	44.6	28.5	22.8	31.3
Railroads	128.0	90.7	59.2	43.7
Leather and leather products	25.1	19.9	13.9	6.8
Meat products	46.1	25.5	22.7	18.0
Apparel	62.1	45.7	35.9	22.6
Growth Industries:				
Trucking and warehousing	51.6	64.9	70.2	74.8
Construction (until the 70s)	137.4	169.3	188.1	188.4
Fabricated metal (until the 70s)	118.9	127.9	143.9	135.4
Machinery, except electrical	176.6	183.4	221.8	225.5
Retail trade	465.8	529.0	663.4	787.4
State and local government	219.7	315.1	522.0	658.0

Source: *Employment and Earnings, States and Areas*, BLS, Bulletin 1370 and Supplement.

The State Federation of Labor, formed in 1883, was dominated in the postwar period by the Construction Trades Unions and, until their expulsion in 1957, the Teamsters; the former represented about a fifth, and the latter about a seventh of the affiliated members.[2] Other prominent union organizations included those for machinists, electrical workers (IBEW), various railway crafts, the musicians, the building and service employees, the printing trades, and the ladies garment workers. More than half of the AFL unions in the state were located in Chicago (in 1951 the president of the Chicago Federation of Labor, William A. Lee, claimed that AFL affiliates in Chicago represented some 450,000 members), but unionism was distributed among more than 250 cities and towns.[3]

The State Industrial Union Council (the CIO body), formed in 1941, was much more concentrated than the State Federation of Labor. At the thirteenth convention in 1956, the Steelworkers had 404 delegates from 152 locals and the Autoworkers had 322 delegates from 74 locals out of a total of 981 delegates from 315 locals. The Packinghouse Workers with 56 delegates from 12 locals, and the Amalgamated Clothing Workers with 36 delegates from 19 locals were the most significant of the remaining 19 international unions.

When the merger of the two state bodies was finally achieved in 1958, the State Federation of Labor delegates included representatives from 32 local central bodies, 20 building, metal, and printing trades councils, 7 local unions, and 60 international unions with 612 local and other units. The CIO delegates came from 9 central bodies and 17 internationals with 197 local and other units. Two hundred and thirty AFL locals and 110 CIO locals came from Chicago. Conspicuously absent were the United Mine Workers, who had withdrawn from the CIO; the Teamsters, who had been expelled from the

Labor in Illinois

AFL on charges of corruption; and the United Electrical and Radio Workers, who had been expelled by the CIO on grounds of Communist domination.

Since the state bodies of the AFL and the CIO were primarily concerned with political action, they will be discussed in a later chapter on that subject. Here they are introduced mainly as a device to identify the diverse elements of unionism in Illinois and their changing character.

The per capita taxes received by the state AFL–CIO reflect some of the shifting fortunes of unions in various occupations and industries, although they also reflect the internal politics of the labor movement. The withdrawal of the Mine Workers and Auto Workers and the expulsion of the Teamsters were major examples of the political factor. The amount of per capita paid was also a matter of union discretion. Hence, the absolute payments recorded are less indicative of membership than the rank orders. Table 7 provides the top fifteen rankings based on per capita payments for 1960–61, 1970–71, and 1979–80.

Between 1960 and 1970, there was exceptional stability in the rankings. The only new member of the top fifteen was the American Federation of State, County, and Municipal Employees (AFSCME), which, together with the Illinois Federation of Teachers, led the advance in the public sector. Only one other union, the International Brotherhood of Electrical Workers (IBEW) gained (or lost) more than two positions. The building trades unions and their traditional allies, the Service Employees International Union (SEIU), the Retail Clerks International Union, and the Hotel and Restaurant Employees and Bartenders International Union formed the dominant group. Apart from the United Steelworkers of America and some mixed unions such as the IBEW and the International Association of Machinists (IAM), the factory unions were conspicuously absent from the leaders. Although the IBEW was an important unit among the building trades, it was also highly important in public utilities, (i.e., telephone, radio, and television) and manufacturing (i.e., electrical and electronics products). Likewise, the International Association of Machinists represented, in addition to construction workers, numerous manufacturing and maintenance employees in metal-working establishments throughout the smaller cities of downstate Illinois as well as in the Chicago metropolitan area.

During the seventies, the Teachers and AFSCME again advanced in enrollment, as did the newly merged Railroad union and the Transit union. The traditional leaders, however, maintained most of their relative positions in membership.

Until the recession of the mid-seventies, the union enrollment pretty much held its own. Membership losses tended to be associated primarily with employment declines rather than antiunion sentiment, although NLRB election data reflected some loss of support for unions among workers, as well as

Table 7. Rankings of Unions Affiliated with the Illinois AFL–CIO, 1960–80

Ranking	1960–61		1970–71		1979–80	
1	Auto Workers	$27,342	Steelworkers	$29,339	Steelworkers	$55,072
2	Steelworkers	21,683	Electricians	19,114	Electricians	53,555
3	Carpenters	15,872	Carpenters	19,045	Carpenters	48,330
4	Machinists	11,481	Machinists	18,270	Teachers	47,899
5	Laborers	11,190	Service Employees	12,569	Machinists	39,635
6	Electricians	11,173	Laborers	12,352	Laborers	30,285
7	Building Service	9,967	Retail Clerks	11,044	Food & Commercial	24,672
8	Retail Clerk	7,891	Teachers	9,800	Service Employees	23,714
9	Hotel & Restaurant	7,775	Meat Cutters	7,659	State, County	16,536
10	Plumbers	5,129	Hotel & Restaurant	7,436	Plumbers	16,085
11	Teachers	4,606	Plumbers	6,456	United Transportation	14,086
12	Meat Cutters	4,248	State, County	5,944	Transit	11,186
13	Painters	4,246	Printing Pressmen	4,441	Painters	10,478
14	St. Railway	3,848	Painters	4,366	Boilermakers	10,271
15	Printing Pressmen	3,292	Transit	4,158	Graphic Arts	10,168

Source: *Annual Proceedings*, Report of the secretary-treasurer.

more aggressive and more sophisticated tactics on the part of employers to dissuade employees from supporting unions.[4]

NOTES

1. Leo Troy, *Distribution of Union Membership Among the States, 1939 and 1953* (New York: National Bureau of Economic Research, 1957).

2. Keith Hindell, "Union Political Action in Illinois, 1944–1959," Bachelor of Letters thesis, Oxford University, April 1962, p. 70.

3. Hindell, "Union Political Action," pp. 91, 70.

4. See, for example, Ronald L. Seeber and William N. Cooke, "The Decline in Union Success in NLRB Representation Elections," *Industrial Relations* 22 (Winter 1983):34–44. On a national basis, the percent of elections won fell from 74.5 in 1950 to 46 in 1978.

4

Unions and Collective Bargaining:
Selected Cases

Individual unions fared very differently after World War II. Although it can be argued that each union is unique, most of them fell into one of the following three classifications:

1. Those that were once part of the mainstream leadership group but that seriously declined in membership and influence because of changing industrial, technological, or market conditions such as the clothing unions, the packinghouse workers unions, the railroad unions, the miners, and the graphic arts unions.

2. Those that prospered, reached maturity, and then more or less stabilized until the severe recessions of the seventies, including such dominant mainstream organizations as the Carpenters, Electricians, Machinists, Teamsters, Autoworkers, and Steelworkers that had epitomized the Big Unionism of the war and postwar years.

3. Those new "service-producing unions" that had sought unsuccessfully for many years to win recognition and now gained a momentum that propelled them into the leadership ranks. In the public sector, these included the Illinois Federation of Teachers and AFSCME; in the private sector, the Food and Commercial Workers Union, the IBEW, and the Communication Workers Union in the telephone industry were representative. Paralleling these unions were organizations well established in other jurisdictions that expanded into the public sector—for example, the Teamsters and the Service Employees—as well as a variety of associations unaffiliated with organized labor that turned from purely professional to unionlike behavior. The Illinois Education Association, the Illinois Nurses Association, and the Illinois State Employees Association were examples of the latter.

In the pages that follow, case studies of important unions from each of these three classes are presented. Most of these studies were conducted in the Chicago metropolitan area because of the unions' size and significance. However, the downstate experience is portrayed in the segment on public unionism and in the five community studies presented in Part IV.

The case studies were not designed to yield quantitative sampling results. Each was treated as a unique example within a fairly broad category. The aim was to catch the basic spirit and qualities of each organization, not to produce generalizations. Hence the studies varied in the dimensions covered and did not generate strict comparative analysis.

The stories of the clothing workers (in section A) and the packinghouse workers (in chapter 8) record the rise and fall of two pioneering models in the realm of trade unionism and collective bargaining. The Amalgamated Clothing Workers epitomized the new social unionism of the twenties and thirties. They reflected, among other things, the contributions of Jewish immigrant labor (socialist and social welfare) to the American labor movement. The Packinghouse Workers Union emerged out of the labor struggles of the thirties. More than any other important Illinois union, it mobilized the energies and loyalty of black workers long before the civil rights movement took hold. It demonstrated to blacks their capacity for leadership in the labor movement and their potential for economic achievement. In the case of the Clothing Workers, low-cost foreign competition had a devastating effect on business and employment. In the case of the Packinghouse Workers, domestic economic and technological forces led to the virtual elimination of meat processing in Illinois.

Four case studies represent mainstream developments. The Chicago Building Trades Council and the Teamsters were the heart of the old American Federation of Labor (AFL), and the former continued to dominate the State Federation of Labor, the Chicago Federation of Labor, and many of the central labor bodies in downstate Illinois. The Teamsters continued to maintain close and influential ties with the Building Trades Council and other AFL affiliates even after the Teamsters' expulsion from the AFL in 1957. "Business unionism" was the prevailing ideology. The Chicago Building Trades Council was the coordinating mechanism and the public voice of the building and construction unions. Teamsters Local 743 was not a truck drivers' local, but its thirty thousand members comprised the largest local in the international union, and its leadership shared many of the values of the organization. In certain respects, however, it was distinctive among Teamster locals, principally in the treatment of blacks and women.

The Steelworkers and the Autoworkers were the equivalent giants of the CIO, dominating the State Industrial Union Council, the Chicago Industrial Union Council, and several downstate central bodies including those in Peoria (Caterpillar local), Moline and Rockford (farm equipment) and (general manufacturing), and the Alton–Granite City area (steel). After the UAW withdrew from the merged AFL–CIO, the Steelworkers shared hegemony in the Chicago and State Federations of Labor with the Building Trades. District 31 of the Steelworkers was the largest subdivision of its international; Local 6 of the UAW at International Harvester's Melrose Park plant was much smaller, but it was widely regarded as a model of UAW achievement. The UAW and the Steelworkers were the major innovators of collective bargaining practice throughout the country after World War II.

All four of the dominant unions—the Building Trades, the Teamsters, the Steelworkers, and the Autoworkers—were in the forefront of organized labor during the nearly thirty years between 1945 and 1973. During the severe recession of 1974–75 and in the disruptive years of stagflation that followed, they were to suffer serious setbacks.

The rise of public and quasipublic service unionism was the theme of the case studies representing the third class. At the state level, AFSCME overcame long-imbedded barriers to acquire both collective bargaining and political status. The Hospital Employees Labor Program (HELP) jointly sponsored by Teamsters Local 743 and the equally powerful Local 73 of the Service Employees Union, demonstrated the possibilities and problems of organization among the semiskilled and unskilled employees of the expanding health care field. The story of the Chicago Teachers Union is described briefly in chapter 8.

4A

The Amalgamated Clothing and Textile Workers Union

The first chapter in the history of the "Amalgamated" starts with the historic 1910–11 strike at Hart, Schaffner, and Marx. That four-month strike at "Hart," the city's largest manufacturer of men's clothing, not only resulted in the first union contract in the local industry, but it also led to the founding of a new and aggressive international union four years later, to important institutional innovations in the arbitration of workers' grievances, and to a long and mutually productive bargaining relationship that was the object of much praise over the years.

Many of the leading figures in the strike went on to become leaders in the national affairs of their new union. Sidney Hillman, international president of the Amalgamated from its founding in 1914 until 1946, who was equally prominent as a CIO leader and as a New Dealer, began his career as a bargaining representative in the Hart's plant. Jacob Potofsky, Hillman's successor as international president, served in the post almost as long as Hillman himself—from 1946 to 1972. Frank Rosenblum was a key figure in the promotion of the Amalgamated's innovative system of social insurance benefits, a vice-president of the CIO, and secretary-treasurer of the Amalgamated during Potofsky's twenty-six years as president.

Under the guidance of Samuel Levin, manager of the Chicago Joint Board from its establishment in 1910 until shortly after World War II, the Chicago union won union security provisions in virtually all of the Chicago market and a forty-four-hour work week (along with New York) in 1919; established in 1922 the Amalgamated Trust and Savings Bank, which was a pioneer in the granting of small loans to workers and the only labor venture in banking that survived the depression; secured (also in 1922) a Chicago contract that established a local unemployment insurance fund into which employers and employees each contributed 1.5 percent of the employee's earnings, and which later served as a model for New Deal planners; and in 1940, created an Amalgamated Life and Health Insurance Co. that provided death benefits and health and accident insurance and was also a model, this time for the

Amalgamated's national insurance plan instituted shortly after the Chicago innovation.

However, this impressive record was impaired by a serious economic development—a rapid decline of the Chicago men's clothing market. Official union histories claim that forty thousand workers in the industry took part in the 1910–11 general strike, and that twenty-five thousand took part in the dramatic, but largely unsuccessful, strike of 1915.[1] When the entire Chicago market came into the Amalgamated fold in 1919, membership stood at 30,800.[2] When the headquarters building, Amalgamated Center, was built in 1927, membership had dropped to 19,800, before stabilizing around 18,000 in the thirties.[3] The Chicago Joint Board locals emerged from World War II with only 15,000 members.[4]

In 1940, Samuel Levin attributed the precipitous membership decline to the "liquidation of a number of firms, to technological improvements, and 'but very little' to runaway shops."[5] Barbara Newell elaborated upon the first factor mentioned by Levin: "Since 1914 Chicago's comet has been fading. New production centers in New Orleans, St. Louis, Dallas and Los Angeles have begun to serve what had been a Chicago market. Even more basic to the whole industry, the American consumer has chosen to put less of his dollar on his back. Chicago's reputation for quality clothes meant that as consumers bought fewer and lower price clothes they began discriminating against Chicago producers."[6]

Local membership continued to decline—from 15,000 in 1945[7] to approximately 5,000–6,000 in 1980.[8] Union members in the traditional heart of the Chicago industry, men's suits and coats, decreased from more than 8,000 in 1948 to some 3,000–4,000 in the late seventies.[9] These employment declines were not unique to Chicago, but also occurred in most of the other traditional centers of the garment industry in the face of a massive onslaught of inexpensive imports and changing consumer tastes.

Despite its losses in membership, Chicago did not diminish the quality of the Amalgamated's contributions to the international union as well as to the Chicago labor movement. Murray Finley became the international president after Potofsky's resignation in 1972, and Joyce Miller became international vice-president and director of social services, president of the Coalition of Labor Union Women (CLUW), and in 1980 became the first woman to sit on the Executive Council of the AFL–CIO.

The dynamism of the Chicago leadership radiated throughout the Midwest. As Sol Brandzel, then manager of the Chicago Joint Board, explained in 1977, "In the early years, organizers from Chicago, one of the first markets organized, spread out across the country to help fellow workers in other cities. They provided leadership in quality and quantity far out of proportion to their numbers."[10]

Rosenblum's Western Organizing Department, formed in 1922, remained one of the premiere units of the Amalgamated until a reorganization in 1964 divided most of the locals under the department's jurisdiction into a Midwest Regional Joint Board in Chicago, with eighty-one locals concentrated in Illinois, Indiana, Michigan, Wisconsin, and Iowa, and a Southwest Regional Joint Board headquartered in St. Louis and that was concentrated in Missouri, Kansas, and Arkansas.[11] The Midwest Regional Joint Board included, in addition to the Chicago Joint Board, the smaller Milwaukee and South End Boards, but it was headquartered in the Amalgamated Center, and the successive managers of the Chicago Joint Board also served as managers of the regional board. On October 1, 1977, this board became known as the Chicago and Central States Joint Board, following the merger of the Chicago and other midwestern locals with the Central States Joint Board of Detroit.[12]

In reviewing the union's local history, the men and women who over the years made up the local membership should be discussed. It was said that by the 1890s a Chicago-made suit consisted "of a coat made by Bohemians, a vest made by Swedes, and pants made by German and Jewish workers".[13] Almost a century later, the ethnic diversity of the Chicago work force in men's clothing remained a living tradition. Robert Myers, the author of a 1937 dissertation on the Chicago industry, estimated that at that time about 25 percent of workers were Bohemian, 20 percent were Polish, 20 percent Jewish, 15 percent Italian, and 20 percent were of other nationalities (comparable nationwide figures were that 40 percent of workers were Italian, 35 percent, Jewish, 10 percent, Polish, 5 percent, Lithuanian, and 10 percent of other nationalities).

During the postwar years, the Eastern European presence diminished in Chicago with the demise of Local 6, the Bohemian Coatmakers, and the mergers, in 1959 and 1961 respectively, of Local 38, the Polish Coatmakers, and Local 269, the Lithuanian Coatmakers, into Local 39, the largest Amalgamated local in the city. However in 1973, it was reported that members of Local 39, which represented the sewing machine operatives working on Hart's coat production, spoke "Greek, Italian, Spanish, and Polish"; its members also included scores of Chinese immigrants and blacks who were brought to the Hart's plant on Jackson Boulevard by van from their communities on the South Side.[15]

The number of Jewish workers in Chicago likewise declined, as they did nationally. In 1981, the business agent of Local 61, the cutters' local at Hart's and some smaller shops, noted that few Jews were left among the cutters, the most skilled workers in the industry and a traditional stronghold for immigrant Jews. He stated that about 65 percent of the local's membership was Italian, with Eastern Europeans, Latinos, and blacks making up most of the remaining third. He also reported that there were only 123 cutters left in Local 61, compared with some 750 in the 1950s.[16]

Arthur Loevy, the Joint Board manager in the early eighties, estimated that 17–18 percent of workers in Chicago were black, 12 percent were Latino, and 10 percent were Asian. According to a top executive at Hart, Schaffner, and Marx, of the 3,980 employees in Hart's Clothing Division in 1979, 528 were black (13 percent), 461 were Latino (12 percent), and 233 were Asian (5 percent). Of the 881 employees in the company's twenty-three Baskin's retail stores scattered throughout the metropolitan area and a few outlying communities, 174 were black (19 percent) and only 24 were Latino.[17]

One other significant trend in the local membership composition was the gradual displacement of male workers by women. Of the suits and coats production workers surveyed periodically by the Bureau of Labor Statistics, 43 percent were men in 1958, 39 percent in 1963, and 33 percent in 1973.[18] By 1979, only 27 percent of the Hart's manufacturing employees were men. Approximately 80 percent of the workers at Oxxford's were women.[19] Two other Chicago locals were overwhelmingly female: Local 83, which represented perhaps 200–300 pants makers at the East Chicago and Michigan City, Indiana, shops of Jaymar–Ruby, a Hart's subsidiary, and Local 223, which represented outerwear workers at Rubin Grais, a producer of high quality leather, cloth, and rain coats, with a workforce of more than three hundred and fifteen other much smaller shops in 1973.

Although the Chicago Amalgamated was to become a strong supporter of day care and other causes important to working women, sexual segregation persisted on the shop floor. In a BLS wage survey conducted in 1973, male workers in the city averaged $4.51 in hourly wages, while women averaged only $3.56, or 79 percent of the men's wages, due largely to the predominance of men in higher-paying jobs and women in lower-paying ones.[20] For example, 106 of 136 cutters were men, as were 169 of the 202 pressers, while 841 of the 907 sewing-machine operators were women, as were 176 of 195 basters, 347 of the 350 hand finishers, and 120 of the 124 "thread trimmers and basting pullers."[21]

Although ACTWU's national reputation for decades centered on its commitment to social benefits for its members, wage rates were always of primary importance for average union members in Chicago and elsewhere. Over the postwar period Amalgamated members enjoyed relatively strong advances in the level of real wages negotiated by their leaders; one author has calculated that between 1941 and 1968 wages in the industry rose 313 percent, while the consumer's price index increased 144 percent.[22] From 1941 on, negotiations covering workers in the men's tailored clothing industry were on a nationwide basis with the Clothing Manufacturers' Association of the USA. These negotiations, which covered a large majority of the Chicago membership (e.g., 8,000 in 1969 and 5,00 in the mid-seventies), set minimum wage rates (in 1980 about 25 cents above the federal minimum wage), hourly wage increases, and cost of living adjustment formulas. However, because the base rate for most workers (75 percent nationwide and 86 percent in Chicago in 1973)[23] was a piece rate settled jointly by a shop chairperson or business agent and a company representative, average wage rates varied significantly among the major cities and regions producing men's clothing.

According to the three available BLS wage surveys, Chicago's relative ranking in wages improved during the period. In 1958, wages in the local tailored clothing industry were 103 percent of the national average (compared with 117 percent in New York, 115 percent in Los Angeles, and 105 percent in Rochester), while wages in the Great Lakes region, including Illinois, Indiana, Michigan, and Wisconsin, were 98 percent of the national average. These relative figures for Chicago and the surrounding region were virtually unchanged in 1968, but in the 1973 survey, the Great Lakes region fell one penny short of tying the Middle Atlantic states for the highest average hourly wage ($3.48 to $3.49). Most significantly, Chicago narrowly surpassed New York City ($3.88 to $3.79) as the highest-wage city in the country. By 1973, average wages in Chicago stood at 118 percent of the national average.[24] According to the head of the Human Resources Division at Hart, Schaffner, and Marx, average wages for production workers, excluding cutters, before the 1980 negotiations were in the $5.75–$6.00 range; the local's business agent stated that after these negotiations Hart's cutters were averaging more than $11 an hour.[25]

Another important characteristic of the union was its commitment to expeditious resolution of shop-floor grievances. In 1973, the *Midwest News* ran two articles featuring the roles of the shop chairpersons and business agents at Hart's and Rubin Grais; these articles emphasized the critical role in union affairs played by this front line of union officials. "Most of the business of Local 39 is conducted not from the union office or by administrators and bureaucrats. It is conducted by the shop floor and it is conducted by the shop chairman and the assistant chairman with the help and supervision of the business agent."[26]

It was the duty of the chairpersons and the business agents who appointed them to keep the workers informed of the union benefits available to them, to rally their support for political causes such as anti-import rallies in the Loop, to assure a smooth flow of work among the various departments of a larger plant such as Hart's, and, most important, to approve any changes in piece rates received by individual workers. In an industry involving thousands of separate, intricate work operations, frequent style changes in the product line, and periodic technological change, negotiating piece-rate disputes demanded that the shop chairpersons and business agents be long-time veterans of the shops, with virtually encyclopedic knowledge of the operations on every machine in his or her shop.

It is significant that union officials can remember only one grievance during the postwar period that actually proceeded to the stage of formal arbitration. As the impartial arbitrator Millard Cass wrote in his order, of January 22, 1973:

> The Company [Hart's] and the Union have had amicable collective bargaining relationships for more than fifty years. Indeed, it was these two parties who instituted in this industry the salutary principle of arbitration of labor disputes rather than resort to economic warfare. That principle has now become a respected practice in this industry. This Company and this Union have not required the assistance of an Impartial Arbitrator to settle their differences during the 54 years in which they have had collective bargaining relations. This demonstrates a high degree of industrial relations statesmanship on the part of both parties. It also, however, underscores the importance of the issue presented to the Impartial Arbitrator in this case.[27]

What was involved in the arbitration case was the determination of Hart, Schaffner, and Marx management to introduce substantial mechanization into its cutting department "for (the sake of) efficiency and to meet domestic and foreign competition." The Amalgamated protested, arguing that the changes were unnecessary and that they "would destroy the skill content of these jobs, break down a recognized craft, impair working conditions, and destroy the cutters' morale and pride in their work." The arbitrator (in 1973) expressed his sympathy for the cutters, the traditional "aristocracy" of the industry's work force, but ruled that under Article 22 of the National Men's Clothing Collective Bargaining Agreement governing technological change Hart's clearly had the right to mechanize its cutting operations. The company was directed not to reduce the wages of the affected workers and not to remove them from employment by reason of the approved changes, and the company and union were ordered to negotiate new incentive rates and production standards appropriate to the new machines.[28] According to the business agent for the Hart's cutters, after this arbitration decision, the cutters shifted from a standards (essentially hourly) method of payment to incentive rates under which they became the highest-paid cutters in the U.S.[29]

As the jobs of cutters and other workers in the traditional shops dwindled due to increased mechanization and firm liquidations, the union at least partially compensated for these membership losses through the organization of many workers who, at first glance, might not seem to be likely Amalgamated members. One of the locals to emerge from these organizing efforts was Local 108, which included clerical and warehouse employees at Hart's and union staff employees from the Amalgamated Center. This local actually dated back to before the war; according to a local president, it was first organized in 1934 and chartered in 1936,[30] but the Joint Board reported to the national convention in 1944 that "a new local was chartered in Chicago in December, 1942, when office and sundry workers throughout the market joined with the already organized Hart, Schaffner, and Marx office employees to form Local 108."[31] Of the 450 local members in 1973, 250 were Hart's employees.[32]

Typical organizing efforts were reported by the Joint Board to the 1958 national convention: "Since the last Convention, the Chicago Joint Board has been successful in its new organizing efforts. Among the new shops organized was the largest remaining 'open shop' neckware company. This shop joined the Amalgamated despite stiff opposition from management. In addition, a company manufacturing quilting materials was organized, the first such manufacturer in Chicago to sign with the Union. Organizing efforts were started and are continuing among bushelmen, retail stores, and related needle trades shops. Some inroads have been made in organizing salesmen, primarily in clothing stores."[33]

However, it was not until the late sixties and seventies that the union initiated the organizing drives that were to result in two new types of Chicago locals: 969, the Retail and Department Store Employees local, and 1062, the Bank Employees local. Organization of retail clothing sales personnel began in 1966 and 1967 and built on the long-established Amalgamated presence in many Chicago stores through Local 5, the "bushelmen" or tailors' local. In the late seventies, Local 5 claimed 500 members, compared with the 800 or so members in the much younger Local 969.[34]

Local 969 received its charter in the spring of 1967, after card checks of employees in the Baskin, Rothschild, and Benson and Rixon men's clothing stores revealed substantial majority support for the Amalgamated.[35] Their ranks were supplemented by eighty employees in four Erie Clothing Company stores in May 1969,[36] but it was not until 1971 that Joint Board manager Murray Finley announced in the pages of the *Midwest News* that "now the Chicago Joint Board has undertaken a systematic retail organizing campaign."

Finley explained that:

> There are hundreds of retail clothing sales and non-selling workers in large and small stores throughout the Chicago Metropolitan area. . . . Often these are not the stores in the fancy suburban shopping malls, but are located in inner-city neighborhoods, close to the customers they serve, and close to where their employees live. Hundreds of workers in Chicago and thousands nationwide are being cruelly exploited by the retail industry for essential work involving long hours. . . . Their wages are low, most of them falling just at the federal minimum wage, and many of them below the minimum wage due to cheating by the employer. . . . In some of the stores, the 60 or 70 hour week is not uncommon— while fringe benefits are virtually non-existent. These workers in unorganized stores do not get paid vacations or holidays, sick days or health insurance or pensions. They are not protected by seniority or a grievance procedure.
>
> Many of these workers are members of ethnic minority groups. . . . They are ripe for exploitation, because they have nowhere else to turn for a livelihood

than to these low-wage retail establishments. . . . They need unionism, they want it, and they're entitled to it.[37]

Further small organizational victories followed Finley's proclamation, with the addition of perhaps a hundred employees at several stores (Lelewear, Tom Oleshar, Beautiful Things, Second Place, Maybrook, and National) in late 1971 and a hundred employees of five Fashion Plate Stores (women's clothing) in late 1972.[38] Negotiations for these workers were on a store-by-store basis.

The bulk of Local 969's membership, however, was still employed at the Hart's subsidiary, Baskin's. According to a senior official of Hart's, there was an off-the-record agreement that Hart's would not resist ACTWU organizing efforts at any new manufacturing facility if the union would refrain from attempts to organize any more of the many Hart's retail chains besides the two where it was already established—the 23 Baskin's stores in the Chicago area and the 27 Wallach's stores in the New York area. For this reason, Hart's five Capper and Capper Stores in Chicago and, more important, its 24 Chas. A. Stevens' stores (women's clothing), with almost 1,000 employees in the Chicago area, were not represented by ACTWU.[39]

Some of the same working conditions that prompted ACTWU organizing efforts in retail stores also prevailed in Chicago banks. According to a *Chicago Tribune* article in the mid-seventies, female bank employees in Chicago earned on average just $4,766 a year compared with $9,058 for male employees; furthermore, 90 percent of the women employees held clerical positions, whereas 36 percent of the males held managerial jobs.[40] Although the Amalgamated sold its pioneering Chicago bank to private interests in 1966, its employees remained union members after the sale; they were, in fact, the only unionized bank employees in the city until November 1975, when the Amalgamated won a 7–4 NLRB election victory at the Midtown Bank of Chicago.[41]

Another small unit followed at the First National Bank in McHenry, a small town northwest of Chicago, in April 1976,[42] and then a larger unit of fifty employees at Metropolitan Bank and Trust Company on the city's Southwest Side in January 1977.[43] Two more banks were organized by ACTWU in 1978—the North Federal Savings and Loan Association and the Guardian Savings and Loan Association,[44] but the union's most publicized organizing effort at a bank occurred in 1976, at the State Bank of India on LaSalle Street. The union enrolled all fifteen employees at the bank, but it declined to recognize ACTWU because it was owned by the Indian government and thus, it maintained, exempt from the NLRA. The Regional Labor Board ruled in favor of the Indian bank, but on appeal in May 1977 the National Board ruled unanimously that employees of businesses owned by foreign governments were entitled to union representation.[45] An initial contract with the State Bank of India was finally negotiated in late 1977.

Finally, brief mention should be made of the Amalgamated's Xerox locals in suburban Chicago. The unique Xerox–Amalgamated relationship dated back to the thirties in Rochester, New York, home of the firm and a traditional Amalgamated clothing market. When Xerox expanded its operations in the Chicago area in the late sixties, two new locals were formed: 14–E, covering employees at the reconditioning plant in Oak Brook, and 14–M, covering workers at a Des Plaines warehouse and an Elk Grove Village plant. Membership in the two locals stood at 550 in 1972, but was down to 400 in 1976, when the Elk Grove Village and Oak Brook plants' operations were consolidated and the two locals merged, with a further loss of seventy jobs.[46]

Despite the decline in Xerox employment, ACTWU's suburban presence grew, with three subsequent organizational victories at workplaces far removed in every sense from the traditional garment shops in the loop: Aurora Bleachery in Aurora (organized in October 1979); Modern Filters, Inc. (fifty-five employees producing cloth filter bags for vacuum cleaners) in Joliet (May 1980), and Automatic Switch Co. (forty employees producing pressure switches) in Elk Grove Village (August 1980).[47] The "suburbanization" of the Chicago union received one final impetus in late 1981, when Hart, Schaffner, and Marx closed its long-time headquarters on South Franklin Street and moved 270 ACTWU members to a new production facility built beside the company's warehouse in Des Plaines.

As important as wage gains, shop-floor governance, and organizing victories were for the Joint Board locals, the Joint Board leadership stressed the original vision of progressive social unionism. Upon his election as the Joint Board manager in 1972, Sol Brandzel explained this concept of social unionism and Chicago's historic role in promoting it. "We have tried, throughout the Amalgamated, as a union, to improve the standards of our members. We wanted to do more than get wage increases. Our goal was to uplift the living conditions of our people, both in the shop and also in their personal lives. The Chicago Joint Board was the cradle of the Amalgamated, supplying the pioneers and great philosophies that have advanced the goals of the union since the 1910 strike. The Chicago Joint Board was always a factor in setting the policies of the organization."[48]

The union's commitment to social and political activism was evident during the tenure of Murray Finley's three predecessors—Samuel Levin, who resigned shortly before his death in 1948 after thirty-eight years as Joint Board manager; Reuben Block, also a veteran of the earliest union days in Chicago, who returned from Allentown, Pennsylvania to serve out the remainder of Levin's last two-year term and who remained Joint Board manager until 1953; and Samuel Smith, a veteran business agent who served until 1961. The Amalgamated made annual contributions to such groups as the Community Chest, the Red Cross, the United Jewish Appeal, and Roosevelt University;

and the Amalgamated Center carried on its prewar tradition of offering an array of activities for the workers and their family members. An achievement of these years was the opening of the million-dollar Sidney Hillman Health Center in September 1955. The center was not unique; the Amalgamated could boast of two such centers in New York, one in Philadelphia, and later one in Rochester; the Chicago International Ladies Garment Workers Union (ILGWU), the Amalgamated's "sister union," sponsored a similar health center for its members. Nonetheless, the Sidney Hillman Health Center quickly became a source of particular pride for the Chicago Amalgamated. By 1960, the center was averaging six thousand clinical visits and services a month,[49] and in 1961, low-cost dental care was added to the many other services provided by the center.[50]

However, neither Reuben Block nor Samuel Smith left as much of an imprint upon the affairs of the union as Levin before them or Finley afterward. Finley, a Michigan native and graduate of the University of Michigan and Northwestern Law School, began his service with the Amalgamated in 1949 under Frank Rosenblum in the Western Organizing Department; he then served as assistant manager of the Detroit Joint Board before returning to Chicago in 1961 as Smith's successor. He served as Joint Board manager in Chicago for a decade before becoming international president in 1972. As a *Midwest News* editorial noted upon his departure for New York, besides Finley's creation of the Midwest Regional Joint Board, which "helped to weld a widely scattered group of locals into a single, unified organization,"

> Under his direction, the Retiree Center, the Day Care Center, Harper Square cooperative housing, the Personal Service Counselor, the Legal Service Program, the Education Programs, School, and Conferences, the Education Plan, expanded Health Center benefits, free prescription drugs, were all established as part of an integrated program of activities and benefits. Many of these programs were started in the Chicago Joint Board where 98% of the market is organized. Gradually, more and more of these programs have been established in the locals of the Midwest Regional Joint Board as well. Now he is leaving Chicago and the Midwest to become the General President of the Union. If he can do what he accomplished in Chicago and the Midwest, he will do an outstanding job.[51]

As Joint Board manager, Finley lost no time in demonstrating his commitment to an expansion of the social benefits offered by the Amalgamated. During 1962, his first year in office, he inaugurated a new education department under the direction of Joyce Miller and opened of a new Retiree Center. Secretary of Labor Willard Wirtz presided over the ribbon-cutting for the Samuel Levin Retiree Center, which provided an active schedule of programs to assure that the rapidly aging work force in Chicago remained integrated in the life of the union. Dancing, singing, orchestral concerts, arts and crafts classes, monthly visits to mentally ill patients at Chicago State Hospital, annual picnics, trips to Hawaii, Washington, Israel, and elsewhere, letter-writing campaigns on critical legislative issues, even picketing in support of the Farah boycott during the early seventies were all sponsored by the Retiree Center.[52] In addition, in 1969, after years of stubborn campaigning by Finley, Miller, and the retirees themselves, the Amalgamated, together with other unions, finally succeeded in having reduced bus and subway fares for senior citizens instituted by the Chicago Transit Authority following a meeting instigated by Finley between Chicago Federation of Labor President Bill Lee and Mayor Daley.[53]

In 1962, the facilities of the Amalgamated Center were turned over to the local officials of the new Office of Economic Opportunity (OEO) program for a full schedule of classes and seminars, including training programs for the teaching staff of Project Head Start. The following year, the Joint Board announced the creation of a unique program called simply the Education Plan. Under the plan the children of all Amalgamated members who had thirteen or more years in the union would receive $600 a year (an amount later raised to $700) to apply toward expenses for four years at any accredited college or approved technical school.

In 1967, Miller also began, in conjunction with the Education Plan, annual conferences on higher education opportunities in the area for children of Amalgamated members. Expanded class offerings in citizenship, English, preretirement education, new membership training, and leadership training also became hallmarks of her tenure as education director.[54]

Miller also served as editor of the Midwest *Regional News*—which was called the *Midwest News* in 1972, then *Labor Times* in 1977—from its first edition in 1964 until 1971. With lively and detailed coverage of the activities of locals under the Joint Board, of local and national politics, and of the daily work life within the Amalgamated shops, this paper lent unity to the approximately a hundred locals it served over the years while setting high standards of journalistic excellence. Under the guidance of Tom Herriwan, Miller's successor as editor from 1972 to 1976, when he became editor of ACTWU's national paper *Labor Unity,* the *Midwest News* won top honors four years in a row in competition sponsored by the International Labor Press Association.[55]

Two other programs also promoted the general welfare of local members. The Community Services Department, established in 1966 under Counselor Jeanne Labiman, provided members with counseling and referral services concerning financial, legal, emotional, or any other "out-of-shop" problems (this program was known as the Personal Service Program after 1971).[56] When union leaders realized that half of the problems members brought to the community services counsellor were legal problems, they established a Legal Service Program in April 1972. This program provided help on such legal matters as adoption, house purchase, wills, and uncontested divorces (but not criminal matters) and included the services of an outside law firm if necessary.[57] Six thousand union members in the Chicago area registered for the legal services at the nominal fee of 50 cents a month, even before the program began offering services.

Expanded services, including the introduction of free prescription drugs in 1969, were also offered at the Sidney Hillman Health Center, which was named in 1971 as "the outstanding ambulatory outpatient medical center in the Chicago Metropolitan Area" by the city's Department of Health.[58] In March 1970, the union opened Chicago's first union-sponsored day-care center next door to the Amalgamated Center, and in October 1971, after five years of sometimes difficult planning, the Amalgamated opened Chicago's first union-sponsored cooperative housing project, the Harper Square complex overlooking Lake Michigan in the Hyde Park-Kenwood neighborhood.

The day-care center on Ashland Avenue was not the first such venture in the United States for the Amalgamated. Since 1968, the Baltimore Joint Board had sponsored a network of such centers that could accommodate a thousand children. Thus, when the Chicago Joint Board opened its center, which had a maximum capacity of seventy-five children, union leaders expressed the hope that it would be merely "the first building among many to provide day care center services for children of our members." Unfortunately such hopes were not realized in subsequent years, although ACTWU leaders in Chicago remained vocal advocates of expanded day-care services for all working mothers. In June 1979, the Amalgamated Center was the site for a conference on Labor Unions and Child Care co-sponsored by the Joint Board and the Chicago chapter of the Coalition of Labor Union Women.

The model for the union's Harper Square housing project was in New York, where the Amalgamated's United Housing Foundation had constructed some thirty thousand units of moderate-income housing since 1926. Potofsky, head of the New York housing program, was present on November 27, 1966, when Finley announced the formation of a United Dwellings Foundation to sponsor similar housing in Chicago.[59] The city's Department of Urban Renewal finally approved the foundation purchase of a seven-acre renewal site near the University of Chicago for the price of $580,000 in early 1968, and in April a gala groundbreaking ceremony was held, attended by Mayor Daley, Potofsky, Rosenblum, John Gray of Hart, Schaffner, and Marx, and other dignitaries who celebrated the beginning of construction on the $16 million project consisting of two 25-story buildings with 554 apartments and 22 low-rise townhouses.[60]

However, the optimism of the moment was soon dissipated by financing problems. Originally, Finley had intended to finance the project with Amalgamated pension funds, but they proved insufficient when interest rates grew too high to permit construction of moderately priced units. When the union failed to submit the required financing plan to the Department of Urban Renewal, the agency, in November 1969, declared the Amalgamated to be in default on its contract to develop the site.[61] Finally, in January 1970, Finley was able to announce to the city government that financing was being arranged with the Illinois Housing Development Authority, which had agreed to finance 90 percent of the project's costs through the sale of bonds, and the U.S. Department of Housing and Urban Development, which agreed to provide a subsidy so that one-third of the units could be rented to low-income families.[62]

Although Finley had once remarked that "if employers can live near the lake, so should Amalgamated members be able to look out their windows at Lake Michigan," Harper Square was never intended primarily for union members; rather, it was viewed as a community project open to both union members and the general public. As in the case of the day-care center, the aspirations for future United Dwelling Foundation projects were not realized. The first Harper Square apartments were opened on October 1, 1971; in December 1973, a day-care center was opened there under the supervision of Muriel Tuteur, and in February 1974, it became a full-fledged coop when more than three hundred residents attended a meeting chaired by the new Joint Board manager Sol Brandzel and elected their first permanent board of directors.[63]

After November 1972, when Finley and Joyce Miller left Chicago for the New York headquarters, the Chicago Joint Board was led by Sol Brandzel, a Local 39 member and long-time assistant to Frank Rosenblum, and by Arthur Loevy, Brandzel's administrative assistant, who succeeded him as manager in 1978 at the age of thirty-nine. This decade of ACTWU history in Chicago seemed in many ways to be an extension of the Finley years rather than a distinctive period. For example, new services were added to the Health Center, including a sickle cell anemia counseling program and cancer prevention clinics in 1974, and twenty-four-hour daily health emergency telephone service and high blood pressure screening tests at the members' workplaces in 1979.[64] In 1974, the Education Department held its first annual urban studies course for fifty-three members, featuring sessions on city crime and politics, Chicago ethnic history, and discriminatory mortage-lending practices.[65] The Social Services Department in Chicago was extended throughout the Midwest in 1977 by having outlying locals elect their own social services committees.[66] Also the Joint Board Locals continued and expanded their large demonstrations against cheap apparel imports and in support of three thousand striking Hispanic workers at the Farah Company's men's pants factories in El Paso and San Antonio.

According to Brandzel's comments and the opinions of other union officials, the "import problem" was first acutely felt in the Chicago market around

1970. At an anti-import rally at the Civic Center Plaza attended by Mayor Daley, Chicago Federation of Labor president Bill Lee, U.S. Congressman Ralph Metcalfe, and some three thousand demonstrators, Brandzel protested that: "Our industry is reeling from the impact of imports which have tripled and in some cases quadrupled in the last five years. In 1968, 500,000 foreign made suits were shipped into the U.S., in 1973, 2,000,000 suits, nearly 15 percent of American production. Nearly 1,000,000 of these suits come from one country, Korea. The U.S. has lost 300,000 job opportunities to imports in the last five years. Today there are 6,000 jobs in apparel factories in Chicago. We cannot afford to close Chicago factories and export these jobs to a Korean police state."[67]

This was not, however, the first major Chicago demonstration over imports. On August 2, 1969, nearly a thousand union pickets surrounded the State Street Marshall Fields' store to protest its sale of imported tailored clothing. This effort was called off by the end of the year after an informal agreement was reached with Fields' management to reduce the importation of men's suits.[68] Only a few weeks later, on March 19, 1970, more than eight thousand Amalgamated members and supporters participated in the National Impact Protest Day at Civic Center Plaza, where they were addressed by Finley, Daley, Metcalfe, and State-Treasurer Adlai Stevenson III.[69]

It is noteworthy that the loss of Chicago jobs to Asian imports produced at least two examples of cooperation between ACTWU and the ILGWU, which had traditionally had relatively little to do with one another locally. In 1976, Finley and Brandzel together with Joint Board Manager Joseph Schwartz and Assistant Manager Louis Montenegro from the ILGWU led a picket line in front of Goldblatt's department store to protest Korean imports. And in 1977, officials of the two clothing unions, along with representatives of the Church Committee on Human Rights in Asia, picketed a seminar on "Business Opportunities in Korea" sponsored by the Chicago Chamber of Commerce.

The cause of the striking Hispanic Farah employees in Texas, including the national consumer boycott against the company sponsored by the Amalgamated, was supported with vigor by Brandzel and the Chicago locals from the beginning of the strike in April 1972 until Farah granted union recognition and a three-year contract in February 1974. Amalgamated day-care center employees contributed $50 a month each to a striker's family; collections were taken at the Retiree Center; and on December 11, 1972, eight thousand union members picketed five locations of Wieboldt's department store, which had Chicago's largest Farah account.[70] In 1974, the Chicago union received an award from Jesse Jackson's Operation PUSH "for carrying on the unfinished work of Dr. Martin Luther King" in regard to its support for the Farah strikers.[71]

Sol Brandzel was also a leading advocate of nationalized health insurance during his tenure as Joint Board manager. As chairman of the Illinois Committee on Health Security, Brandzel had pushed for passage of the Kennedy–Griffiths Health Security Bill by the U.S. Congress and even roundly criticized Senator Edward Kennedy when he switched his support to a compromise measure in April 1974.[72] In 1975, Brandzel presented a petition of four thousand signatures for national health insurance to Chicago Congressman Dan Rostenkowski's committee. When Brandzel resigned as Joint Board manager in November 1978, he became temporarily the coordinator for national health insurance legislative activities at ACTWU's Legislation Department in Washington[73] and served as member and president of the Chicago Board of Education.

To a great extent, the union's prospects under Arthur Loevy depended critically on the local plans of Hart, Schaffner, and Marx. Since early in the century, Hart's plants in Chicago (and their retail stores in later decades) provided a certain measure of employment stability to a union operating in a rapidly declining market. This was particularly true during the decade following the August 1972 closing of the B. Kuppenheimer plant, which left Hart's as the only large-scale clothing employer in the Chicago market.

Although the future of Hart's itself appeared bright, prospects for its two to three thousand production employees in Chicago were much more threatening. Hart's had earned a reputation as a "very conservatively financial, well-run company" about which financial analysts "have a hard time finding something bad to say."[74] If its internal financing policies were conservative, its postwar history of acquisitions was not; even before the 1980 expiration of a Justice Department consent decree forbidding it from buying out any men's clothing retail stores for ten years, Hart's owned 274 retail stores in sixty-six cities throughout the United States. The retail division accounted in 1980 for 60 percent of the company's revenues and 45 percent of pre-tax earnings.[75] The probable future directions of the firm were indicated by chief executive Jerome Gore when he discussed acquisition possibilities. "We want to reduce our dependence on men's apparel. We also want stronger sales of apparel to women. We'd like to get into consumer businesses that have better growth potential."[76]

Corporate vice-president Sherman Rosen stated that "to the extent" Hart's stayed in manufacturing, it would be more in women's clothing, which already constituted one-fifth of its clothing production, than in men's tailored clothing. "The long-range corporate strategy is to move manufacturing operations out of the city within the next ten to fifteen years, due to considerations of plant efficiency and high wages." He cited in particular high company payments (approximately 16 percent of payroll) to the local pension and social benefits funds as an obstacle to a continuing presence in Chicago. And

Rosen admitted that the ability to negotiate more favorable wage settlements in communities outside Chicago was an "important consideration" for the firm.

In later years, almost all of Hart's expansion had been in the mid-South (e.g., Missouri, Arkansas, Kentucky, and North Carolina). When it bought out a clothing factory in Winchester, Kentucky—a shop with a long history of employer resistance to unionization—and rehired the old work force to produce coats under the Austin Reed label—for years a high quality, "Chicago" label—Hart's not only agreed to a union security clause with ACTWU, but also to place the new local under the jurisdiction of the Chicago Joint Board. Another mid-South plant was a good illustration of the dimming prospects for the Chicago work force producing high quality suits and coats under Hart's most prestigious labels: Hart's Whiteville, North Carolina plant, "probably the most modern clothing plant in the country" according to Jerome Gore, produced $100 suits under the Playboy label.

Despite its declining Chicago work force, there was no doubt that Hart, Schaffner, and Marx would continue to play a large role in the national clothing industry, and particularly in the industry's labor-management negotiations. The Chicago union's future, however, rested with its ability to adjust to the dislocations created by low-cost domestic and foreign competition. As its historical experience indicated, the Amalgamated had been gifted with a succession of creative and energetic leaders. It had established close, harmonious working relations with the major employers of the men's apparel industry. It had won for its members relatively favorable wage levels and had been a pioneer in promoting a wide array of fringe benefits. But it could not insulate its "job territory" (to adopt Selig Perlman's celebrated concept) from the forces of outside competition. For many years (until the fifties) the competition came primarily from low-cost employers in other sections of the United States. Some of this competition was unionized, but only after the most strenuous campaigning. However, the competitors from abroad (e.g., in Hong Kong, Korea, Poland, and Mexico) proved more formidable because their production costs were less amenable to American regulating controls, and they could not be organized by American unions. The result was a serious decline in union membership offset only to a limited degree by an expansion of jurisdictional boundaries into retailing, banking, and miscellaneous fields.

NOTES

This section is a condensation and revision of a report researched and written by David Nicolai.

1. *1956 Amalgamated Clothing Workers Union Convention Proceedings* (Special 50th Anniversary Issue) (New York, May 9–15, 1964), pp. 265 and 268.

2. Robert J. Myers, "The Economic Aspects of the Production of Men's Clothing," Ph.D. diss., University of Chicago, 1937, p. 26, cited in Barbara Newell, *Chicago and the Labor Movement: Metropolitan Unionism in the 1930's* (Urbana: University of Illinois Press, 1961, p. 58

3. Myers, "The Economic Aspects."

4. *Chicago Tribune*, February 6, 1940; May 18, 1944.

5. Ibid., February 6, 1940.

6. Newell, *Chicago and the Labor Movement*, p. 58.

7. The 15,000 figure is from Anglo-American Council on Productivity, *Productivity Team Report on Mens Clothing*, London 1950, p. 37.

8. The 5,000–6,000 figure is from Arthur Loevy, current Joint Board manager.

9. 1958 figure, BLS wage survey, "Wage Structure: Men's and Boy's Suits and Coats," March 1958, p. 45; 3,000–4,000 figure, BLS wage survey, "Men's and Boys' Suits and Coats," *BLS Bulletin* 1843, 1975, p. 82, and Arthur Loevy.

10. *Labor Times*, November 1977, p. 10.

11. 1966 ACWU Convention Proceedings, Atlantic City, pp. 144–45.

12. *Labor Times*, November 1977, p. 10.

13. Newell, *Chicago and the Labor Movement*, pp. 60–61.

14. Ibid., p. 61.

15. *Midwest News*, June 1973, pp. 13 and 15.

16. Interview with Michael Bugel, Local 61 business agent, March 27, 1981.

17. Interview with Sherman Rosen, Hart, Schaffner, and Marx corporate vice-president for human resources, June 1981.

18. BLS Wage Surveys, "Men's and Boys' Suits and Coats."

19. Interviews with Sherman Rosen and Attilio DiNello (business agent serving Oxxford plant), March 27, 1981.

20. BLS Wage Survey, "Men's and Boys' Suits and Coats." p. 36.

21. Ibid., pp. 36–37.

22. Harry Corbin, *The Men's Clothing Industry: Colonial through Modern Times* (New York: Fairchild Publishers, 1970), pp. 327–28.

23. BLS Wage Survey, "Men's and Boys' Suits and Coats," p. 72.

24. All figures from BLS wage surveys for 1958, 1968, and 1973.

25. Interviews with Sherman Rosen and Michael Bugel.

26. *Midwest News*, June 1973, p. 13.

27. Order of Impartial Arbitrator, original document, January 22, 1973, p. 1.

28. Ibid., pp. 2–4.

29. Interview with Michael Bugel.

30. *Midwest News*, December 1973, p. 13.

31. 1944 ACWU Convention Proceedings, p. 264.

32. *Midwest News*, December 1973, pp. 14–16.

33. 1958 ACWU Convention Proceedings, p. 155.

34. *Midwest News*, June 1977, p. 14.

35. Ibid., January 1970, p. 8.

36. Ibid., June 1969, p. 1.

37. Ibid., January 1971.

38. Ibid., January 1972, p. 1; February 1973, p. 6.

39. Interview with Sherman Rosen.

40. Reprinted in *Midwest News*, February 1977.

41. Ibid., December 1975; November 1976.

42. Ibid., June 1976.

43. Ibid., February 1977; *Chicago Tribune*, January 10, 1977.

44. *Chicago Tribune*, January 10, 1978; *Labor Times* (successor title to *Midwest News*), July 1979, p. 5.

45. *Midwest News*, February 1977; *Chicago Tribune*, February 15, 1977; May 27, 1977; *Labor Times*, November 1977.

46. *Midwest News*, June 1968; April 1972; February 1973; April 1976.

47. *Labor Times*, December 1979; June 1980; October 1980.

48. *Midwest News*, December 1972, p. 20.

49. 1960 ACWU Convention Proceedings, pp. 159–60.

50. 1962 ACWU Convention Proceedings, p. 149.

51. *Midwest News*, December 1972.

52. Ibid., March 1974.

53. Ibid., June 1969.

54. 1964 ACWU Convention Proceedings, p. 271; 1968 ACWU Convention Proceedings, p. 151.

55. *Midwest News*, September 1974; December 1975; November 1976.

56. Ibid., November 1967; June 1971.

57. Ibid., January 1972; February 1972.

58. Ibid., June 1969; November 1971.

59. *Chicago Tribune*, October 28, 1966.

60. Ibid., April 21, 1968; *Midwest News*, June 1968.

61. *Chicago Tribune*, September 14, 1969; November 19, 1969; November 30, 1969.

62. Ibid., January 21, 1970.

63. *Midwest News*, December 1973; March 1974.

64. Ibid., June 1974; July 1979.

65. Ibid., September 1974.

66. Ibid., November 1977.

67. Ibid., December 1974.

68. Ibid., October 1969; January 1970.

69. Ibid., April 1970.

70. Ibid., April 1972; December 1972; February 1973; April 1973.

71. Ibid., June 1974.

72. Ibid., March 1974.

73. Ibid., January 1979.

74. *Chicago Sun-Times*, February 22, 1981.

75. Ibid.

76. *Chicago Tribune*, April 29, 1979.

4B

The Chicago Building Trades Council

For many Americans, the two outstanding symbols of postwar Chicago were the city's awesome skyline and its legendary mayor, Richard J. Daley. The two popular symbols were not unrelated. Mayor Daley presided over the city from 1955 to 1976, a period that saw the construction of the nation's tallest building (the Sears tower), busiest airport (O'Hare International), and busiest expressway (the Dan Ryan). As Milton Rakove, one of Mayor Daley's fairest critics, wrote, "Daley is a builder, the greatest builder in Chicago's history, outstripping even former Mayor ('Big Bill the Builder') Thompson, who also left his mark on Chicago's physical appearance. 'Daley likes to build big things,' according to *Chicago Daily News* columnist Mike Royko. 'He likes highrises, expressways, parking garages, municipal buildings, and anything else that requires a ribbon-cutting ceremony and can be financed through federal funds'."[1]

Most Chicago residents shared Daley's pride in their city's great building accomplishments of the past twenty-five years, but perhaps no group was more enthusiastic about, or benefitted more from, these activities than the members of the Chicago Building Trades Council (CBTC). These construction workers, numbering 90,000 to 120,000 during the postwar years and representing more than a hundred separate locals of some nineteen international unions, provided the essential brawn and skills for the city's building projects. Equally important, their leaders provided the necessary foresight and influence to preserve Chicago's reputation as a union town, even during the late seventies when many other American cities were witnessing major incursions of nonunion construction.

Leaders of the CBTC took particular pride in their commitment to harmonious labor-management relations, best exemplified in the continuous operation of the Joint Conference Board, which, since its establishment in 1913, spared the Chicago area construction industry costly interunion jurisdictional disputes. The Joint Conference Board was not unique to Chicago—Boston and New York also had such boards—but the Chicago board compiled an outstanding record of formal and informal resolution of jurisdictional disputes.

After World War II, the Chicago building trades also produced a disproportionate number of union leaders who achieved top positions in the national labor movement. Robert Georgine, president of the AFL–CIO's Building and Construction Trade Department since 1974 and a product of Chicago's Lathers' Local 74, was only one prominent example. The laborers, operating engineers, bricklayers, cement masons, lathers, and plumbers international unions all selected Chicagoans as their presidents after 1945. Although he was largely absent from the Chicago scene after the war, Joseph Keenan, from Chicago's powerful Local 134 of the International Brotherhood of Electrical Workers, was a prominent labor statesman in many different capacities—as a participant in the reorganization of the German trade union movement immediately after the war, as the first director of the AFL's Labor League for Political Education, as the secretary of the IBEW, and as a vice-president of the AFL–CIO.

The postwar leaders of the CBTC—Patrick Sullivan (1925–58), Earl McMahon (1958–66), Thomas Murray (1966–71), and Thomas Nayder (1971–present) also enjoyed exceptionally close working relations with Mayor Daley. Their ties to Daley were based on more than their common Irish ancestry or on Daley's family ties to the building trades (his father was a long-time member of Sheet Metal Workers Local 73, and his son Michael later served as the local's attorney). The ties between Daley and the building trades leaders were based, most of all, on the mayor's firm commitment to the controversial "prevailing wage" policy for tradesmen employed by the city government. On its surface, the prevailing wage policy, which first became effective in Chicago during the thirties under Mayor Edward Kelly, merely assured that city tradesmen would receive, under an informal handshake agreement with the mayor, the same wage rates as those formally negotiated by their unions with private contractor associations in Chicago. Although building trades spokesmen staunchly defended the prevailing wage as essential to the maintenance of union conditions and as a matter of simple equity for their public-sector members, this policy was assailed over the years by diverse critics on a number of grounds: that city employees who were assured of year-round employment should not be paid hourly rates that were negotiated at high levels to compensate for the intermittent nature of most construction work; that construction wages were inappropriate for city tradesmen who allegedly performed primarily maintenance work; that the city trades jobs were an integral part of the well-known Daley-era patronage system; and, perhaps most important, that the coziness of the prevailing wage agreement was an important factor in denying the majority of city employees the benefits of bona fide collective bargaining.

Leaders of Chicago's large minority communities were particularly unhappy with their outsider status. Although the history of public controversy over the racial policies of the Chicago building trades dates back to at least 1954, when eight blacks sued Lathers Local 74 over alleged racial discrimination, the issue did not come to the forefront until the summer of 1969, when a series of dramatic confrontations between civil rights leaders, black youth groups, building trades leaders, and influential outsiders, including Mayor Daley, led to months of tense negotiations and, finally, agreement on a voluntary plan to integrate the building trades. During the next decade, despite significant progress made by several of the trades in opening their ranks to black and Latino Chicagoans, the building trades remained embroiled in often bitter controversy over their allegedly exclusionist nature.

The affiliated bodies of the CBTC all predated World War II by many years. The four district councils, which each united locals from the same international union in order to coordinate collective bargaining, apprenticeship programs, and representation to the CBTC, all dated back to the late nineteenth and early twentieth century. They were the Carpenters' District Council, with a postwar average of 30,000 members in some 45 locals; the Laborers' District Council, with some 20–25 locals whose exceptionally seasonal membership was variously reported at 15,000 to 40,000 workers; the Painters' District Council, with about 20 locals and approximately 10,000 members; and the Ironworkers' District Council, composed of 4 locals with a combined membership of perhaps 4,000–5,000 workers. The larger locals affiliated directly with the CBTC, each with an average membership in the 5,000–7,000 range, included IBEW Local 134, Operating Engineers Local 150, Plumbers Local 130, Sheet Metal Workers Local 73, Bricklayers Local 21, and Pipefitters Local 597. Smaller locals, with membership in the 1,000 to 2,000 range, included Asbestos Workers Local 17, Elevator Constructors Local 2, Lathers Local 74, Plasterers' Local 5, Cement Masons Local 502, and Composition Roofers Local 11.[2]

Earl McMahan's description of the functions of the CGTC, although written in 1947, remained true throughout the postwar period:

> The Chicago and Cook County Building and Construction Trades Council is the representative arm of the Building and Construction Trades Department [of the AFL] in the Chicago and Cook County area, and is the regional "central body" representing all building trades organizations within the Chicago and Cook County jurisdiction. . . .
>
> The Chicago Building Trades Council is in reality a "buffer." It acts on most questions involving the labor union and its critics, and on any problem affecting the trade unionist in the construction industry. It has enjoyed much success, protecting its affiliated organizations against unfair legislation, and in sponsoring legislation beneficial to the public. It has protected the buying public against faulty construction methods, and represents the building and construction mechanics on questions of civic and national character and of patriotic and common good. It also uses its best efforts to have knowledge of any problem affecting the industry in the present or the future.[3]

Some thirty-five years later, CBTC president Thomas Nayder described the main functions of the council as keeping the area locals "in tune" with the AFL–CIO's Building Trades Department, serving as a "focus" for the locals and as their central "spokesman," acting as an umbrella organization in dealings with its management counterpart, the Building Construction Employers Association of Chicago (founded in 1911), and conducting liaison work with various labor federations (e.g., the Chicago and State "Feds"). Nayder also emphasized that the CBTC does not have the authority to regulate or dictate the internal affairs or collective bargaining behavior of its affiliates; rather, the primary functions of the council fall in the realms of education and mediation.[4]

Apparently the manner of CBTC leadership varied considerably with the four postwar presidents. Nayder described Patrick Sullivan as an "autocratic" leader and noted that the chaotic conditions in the local industry before the war required such leadership. Les Asher, the long-time counsel to many of the building trades in the city, described Sullivan as a "tough guy who ran a tough union" and as a "hard-fisted" leader who "didn't care about anything but the Chicago building trades." Earl McMahon, who served as secretary of the council from 1935 and became president in 1958 at the age of sixty-four upon Sullivan's death, was described by Nayder as a "very mild" leader who "wiped away much of Sullivan's autocratic stature." Asher termed McMahon, who had originally come out of Lathers Local 74, as a "fine" leader, "understanding, very decent, and with a broader perspective [on labor issues] than Sullivan." Both men spoke less highly of McMahon's successor, Thomas Murray, a business representative from IBEW Local 134, who became president in 1966 at the age of seventy-four and served until his death in 1971. Murray served as president for only five years, but these were critical years, perhaps the most critical in the postwar history of the Chicago building trades, dominated as they were by the explosive issue of racial segregation in the trades. Nayder described it as a "very difficult" period for the aging Murray, who was from the "old line" school of business agents and who displayed "very little interest in sociological change." Asher described Murray as "more limited" than the other postwar presidents. Nayder, who was elected to his first full four-year term in 1972 at the age of fifty, was from Glaziers Local 27 and had acted as secretary-treasurer of the Council since 1958. John Boland, a veteran officer of Plasterers Local 5, considered Nayder "low-key, but firmly in control."[5]

The most important area of union activity in which the CBTC exercised minimal interference was collective bargaining. Postwar bargaining developments in the Chicago area construction industry can be analyzed in three main areas: negotiated wages and fringes, local work stoppages, and changes in collective bargaining structure, especially the emergence in 1972 of the Mid-American Regional Bargaining Association (MARBA), fourteen contractors' associations representing more than a thousand contractors from nine counties in the greater Chicago area. In the area of wages and fringe benefits, Bureau of Labor Statistics figures indicate that Chicago construction workers, like their counterparts around the country, scored impressive gains in real (inflation-adjusted) wage levels. From 1945 to 1980, when the Consumer Price Index (CPI) increased by about 333 percent, the average journeyman's wages in Chicago increased by 779 percent, from $1.79 per hour to $13.96, while helpers' and laborers' wages increased during the same period from $1.21 per hour to $11.09 or an increase of 916 percent. The wage increases for Chicago journeymen were very close to the national average, but the increases for helpers and laborers lagged somewhat behind the national average.[6]

Chicago's wages were fully 22 percent above the national average in 1945, but only 13 percent in 1980. In 1945, only three American cities had journeymen's wages higher than Chicago's average of $1.79. But by 1980, Chicago's average hourly rate of $13.41 (averaging in both journeymen and helpers and laborers) was exceeded by three Great Lake cities (Toledo, $14.23; Cleveland, $13.69; and Cincinnati, $13.51) and two West Coast cities (San Francisco, $14.87; Seattle, $14.77).[7]

More significantly for a high-wage area, Chicago building trades unions lagged behind national trends in the negotiations of fringe benefits (e.g., health and welfare funds, pension funds, and paid vacation). For example, in 1970, the average employer contribution per hour to fringe benefits in Chicago was 61 cents, whereas nationwide it was 80 cents; the corresponding 1980 figures were $2.33 and $2.83. By 1980, workers in nineteen cities were ahead of their Chicago counterparts in total compensation."[8]

Top union and management officials in the Chicago construction industry were particularly proud about the so-called "Chicago Labor Peace Formula." The twelve representatives of the Building Construction Employers' Association (BCEA) and the twelve representatives of the CBTC who comprised the Joint Board issued a total of 312 official resolutions of jurisdictional disputes between 1946 and 1977, or approximately ten per year (compared with only 167 between the board's establishment in 1913 and 1945).[9] Many more disputes were settled informally on the job.

Once a dispute reached the Joint Board and a decision had been handed down, Chicago building trades unions could appeal the local decision to the National Joint Board for the Settlement of Jurisdictional Disputes, which was established by the AFL's Building and Construction Trades Department in 1948. A 1963 article in the *Federation News* noted that in the local board's first fifty years of existence only six out of its 377 decisions had been reversed by the national board.[10] However, between 1970 and 1977, the national board affirmed only four of the Chicago board's determinations, while reversing nine of them.[11]

The success of the Chicago Joint Board in eliminating jurisdictional strikes is best reflected in the fact that such strikes accounted for a fifth of all strikes in the national construction industry. But the elimination of jurisdictional strikes did not mean that the Chicago building trades were immune from more customary work stoppages over wages and working conditions. The best estimate is that some thirty strikes or lockouts occurred in the Chicago industry between 1945 and 1980. These work stoppages occurred more frequently in the later part of the period than in the earlier part. A ten-week strike/lockout involving Lathers Local 74 in 1950 was reliably described as the first major work stoppage in the local industry in thirty-one years;[12] three more strikes took place in the fifties, while eight occurred in the sixties, and nineteen in the seventies. The most disruptive period for the local industry was unquestionably the late sixties and early seventies, when strikes over traditional economic demands, safety conditions, and the insistence by some contractors' associations on regional bargaining, plus continuing controversies over racial segregation in the trades, combined to produce an exceptional number of work stoppages. During this period the construction of such well-known Chicago buildings as the Daley Center, the Federal Center, the John Hancock Building, and the Sears Tower was hampered by work stoppages.

Perhaps a third of all the postwar strikes were quite short (five working days or less); most of the longer strikes did not involve any efforts to close down the entire local industry; and the vast majority of the strikes, whether long or short, revolved around bread-and-butter issues of wage increases or changes in work rules.

With the exception of two nationwide strikes by the International Union of Elevator Constructors, which lasted 53 days in 1966 and 101 days in 1972,[13] the longest work stoppages to hit the Chicago industry were the aforementioned 68-day strike by Lathers Local 74 in 1950, a 55-day strike by Plumbers Local 130 in 1954, a 49-day strike by Operating Engineers Local 150 in 1966, a 47-day strike by Cement Masons Local 502 in 1970, and a 57-day strike by six Teamster locals representing drivers who transported construction materials in 1974. All these lengthy work stoppages, with the exception of the unique Lathers dispute in 1950, concerned wage and/or rule demands.

According to William McCabe, the executive director of MARBA, the unprecedented size of the 1970 settlements with the Operating Engineers and the Cement Masons—along with a ten-week strike the same year by the Will County District Council of Carpenters that resulted in hourly rates $1.42 higher than those in Cook County—convinced leading Chicago contractors and business figures that steps to counteract inflationary wage settlements in the local industry were urgent.[14] Clearly their concern over inflationary contracts was not without basis; wage increases in Chicago and nationwide set postwar records in both 1970 and 1971. Chicago construction wages increased

13.6 percent on average in 1970 (13 percent nationwide) and 14.8 percent in 1971 (12.2 percent nationwide).[15] These levels of wage increase led to the imposition of direct wage controls on the construction industry (and later on the rest of the economy) by the Nixon administration through the establishment of the Construction Industry Stabilization Committee in March 1971. This period was, moreover, characterized by a record building boom in Chicago; in 1971, the value of building permits for the city easily set a postwar high of $801 million, while the value of permits for the years 1968, 1969, 1970, and 1972 was also extremely high, in the $500–575 million range each year.[16]

On July 6, 1970, while the Operating Engineers' and Cement Masons' walkouts were still underway, Robert C. Gunness, president of Standard Oil (Indiana) promoted the formation of the Chicago Construction Users' Council, with the cooperation of top officers of nine major Chicago firms including Commonwealth Edison, International Harvester, Illinois Bell, Inland Steel, and Sears-Roebuck.[17] As Franke and Hartman have noted, more than fifty-five such users' councils were formed by mid–1975 through the construction section of the Business Roundtable.[18]

Gunness stated the Chicago Users' Council's goals to be the support of contractors during negotiations in order to avoid excessive wage increases, encouragement of "expanded trade membership" (i.e., encouraging certain trades to train more apprentices in order to avoid skilled labor shortages), the elimination of both overtime work (except in emergencies) and restrictive work rules, and the establishment of reasonable completion dates for construction work. He noted that "construction users, contractors, and building trades unions all share the blame for the excessive increases in building costs." He criticized major construction users, who were eager to see their projects completed on a timely basis, for condoning the payment of excessive overtime pay and high wage rates. As a consequence, Gunness concluded, "building contractors have been under little pressure to bargain more effectively with the unions."[19]

According to McCabe, Gunness and Frederick Jaicks, chairman of Inland Steel and Gunness's successor in 1973 as chairman of the local users' council, were instrumental in the formation of MARBA in December 1971.[20] Robert E. Nielsen, vice-president of the Builders' Association and the first chairman of MARBA, stated that MARBA members intended to unite in negotiations in order to achieve common wage rates, work rules, and contract expiration dates for individual trades in the nine-county area.

In April 1972, William McCabe announced that MARBA intended to negotiate regional contracts in the spring bargaining season with four trades— the cement masons, bricklayers, carpenters, and laborers. He warned that unless the Chicago industry introduced regional bargaining, open-shop construction, factory-produced buildings, and government intervention would threaten the future of both unions and contractors in the Chicago area.[21]

Robert Wilke, secretary-treasurer of the CBTC under Nayder, noted that MARBA came on "very strong" during this initial attempt at wide-area bargaining.[22] Nayder and Wilke co-authored a long *Federation News* article condemning MARBA's "bullish approach to labor relations." Their criticisms centered not so much on regional bargaining per se, which they admitted had "some advantages," but rather on McCabe's alleged failure to discuss the possibility of regional bargaining with leading union and contractor representatives before issuing an ultimatum to the unions at his well-publicized April press conference.

The Construction and General Laborers District Council of Chicago and vicinity was the first local union to reach agreement with MARBA negotiators in 1972. The one-year pact signed on June 3, 1972 provided a 50 cent (7 percent) increase in wages and benefits and, according to a MARBA report, "important work rule concessions . . . which still remain goals in other MARBA trades . . . [including] eight hours of overtime at time and one-half rates on Saturday and a flexible starting time."[23] Speaking to the 1972 operating engineers convention, the international president of the Laborers Union, Peter Fosco, strongly endorsed regional bargaining in order to end "the competition among unions . . . to outdo each other at the bargaining table" that was inherent in the fragmented bargaining structure of the industry.[24] Although MARBA continued to sign twelve separate agreements with the Laborers Union in the nine-county region, according to McCabe, who labelled it "coordinated bargaining," "all [were] bargained at one table and at the same time."[25]

The 1972 negotiations between MARBA and the other three basic trades were all marked by serious work stoppages. On June 5, Bricklayers Local 21, which represented about 5,000 bricklayers in Cook County and which had already signed a one-year pact providing a 51 cent increase with one MARBA affiliate, the Builders' Association, began selective strikes against contractors belonging to another MARBA association, the Mason Contractors Association of Greater Chicago, which employed around 40 percent of Cook County bricklayers. The selective strikes escalated two days later into an employer lock-out, and the next day into blanket picketing by Local 21, idling an estimated $60 million in Cook County construction before the strike was called off on June 9. The cause of the strike was not pay, but rather the mason contractors' insistence on numerous work rule changes and on the union's desire for the establishment of a local industry promotion fund. Apparently, the 1972 strike was settled without agreement on these issues, which were not resolved until 1973, when the mason contractors joined in unified MARBA negotiations.

The one-week Bricklayers' strike in 1972 was only a prelude to the two more lengthy MARBA-related strikes that year. Cement Masons Local 50 began a three-week strike on June 19, and on June 21, the Chicago District Council of Carpenters walked out, also for a three-week strike—the first strike by that body since 1919. Again the key issues were MARBA's demands for work-rule changes involving, among others, lunch hour scheduling, crew sizes, and starting times.[26]

The Cement Masons and Carpenters initiated selective picketing on June 21 at such major job sites as the Sears Tower, the Standard Oil Building, and the new Federal Building downtown, and on July 26 MARBA contractors retaliated with a nine-county lock-out of the two trades.

The three-week work stoppages reportedly idled at times as many as 70,000–80,000 building tradesmen in the area and more than $15 billion worth of new construction before settlements were reached with both trades on July 6. The Carpenter District Council approved, 136 to 3, a one-year pact providing $1.15 in wage and benefit increases (13 percent) and various work rule changes including no restrictions on the introduction of new tools and machinery into the local industry—a significant breakthrough for the MARBA negotiators.[27] The Cement Masons' contract contained a much smaller wage increase—at 5.5 percent it exactly met the guidelines used by the Construction Industry Stabilization Committee, but the union was able to maintain all existing work rules including the bitterly disputed provision for double-time pay for all work done during the customary lunch period of 12:00–12:30 p.m.[28]

For Operating Engineers Local 150, 1973 was their first year of negotiations with MARBA. These negotiations resulted in moderate wage increases—55 cents (5.2 percent) in 1973 and 50 cents (4.5 percent) in 1974—and some MARBA-proposed work rule changes.[29] In striking contrast with its prior history, Local 150 began a strike-free bargaining relationship with MARBA that lasted throughout the remainder of the seventies. As in the case of the Laborers, both international presidents during the seventies, Hunter Wharton and J. D. Turner, were vocal advocates of regional bargaining.[30]

Despite a short 1973 strike, the Laborers and MARBA achieved what many observers hailed as a milestone in statesmanlike bargaining for the Chicago area in 1975. On January 9, almost six months before the expiration of the existing contract, District Council president Joseph Spignola announced agreement on a one-year pact, effective June 1, providing no wage increase and only a 25 cent increase in pension fund contributions. Spignola stated that the decision to forego a wage increase was approved unanimously by the District Council representatives of the twenty-four local laborers' unions. "We hope that this restraint of wage demand will be reflected by a renewed

end to the city's payment of construction wages to maintenance workers. The bill apparently died in the Council Finance Committee headed by Alderman Thomas Keane, the floor leader of the city council and reputedly the "'second-in-command' of the [Daley] machine."[39] The Civic Federation estimated that the Hoellen Bill would have saved the city about $6,000,000 in its 1964 budget.[40]

In 1969, Judge P. J. Trapp of the Illinois Appellate Court for the Fourth District handed down the final court decision involving the coverage of the prevailing wage law. *Mahin v. Myers* (108 Ill. App. 2nd 416) stemmed from a suit brought by the Illinois Association for Mental Health, the Better Government Association, and six citizens against the directors of the state Department of Personnel and Mental Health, protesting the payment of 514 maintenance employees of the Mental Health Department at the prevailing construction wage for their trades. Judge Trapp dismissed the plaintiffs' suit, holding that the combined effect of *Bradley v. Casey* and *Monmouth v. Lorenz* was to find that no government unit in Illinois could be required to pay the prevailing wage, but none was prohibited from doing so.[41]

Thus under the Supreme Court and Appellate Court decisions, the legality of Chicago prevailing wage practices appeared to be uncertain. But the city's policy actually predated state regulations by eight years and obviously enjoyed strong support in later years regardless of the court challenges to the state law. The Civic Federation reported that the local practice dated back to 1933, the inaugural year of Mayor Edward Kelly.

Nayder believed that the later years of Mayor Kelly, who left office in 1947, were when "the prevailing wage understanding really took hold." Nonetheless, it was Mayor Daley who became the best-known practitioner of the prevailing wage handshake agreement during the postwar period. Throughout his twenty-one year reign as mayor, Daley consistently rebuffed the criticisms of the prevailing wage offered by the Civic Federation, the Better Government Association, the daily papers, anti-machine aldermen, and others, by insisting that it was not city policy to pay its maintenance workers wages above those in the private sector. When critics cited BLS wage surveys showing that city wages for maintenance and custodial workers were as much as 26 percent above those in private industry,[42] Daley responded by noting that the private-sector wage average was lowered by the presence of nonunionized employees, although this could hardly have been a significant factor in the virtually 100 percent unionized building trades (or building maintenance).[43]

Building trades spokesmen, on the other hand, maintained that the distinction between construction and maintenance work was a "stupid, childish argument." Also, as the building trades unions steadily negotiated substantial fringe benefits into their contracts, including health and pension benefits and paid holidays and vacations, it was no longer clearly the case that the city's benefits were superior to those of tradesmen entitled to contractual fringes. In 1963, both Stephen Bailey of the Plumbers and Francis X. McCurtin, business manager of Pipefitters Local 597, maintained that their members employed by private contractors received better benefits than their counterparts employed by the city.[44] Finally, it was not definitely the case that the vast majority of city tradesmen enjoyed steady, year-round employment. Arthur Lindell, director of the city budget, stated in 1964 that city prevailing-wage workers averaged 194 days of work a year, whereas non-city tradesmen averaged 200 days a year.[45]

In Chicago, the prevailing wage system also played a political role that may well have far outweighed in significance the policy's economic impact on local governments. That role was "to consummate a marriage," as Sidney Lens put it, between the business unionists who dominated the Chicago Federation of Labor and the patronage-oriented local Democratic party leaders. In his widely read 1969 study, *Labor in American Politics*, David Greenstone analyzed the relations between the leaders of the CFL and of the local party—two elites bound by a preference for "relatively narrow politics of group and individual interests" in a city "where politics was most fundamentally not a contest for power and therefore control over public policy, but a primary source of livelihood and only secondarily a contest for power."[46]

Lens believed that the "10,000–12,000 jobs covered by the prevailing wage system [were] choice," and Daley "for his own reasons, wanted them to remain choice." Not only did the jobs gain Daley the loyalty of important union leaders, but also, in turn,

> craft-union leaders were able to place a sizable number of their favored members in choice city jobs, the *quid pro quo* was that those members found a nucleus of support for their benefactors in inner-union affairs. Daley has institutionalized and modernized this system, eliminating some of its gross features, such as patronage in the hospital, but the power of old-line unionists (called business unionists by labor writers) has never been greater. They serve on licensing boards for certain skilled tradesmen, they have a voice in the operation of craft schools like Washburne, and because of their long established ties to politicians, they still have a major input in hiring and firing.[47]

Greenstone cited three main factors that strengthened the CFL–Democratic party alliance in Chicago. First, there was a "complex exchange of special favors and benefits." Second, there was "an informal elite network, [which] by cutting across formal party and union structures, permitted individual leaders to pyramid or multiply their power."

The third factor was that "the CFL leadership shared with most party leaders a lower-class, usually Irish Catholic background, and the native ability and toughness that helped both groups achieve organizational and economic success."[48] The leadership on both sides of the CFL-party alliance was

thoroughly dominated by Irish-American natives of the city—many of t
from Daley's own neighborhood, Bridgeport, the adjacent Back-of-the-Yar
district, or other southwest side working-class neighborhoods.

Many top building trades leaders did not hesitate to display their sincere
enthusiasm for their Irish Catholic heritage. For example, Stephen Bailey,
and then his nephew and successor as business manager of Plumbers Local
130, Stephen Lamb, served each year as chairman of the St. Patrick's Day
Parade. An annual Labor Mass, begun by the Building Trades Council in
1940, was faithfully attended by a who's who, primarily of Irish union and
party leaders, in addition to thousands of building trades members.[49] The
Reverend Joseph Donahue, the council's chaplain and a former lather, wrote
a column for the building trades edition of the *Federation News* for twenty
years; in 1970, he was appointed a special assistant to Thomas Nayder after
being fired as chaplain at a state mental institution whose "deplorable" conditions he publicly condemned.[50]

The prevailing wage agreement was considered a major factor in determin-
ing the overall political orientation of top CFL and building trades leaders.
It promoted an emphasis on both local and state politics over national politics.
However, Chicago building trades leaders did not completely ignore national
politics. For example, in the early sixties, McMahan, Nayder, Asher and
Stanley Johnson led delegations of local union leaders during the annual
AFL–CIO Building Trades Department's legislative conferences in
Washington. They visited the offices of every member of Congress from
Illinois to inquire about positions on such federal legislation as the Davis–
Bacon Act, on-site picketing, and federal aid to education.[51]

At least since the local AFL–CIO merger in the early sixties, such efforts
primarily benefitted Democratic candidates; according to Nayder, the council
usually passed a general "supportive resolution" for all candidates endorsed
by the Committee on Political Education (COPE). But building trades politics
on the state level could be surprisingly bipartisan. Three Republican governors—Dwight Green (1940–48), William Stratton (1952–60), and Richard
Ogilvie (1968–72) — enjoyed strong support within the building trades.
Green, in fact, placed Earl McMahan on the state payroll for two years
(1944–46) at $200 a month as a representative of the state Labor Department
scouting employment opportunities for returning GIs. Roy Cummins from
IBEW Local 134 served for eight years as director of labor under Governor
Stratton, who maintained a "very open door relationship" with state labor
leaders, according to Nayder.[52] Even a Republican with a reformist "anti-
machine" reputation such as Ogilvie could gain building trades support,
perhaps because of his working relations with local union leaders when he
served as president of the Cook County Board, whereas his successor, Daniel
Walker, a Democrat with similar anti-machine credentials, could count on no

ng trades leaders enthusiastically supported Michael
vith close family ties to the building trades, in the 1976
atic primary against the incumbent Walker.[53] Many
ades leaders were active Republicans in their com-

...oned "favorable ordinances governing the construction
...mportant favor granted the union by Chicago party leaders,
and another political scientist, William Grimshaw, wrote that "the City's
endlessly elaborate, highly restrictive, and cost-escalating building code tes-
tifies to the considerable strength of organized labor." But there is scant
historical evidence of public controversies over the code. A 1967 *Chicago
Sun-Times* article reported that the code had undergone its last major revision
in 1949. Every attempt to modernize the code brought forth the bitter and
militant opposition of the building trades unions, and less openly, certain
monopolistic building materials interests.[54] No further mention of the building
code can be found until the late seventies, when the nationwide trend of
revitalizing innercity areas through the rehabilitation of older buildings became noticeable in Chicago. *Chicago Sun-Times* editorials in 1978 and 1979
condemned the code as "an 800-page mares' nest that facilitates graft . . . and,
in its protection of construction union interests, kites costs by forbidding the
use of modern, money-saving materials like plastic waste pipes, non-metallic
sheeted electrical cable and fiberglass bathtubs." The code, according to the
paper, raised the costs of renovating a Chicago home by $2,000–4,000.[55]

Whether or not Chicago actually had the nation's strictest building codes,
as critics alleged, it was clear that local politicians did not consider it necessary to remove the code's enforcement from union influence. The city employed a large number of building inspectors (approximately 370 in 1978),
all of them allegedly members of building trades unions, to enforce the code.
Most of these workers were paid the prevailing wage, although some, including the electrical and plumbing inspectors, were reportedly paid at the high
union wage for private construction foremen. These jobs were considered
choice patronage positions.[56]

Many union officials also headed the public agencies that supervised areas
of interest to their trades. Although it was not possible to compile a complete
list of such officials, a few examples were James Cusack from Sheet Metal
Worker Local 73, who was chief of the City Bureau of Heating, Ventilation,
and Industrial Sanitation; Gerald Sullivan, treasurer of IBEW Local 134 and
superintendent of the Cook County Department of Construction, Maintenance, and Operations; and Michael Kennedy, Boyles's successor as business
manager of Local 134 and City Commissioner of Gas and Electricity.[57]
Perhaps the most prominent example was William Hogan, Thomas Murray's
successor as president of Local 134 and chief of the city Bureau of Electrical

Inspection until his resignation under fire in March 1980 following a three-year investigation of the department by U.S. Attorney Thomas P. Sullivan and FBI agents; the investigation resulted in 25 out of the city's 70 electrical inspectors being convicted of charges of accepting bribes.[58]

The first known legal protest against discriminating practices in the local building trades came in 1953, when eight black applicants for membership in Lathers Local 74 filed a lawsuit alleging that they had been denied admission solely on the basis of their race. The suit was not settled until March 1958, when U.S. District Judge Joseph Perry issued a consent decree forbidding racial discrimination by either the local or the Employing Lathers' Association of Chicago. Although the union's attorney acknowledged that only nine out of Local 74's nine hundred members were black, and although the union agreed to pay $500 in damages to each of the eight plaintiffs and $6,000 in legal expenses, the union did not concede that it was guilty of discrimination, contending instead that it agreed to the decree in order to avoid a lengthy and expensive trial. Five years later, Local 74 reported only seven black journeymen.[59]

With the exception of this one isolated and ineffective consent decree, challenges to the building trades' methods of recruitment were not raised until 1961. These challenges were raised by the Negro American Labor Council and centered on admissions policies to Washburne Trade School. Washburne, founded in 1919 and operated by the Chicago Board of Education, had for years trained the large majority of skilled trades apprentices in the metropolitan area, while acquiring a nationwide reputation for producing highly skilled journeymen. Students entered Washburne only after already receiving their high school diploma and attended classes only one day a week while working as paid apprentices during the remainder of the week. By far the most important distinction between Washburne and more conventional trade schools was the fact that admission to Washburne was controlled not by the Chicago Board of Education or Washburne administrators, but rather by the joint apprenticeship committees of the twelve skilled trades that utilized the school's facilities. These committees were composed of an equal number of representatives from the union and the contractors in each trade.

For many outsiders, however, it was difficult to determine whether the board of education, the unions, or the contractors were most responsible for any discrimination that did occur in apprenticeship programs.[60] In 1961, after representatives of the Negro American Labor Council presented at public hearings of the board of education the results of a survey they had conducted showing that only 1 percent of Washburne's 2,600 students were black, the superintendent of education simply responded "no comment" when asked if the board had any responsibility to combat segregation at the facility. At the same hearings, Thomas Murray, board member and future president of the

CBTC, stated that "it was in the tradition of the skilled trades to admit whom they pleased, and that only incidentally were Negroes the victims more than whites. If there were Negroes in the skilled trades, they would have the same privileges of using discrimination as the whites now enjoyed."[61]

Approximately one week after the Chicago Board of Education hearings and one week after the Illinois AFL–CIO convention adopted—following "hot and heavy" debate—a resolution calling for the appointment or election of a racially integrated committee to work toward the goal of racially integrated apprenticeship programs,[62] members of the U.S. House of Representatives Subcommittee on Labor, chaired by Congressman James Roosevelt convened two days of hearings in Chicago to explore the dimensions of local employment discrimination and the need for a federal equal employment opportunity statute.

During these hearings Mayor Daley spoke with particular pride about the work of the Chicago Commission on Human Relations (CCHR), which had been established in 1947 under Mayor Kelly as the first such municipal antidiscrimination agency in the United States. Indeed, during the early sixties, this commission did play a leading role in trying to combat segregation in the local building trades. It joined hands with the Chicago Urban League in pleading privately with the Board of Education to exert more control over admissions to Washburne, but, according to a study by Jo An Chandler, the board members' belief that there was absolutely nothing they could or should do about the situation controlled the board's actions for almost six years.[63]

More positively, the CCHR began to correct perhaps the most important barrier to significant antidiscrimination efforts, that is, the lack of reliable information. In 1962, it began gathering statistics on minority involvement in apprenticeship programs and overall minority membership in the trades. That year, it was also responsible for beginning a semimonthly, trade-by-trade reporting system for minority employment on both the new Federal Center and Civic Center downtown.[64] And in December 1963, Edward Marciniak, the executive director of CCHR, reported to the city council that a commission survey showed that twelve unions covered by the city's prevailing wage agreement—eight of them in the building trades—had no black members.[65]

On July 16, 1963, shortly after announcing to the city council his conviction that the Chicago building trades would soon be the first in the United States to achieve racial integration, Mayor Daley met privately with leading figures from the unions to secure their cooperation in opening up apprenticeship opportunities to black youths. Daley termed the meeting "fine and cooperative," and the following day the members of the CBTC voted "to use every effort to implement the Mayor's program." Unfortunately, it was never publicly stated exactly what Daley's program was, and nothing more was ever heard of efforts stemming from this meeting.[66]

The acquiescence of the board of education, the union, and the Department of Labor in a discriminatory apprenticeship program was condemned in an October 1963 court decision, *Todd v. Joint Apprenticeship Committee.* Federal District Judge William Campbell ordered Structural Ironworkers Local 1 to accept as apprentices two black applicants and certify them for work on the Federal Center. Judge Campbell noted that none of the eight hundred apprentices accepted by the Joint Apprenticeship Committee of the Steelworkers (i.e., Ironworkers) since 1952 had been black; moreover, few blacks had ever applied to the committee because of the "potent futility" of their application. The decision also criticized the board of education for making its facilities available to an "invidiously discriminatory" scheme and the Chicago office of the Department of Labor's Bureau of Apprenticeship and Training for its "overall apathy to the problem."[67]

The year 1964, which saw the enactment of the Federal Civil Rights Act in Washington, was marked in Chicago by the establishment of an Apprenticeship Information Center in March and the appointment of a "Washburne subcommittee" by the board of education in August. According to Raymond Scannell, then director of employment services for the CCHR, the groups most opposed to the establishment of the center were the joint apprenticeship committees, the board of education, and the U.S. Department of Labor's Bureau of Apprenticeship and Training. Whereas the sponsors of the center hoped to see it actively involved in recruiting functions in the black community, the center's opponents wanted it to exist for information purposes only. Recruitment by the center in Chicago's black communities did not become substantial until 1967.[68]

The formation of the Washburne subcommittee by the board of education was a response to a June 1964 letter from the CCHR to the board listing four trades that had never had a black participant in their Washburne programs — sheet metal workers, structural ironworkers, ornamental ironworkers, and pipe fitters — and requesting that public funds and facilities be withdrawn from any trades that persisted in such discrimination. Subcommittee members Thomas Murray and Thomas Nayder stated that the board would be going "far afield" from its responsibilities if it began demanding that a certain number of Washburne apprentices be black. Murray also claimed that interference from the board would lead the unions to abandon Washburne and set up their own schools, and he suggested that the federal government or the CCHR should be responsible for eliminating any discrimination.[69] It was not until July 1965, following further prodding by the CCHR, that the board adopted a policy of "requiring unions wishing to use public trade or vocational schools to attest in writing that their employment practices adhered to the 1964 Civil Rights Act."

Perhaps motivated by the board of education's continuing failure to address this problem aggressively, Mayor Daley announced in December 1965 a "Plan for Chicago,"

A joint venture by the unions, employers, the Board of Education, the Illinois State Employment Service, the Manpower Administration of the Department of Labor, the Urban League, and other civil rights groups . . . [involving] four main areas of activities: active recruitment by unions and employers from minority groups; surveys by the public schools to locate potential applicants from the vocational schools; processing and referral by the Apprenticeship Information Center; and coordination and technical personnel services to be provided by the manpower administration, and the Board of Education to provide remedial courses for those interested but not qualified for the programs.[70]

In September 1966, Edward Marciniak announced that, with the acceptance of a black apprentice by the Structural Ironworkers' apprenticeship committee, Chicago had become the first city in the United States in which all the building trades had accepted black apprentices.

Progress, however, was uneven among the trades, undoubtedly because of the autonomy of the individual trade's joint apprenticeship committees; by 1969, for example, blacks constituted fully 40 percent of the apprentices in the plastering program at Washburne, 15 percent in painting and cement masonry, 11 percent in lathing, 8 percent in structural ironworking, 6 percent in carpentry, plumbing, and electrical work, and only 2 percent in pipe fitting, architectural ironworking, and sprinkler fitting.[71]

Nonetheless, much had been accomplished by the late sixties. Perhaps the most important was, in the words of a BCEA report, simply "the coming together of groups that literally had no [prior] knowledge of each other's interests or concern."[72] Chandler reported that the recruiting efforts of both the Apprenticeship Information Center and Urban League had become increasingly aggressive by 1969, and that the board of education with its new superintendent, James Redmond, was increasingly cooperative about disseminating the necessary information on opportunities at Washburne to officials at other Chicago public schools.[73]

Meanwhile, the CCHR had begun concentrating most of its resources on its Contractor's Compliance Program, which had been initiated in the mid-sixties and which was recommended by the U.S. Conference of Mayors in 1966 as a model for other American cities. This program used voluntary means to encourage contractors doing business with the city to increase the number of their minority employees and to raise the number of black contractors holding contracts with the city government.

However, a 1969 CCHR report concluded, "The current system of employment by the construction industry has worked in the past but unfortunately some individual trades and contractors have not presented full economic participation to the black community. Any future efforts must demonstrate that the construction industry actively encourages employment of minority groups and finds ways to qualify people.[74]

These words were written approximately two months after major protests over building trades segregation had occurred in Chicago. On July 2, 1969, seventeen black youths occupied and barricaded the entrances to the CBTC offices at 130 North Wells Street, following a demonstration by 100–200 protesters who picketed the nearby First National Bank Building site to demand immediate union jobs for blacks.

The following day, pickets halted rehabilitation work on three apartment buildings in Lawndale, one of the most devastated black neighborhoods on the West Side. A coalition of sixty-one black community organizations and "street gangs," named the Coalition for United Community Action (CUCA) and headed by the Reverend C. T. Vivian, announced at a press conference that the Lawndale picketing was prompted by the failure of the projects' general contractor to honor the agreement to award $1,900,000 in subcontracts to members of the West Side Builders' Association, a group of eighty black contractors. According to a spokesman for these builders, they had actually received only $75,000 in subcontracts.

Within a week young blacks had halted perhaps $80 million worth of construction on the city's south and west sides, including a number of major buildings at the University of Chicago and stations on the Dan Ryan rapid transit system. Following two unsuccessful meetings between representatives of CUCA, CBTC, and BCEA, a five-hour meeting on August 21 ended with representatives from all three groups reporting that "definite areas of agreement had been found in the month-long dispute."[75]

On August 26, the Reverend Ralph Abernathy, head of the Southern Christian Leadership Conference (SCLC), which sponsored one of the constituent organizations of CUCA, Operation Breadbasket, addressed 2,400 delegates attending the annual Illinois AFL–CIO conference at the Conrad Hilton Hotel. Abernathy expressed full SCLC support for the CUCA protestors, who "have put aside the slogan, 'Burn, Baby, Burn,' and have replaced it with the slogan, 'Build, Baby, Build.'" "Young blacks, uneducated though they may be, poor though they may be, if they can learn to fight and kill in Vietnam for Democracy, can learn to be plumbers and electricians in the building trades industry."[76]

Whatever goodwill Abernathy had created with the union delegates must have been severely damaged two days later, when the convention was disrupted by a dozen blacks led by Meredith Gilbert of the Lawndale People's Planning and Action Committee, who reportedly "mounted the speakers' stand, pushed aside Reuben Soderstrom [the 82-year-old president of the State Federation], and assailed the delegates" for the alleged weakness of a resolution they had adopted supporting blacks in their efforts to achieve equal employment opportunity and job-training programs.[77]

The disruption of the convention, along with escalating CUCA demands including full CUCA control of a training program, funded by "labor and management," open to trainees "without testing or prior experience, with or without a police record," and operative until 30 percent of the members of each trade were black, led to another breakdown in negotiations between CUCA, CBTC, and BCEA.[78] Public demonstrations also resumed on September 8 for the first time since a circuit court judge had enjoined picketing of construction sites in mid-August. A confrontation between around five hundred black demonstrators and two hundred policemen at a building site on the Chicago Circle campus of the University of Illinois involved some shoving and rock throwing, but no serious violence, although the Reverend Jesse Jackson, the 27-year-old director of Operation Breadbasket, and four other demonstrators were arrested for trespassing.[79]

Negotiations dragged on for another four months before an agreement for a new "Chicago Plan" was signed on January 12, 1970. The agreement contained the following provisions:

1. The unions and contractors would bring 4,000 blacks into the industry as soon as possible by hiring and admitting to union membership 1,000 tradesmen already fully qualified, enrolling 1,000 partially skilled blacks in abbreviated apprenticeship programs, giving free apprenticeship training to 1,000 youths to enable them to meet entrance requirements, and employing 1,000 others as on-the-job trainees.
2. Unions and employers would attempt to increase black representation in the 90,000 industry work force "at least proportionate to their percentage in the community-at-large" (estimated at 20 percent) within five years.
3. None of the nineteen building trades unions would be required to participate in a training program; those that do would work with CUCA representatives to devise a training program.
4. Where possible, the training programs would be operated separately from the existing apprentice programs and on an accelerated basis.
5. A committee consisting of two blacks, two union officials, two contractors, and Mayor Daley or his representative would work to implement training programs agreed upon by each participating union and would seek government funding for such programs. This committee would act only upon the vote of five out of the seven members.[80]

Any hopes that the January agreement would end public controversy over the racial situation in the building trades were not long-lived. On July 22, 1970, John Wilks, head of the U.S. Department of Labor's Office of Federal Contract Compliance Program, announced that his office was conducting an investigation based on charges made by minority groups that there had not been a good-faith effort to move forward with the plan. Wilks charged that not one person had been trained under the program during its first six months and explained that, in his opinion, "a major cause that the program is not moving ahead is because of the conduct of the craft unions which have never committed themselves to accept a given number of trainees." The one exception, Wilks noted, was the operating engineers.[81]

On July 28, following a two-day investigation of the Chicago Plan by some of his colleagues, Herbert Hill, the national labor director of the NAACP and a long-time (and harsh) critic of craft union exclusionism, announced that the plan was not working and that he was sending a telegram to U.S. Secretary of Labor James Hodgson urging the end to all federal funding of construction projects in Chicago and two sweeping revisions in the Chicago Plan: a specified minimum number of minority workers would be employed in each craft and at each stage of construction and union membership would not be required of minority participants. Alderman Fred Hubbard (D.-2nd Ward), Mayor Daley's appointee as administrative head of the plan, rebutted Hill's charge with a claim that the plan would be responsible for the employment of five hundred new workers by the end of October.[82] However, in late May, it was discovered that Alderman Hubbard had fled from Chicago after apparently embezzling $100,000 of Chicago Plan funds by forging Thomas Nayder's signature on a number of checks. Hubbard was eventually apprehended by FBI agents in a gambling establishment outside Los Angeles in August 1972 and found guilty of sixteen federal counts of embezzlement. He had been widely regarded as one of Chicago's most promising young black politicians before his conviction and fifteen-month stay in federal prison. His actions not only destroyed his political career, but also resulted in the Department of Labor's refusal to grant further funds to the Chicago Plan, which terminated on June 30, 1971.[83]

The second Chicago Plan took even longer to negotiate and was in effect for an even shorter period than the first one. Donald Irwin began to lead efforts to negotiate a new plan soon after his appointment as the Chicago area regional director of the U.S. Department of Labor in January 1972. However, final agreement was delayed until October because of controversy over the Urban League's central role in the plan.

CUCA leaders were extremely dissatisfied with the designation of the Urban League as the sole representative of minority interests in the new plan proposed by Irwin. In June and July of 1972, CUCA members decided once again to take direct action on job discrimination with a "summer offensive" of visiting construction sites throughout the city and halting work, if necessary, until the contractors agreed to increase the percentage of minority workers to 50 percent.[84] Although the basic thrust of these efforts, which met with varying success, appears to have been the hiring of black workers, it is significant that in their negotiations with the People's Gas Company, the main target of the "summer offensive," CUCA representatives demanded that 49 percent of the company's construction work force be "*black* and *brown*" workers, which they broke down into 33 percent black, 12 percent "Latin," and 4 percent "Oriental."[85] Simultaneously, the protest over the Urban League's role in the new plan appeared to mark the first significant involvement by representatives of the city's growing Latino community in the building trades integration struggle, as spokesmen for the Spanish Coalition for Jobs, a CUCA affiliate, and the Latin American Task Force joined in the criticism that the Urban League could not adequately represent minority interests. One account also stated that CUCA's demands during the 1972 negotiations were for "31% black and 12% brown construction workers."[86]

On July 18, the executive board of the Urban League voted not to sign a $1.2 million contract with the Department of Labor to administer the proposed program after demonstrators from CUCA and the Spanish Coalition for Jobs disrupted the board's meeting with demands that the league not sign the contract and that their organizations be included in the decision-making structure of any program eventually agreed to.[87] These demands were met, more or less, in the plan that Irwin finally announced on October 18.

The 1972 Chicago Plan agreement, with specific minority percentages for each of fifteen crafts, was obviously a much more carefully crafted document than its 1970 predecessor; nonetheless, the program it created began to unravel publicly within eight months. The Urban League was reportedly threatening to withdraw from the plan during the summer of 1973 because of an alleged lack of cooperation by unions and contractors.[88] However, in July, Nayder reported that 668 minority workers had been accepted for training or employment, or 47 percent of the first year's goal, and although three-fourths of the plan's first year had already expired, he expressed confidence that the entire goal would be met by September 30.[89] By mid-August, union and contractor officials claimed 754 placements, still only 51 percent of the goal, but soon afterward it was reported that investigators from the Office of Federal Contract Compliance were able to confirm the employment or address of only a fraction of the workers supposedly placed through the program.[90]

On October 18, 1973, its first year anniversary, the second Chicago Plan was pronounced dead by Assistant Secretary of Labor Bernard DeLury, who asserted that "Chicago is just not susceptible to a voluntary solution." DeLury announced the replacement of this hometown plan with a "Philadelphia Plan" under which all local contractors on federally financed projects would face strict requirements to hire specified numbers of minority workers.[91] The new plan, the seventh such "imposed" plan in the United States, applied to all construction work in Cook, DuPage, Kane, Lake, McHenry, and Will counties, and to all contractors and subcontractors bidding on federal contracts exceeding $10,000 on projects worth $500,000 or more. The plan was to run for five years. However, it was not able to survive the 1974–75 recession.

The seventies were to reveal some important shifts in the underlying forces affecting the discrimination problem. On the one hand, two severe recessions in the mid- and late-seventies reduced construction employment sharply and thereby made affirmative action extremely difficult to effectuate. According to the Illinois Bureau of Employment Security, construction employment in the Chicago metropolitan area fell from 124,600 in April 1969 to 99,000 in April 1981. Opportunities for new employees were obviously limited. At Washburne, apprenticeship enrollment fell from 3,746 in 1969 to 1,620 in 1981. On the other hand, the number of black apprentices at Washburne declined only from 275 to 263, and the number of other minorities increased from 84 to 133. As a result, the percentage of minority apprentices rose from 9.5 to 24.4. Although the absolute numbers were small, they could be interpreted to suggest that some attitudes were changing and to raise hopes for the future.[92] A 1984 study for the Senate Committee on Higher Education, in contrast, concluded that "the struggle to increase minority access to Washburne has gone on since the early 1960's and today remains illusory."[93]

The unions comprising the Chicago Building Trades Council had a semisheltered status insofar as competition from lower-cost construction was concerned. Unlike manufactured products, the potential impact of outside competition was limited. As noted at the outset, even during the late seventies, Chicago construction continued largely "union." The recessions of the seventies, of course, reduced the demand for new construction and employment, and there was some increase in nonunion projects. The union leaders, however, were sensitive to the cost problem, and relations with the employers remained generally firm despite an increase in strikes. Notwithstanding the death of Mayor Daley in 1976, the unions maintained their considerable political influence with his immediate successors, Mayors Bilandic and Byrne, as well as with Republican Governor James Thompson. Apart from the impact of recession, the major problem of the seventies was the mounting pressure from Chicago's expanding black and Hispanic communities. Within the labor movement itself, both in Chicago and on the state level, the Building Trades Unions continued to maintain a leading position.

NOTES

This section is a condensation and revision of a report researched and written by David Nicolai.

1. Milton Rakove, *Don't Make No Waves, Don't Back No Losers* (Bloomington: Indiana University Press, 1975), p. 77.

2. All membership figures are, of necessity, highly approximate because of employment fluctuations stemming from seasonality, cyclical trends in the construction industry, and the impact of technological change on each trade.

3. Earl McMahon, *The Chicago Building Trades Council: Yesterday, and Today* (Chicago: Chicago Building Trades Council, 1947), pp. 23–25.

4. Interview with Thomas Nayder, November 6, 1982.

5. Interviews with Thomas Nayder; Lester Asher, July 28, 1982; and John Boland, November 12, 1982.

6. *BLS Bulletin* 862 (1946), pp. 16–17; *BLS Bulletin* 1011 (1951), pp. 8–9; *BLS Bulletin* 2091 (1981), pp. 19–20.

7. *BLS Bulletin* 862, pp. 16–17; *BLS Bulletin* 2091, pp. 19–20.

8. *BLS Bulletin* 1709 (1971), p. 15; *BLS Bulletin* 2091, p. 19.

9. *Directory and Guide to the Building Construction Employers' Association* (Chicago: BCEA, 1978), pp. 103–243.

10. *Federation News*, September 28, 1963, p. 1.

11. *Directory and Guide to the BCEA*, pp. 217–43.

12. *Chicago Tribune*, September 1, 1950, p. 1.

13. Gary Fink, ed., *Labor Unions* (Westport, Conn.: Greenwood Press, 1977), p. 86.

14. Interview with William McCabe conducted by Walter Franke and Paul Hartman, August 18, 1978.

15. *BLS Bulletin* 1709, p. 15; *BLS Bulletin* 1747 (1972), p. 15.

16. *Directory and Guide to the BCEA*, p. 42.

17. *Chicago Tribune*, July 7, 1970, sec. 3, p. 7.

18. Paul Hartman and Walter Franke, "The Changing Bargaining Structure in Construction: Wide-Area and Multicraft Bargaining," *Industrial and Labor Relations Review* 33 (January 1980): 179.

19. *Chicago Tribune*, July 7, 1970, sec. 3, p. 7.

20. Interview with William McCabe; and "MARBA: Report of the Chairman, 1972–76, Acknowledgements."

21. *Chicago Tribune*, April 17, 1972, p. 3; *Chicago Sun-Times*, April 18, 1972, p. 25.

22. Interview with Robert Wilke conducted by Paul Hartman and Walter Franke, August 8, 1978.

23. *Chicago Tribune*, June 4, 1972, p. 19; and "MARBA: Report of the Chairman, 1972."

24. Hartman and Franke, "The Changing Bargaining Structure," pp. 173 and 174.

25. Interview with William McCabe.

26. *Chicago Sun-Times*, June 20, 1972, p. 30; *Chicago Tribune*, June 20, 1972.

27. "MARBA: Report of the Chairman, 1972–76"; *Chicago Tribune*, July 7, 1972, p. 1; *Chicago Sun-Times*, July 7, 1972.

28. *Chicago Sun-Times*, July 7, 1972.

29. Ibid.

30. Hartman and Franke, "The Changing Bargaining Structure," p. 173.

31. *Chicago Daily News*, January 10, 1975; *Chicago Tribune*, January 10, 1975.

32. *BLS Bulletin* 1972 (1977), p. 22.

33. *Chicago Sun-Times*, June 1, 1979, p. 3; June 7, 1979.

34. Interview with Thomas Nayder; Oberman estimates, *Chicago Tribune*, April 1, 1980.

35. Chicago Civic Federation, "A Study of Prevailing Wage Rates Paid by Chicago's Major Government Units" (Chicago: Civic Federation, 1964), pp. 43–45.

36. "A Study of Prevailing Wage Rates," p. 46.

37. *City of Monmouth v. Lorenz*, 30 Ill., 2nd 60.

38. *Chicago Tribune*, October 2, 1963, p. 18.

4c

Steelworkers District 31

One of this nation's oldest and mightiest centers of heavy industry straddled the state border between Illinois and Indiana at the southern tip of Lake Michigan. Throughout the post-World War II era, only the Pittsburgh area rivalled the Calumet region—the name comes from the Calumet River, whose two branches flow through South Chicago, Hammond, East Chicago, and Gary—as a center of the American steel industry. By the 1970s, the combined steel output of Illinois and Indiana, running at 30–35 million net tons a year and overwhelmingly concentrated in the Calumet area, exceeded that of the state of Pennsylvania by increasingly wide margins.[1] The largest steel mill in the nation, U.S. Steel's Gary Works, was located in the region, as were the fourth and fifth largest mills, U.S. Steel's South Works in Chicago and Inland Steel's Indiana Harbor mill in East Chicago.[2]

Both the large mills owned by some of the major American corporations and the hundreds of small foundries and fabricating plants scattered throughout the metropolitan area provided employment to well over 100,000 workers during most of the postwar period. From the Steel Workers' Organizing Committee (SWOC) drives of the late thirties and early forties, these thousands of workers were members of District 31, United Steelworkers of America (USWA). District 31 membership grew rapidly during the war from perhaps 18,000 members in 1940 to 90,000–100,000 in 1945, and then stabilized between 100,000–125,000 for the next thirty years. The number of USWA locals in the district doubled during this time, from about 140 at war's end to approximately 290, falling into eight separate subdistricts in the 1970s.

On average, about 60 percent of District 31 members worked in the basic steel industry. At times more than ten thousand were employed in the steel can industry at the dozen or so local plants of the American Can Company and the Continental Can Company. Another five to eight thousand were members of Local 2047 at Crane Plumbing Company in South Chicago, the world's largest manufacturer of plumbing fixtures, and some two thousand workers were employed at two local aluminum plants owned by the Kaiser and Reynolds corporations. Virtually all other members of the district either worked at local foundries and metal fabricating or heavy machinery shops, with the major exception of more than four thousand utilities workers employed by Northern Indiana Public Service Company (NIPSCO), who became district members when the USWA negotiated a nationwide merger in 1972 with District 50, Allied and Technical Workers.

For more than thirty years this vast "union empire" was presided over by one man—Joseph Germano—with the assistance of an extremely able staff including Samuel Evett, Lester Thornton, Joseph Cesario, Raymond Pasnick, and Larry Keller. A second-generation Italian-American native of South Chicago and a veteran of the Amalgamated Association of Iron, Steel, and Tin Workers before the arrival of SWOC organizers in the Midwest, Germano ruled the district from 1940 until 1973, when he reached the mandatory retirement age of sixty-nine. The international's constitution, adopted at the 1942 Cleveland convention when SWOC became the United Steelworkers of America, allowed all of the thirty or so district directors a great deal of leeway in the running of district affairs and a significant say, through their seats on the international Executive Board, in the determination of national union policy. No district director benefitted more from this arrangement than Germano, whose leadership of more than 120,000 union members, or about one-tenth of the entire international's membership allowed him to wield great influence over the USWA's international officers. His status as "the union's most powerful wirepuller,"[3] in the words of a knowledgeable CIO veteran, was most obvious in 1965, when Germano led the dramatic struggle to topple David McDonald as international president, but his influence at USWA headquarters in Pittsburgh was reputedly just as great in other, less tumultuous, times.

The political legacy of the Germano years was ambiguous. On the one hand, as the head of the largest CIO union in the state, Germano often mustered his political resources in enthusiastic support of a long list of progressive causes—civil rights, state constitutional reform, and environmental issues, for example. On the other hand, Germano's behavior often appeared to be that of a prototypical machine politician, much in the manner of his close political ally, Chicago mayor Richard Daley. He obviously valued close ties with important political figures, sometimes regardless of their stands on issues, and the benefits that often accrued from such ties. The workings of the political machine that Germano headed resulted, among other things, in the fact that after 1947 he never faced an opponent for his post as district director. A militant anticommunist in the postwar years, Germano had little use for leftist dissidents. However, if Germano successfully countered dissent for some three decades, the accumulated discontent erupted dramatically after his departure, when insurgent and old-line leaders in District 31 fought for control of both the district and international union.

For a proper understanding of postwar events in District 31, the development of the Steelworkers' union in the decade before the war's end is important. As a U.S. Department of Labor report has emphasized, from its founding in 1936, "The SWOC was not an autonomous, member-controlled union. Its affairs were shepherded by the United Mine Workers of America who furnished the greater part of its finances and staff, and the imprint of the miners was discernible in its early leadership attitudes, and tactics. There was a tight control from the top which took the form of a benevolent autocracy."[4]

For the all-important Midwest Region, Phillip Murray, the head of SWOC and a UMWA vice-president, appointed as regional director one of his closest allies, Van Bittner, a Pennsylvania coal miner who had organized thousands of miners in the South and who had served as president of UMWA's District 17 in West Virginia since 1924. Bittner presided over the initial organizing drives in the Calumet region and elsewhere in the Midwest from 1936 to 1940 (he also played a leading role in organizing the city's important packinghouse industry during these years). If any of the district officers deviated from the standard SWOC pattern of strict obedience to UMWA-dominated leadership, it was definitely not Bittner's Chicago office.

Germano was active from the outset of the New Deal era, first within the long-established but feeble Amalgamated Association of Iron, Steel, and Tin Workers, AFL. In 1936, the thirty-two-year-old Germano, a millwright who had in 1933 organized Amalgamated Lodge 56 at the small Youngstown Sheet and Tube Plant in South Chicago and then served as its president, attended the Cannonsburg, Pennsylvania, convention of the Amalgamated. There he and James Thimmes, the only other delegate from Chicago and a future vice-president of the USWA, drafted a resolution accepting the CIO's offer of the necessary men and funds to organize the steel industry. Despite the Amalgamated's perennially weak status in the industry, there was significant resistance to the CIO offer by many delegates, but after Germano personally introduced the pro–CIO resolution on the convention floor, a bit of parliamentary maneuvering assured victory for this position.[5]

By 1939, Germano was on the staff of SWOC and was placed in charge of organizing in the important Indiana Harbor area of East Chicago, site of the huge Inland and Youngstown Sheet and Tube mills, with a combined employment of eighteen to twenty thousand workers. These two targets were critical to the fortunes of the local SWOC drive.

Following the combined impact of the Little Steel strike failure in 1937 and a renewed economic depression in late 1937 and 1938, SWOC was struggling for its very existence in the Chicago area. SWOC had been unable to negotiate any union security provisions anywhere in the United States, so it was a constant struggle to maintain membership levels and dues revenues at satisfactory levels. Barbara Newell's inspection of District 31 files indicated that SWOC contracts in 1938 covered only one-fourth of all the steel workers in the Calumet district—a number between 25,000 and 30,000 workers. Newell also estimated dues-paying membership as fluctuating broadly within the range of 7,000–10,000 members in 1938, and 15,000–25,000 in 1939.

Early in 1939, SWOC organizers under Gary subdistrict director Frank Grider undertook a membership drive that reportedly resulted in almost complete unionization by the three major U.S. Steel locals in Gary (1014, 1066, and 1117) and Local 65 in South Chicago. In September 1939, Germano led 500 volunteer organizers at Inland in signing up 1,500 workers and absorbing the long-established Employee Representation Plans for a total of 8,000 new members. Murray appointed Germano as district director in late 1940, when Bittner left Chicago to become national head of the Bethelem Steel organizing drive.

Besides winning formal bargaining rights and union security in basic steel, during the war SWOC was also busy organizing outside basic steel and undergoing the transformation from an ad hoc organizing committee under the aegis of John L. Lewis's CIO to an autonomous international union. A rough estimate is that the Chicago–Gary district staff members and volunteers were organizing perhaps thirty new locals a year on average during the war and immediately thereafter.[6] Some ten of these new locals were clerical units in basic steel.

Except for the clerical locals, all the area organizing occurred outside basic steel in the numerous steel forges, rolling plants, wire mills, slag and ballast companies, canning plants, and fabricating plants spread throughout the industrial towns of northwest Indiana, the entire city of Chicago, and a number of blue-collar suburbs and outlying areas on the southern and western edges of the city. (The northern suburbs were part of District 32, with headquarters in Milwaukee.) Many of these bargaining units had less than 50 members, and 100–300 workers was the typical range, but some larger locals were also organized in the early and mid-forties, including 2,300 employees at General American Transportation Company in Gary (first contract, July 1942), 3,000 Pullman-Standard employees in Hammond (NLRB election won in June 1943), more than 1,500 workers at Pullman-Standard shipyards in South Chicago (NLRB elction won June 1943), and 2,500 workers at the Pullman plant in South Chicago, where the NLRB election was won in February 1944.[7]

The union also won a string of NLRB elections at the Chicago area can plants; by August 1943, the USWA had organized all six Continental Can plants, with some 5,000 employees, and the approximately 3,500 employees in the three local American Can Company plants were also organized during the war. By far the largest local outside basic steel joined the USWA at the war's end, in September 1945, when the 7,000 employees of Crane Plumbing

Company in South Chicago voted overwhelmingly for the Steelworkers in an NLRB election. By the seventies, the non-basic steel membership probably outnumbered those in basic steel.

The years 1942–47 were also important because of the transformation of SWOC into the United Steelworkers of America, with constitutional arrangements that would allow Germano to consolidate his political control of the district and influence within the international by the immediate postwar years. During SWOC's second annual national Wage and Policy Convention, held in Chicago in May 1940, the 834 delegates voted unanimously to hold in 1942 a constitutional convention to unite SWOC and Amalgamated into a new international union with a new constitution. The delegates to the 1942 Constitutional Convention in Cleveland adopted the new constitution and elected Phillip Murray as the first president of the new USWA, David McDonald as secretary-treasurer, and thirty-nine district directors, including Germano. The district directors were elected by the direct vote of delegates from their own districts.

Germano had faced stiff opposition for this post during the 1942 convention, when most of the district directors were elected either by acclamation or by large electoral margins. His opponent was a former president of a company union, George Patterson, who was rumored among Germano supporters to be a communist or communist sympathizer and was one of the heroes of the Memorial Day Massacre, during which he lost an eye.

When the election of district directors was shifted from convention delegates to a district membership referendum, in 1945, Germano found himself challenged by Patterson again. Patterson was serving in the American armed service in India when he learned that the election, in which his supposedly communist leanings were turned into a major issue by Germano and his supporters, had been won by Germano on February 13, 1945, by a vote of 31,294 to 7,228. Patterson lamented years later that "I was no more a red than he [Germano] was, but this is the dope, you know. That's the way they worked."[8] A few years later, Patterson was transferred to the union's staff in Wisconsin, where he spent the next thirty-five years of his career in the Steelworkers.

Germano faced his final election challenge in December 1946. The challenger was John Mayerick, president of the large U.S. Steel Local 1014 at the time. Some newspaper accounts described Mayerick as a "leftist," but Samuel Evett, a longtime Germano assistant, described him as an independent, both "anti-Communist and anti-administration." Germano won by a large 5–1 margin.

Because of its huge size, District 31 had six subdistricts until 1973 and eight by 1975. Perhaps the main significance of the subdistricts was the development of a secondary level of union leaders between the district director and the local union leaders. Many of Germano's most trusted lieutenants served as subdistrict directors, including Joseph Jeneske, Lester Thornton, and Orval Kincaid in Indiana, and Raymond Sarocco, Sam Perish, and Joseph Cesario in Illinois. Their duties included organizing subdistrict conferences on legislative politics, grievance procedures, workers' compensation, community services, and similar topics; leading unionization drives at nonunionized workplaces; overseeing contract administration (including arbitration cases); contract negotiations at the non-basic steel firms; and supervision of the international representatives working in their subdistricts. Most of the larger locals had full-time elected presidents and grievance committee chairmen.

By 1945, the USWA and the major basic steel companies were well on their way to highly centralized, industrywide bargaining. And District 31 exerted an influence proportionate to its large membership on the formulation of bargaining demands and on strike settlements. This influence came through the representation of its locals on the Wage Policy Committee and the separate negotiating committees that the USWA established for each basic steel firm. The Wage Policy Committee was formally established by the 1944 convention "to execute the best agreements available." It was composed of all international Executive Board members, plus 130 committeemen elected at district conferences, with each district assigned a specific quota of delegates according to its share of the national membership (District 31's delegation was thus usually thirteen or fourteen). The primary functions of the Wage Policy Committee, according to Lloyd Ulman,[9] were to issue a written set of instructions to the union's negotiators based upon hundreds of resolutions on bargaining demands submitted by district conferences and local unions; to back up the negotiators during strategic points in the negotiations; and to vote on the settlement reported to it by the international president and his chief assistants.

The actual bargaining was carried on by the company negotiating committees appointed by the international president and consisting of one or more international officers, district directors, or members of the technical or organizing staff, and representatives of all the local unions in the firm's workplaces. Although these committees met and negotiated separately at each company's principal location, according to Jack Stieber, "in practice, the committees generally marked time until a settlement was reached between the union and U.S. Steel. This settlement was then followed, possibly with minor adaptations, by each of the major companies."[10]

Although other basic steel locals in District 31 showed little deviation from the industrywide patterns in contract negotiations and strikes, this was most definitely not the case with Local 1010 at Inland Steel. As Bernard Karsh's research in the fifties indicated, 1010's reputation as a local of unusual militancy (James Balanoff, later a district director, referred to his home local as the "red local") was borne out by "its long history of aggressive job actions"

toward Inland management at Indiana Harbor and by its "conspicuous . . .
opposition to the policies of the [union's] national officers."[11]

Although Karsh noted that "there have been no slowdowns in the plant
since early in 1953," it is clear that Local 1010's aggressiveness extended
from at least the mid-forties all the way through the fifties. In August 1945,
strike leaders at 1010 defied two separate War Labor Board orders to return
to work during a wildcat strike called "to compel the reinstatement of its [the
union's] president, who had been discharged for taking an unauthorized vacation."[12] The strikers also defied Germano, who delivered a demand from
Murray that they return to work (wildcat strikes had been outlawed at the
1942 convention, and only the USWA president could authorize a strike).

Two years later, during the otherwise peaceful 1947 basic steel negotiations
considered "a high-water mark in relations between the parties which was not
to be duplicated for many years to come,"[13] the workers at Inland went out
on a one-week strike in May over a "union responsibility" clause proposed
by management. But the strike was settled, according to Jack Stieber, "with
language providing for protection against wildcat strikes."

In contrast to the usual practice of limited union picketing and free passage
of essential supervisory personnel in and out of the plant, during the 1949
industrywide strike Local 1010 initiated twenty-four-hour "shoulder-to-shoul-
der" picketing that denied plant entry to any top Inland officers and interfered
with food supplies to the seven hundred foremen and other supervisors inside
the plant.

Another plantwide wildcat strike occurred at Inland in October 1951, despite the Korean War production effort then underway and despite the fact
that industrywide negotiations had just begun. The wildcat began when
ninety-six "pickling" or cleaning department employees walked out in a dispute over the application of incentive rates to a new pickling process. Following a day or two of mass picketing, a statement by Inland president Clarence
Randall that "the strike is Communist-inspired," an admission by Local 1010
president William Maihofer that the dispute directly involved only twenty-one
employees and $2,500 total incentive pay, and meetings with a Federal Medi-
ation and Conciliation Service official, the strike ended on October 18, 1951.
The company agreed to send the twenty-one men back to work and to submit
their rates to immediate arbitration; the union gave assurance that it would
make every effort to increase production on the pickling line in question.

During the 1952 basic steel strike that followed the Supreme Court's decision that President Truman's seizure of the steel mills was unconstitutional,
Inland strikers once again proved to be the most aggressive in the district.
The *Tribune* reported that, contrary to Germano's orders, Local 1010 pickets
refused to let a hundred key supervisory personnel into the mill despite the
possibility that untold damage would be done to the plant's hearths, furnaces,

and ovens if they were cooled improperly because of the lack of qualified personnel. In addition, approximately three hundred steelworkers reportedly swarmed onto the East Chicago bridge and took keys from scores of truck drivers in order to stall them on the bridge so that it could not be raised to let an Inland ore boat unload at the mill. Local 1010 also voted that the eight hundred supervisory men confined in the plant could not receive visits at the plant gate from their families, because "the women and kids were making a holiday of it . . . [and thus] breaking the morale of the pickets."[14] No similar incidents were reported at other District 31 mills during the 1952 strike.

Two final wildcat strikes at Inland during the fifties should be mentioned. One was a five-day strike from January 30 to February 4, 1953, which followed the twenty-day suspension of two workers who refused a foreman's order to work overtime and the ten-day suspension of a grievanceman for the manner in which he protested the two suspensions. This dispute was resolved when the parties agreed to expedited processing of the suspensions through the contract's grievance and arbitration procedures. The second was a forty-eight-hour strike in September 1958 by 207 garage workers protesting inadequate bus service to the plant's new garage; the strike ended with three-day suspensions without pay for the striking employees.

Local 1010 was not alone in its willingness to call wildcat strikes. For example, Local 1066 at U.S. Steel's sheet and tin mill in Gary engaged in a two-day wildcat in August 1949 to protest the death of a union member crushed by an eleven-ton wire coil. Approximately a thousand members of Local 1066 were back out on a strike in February 1951, and again in April, over another fatal in-plant accident in addition to incentive-rate disputes. The two thousand employees at the Joliet plant of the American Steel and Wire Company (a U.S. Steel subsidiary) engaged in a week-long wildcat over incentive rates in September 1950. A three-day walkout by the ten thousand members of Local 1011 at the Youngstown Sheet and Tin mill occurred in March 1958 following the suspension of a shop steward protesting the job reclassification of one employee.

Other examples of large-scale wildcats during the fifties—at Republic Steel, at Crane Plumbing, at the South Works, and elsewhere—could be cited, but the fact remains that no other local came close to equalling Local 1010's record in this regard. But why Local 1010, and why Inland? Most observers over the years have concurred in Karsh's judgment that Inland had been a "progressive and efficient" firm, and former Inland executives William Caples and Frank Cassell (admittedly, not the most objective sources, as both played key roles in shaping the firm's new Industrial Relations Department during the postwar years) spoke of the company as being the most advanced basic steel firm in regard to industrial relations. Both officials also spoke of the continuing influence on the firm of its two founding families, the Blochs and the Ryersons, the former Jewish and the latter Episcopalian but both "strongly religious" and committed to humane personnel policies (although not necessarily to the recognition of the union during the SWOC drives) and to civic improvements in the East Chicago community.

Cassell speculated that it might have been the very "liberalism" of Inland management, as evidenced in its early hiring and promotion of minority employees, which prompted the local's militancy, that is, unionists tended to be more militant when they perceived real possibilities for improvement. Caples mentioned the inconsistency in labor relations policy between top management and lower management as a prime cause for the workers' militancy—an observation confirmed by Cassell's belief that there was considerable resistance among plant foremen when Inland president Clarence Randall was strongly pushing the firm from a stance of outright opposition to the union to one of general accommodation during the forties and fifties.

A third factor that Caples cited may be the most valid—that is, "the presence of genuine Communists in the Local." Regardless of whether or not individual leaders of Local 1010 were actually party members or members of other radical factions (the USWA constitution forbade communists from holding union office after 1948), probably few observers would disagree with Caples's statement that "radicals . . . who never really accepted the right of management to run the mill . . . had complete control of Local 1010 for years and years." Caples referred to continual visits by FBI officers to rifle through personnel files in a search for communists, and Cassell spoke of plant sabotage occurring due to rivalries between the three main factions of communists in Local 1010: Stalinists, Trotskyists, and (to a smaller degree) Titoists. With such lively internal politics, it was always possible that the wildcats were as much directed against top union officials as against Inland management.[15]

Finally, mention should should be made of one chapter in Local 1010's early bargaining history that had enormous repercussions on the future course of contract negotiations in basic steel and many other American industries. After the 1946 strike, Inland management instituted a new policy of compulsory retirement at age sixty-five as part of the contributory pension plan begun by the company in 1943. Union officials, guided by General Counsel Arthur Goldberg, immediately filed charges with the National Labor Relations Board, claiming that such actions violated both the seniority and discharge sections of the contract and that Inland management had refused to bargain with the union on the issue of pensions and a mandatory retirement age. On April 13, 1948, the NLRB ruled that pension payments are a form of wage and that the terms under which pensions are to be paid, including a mandatory retirement age, fall within the meaning of "conditions of employment" under the National Labor Relations Act and thus are mandatory topics of collective bargaining.

This NLRB decision was affirmed by the U.S. Circuit Court of Appeals in Chicago in September 1948 and then by the U.S. Supreme Court, which in April 1949 declined to review the appellate court decision. This legal action on behalf of Local 1010 and Local 64, a small Inland Container Corporation local in Chicago Heights, not only paved the way for the noncontributory pension plan won in the 1949 industrywide negotiations, but also was a landmark in the postwar development of negotiating even more complex retirement and insurance plans and other fringe benefits.

Like the Clothing Workers and a number of other unions, the Steelworkers placed considerable emphasis on education and community services. District 31 was one of the first Illinois unions to take advantage of the labor education facilities of the University of Illinois in Champaign-Urbana and Chicago and each summer starting in 1947 sent a sizable contingent of local leaders and active members to week-long study programs. Steelworkers also were enrolled in classes at Roosevelt University and the University of Chicago. District 31 conducted its own education sessions in the areas of political action and community services. With the encouragement and assistance of both the international Union and District 31, many larger locals printed newspapers. District 31 was also an active sponsor of community services such as the United Way, and it provided assistance to members and their families in need.

Along with District 32 (northern Illinois) and District 34 (southern Illinois), District 31 wielded considerable political influence in both Chicago and Springfield. They also worked closely with other CIO unions in the early years and with such AFL affiliates as the Machinists, AFSCME, the International Ladies Garment Workers, and the IBEW after merger.

District 31's political actions in these years can be associated with the names of two of Germano's closest political aides, Frank Annunzio (later a long-time member of Congress) and John Alesia. Germano, Annunzio, and Alesia shared more than Italian surnames; all three were brothers-in-law (according to Sam Evett,[16] Annunzio married Germano's wife's sister, while Alesia was Germano's wife's brother). Frank Cassell also stated that the three shared a devout adherence to Catholicism, had close ties with Cardinal Samuel Stritch of Chicago, and held deeply anticommunist views that may have stemmed from their Catholic beliefs.

There was considerable stimulus to these leaders' anticommunism in the two or three years immediately after the war. Agitation between the communists and anticommunists from District 31 came to a head at the various national conventions in 1946 and 1948. The anticommunists dominated the procommunist delegates from District 31 by a 5–1 margin at the 1946 convention, where the antagonism between the two groups culminated, according to the *Tribune*, in a fist fight between District 31 international representative Norman Harris and Nicholas Migas, a self-professed communist and president of Local 1010. The brawl between Harris and Migas was reportedly followed by a fifteen-minute free-for-all that Murray could hardly quell.[17] Two years later, at the Boston convention where the prohibition of communist officers was finally passed, Migas was again the center of attention. He passed out a circular attacking the international officers in language similar to that in the Communist party publication, the *Daily Worker*, and was consequently condemned by both Murray and Germano.

Just weeks after this convention, a trial committee at 1010 tried Migas on the grounds that his holding the office of a grievance committeeman in the local violated the new constitutional ban on communists. The committee voted 44–1 not to remove Migas from office despite his statement that "I am a Communist and I might say that I'm very proud of being one"; however, upon appeal the international Executive Board reversed the local's decision in fall 1948 and removed Migas from office under threat of receivership.[18]

A similar case occurred in 1950, when the international convention refused to seat delegate Charles Figer, a former president and secretary at Local 1011 whom Murray personally identified as a communist. When Figer was elected financial secretary of 1011 by a 2–1 margin one month after this convention, the international Executive Board ordered him removed from office. But local president William Christy vowed to fight the order, stating that "Figer resigned from the Communist Party about four years ago and has signed a non-Communist affadavit. The local is overwhelmingly for him."[19]

One should not, however, overestimate the number or influence of communists in District 31 during the late forties. Anticommunist feeling apparently ran high at a large number of locals. Local 65 at the South Works and Local 1834, the "Eugene Debs local" at the Pullman plant, were among five South Chicago locals whose members passed resolutions before the 1946 convention demanding the removal of communists from the USWA.[20] Also in 1946, just two years before the Figer affair, Local 1011 passed a resolution adjuring the United States "to cease appeasing Russia and take a firm stand against Russian methods."[21]

One should also not misunderstand the role of communists or other leftists within the mills. Although Evett complained that they used to wear down the rank and file at local meetings until they would leave so that the "communist clique" could then pass its own political resolutions, he admitted that the radicals were articulate leaders and good organizers. Cassell believed that the leftists excelled above all at being good bread-and-butter unionists, aggressive in pursuing grievances or fighting arbitrary treatment by foremen. Caples believed that the rank and file allowed leftists to run the locals without interference, as "they just wanted good pay."[22]

None of these considerations, however, appeared to lessen Germano's determination to ferret out communist or leftist influence in Chicago. The most dramatic struggle for Germano came at the turbulent Illinois CIO convention in August 1947, when Germano was elected president of the body, succeeding the aged Samuel Levin of the Amalgamated Clothing Workers. A Chicago paper reported that "the CIO convention was the stormiest in the council's seven-year history, split between bitter right- and left-wing factions."[23] Left-wingers were led by Robert Travis of the United Auto Workers, Ernest DiMaio of the United Electrical Workers, and delegates from the Packinghouse Workers and the Fur and Leather Workers. Besides the Steelworkers, the anti-left majority included the Amalgamated Clothing Workers, the Flat Glass Workers, and some delegates from both the UAW and the Packinghouse Workers. The worst fighting occurred not over election of officers, but over the recommendation of the "right-wing dominated" Constitutional Committee to reduce the size of the State Board from thirty members to nine, all to be elected at large. Leftists charged that this recommendation was "an attempt to prevent majority opinion in many international unions from having voice and vote, thus making an unrepresentative body," and also "an effort to capture control of the state CIO machinery by the right-wing leaders of the Steelworkers."[24] The Steelworkers, with more than three hundred delegates out of a total of 544, obviously dominated the convention.

After Germano, whose forces won all seats but one on the newly constituted State Board, defeated Charles Winter, a UAW legislative aide who denounced "right-wing efforts to capture the CIO machinery by strong-arm methods," Germano announced: "I do not like Communists, and I shall do everything possible to see that Communists not only do not control our union, but that they do not get control in this country."[25]

The struggle over domination of the CIO state convention spilled over to the Cook County Industrial Union Council. Controversy in the Cook County Council arose over whom it should nominate for the Chicago Board of Education seat previously reserved for a CIO leader. John Doherty, midwest representative of the USWA, had held the seat from 1946 to 1954. When Mayor Edward Kelly appointed him to the school board, Doherty said that he regarded his appointment as a "tribute to the prestige the USA–CIO now enjoys in community affairs." But Doherty lost his seat in 1954, when Mayor Martin Kennelly did not reappoint him after the citizens' nominating committee failed to renominate him. The *Chicago Tribune* reported that Kennelly's failure to support Doherty was a factor in the CIO's decision to abandon him and support Richard Daley in the 1955 mayoral campaign.

In April 1955, the Executive Board of the county CIO voted unanimously to nominate Ralph Helstein, the international president of the United Packinghouse Workers, to the vacant seat; however, only eight of the fifteen board members were present for the vote, with all five USWA representatives absent including Albert Towers, president of Local 65, chairman of the county council, and a confirmed Germano loyalist. Mayor Daley eventually resolved the dispute in favor of the Steelworkers; in early 1956, he appointed Raymond Pasnick, District 31's publicity director and midwest editor of *Steel Labor*, to the school board. Pasnick served on the board for ten years before moving on to Pittsburgh to become the USWA's director of public relations under the I. W. Abel administration.

Despite the evidence of extensive resentment toward Steelworker leaders such as Germano, Annunzio, and Alesia on the part of many prominent CIO unionists in the state, including Duane (Pat) Greathouse, regional director of the UAW, it should not be assumed that the USWA leaders were apathetic toward progressive, CIO-endorsed political goals. Whereas Annunzio's political career personified their involvement in the non-issue-oriented, patronage-centered machine politics for which Chicago had a nationwide reputation, Alesia's long career as legislative director for District 31 personified the opposite tendency of a strong commitment toward more issue-oriented, social-welfare politics. In his 1969 study, *Labor in American Politics*, J. David Greenstone noted that "like Germano, Alesia enjoyed the accumulation and exercise of power and usually employed it for liberal ends. . . . In fact, on most issues, Alesia was widely considered during the early 1960's to be the most effective labor lobbyist for liberal legislation in Springfield. By all odds, for example, he worked harder than any other union lobbyist for the state fair employment practices act that finally passed in 1961. . . ."[26]

Germano served for many years as chairman, and Alesia as executive director, of the statewide Steelworkers' political education committee, which represented about a hundred thousand union members (around seventy thousand from District 31 and thirty thousand from both District 32 in northern Illinois and District 34 in the remainder of the state). In February 1959, Germano promised the four hundred delegates attending the political education committee's first annual conference in Springfield that their agenda "will go far beyond the program of the Illinois AFL–CIO."[27] By 1962, George Bliss, the longtime labor affairs reporter for the *Chicago Tribune*, wrote that the Steelworkers had "the most potent and militant political machine of any union in Illinois."[28]

Although Greenstone believed that "by comparison with UAW officials in Chicago, most of Germano's officials did not as easily command a liberal ideological rhetoric,"[29] his discussion of the two unions' stances during the Democratic primary for the 1960 gubernatorial race indicated that their political inclinations were not always predictable. In this campaign, the Chicago Democratic organization picked Cook County Judge Otto Kerner as its preferred candidate, but he was challenged by State Treasurer Joseph Lohman, whom Greenstone describes as much more liberal than Kerner.

Germano and other USWA leaders, in addition to a minority of UAW activists, supported Lohman, while the UAW leadership, "bent on improving its relations with the party," endorsed Kerner. Both unions were miffed that the local party had chosen Kerner without consulting them, and the Steelworkers hoped "that an independent stand would elicit more respectful treatment from the party," and that they "would have dominated labor politics in the state for many years" if Lohman won. Kerner won both the primary and general elections easily, and afterward "he handsomely rewarded the UAW for its support [including appointing UAW official Robert Johnston as state director of labor] and pointedly ignored USWA."[30] At the 1961 state AFL–CIO convention, Germano denounced Kerner: "In all the years I've been in the labor movement, I can't recall a governor as uncooperative with labor as Kerner. Others here agree with me, in that we had much better relations with Republican governors such as Governor Stratton and Governor Green."[31]

Influential labor leaders' approach to the 1960 gubernatorial race, the basis of Germano's support for Stevenson in 1948, and other examples serve to corroborate Greenstone's thesis that issue-oriented, social-welfare politics that motivated industrial unions nationwide always remained subordinate in Chicago, where the Democratic party organization and the top leadership of the Chicago Federation of Labor (to which the UAW was not affiliated) dominated the local party-labor political alliance.

Regardless of their tie with mainstream machine politicians, the Steelworkers were among the leaders on behalf of two long-overdue reforms of the state government achieved in the sixties: reapportionment of the state senate on a population basis and introduction of the state's first income tax. After delegates to the annual political education committee conference passed a resolution in support of a test case concerning legislative reapportionment, Germano, Alesia, and other USWA leaders filed a lawsuit in February 1963 against top state officials charging that state senators should be elected from districts substantially equal in population rather than land area. When the federal district judges, by a 2–1 vote, upheld the 1954 amendment to the state constitution that allowed senatorial districts to be drawn on the basis of land area, the case, together with others, was appealed to the U.S. Supreme Court, which in June 1964 ruled in *Reynolds v. Sims* that both houses of legislatures must be apportioned on the basis of population under the "equal protection of the laws" clause of the Fourteenth Amendment.

Although this famous one-man, one-vote decision by the Supreme Court was a response to more than thirty reapportionment suits, *Steel Labor* claimed that only in Illinois and Michigan were the suits "initiated and carried to their conclusion by union officials." Germano's prediction that "this [decision] will end the present senate districting in Illinois which has created a system of government by a minority largely unfriendly to labor" proved to be accurate. As Neal Peirce observed in 1972, "the old rural GOP oligarchy that long held sway has been dispersed, and the Democrats in 1970 were actually able to win control of the [Senate] for the first time in thirty years."[32]

While arguing the reapportionment case, Steelworkers' national counsel Bernard Kleiman made the argument that state revenue needs had not been met in most states because of the disproportionate number of rural lawmakers; he added that "a legislature responsive to the people could put our state on a sound financial footing by enacting a state income tax."[33] The Steelworkers had been fighting for the replacement of the Illinois state sales tax by a graduated income tax ever since the first political education committee conference in 1959. Greenstone notes that, "labor's traditional opposition to the sales tax as a regressive burden on the poor best explains the USWA's vehement opposition . . . to the new Kerner administration's 1961 sales tax increase—an increase the UAW supported."[34] The Steelworkers also opposed a constitutional amendment passed by the legislature in 1965 and endorsed by Governor Kerner but not adopted by the voters, because this revenue amendment called for a limited, flat-rate income tax, whereas the Steelworkers had long pushed for a graduated tax.

Their efforts, supported by other unions as well as nonunion groups, were finally rewarded in 1969, when Governor Richard Ogilvie pushed the first income tax in Illinois history through a reluctant legislature. Ogilvie orginally proposed a flat 4 percent rate for the income tax, but the legislature modified it to 2.5 percent for individuals and 4 percent for corporations; moreover, the tax was somewhat progressive because it provided for a liberal $1,000 personal exemption for each taxpayer and each of his or her dependents, thus allowing poor families to pay little or no tax. The new tax doubled the state's revenues between 1968 and 1971.

As important as was the involvement of Germano, Alesia, and other Steelworkers officials in Illinois politics, another, separate level of union politics revolved around the union locals and, for many members of District 31, was of more immediate importance than either gubernatorial races or legislative reform. This level of union politics was ably analyzed by sociologist William Kornblum in his study of South Chicago's Steelworkers, *Blue Collar Community.* Kornblum, who lived in South Chicago from 1968 to 1970 and worked in a steel mill there, investigated both local union politics and city ward politics as community institutions whose dynamics are dominated by ethnic/racial mobility and succession. He observed about the steel locals:

> Outsiders to industrial communities often judge local labor unions according to their feelings about the development of the national labor movement since the 1930s. The industrial unions have discouraged many intellectuals who once saw in them the hope for a working class which would be conscious of its common interests and would select leaders who could best articulate those interests. In general, the disappointment over the unions' failure to unify blue collar America behind socialist or progressive political programs has resulted in an ignorance of the role local unions do play in the life of working-class people. More specifi-

cally, most observers have neglected the unions' success at forming committees in the segmented industrial areas of the country. It is true that local unionists operate within limits established by the relationship between national corporations and union bureaucracies. Also, in South Chicago as in most industrial communities, the early histories of labor-management conflict established patterns of local union politics which persist today. Even in South Chicago's "glorious" decades of labor organization, politics in the steel mills often combined well-articulated class issues with an overriding concern for ethnic and racial mobility through union leadership.[35]

During the post-World War II period, the aggregation of ethnic or racial groups into the South Chicago community institutions was largely a story of the large-scale entrance of blacks and Hispanics into the neighborhoods, union locals, and ward politics. At the time of Kornblum's research, he could still write that strong resistance on the part of white residents had made it impossible for the majority of the mills' black employees to live in the traditional mill neighborhoods, thus "limiting their influence in both union and local politics far more than would be expected on the basis of their numbers in the mills." But he noted that "most white residents perceive that the racial composition of these neighborhoods is destined to change in the next decade [the 70's]."[36] They were correct. As the 1980 *Almanac of American Politics* notes about South Chicago's second congressional district, which included all the mill neighborhoods, "Both parts of the second district [east and west of the mills] have one thing in common: they have been the site of Chicago's—and the nation's—most massive neighborhood racial change in recent years. In 1960 less than 20% of the population . . . was black; in 1970 it was 40%, and today blacks form a solid majority."[37] The growth of the Hispanic population in these South Chicago neighborhoods was less dramatic—from 5 percent in 1970 to 8 percent in 1980.

The residents of South Chicago possessed in their labor unions a system of negotiation through which they could transcend the physical and cultural isolation of their neighborhoods. Although employees tended to work in the mill nearest to their place of residence, the mills drew on population from the entire area as well. Steel mills then brought together the diverse elements of different neighborhoods into work groups that in turn were aggregated into union politics. This pattern of aggregation built upon primary relations and ethnic loyalties created in both place of work and place of residence.

Kornblum, who believed that "in the decades since World War II, status rather than class conflict has become almost the distinguishing feature of blue-collar community life,"[38] was quite concerned about the extent to which the preoccupation with ethnic succession in the steel locals impeded the emergence of more class-based, issue-oriented politics in South Chicago. He concluded that in the context of an ethnically heterogeneous, blue-collar community like South Chicago issues of class were essentially inseparable from those of ethnic succession to community leadership.

The near victory of the progressive coalition in the local at Republic Steel in 1970, along with the election of the first black local president, Robert Hatch, at South Works Local 65 that year, were clear signs that a new generation of leadership had finally arrived in District 31. Blacks had become presidents of some non-basic steel locals by the sixties. There were other signs by the mid-sixties that Germano's political machinery was losing a bit of its clout among the rank and file of District 31. For example, in 1964, two men, William Kranz and Stephen Bazin, who were reliably reported to be vocal opponents of Gary Subdistrict director Orval Kincaid, were elected presidents of the two largest locals in Gary—1066 and 1014, respectively. The election of these two men, along with Bazin's outspoken black vice-president Curtis Strong, was viewed widely as a repudiation of Kincaid, who had been one of Germano's closest aides since 1948 and who was accused in 1964 of "controlling elections" in Gary since the early fifties.[39]

In addition, important concentrations of young steelworkers developed at the two new basic steel mills built in District 31 during the sixties. *Steel Labor* reported in 1966 that the average age of the workers at Bethlehem Steel's new Burns Harbor plant was twenty-nine years.

Local 6787's history of wildcat strikes during it first five years of existence at Burns Harbor also must be seen as a testament of the youthful impatience of its members. After the lengthy steel strike in 1959, District 31 did not experience any authorized, industrywide strikes or many significant wildcats, not even at Local 1010. But Local 6787 members were out on a wildcat strike in November 1965, two months after the mill opened, over an alleged management plan to introduce a four-day work week; in January 1966, over the use of outside contractors; in June 1966, over hiring procedures; in April 1967, over the alleged lack of a break during an eight-hour shift; in July 1967, over the discipline of an employee who supposedly set off a firecracker in the mill; and again in May 1970, over the lack of incentive rate increases in the prior two years.

In 1973, Germano's career as District 31 leader ended with his retirement. He decided to support his long-time personal assistant, Sam Evett, for the succession. Evett's challenger was an energetic and outspoken young radical. Edward Sadlowski, thirty-four, who had been elected president of Local 65 in 1965 at the age of twenty-five.

The election campaign between Sadlowski and Evett featured little debate on substantive issues. Rather, the election "tended to set a generation of steel unionists, who had maintained their power in the district since the 1930's, against a large coalition of generally younger and more progressive local unionists throughout the vast Calumet Steel-producing region."[40] In addition, two disaffected long-time members of the District 31 staff decided to support Sadlowski.

Although the initial count showed Evett defeating Sadlowski by a slim margin of 23,394 votes to 21,606, Sadlowski won the South Chicago and Indiana Harbor subdistricts, both dominated by big basic steel locals, by 2–1 margins. In fact, the dissidents "won the election in almost all the large mills of the district, but they saw their lead whittled away in the smaller shops, where they had often been unable to campaign, or where their campaign workers were barred from entry on election day."[41]

Evett's electoral victory did not stand for long. Two weeks after the election, Sadlowski charged his opponent with widespread election violations including the stuffing of ballot boxes, denial of some members' rights to a secret ballot, and even no election at all in several locals. After USWA officials in Pittsburgh ruled Evett's election legitimate, Sadlowski appealed to the U.S. Labor Department. On November 8, 1973, the U.S. Justice Department filed a suit in the federal district court in Pittsburgh, seeking the removal from office of Evett and a new election in District 31. The suit, filed on behalf of Secretary of Labor Peter Brennan after an exhaustive investigation by Labor Department investigators in Chicago, alleged that some members were denied the right to vote, that Sadlowski was denied poll observers, that some returns were not counted, and that the Evett forces had engaged in shakedowns of staff personnel for campaign funds. The suit never came to trial; on July 12, 1974, Evett himself called for a new election to "show that the members of this district reject the promoters of dissent," and on July 21, Judge Louis Rosenberg in Pittsburgh set November 19 as the deadline for a new election. As many as two hundred Labor Department observers supervised the rerun election held between November 12 and November 15, in which Sadlowski beat Evett by a 2–1 margin, or 39,639 votes to 20,158.

Sadlowski served as director of District 31 for only a little more than two years before relinquishing his post to his close ally, James Balanoff, a local 1010 leader, in order to run for the international presidency against Lloyd McBride in 1977. Under Sadlowski, the once powerful political machinery built up by Germano dwindled considerably in its impact on state and local politics, although Sadlowski had made almost no allies on the District 31 executive board. This was perhaps inevitable under a maverick leader who explicitly repudiated Germano's legacy of cozy ties with prominent Illinois Democrats regardless of their political ideologies, and whose own ideology downgraded the importance of political programs. Sadlowski, for example, endorsed Mayor Daley's opponent, Alderman William Singer, in the mayor's last electoral race. The young leader's inability to gain control of the Steelworkers' political resources was more evident in January 1975 at the annual meeting of the union's Illinois Political Education Committee, where the recently defeated Evett announced his resignation as the committee chairman. Sadlowski hoped to replace Evett, but during a "long and angry" meeting of the executive board, members voted 6 to 5 to name Buddy Davis, then legislative director for District 34 and future district director of District 34, to the post; they also voted 6 to 5 to repudiate Sadlowski's efforts to dump the veteran union lobbyist John Alesia.

During local elections in 1976, the pro-national administration candidate Jack Parton, won the presidency of Local 1014, although Sadlowski supporters won the elections at the three other largest locals in the district: at his home Local 65, the Hispanic financial secretary, John Chico, who had served as Sadlowski's financial chairman during the 1973 and 1974 campaigns, defeated the pro-national administration incumbent, Frank Mirocha; at Locals 1010 and 1011 in Indiana, two Hispanic incumbents were defeated by pro-Sadlowski candidates. Besides the usual ethnic considerations and the relative strengths of pro- and anti-Sadlowski sentiments that certainly played large roles in the outcome of these two Indiana races, allegations of financial abuses by incumbent officers also were a factor. Most officers elected in other locals in District 31, however, were not close to Sadlowski.

The contest for international president between Sadlowski and Lloyd McBride, director of District 32 (Southern Illinois, Missouri, and Iowa), drew an extraordinary amount of nationwide publicity. Essentially, Sadlowski ran against the no-strike provision of the Experimental Negotiating Agreement (ENA) in the basic steel industry and for membership ratification of industrywide contracts; McBride defended the impressive economic gains made by USWA members under the existing collective bargaining arrangements. Sadlowski and Balanoff, who was running to succeed Sadlowski as District 31 director, also called, in general, for a return to a more militant attitude toward steel management reminiscent of the organizing days of the thirties and forties; McBride defended the necessity of "mature unionism," as represented by the ENA, in a transformed industrial environment.

Finally, both sides made major issues over the nature of each others' campaign resources. Sadlowski supporters maintained that at the 1976 international convention in Las Vegas, which marked the beginning of the campaign season, USWA president Abel, on behalf of McBride, was able to use the traditionally rigid procedural rules to deny the insurgents any opportunity for real floor debate and to secure passage of a pro-ENA resolution. In November, Sadlowski filed a suit in Pittsburgh claiming that the Abel administration had failed to provide him with a list of the polling places for the union's 5,400 locals, thus making it impossible for his supporters to monitor the vote effectively, and also that the USWA's monthly publication, *Steel Labor,* was being used to attack him and his candidacy. Also, as the *Wall Street Journal* reported, McBride's greatest asset in the campaign was "the overwhelming support he enjoyed from the union's 850 field staff representatives."[42]

McBride supporters countered Sadlowski's allegations of staff shakedowns with repeated charges that his opponent's campaign was being funded by "limousine liberals," "radicals," and "outside meddlers." Sadlowski admitted receiving contributions from such figures as John Kenneth Galbraith, Xerox president Max Palewsky, some other corporate executives, and many prominent Chicagoans including the antiwar labor activist Sidney Lens, the architect Bertram Goldberg, and his own attorney, former alderman Leon Despres. He claimed, however, that such contributions represented only 20 percent of his funds, with the remainder coming from union members; McBride spokesmen, however, charged that only 5–6 percent of Sadlowski's contributions came from steelworkers. The year after McBride's defeat of Sadlowski by a vote of 328,861 to 249,281, the new administration imposed a ban on any candidate for USWA office receiving outside contributions—a ban that was challenged in court and that resulted in a 5–4 Supreme Court decision upholding the policy.

Although he lost nationally, Sadlowski did much better in District 31, winning 34,658 votes to McBride's 21,964. Thus Sadlowski won some 61 percent of his district's votes, although he carried somewhat less than 40 percent nationwide. In the eight largest locals in District 31—the huge basic steel locals in which discontent with the national union leaders was reportedly the most acute and Sadlowski's support the most solid—he carried 64 percent of the vote, only a slightly larger percentage than that received in the numerous small locals.[43]

In the election for the directorship of District 31, which was left vacant by Sadlowski's quest for higher office, district members also reaffirmed support for the dissidents. In a five-man race, Balanoff won by polling 19,540 votes (or about 37 percent of the total); his strongest opponent, Harry Piasecki, former president of Local 1014, garnered 13,750 votes, while James Baker the black subdistrict director from Gary, received 8,996; Emmet Palmer, a staff representative from Subdistrict 5, gained 6,512; and Paul Markonni, Subdistrict 5 director, won 3,571.[44] When Balanoff resigned as Local 1010 president in order to become district director, his post was filled by his vice-president, William Andrews, who became the first black president of the 18,000 member local.

However, two years later, John Parton, a self-described "hill-billy" from West Virginia and two-time president of Local 1014, defeated Balanoff for the District 31 directorship on May 28, 1981. Parton collected 24,281 votes, or 52 percent of the total, to Balanoff's 22,237. Only 46 percent of the district's membership voted in the bitterly fought election. Despite differing interpretations of the election results, it seemed irrefutable by the 1981 race that the dissidents' fight-back focus had not won the full support of the majority of District members.

One aspect of this election concerned the seriousness of the talk about industrial decline, mill closings, and job losses in the region. The concern of local steelworkers and their leaders about declining employment in District 31 was certainly justified. Many small metal fabricating plants had either closed or moved to the South, and employment in can manufacturing had shrunk drastically because of new technology. In August 1977, after U.S. Steel issued an ominous statement that the South Works were in an "acute financial squeeze," rumors began circulating that the corporation was on the verge of closing the historic 8,000-worker mill. J. Bruce Johnson, vice-president of labor relations for U.S. Steel, wrote a letter to the *Chicago Tribune* on September 8, 1977, concluding that "unless there are changes, the prospects for South Works and other older Steel mills communities are not good."[45] For the remainder of the seventies, the bitter talk about an imminent South Works closure continued unabated while the steel industry as a whole faced increasing foreign competition from Europe and Asia. Hardly mentioned was the emerging growth of domestic competition from specialized, nonunion, low-cost "mini-mills."

In January 1980, a few months after the faltering International Harvester Corporation closed its Wisconsin Steel Works and idled 3,500 workers, United States Steel announced that it would close its 750-employee fabricated steel plant in Gary (American Bridge Division of U.S. Steel) in the wake of the workers' refusal to accept a three-year wage freeze.[46]

By late 1980, more than 8,000 Steelworkers in the Chicago area were unemployed, and many of these were losing their Supplemental Unemployment Benefits (SUB) as U.S. Steel, Bethlehem, and other major companies' SUB funds became depleted. The usually cited figure for district membership was 100,000, down from the 125,000 often reported during the last of the Germano years. Balanoff estimated that actual dues-paying membership was around 90,000 when he was director, perhaps even closer to 80,000 in the early eighties. Yet even the pessimists failed to envision the dismal future that lay ahead.

This account of District 31 is primarily concerned with internal union politics. Collective bargaining was highly important to steelworkers, as it was to members of most other unions, but the core decisions were made at the international level within the framework of a highly centralized, industrywide bargaining system. District 31's top leadership played an important role in this system; for the rank and file, the system's workings were quite remote.

In contrast, local plant, local union, and community politics were of direct and immediate significance. The three interrelated zones of activity offered numerous opportunities for individuals to enrich their personal and work lives. They enabled activists to overcome the hazards and tedium of industrial work.

For most of the period under review, the plants and locals of District 31 witnessed an exceptional variety of ideological and ethnic worker behavior, combined with impressive advances in economic benefits. Concurrently, however, industrial environment was undergoing insidious challenge from technological and competitive forces that threatened to undermine the accomplishments of several decades. Signs of these challenges became widely visible only in the middle seventies, but few unionists could anticipate the depressing conditions that lay ahead for them and their organizations.

NOTES

This section is a condensation and revision of a report researched and written by David Nicolai.

1. *Annual Statistical Reports* of the American Iron and Steel Institute (Washington, D.C.): 1970, p. 41; 1975, p. 55, and 1980, p. 57.

2. *Chicago Tribune,* October 16, 1953, sec. F, p. 4.

3. Len DeCaux, *Labor Radical: From the Wobblies to the CIO* (Boston: Beacon Press, 1970), p. 507.

4. U.S. Department of Labor, *Collective Bargaining in the Basic Steel Industry* (the Livernash Report), 1961, p. 80.

5. Germano's own account of his role at the Cannonsburg Convention is in *Steel Labor,* June 1961, pp. 6–7.

6. *Steel Labor,* October 1944, p. 4 reported forty-five NLRB elections won during the previous one and a half years; *Official Proceedings* of the 1947 District 31 Conference reported twenty-six new workplaces organized during that year (p. 7).

7. *Steel Labor,* August 23, 1942, p. 6; June 24, 1943, p. 9; February 25, 1944, p. 9.

8. Linnet Myers, "Birth of USWA Local 65," unpub. paper in file of Southeast Chicago Historical Project, p. 71.

9. Lloyd Ulman, *The Government of the Steel Workers' Union* (New York: John Wiley, 1962), pp. 56 ff.

10. Jack Stieber, "Steel" in *Collective Bargaining: Contemporary American Experience,* ed. Gerald D. Somers (Madison: IRRA, 1981), p. 165.

11. Bernard Karsh, "Steelworkers: Militant Unionism," in *The Worker Views His Union,* ed. Joel Seidman et al., (Chicago: University of Chicago Press, 1958), pp. 69–70.

12. Karsh, "Steelworkers," p. 67.

13. Stieber, "Steel," p. 178.

14. *Chicago Tribune,* April 30, 1952, p. F3; June 19, 1952, p. F3.

15. Interviews with William Caples and Frank Cassell, April 16, 1982.

16. Interview with Samuel Evett, April 17, 1982.

17. *Chicago Tribune,* May 19, 1946, p. F2.

18. *Steel Labor,* November 1948, p. 5.

19. *Chicago Tribune,* May 12, 1950, p. F3; June 18, 1950, p. F2; July 22, 1950, p. F3.

20. Harvey Levenstein, *Communism, Anti-Communism, and the CIO* (Westport, Conn.: Greenwood Press, 1981), p. 51.

21. *Chicago Tribune,* April 13, 1946, p. F3.

22. See notes 15 and 16.

23. *Chicago Sunday Times,* August 24, 1947.

24. *Chicago Star,* August 30, 1947.

25. Ibid.

26. J. David Greenstone, *Labor in American Politics* (Chicago: University of Chicago Press, 1969), pp. 200–1.

27. *Chicago Tribune,* February 2, 1959, p. F3.

28. Ibid., January 28, 1962, p. F2.

29. Greenstone, *Labor in American Politics,* p. 200.

30. Ibid., pp. 269–70.

31. *Chicago Tribune,* October 11, 1961.

32. Neal Peirce, *The Megastates of America* (New York: W. W. Norton, 1972), p. 307.

33. *Chicago Tribune,* February 4, 1964, p. 3; September 10, 1964, p. 3.

34. Greenstone, *Labor in American Politics,* p. 201.

35. William Kornblum, *Blue Collar Community* (Chicago: University of Chicago Press, 1974), pp. 90–91.

36. Kornblum, *Blue Collar Community,* p. 13, 31.

37. Michael Barone, Grant Ujifusa, and Douglas Matthews, *Almanac of American Politics: 1980,* (New York: E. P. Dutton, 1979), p. 241.

38. Kornblum, *Blue Collar Community,* p. 207.

39. *Gary Sunday Post Tribune,* June 28, 1964.

40. Kornblum, *Blue Collar Community,* pp. 221.

41. Ibid., pp. 227–28.

42. *Wall Street Journal,* December 31, 1976, pp. 1 and 10.

43. *Report on International Election of February 8, 1977* (Pittsburgh: USWA International Tellers, 1977).

44. *Report on International Election;* District 31 tally sheets; *Report on International Election.*

45. *Chicago Tribune,* August 26, 1977, p. 4; August 31, 1977, p. 4; September 8, 1977, p. 4.

46. Ibid., January 1, 1980, p. 5.

4D

United Auto Workers Local 6

United Auto Workers Local 6 in Melrose Park, Illinois, was first organized in 1941 at a new Buick Motors plant that produced engines for World War II bombers. Three months after the war ended, the sprawling plant located at a busy suburban intersection thirteen miles west of the Chicago lake front, was purchased by one of the city's industrial giants, the International Harvester Corporation, for the manufacture of diesel engines and crawler (construction) tractors. With a nucleus of veterans from the Buick days, the UAW quickly reestablished its presence in the plant, and after an NLRB election victory in November 1946, Local 6 represented the workers at Melrose Park continuously for the next thirty-five years.

With an average membership over the years of 3,000–3,500 workers, Local 6 never constituted a significant numerical percentage of the membership of its huge international union, the UAW, nor of the 125,000 UAW members employed in the "ag imp" (agricultural implement or equipment) industry. The local also did not represent more than 10 percent of the 30,000–40,000 production workers employed by Harvester throughout the country. Thus, the fortunes of Local 6, at least since the emergence of centralized contract negotiations after 1950, were determined to a great extent by the national policies of Harvester and the UAW, especially by the national collective bargaining relationship between the two.

With the advantages of representation by a large and powerful industrial union, of pattern bargaining based on auto industry settlements, and of a long tradition of aggressive bargaining and militant leadership, Harvester workers at Melrose Park achieved contracts that were envied by most industrial workers in the United States. For example, average wages at Local 6 rose from $1.71 per hour in 1949 to $9.21 per hour in 1979—a rise of some 540 percent during a period when the Consumer Price Index for Chicago rose by about 260 percent.[1] The benefits won included three to five weeks of paid vacation leave; fourteen regular holidays and five personal holidays; and drug, dental, and vision-care benefits, in addition to the usual medical and hospitalization insurance pensions of $950 per month after thirty years of service and "optional" and preretirement leave programs.

However, the history of continuous contract gains in wages and benefits drew to a close for Local 6 in the late seventies. By that time, International Harvester was being branded a "severely undercapitalized, overstaffed, disor-ganized, and inefficient company."[2] From the beginning of the 1979–80 strike, whose settlement produced few, if any, of the desired concessions for management, Harvester amassed losses totaling a staggering $503.7 million, the largest five-quarter loss in American corporate history outside the auto industry. For a time the company discussed possible closure of the Melrose Park plant.

One of the distinctions of Local 6 from its outset was the calibre of its leadership. From the very first Buick days, Local 6 produced a long line of exceptionally competent leaders, many of whom went on to important positions in the UAW's Harvester Department or Agricultural Implement Council, at international headquarters in Detroit, in university labor education programs, and in progressive political organizations in Washington.

The leadership for years had the reputation of being loyal adherents to UAW President Walter Reuther and his concept of social unionism; of strong opposition, during the first years, to the rival caucus led by R. J. Thomas and George Addes within the UAW and to the communist-dominated Farm Equipment Workers Union, which represented many Harvester Workers until 1955; of great commitment to union democracy at the Melrose Parks works; and of unflagging militancy in its relations with local management. These traits were evident in the vigorously contested local elections, which usually drew turnouts as high as 70–85 percent of the membership, and in the scrupulous reporting on both developments within the plant and national union and social issues in the weekly newspaper, the *Union Voice*. But perhaps most important for the rank and file of Local 6, the ideal of industrial democracy was expressed most forcefully in the daily workings of the shop committee, a body considerably more powerful than the local's executive board. In the early years, the shop committee, comprised of representatives or "zonemen" from each major zone or department in the plant (including a chairman elected among the committee members), was responsible for contract negotiations, but after 1950, it concentrated on grievance processing and other aspects of supplemental contract negotiations. Its weekly meetings with local management officers centered on disputes over piecework rates, production standards, seniority rights, layoff procedures, and other contractual matters whose enforcement by the shop committee was believed to guarantee Local 6 members both dignity and security at their workplace.

In his 1950 master's thesis on grievance processing at the Buick plant, Bernard Karsh wrote that the work force was characterized by a "great preponderance of untrained, unskilled workers," most of whom had had little, if any, previous experience with industrial jobs or unions.[3] Perhaps a quarter of these workers were women, and according to some old-time UAW activists, "hookers, gamblers, the Mob, and politicos representing every faction in Chicago" were also well-represented at Buick.[4] However, as Karsh emphasized, the majority of unskilled and inexperienced workers was complemented by a small core of skilled veterans from both GM and the UAW. Shortly after the UAW first won recognition from GM in the late thirties, the firm's conversion to wartime production caused substantial temporary unemployment among GM workers; GM encouraged them to seek employment in their war production plants, including the one at Melrose Park. Their skills were in demand at the plant, and the Melrose Park personnel department accepted the demands of the new UAW organizers that the workers be hired on.[5]

The core of veteran unionists from the auto plants, along with a coterie of "worker-intellectuals," university graduates, assorted radicals, and other non-GM veterans, provided the leadership for the Buick local. For example, Robert Stack, who before the war was a reporter and member of the Chicago Newspaper Guild, had been fired in a newspaper strike, was president of Local 6 when it temporarily folded in 1945, and later chairman of the Shop Committee for many years after the war. Carl Shier held a number of local offices, including shop committee chairman, before becoming the international representative in 1967; later he was a national vice-chair of the Democratic Socialist Organizing Committee. Jack London subsequently became a professor of sociology and adult education at the University of California, Berkeley, and William Dodds was a University of Chicago student who worked at Buick at night and was urged to become a union activist by his professor Paul Douglas. Dodds, who subsequently earned a master's degree in economics from Columbia University, left Local 6 after the war to hold a number of UAW posts in political education; he also served as executive director of the Democratic National Committee and of Douglas Fraser's short-lived Progressive Alliance, and long held the post of political action director of the UAW.[6]

Also coming from a university setting were Jack Conway and Ralph Showalter, both from working-class backgrounds in Seattle but associates at the University of Washington,[7] where Conway, a University of Chicago graduate, taught and Showalter was one of his students. They decided to move to Chicago and hire on at Buick, where Conway became chairman of the Shop Committee and leader of the Reuther caucus. He left after the war to serve for many years as administrative assistant to Walter Reuther and as executive director of the AFL–CIO's Industrial Union Department. Later he served as deputy director of the federal government's Housing and Home Finance Agency and of the Office of Economic Opportunity under the Kennedy and Johnson administrations.[8] Showalter later served for many years as a UAW legislative representative and was a prominent civil rights activist.[9]

With the leadership of the Reuther caucus in the hands of Conway, who was remembered by his colleagues as an extraordinarily skilled negotiator, Local 6 established itself as a progressive and militant union during the war. Two of Conway's major efforts were aimed at ending discrimination against the many black and women members. Although blacks were employed from the very first in janitorial and other menial jobs, Conway was responsible for seeing that the plant's first black employee worked on a machine. Conway was also responsible for pursuing a grievance for two-and-a-half years on behalf of a woman supervisor who was paid 10 cents per hour less than a male counterpart. According to Carl Shier, the women employees in the plant were quite insistent that Local 6 leaders persist for a favorable determination, first with the GM umpire (arbitrator) and then with the National War Labor Board during World War II. After receiving such a decision on this early equal pay for equal work case, women workers held a party for the union men and apologized for the harsh treatment they had meted out over the case.[10]

Another example of the local's bargaining militancy was its opposition to the wartime no-strike pledge adhered to by the UAW and other unions. Local 6 delegates at the 1943 and 1944 Constitutional Conventions of the UAW urged repudiation of the pledge, and its leaders fought, also without success, for a "no" vote in the 1944 membership referendum held by the UAW on the issue. In early 1945, Local 6 took a strike vote over management's refusal to resolve seniority grievances, but according to Karsh, Buick bargained swiftly, and the strike was averted until the war's end.[11]

Carl Shier also remembered that a Trotskyite faction from the Socialist Workers' party was responsible for Local 6 being one of the first two or three UAW locals to press for a convention resolution based on Trotsky's article, "Transitional Demands." Trotsky had advocated that during inflationary times organized labor should demand a wage escalation clause, and during a depression should demand a deescalation clause providing for the reduction of work hours. As Shier said, "we were way ahead of everyone else on the escalator clause, which is today's cost-of-living allowance."[12]

Karsh contended that extreme distrust pervaded local union-management relations at Buick, primarily due to the hostility of the UAW veterans who had experienced firsthand the verbal and physical violence of the GM organizing drives in the thirties. The distrust was most evident in the union's aggressive approach to grievance processing, which finally caused the grievance machinery to break down completely in April 1945 after being flooded with seniority rights grievances. But it was also evident in the squabbling between Local 6 and Melrose Park managers over such innocent matters as blood donations, baseball games, a victory dance, and even a cash collection for cigarettes for Local 6 members in the services.[13]

When Harvester bought the plant from the government for $13.7 million and occupied it on January 1, 1946, it brought to Melrose Park a long and well-known history of bitter resistance to unions. Harvester was also burdened by its acrimonious relations with the radical Farm Equipment Workers Union (the FE), which represented about thirty thousand Harvester workers in eleven plants at war's end, and with the UAW's seventeen thousand employees in six plants.[14] The union, for its part, brought back many of the veteran Buick militants, Shier, Stack, and the first three local presidents under Harvester,— Edward Thompson, Roy Dahlke, and Ray Cluts—and added to them new militants who hired on in 1946 and 1947. These included Seymour Kahan, who served as assistant director of the UAW's Agricultural Implement Council after leaving Melrose Park; Norman Roth, an acquaintance of Kahan's and Carl Shier's during their adolescence in Chicago, a leading opponent of the Reuther caucus at Local 6 in the forties, and years later three-term president of the local; and Robert Jones, the local's first (and only) black president, who, upon his election in 1957, reportedly became the first black president of any predominantly white union local in Chicago.

The only sustained challenges to the Reutherites at Local 6 from the FE or the UAW's Thomas–Addes caucus came during the first months of Harvester's operations. At this time, according to Stack, Joseph Mattson, Region 4 director for the UAW, relied heavily on the support of communist unionists within the UAW; he put up a candidate for directorship of the Chicago Industrial Union Council. After his candidate lost, Mattson harbored considerable ill-will against Stack and other anticommunist Local 6 activists who had fought the candidacy. In April 1946, Mattson placed staff representative Harry Mays in charge of Local 6. This was a retaliatory action, because Mays was a Thomas–Addes supporter and thus not acceptable to Local 6 leadership.

The FE, which already represented the workers at the other Harvester plants in Chicago—the McCormick, Tractor, and West Pullman works—was also present in Melrose Park in 1946. One of its leaders was Norman Roth, who was allied with the FE until its decisive defeat in the NLRB election. Afterward Roth became a leader in the Thomas–Addes caucus' Committee to Build Local 6.[15]

The details of the first decade or so of Local 6's relations with Harvester are not as well-known as later events because the existing copies of the weekly paper, the *Union Voice,* were only available beginning in 1951, and then only very irregularly until 1954. However, the broad outlines of the bargaining relationship up to 1955 are clear enough; it was characterized by continuing guerilla warfare between the union and management, particularly over piecework rate grievances, and by the local's struggle for union security and a master contract covering all Harvester workers represented by the UAW. Robert Ozanne observed that: "The years from 1945 through 1958 witnessed more prolonged labor-management strife than had any other period. With the exception of 1949, every contract negotiation of this period was accompanied by strikes, in 1946, 1947, 1948, 1950, 1952, 1955, and 1958. The signing of the agreements signified little, as the unresolved conflict raged unabated through the media of the grievance procedure and local work stoppages in Harvester plants. From 1954 to 1959 more than 48,000 grievances went to the last stage of the grievance procedure. At one time during the 1955–1958 agreement, 12,000 grievances were awaiting arbitration."[16]

Harvester's success in maintaining labor peace with employees' works councils in the thirties had sold management on the merits of company unionism, so that by 1941, it was one of the few large corporations still holding outside unionism at bay. Only during the war, under the pressure of National Defense Mediation Board and National War Labor Board orders to agree to representation elections and to grant union security, did the company first experience powerful, independent unions. By then, according to Ozanne, the indigenous conservative trade union leadership had long since been destroyed, replaced by the more docile works council leadership so that the leaders who emerged in both the FE and UAW were generally young, able radicals. They were also warring radicals; the communist leaders of the FE and the anticommunist Reutherites in the UAW were engaged, during the first decade after the war, in bitter ideological struggles, raids on each other's Harvester plants, and intense internal debates on proposed mergers.

The intra-Harvester rivalry between the FE and UAW was intensified by management's decision to revoke or resist union security in the immediate postwar years. Without security, even locals such as the one in Melrose Park, where one union was never seriously threatened by the other, were not immune from the influences of bitter union rivalry. Until the FE was so weakened by a disastrous 1952 strike that the UAW could absorb its remaining locals through decertification elections in 1954 and 1955, and until the UAW locals won full union security in their 1955 master contract, all local leaders felt obliged to prove their superior militancy to their members.

Among other tactics, Local 6 flooded the grievance machinery, deliberately walked out of grievance meetings, organized employees against working overtime, held back production to the minimum guaranteed rate, and called "quickie walkouts."[17] The guerilla skirmishes most often involved grievances over the company's complicated system of production standards, or piece and time rates. At Melrose Park and chainwide, somewhat less than one-half of the production workers were piece workers.[18]

Most observers agree that piece rates did not mean low wages after the war. Karsh observed in 1952 that "Local 6's militancy, directed against a fairly profitable company, has helped to bring piece rates and working conditions to very high levels, equal to the best in the industry."[19] Carl Shier also acknowledged that the piece rates determined by the NWLB had allowed

Harvester workers to do very well in wages compared with other workers. Nonetheless, grievances continued to mount, and when the company began its efforts to tighten up piece rates and to downgrade job classifications for day workers, Local 6's reaction was predictable. In 1948 and 1950, it and other Harvester locals went out on strike over these and union security issues, and in 1952 it called a major strike, independent of the other UAW locals, over piece and time rates.

The 1948 strike, called on August 17 and involving some twenty-four thousand Harvester workers, centered on "disagreements over grievances, time-studies, standards of wage rates, and holiday pay," according to the *Chicago Tribune.*[20] But Karsh also believed that at issue was "the desire of the various UAW locals in the company's plants to obtain a master contract."[21] The strike ended on September 2, when Harvester granted a number of uniform contract provisions, rather than a master contract, and a substantial wage increase. A Local 6 pamphlet claimed a 10 percent wage increase and also a maintenance-of-membership clause.[22]

On May 4, 1950, some seven months of negotiations over new pension and health and welfare benefit plans ended in agreement. Covering twenty-one thousand UAW members at Harvester, the noncontributory pension plan and contributory health and welfare plan, funded at $12,000,000 a year, were modeled after a plan negotiated by the UAW and Chrysler. Harvester would pay 7.5 cents per hour per employee into the pension fund and 2.71 cents per hour into the health and welfare fund, while each employee would contribute 3.6 cents per hour to the latter. The plans provided for monthly pensions of $100, including social security after 25 years of service, disability benefits of $50–$100 a month at age 55 with fifteen or more years of service, life insurance up to $28,000, accidental death benefits of $1,500, and hospitalization and medical benefits.[23]

But just a few months after this agreement was signed, the Harvester locals were out on a seventy-seven-day strike. The UAW demanded settlement on terms patterned after the pact signed with GM, including a modified union shop, an annual improvement factor (4 cents), and a cost-of-living escalator (6 cents), while management asked for a five-year contract.[24] The modified union shop was gained approximately one year after 85 percent of Local 6 members had voted in an NLRB-supervised election to authorized their leaders to seek a union shop. The union security clause "while not compelling old employees to join the union, required new workers to join upon the completion of their three-month probationary period. At the end of a year they had the privilege of withdrawing from the union, though their failure to do so at that time bound them to remain members for the duration of the contract. Workers who were union members when the contract was signed were similarly required to maintain their membership. This union security clause was in effect in 1952, when Local 6 had approximately thirty-four hundred members, representing over 99% of those in the bargaining unit."[25]

While the 1950 contract was the first UAW–Harvester contract to be negotiated centrally, the UAW spokesmen consisted of four regional directors who found it difficult to agree on a uniform contract.[26] Whether because of the lack of central union direction or because of the inherent complexity of the issues, the UAW and Harvester were unable to reach agreement on a new rationalized structure for piece and time rates. These issues were referred to local negotiations, with the provision that any local could strike legally over production standards during the life of the contract.

Not surprisingly, Local 6 was one of a few UAW locals to exercise this contractual right. Tensions at Melrose Park had been exceptionally high during the year preceding the strike. On September 28, 1951, shop committeeman Robert Stack was discharged for insubordination while he was conducting a time study, supposedly in violation of the contract. When faced with a membership meeting scheduled two days after the discharge for a strike vote, management immediately changed Stack's discharge to a thirty-day suspension. Local 6 member then voted to agree to take the suspension to arbitration and also to pay Stack's wages for the month out of work.

Local tensions were further exacerbated in 1951, when Harvester established a standards department in Melrose Park and every other plant.[27] In February 1952, a writer in the *Union Voice wrote:* "In a move unmatched by audacity and gall, the company is trying to cut a daywork classification in half! They want to cut it from group 6 down to group 3! If they can get away with this, no classification in the plant is safe. If we lose this one it will be an open invitation to start chiseling on anyone's and everyone's job."[28] Matters worsened when Harvester fired the permanent arbitrator in early March.

But it was not until August 4, after two workers were discharged for an alleged slowdown, that Local 6 went out on its second seventy-seven-day strike. The strike occurred in the middle of continuing intense rivalry between the FE and UAW. It was a sign of exceptional militancy on the part of Local 6 to undertake a long-term strike during Harvester's all-out battle against the FE, which was engaged in a disastrous thirteen-week strike.

The strike ended in October 1952, when management agreed to higher job classifications on every daywork job that the local had demanded be raised, using a formula by which piece rates were raised on more than a thousand jobs in the plant by an average of 25 percent, to reinstating the two fired employees, and to not penalizing workers for any actions taken during the strike.

In many ways, the 1952 strike marked the closing of Local 6's first postwar period. It was the last strike undertaken when rival FE locals still threatened the UAW; it was the only independent strike Local 6 brought against Harvester until a two-day walkout in 1970; and it was the last strike specifically over the company's postwar efforts to tighten production standards. Local 6 and Harvester were groping toward a new bargaining relationship, one dominated by centralized contract negotiations and by pattern bargaining based on the UAW's Detroit contracts.

The UAW's establishment of a Harvester Department (or council) uniting all its locals in the chain, the merger between the UAW and the FE, and the emergence of a central labor relations staff at Harvester were the chief factors behind the rationalization of labor relations in the mid-fifties. In January 1954, with the aid of the new permanent arbitrator David Cole, the union and Harvester reached agreement on a central organization for the UAW, the Harvester Department, "an arrangement long sought by management to deal with a few union officers on major policy matters rather than with a number of regional directors."[29] The Harvester Department consisted of a chairman, who was then Vice-President Leonard Woodcock, and four regional directors.

In June 1954, the UAW supplanted for the first time a former FE local in East Moline, and similar victories followed at the remaining nine FE plants in early 1955. By May, the UAW–FE merger, in which many former FE leaders became UAW leaders, had been worked out with the participation of Seymour Kahan, and Ray Dahlke from Local 6. The UAW now represented about forty thousand Harvester workers, 95 percent of all production and maintenance personnel.[30]

In 1947, Harvester had created a new position of vice-president for industrial relations, to whom the central labor relations staff organized in the early forties would report. This position passed in 1952 to William J. Reilly, who became "without question . . . the most influential management representative in Harvester labor relations from the postwar period into the present decade, the 1960's."[31] Shier described Reilly as a "very smart, skillful negotiator" who was much easier to work with than most management representatives— an opinion also held by Stack. Shier also described the local's relation with Reilly as "respectful, somewhat friendly."

The culmination of the centralizing process came in the 1955 negotiations in which both Shier and Kahan participated, the latter as the newly elected head of the Harvester Department. Despite a three-week strike, the outcome of these negotiations was to lead to a substantial improvement in local and national relations. In early 1955, top company and union officials met to resolve policies over incentive, classification, and overtime issues. Basing their decisions on guidelines by David Cole, they were able to formulate agreements that resolved hundreds of grievances. They also held meetings to explain the guidelines to plant managers and shop committees, who were then able to settle many other grievances. In this manner the estimated number of grievances awaiting arbitration was reduced from twelve thousand to two thousand during the first half of 1955 (specific figures for Melrose Park were unavailable). During the negotiations that year, which began on June 30, Harvester pushed for the abandonment of the second step in the grievance process, involving the local committeemen and plant management, because management believed that this step had only impeded the processing of grievances.[32]

This proposal and one on production standards were the only unresolved issues when the UAW strike began on August 23. In the three-year master contract announced on September 16, the UAW agreed to a simplified two-step grievance machinery (employee-foreman conference, then top union and management officials, backed by final arbitration) and a provision to have the union's Harvester Department screen many backlogged grievances. These provisions resulted in a drop in the number of grievances processed by the average UAW local from a hundred per week to six or seven by the summer of 1956.[33] In line with the Detroit pattern, the UAW won the union shop, a wage increase of 11 cents per hour, supplemental unemployment benefits, and other economic benefits. More important, it obtained agreement on substantially its own terms over the right of Harvester piece and day workers to retain the wage advantages they had accrued since World War II.[34]

While Local 6 leaders and others were thus pushing for centralized bargaining machinery that would closely follow the Detroit lead in contract provisions, they were also maintaining their strong support for Walter Reuther and for his advocacy of social unionism. The resolutions passed by Local 6 under President Ray Cluts for presentation to the UAW's 14th Constitutional Convention in 1953 provided an excellent example of the local's progressive thinking. They called for the founding of a new farmer-union-liberal political party that would fight for national health insurance, more generous workers' compensation, unemployment and social security benefits, strong civil rights legislation, and an end to American support to authoritarian rulers such as Francisco Franco and Antonio Salazar in Europe and Syngman Rhee and Chiang Kai-shek in Asia. Other resolutions called for a national daily labor newspaper, for unification of the AFL and CIO, for the establishment of union hospitals where workers could go for periodic checks on occupational and other diseases, for a UAW nonprofit health insurance company, and for the teaching of the ideals of industrial democracy to American school children. Finally, one resolution called for maintaining annual local elections rather than going to a biennial election as many Harvester locals had done, for the establishment of the Harvester Department to facilitate the exchange of information between locals, for rank-and-file election of delegates to CIO conventions, and for opposition to any extension of the terms for regional directors or international representatives.[35]

At the 1955 convention, where Local 6 boasted of being the only local to provide the shop with daily bulletins on the convention proceedings, its delegates helped block an administration-proposed loyalty pledge for candidates in local elections and another administration proposal for compulsory two-year terms for local officers.[36]

By the end of World War II, both company and union had displayed exceptional support for nondiscriminatory hiring and promotion. Harvester had in wartime begun a program of nondiscrimination in employment that "went far beyond the dictates of the President's order" [Executive Order 8802 of June 1941, requiring a nondiscrimination clause in all defense contracts and establishing a Fair Employment Practices Committee]. Black employment nationwide at Harvester jumped from 4.5 percent in 1940 to 13.8 percent in 1959. At Melrose Park, black employment rose from 4 percent in 1946 to 14 percent in 1952, and then stabilized between 14 and 19 percent through the remainder of the decade according to company files.[37] The progress toward full employment opportunities at Melrose Park was facilitated by the local's formation of a Fair Practices Committee (FPC) in 1952.[38] According to Stack, the chairman of the FPC along with the shop committee chairman met with plant management once a month to discuss all cases of alleged discrimination.

The only time a significant alteration in the makeup of the Melrose Park work force occurred was in 1970, when Harvester closed down its Tractor Works plant on Chicago's South Side. The works had employed many black and Hispanic workers, who made up a large percentage of the seven hundred or so men who were able to transfer to Melrose Park. Under the Tractor Works agreement signed February 14 by Harvester and the UAW, these workers were able to hire in, with guaranteed master seniority back to November 1, 1961, on any open job (one posted and not filled by a seniority employee).[39]

According to local officers David Ryan, vice-president of Local 6 and Alex Duarte, sergeant at arms, because of the Tractor Works' transfer and also because of a gradual rise at other times in minority employment, slightly under half of the workers were black in 1982, and perhaps 17 percent were Latino. Women were still a relatively small minority of the workers; they only began entering the plant in any numbers at all in the seventies, and they entered into the life of Local 6 only on a limited scale. A women's committee was in existence in November 1978, but the only mention of its activities in the *Union Voice* was a passing notice: "members of the women's committee womaned the stoves in a fund-raising effort"![40]

Otherwise, the history of Local 6 during the sixties and seventies reflected the emphasis on local contract administration which followed the introduction in 1960 of the "New Look" policy of speedy oral grievance settlement in Harvester plants. Robert McKersie, who examined structural factors in the UAW–Harvester bargaining relationship shortly after the New Look was implemented, concluded that "by far the most important structural development has been the shift to local contract administration that the grievance prevention program has fostered."[41] Although there were subsequent minor eruptions over production standards grievances at Melrose Park, the policy of preventing written grievances was effective enough there to free the local's attention to other local issues. Plant shutdowns and layoff arrangements, technical displacement and on-the-job training, the use or abuse of preemployment testing, and the reliability of the plant's medical services were among the important shop issues concerning Local 6 leaders in the sixties and seventies. But most important were issues of safety and health within the plant—concerns that received constant union attention after 1962 and that led to a two-day wildcat strike in 1971. Besides this trend in contract administration, the two decades were marked by the complete dominance of national-level contract negotiations and by an internal political life that largely carried forth the earlier traditions of progressive leadership and lively internal democracy.

At least until the late seventies, Robert Ozanne's conclusions, written in 1966 about the impact of the New Look policies, apparently applied to Melrose Park and other plants: "Certainly there is a greater degree of confidence between union and management at Harvester than ever existed in the earlier history of the company. The company-union relationship is today typical of that in other large manufacturing firms, most of which fit [Richard] Lester's description of the third stage of development [in management's labor relations policy]: acceptance and accommodation."[42]

An especially contentious issue was management's decision in February 1969 to install an experimental management information and control system (MICS) at Melrose Park. The MICS was designed to improve the scheduling of workers and materials and involved the use of employee identity cards and job assignment cards with electronic tuning and recording devices alongside each machine. The reaction of Local 6 leaders to these "electronic stool pidgeons" was immediately hostile. In May, Seymour Kahan warned Robert Crowell, Reilly's successor as head of industrial relations at Harvester, that "the UAW would be less than men, less than unionists if they permitted IH to install the electronic recording devices. He [Kahan] added that he wasn't making idle threats and that the UAW would not sit still while I-H attempted to turn its members into robots. He also stated that the electronic system I-H proposed to use was more vicious than a TV scanning camera used to keep workers under surveillance. The I-H electronic system, he added, would tie workers to their machines as though they were lashed with ropes."[43]

Nonetheless, the MICS was finally installed at Melrose Park in the summer of 1972. At this time, the company provided Local 6 with the following assurances about its operations: its purposes included providing a record of employee attendance and overtime hours, identity of an employee, the part number being produced, the number of pieces produced, etc., and using information for inventory control, job scheduling, and piece workers' pay. The MICS would not be used to establish or change new or existing production standards, to monitor the employees' work or personal activities for disciplinary purposes, to record the time used to make individual pieces, or to report on employee absences or job stoppages of less than ten minutes. Time-study personnel would not be allowed access to the MICS central room, whereas a union representative would with permission from the work's industrial relations manager and changes in the system that affected employees would be discussed with the union well in advance of their introduction.[44] Evidently Harvester subsequently kept these commitments because the MICS was never again an issue with Local 6.

Local questions of occupational safety and health were, however, far more important than the MICS or other plant issues. The first mention of a safety program in the *Voice* concerned a "floor-level safety and good housekeeping program" that was introduced in 1962. The program called for the policing of the plant by two "action committees" composed of management and union officials. According to Stack, Plant Manager Peter Becker "convinced members of the Safety Committee, both Management and Union, that he means business and the Union members of the Committee fully intend to see that his plans are carried out."[45] Still, in 1964 the Shop Committee complained bitterly to plant management about the breakdown in safety and sanitation and threatened to call in government inspectors. Management's response was a clean-up, which was described by Stack: "Work is now in progress to make Melrose Park Works one of the safest and cleanest plants in the I-H chain. Aisles are going to be striped; each Supervisor is now compelled to contact at least two employees each day regarding safety and housekeeping; an inspection of the plant by the joint Union-Management Safety Committee will be made each month; and other programs are under development."[46]

In December 1966, however, Local 6 decided to call in an official from the U.S. Department of Labor to enforce the safety provisions of the Walsh–Healy Public Contracts Act. Bernard Culleran, a safety engineer with the Bureau of Labor Standards, heard complaints of "lack of proper ventilation and smoke fumes; blocked and narrow aisles; blocked stairways, broken, dirty, and oil-soaked floors; and use of combustible material without adequate ventilation," from Melrose Park workers. According to the *Voice,* Culleran "ordered numerous violations corrected."[47] In September 1968, Local 6 alleged "hundreds" of violations of the Illinois Factory Code and called in the state factory inspectors.

By this time Local 6 was also pushing for safety and health rights in both legislation and contracts. In 1968, members were encouraged to write to their congressional representatives in support of the Johnson administration's Occupational Safety and Health Act. In March 1969, Carl Carlson, chairman of Local 6's Safety Committee, prepared several portfolios containing "documented evidence of the poor safety and sanitation conditions" at Melrose Park for distribution to congressional representatives by Local 6 members attending a UAW conference in Washington. This action came at the same time that about a dozen Local 6 members picketed the plant over safety and health violations. As local management hosted the board of directors of International Harvester, the workers picketed outside the plant, carrying placards alleging that the plant was in violation of federal, state, and county safety codes.[48]

The strife over safety grievances came to a head on February 6, 1970, when a two-day strike, the first grievance strike at Melrose Park in more than ten years, began. Complaints over safety grievances, production standards grievances, job classifications, noise and air pollution, equalization of overtime, and insurance benefits prompted the short stoppage. The union leaders' rhetoric during the days before the strike was rather vague about why a general labor-management crisis had arisen at Melrose Park, or why this backlog of grievances, which had grown to about 175, differed from other buildups of the postwar era. Although the settlement at Melrose Park included provisions on all the issues, the *Voice* only carried details of the improvements in the safety program. These included having the works manager or assistant works manager attend the monthly meeting of the joint union-management Safety Committee, developing a safety awareness program for foremen and stewards, establishing a noise abatement and hearing conservation program that would arrange joint investigations of all noise and smoke areas, and the inspection of overhead hoisting equipment. The union members voted to accept the settlement, 586–32.[49]

Although safety concerns continued to fill the pages of the *Voice* throughout the decade, the only other major eruption occurred in July 1975, when local union and management officials narrowly averted a strike with a settlement listing a large number of improvements in the safety program. The July 26, 1975, *Voice* listed all these provisions, including the right to a medical examination by all workers who might be exposed to toxic chemicals, the removal of most asbestos from the plant, and the distribution throughout the plant of a list of 560 hazardous materials.

It is difficult to assess whether the contentiousness during these years over safety issues resulted more from genuinely poor safety conditions within the plant or from Local 6's living tradition of guerilla warfare with the plant managers. When the union brought in the state factory inspectors in 1968, Robert Stack commented that "The ironic tragedy of this whole safety episode is that the local management views it as a clash and power struggle between it and the Shop Committee. The fact that the health and safety of International Harvester employees is at stake seems to have been overlooked by management. This is not conjecture on the part of this reporter. The State inspectors were told by certain management people that the Union was only raising the safety problems as a pressure to win grievances."[50]

Judging from Stack's observation, both union and management considered the other one guilty of approaching safety issues as pressure points in their relationship. There also does not appear to be overwhelming evidence of exceptionally poor safety conditions. There were only ten lost-time work accidents at Melrose Park in 1977, according to the *Voice*—certainly not a large number for such a large plant.[51] From 1946, only one Melrose Park worker had died as a result of an on-the-job accident. Also, the fact that the demands in the 1970 strike had safety concerns listed first on a rather long list of traditionally acrimonious issues such as backlogged grievances and production standards lent credence to the belief that Local 6 leaders were approaching safety complaints as aggressively as they had the earlier shop issues of the forties and fifties.

Following a two-month strike in 1959 and a settlement that did not please Local 6 leaders, the history of contract negotiations for the next twenty years until the 1979–80 strike was as unremarkable as the earlier negotiations had been turbulent. New three-year pacts were signed without strikes in 1961 and 1964, after a one-day stoppage in 1968, after a two-and-a-half week strike in 1971, after a two-week strike in 1973, and a one-day walkout in 1976. Robert McKersie stated that the primary determinant of the UAW's bargaining strategy in later negotiations was "the pressure within the union for obtaining uniform settlement terms both within the farm equipment industry and with respect to the auto industry." He also noted that "the ability of the UAW during recent negotiations, especially during 1958, to whipsaw the companies within the farm-equipment industry has been an important factor in precipitating strikes."[52]

Examples of some of the innovative benefits workers at Melrose Park and throughout the industry enjoyed before they reached Detroit included a full week of extra vacation time or pay above the Detroit provisions (1964); a one-week Christmas vacation shutdown (1967); revision of the cost-of-living escalator clause to provide for no ceiling wage adjustments; and a comprehensive, nondeductible dental plan for employees and their dependents innovated by Harvester in 1970–71. Three new types of paid time off were won in 1976: the "attendance bonus," in which employees earned one-half hour off for each week in which they worked all scheduled hours; the "pre-retirement leave program," in which employees with more than thirty years' service could take from one to four weeks of extra vacation a year, depending on their age, and be paid at the level of their applicable disability benefits; and the "optional leave program," in which workers with ten or more years of seniority could elect to take a layoff of from eight to thirteen weeks after the layoff of all workers with less than one year of service if the company deemed further layoffs necessary. The 1976 and 1980 Harvester pacts dropped the attendance bonus plan in preference for an additional week's vacation.[53]

Carol J. Loomis, writing in *Fortune* magazine, believed that one problem with the twenty years of relative labor peace enjoyed by Harvester after the 1958 negotiations was that "contracts were renewed with relative ease only because the company buckled on work-rule issues that it was beginning to think were increasingly impairing Harvester's ability to compete." The first significant attempt at tightening work rules occurred during the 1973 negotiations, when Brooks McCormick, chief executive officer and a descendant of Harvester's founding family, insisted on the company's right to schedule Saturday work. A fifteen-day strike ensued, at the end of which "the union gave an inch," acceding to the insertion of a letter into the contract that said the union would cooperate with the company in "encouraging" employees to work, provided they received advance notice, on up to seven Saturdays a year (later raised to fourteen). Loomis also stated that one purpose of the letter was "to discourage overtime strikes, a prevalent practice in which whole departments or even plants would refuse to volunteer for overtime, because they were trying to punish the company for one thing or another." As she concluded, "The letter didn't work, in part no doubt because its aims collided with a rising desire among workers everywhere for more leisure time, not less."[54]

Charles Bryant, Stack's successor as chairman of the Shop Committee, acknowledged in a June 1979 *Voice* that the last few suspensions and/or discharges issued for absenteeism and tardiness concerned overtime workers who came in late or not at all.

In October 1979, in the weeks before a 172-day strike began, Bryant and the new Local 6 President Robert Tinker were again faced with the threat of a wildcat overtime strike by Local 6 members. The threatened strike came when top UAW negotiators (including Cletus [Horace] Williams, head of the UAW bargaining team and a Local 6 alumnus) were engaged in critical negotiations and/or strikes with all of the Big Three companies. It also came shortly after the international union had authorized an extension of the contract beyond the October 1 expiration date, much to the dismay of many Local 6 leaders and members.

When the strike began on November 1, mandatory overtime was the one over-riding issue. The attempts to tighten work rules by Harvester's controversial new chief executive officer Archie McCardell were the fighting concerns. McCardell, formerly with Ford and Xerox, came to Harvester in 1977 as Brooks McCormick's successor, with an extraordinary compensation package including a base salary of $460,000, annual incentive income of $300,000, and a loan of about $1.8 million to purchase 60,000 shares of

Harvester stock, the loan to be forgiven if he succeeded in raising the firm's lackluster financial performance to the level of its competitors. McCardell had a driving ambition from the beginning to hammer down costs "whose excessive character can be seen in Harvester's low return on sales: 3.4 percent in 1977, versus better than 7 percent for Caterpillar and Deere."[55]

One of McCardell's chief demands on work rules, concerning the temporary layoff problem, was settled before the strike, with each side getting something it wanted:

> The problem concerned a right of seniority, which, in the case of a short departmental layoff (caused, say, by a parts shortage), allowed workers with sufficient tenure to avoid the layoff by moving out into the rest of the plant and bumping workers junior to them (who might then bump someone else). The chain reaction was very costly to the company. Meanwhile, the UAW believed that most of the senior workers would have preferred another kind of prerogative: an option of being laid off first (ahead of junior workers) when only part of a department was going out. Why would a senior worker want to be the first out the door? Because he could get a short vacation and meanwhile draw down, through regular and supplemental unemployment benefits, about 95 percent of his regular take-home pay. The union gave up its old right for this new one, and both sides emerged satisfied.[56]

This compromise (the provisions of which Local 6 was to utilize only a year after the strike, when nine hundred Melrose Park workers were laid off from November 1, 1980 to January 5, 1981 at 95 percent of their regular pay) cleared the way for dealing with the two most contentious work-rule issues—the company's demands that it be allowed to schedule work on fourteen Saturdays a year, and that an employee's right to transfer to another job be limited to two moves a year.

Although Harvester was eager to blanket restrictions on job transfers, UAW vice-president Duane "Pat" Greathouse convinced management negotiators that the transfer arrangements at the plants were too diverse to allow a companywide settlement, so the issue was sent back to the locals. After examining some of the very minor revisions in seniority transfer rights negotiated locally in the last month of the strike, Loomis concluded that "even the company's biggest gains [e.g., a three-month freeze in each job] were slivers compared to the log it had begun negotiations trying to cut: a maximum of two transfers a year."[57]

In the end, management's concessions on mandatory overtime were at least as great as those on job transfers. A settlement was signed and ratified on April 20, 1980, by the UAW members, 11,000–2,000. Much was written and said at the time of the settlement about the significance of the 172-day strike over work rules. Local 6's Cletus Williams and Carl Shier both emphasized the union's bitterness at McCardell's attempted work-rule takeaways. Shier called the union's tenacity "a message to the companies that conditions that have existed for decades are almost impossible to take away from American workers. They're the greatest defensive fighters in the world."[58] Shier also mentioned Harvester's record profits in 1979 as further stiffening the workers' resistance to management takeaways, and Williams blamed the "new atmosphere" at Harvester since McCardell came. McCardell and other top management officials at first tried to defend the contract as the first step in achieving competitive labor costs, but such claims became virtually irrelevant in the context of the company's subsequent profound financial problems.

Despite the Reutherite vision of American trade unionism held by most Local 6 leaders since the war, the main significance of their militancy to the thousands of Melrose Park workers was probably its guarantee of high wages, excellent hours, and acceptable work rules. Unfortunately, recession and foreign competition were soon to undermine these achievements.

Local 6's dynamic experience epitomized the social unionism of the UAW. It was expressed along three dimensions. Within the organization itself, ideology became the basis of the struggle for control. At one level the struggle pitted the anticommunist Reutherites against the radical supporters of the Thomas–Addes caucus. Similarly, it was involved in the conflict between the dominant Reuther faction and the communist leaders of the competing Farm Equipment Workers Union. Other strands of pressure were exerted by Trotskyites, black and Hispanic ethnic groups, and women workers. Even though the Reutherites controlled the positions of leadership, they were constantly impelled to adopt more militant stances by the pressure of rival factions.

Militancy extended to Local 6's relationship to the International Union. On numerous issues, such as the wartime no-strike pledge and wage escalation, Local 6 tended to urge more aggressive postures upon the International leadership. At the same time, many of the local's top officials moved up to join the ranks of the central Reuther organization in Detroit and Washington. Although the local was a tiny cog in the Reuther machine, its leaders influenced UAW policy not only in the politics of Chicago and of Illinois, but also in the national scene.

The third major dimension of Local 6's history was the relationship with plant and company management. Three periods are discernible. The first covered the years between 1941 and 1955 and was characterized by highly competent observers as guerilla warfare. The second extended from the mid-fifties until the late seventies, during which time new top company personnel worked out an impressive system of accommodation with the local. The new approach to grievance handling attracted national attention. The third period began in the late seventies as the company attempted unsuccessfully to regain its national and world competitive positions by cutting labor costs and eliminating what it regarded as unduly restrictive work rules. The 172-day strike of 1979, which reflected the new conflict state, was focussed on the company's right to schedule overtime work. The company failed to achieve its objective. Meantime, its competitive condition steadily worsened. The very survival of the company and of Local 6 was in question.

NOTES

This section is a condensation and a revision of a report researched and written by David Nicolai.

1. 1949 wage figure from *Union Voice;* 1979 wage figure from *Chicago Tribune* March, 19, 1980; CPI figures from BLS, *Handbook of Labor Statistics,* Bulletin 2070, (Washington: BLS, 1980), p. 326.

2. *Chicago Tribune,* May 3, 1981.

3. Bernard Karsh, "The Grievance Process in Union-Management Relations: Buick Melrose Park and the UAW-CIO Local 6," master's thesis, University of Chicago, 1950, pp. 42, 45.

4. Interviews with Carl Shier, October 30, 1980 and William Dodds, April 25, 1981.

5. Karsh, "The Grievance Process," p. 44.

6. *Union Voice,* May 18, 1979; interview with William Dodds.

7. Shier said Washington State University, Dodds said University of Washington.

8. *Union Voice,* February 22, 1963; June 19, 1963; March 19, 1965.

9. *Union Voice,* December 7, 1962.

10. Interview with Carl Shier, October 30, 1980.

11. Bernard Karsh, "Metalworkers: Factionalism and Conflict," in *The Worker Views His Union,* ed. Joel Seidman et al. (Chicago: University of Chicago Press, 1958), p. 92.

12. Interview with Carl Shier.

13. Karsh, "The Grievance Process."

14. See Robert Ozanne's *A Century of Labor-Management Relations at McCormick and International Harvester* (Madison: University of Wisconsin Press, 1967), p. 209.

15. Interview with Robert Stack and Norman Roth, April 25, 1981.

16. Ozanne, *A Century of Labor-Management Relations,* pp. 208–9.

17. Karsh, *"Metalworkers,"* p. 95.

18. Companywide proportion—45 percent, Ozanne, *A Century of Labor-Management Relations,* p. 221; "somewhat less than half" at Melrose Park, interview with Robert Stack.

19. Karsh, *"Metalworkers,"* p. 95.

20. *Chicago Tribune,* August 18, 1948.

21. Karsh, *"Metalworkers,"* p. 94.

22. "Solidarity thru Progress: Local 6" (ten-year anniversary pamphlet), no page number.

23. *New York Times,* November 12, 1949; April 21, 1950; June 4, 1950.

24. Benjamin Selekman et al., *Problems in Labor Relations* (New York: McGraw-Hill, 1958), p. 483.

25. Karsh, *"Metalworkers,"* p. 94.

26. Robert McKersie, "Structural Factors and Negotiations in the International Harvester Co.," in *The Structure of Collective Bargaining,* ed. Arnold Weber (Chicago: University of Chicago Press, 1961), p. 291.

27. *Union Voice,* October 1, 1951.

28. Ibid., February 15, 1952.

29. Selekman, *Problems in Labor Relations,* p. 484.

30. Ibid.

31. Ozanne, *A Century of Labor-Management Relations,* p. 180.

32. Selekman, *Problems in Labor Relations,* p. 486; McKersie, "Structural Factors and Negotiations," p. 298.

33. Selekman, *Problems in Labor Relations,* p. 494.

34. Ibid., p. 492.

35. 1953 Local 6 Resolutions to UAW Convention (unpub. document, vertical files, University of Illinois Institute of Labor and Industrial Relations).

36. *Union Voice,* April 8, 1955.

37. Ozanne, *A Century of Labor-Management Relations,* pp. 188, 192, 193.

38. 1952 Annual Report to Membership.

39. *Union Voice,* April 10, 1970; April 17, 1970.

40. Interviews with Carl Shier, Robert Stack, and others; *Union Voice,* November 3, 1978; June 8, 1979.

41. McKersie, "Structural Factors and Negotiations," p. 302.

42. Ozanne, *A Century of Labor-Management Relations,* p. 232.

43. *Union Voice,* May 2, 1969.

44. Ibid., February 16, 1962.

45. Ibid, February 21, 1962.

46. Ibid., April 24, 1964.

47. Ibid., December 9, 1966; October 4, 1968.

48. Ibid., March 11, 1969.

49. *Chicago Tribune,* February 4, 1970; February 10, 1970; February 15, 1970; *Chicago Sun-Times,* February 10, 1970; *Chicago Daily News,* February 9, 1970.

50. *Union Voice,* October 4, 1968.

51. Ibid., January 19, 1979.

52. McKersie, "Structural Factors and Negotiations," p. 287.

53. *Daily Labor Report,* May 6, 1980, p. C–1; BLS *Wage Chronology International Harvester Company and the Auto Workers: February 1946—September, 1976,* Bulletin 1887 (Washington: BLS, 1976).

54. Carol J. Loomis, "The Strike That Rained on Archie McCardell's Parade," *Fortune,* May 19, 1980, pp. 91–99.

55. Loomis, "The Strike That Rained," p. 93.

56. Ibid., pp. 96–97.

57. Ibid.

58. *Chicago Sun-Times,* April 21, 1980.

4E

Teamsters Local 743

The Teamsters had achieved exceptional strength in Chicago by the twenties. One estimate cited by Newell was that by 1929, 77 percent of the "teamsters, chauffeurs, and allied occupations" in Chicago were unionized, although the following year witnessed a serious factional division that led to the formation by part of the membership of the Independent Chicago Teamsters Union as a breakaway fragment of the International Brotherhood of Teamsters.[1] Although the nucleus of the IBT was well established before the start of the postwar era, this section will deal with a nontrucking branch of the union that was in its infancy in 1945 and was to grow into the international's largest local with some thirty thousand members.

In 1945, Local 743 represented some five hundred workers in a handful of Chicago warehouses. The local was just four years old, having been created in 1941, when the American Federation of Labor granted jurisdiction over warehouse workers to the International Brotherhood of Teamsters and two independent AFL warehouse locals in Chicago merged to become Local 743: Wholesale Dry Goods Warehousemen Local 20475 at Butler Brothers, and Wholesale Hardware Warehousemen Local 20549 at Hibbard, Spencer, and Bartlett.[2] Details of the local's early years are not available, but a short history published by Local 743 states that with the organization during 1942 of warehousemen employed by Alden's mail-order firm, membership shot up to 1,200, only to decline to 500 three years later because of the wartime mobilization.[3] However, under the exceptional leadership of Donald Peters, who served as president from 1946 throughout the entire period of this study, the local was to become not only the Teamsters' largest affiliate, but also the largest unit of women workers (with the possible exception of some teachers and communications unions) in the country.

The local's two most important organizing victories during the decade following the war came in the mail-order industry, which was centered in Chicago. The Teamsters organized the third-largest mail-order firm, Spiegel's, in 1946, and the second-ranking firm, Montgomery Ward's, some nine years later. Their subsequent efforts to unionize Sears, Roebuck, the industry leader, were not successful. Recognition by Spiegel's came after a strike from

May 28 to June 14, 1946 by some 800 employees organized by Local 743; management agreed to recognize 743 as the bargaining agent for 3,500 of its employees in fourteen warehouses and to grant a $4 per week raise.[4]

The strike and new contract at Spiegel's did not attract much outside interest compared with the 1955 strike at Montgomery Ward's, which ended with Ward's announcement, amid controversial circumstances, that it would sign Teamsters' contracts for 15,000 warehouse employees nationwide. The three-week strike in March ended over a year of fruitless contract negotiations following NLRB election victories for the Teamsters in January 1954. According to the local's history, 88 percent of Chicago Ward's employees voted in favor of Local 743 in these elections.[5] The negotiations had been led nationally by Jimmy Hoffa, then a Teamsters' international vice-president and the head of its over-the-road drivers' Central States Conference, and, for the 5,000 warehouse employees of Ward's in Chicago, by Donald Peters. On March 9, two days before the strike began, Teamsters Joint Council 25, representing approximately 40 different locals and 120,000–140,000 union members in the Chicago area, pledged its support to Local 743 in the Ward's negotiations.

The Teamsters' negotiations with Ward's management aroused controversy not only at the time, but also two years later, when they were examined during the U.S. Senate's McClellan Committee's investigation of labor racketeering. The controversy dated back to January 1955, when Teamsters' President Dave Beck announced the Ward's drive in Miami Beach and stated that it was "pure coincidence that the welfare fund of the central states conference of the Teamsters, a subsidiary of the international, has recently invested one million dollars in Ward's common stock and has arranged to put in another million."[6]

However, by the beginning of the strike in March, George Bliss, the veteran labor correspondent for the *Chicago Tribune,* reported widespread speculation in Chicago over the possibility of the Teamsters' shares being wielded in an upcoming proxy struggle for control of Montgomery Ward's. Bliss stated that $2 million had already been invested in Ward's stock by Hoffa on behalf of the Michigan Teamsters' Health and Welfare Fund; he also reported that some local Teamsters and businessmen were concerned that the trust arrangement for the new Central States Fund would leave Hoffa in complete control of it. These concerns were fueled by rumors that Dave Beck had struck a deal with New York industrialist Louis Wolfson, calling for the union's shares to be voted in support of Wolfson in his proxy battle with the incumbent Ward's chairman, Sewell Avery, in exchange for complete freedom to unionize Ward's employees should Wolfson win.[7]

On March 31 it was Avery, not Wolfson, who triumphantly announced an agreement with the Teamsters. The 81-year-old Avery had incurred considerable notoriety during World War II when his defiance of War Labor Board and presidential directives to grant union recognition and union-security provisions to organized Ward's employees led to Avery's physical removal from his Chicago office by U.S. marshals and the eventual seizure of all Ward's facilities by the federal government. Avery had obviously undergone quite a change of heart toward unions by 1955. Dave Beck announced that he would urge the Teamsters' trustees to vote for Avery at the April 22 shareholders' meeting, although Hoffa reminded reporters that the union only held $1 million worth of Ward's stock, and that this represented only a minute portion of the firm's outstanding shares. Nevertheless, Avery won the proxy battle with Wolfson, 4,100,000 shares to 1,700,000.[8]

Suspicions were immediately aired that this sequence of events represented a large-scale "sweetheart," or collusive, contract, and two years later members of the McClellan Committee, particularly Senator John F. Kennedy, pursued this possibility with great interest. In May 1957, Alfons Landa, a business attorney, testified that he had run into Dave Beck shortly after reading that he was siding with Wolfson in the proxy struggle and had suggested to Beck that if he switched the Teamsters' shares to Avery's side, the Ward's chairman would end his bitter resistance of unionization. Landa testified that Beck approved of the idea, and that it was "passed on" to the appropriate officials at Ward's.[9]

The committee heard no specific testimony on the roles played by Jimmy Hoffa or Donald Peters during the 1955 negotiations; however, in 1957, at the same time the Senate was investigating these affairs, Hoffa and Peters were leading negotiations for a new Ward's contract in Chicago. Peters was then serving as head of the union's Montgomery Ward's Council, which negotiated on behalf of some twenty thousand employees in about sixty Ward's facilities nationwide. He and Hoffa announced the ratification of a one-year contract on July 31, two months after the expiration of the old pact; it provided for wage increases ranging from 7 to 24 cents an hour; shorter hours, and arbitration of grievances.[10]

This contract was followed by a five-year pact negotiated in 1958, which appeared to mark the beginning of stable bargaining relations between the company and union. For the first and last time, the 1958 Ward's contract was negotiated jointly by Peters and Hoffa for the Teamsters and by James Suffridge, president of the Retail Clerks International Association; it covered around 22,000 teamsters and 8,000–9,000 clerks nationwide. The Teamsters and Clerks unions had been involved in bitter jurisdictional disputes at Ward's dating back to 1945; the Teamsters accused the Retail Clerks of a refusal to cooperate or bargain jointly during the 1956 negotiations, when the Teamsters had to work for two months without a contract. The Teamsters, with Hoffa as their new international president, refused to honor picket lines when the Clerks went on strike in January 1958. In their first show of overt hostility toward an AFL–CIO affiliate since their expulsion from the federation one month earlier, the Teamsters accused the Clerks' union leaders of "stupidity and self-interest" in calling the strike.[11] Nonetheless, Peters, Hoffa, and Suffridge joined together to end the Clerks' strike and sign, on May 26, a joint contract providing for wage increases, a cost-of-living clause, and a wage equalization agreement for the Clerks, who had received no increase the previous year. The contract also called for a modified union shop, which Hoffa described as "fundamental departure" from traditional Ward's policy (the controversial 1955 contract had contained a maintenance-of-membership clause).[12] A full union shop was not gained until the 1963 negotiations, which Peters and Hoffa again led in Chicago; the fifty-month contract also provided for wage increases averaging 26.3 cents per hour over the contract period, a profit-sharing plan, and numerous benefit improvements.[13]

Besides their work together during the fifties on the Ward's negotiations, Don Peters and Jimmy Hoffa had more questionable ties that were examined by the McClellan Committee. In January 1959, the senators heard extensive testimony on Peters's associations both with Hoffa and with two influential Chicago figures with reputed syndicate ties, Paul Dorfman and his son Allen. On January 22, Hoffa testified that Peters had been with him during his 1957 trial in Washington on corruption charges to discuss the Ward's negotiations and to "stay and observe the trial."[14] Committee Counsel Robert Kennedy later revealed subpoenaed records showing that Local 743 funds had paid for the one-night Washington hotel bill of the retired prizefighter Joe Louis during Hoffa's trial. This information came amid press allegations that Hoffa had paid Louis to "come down here and shake hands with him, and call him his friend" during the trial.

On January 27, 1959, Martin Uhlmann, a committee staff investigator, testified that the first contract signed by Allen Dorfman to provide insurance to a Teamsters' local came in December 1949, when Local 743 signed with the Dorfman family's Union Casualty Company.[15] Dorfman, who had been set up in the insurance business in 1948 by his father, Paul, the alleged gambling boss of Chicago's North Side, was under investigation by the committee for the $86,000,000 insurance business that he conducted with unions. Years later, Labor Department investigations would reveal that "hundreds of millions" of dollars in union funds flowed through Allen Dorfman's companies throughout the postwar period.[16] Uhlmann further testified to the committee that one year after signing up Local 743 Dorfman added the entire Central States Teamsters Fund to his insurance business. Uhlmann's documents showed that the insurance was awarded on a noncompetitive basis, and that Jimmy Hoffa was instrumental in arranging the deal.[17]

Two days, later, Daniel Healy, director of Region 14, AFL–CIO (Illinois and Iowa), testified concerning alleged colusive arrangements between

Dorfman, Local 743, and the waste trade industry in Chicago. Healy had been appointed in July 1957 as trustee of Waste Material Handlers Local Union 20467, which George Meany had put under direct AFL–CIO trusteeship in December 1956, after the discovery that its health and welfare funds were being transferred to a personal checking account of Paul Dorfman. Dorfman, according to Healy, was also drawing salaries from both the general fund and the health and welfare fund of the waste handlers' local. Healy had also discovered that some of the terms of the prior contract negotiated by Dorfman, including overtime and holiday pay provisions, were being violated by the employers with Dorfman's consent.[18] Also, "the president of the union had very, very seldom run a meeting and Mr. Dorfman always chaired the meeting."[19]

Sometime after Healy, as trustee of the local, notified the waste industry employers' association that he wished to negotiate a new contract, he learned that Paul Dorfman was busy organizing waste handlers for Local 743:

> On February 27, 1958, as I said before, we notified the association that we wished to amend, modify and renew the agreement. We went into negotiations some 30 days later, and right along around that same time Mr. Paul Dorfman conducted an organizational campaign. Our first knowledge was at B. Cohn & Sons, who is not a member of the association where Mr. Dorfman went in with the knowledge of the employer and organized or signed up the employees on cards for Local 743 of the International Brotherhood of Teamsters.
>
> At the time it was called to our attention that the authorization cards carried the designation of AFL–CIO after the local, and as a result of that unfair labor practice, charges were filed which were dismissed by the Board after investigation, mainly because the contract was an independent contract outside of the association and as such the expiration date was September 1, so that the move on Mr. Dorfman's part would be premature as far as that agreement was concerned.
>
> *Mr. Kennedy.* So what happened was that Mr. Dorfman had been expelled from the AFL–CIO, and you had found, or learned, that there had been misuse of union funds and a violation of the trust agreement regarding the welfare fund, and the contract that had been written with the association had not been enforced. After this information you started to enter into negotiations to sign a contract with the Waste Trade Industry of Chicago, and you found the same Paul Dorfman was then going to work for the Teamsters?
>
> *Mr. Healy.* That is correct.[20]

Healy finally negotiated a new contract for the waste handlers in November 1958, six months after the expiration of the old contract—a period of time during which "the employers were used rather roughly by various members of the association." Healy described the new contract as "not as good an agreement as I would like to have seen in there . . . we negotiated at a time when we had an economic recession as far as the waste industry was concerned, plus the fact that we had this continual harassment from Mr. Dorfman that certainly was not the best atmosphere to negotiate a decent agreement in."[21]

The next witness before the committee on January 29 was Don Peters, who pleaded the Fifth Amendment forty-four times under quite hostile questioning by Senators McClellan, Kennedy, and Ervin. Peters first took the Fifth when asked the amount of the salary he received from Local 743. After Senator McClellan reprimanded the witness for his failure to answer the question, Senator Kennedy stated that the committee's figures showed that Peters's salary had jumped from $11,000 in 1954 to $27,000 in 1958. Senator Ervin noted, with some outrage, that the latter figure was then higher than a U.S. senator's, and demanded of Peters that he explain what services he provided Local 743 that would justify such a high salary, but Peters declined to answer.[22] (High, multiple salaries were a common phenomenon among top Teamsters officials and not unique to Peters.)

Senator Kennedy continued the investigation with a statement that the committee had learned that the collusive waste trade agreement was arranged in February 1958 at Miami Beach's Castaways Hotel by Paul and Allen Dorfman, Hoffa, Peters, and Ted Schulman, head of the employers' association. Peters repeatedly pleaded self-incrimination when the senators inquired about motel bills for Peters and the Dorfmans from the Castaways and about a Local 743 check paying for Peters's air fare to Miami.[23]

The McClellan Committee inquiries and Peters's relations with the Dorfmans and Hoffa were to mar Peters's public image throughout his career. But, as *Chicago Tribune* writer James Warren was to state much later, Peters was a complex figure who also displayed a "deeply progressive streak."[24] Besides his remarkable organizational and administrative abilities, Peters demonstrated a lively interest in advancing the welfare of minority groups, strongly encouraged and supported labor education programs for his members, and sometimes took liberal political positions contrary to those of the international union's leadership.

The late fifties were significant years for Local 743 not just because of the attention its president received from the McClellan Committee. It was during this period that it became one of the fastest growing union locals in the United States, despite the failure of the Teamsters' efforts to organize the majority of the employees at the nation's retail giant, Sears, Roebuck.

On July 10, 1958, Hoffa announced in Washington the beginning of a campaign to organize seventy thousand Sears mail-order, warehouse, repair, and service workers. A week earlier, A. H. Raskin had reported in the *New York Times* that Hoffa and his "chief braintruster" Harold Gibbons of St. Louis had mapped out plans for what Raskin described as "the biggest organizing campaign undertaken by any union since World War II."[25] Three days before the Washington announcement Hoffa had been in Chicago, where, according to the *Tribune*'s George Bliss, he laid out an organizing drive among fifty thousand warehouse workers in Chicago, including fifteen thousand employed by Sears; Hoffa gave Peters a $23,000 check to begin the campaign, with the understanding that Local 743 would match this amount.[26]

The Teamsters' Sears campaign officially got under way on January 5, 1959. On January 8, Peters, as head of the drive in the central states, presided over a Chicago meeting of union officials from fifty locals in the thirteen-state area.[27] A brief report in the *New York Times* in December 1959 stated that "although no representation elections have been held, the Teamsters are claiming progress." Chicago and national publications remained silent on the union's efforts.[28] Apparently the company's policies of paying competitive wage rates and offering a pioneering profit-sharing plan and a relatively generous retirement plan to its employees paid off; Peters later said of Sears that "everytime we make a move, they give all their people a raise."[29]

Whether rivalry with the Retail Clerks International was a factor in the Teamsters' defeats is also speculative. Before the campaign, only 14,000 of Sears' 205,000 employees were reported to be unionized, about half by the Teamsters and half by the Clerks' union. Hoffa announced in July 1958 that he had discussed the campaign with James Suffridge, and that the Teamsters' executive board had authorized him to negotiate a mutual assistance pact with Suffridge's union.[30] Nothing more is known about relations between the two unions during the Sears drive, although the *Tribune* did report in March 1959 that Chicago's Local 1550 of the Retail Clerks and the Teamsters (Local 743) had started "dual" organizational drives for Sears' employees.[31]

New York Times journalist A. H. Raskin had anticipated a more favorable result:

> Ironically, Mr. Hoffa's critics in the Senate Select Committee on Improper Activities in the Labor or Management Field may have created a more favorable setting for the Sears unionization effort than had existed before the Committee's formation. In past years the company received union-busting advice from Nathan W. Shefferman, a management consultant who acted as "chancellor of the exchequer" for Mr. Hoffa's predecessor, Dave Beck. The consultant's technique was to lavish favors on labor leaders while advising employers on how to keep the leaders' unions out. After the Shefferman tactics had been exposed [by the McClellan Committee in 1956], Sears denounced them as "disgraceful" and promised the Senators that such anti-union acts would not be repeated.[32]

Despite the failure of the Sears drive, Local 743 in the late fifties added to its previous base of a few large mail-order locals thousands of workers in Chicago's many small manufacturing firms. In the words of 743's own history, "The union's membership is as varied as all America. Workers in 536 companies make Christmas trees and toys, fill mail orders and manufacture cameras, tape recorders, lamps, plastic products, school supplies, and thousands of other items. . . . Members are people of every type of skill . . . shipping clerks . . . lathe hands . . . artists . . . insurance claim processors . . . fork-lift operators . . . assemblers . . . sales personnel . . . mail clerks . . . more occupations than in any other union in the country."[33]

By 1960, Local 743 and two other Chicago locals had become the three largest Teamsters' locals in the country, pushing Local 299 in Detroit, Hoffa's home local, into fourth place. That year John F. English, the Teamsters' secretary-treasurer, announced that Local 705 (truck drivers, oil drivers, filling station, and platform workers) had more than 19,500 members in Chicago; Local 743 had 18,000; and Local 710 (meat and highway drivers, dockmen, helpers, and miscellaneous truck terminal employees) had 16,400 members. English specifically cited 743's gain of 3,600 new members in 1959—a figure that reportedly made 743 the fastest growing local in the United States.[34]

These three locals were fast becoming powerful members of Chicago's Joint Council 25, whose total membership of 140,000 made it the largest such Teamsters' council in the country. The council was then headed by Ray Schoessling, who was later to become head of the Central Conference of Teamsters (Hoffa's post before he became president) and then international secretary-treasurer, second in rank to Frank Fitzsimmons.

It was these three locals, 743, 705, and 710, whose announcements of support for Hoffa in September 1957 assured the Joint Council's endorsement of him over Thomas J. Haggerty in his bid to succeed Dave Beck as international president. When asked why, at a time when the AFL–CIO's Ethical Practices Committee was recommending the expulsion of the Teamsters to the federation's executive board, these locals supported Hoffa over Haggerty, who was secretary-treasurer of Milk Drivers' Local 75, a member of the Chicago Board of Education, and a reformist candidate committed to cleaning up the Teamsters, Donald Peters replied: "We pledged ourselves to Hoffa and we have a habit of keeping our word. Hoffa's proven ability to organize and negotiate the best contracts for labor makes him the outstanding candidate for the job."[35]

The rise of 743 to prominence during the late fifties and early sixties did not occur without some violent incidents and adverse publicity in the Chicago papers. Four such publicized events were recorded in Chicago: in 1959 at Drake Manufacturing Corporation and at Aetna Plywood and Veneer Company; in 1961 at Spectator Sportswear Company; and in 1962 at Phil-Mail Lingerie Company. The Aetna case is illustrative.

On March 26, 1959, Donald Peters and two 743 organizers, James Galineas and Russell Anderson, were arrested on assault charges after an incident at Aetna Plywood and Veneer Company. Albert Suggett, Jr., a nonunion salesman who volunteered to drive company trucks during a strike that began on July 22, 1958, alleged that he was approached by twelve members of 743 on the loading dock, threatened, struck in the face, pushed against the truck, and kicked.

Although these charges were subsequently dismissed on technical grounds in criminal court, the Cook County Grand Jury, on July 15, 1959, issued an indictment of conspiracy to boycott and injure the business, interference in employment through threats, preventing persons from working on such terms as they see fit, and entering the company premises to cause employees to leave their jobs. During the strike, according to the *Tribune*, two 743 members poured sugar and iron filings into the gas tank of an Aetna truck, the plant mysteriously caught fire and a stairway was destroyed, and a company truck was damaged by fire at the home of a company officer. On February 15, 1960, four of the union men were convicted on the conspiracy charges and fined a total of $6,500, while eight other defendants, including Peters, were acquitted for lack of evidence linking them conclusively to the conspiracy (two of the defendants could not be located to stand trial).[36]

The Aetna strike was not finally resolved until 1963. The continuing controversy revolved around Aetna's firing of fifteen striking 743 members on March 23, 1959, the same date it filed a petition with the NLRB seeking an election to determine if 743 still represented a majority of its employees. Shortly thereafter, 743 filed a charge with the board alleging that Aetna had failed to bargain and had illegally fired the strikers. The NLRB eventually dismissed both charges filed by 743 and held an election in which no votes were cast for the union, eight were against, and nine ballots were challenged. On March 6, 1962, the board overruled 743's objections to the election and determined that the majority of Aetna employees had not chosen 743 as their representative.[37]

But the Teamsters continued their picketing after that date, arguing that the sole object of the picketing was now to get Aetna to rehire the fired warehousemen. The board, however, disagreed, and in a decision and order dated January 22, 1963, ruled that forcing Aetna to recognize it as a bargaining agent remained an object of 743's picketing; therefore, the picketing violated Section 8(b)(7)(B) of the NLRA, which proscribes recognitional picketing within one year after a valid NLRB election. The board ordered Local 743 to cease the picketing, and four-and-a-half years of bitter struggle between 743 and Aetna ended in defeat for the union.[38]

It is difficult to judge, on the basis of sporadic newspaper coverage, whether resort to verbal and physical threats against company employees and disregard for NLRB election results represented isolated occurrences in the history of 743 or a more serious, long-term pattern. The fact that all four such incidents reported in the papers occurred only between 1959 and 1963 probably indicates a turbulent period in 743's affairs that stands apart from earlier and later periods. Violence has often been a characteristic of organizing campaigns in American labor history, and employers have contributed significantly to it.

It is more important to examine the quality of representation that Local 743 offered its members after gaining bargaining rights in a workplace. Specifically, did the hundreds of 743 contracts provide improved wages, benefits, and working conditions? Also, did 743 procedures allow a meaningful degree of union democracy for its thirty thousand members? In a 1979 piece of investigative reporting, Steve Askin of the *Chicago Reporter,* a monthly paper covering minority affairs in the city, concluded that "Local 743's bargaining record, its tolerance of membership participation, and its unique (among Chicago Teamsters locals) record on civil rights and community outreach, make it a good yardstick for measuring the performance of other Teamster bodies."[39]

Askin estimated that approximately 40–45 percent of all Chicago Teamsters were black or Latino, and that about 60–70 percent of the membership in the nontrucking locals were composed of minorities. Also, about a fifth of all Chicago Teamsters members were women. Local 743's 20,300 black and Latino members and 17,000 women members constituted the highest percentages of racial minorities and women for any Teamsters' local in Chicago. As to the officialdom, the Chicago Joint Council's Executive Board consisted of seven white men; all the locals were headed by white men; and only ten blacks and no Latinos were among the 119 Executive Board members paid full-time salaries by Chicago locals in 1977.[40] Furthermore, out of 91 organizers, business representatives, and business agents on union salary and not on the Executive Board, only fifteen were black, three were Latino, and eight were women. It is worth noting, however, that more than half the nonwhite staff members and all but one of the women worked for Local 743.

The staff of 743 included Recording Secretary Robert Simpson, "one of the workers' most outspoken black Teamsters officials" and an activist in Chicago's Coalition of Black Trade Unionists. In 1971, Simpson gained considerable attention when he appeared at a Chicago press conference called by Jesse Jackson to protest the Nixon administration's wage-price freeze and its plea for an end to labor strikes. Appearing only days after Frank Fitzsimmons had pledged the Teamster's full cooperation with Nixon's economic policies, Simpson announced that 743 would not call off any strikes and also endorsed Jackson's call for work slow-downs to protest Nixon's initiatives. When asked if he was speaking for his local, Simpson said that he was, and that 743 had the autonomy to ignore Fitzsimmons' pledge.[41]

Another 743 official was Executive Board member Clara Day, described in the *Reporter* as the Teamsters' "most visible woman leader" in Chicago. A member of the city's Commission on Human Relations and the Illinois Commission on the Status of Women, Day, who was black, was elected Midwest regional vice-president of the Coalition of Labor Union Women (CLUW) at its founding convention in Chicago in 1974.

When Donald Peters, who served as a vice-president of the Chicago Urban League, was designated that organization's man of the year in 1968, he was cited for "financial aid to those who are struggling for an education with determination" (he had given both personal and union financial assistance to black students), and for his "courageous leadership which has inspired others to join the on-going battle for interracial justice and equitable relations between people of all colors." According to Peters, 743 was among the first locals to obtain antidiscrimination clauses in its contracts after World War II, and among the first to gain a paid holiday on Martin Luther King's birthday in the late sixties.[42]

Perhaps the most concrete contribution 743 leaders could make to the welfare of its thousands of minority and female members would be the provision of competitive wages, decent benefits, and the other traditional goals of American trade unionism. In this regard, the *Reporter* article concluded that wages and working conditions had actually worsened through union action or inaction in three of the other heavily minority, nontrucking Teamster locals in Chicago: 703, 727, and 777. As for 743, however, Askin concluded that although "the effectiveness of so vast a union is difficult to gauge, it appears that Local 743 has boosted the living standard of many thousands of workers in traditionally low-paying jobs."[43] Unfortunately, his conclusion was based on a limited statistical comparison between wages provided in hospital employee contracts and wages in nonunion health facilities in Chicago, where starting pay was approximately 5 percent below that earned by workers represented by the Hospital Employees Labor Program (HELP), the joint affiliate of 743 and local 743 of the Service Employees. It has been impossible to determine, without the cooperation of 743 officials, how the local members who were not covered by HELP contracts fared on wages and working conditions.

In October 1979, Peters unsuccessfully challenged Joseph Bernstein, head of Local 781, for the vice-presidency of Joint Council 25; he allied himself with Dominic Senese, president of Local 703 (produce drivers and landscape workers), who challenged council president Lewis Peick, also unsuccessfully. In fairness to Peters, it should be noted that the incumbent vice-president he sought to oust, Bernstein, and his two sons were reputed to run Local 781 as a personal fiefdom, that one management official described as an "absolute catastrophe for workers."[44]

However, Peters's choice of an ally in their challenge to the leadership was also suspect. Senese had gained considerable attention during the fifties for the strong-arm tactics he used to maintain control of the Fulton Street Produce Market, and his ties to syndicate figures were an open secret in Chicago. Moreover, members of his local, two-thirds of whom were Latino migrant landscape workers, were reportedly as abused by their union leadership as any Teamsters in Chicago.[45] Peick, on the other hand, was a longtime political ally of Mayor Daley, a powerful, independent unionist who had successfully resisted Hoffa's attempt to encroach on his jurisdiction, and he had a reputation for strong, honest leadership.

On the positive side, the *Chicago Reporter* concluded that among the Teamsters' nontrucking locals, only 743 and 738 (composed primarily of food industry workers) allowed members to elect stewards and negotiating committee members, have regular training programs for stewards and distribute local newspapers. Local 743 took particular pride in its steward-training program, which was conducted continuously from the late fifties in cooperation with the labor extension program of the University of Illinois' Institute of Labor and Industrial Relations. They claimed it was the largest such program in the American labor movement.[46] And *The Voice of 743*, the monthly newspaper begun in 1957, carried Spanish articles in contrast with some of the other Teamsters' locals whose officials allegedly exploited their Latino members' ignorance of English.

The *Reporter* also noted that:

> Local 743 is one of the few locals that encourages members to attend its meetings. Only a tiny fraction of the members attend, however, and announcements in the *Voice of 743* rarely say what business will be considered.
>
> As in most non-trucking locals, elections for union offices are almost never contested and new officeholders are usually recruited by those who already hold power. Dispersal among hundreds of unrelated workplaces makes it difficult for members to have power in union politics.[47]

A longtime labor educator, Herman Erickson, who was extremely knowledgeable of Local 743's internal organization confirmed that the stewards and active members were encouraged by the union's top leaders to participate in the educational programs as well as in the local's unit meetings that often followed such programs. Contrary to the *Reporter*'s observations, he felt that the union activists played an influential role in the life of the local and often helped to shape policy, sometimes causing a reversal of initial leadership proposals (e.g., to raise dues). He also emphasized the importance of the stewards in continuing communications between the members and leaders.[48]

This brief account of Donald Peters and Local 743 is full of ambiguities and contradictions. An exceptional organizer and administrator with an attractive and forceful personality, Peters combined an apparently avid appetite for high rewards with a broad social interest in improving the employment and living standards of some of the most downtrodden members of the labor force. In view of the dismal civil rights records of other heavily minority Teamsters' locals, the prominent roles achieved by blacks, Latinos, and women on 743's Executive Board and paid staff must have reflected a deep personal commitment on Peters's part to the rights of minorities. Yet he associated, in apparently equal sincerity, with some of Chicago's most notorious underworld figures as well as with the most respected leaders of minority groups. He was involved in dubious loans and investments and was supportive of an elaborate program of workers' education and training. In a sense, he combined the extreme currents of the great metropolitan center of which he was a significant part.

NOTES

This section is a condensation and a revision of a report researched and written by David Nicolai.

1. Barbara Newell, *Chicago and the Labor Movement: Metropolitan Unionism in the 1930's* (Urbana: University of Illinois Press, 1961), pp. 209–10.

2. *Local 743: Portrait of a Union* [information booklet published by Local 743 c. 1968], (vertical files, Institute of Labor and Industrial Relations, University of Illinois at Urbana-Champaign, pp. 4–6).

3. *Local 743*.

4. Ibid., pp. 6–7; *Chicago Tribune*, June 12, 1946; June 14, 1946.

5. *Local 743: Portrait of a Union*, p. 7.

6. *Chicago Tribune*, January 27, 1955.

7. Ibid., March 10, 1955; April 1, 1955.

8. Ibid., April 1, 1955.

9. U.S. Congress, Senate, Select Committee on Improper Activities in the Labor or Management Field, *Investigation of Improper Activities in the Labor or Management Field* (hereafter referred to as the "McClellan hearings"), 85th Cong., 1st sess., May 14, 1957, pp. 2275–76.

10. *Chicago Tribune*, May 20, 1956; July 23, 1957; July 31, 1956.

11. Ibid., January 16, 1958.

12. Ibid., May 27, 1958.

13. Ibid., May 7, 1958.

14. McClellan hearings, pp. 5133–34.

15. McClellan hearings, pp. 15993–94.

16. *Chicago Tribune*, November 27, 1979.

17. McClellan hearings, p. 15994.

18. Ibid., pp. 16091–93.

19. Ibid., p. 16095.

20. Ibid., pp. 16093–94

21. Ibid., p. 16095.

22. Ibid., pp. 16098–99.

23. Ibid., pp. 16098–99.

24. *Chicago Tribune*, January 28, 1985.

25. *New York Times*, July 3, 1958.

26. *Chicago Tribune*, July 11, 1958.

27. *Chicago Daily News*, December 3, 1958; *Chicago Tribune*, January 7, 1959.

28. *New York Times*, December 18, 1959.

29. *Wall Street Journal*, December 29, 1958; *Chicago Sun-Times*, September 5, 1982.

30. *New York Times*, July 3, 1958.

31. *Chicago Tribune*, March 14, 1959.

32. *New York Times*, July 3, 1958.

33. *Local 743*, p. 8.

34. *Chicago Tribune*, August 8, 1960.

35. Ibid., September 1, 1957; September 9, 1957.

36. *Chicago Tribune*, February 16, 1960; *Chicago Sun-Times*, February 16, 1960; *Chicago Daily News*, February 16, 1960.

37. NLRB Decision and Order, Case #13-CP-44, January 22, 1963 (vol. 140 of NLRB D&Os), pp. 707–12.

38. Ibid.

39. Steve Askin, "Minority Workers Hit Hardest by Teamsters Union Corruption," and "Some Locals Fight for Higher Pay; Others Keep Wages Low," *Chicago Reporter*, March 1979, p. 7.

40. Askin, "Some Locals Fight," pp. 6–7.

41. *Chicago Tribune*, August 21, 1971.

42. Hoke Norris, "Union Man," *Chicagoland 7* (January 1970), p. 34.

43. Askin, "Some Locals Fight," p. 7.

44. Ibid., p. 8.

45. Ibid.

46. *Local 743*, p. 16.

47. Askin, "Some Locals Fight," p. 8.

48. Interview with Herman Erickson, March 11, 1985.

4F

Hospital Employees Labor Program

An unusual and distinctive offshoot of Teamsters' Local 743's history was the Hospital Employees Labor Program (HELP). HELP was a joint venture between Local 743 and Service Employees Local 73, headed by John Coleman, its founder in 1941. Coleman, like Donald Peters, had personally presided over the spectacular growth of his local from four hundred members in 1941 to four thousand in 1946, ten thousand in the late sixties, and eighteen thousand by 1980. Local 73 was not only the largest Service Employees' local in the state, but the largest of all AFL–CIO locals in Illinois. With this important base, Coleman in 1968 assumed the position of international vice-president as well as president of Chicago's Service Employees Joint Council No. 1, which was comprised of twenty-one service employees locals in Chicago representing some seventy thousand workers, or about one-seventh of the international's nationwide membership. The SEIU, which was known as the Building Service Employees Union until 1968, had been founded in Chicago in 1921 and had grown to one of the largest international unions in the United States during the forties and fifties under the astute and vigorous leadership of Chicagoan William McFetridge, the powerful past president of Flat Janitors Local 1 and a close friend and ally of Mayor Daley, despite his active support for the Republican party nationally.

HELP was initiated in 1966, when Peters and Coleman "established a joint council of the two local unions called HELP, the Hospital Employees Labor Program of Metropolitan Chicago."[1]

HELP was considered to be the largest cooperative organizing venture in the United States between two unions in the health care industry, as well as the largest cooperative venture of any sort uniting an AFL–CIO affiliate with the Teamsters since that union's expulsion from the federation in 1957. With the goal of organizing an estimated sixty thousand nonprofessional workers in more than a hundred hospitals in the Chicago area, HELP officials did not hesitate to describe their campaign as the largest in the area since the historic CIO drives of the thirties.

After five years of court battles, a number of dramatic strikes and near-strikes, and the reported expenditure of $1,000,000 by the leaders of Locals

73 and 743, HELP was able to claim that it had brought some seven thousand employees in twenty Chicago hospitals under contract. Organizing results, however, were less impressive after 1971, despite congressional enactment of the 1974 amendments to the National Labor Relations Act, which endorsed collective bargaining in the health care industry by rescinding the previous exemption of nonprofit hospitals from the act's jurisdiction. In the seventies, HELP organized only four thousand additional workers, and two thousand of these were gained in a single NLRB election victory in 1978.

The latter was a dramatic board election that pitted HELP organizers against the management, not of a Chicago hospital, but of the renowned University of Chicago. The drive to organize the university's two thousand clerical employees was officially sponsored by HELP, but the basis for operation was a five-hundred-member unit of Local 743 that represented service and mainte- nance employees at the university hospitals. Donald Peters personally led Teamsters' organizers in the hotly contested battle against the university's new president, Hanna Holborn Gray, and other top administrators of the elite, but then financially troubled, institution. NLBR officials spent four months investigating the status of eighty-seven challenged ballots after the November 1978 election, which had produced a narrow initial 712–706 margin in favor of HELP; board officials finally announced the union the winner in March 1979 by an official tally of 744–723.

Peters actually first entered the field of organizing hospital workers during the late fifties, a few years before the formation of HELP. Peters and his friend John Coleman became active in Chicago hospitals in 1959 during a nationwide upsurge in health care organizing, but only after the city's first hospital strike was called by another union leader, Victor Gotbaum, later the top official of the American Federation of State, County, and Municipal Employees (AFSCME) in New York City. On June 2, 1959, the same day that a 46-day, eight-hospital strike in New York City was settled with a partial victory for Local 1199 of the Retail Drug and Hospital Employees Union, Gotbaum began an organizing drive at Chicago's Mt. Sinai Hospital and the much smaller Chicago Home for the Incurable. Gotbaum, then district direc- tor of AFSCME in Chicago, headed the drive among Mt. Sinai's four hundred nonprofessional employees on behalf of AFSCME Local 1657.

By mid-August, Gotbaum claimed that 85 percent of the nonprofessional employees at Mt. Sinai had signed union cards, that 80 percent had signed at the Home for the Incurable, and that he also had majorities at Wesley Memorial, Chicago Osteopathic, and Columbus Hospitals.[2] Mt. Sinai, how- ever, remained the focus of his efforts. Management officials repeatedly re- fused to negotiate with Gotbaum, but in August they announced that improve- ments for employees would take effect in October, including a general wage increase, a grievance procedure, reduction of the work week to forty hours, time-and-a-half for overtime, and revision of the maximum vacation from one to two weeks. Management still refused to consider union recognition or bargaining rights, and on August 20, employees at both hospitals voted to begin a strike on August 27. The union offered to accept arbitration from any impartial group, but as the strike deadline approached, Mt. Sinai management declined to meet with the director of the Illinois Department of Labor, and Mayor Richard Daley did not respond to requests for intervention by officials of other unions.[3]

The strike lasted five months; during this period, Locals 73 and 743 entered the scene. In September, John Coleman announced his local's plan to conduct a membership drive among a hundred thousand hospital workers in the Chicago area. Local 743 followed suit in late October with a similar announcement. In December, Donald Peters announced that he would send out a hundred organizers, including many "borrowed or hired" from other unions, to sign up nonprofessional employees in Chicago's forty-five largest hospitals.[4]

Peters also announced that 743 was petitioning the NLRB to hold representation elections at seven hospitals. AFSCME Local 1657 filed a similar petition regarding the five hospitals it was organizing.[5] These petitions were meant to clarify the unions' rights in Illinois, one of thirty-eight states that had not provided, after the passage of the Taft–Hartley Act, any regulation of bargaining in nonprofit hospitals by statute or agency. Management at all the affected hospitals had been justifying their refusal to bargain by simply asserting their right not to do so under federal or state law.

On January 21, 1960, Ross Madden, director of the NLRB's Thirteenth Region, dismissed the petitions, referring to a recent NLRB decision in Washington that affirmed the Taft–Hartley exemption of nonprofit hospitals from the NLRA and that declined to assert jurisdiction over a proprietary hospital unless it was located in the District of Columbia, vitally affected national defense, or was an integral part of a commercial concern falling within the board's jurisdiction.[6]

Ten days later, the AFSCME strike was finally terminated by the union without any concessions from management. Gotbaum's strong commitment to nonviolence on the picket lines had allowed the hospitals to hire many replacements and volunteers, and with extra effort by nonstriking personnel, hospital operations were never affected seriously. In their analysis of the Mt. Sinai strike, Robert McKersie and Montague Brown emphasized the lack of support for AFSCME's efforts by other Chicago unions.[7] The historical record is unclear over whether the relations between the three unions active in Chicago hospitals were characterized more by rivalry or by cooperation.

In an analysis of the national upsurge in hospital organizing drives during 1959 and 1960, the labor reporter Sanford Gottlieb noted the close cooperation between Teamsters and AFSCME locals in New York City and added "in

Chicago, too, AFSCME and the Teamsters apparently had a close working relationship . . . further progress of the unionization drive in Chicago would seem to hinge on whether the Teamsters decided to throw in additional resources. Since the public employee union is unable to make further financial commitments, only the Teamsters are in a position to continue the struggle. That decision must apparently be made at the top echelons of the union."[8] Gottlieb also aired reports that a Building Service Employees representative had tried behind the scenes to prevent some hospitals in Chicago from recognizing rival unions, but he concluded that evidence to support such a claim was lacking.[9]

The first unionization drives in Chicago hospitals had apparently ended in complete failure with the NLRB's dismissal of the unions' petitions and the calling off of the AFSCME strike. However, in the judgment of Leo Osterhaus, who conducted a survey of labor relations in Chicago hospitals in 1965, "the threat of unionization helped to change the working conditions, increase the wages, and increase the fringe benefits, and it awoke the public in general to the employees' poor working conditions in the hospitals."[10] In 1956–57, average weekly wages for nonprofessional employees in Chicago hospitals were 5.5 percent higher than the average in fifteen other metropolitan areas surveyed by the Bureau of Labor Statistics, but in 1960 and 1963 surveys, the wage differential had increased to 12 percent. Osterhaus's figures also showed a significant narrowing of the traditionally large gap in nonprofessional wages between the higher-paying government hospitals and the lower-wage private hospitals in Chicago during this period.[11]

The preponderance of black and female employees among nonprofessional hospital employees; the lack of legal protection for their bargaining rights under the Taft–Hartley Act; internal hospital occupational structures, with an extraordinarily wide array of skill levels and job assignments among employees who often had little contact with their diverse co-workers; the nonprofit status of most private hospitals, which for many served to justify low wages and which led to the belief that an overriding concern for service to the ill should outweigh any consideration of the worker's welfare—all these factors continued to make organizing in the hospitals a difficult field throughout the sixties. Organizing virtually ground to a halt in Chicago and elsewhere after the events of 1959 and 1960.

Finally, in the summer of 1966, Peters and Coleman began discussing the possibility of a renewed drive in Chicago hospitals. The close personal friendship and working ties between Coleman and Peters were probably most responsible for their decision to merge the financial assets and organizing personnel of their locals into a unique "organic unity," in the words of Harry Kurshenbaum, a HELP official.[12] The formation of HELP was definitely not prompted by any suggestions of higher-ranking AFL–CIO officials. As

Labor in Illinois

George Bliss wrote in the *Tribune* at the time, "Officials of the two locals concede that George Meany, AFL–CIO president, could object to the relationship between the two locals (one belonging to the expelled Teamsters) but they said the drive for hospital workers will continue despite what Meany might try to do."[13] Jimmy Hoffa, on the other hand, gave his "total blessings" to the initiation of HELP, according to Kurshenbaum.

On October 27, 1966, twenty-five or thirty paid staff organizers from the two locals and approximately 350 worker activists launched the HELP drive by distributing literature and membership cards at the entrances of twenty-five hospitals. Kurshenbaum summed up the heady atmosphere that prevailed among the organizers with this statement of their attitudes: "Let's pull out all the stops. We'll hit the streets like commandos . . . like with the CIO."[14]

Predictably, HELP officials claimed an overwhelmingly positive response by workers in the first weeks, whereas hospital administrators insisted that "hospital wastebaskets are full of HELP literature with membership cards attached."[15] The real response was evidently somewhere between overwhelming and negligible, judging from Peters's statement in late December that HELP had organized about three thousand workers, including the majority of employees at seven hospitals: Presbyterian–St. Luke's, Jackson Park, Norwegian–American, St. Bernard's, South Chicago Community, Drexel Home for the Aged, and Fairview.[16]

HELP's second victory, following a successful election in March 1967, at a very small unit in Louise Burg Hospital, was a significant one. It occurred in May 1967 at the city's largest private hospital, Presbyterian–St. Luke's Medical Center, where, in an agreed-upon election, 659 service and maintenance employees voted for HELP representation, and 118 voted against the union. The bargaining unit at Rush–Presbyterian–St. Luke's, as the medical center was later known, was to rank as one of the two largest units in HELP—both it and the unit at Wesley Memorial Hospital, the third largest private hospital in Chicago, having approximately 1,200 members.[17]

The Presbyterian–St. Luke's victory set the momentum for the next four-and-a-half years of successful organizing by HELP. The union won an impressive sixteen elections out of the twenty-five held between May 1967 and November 1971. These election results included a number of decisive wins at some of the largest Chicago hospitals, among them Mt. Sinai in November 1967 (332 votes for HELP, 38 against), Michael Reese in April 1968 (440–261), Chicago Wesley in February 1970 (472–110) and Oak Forest in November 1970 (913–174).[18]

It is noteworthy that all of the units organized by HELP during its first five years were service and maintenance units. In fact, HELP's first nonservice and maintenance unit was not organized until May 1977, when clerical workers at Michael Reese voted to join HELP. Although Donald Peters had originally announced that only doctors and hospital administrators would be exempted from HELP's efforts, he and his colleagues soon realized that at least initially their efforts would have to be concentrated on the lowest-paid, heavily minority and female, service and maintenance employees. From that base they hoped to extend their representation to clerical and technical employees and eventually to registered nurses and other professionals. Unfortunately, as Harry Kurshenbaum explained, HELP soon became labeled a "nigger union" by its detractors, and its identity as a heavily black, exclusively nonprofessional union impeded its growth among higher-ranking workers and in suburban hospitals.

During these early years before the passage of the 1974 health care amendments, HELP sought representation elections through one of three means: voluntary agreement with management, the use of legal pressure, or the threat of a strike. The two notable examples of the first method were Presbyterian–St. Luke's and Mt. Sinai. The administrator of Presbyterian–St. Luke's was Dr. James Campbell, whom Kurshenbaum described as one of the best men in his field and a "Jeffersonian democrat" who sincerely believed that hospital employees had as much a right to vote for union representation as the millions of American workers covered by the Wagner Act. The same attitude prevailed among the administrators at Mt. Sinai, who answered to the Jewish Federation of Chicago, an organization that had had a master contract with Local 73 covering its social workers for many years. Kurshenbaum cited as typical of Mt. Sinai management Ruth Rothstein, executive director of the hospital, whose husband was a labor lawyer and whose son was house counsel to Local 73.[19]

The first court decision regarding HELP's right to hold representation elections involved Norwegian–American and South Chicago Community Hospitals. HELP brought the case to equity court, where remedies were sought when there was no specific applicable law, as was the case with hospital organizing in Illinois before 1974.[20] In February 1967, Circuit Court Judge Daniel Covelli ordered the two hospitals to hold representation elections, but also issued an injunction against striking at either hospital. Judge Covelli further directed HELP and the hospitals to agree to an impartial agency or person to conduct the elections.

About a year later, on February 1, 1968, the First District Appellate Court reversed Judge Covelli's decision. This decision rested on two main arguments: first, "This court may not formulate labor rules or policies when the legislature has failed to do so. The consequences of such an action would be far-reaching indeed, and would convert our courts into labor boards. . . . "; second, "the rights of those who labor must be respected but the operation of a hospital involves a public interest of such urgency that labor's right to strike must yield to the greater importance of the uninterrupted and efficient operation of hospitals."[21]

The final word on these cases was expressed by the Illinois Supreme Court. In December 1969, the high court ruled that employees of nonprofit hospitals have a right to peaceful picketing and to strike. It ruled that the appellate court's decision had been based on an article of the state constitution that provided for a thorough and efficient system of free schools, but that no such provision existed regarding hospitals. The court further ruled that any exceptions to the Illinois Anti-Injunction Act, which prohibited the issuance of injunctions against peaceful picketing or strikes growing out of bona fide labor disputes, must be granted by the state legislature and not the court. The Illinois legislature declined to act on the court's suggestion.[22]

Ironically, after the supreme court decision, HELP lost the elections at both Norwegian–American and South Chicago Community Hospitals. Also, union officials discounted the importance of the final court decision. It appears that while the appeals were winding their ways through the courts, HELP leaders had learned that both strike threats and actual strikes could produce much faster results than court decisions.

In most cases the mere threat of a strike, which hospital administrators generally considered an intolerable eventuality, was sufficient to prompt negotiations between the administrators and HELP. In such cases HELP would approach management with a "pre-election agreement" modeled after the original one at Presbyterian–St. Luke's and providing specifications on the determination of the bargaining unit; the mechanics of the election; the arbitration of all disputes arising out of the election process, contract negotiation, and grievances; and a no-strike, no-lockout agreement. These elections were supervised by one of three parties: the Illinois Department of Labor, the American Arbitration Association, or Ann Miller, a private attorney in Chicago.[23] Such pre-election agreements were used by HELP more than thirty-one times before federal jurisdiction was assumed in 1974.[24]

Although HELP would agree to no-strike, no-lockout provisions once contracts had been signed, its leaders made clear from the very beginning that it would not relinquish the right to recognition strikes. On October 28, 1966, the day after HELP organizers first appeared at local hospitals, Harry Kurshenbaum announced that HELP would consider calling strikes and, if necessary, arrange for emergency crews to care for patients in the event of one.[25]

HELP's first strike began at Walther Memorial Hospital, in the city's West Side ghetto, on February 19, 1969. Estimates in the newspaper accounts vary, but perhaps one-half to two-thirds of Walther's approximately two hundred nonprofessional employees either failed to report to work or picketed actively during the strike. Circuit Court Judge Walter R. Dahl refused to issue an injunction because he found insufficient evidence of the alleged acts of intimidation by pickets. Judge Dahl also met with union and hospital attorneys to establish procedures that would allow the hospital to receive any emergency medical supplies it needed. Although Walther officials claimed that the use of forty volunteers enabled them to maintain operations at near-normal levels, they capitulated to HELP on the seventeenth day of the strike and agreed to a representation election. HELP won, 131–53.[26]

The most prolonged and most bitter strike action taken by HELP occurred in 1970 at Wesley Memorial Hospital (later part of the Northwestern University Medical Center). At a January 16 press conference, Peters and Coleman threatened strikes at both Wesley and Mercy Hospitals. They claimed majority status among the 700–800 nonprofessional employees at Wesley and charged that the hospital administrators had repeatedly refused to hold an election to confirm their status. At Mercy, Coleman explained, management refused to accept an arbitrator's decision favorable to the union concerning negotiation impasses that had developed after HELP won a representation election among the four hundred nonprofessional employees in October 1968. They warned that all services to the hospital could be shut off by their picket lines.[27]

The threat of a Mercy strike was averted when the hospital board met and agreed to a new contract with HELP in early February. Wesley officials made a last minute effort to avoid a strike by sponsoring a secret ballot election among their employees. HELP, however, did not actively participate in the election, which was held January 27–28 and supervised by eight clergymen and hospital employees. The outcome was 439–120 against the union, but Coleman's response was simply, "We will prove we represent the majority of the employees when we pull them out on the street."[28]

The strike and picketing began on February 5, 1970. The hospital reported 153 absent workers, and the *Tribune* asserted that 125–30 workers were on the picket lines, which stopped the delivery of food and medical supplies and garbage service to the hospital and its seven hundred patients. But HELP spokesman Irving Kurasch announced that a plan had been worked out through the labor relations unit of the Chicago police to allow the delivery of infant formula and radioactive isotopes used in cancer treatment.[29]

The five-day strike ended after Circuit Court Judge Nathan Cohen refused to enjoin the picketing unless representatives of the union and hospital attempted to work out an election agreement. The parties agreed that the election would be held on February 24–26 and be supervised by the Illinois Department of Labor under NLRB procedures.

According to the Chicago Hospital Council summary of HELP elections, the election was held and won by HELP, 472–110. But apparently Wesley administrators still refused to bargain with HELP because by October 2, pickets were back out in front of the hospital. On November 24, two Local

743 organizers and five women strikers were arrested for obstructing traffic when they denied a delivery truck access to the hospital.[30]

On December 9, 1970, Judge Covelli appointed Charles Swibel, chairman of the Chicago Housing Authority, to arbitrate the year-long dispute and to attempt to curb the violence and intimidation that had marked the recent picketing.[31] The result of Swibel's arbitration was an agreement to conduct a card check in order to determine HELP's status among the employees. The result confirmed its majority status, but Wesley still resisted by challenging the card check outcome in the courts. Finally, Judge Cohen overruled the hospital's objections, and a contract was negotiated. According to Kurshenbaum, once Wesley officials finally dropped their bitter resistance to unionization, the bargaining relationship between HELP and Wesley became a very good one "overnight."

The two other HELP strikes that included significant incidents of violence came in 1972 at Woodlawn and Norwegian–American Hospitals. On June 15, the first day of the Woodlawn strike, Robert Simpson, the black activist official of Local 743, and James Hoskins, a 743 business agent, were arrested on aggravated battery charges after allegedly beating two hospital employees who attempted to cross the HELP picket line. Broken hospital windows and other incidents of physical and verbal abuse by pickets continued until a neighborhood group offered to arbitrate the dispute in order to avert a health care crisis in the impoverished black Woodlawn community.[32] But the strike, which involved some eighty workers and pickets from the NAACP and Operation Breadbasket, dragged on for more than two years, according to Kurshenbaum. After the passage of the 1974 NLRA health care amendments, HELP brought unfair labor practice charges against Woodlawn management, but without avail.

The seventeen-day strike at Norwegian–American (April 19, 1972 to May 5, 1972) was unruly enough to result in a temporary restraining order that forbade interference with the delivery of goods and services, including garbage removal. Police escorts accompanied garbage trucks one day during the strike, but that did not deter the pickets from puncturing the tires of a garbage truck the next day. Professional employees had to resort to smuggling vital supplies such as baby formula and blood into the hospital. When the hospital finally agreed to an election, HELP lost, 90–98.[33]

Perhaps its election loss after the Norwegian–American strike in May 1972 marked an end to HELP's "heroic" years of organizing. From 1966 to 1972, HELP had enrolled approximately seven thousand workers in about twenty Chicago-area hospitals through a strategy of using strikes and strike threats to force preelection agreements from the hospitals. In August 1972, Harry Kurshenbaum recalled the progress of this strategy as "pure brinkmanship."[34]

But six years later he spoke from an utterly different perspective when comparing the early years of brinksmanship with the following years under the amended NLRA:

> During this [the early] period we discovered two curious things. First, even though in many instances we could not pull out an entire hospital by a strike of any one group, the mere threat of a strike triggered forces within the community (politicians, civil rights leaders, people of good will) to work to get both sides together to avoid a work stoppage. Second when hospitals sought injunctions against our pickets many judges were willing to grant injunctions only after the hospitals demonstrated good faith bargaining. In this peculiar fashion (judges forcing employers to the table), major hospitals in this city were organized.

> In 1972 when I was testifying before [the Senate Committee] . . . it occurred to me at the time that with these amendments we [the unions] might be stepping into a mine field. Lo and behold that is exactly what we've done, with devastating results.[35]

"Devastating" may be too strong a term, but the picture indeed changed. HELP's growth since shortly before the 1974 amendments was slower and of a different sort than during its first years. HELP added about four thousand members to its 1972 membership total of seven thousand.[36] Whereas its pre–1974 membership came almost entirely from service and maintenance units in private Chicago hospitals (Oak Forest being the notable public-owned exception), some 350 of the 4,000 workers organized after 1974 were members of a clerical unit at Michael Reese; another 350 were members of a technician's unit at Riveredge Hospital (the largest such hospital technicians unit in the United States, according to HELP officials), and, most strikingly, about 2,000 were members of a single clerical unit at the University of Chicago.

These large nonservice and maintenance units represented major victories for HELP and important potential areas for its future growth. But its overall record in representation elections during the eight years after 1972 was not encouraging. From the Norwegian–American defeat in May 1972 until the University of Chicago victory in November 1978, HELP lost eighteen out of twenty-six elections.[37] Nor were there strong indications that the tide had turned after the University of Chicago election. When asked about the most recent efforts of HELP, Kurshenbaum cited three consecutive defeats and acknowledged "they [management] are beating us bad."

A number of diverse factors might have contributed to HELP's general lack of success: the unique structure of the organization and its implications for the basic identity of the union; the related issue of HELP's response, or lack of response, to the civil rights movement; the possibility that its bargaining posture in contract negotiations had not been particularly militant; management's response to both the unionization threat and to the changed conditions under the amended act; and even the inherent difficulties of union organizing among hospital employees.

In their excellent 1979 study, *The Impact of Collective Bargaining on Hospitals,* Richard Miller, Brian Becker, and Edward Krinsky offered this summary of HELP's organizational structure: "HELP constitutes an independent labor organization, unaffiliated, with its own Constitution, bylaws, and officers. It is controlled totally, however, by the founding unions, which supply its executive board members and its administrative officers. For example, it is customary to alternate the president and secretary-treasurer positions between Locals 743 and 73. In addition, as hospitals are unionized, the new union members are divided equally between the two locals. If these new members are to influence the bargaining policy of HELP, they must do so through the parent Locals 743 or 73."[38]

The HELP Constitution, dated December 1, 1967, indicated how closely Locals 743 and 73 officers controlled the affairs of the union. A delegate body comprised of seven members from each union—its president, vice-president, secretary-treasurer, recording secretary, and three other Executive Board members—was entitled to elect HELP officers, and only delegates were eligible for office. Four officers, the president, vice-president, secretary-treasurer, and recording secretary, made up HELP's Executive Board, which conducted all affairs between sessions of the delegate body and "is empowered to transact any and all acts which it may determine to be necessary and proper to achieve the objectives of this organization. . . ." Two members of the Executive Board, one from each of the sponsoring unions, constituted a quorum, and the affirmative vote of at least one board member from each union was required for board action.[39] Over the years the four Executive Board positions were effectively monopolized by Donald Peters from 743 and John Coleman, Irving Kurasch, and Harry Kurshenbaum from 73.

A preexisting tradition of paternalistic leadership was transferred to HELP when Peters and Coleman founded it in 1966. Equally important was the fact that workers organized by HELP became members of one of the two locals after certification of their unit, thus greatly reducing the potential for rank-and-file control over the officers. Kurshenbaum stated that HELP originally divided its members between the two locals on a one-by-one basis within units, but when this arrangement proved untenable, it was decided that Locals 743 and 73 would divide the membership unit-by-unit. In 1980, perhaps 7,000 of 743's 30,000 members were HELP workers, and likewise about 6,000 of 73's 17,000 members were from HELP. Any influence they wished to wield over HELP affairs had to be achieved as distinct minorities within two exceptionally large union locals. They paid their dues, amounting to about two hours of pay a month, to their respective locals and attended the membership meetings of Locals 743 and 73. The other members of the two locals had no connection to the hospital industry and presumably little understanding of the many workplace problems unique to the hospital industry.

Both Locals 743 and 73 for many years provided ambitious steward training programs through the labor education programs of the University of Illinois and Roosevelt University, respectively. Undoubtedly, many HELP stewards who benefitted from such training provided valuable representation in the hospitals for their fellow workers. However, the constitution placed severe limitations on the stewards' potential autonomy from the HELP leadership.[40] The same sort of situation prevailed among HELP negotiating committees, which were elected by bargaining unit members, but which were always led by "Harry or Irv."[41]

According to Kurshenbaum, the leaders of HELP had originally aspired to play a more socially significant role in the hospital industry, including involvement in such issues as patient-care quality and hospital financing. But early on "HELP's own [rank and file] activists pushed us into a bread-and-butter position, and we never did climb out of it." He described many of HELP's women members as "breadwinners," raising families and often divorced, and concluded that they were simply "too goddamned tired to take a philosophical position" on women's rights, for example. Kurshenbaum did say that the women were responsive to HELP's demand for child-care centers in their last negotiations—demands adamantly refused by the hospital. But he concluded, "we somehow have retreated. Maybe we can be criticized that we didn't create the leadership concept, but we have simply retreated."[42]

Miller, Becker, and Krinsky also note the extremely high rates of mobility among all hospital workers and in particular, the large number of young, female hospital workers who saw themselves as only temporary members of the work force and thus had comparatively little to gain from active participation in union activities.[43]

Because HELP did "retreat" from initial aspirations for a socially conscious unionism to the usual bread-and-butter emphasis of American unions, a critical question concerns how effective HELP was in pursuing higher wages and other traditional union goals. Here the picture appears to be one of steady, if not spectacular, HELP gains.

Bureau of Labor Statistics figures compiled in September 1978 indicate that nonprofessional hospital wages in the Chicago area were high by national standards, but not exceptionally so. For example, in Chicago, the average hourly wage paid for ten representative nonprofessional job categories was $4.70. This was significantly higher than such cities as Houston ($3.58), Kansas City ($3.72), or St. Louis ($4.05), where little hospital organization had occurred, but it was still significantly behind the rates in the two American centers of aggressive hospital unionism, New York ($5.90) and San Francisco ($5.87).[44]

Chicago's average nonprofessional hospital wage in 1978 was only 4.7 percent higher than the $4.49 average for all twenty-two surveyed cities. Interestingly enough, earlier BLS figures showed Chicago's relative wage advantage to be 12 percent in 1966, at the time of HELP's founding, and 8 percent in 1972, at the conclusion of its series of early organizing successes.[45]

Union/nonunion wage differentials in Chicago hospitals were not great in 1978; the average nonprofessional employee's wage in a unionized hospital was $4.85 per hour, or 5.9 percent greater than his or her counterpart's wage of $4.58 in nonunionized facilities.[46] This figure was in keeping with Miller, Becker, and Krinsky's finding for the tri-state area they surveyed (Minnesota, Wisconsin, and Illinois), that unionism raised hospital wages 5 percent (and raised fringe benefits 10.9 percent).[47]

While Miller, Becker, and Krinsky emphasize the union's nonmilitant bargaining stance, one must not underestimate the importance of management's independent response to the unionization threat. As Leo Osterhaus pointed out, Chicago's period of greatest relative wage advantage came in the early sixties, when there was no active organizing but local hospital administrators were clearly frightened by the spectre of the dramatic 1959–60 Mt. Sinai strike. Chicago hospitals obviously did not lose sight of this lesson. HELP organizer Fisher believed that competitive wage rates at nonunion hospitals were the main reason for HELP's many election losses during the seventies.[48]

Raising wages was but one aspect of a complete management strategy to counter hospital unionization in Chicago and other American cities:

> Strenuous efforts are being made to counter union-organizing drives and to resolve employee problems quickly. Administrators with labor relations experience are being hired, grievance procedures even in non-union hospitals are being created, personnel supervisors are being retained to advise and represent the hospital on union-related issues. In general, the personnel function is being greatly expanded and updated, often at the expense of other functional areas.
>
> In addition, the practice of granting salary and benefit increases achieved in bargaining to non-union employees in unionized or non-unionized hospitals is widespread. Labeled as the "threat effect", this policy may result in compensation levels in the non-union sector that not only equal but in fact may exceed those of the unionized hospital sector [during the early eighties, the case in such cities as Boston, St. Louis, and even San Francisco].[49]

This management strategy was perhaps pursued even more effectively in Chicago hospitals than elsewhere. Osterhaus pointed out as early as 1966 that local hospitals, in addition to their relatively high wages, offered good fringe benefits and "very good" personnel policies:

A great deal of the credit for good personnel policies and procedures in the Chicago area could be attributed to two organizations. The American Hospital Association conducted many seminars and group discussions on this subject and on the problems of labor-management relations. Being in the same city, many of the administrators and personnel officers attended these sessions and gained a vast amount of knowledge and an accumulation of experience from all over the United States.

The Chicago Hospital Council also worked very closely with the hospitals on personnel policies. The council sent out various suggestions and guidelines and arranged for administrators and personnel directors to attend seminars and meetings conducted by the AHA. They also conducted some meetings of their own on labor-management problems peculiar to the Chicago area.[50]

Many Chicago hospitals were thus probably capable of mounting an antiunion campaign as sophisticated as any found in the United States. Fisher acknowledged that "Madison Avenue-style counter-campaigns were the administrators' strongest suit against HELP."[51] He thought that these campaigns had been much more significant obstacles to union organizing than any delaying tactics used by management attorneys before the National Labor Relations Board, which were much more emphasized by Kurshenbaum and other union leaders. Fisher's contention is supported to some extent by Miller, Becker, and Krinsky's observation that "hospital managements increasingly resorted to outside consultants to counter union-organizing drives. Where consultants were used, hospitals won over two-thirds of the elections."[52]

Unionists' complaints about the 1974 health care amendments to the NLRA centered on the board's controversial rulings concerning proper bargaining units within a hospital. The evidence on HELP's election wins and losses since 1974 did not, however, indicate that the board's process of unit delineation was a major problem for the union. As we have seen, HELP's losses continued in its former stronghold, the service and maintenance units, whereas its big wins were in one technical and two clerical units.

The extremely narrow margin of HELP's victory at the University of Chicago displayed the tenuous hold it had over certain categories of clerical workers. In November 1977, the latter voted 1,174–168 to reject the first contract offer to emerge from negotiations between the university and the union. It is unclear whether this vote represented an angry rejection of HELP's bargaining position or a positive show of support, specifically an authorization to strike, as some union leaders claimed. Regardless, on November 12, 1979, the employees voted 926–90 in favor of a new and improved contract proposal. The successful proposal included a 25 percent wage increase for all employees over two years, retroactive classification upgrading of nearly 1,000 employees in the lowest job grade, the end of most merit pay increases, a standard seniority clause, and binding grievance arbitration.[53]

Donald Peters had said that the University of Chicago victory would prompt further efforts to organize in academic and related fields in Chicago, but Harry Kurshenbaum asserted that any such efforts outside the health care industry would not be conducted by HELP as such. Most of HELP's time and resources were going into organizing registered nurses. HELP won a unit for RNs at Riveredge Hospital in March 1978, but was subsequently decertified before it could negotiate a contract. HELP also withdrew from an RN campaign at Michael Reese because of the lack of a positive response among the nurses. Fisher conceded that Chicago nurses' wages were competitive by national standards and that a "huge" labor shortage existed for Chicago nurses.[54]

With the exception of Riveredge, the RN drives were only begun in 1980, and at the time of this study, it was still much too early to surmise whether RNs would provide HELP with the steady election victories it needed in order to maintain the momentum gained at the University of Chicago. When Kurshenbaum mentioned the new trend toward concentrating on the organization of nurses' and technicians' units, he spoke of the need to enlist "more articulate" professional employees, in the hope that they might revitalize HELP.

HELP was a unique variant of the new unionism of the 1960s—the effort to extend the union movement to some of the most rapidly expanding sectors of the economy. With the organizations of teachers and government employees, it shared the drive to raise the employment standards of the public and nonprofit sectors to the levels of the industrial work force. The initial success was impressive. The slow-down after 1971 emphasized the difficulties of organizing largely unskilled, female, minority hospital employees, especially in those cases in which management was determined to resist with the most sophisticated techniques available.

The unionization process was complex. Nevertheless, the unions involved—Teamsters Local 743 and Service Employees 73—were two of the most successful organizations of female and minority employees in Illinois. They had sizable economic and organizational resources at their command. They could call on influential political relationships if necessary. Their reputations in the black and Hispanic communities were strong and positive. On the other hand, the new members were an extremely difficult group to keep interested and involved in organization. They had little or no means of formulating or even influencing policies. Incentives for new leaders to rise from the ranks were limited. It remained to be seen whether HELP could provide an adequate structural basis for hospital employee organization.

NOTES

This section is a condensation and a revision of a report researched and written by David Nicolai.

1. Richard U. Miller, Brian E. Becker, and Edward B. Krinsky, *The Impact of Collective Bargaining on Hospitals*, (New York, Praeger Publishers 1979), p. 35.

2. "Employees Vote to Strike at Two Chicago Hospitals," *Hospitals*, January 26, 1960, p. 19.

3. Robert B. McKersie and Montague Brown, "Nonprofessional Hospital Workers and a Union Organizing Drive," *Quarterly Journal of Economics* (August 1963): 374–76.

4. "Strike Against Two Chicago Hospitals Continues as Another Union Announces Organization Drive," *Modern Hospital* (October 1959): 64; "Teamsters Drive in Chicago Gains in Intensity," *Hospitals*, January 16, 1960, p. 110.

5. *Chicago Daily News*, December 2, 1959; *Hospitals*, January 16, 1960, p. 110.

6. *Chicago Tribune*, January 22, 1960; *Hospitals*, February 16, 1960, pp. 107–8.

7. McKersie and Brown, "Nonprofessional Hospital Workers," pp. 379–80.

8. Sanford Gottlieb, "How Unions Are Doing in Hospital Campaign," *Modern Hospital* (March 1960): 109.

9. Gottlieb, "How Unions Are Doing," p. 110.

10. Leo Osterhaus, "Labor Unions in the Hospital and Their Effect on Management," Ph.D. diss., University of Texas, 1966, p. 203.

11. Osterhaus, "Labor Unions in the Hospital," p. 171.

12. Interview with Harry Kurshenbaum, January 31, 1981.

13. *Chicago Tribune*, October 28, 1966.

14. Interview with Harry Kurshenbaum.

15. *Chicago Tribune*, October 29, 1966.

16. Ibid., December 20, 1966.

17. Unpublished history of HELP by the Chicago Hospital Council, p. 6.

18. Ibid., p. 5.

19. Interview with Harry Kurshenbaum.

20. *Chicago Daily News*, February 11, 1967.

21. *Chicago Tribune*, February 2, 1968; *Service Employee*, February 1970, p. 7.

22. *Service Employee*, February 1970, p. 7; Miller, Becker, and Krinsky, *The Impact of Collective Bargaining*, p. 18.

23. Ronald L. Miller, "Collective Bargaining in Non-Profit Hospitals," Ph.D. diss., University of Pennsylvania, 1969, pp. 274–77.

24. Miller, Becker, and Krinsky, *The Impact of Collective Bargaining*, p. 19.

25. *Chicago Tribune*, October 29, 1966.

26. *Chicago Tribune*, and *Chicago Daily News*, February 20, February 21, February 23, and February 24, 1969; Miller, Becker, and Krinsky, *The Impact of Collective Bargaining*, p. 19; Chicago Hospital Council History of HELP, p. 5; *Hospitals*, April 1, 1969, p. 205.

27. *Chicago Tribune*, January 17, 1970.

28. Ibid., January 29, 1970.

29. Ibid., January 6, 1970; January 7, 1970.

30. Ibid., October 3, 1970; November 25, 1970.

31. Ibid., December 10, 1970.

32. Ibid., June 16, 1972; July 22, 1972.

33. Ibid., May 6, 1972; June 25, 1972.

34. Kurshenbaum testimony before the Senate Subcommittee on Labor, Committee

on Labor and Public Welfare, "Coverage on Non-Profit Hospitals under the NLRA, 1972," (Washington: Government Printing Office, August 16, 1972), pp. 8–9.

35. Kurshenbaum speech, University of Illinois Labor Education Conference "Unionization and the Health Care Industry," November 29-December 1, 1978.

36. Figures from Kurshenbaum interview and Chicago Hospital Council tables.

37. Chicago Hospital Council figures.

38. Miller, Becker, and Krinsky, *The Impact of Collective Bargaining*, p. 53.

39. HELP Constitution, pp. 4, 5, and 7.

40. Ibid., p. 11.

41. Interview with Jeffrey Fisher, HELP organizer, February 20, 1981.

42. Interview with Harry Kurshenbaum.

43. Miller, Becker, and Krinsky, *The Impact of Collective Bargaining*, pp. 77–78.

44. BLS *Bulletin* 2069 (September 1978): 14.

45. Osterhaus, "Labor Unions in the Hospital," p. 168; BLS *Bulletin* 1829 (August 1972): 11.

46. BLS *Bulletin* 2069, p. 18.

47. Miller, Becker, and Krinsky, *The Impact of Collective Bargaining*, p. 106.

48. Interview with Jeffrey Fisher.

49. Miller, Becker, and Krinsky, *The Impact of Collective Bargaining*, p. 78.

50. Osterhaus, "Labor Unions in the Hospital," pp. 154–55.

51. Interview with Jeffrey Fisher.

52. Miller, Becker, and Krinsky, *The Impact of Collective Bargaining*, p. 31.

53. *The Maroon* [student newspaper], November 13, 1979.

54. Interview with Jeffrey Fisher.

4G

American Federation of State, County, and Municipal Employees

For most Illinois unions, the sixties were at best a decade of stability or mild growth and the seventies a decade of decline. The major exceptions were found in the public sector; within this sector, two teachers' organizations, the Illinois Federation of Teachers (IFT) and the Illinois Education Association (IEA) and the American Federation of State, County, and Municipal Employees (AFSCME) stood out for their growth and militancy. This section deals with the latter.

AFSCME originated in the early thirties in Wisconsin as a civil service association. It was not until the second half of the fifties and the first half of the sixties that it shifted its focus toward collective bargaining. This shift was affirmed nationally in 1964 when a militant and aggressive Jerry Wurf supplanted Arnold Zander as president. By mid-1970, the union had reached an average annual membership of 470,000, double the size when Wurf took office, and was the largest AFL–CIO affiliate in the public sector.[1]

The Illinois AFSCME lagged behind other industrial states like New York, California, Michigan, and Wisconsin in its development. Part of the reason was its inability to break through the barriers imposed by the Chicago and Cook County Democratic political machine, first of Edward J. Kelly and Patrick Nash, and later of Richard Daley. The machine had established an informal but extremely tight political network of relations with the leaders of several key craft unions—the Teamsters, Service Employees, and Building Trades Council—which placed other organizations at a disadvantage. The other main reason for AFSCME's slow progress in organizing public employees was the absence of statutory support in Illinois for the concept of collective bargaining.

But some organization did occur because other conditions were extremely favorable to unionism, notably the rapid growth of employment in the public sector and the lag of pay and other employment conditions behind those in the private sector. Government employment in the state (local, state, and federal) rose continuously from 284,000 in 1947 to 740,000 in 1980. Because federal employment in Illinois throughout the period remained almost stationary (at around 100,000), the vast upsurge existed in the public schools and in state and local employment.

In the early fifties, when reliable data on union membership were lacking, a University of Illinois study of state government estimated that about 20 percent of all state employees, excluding state universities and colleges, were organized.[2] The state then employed about 32,000 people, excluding those in education. AFSCME reportedly represented the largest organized group of state employees in Illinois, primarily blue-collar and service workers in the Department of Public Welfare and the Department of Public Safety—attendants, institutional and maintenance workers, food service employees, therapy and recreational aids, and guards at penal institutions.[3] It also claimed members among some institutional nurses and some white-collar employees in the Division of State Employment and Unemployment Compensation of the Department of Labor and in the Public Aid Commission. Perhaps its major success at this point was the organization of a large segment of nonacademic, noncraft personnel at the state colleges and universities, including the University of Illinois.

AFSCME was not the only organization reporting state government membership at this time.[4] The CIO's United Public Workers of America claimed a sizable group of members in the Division of Employment and Unemployment Compensation in Chicago. After this union was expelled from the CIO on grounds of being communist-dominated in early 1950, it was succeeded by the Government and Civic Employees Organizing Committee, CIO. Teamsters Local 726 represented about three hundred field maintenance employees in the State Division of Highways in Cook County and a small unit of nineteen maintenance equipment operators in the Department of Public Welfare. One of the chief rivals of AFSCME, the Building Service Employees International Union, organized janitors, elevator operators, and other building service employees employed to service state-owned buildings, especially in Chicago and Springfield. Also some nineteen AFL craft unions represented about four thousand blue-collar workers, including 650 in the building trades and the rest among barbers and beauticians, bakers, firemen, motion picture operators, automotive service employees, and truck drivers. Finally, there were three associations—the Illinois State Nurses Association, the Illinois State Employees Association, and the Civil Service Protective Association—which functioned primarily as lobbying organizations but were soon (in the case of the first two) to assume many of the aspects of trade unions.

In the absence of general statutory guidelines, there was little genuine collective bargaining in state or local government in 1950. A wide array of policies and practices could be found from agency to agency and even within agencies.[5] The crafts, for example, relied primarily on the prevailing wage principle and were concerned primarily with pay rates. AFSCME, the CIO Government and Civic Employees Organizing Committee, and various locals of the Building Service Employees International Union received informal recognition of a consultative nature under which they discussed grievances with management, represented members in Civil Service discharge and other grievance hearings, and worked out general policy understandings regarding such issues as promotions and job assignments. A few unions, including the Teamsters and Machinists, negotiated written memoranda of understanding for their members, formalized in a letter from the state director of finance to the union representative. Bargaining representatives were determined by membership card checks or, where competing unions existed, by secret ballot elections.

In 1945, when the Chicago Transit System was transferred from the private to the public domain, the Illinois General Assembly authorized the continuation of the longtime collective bargaining system, including voluntary binding arbitration in disputes over the terms of new contracts. AFSCME was not affected by this action. However when the General Assembly, in 1951, authorized the State University Civil Service System to enter into negotiations on wages and other conditions of employment with employee organizations representing nonacademic employees, AFSCME was one of the chief beneficiaries. AFSCME had successfully organized large numbers of food service, janitorial, and other employees in higher education institutions throughout the state, and the new statutory provision enabled it to enter into formal collective bargaining agreements. AFSCME also benefitted from the revision of the State Personnel Code in 1955 when the state director of personnel was authorized to conduct negotiations affecting pay, hours of work, or other working conditions of employees subject to the code. In 1961 and 1963, the state legislature authorized the voluntary check off of union dues for state and local employees.

Despite these organizational gains, progress was slow toward a full-blown system of collective bargaining for public employees. The Daley patronage organization in Chicago and Cook County had been honed to a fine point in the late fifties and sixties and rejected outside unionism as a serious threat. Many state and local government agencies outside of Chicago were equally resistant, although a variety of municipalities, including Bloomington, Decatur, Springfield, Champaign-Urbana, the Quad Cities, and Alton, negotiated collective bargaining contracts.

Nonetheless, Governor Otto Kerner, a Daley-supported Democrat, sensed that Illinois was lagging behind most of the nation's major states. In 1966, he appointed a distinguished multiparty advisory commission to study the issue of labor-management policy for public employees and to produce a report with recommendations for action.[6] The commission was headed by one of the state's most experienced and insightful labor relations experts, Martin Wagner of the Institute of Labor and Industrial Relations at the University of Illinois. Other members included top representatives of labor, management, the state administration and the legislature, and the academic community. After six months of public hearings, staff research, and deliberations, the commission produced a report that recommended legislature enactment of a comprehensive collective bargaining law for public employment in Illinois.[7]

Despite several serious limitations from its point of view, including a prohibition of the right to strike, AFSCME strongly supported a compromise proposal as "a foot in the door." However, all of the other major AFL–CIO unions with public-sector interests opposed the compromise because it banned the right to strike over new contracts, it excluded the union and agency shops, and it allowed any citizen or organization to intervene through court action in a strike situation if an injunction was being violated or if the public employer did not seek an injunction within forty-five hours after the occurrence of a strike. The Illinois Federation of Teachers and the influential independent Illinois Education Association called for separate legislation for teachers.

The result of the split in labor's ranks, the hostility of the Chicago Democrats to any legislation affecting Chicago, and the skeptical feelings toward public unionism and collective bargaining of many downstate Republicans was that two very different bills were passed in the house and senate. In the final week of the legislative session, a joint conference committee was unable to compromise the disputed issues, and each chamber firmly adhered to its own bill, thereby killing the prospect of legislation.

The momentum toward collective bargaining for public employees was checked but did not come to a halt. AFSCME reported to the Kerner Commission that in late 1966 it had some eighteen thousand members in state hospitals, public aid offices, penal institutions, and universities, about equally divided between downstate and Cook County.[8] It had active lobbying and steward training programs. The Building Service Employees International Union claimed more than twenty thousand members, primarily in the Cook County area. The Illinois State Employees Association, which was still primarily a lobbying and consultative organization, claimed some ten thousand members. The Independent Union of Public Aid Employees was the bargaining agent for some 4,200 employees, mostly professional social workers and support staff, of the Cook County Department of Public Aid. The Teamsters, Building Trades, Teachers, Nurses, Firemen, and Police were other important organized groups.

Legal support came from several sources other than statutory enactment. In 1966, in *Broman v. Board of Education of the City of Chicago and Fewkes* (Ill. App. Co., First District, No. 51378, November 9, 1966), two lower courts upheld the right of the Chicago Board of Education to enter into an exclusive collective bargaining relationship with a union that demonstrated its majority status in a secret-ballot election. The Illinois Supreme Court subsequently rejected an appeal from the Chamber of Commerce to overturn the decision.

In 1970, a legislative commission on labor laws conducted a new inquiry into public-sector bargaining policy. The commission started with the report of the Kerner Commission but then took into account developments throughout the country as well as changing political and economic attitudes in Illinois. The result was a set of recommendations that borrowed key ideas from the Pennsylvania law, including a limited right to strike, and the union shop for voluntary nonprofit hospitals or nursing homes.[9] The report stated: "The passage of legislation is even more imperative now than it was four years ago." It cited a statement received from Lee C. Shaw, a prominent management labor relations lawyer on the Kerner Commission:

> The circumstances which give rise to the establishment of this Advisory Commission are more compelling today than they were in 1966. In 1966, there were 400,000 state and local employees in Illinois; today there are approximately 500,000. In 1966 there were 11 public employee strikes in Illinois; in 1968, the latest year for which statistics are available, there were 22. In 1966, 13 states had legislation covering some or all categories of public employees; today 29 states have such legislation. As a result of inaction by the Legislature, Illinois now finds itself one of a rapidly diminishing number of states that has *not* enacted legislature guidelines for collective bargaining in the public sector.[10]

Despite the Labor Laws Commission's influential membership and the strength of its report, the effort to pass a bargaining law again failed. However, pressure for a legal public policy mounted. AFSCME was in the forefront of the drive. During the 1972 gubernatorial election it threw its lot behind maverick Democrat Daniel Walker who challenged the Daley-controlled state organization, defeated its candidate, Paul Simon, in the primary, and then upset Republican Richard Ogilvie in his drive for reelection. During the campaign Walker committed himself to the principle of collective bargaining for public employees.

Walker was true to his word. When his effort to persuade the General Assembly, which was controlled by his Democratic foes, failed, he emulated President John Kennedy of a decade earlier and issued Executive Order 6 in September 1973, giving state employees under his jurisdiction (about two-thirds of state employment outside of higher education) the right to form or belong to unions of their own choice without interference from management and to engage in collective bargaining with the state administration. An Office of Collective Bargaining, consisting of three part-time public members and a small staff of labor lawyers and industrial relations specialists under an executive director, was established to administer the order.[11]

In anticipation of the executive order, AFSCME launched a major membership drive in January 1973 and added about 2,500 members by September 1973. In the series of representation elections that ensued, it quickly established itself as the dominant representative of state employees in Illinois.[12] It won the first election in September 1974 to represent 2,500 correctional employees with 97 percent of the vote, and in December 1974, it defeated the Illinois State Employees Association (ISEA) by a 5–1 margin to represent some 12,000 institutional service employees. In the fall of 1975, AFSCME defeated ISEA by a 3–2 margin to represent 12,100 state clerical employees. ISEA attempted to get the courts to declare the executive order illegal and to set aside the elections, but was unsuccessful in both challenges. By 1980, AFSCME was the exclusive bargaining representative of the great bulk of the 55–60,000 state employees covered by the executive order, which was continued in effect by Republican Governor James R. Thompson when he replaced Dan Walker in 1976. A variety of small craft or professional units were organized by the Teamsters, Machinists, Nurses, Firefighters, and Teachers.

The coverage of the executive order extended to only about a third of all state government employment (including higher education) and to only about 8 percent of state and local employment combined. Despite the absence of comparable legal guidelines, however, considerable organization and many bargaining relationships were effected by AFSCME (chiefly among nonacademic personnel in higher education and municipal employees other than police and firefighters) as well as by the two teachers organizations, the Service Employees, the Building Trades, the Teamsters, and others. Despite a slackening of unionization during the economically troubled late seventies, AFSCME claimed about thirty thousand members in 1980 compared to the eighteen thousand of the late sixties. The next major breakthrough was to come after 1980 when the power of the Chicago Democratic organization was shattered by a series of defeats, including the mayoralty elections of Jane Bryne and Harold Washington and the passage in 1983 of two comprehensive public-sector bargaining laws—one for education, the other for remaining public employees—that supplanted Executive Order 6 and an ineffective Education Labor Relations Law of 1981 and covered all state and local government employees except police and firefighters.[13]

AFSCME's first official state unit under Executive Order 6 covered prison workers. McFadden's 1954 study of the state service noted that AFSCME was particularly active in the Department of Public Safety and the Department of Public Welfare.[14] Public safety encompassed the various penal and correctional units of the state, of which the focal employees were the guards. At this point, the union did not have collective bargaining rights, but they were given consultative rights with respect to their members to discuss individual and group grievances, to take up general policies and rules, and to represent employees in Civil Service proceedings. When the Kerner Commission surveyed the scene in 1966, it found that this informal system was still in effect. Decision-making power remained with management. The situation was clearly unsatisfactory to AFSCME, which devoted much of its resources to lobbying in the state legislature for collective rights.

With Executive Order 6, AFSCME moved quickly to organize the eligible workers and by 1975, despite opposition from the Teamsters and the Service Employees Union, it had been certified by the governor's Office of Collective Bargaining as the exclusive bargaining representative for prison employees. When Jeffrey Delaney conducted his study of Illinois prisonworkers in the early eighties, he was informed that AFSCME represented more than six thousand, including three thousand guards.[15] In December 1975, the first contract was negotiated and signed.

As Delaney reported, in the two years immediately preceding the issuance of the executive order, several correctional unit locals became so exercised over prison conditions that they resorted to job action. Most of the guards' militancy stemmed from violence in the prisons. At least one major riot occurred at each of the state's largest high-security prisons: Stateville, Pontiac, and Menard. In early 1973, a correctional employee was killed by an inmate at Stateville. The prison was immediately placed on twenty-four hour lock-up. When the warden decided to end the deadlock, 75 percent of the three hundred guards went out on strike. This marked the first time that Illinois prison guards had struck over security conditions. The warden was forced to negotiate with the union to end the strike, and no action was taken against the strikers. Prisoner violence became a major factor in further guard unionization.

Initially, bargaining took place on a department basis with a representative of the governor's office acting for management and an international AFSCME officer representing the employees. Because of Governor Walker's close relations with the union, AFSCME won important concessions, such as prohibition of subcontracting, restrictions on overtime, and reliance on seniority in the case of layoffs.

When Governor Thompson assumed office in 1976, the state adopted a firmer position. It was determined to establish statewide, uniform policies and attempted to win back some of the earlier concessions. The parties agreed to negotiate a master contract for all state bargaining units represented by AFSCME (including prisons) with supplementary departmental agreements negotiated as needed. The state's chief spokesman was a representative of the director of personnel. An experienced labor negotiator from Wisconsin state government, Peter Vallone, was recruited as labor relations director. AFSCME also changed its bargaining structure by setting up a District Council whose executive director was to serve as chief spokesman during negotiations. The first executive director, Larry Marquardt, was a strong advocate of prison reform and believed in political activism as a way of obtaining changes in prison conditions.

The master agreement primarily concerned pay, seniority provisions, fringe benefits, and the grievance procedure. Supplemental agreements were limited by the State Office of Personnel to the number of union stewards in each facility, union access to bulletin boards, and shift hours. However, the role of the Department of Corrections (formerly Public Safety) was substantially enhanced by the establishment of a standing Labor-Management Committee designed to improve relations and to resolve problems as they arose. The twenty-two-member committee consisted of eleven wardens and assistant wardens selected by the Correction Department's supervisor of labor relations and of eleven union representatives chosen by the local union presidents and stewards. At the same time, the Office of Personnel and the Corrections Department tightened their relationship in order to prevent the union from seeking to get from one agency what it was unable to obtain from the other. In turn, the union shifted to political activism at the levels of the governor's office and the General Assembly to try to obtain objectives that could not be obtained at the formal bargaining table or through informal dialogue with the Office of Personnel or the Corrections Department.

Three major issues were particularly subject to political activism. One was the problem of prison overcrowding. By the late seventies, all of the major prisons were crowded to capacity. In addition, Illinois had the second highest percentage in the country (78 percent) of inmates incarcerated for violent crime. As public pressure against crime in the streets mounted, judges imposed more and longer sentences. Despite strenuous governmental efforts, the state was unable to construct sufficient new facilities and to improve old ones to keep pace with the growing inmate population. Violence in the largest prisons broke out, and the guards were placed under severe pressure. Adequate staffing became a major issue as a consequence of deteriorating environmental conditions. AFSCME called for improvements on both scores—eliminate the overcrowding, control violence, and improve staffing and staff pay, benefits, and job security. In 1977, a law was passed providing for the death penalty for persons convicted of killing law enforcement officers. For a number of years the guards were in open conflict with prison administrators over these and related matters.

A second source of conflict and political activism arose from prison reform agitation that came from the inmates and civil liberty groups. This was closely tied to the overcrowding and violence issue. AFSCME supported some of the proposals, as did the prison authorities. But suggestions for freer movements by inmates and other proposed reforms posed problems of safety and security for guards that often raised their apprehension. Thus reform itself became a cause of tension among guards, administrators, and inmates that required action at both the bargaining table and the legislative arena.

A third major issue had to do with the racial integration of the guard force. The major prisons were located in rural areas inhabited mainly by whites. As a result, most guards were white. Until the fifties, this posed no problem because most of the inmates were also white. But by the sixties, the inmate population had become predominately black, and friction developed. Pressure from civil rights groups added to the problem. When the Corrections Department adopted an affirmative action program, tension mounted between the veteran white guards and the new minority recruits who came from the same minority neighborhoods as many of the prisoners. White guards in some of the Southern Illinois facilities often had ties with white supremacy groups, which exacerbated the situation. By the end of the seventies, the percentage of black guards had risen significantly, and promotional opportunities for them had improved significantly. As the seventies ended, a new potential source of conflict loomed—women guards. AFSCME, a longtime advocate of civil rights, was in the forefront of the new issue.

The story of the social workers in Cook County concerns another interesting dimension of AFSCME's development.[16] According to Arnold Weber, between 1953 and 1966, representatives of Local 73 of the Building Service Employees International Union (BSEIU) were the chief spokesmen of employees in the Cook County Department of Public Aid. Like other labor relationships controlled by the Democratic organization, no formal representation or contractual system existed. The union took up complaints or grievances from time to time with management and met periodically to discuss pay and general policy. There appeared to be little employee involvement. In 1965, however, a group of employees established an Independent Union of Public Aid Employees (IUPAE), primarily for social workers, and requested recognition and exclusive bargaining rights. In Weber's words, "the refusal of the agency to accede to these demands precipitated a series of skirmishes, culminating a full-scale strike by the IUPAE in May 1966."[17] Intervention by Mayor Daley led to the end of the strike, the appointment of a tripartite fact-finding board to study the feasibility of a representation election, and in October 1966, by the Cook County Board of Commissioners' approval of an election. When the unit was defined to cover most social workers and clerical employees and to exclude supervisory and blue-collar workers, BSEIU withdrew. The election of December 14, 1966, arranged by Weber and conducted by the American Arbitration Association resulted in a 2,677–1,056 vote for the IUPAE.

Negotiating a contract, however, proved to be a complex and frustrating matter. Although the Department of Public Aid was technically under the authority of the Cook County Board of Commissioners, it was created and governed by the state legislature and subject to certain rules and guidelines promulgated by the state Department of Public Aid. In addition, the Cook County Civil Service Commission and the U.S. Department of Health, Education and Welfare imposed other standards. Funds came from a property tax levied in Chicago, from county and state general revenues, and about 65 percent came from federal government appropriations. Both structural and political considerations affected negotiations, including the need to appoint a new department director following the death of his long-time predecessor. Bargaining went on from January 1967 to April, but deadlocked over which agency had the power to set up a new salary plan; a demand for medical insurance; issues of union security, advisory grievance arbitration, and automatic progression that raised possible conflicts with civil service rules; and the question of "temporary employees." Further complications came from a militant group in the union that wanted to reform the welfare system through collective bargaining. On April 27, 1967, the IUPAE called a strike. About 1,200 employees, or 29 percent of the 4,200 in the bargaining unit, struck, but they included a majority of the professional social workers. The IUPAE was able to muster only limited financial support from a few industrial unions and none from the politically influential crafts. Nor could it win the backing of their welfare clients and the black community. A few unauthorized sit-ins and instances of violence also proved harmful. A tentative agreement, however, was finally achieved and the strike ended after five weeks. But despite public support from the departmental director, William Robinson, the Cook County Board of Commissioners refused to approve the agreement, apparently on the grounds that many of the provisions were not within its jurisdiction. Mass picketing, lobbying, consultation with Mayor Daley, and renewal of the strike all proved futile. The union was not broken, and some pay gains and other benefits were secured. A grievance procedure, without any form of arbitration, was put into effect. However, no formal collective bargaining or signed contract was achieved.

As the union president, Max R. Liberles, later put it in an affidavit to the Office of Collective Bargaining (OCB), "The formal collective bargaining apparatus then fell into disuse and the Union for the next eight years bargained informally with the County and, after 1974, (when the agency was shifted to state authority) with the state."[18]

The next turning point came with the issuance of Governor Walker's Executive Order 6. Under this order, the OCB was instructed to set up bargaining units on a statewide basis and "(1) avoid artificial distinctions between groups of employees whose functions and community of interests are similar, without regard to the statutory jurisdiction of any agency; and (2) promote the interest of the State in bargaining on a statewide basis by considering statewide units presumptively appropriate."[19] IUPAE was placed in an untenable position as an isolated local organization. To avoid elimination, it merged with AFSCME and became Local 2000. In this position it gained formal collective bargaining status and assumed a significant and vigorous place in AFSCME's expanding structure. Local 2000 demonstrated that, given legal support, professional employees could act as militant unionists just as prison guards and blue-collar service and craft workers had done. In the remaining years of the decade, relations between local 2000 and the Department of Public Aid were often contentious and controversial, partly because DPA management adopted a hard barganing posture and resisted union efforts to widen its participative role, and partly because Local 2000 conceived of its function as encompassing professional as well as the traditional bargaining objectives.

As the preceding discussion suggests, public employee unions and associations devoted considerable effort and resources to political action.[20] Before the introduction of collective bargaining, AFSCME, like its rivals, lobbied extensively for economic and civil service goals at the state and local government levels. It also engaged in electoral politics, from time to time endorsing candidates for local, state, and federal office. Under the leadership of International President Jerry Wurf, AFSCME was a leading union spokesman for liberal causes, often deviating from AFL–CIO policy. Thus it endorsed Senator George McGovern for president in 1972 while the AFL–CIO took a neutral stance; it split between Dan Walker and Paul Simon for governor in the Democratic primary in the same year despite the pro-Simon position of the state Democratic organization under Mayor Daley's control and then strongly supported Walker in the main election; and it was among the few unions that opposed the Vietnam War. AFSCME officers also played a leading role in the formation of the Coalition of Black Trade Unionists and the Coalition of Labor Union Women.[21]

Much of the politics was job-oriented, either to secure collective bargaining rights or to enlist executive or legislative support for AFSCME economic goals when it could not achieve them through direct bargaining. Resort to the so-called end run was one tactic that sometimes lead to tougher bargaining tactics on the part of the state administration or municipal authorities. But AFSCME also agitated for policies in behalf of its clients who were among the most disadvantaged in American society. Substantial proportions of its members were low-paid blacks, Hispanics, and women for whom public assistance programs such as low-income housing and medicare were important topics. As one of the nation's most rapidly growing labor organizations and as advocate for the working poor as well as the unemployed, AFSCME in 1980 symbolized the new unionism.

The rise of AFSCME to a prominent role in the representation of and collective bargaining for state and local employees in Illinois is one of the major success stories among unions in the sixties and seventies. Whereas the leading craft unions of the building trades and the two principal industrial unions—the United Steelworkers and the United Automobile Workers—encountered serious organizational problems in the mid and late seventies, AFSCME continued its advance.

State and local government unionism originated before and during World War II without formal legal support. However, significant success was achieved only after the issuance of a gubernatorial executive order in 1973 and later passage of statutory law in 1983. Legal support was reinforced by and dependent upon effective political action. A sympathetic Governor Dan Walker, for example, contrasted markedly with a reluctant Mayor Richard Daley. Whereas private-sector unionism was primarily concerned with economic forces and only secondarily involved in political action, public-sector unionism found it essential to give top priority to political and legal factors.

NOTES

1. Richard A. Dobb, "AFSCME, an Emerging Trade Union in the Public Sector, 1960–1970: A Case Study," A.M. thesis, University of Illinois, 1971.

2. Richard C. McFadden, *Labor-Management Relations in the Illinois State Service*, (Urbana: University of Illinois Institute of Labor and Industrial Relations and Institute of Government and Public Affairs, 1954), p. 13.

3. McFadden, *Labor-Management Relations,* p. 11.

4. Ibid., pp. 12–17.

5. Ibid., pp. 18ff.

6. For a detailed discussion of the work of the commission, see Milton Derber, "Labor-Management Policy for Public Employees in Illinois: The Experience of the Governor's Commission, 1966–1967," *Industrial and Labor Relations Review* 21 (July 1968).

7. *Report and Recommendations,* Governor's Advisory Commission on Labor-Management Policy for Public Employees, Springfield, Ill., March 1967.

8. *Report and Recommendations,* pp. 45–47.

9. Commission on Labor Laws, *Report and Recommendations to the Governor and the General Assembly,* April 1971, pp. 19–42.

10. Ibid., p. 20.

11. Milton Derber, Peter Pashler, and Mary Beth Ryan, *Collective Bargaining by State Governments in the Twelve Midwestern States* (Urbana: University of Illinois Institute of Labor and Industrial Relations, December 1974), pp. 16–18.

12. James E. Martin, "Winning a Representation Election in a Public Sector Bargaining Unit," mimeographed, undated, pp. 4ff.

13. According to *Crain's Chicago,* June 25, 1984, AFSCME claimed 57,000 members, including nearly 7,000 in Chicago.

14. McFadden, *Labor-Management Relations,* p. 11.

15. Jeffrey Delaney, "Illinois Correctional Employees Union Response to Prison Conditions" (Urbana: University of Illinois Institute of Labor and Industrial Relations,

typed manuscript, March 16, 1982), p. 12. The remainder of this discussion on correctional employees is based primarily on Delaney's paper.

16. Most of this account is based on Arnold R. Weber, "Paradise Lost: Or Whatever Happened to the Chicago Social Workers," *Industrial and Labor Relations Review* 22 (April 1969).

17. Weber, "Paradise Lost," p. 325.

18. In the matter of State of Illinois, Department of Personnel, and AFSCME, Case No. UC-80-86D-OCB, March 30, 1981, Affidavit, p. 2.

19. Executive Order No. 6 (1973) and *Rules and Regulations of the Director of Personnel for Public Employee Collective Bargaining* (Springfield: Illinois Office of Collective Bargaining, 1980), p. iii.

20. This discussion is based primarily on Ian Charles McAndrew, "The Politics of the Public Workers Union: A Case Study of AFSCME in Illinois," Ph.D. diss., University of Illinois, 1975; Keith Hindell, "Union Political Action in Illinois, 1944–1959," bachelor's thesis, Oxford University, April 1962; and Anthony M. Halmos, "Public Sector Collective Bargaining Legislation in Illinois," tutorial paper, University of Illinois Institute of Labor and Industrial Relations, March 1979.

21. McAndrew, "The Politics of the Public Workers Union," p. 212.

PART III

Labor, Politics, and the Law

Illinois Labor was deeply involved in state and local politics for many decades. Its activities can be traced along three dimensions: efforts to elect sympathetic candidates, efforts to enact favorable laws and to defeat hostile proposals, and efforts to influence the administrative and judicial systems responsible for the interpretation and application of laws.

In the early post-World War II years, the division between the state AFL and the state CIO hampered these efforts and sometimes created serious political conflicts. After the merger movements got underway, intra-labor cooperation gradually replaced competition despite the absence of the Mine Workers, Teamsters, and Auto Workers (among others) from the AFL–CIO. Labor support for the Democratic party increased as it decreased for the Republican party, although a few individual Republican candidates such as Governor William Stratton in 1956 and Senator Charles Percy in 1978 won Labor endorsement. Individual unions and leaders, within the AFL–CIO ranks as well as outside of it, sometimes diverged from federaion policy. At the municipal level, Labor's involvement in politics varied from the tight integration of the Building Trades Unions with the Daley machine in Chicago and with the Fields machine in East St. Louis to the influential role of the UAW in Rockford and Moline and the Steelworkers in South Chicago to the relative inactivity of Labor in Peoria and most smaller downstate communities. The Building Trades at the local level were frequently close to the Republican organizations.

The impact of Labor on legislation, however, was less in terms of positive achievement than in preventing the passage of hostile laws. The explanation lay chiefly in the formidable opposition of the state's business and industrial associations such as the Chamber of Commerce and the Manufacturers' Association, as well as farm groups. It also inhered in the Illinois constitutional provision that a law had to receive a majority of votes of the legislative body, not simply a majority of votes cast. The result was that relatively few direct labor laws (especially labor relations laws) got on the books. One of the other interesting features of the legislative process was the long-term use of the agreed-bill concept (that is, an agreement reached among labor, employer, and legislative leaders before enactment) for laws dealing with unemployment compensation, workmen's compensation, and occupational health and safety.

The state courts played an unusually important role, not only in interpreting statutory law, but also in filling the gaps resulting from legislative inaction, such as the right of public employees to strike. Some district courts, for example, adopted surprisingly activist and interventionist policies in labor disputes. However, most appellate courts and the state supreme court tended to adopt highly conservative positions in interpretation and application. It was no accident that Labor strongly advocated the election of judges and resisted appointment proposals.

5

Electoral Politics

Illinois Labor has long been involved in the state's political life. The post-World War II era, however, provided a dramatic expansion of such activities in no small part because of the rapid legalization of the national industrial relations system. Not only did many of Labor's goals seem most realizable through the political route, but also the growth of labor organization led to widespread public desires, reinforced by employer interests, to regulate the new giant to protect individual and minority workers against possible abuses by union controllers.

This multisided and complex subject requires analysis along three different lines, which are presented in this and the following two chapters:
1. Labor's efforts to elect federal, state, and local officials who could be counted on to support Labor's legislative and administrative aspirations and to defeat Labor's opponents whenever possible;
2. The network of laws (state and local) that impinged directly and indirectly on Labor's goals and on the interests of employers and other groups who desired to limit or control labor's activities;
3. The administrative and judicial systems responsible for the interpretation and application of the laws.

In the beginning of the period, Labor was divided politically as well as organizationally. Reuben G. Soderstrom, president from 1930 of the Illinois Federation of Labor and, after the 1958 merger, of the state IFL-CIO until his death in 1970, had been a lifelong Republican, had served eight terms in the state legislature as a Republican, and had numerous Republican friends in government. In 1948, Soderstrom personally endorsed Republican Governor Dwight Green for a third term in Green's unsuccessful race against Adlai Stevenson, and the federation followed suit.

As Green's biographers noted, his enthusiastic support from the IFL was due in no small measure to the enactment during his tenure of such legislation as the prevailing wage law for state employees and contract workers (particularly coveted by the building and construction unions), an equal pay law for women, and substantial improvements in workmen's compensation and unemployment insurance.[1] In addition, he had called for labor-management cooperation and opposed restrictive legislation at a time when the federal government and many states were turning to regulation and restrictionism. In contrast, the state CIO strongly supported Stevenson and upon his election was rewarded by the appointment of the first CIO official (Frank Annunzio of the Steelworkers Union and brother-in-law of the state CIO head, Joseph Germano) as director of labor.

There were later examples of Labor's support for individual Republican candidates as well, most notably Governor William Stratton in 1956 and U.S. Senator Charles Percy in 1978, but also for state legislators and other office candidates. The Stratton case was similar to Green's. In his presidential address to the 74th Annual Convention of the IFL, Soderstrom extolled Governor Stratton "who has signed a large number of labor bills for us, and who has assured us again and again, that there will be no anti-union or oppressive legislation enacted as long as he is the Governor. . . ." He also praised the Republican attorney general, Latham Castle, "who recently ruled that Supplemental Unemployment Benefits could be given to wage earners without any deduction from their Social Security Unemployment benefits."[2] In 1978, the IFL–CIO endorsed U.S. Senator Charles Percy rather than his Democratic opponent Alex Seith. Percy's campaign manager James D. Nowlan attributed this unusual action (it was the only endorsement in the postwar period by the federation of a Republican running for the Senate) to three factors.[3] One was a calculated campaign to win Labor's support by courting influential individual labor leaders. A second was to emphasize Percy's Committee on Political Education (COPE) voting record, which was better than that of most Republicans, and that Labor knew where Percy stood on most issues and could depend on his voting for cloture when the question of shutting off debate on the 1978 Labor Reform bill came up in the U.S. Senate. The third factor was Percy's accessibility to labor leaders. For a number of years he had worked with a labor advisory committee and had given Labor an opportunity to express its views to him on important Labor issues. In addition, Percy supporters suggested to Labor that Seith was a political unknown, a corporate lawyer with conservative inclinations.

Overall, however, the central trend of the postwar period was a pronounced shift of Labor support toward the Democrats. This is shown in Table 8, which reveals overwhelming rising support for the Democratic party during the postwar period. After 1958, no Republican candidates were endorsed for federal office, except Senator Percy in 1978. At the state level, Republicans were endorsed only twice for governor (Green in 1948 and Stratton in 1956). The state senate figures show substantial Republican suppoort in the early years but significant decline after 1958 when the state AFL and CIO merged.

Table 8. IFL and IFL–CIO Support for Federal and State Candidates by Party

Date	U.S. President		U.S. Senate		U.S. House		Governer		State Senate		State House	
	R	D	R	D	R	D	R	D	R	D	R	D
1946									13	14	50	61
1948		X		X	3	25		X	17	5	54	63
1950		X		X	1	25			8	14	44	72
1952		X			2	24		X	14	11	52	73
1954				X	1	21			11	17	33	70
1956		X		X	1	22		X	14	23	62	93
1958					3	24			6	17	60	95
1960		X		X	0	24		X	5	21	42	99
1962				X	0	21			4	25	49	97
1964		X			0	24		X	4	26	32	117
1966				X	0	23			3	56	30	111
1968		X		X	0	23		X	0	2	44	100
1970				X	0	24			4	53	60	81
1972		X		X	0	21		X	3	56	36	101
1974				X	0	22			2	19	37	103
1976*		X		X	0	20		X	1	34	23	108
1978				X	0	20		X	1	38	19	107

*In 1976 one independent candidate for state representative was endorsed.
Sources: IFL-CIO *Weekly Newsletter*, the IFL *Newsletter* (prior to the merger), *Illinois Labor* (the CIO newletter), and the *Illinois Blue Book*.

The house figures are less meaningful. Because of the prevailing unique cumulative voting system for representatives, both parties were assured at least one of the three seats in each district. In the Chicago area, however, the Democrats held such a dominant position that many of the Republican officeholders found it expedient to collaborate with them. As Milton Rakove, one of the most knowledgeable students of the Chicago political scene, observed:

> Recognizing the long-term domination of the city by the majority Democratic party and cognizant of the unwillingness of their Republican cohorts in the suburbs and downstate to help them in their wards, they (the Republican representatives) also recognize that the best way in which they can serve their constituents as well as their own interests is to work with the majority party. A Republican committeeman who works well with his Democratic counterpart can get help from the Democrats in getting elected committeeman and can also get help in getting elected as state representative or alderman. . . . A number of Chicago's

Republican ward committeemen hold safe seats in the state legislature with Democratic help.[4]

The explanation for the close Labor tie with the Democrats is clear enough. In the thirties, most Republicans had opposed the Labor policies of the New Deal. In the immediate postwar years, Republicans had successfully led the fight for passage of the Taft–Hartley law, combining with conservative Southern Democrats to override President Truman's veto. In Illinois, the majority of Republicans had consistently been identified with business and farmer interests in opposition to Labor. As was repeatedly stated in federation proceedings and other publications, "recommendations of candidates are based upon the support which they have contributed towards the enactment of labor legislation—that is to say, such recommendations are based upon their voting record on important labor roll calls."[5] Whether a candidate was a Republican or a Democrat was immaterial so long as he or she was friendly to labor legislation.

A more complicated question is how representative the IFL–CIO was of the Illinois working population in the electoral arena. Organizationally, the federation seems to have been the principal institutional leader in expressing organized labor's political sentiments. In order to coordinate its activities with other statewide labor bodies, the federation had joined with the Railroad Brotherhoods, the United Mine Workers, the Chicago Federation of Labor, and others in a Joint Labor Legislative Board formed about 1916. The board was concerned primarily with lobbying for labor legislation, but it also transmitted sentiments and information that aided in determining support for candidates. The board performed the same function at the state level as Labor's League for Political Action and later COPE did nationally. In the postwar period, Soderstrom was chairman of the board, and Clinton Bush, legislative representative of the Locomotive Engineers and Firemen, was secretary.

Before their merger in 1958 (three years after the national merger), the State Federation and the state Industrial Union Council had gone their separate political ways, with the latter more active in elections and more closely tied to the Democrats. In 1956, following the national merger CIO representatives were invited to participate in the meetings of the Joint Labor Legislative Board and came as observers. However, as John Alesia, the director of the CIO Political Action Committee, told the 1949 CIO state convention: "Our policy is a simple one . . . : That we are going to work within the framework of the two major political parties, the Democratic and the Republican parties. We are not endorsing parties, but individual candidates on the record they made."[6]

Alesia went on to praise one Republican, Congressman Cecil W. Bishop, for voting with Labor on the Taft–Hartley law and the Minimum Wage bill; and he severely criticized another Republican, Congressman Richard W.

Hoffman, for being friendly toward Labor before he was elected and voting against Labor after the election. Alesia concluded: "We are not a political arm of the Democratic party, but it seems that the Republican candidates are following the organizational pattern, voting straight against us. And we have no other choice." This view was increasingly shared by the State Federation, although certain downstate unions, particularly in the building and construction trades, often sought and obtained Republican support.

In 1959, the nonpartisan policy was reemphasized on purely pragmatic grounds, but the trend toward the Democrats was noted. The IFL–CIO Executive Board report stated: "We would be less than honest if we did not pay our respects to most of the Democrats for their real service to the cause of equity for all Illinois citizens. We praise those limited numbers of Republicans who believe in full justice for laboring people as well. Without them, Illinois wage earners would be in a sorry plight. Up to date no one party has stood solidly on a highly controversial labor bill. Therefore, we urgently need the help and votes of members of both parties. So we repeat again, look first at the record of the legislator and not his party affiliation."[7]

This policy was still in effect in 1980, as was demonstrated by a lengthy debate at the 23rd Annual Convention over several resolutions proposing the establishment and firm implementation of standards for electoral endorsement.[8] One resolution noted that the Executive Board had ignored a resolution passed several years earlier requiring that a candidate must have a 60 percent favorable voting record. The resolution also voted that two years later, the same 60 percent voting resolution was adopted and followed until 1980, when it was again set aside and a cumulative 60 percent voting record—rather than the immediate legislative session record—was adopted. The resolution further noted that support had been given to four Republican legislators with voting records of 46 percent, 37 percent, 65 percent, and 57 percent and to one Democratic legislator with a 56 percent voting record. The resolution urged enforcement of the 60 percent voting standard.

Another resolution proposed three standards:

1. A candidate seeking reelection must have a past session voting record of 70 percent favorable to Labor.
2. A candidate seeking reelection must have an overall record during his last term of an average of 60 percentage vote in favor of Labor.
3. A candidate seeking his first election to the state legislature must be willing to submit to a screening committee to determine his attitudes on issues important to Labor.

The Committee on Legislation recommended nonconcurrence on the grounds that the standards were too tight and that if they were adopted "our endorsements would be limited to a very few legislators." The resolution was defeated by "over a two to one margin."

To implement its electoral support policy, the IFL–CIO relied on the COPE organization, which emanated from Washington and promoted the establishment of a comprehensive national network of state, county, city, and congressional district COPE committees. However, the individual national and local unions provided most of the staffing and financial resources. Thus candidates got significant labor support or opposition primarily when individual unions and central labor bodies had a strong and direct interest. Relatively few unions were equipped to activate their members politically and to get out the vote. The Auto Workers, Steelworkers, Machinists, some of the Building Trades, the Service Employees, and, in the seventies, the Teachers and State, County, and Municpal Employees were perhaps the most active. Some unions like the Firefighters and Police were effective primarily at the municipal level; others like the Railroad Brotherhoods at the state and national level.

The Chicago experience was particularly important because of the great size of the voting population, the strength of the Labor movement, and the unusual ties with the Democratic party. J. David Greenstone has provided one of the few significant in-depth analyses of Labor's political role.[9] He concluded that in many ways, Labor's role, even after the AFL–CIO merger, was closer to the spirit of the twenties than to the "political ethos" of either the thirties or the sixties. In 1947, the Democratic machine established in the thirties by Edward Kelly (Chicago mayor from 1933–47) and Patrick Nash was ousted by businessman-reformer Martin Kennelly with the aid of national Democratic committeeman Jack Arvey. However, the machine was soon restored to power under the leadership of Richard Daley, who replaced Kennelly in 1955 and ruled for twenty-one years.

COPE's difficulties were similar to the problems of "good government" reformers in dealing with the Daley political machine. Greenstone found that the machine was primarily concerned with specific discrete benefits for particular small groups or individuals and had relatively little concern for welfare-state issues affecting large classes of people. The machine preempted the electoral campaign functions, and COPE activists played a subordinate part in most of the wards.[10]

In dealing with the Chicago politicians, organized Labor actually was divided into three main segments. The powerful CIO unions like the Steelworkers and Auto Workers (and their smaller allies) were guided by New Deal sentiments and goals. They found the machine generally supportive of Labor's federal goals and willing to endorse pro-Labor candidates for high-level federal and state positions. But when it came to local positions (mayor, district attorney, city alderman) in Chicago and Cook County and state legislative positions, machine interests predominated. Thus the Daley machine was able to maintain concurrently the support of the Chicago business community and the CIO unions.

A very different role was enjoyed by certain business-oriented AFL union. that represented a large segment of city employees as well as private-sector employees. These unions had a particularly strong interest in the construction, maintenance, and service trades and took advantage of "prevailing rate" principles to win high levels of pay and conditions for their members as well as material and political benefits for the leaders. William McFetridge, a powerful force in the Building Service Employees Union, shifted his loyalties from the Republicans to the Democrats when his close friend Richard J. Daley succeeded Martin Kennelly as mayor in 1955. As a longtime influential figure in the Chicago Federation of Labor, he was a key advisor to Daley on Labor matters and a primary channel of communications between the machine and the conservative AFL unions.

Even more important as Labor's liaison with Mayor Daley was William Lee, president of the Chicago Bakery Drivers Local 734 from 1927, and president of the Chicago Federation of Labor from 1946.[11] Like McFetridge, Lee was a close, trusted friend of the mayor and had easy access to him. Daley appointed him in 1955 to the important post of president of the City Civil Service Commission, as well as to the mayor's Citizens Committee that advised on the appointment of school board members and other committees. He also held a variety of other civic and union positions so that he was widely known and respected as labor's principal spokesperson in Chicago. Frequently, he assisted the mayor in resolving labor problems.

Not all unionized employees of the city, however, shared the same interests and benefits with the tradesmen. The firefighters, police, transit workers, librarians, and school teachers, for example, who were not beneficiaries of the prevailing rates policy favored by the craft unions, often resented the favored treatment given to the trademen. They were not part of the Daley machine, although they sometimes turned to the mayor when discussions with their agency heads reached an impasse. A Teachers' Union (later Local 1 of the American Federation of Teachers, AFL–CIO) had been in existence since 1902, but it did not win its first collective bargaining contract with the Daley-dominated school board until 1966. The firefighters and police unions were not to obtain contracts until 1982, after Mayor Jane Byrne had assumed office. The city librarians, organized by AFSCME, continued to be unrecognized even then.

The relationships of these organizations were determined by the character of Chicago politics, particularly during the Daley regime. Paul E. Peterson, a close student of the city schools, observed that until 1966 the Chicago Teachers' Union (CTU) worked closely with reform elements in the Citizens Schools Committee and played a significant role in replacing the machine-dominated school board (appointed by the mayor) and superintendent in 1946

.fter they made economic gains in cooperation with reform
lerold Hunt and Benjamin Willis.

.1 his successor, James Redmond, resisted CTU demands for
.iining, and about 1966, the CTU "shifted away from the refor-
, political support from the machine faction on the Board and
.he city."[13] With the dramatic rise of public school collective
ᴜ.   ıationwide in the early sixties, William Lee perceived the growing
importan. / of teacher unionism and urged Mayor Daley to throw his support
to the CTU. Daley's allies on the board overruled Superintendent Willis in
1966, and after a court decision authorizing an election, which the CTU won,
the board entered into its first teachers agreement. Subsequently, Daley frequently intervened to bring about a settlement, and several times (especially
in the early years) assumed the responsibility of raising necessary tax funds
to finance a settlement.

Peterson offered four principal reasons for the shift in policy. The first was
that although organized labor was an important supporter of the Democratic
party, it did not dictate party policy and seldom concerned itself with major
public issues. As long as the CTU was allied with school reformers, the union
leaders associated most closely with Daley (e.g., McFetridge and Lee,
Stephen Bailey of the Plumbers, Thomas Murray of the Electrical Workers
[IBEW], and Thomas Nayder of the Building Trades Council) provided it
with little support. Once the CTU broke with the reformers, Lee and other
craft unionists became staunch supporters of the CTU. The second reason for
the shift, according to Peterson, was that "machine-oriented board members
seemed more interested in 'managing conflict' than in fiscal responsibility or
educational efficiency." This facilitated union bargaining gains. A third reason
was the empathy between the long-time CTU president, John Desmond, and
the Daley people; they were primarily Irish-Catholic, shared the same life-
style, and spoke the same language. The fourth, and perhaps most important
reason was that the Daley machine in the mid-sixties stood to benefit politically by reaching an understanding with the CTU, given the stormy conditions
in education that they confronted, not only from reformer pressure, but also
from the civil rights movement.

Labor's involvement in electoral politics downstate was appreciably less
significant, overall, than in Chicago. As the community studies of Part IV reveal, however, it varied from considerable activity and effectivenesss in
Rockford to limited impact in Peoria. It also fluctuated fairly widely over
time within a community. In East St. Louis, for example, the relationship
during the twenty-year regime of Mayor Alvin Fields closely resembled the
Chicago pattern of Mayor Daley. But after the demise of the Fields's machine
and the victory of a series of black community leaders, the union role diminished. A brief inquiry into labor relations in the small but important

Southern Illinois community of Mt. Vernon indicated that from the mid-thirties to the mid-fifties, Labor was a strong force in both the political and economic arenas and continued to be influential throughout the study period despite a decline in union membership.[14] In contrast, Labor's political role in university communities such as Bloomington and Champaign-Urbana remained comparatively slight, despite a fair degree of unionization.

NOTES

This chapter is based in part on research by Marick Masters and on a series of community studies reported in Part IV. Another helpful source was Keith Hindell, "Union Political Action in Illinois, 1944–1959," bachelor's thesis, Oxford University, April 1962.

1. Robert J. Casey and W.A.S. Douglas, *The Midwesterner: The Story of Dwight H. Green* (Chicago: Wilcox and Follett, 1948), p. 295.

2. *Proceedings* of 74th Annual Convention, Illinois State Federation of Labor, Springfield, October 8–12, 1956, p. 7.

3. Interview with James D. Nowlan, September 17, 1979.

4. Milton Rakove, *Don't Make No Waves, Don't Back No Losers* (Bloomington: Indiana University Press, 1975), p. 175.

5. See, for example, *Proceedings* of 1st Annual Convention, Illinois State Federation of Labor and Congress of Industrial Organizations, Peoria, October 7–9, 1958, p. 73.

6. *Proceedings* of 67th Annual Convention of Illinois State Federation of Labor, Springfield, September 26, 1949, p. 114.

7. *Proceedings* of 2nd Annual Convention, Illinois State Federation of Labor and Congress of Industrial Organizations, Chicago, September 8–11, 1959, p. 124.

8. *Proceedings* of 23rd Annual Convention of Illinois State Federation of Labor and Congress of Industrial Organizations, Rosemont, September 29-October 2, 1980, pp. 298–301.

9. J. David Greenstone, *Labor in American Politics* (New York: Alfred A. Knopf, 1969), chap. 3.

10. Greenstone, *Labor in American Politics*.

11. When the Teamsters were expelled from the AFL in 1957, Lee, who was an international vice-president and an anti-Hoffa leader, joined the Service Employees Union.

12. This discussion of the Chicago Teachers Union is based mainly on Paul E. Peterson, *School Politics Chicago Style* (Chicago: University of Chicago Press, 1976), especially chap. 8.

13. Peterson, *School Politics*.

14. Interviews with the president of the Central Trades Assembly, Loren Scott, and former city attorney, George W. Howard, April 30, 1982.

6

Legislation

Perhaps the central feature of labor law in Illinois in the period under study is how few direct labor laws (especially labor relations laws) got on the books despite the extensive involvement in electoral politics and lobbying described in the previous chapter. This was true of both laws that Labor wanted and laws that Labor opposed. It is important to keep in mind, however, that Labor had an impact not only on laws directly bearing on labor organization and conditions of employment, but also on a wide array of legislation affecting the general public such as tax policy, constitutional reform, selection of judges, mass transit, and equal rights for women. That Labor was less successful than it hoped may be attributed in part to the split between the AFL and CIO, the nonaffiliation of the Teamsters and the UAW after "merger," and divisive interests of AFL–CIO unions.

In this analysis, the focus will be on the activities on the Illinois State Federation of Labor and Congress of Industrial Organizations (state IFL–CIO) for four reasons. First, the State Federation has traditionally been the recognized voice of organized Labor and has been a major (although incomplete) coordinating force among the politically oriented unions in Illinois. Second, when governors and legislative leaders sought an expression of Labor's interests and views, they typically relied on the State Federation to provide it. The federation's role in the so-called agreed-bill process, which will be discussed later in this chapter, is illustrative. Third, the political views of the federation are most easily accessible, thanks to its annual proceedings and other publications such as the weekly *Newsletter*. The printed statements are not always a complete or true representation of Labor's motivations and behind-the-scene behaviors, but they are an excellent starting point. Finally, it is extraordinarily difficult to determine the views of working people in general on legislative issues. Labor does not speak with a single voice. Unions, whether affiliated with the State Federation or not, have varying interests; their rank and file identify with diverse ethnic, occupational, sectional, and other interest groups and institutions. Unorganized workers also express their views in manifold ways or are silent. Hence, in treating the State

Federation as Labor's focal point, care will be taken to note deviations where feasible and to make allowance for alternative views.

A survey of the state's legislative record reveals Labor's sustained interest in enacting laws that dealt with the following topics: unemployment compensation, workmen's compensation for industrial accidents and sickness, health and safety rules, prevailing wages, minimum wages, methods of pay and minimum conditions for public employees, collective bargaining for public employees, public pension systems, and nondiscrimination in employment.

The unemployment compensation and workmen's compensation issues were dealt with at virtually every session and, in testimony to their importance, were the principal, if not the exclusive, subjects of the agreed-bill process during the years of its operation. Each legislative session witnessed Labor attempts to extend the benefits of these laws, attempts that were often successful and that raised the standards in the state to among the most favorable in the nation. Management generally resisted these improvements as too costly, and there were often bitter struggles over efforts to tighten the laws and to reduce benefits. Throughout the period Labor was the more successful, but in 1979 and 1980, recessionary conditions and concern over the movement of industry to lower-cost states resulted in Labor concessions.

Prevailing wage legislation was particularly important to the crafts and trades with members in both the private and public sectors. This legislation, first enacted in 1941 after the model of the federal Davis–Bacon Act of 1932, provided for the payment of rates prevailing in the private sector to state employees and employees on public projects.[1] (Similar policies were adopted at the local level for some municipalities and counties.) For many years after the law was enacted, Labor made efforts, often successfully, to add new categories of employees to the prevailing rate roster. In the seventies, the pendulum shifted, and pressures began to develop to eliminate prevailing wage programs on the grounds that they were unnecessarily costly and that public employees had job security, longer work periods, and fringe benefits that the private sector lacked. It was argued that if the prevailing wage was retained, its computation should make allowance for fringe benefits. Labor was forced into a defensive posture, but as of 1980 had succeeded in retaining the existing law.

Collective bargaining legislation for public employees was a different story. It is interesting to note that some fourteen years before Wisconsin enacted the first public-sector bargaining law, the Illinois General Assembly passed such a bill in 1945. But it was vetoed by Governor Dwight Green, who was then perceived as a friend of organized Labor, on the dual grounds that it would "amount to a usurpation of legislative power" by attempting to bind succeeding legislative bodies, and that it involved "the possibility of serious conflict with the Civil Service Law."[2] In that same legislative session, a law was passed that authorized the continuation of collective bargaining for the employees of the Chicago Transit System, which had been transferred from private to public ownership. In 1951, the State University Civil Service System was authorized to enter into negotiations on wages and other conditions of employment with employee organizations representing nonacademic employees; and municipalities and their firefighters were authorized to resort to advisory arbitration when wage disputes reached impasse.[3]

Despite favorable recommendations for a comprehensive public-sector bargaining statute by a broadly representative commission appointed by Governor Otto Kerner in 1966 and by the legislatively established Commission on Labor Laws in 1971, Labor's efforts to win an acceptable law were frustrated session after session. In 1973, newly elected Governor Dan Walker fulfilled a campaign commitment to the American Federation of State, County, and Municipal Employees (AFSCME), which had strongly supported him against the mainstream of the Democratic party, and issued Executive Order 6 giving collective bargaining rights to some sixty thousand state employees (about half the state's employment) under his direct jurisdiction. This order was modeled on President John Kennedy's federal executive order of 1962 and on various aspects of the Taft–Hartley law. In 1980, the Illinois Education Association was able to persuade the legislature and the governor, James Thompson, to approve a law that provided for nonbinding representation elections for public school teachers, as well as authorizing the agency shop and binding arbitration of grievances. It went through the General Assembly so quietly and quickly that not until after its passage did opponents of the agency shop and grievance arbitration awake to its significance.

But still no comprehensive bargaining statute was adopted until 1983 akin to the laws in most well-unionized states and the federal government (such as the Civil Service Reform Act of 1978). Why, in such a strong union state as Illinois, was there no supportive collective bargaining legislation for public employees—or for that matter, for private employees? The reasons are complex and diverse. First, and probably foremost, was the aversion of the Chicago Democratic machine to a law that would include Chicago and potentially interfere with the smooth operations of the informal party-union system. Not until the 1980 administration of maverick Mayor Jane Bryne and the signing of formal bargaining agreements with the Firefighters' Union and the Police Association did the possibility of Chicago legislative support emerge. Even in the most favorable circumstances, under Democratic Governor Kerner, the Chicago legislators in the state senate refused to go along.

A second factor was division within the labor movement itself. AFSCME, the main driving force for public-sector bargaining legislation, was willing to accept a no-strike provision, if only to get a foot in the door. They had the support of the powerful industrial unions in steel and autos, but the latter had no direct interest in public-sector employment. On the other hand, the building trades and other prevailing rate groups strenuously opposed any ban on strikes and believed that they could achieve their goals without a public bargaining law. Because the prevailing rate law protected their central interest, they saw no benefit in giving up the right to strike (symbolically, because the state supreme court had declared that right illegal in the absence of affirmative legislation) for unneeded representation and unfair labor practice procedures. The internal debate at times became so fierce that AFSCME threatened to disaffiliate from the State Federation. In 1977, however, with support from the Steelworkers, Machinists, and other unions, the convention of the State Federation declared a comprehensive public bargaining statute as their major legislative goal, and Representative Thomas Hanrahan, a union official from Waukegan, successfully steered a bill (which was silent on the strike issue) that all of the unions had agreed upon through the House. The bill, however, died in the senate Labor and Commerce Committee. At the 21st Annual Convention in 1978, a resolution was introduced (although not adopted) that noted that this was not the first time the senate had so acted and accused Chicago Democrats of blocking passage. It called on Mayor Michael Bilandic of Chicago to work for the adoption of a Chicago City ordinance.[4] Another important divisive force was in public education, where the Illinois Federation of Labor (IFL) and the Illinois Education Association (IEA) were bitter rivals. The IFL, secure in Chicago and some of its suburbs and a few downstate areas without legislation, saw limited potential in downstate Illinois; they therefore opposed legislation without a right to strike. The IEA, increasingly aggressive downstate and politically effective in Springfield, pushed for separate legislation for teachers.

Finally, there was the opposition of associated public employers to collective bargaining legislation, especially if strikes were to be permitted. During the Kerner Commission proceedings in 1966 and 1967, the Illinois Manufacturers' Association expressed flat opposition to any affirmative legislation.[5] The state Chamber of Commerce opposed the private-sector model and insisted on a strong strike ban with penalties, safeguards for professional employees, a separate law for teachers, and preservation of fiscal control by the appropriate public authorities. The Illinois Municipal League, representing 1,000 of the 1,200 municipalities in the state, was willing to support permissive legislation if accompanied by provisions advocated by the Chamber of Commerce. The top officials of the city of Chicago and Cook County were silent, but the subsequent behavior of their representatives in Springfield effectively registered their opposition. The Association of School Boards reversed a longstanding policy of opposition and endorsed limited legislation for school employees although they expressed a clear preference for a separate school law. State university administrators were successful in getting their academic employees excluded from any proposed law. In the years following 1967, despite a substantial growth in public-sector unionism and bargaining at all levels of government, management opposition appeared to harden, although the governors of the seventies, Democrat Dan Walker and Republican James Thompson, expressed support and promised to sign affirmative bills if passed by the General Assembly. One of the most active lobbyist organizations in opposition during the late seventies was the National Right to Work Committee.

The failure to enact public-sector bargaining legislation was initially shared by another top priority item—legislation to curb discrimination in employment—but the latter effort finally succeeded (see chapter 13). Illinois was a pioneer in adopting civil rights legislation. Chicago passed a fair employment practices ordinance in 1945, despite an attack by the Illinois Manufacturers' Association that it was unconstitutional. But comparable bills in the state legislature were defeated in 1945, 1947, and 1949, and throughout the fifties. Finally in 1961, with the strong backing of Governor Kerner, a state law was passed although the Republican-controlled senate refused to confirm two of the initial appointments made by the governor to the new commission. Organized labor actively supported this long legislative drive, as it did in the national campaign that was not to reach fruition until 1964.

Health and safety were final examples of legislation that was high on Labor's agenda, dating from pre-World War II days. In 1953, the Department of Labor's compilation of laws relating to labor and employment included the following under health and safety: factory inspection, health and safety, work under the compressed air act, sanitary standards for butterine and ice cream factories, structural work, washrooms in certain employments, and protection of chauffeurs. Separate laws also existed for coal miners and the railroads. Amendments to these latter statutes were passed in the late forties and again in the fifties, reflecting the unions' active interest in these industries. Also in the fifties, laws were enacted for the protection and safety of construction workers, and the first law pertaining to radiation was adopted in the form of a requirement that all radiation installations must be registered with the Department of Public Health. In 1963, the concern with radiation was extended by a law requiring the registration, licensing, inspection, and control of radiation sources. For the first time, laws were passed (in 1961, 1963, and 1965) pertaining to the licensing and regulating of migrant labor camps and the establishment of minimum standards for them. In 1961, a bill was enacted combining the safety education and the factory inspection divisions of the Labor Department.

During the seventies, some additional railroad safety standards and new regulations relative to boilers and elevators were adopted, and the Commerce Commission was authorized to formulate and enforce federal regulations over the transportation of hazardous materials by rail. But the major legislative actions in this decade were the state's attempt to assume responsibility for the enactment of federal OSHA standards and employers' efforts to reduce the cost of unemployment insurance and workmen's compensation.

The following account of OSHA is based largely on a study by Craig Sanders, the only available published report that could be located,[6] and supplemented by some limited personal experience as a hearing officer and miscellaneous documentary sources. When OSHA was enacted by the federal Congress in 1970, it contained a provision that encouraged states to assume responsibility for health and safety conditions provided they established appropriate and adequately funded administrative machinery and enforced standards that were equal to or better than federal standards. Illinois was the twentieth state to receive permission to set up its own program. The process started in 1971 under Governor Richard B. Ogilvie, who authorized both the state Department of Labor and the Industrial Commission to undertake the development of an acceptable plan. Later in 1971, the General Assembly passed an amendment to the 1936 Health and Safety Act giving the Industrial Commission exclusive responsibility for setting state standards and receiving reports of accidents and illnesses. But the plan that was approved by Governor Dan Walker and submitted to OSHA in November 1972 was far from an agreed bill. Labor objected that it was not given an opportunity to participate in the plan's formulation, and although the plan was drafted by an employer consultant firm, the National Loss Control Corporation, employers fretted over internal differences and the resultant need to reach a compromise. According to a Sanders's interview with Robert Gibson, then secretary-treasurer of the State Federation, the national AFL–CIO was opposed to individual state plans. OSHA finally approved the plan on November 1, 1973, for a three-year trial period subject to federal review. The industrial Commission was given rule-making authority; the Department of Labor was charged with the task of conducting inspections and issuing citations and penalties. Appeals were in the jurisdiction of the Industrial Commission and its hearing officers.

The plan proved defective from the start, primarily because the General Assembly was unwilling to appropriate sufficient funds for enforcement and the staff of inspectors was judged by the federal reviewers to be inadequate in numbers, quality, and training. All of the major interest groups found grounds to complain. Employers called for more emphasis on consultation and education rather than penalties. Labor wanted more frequent inspections and firmer penalties. In any event the governor found the program a political embarrassment and decided to discontinue it as of June 30, 1975. Enforcement of OSHA was returned to the federal agency, with both labor and the employers continuing to express dissatisfaction with its status.

The frustrations with OSHA in the seventies were matched by the continuing struggle over the state's unemployment insurance and workmen's compensation and occupational disease programs. In essence, the issue was between costs and benefits. For business, apart from frequent allegations of abuse and inefficiency, the costs were alleged to be too high. Illinois firms were said to be suffering from a competitive disadvantage with out-of-state companies, and the state was allegedly losing old resident firms and failing to attract new ones because of these costs. For Labor, the benefits were said to be inadequate, not commensurate with the economic wealth of Illinois, and failing to keep up with rapidly rising inflation.

Of all the state legislative interests in the employment area, these laws were paramount to the State Federation and the principal employer/business associations. It was not merely because of their intrinsic importance; many other subjects were of at least equal if not greater significance. Rather it was because the fundamental principles involved were perceived as mutually essential and both sides accepted the feasibility and value of agreement. Other issues such as minimum wages, collective bargaining, the right of public employees to strike, and even nondiscrimination in employment continued to be clearly in the adversarial arena. But unemployment insurance, workmen's compensation, and occupational disease had been singled out by the major parties as distinctive subjects for agreed bills.

Not that the agreed-bill process always worked smoothly, mutualistically, or uninterruptedly. Gilbert Steiner's perceptive analysis of the agreed-bill process in unemployment insurance during the late forties noted "even with legislative participation in preliminary activities . . . a successful agreed bill is not guaranteed as may be demonstrated by the two attempts to extend coverage through an agreed bill, both of which were aborted in the legislature."[7] The parties themselves were often divided. The state CIO, for example, was much less enthusiastic about the process than the state AFL, but it lacked the political influence to achieve better results through normal adversarial legislative procedures. Likewise, the five participating business groups including the Chamber of Commerce and the Manufacturers' Association were often divided in viewpoint.

At the tenth annual convention of the state AFL–CIO in 1967, the Executive Council reported that for nearly forty years the agreed-bill process had functioned quite well—yielding slow but orderly advances in workmen's compensation and occupational diseases law. In 1963, however, the parties failed to agree. Two years later an agreed bill was again reached, but in 1967, the process was once more discontinued when the employers submitted their own bills to the General Assembly, Labor lobbied strongly against them and presented countermeasures, and no legislation emerged. In 1969, Governor Ogilvie made a special request to the parties to renew the agreed-bill process. Agreement with modest improvements was reached on the workmen's compensation and occupational diseases bills and became law. But when it came to unemployment compensation, the senate (including both Republicans and Democrats) refused to accept two agreed bills that extended coverage to small employers with fewer than four employees and to state employees. Labor felt that the agreed-bill process had been undermined. The process was not to be restored until 1979 in the case of unemployment compensation, and 1980 in the case of workmen's compensation and occupational diseases.

During the 1975 legislative session, with a Democratic governor in office and Democratic control of both houses of the General Assembly, substantial improvements in coverage and benefits were achieved by Labor, despite strong employer protests, in the workmen's compensation, occupational disease, and unemployment compensation acts. An elated State Federation Executive Board report in 1975 claimed: "We are number one in the Nation on w.c. and o.d. acts. We are right up there with the improvements in the u.c. acts."[8]

The employer associations, however, launched a major counterattack over the next four years, charging that the competitive position of Illinois business had been undermined seriously. In each session the employers not only resisted new Labor proposals, but also introduced their own legislation to trim back the 1975 laws. They were aided in this regard by the 1976 election of a Republican governor, James Thompson, and by the Republicans regaining control of one of the two houses of the General Assembly. In 1979, faced with more than fifty bills each on workmen's compensation and unemployment compensation, the governor and the leaders of the General Assembly asked the employer and labor representatives to try to negotiate agreed bills. The parties felt that they had no choice but to comply. An unemployment insurance bill was adopted after three weeks of hard negotiations;[9] no agreement, however, could be reached on workmen's compensation, and no legislation was passed. In 1980, an unemployment insurance agreed bill was again passed under the auspices of the Employment Security Advisory Board (comprised of three members each from Labor, business, and the public appointed by the governor). Workmen's compensation, however, proved to be the most controversial topic of the legislative session. At one point, when a pro-employer bill appeared to be at the passage stage, Labor marshalled some five hundred members from around the state for an intensive lobbying effort. Faced with seeming defeat, Labor finally worked out a compromise with the legislative leadership that contained concessions trimming back some of the gains obtained in 1975.[10]

Labor law has its negative as well as its positive features, and a good deal of Labor's attention was devoted to opposing the passage of undesirable bills. The two major concerns were bills designed to weaken union organization and bargaining power and bills seeking to reduce or eliminate employment-related benefits. In the first category were the so-called "right-to-work" bills, proposals to limit or ban picketing, efforts to impose binding arbitration, and bills to exclude strikers from unemployment compensation. The second category included bills to tighten up or reduce unemployment insurance, workmen's compensation, and occupational disease standards, bills to relax child labor, women's labor, and prevailing wage laws, and proposals to restrict or diminish civil service benefits (e.g, mandatory retirement). Some of these bills were the expressions of individual legislators' attitudes, lacked organizational support, and were easily killed in committee. In virtually every legislative session, however, some hostile bills were vigorously advanced by the major business organizations and necessitated extensive counterlobbying among Labor supporters. Relatively few such bills were enacted because the opposing parties in Illinois politics tended to be evenly balanced, and the constitution favored a standoff. If a legislator failed to cast a vote, the act had the effect of a negative vote. To pass a bill required a majority of the possible votes, not the votes actually cast. Also hampering the enactment of controversial proposals was the power of the governor to use an item veto, that is, to delete or to revise sections of bills.

Labor's interest in legislation was by no means exclusively confined to labor law, although most of its lobbying was devoted to the laws discussed above. More general public issues were also of concern, perhaps the most important of which were constitutional revision, the Equal Rights Amendment (ERA), tax policy, and public works.

The issue of constitutional revision was an old one. Many efforts had been made in the past to rewrite the state's 1870 constitution, including the convening of a constitutional convention. Labor was strongly opposed to the latter approach because it feared that unfavorable labor provisions, as well as undesirable general provisions, might be adopted. In 1949, it helped to defeat a bill calling for a convention and instead co-sponsored the so-called Gateway Amendment, which eased the amending clause (Article 14) of the constitution by providing that no more than three articles of the constitution might be submitted to referendum oftener than once in four years. The referendum on the Gateway Amendment was passed in November 1950.

In 1947 and 1949 bills for a constitutional convention were again proposed and defeated. However, the forces pressing for a convention were not to be denied. In 1968, the General Assembly approved the convening of a constitutional convention (popularly referred to as "Con-Con"), and a general public referendum ratified the idea in 1969 despite Labor opposition. After a session of more than eight months, the convention adopted a revised constitution on September 3, 1970, which, if ratified in referendum, was to take effect July 1, 1971. For tactical purposes, the convention proposal was divided into several segments: a "general package," judicial selection, legislative voting, the abolition of capital punishment, and lowering the minimum voting age to eighteen. Labor early announced opposition to the general package primarily because it regarded the revenue section as pro-business; it favored the election of judges rather than a merit selection system, retention of the cumulative voting system, and votes for eighteen-year olds; and its was neutral on capital punishment. Later in the referendum campaign, the Chicago Democrats revealed a readiness to support the general package. The ultimate result was electorate approval of the general package; on the other issues, Labor's position, which coincided with that of the Chicago machine and many downstate politicians, was triumphant.

The selection of state and local judges was a particularly sensitive issue because the major associations of lawyers in the state, as well as law school deans and other prominent public figures, were pressing strongly for a merit appointment system. Labor feared that this approach would lead to an elitist judiciary with conservative values more partial to business. Moreover, its close ally, the Chicago Democratic political machine, saw the courts as both an attractive means of rewarding worthy supporters and as a protective shield against challenges from political opponents. The elective process assured the machine of control over the court system in Cook County and gave it considerable influence over the selection of those supreme court judges within its political orbit.

Rubin Cohn has provided an insider's brilliant insights into the struggle that went on at the constitutional convention and during the referendum campaign over the judgeship issue.[11] It was nip-and-tuck, but the merit proposal was defeated. Labor's role in the convention was modest. It apparently relied primarily on the Chicago Democrats with whom it was closely identified and two union delegates, James Kemp of the Building Service Union, and William F. Lennon of the Jewelry Workers.[12] A student of lobbying at the convention, Ian D. Burman, interviewed Stanley Johnson, then executive vice-president of the State Federation and Harl Ray, then president of the Champaign-Urbana Federation of Labor. Johnson said that he had spent many hours in the convention gallery in the early months, but when the General Assembly restarted sessions, he felt it was more important to spend the bulk of his time in the legislative halls. He also expressed the view that "lack of support from union officials hurt the state AFL–CIO's ability to influence convention decisions." Ray, who was particularly interested in pension rights for state and local government employees, noted that just as he was giving up on getting a proposal out of committee, a neutral delegate, Henry Green, agreed to take up the issue and was able to carry it through to a successful conclusion.[13] It is interesting to note that Labor had been expected to lobby extensively but in fact did not, and other groups, such as the League of Women Voters and the bar associations, were far more active.

The Equal Rights Amendment issue produced an interesting shift in Labor's position in the seventies. When the bill for an amendment to the federal constitution was first passed by Congress in 1972, it was opposed by the national AFL–CIO on the grounds that all protective legislation for women would be jeopardized. At the state level, the State Federation neither supported nor opposed two legislative resolutions.[14] Labor was in a dilemma because its women members were divided. The following year, the State Federation abstained from taking a legislative position supporting a neutrality position of the national AFL–CIO. In the meantime, it threw its weight behind a series of bills giving equal status for women in the issuance of credit cards, employment, pay, and housing. In 1975, after a change in national AFL–CIO position, the State Federation for the first time testified affirmatively for ERA. By then, thirty-four of the necessary thirty-eight states had voted approval, and Illinois was virtually the only industrial state that had not. Nevertheless, the federation took a cautious position. It noted that its surveys and communications indicated that "over 50% of our membership do approve."[15] Nevertheless, many members and wives of members were opposed. Moreover, several "of our overall best friends" in the General Assembly were opposed. Hence the State Federation refused to label those legislative opponents as "unfriendly."

From 1975 on the State Federation, in consonance with the national AFL–CIO, took an increasingly supportive position on ERA as emotions throughout the state intensified and lobbying and demonstrations mounted. The Executive Board reporting to the Twenty-first Annual Convention now stated flatly: "ERA was a Labor issue."[16] In 1979, the Executive Board annual report stated: "We are even more persistent in our support for ratification of the Equal Rights Amendment. . . . Only through this Amendment will we finally enact laws which recognize the dignity and individuality of every person and eliminate discrimination on the basis of gender. . . . The officers of the Illinois State AFL–CIO have made it clear in the past and will continue to make it clear in the future: ERA is a Labor issue and a priority in our Legislative Program in Illinois."[17] In 1980, Labor's efforts in behalf of ERA in Illinois reached a peak. On April 26, a reported 1,200 trade unionists from all over the state under the banner of "Labor United for ERA" rallied in Chicago at Plumbers' Hall and listened to a nationally prominent list of union and women's leaders, including Lane Kirkland, AFL–CIO president, endorse the ERA. Kirkland suggested that COPE use the ERA as a measure of support for legislation. The next week Robert Gibson, State Federation president, led a long list of witnesses testifying in behalf of the ERA resolution before the House Judiciary Committee. On May 10, a Mother's Day march of more than fifty thousand persons, including many unionists, was held in Chicago's Grant Park. And on May 13, more than five thousand participated in a national ERA lobbying day in Springfield. Unfortunately, the ERA proponents fell 5 short of convincing the necessary 107 legislators in the house. Two more years of similar fruitless agitation were to elapse before the deadline for ERA expired.[18]

Tax policy and public works represented two other important areas of concern to organized labor. However, no single law occupied center stage; rather, numerous bills dealing with a wide variety of related topics came up for consideration each year. In the forties, for example, bills either supported or opposed by the State Federation or the state CIO included a "repeal of tax limitation" resolution, a strip mine tax, a housing tax exemption, and a Sanitary Board tax. In the fifties, the array of tax bills included tax aid to Chicago and other cities, a proposed resolution to Congress to revise the income tax provision in the U.S. Constitution, an occupation tax on ingredients in tangible property, gasoline tax exemption for municipal transportation systems, a tax increase for public libraries in Chicago, higher tax rates for public schools, authorization of bond referenda for schools and port districts, and several sales tax proposals. During the sixties, franchise sales, gasoline, and income taxes became increasingly important.

State income taxes on individuals and corporations were adopted in 1969 during Governor Ogilvie's administration, an action that was widely believed to have led to his defeat for reelection. A homestead tax exemption of $1,500 on the assessed value of homes of persons sixty-five and over passed with Labor's support. And in the seventies, real estate tax exemptions for senior citizens, a state lottery to alleviate the tax burden, exemptions from the personal property tax, home improvements tax relief, and sales and income tax exemptions reflected the widespread concern with taxes in the state.

In general, Labor's tax position was based on equity arguments. The sales tax, particularly on food and drugs, was opposed as regressive and a burden on workers. Lower individual income tax rates and higher corporate rates were deemed desirable. Exemptions for senior citizens and lower income earners were supported. User taxes for roads and mass transit were preferred to either higher sales or personal income taxes. The State Federation's Executive Board report of 1969 summed up the issue: "The new Illinois Income Tax, which became effective August 1, 1969 on a withholding basis, was not the type of tax we have been projecting on behalf of our membership. First, we wanted a graduated income tax. Failing that, we wanted a sharp differential between the individual and corporate tax. . . . We coupled the above with reduction in the sales tax and eventual abolition of sales taxes, especially on food, clothing and medicine. None of this came to pass."[19]

In the area of public works, Labor was invariably supportive. A review of the bills authorizing public works projects, such as highways, dams, parks, educational facilities, mental institutions, hospitals, prisons, and mass transit, reveals a consistent policy. Bond referenda typically won Labor backing. Such support can clearly be attributed to Labor's concern over jobs. Not only the powerful building and construction trades were the direct beneficiaries; the suppliers of steel, cement, and other materials also benefited in terms of employment. Together with the interested employers, the supporters of public works projects represented a formidable influence on both state and local legislative bodies. Their main adversaries in this area were the various taxpayers' associations, some business groups, and the elected officials who were necessarily sensitive to taxpayer reactions. During the prosperous years of the fifties and sixties, public works were authorized in huge volume. In the seventies, state and local finances became steadily more stringent. The taxpayers began to rebel against the tax burden, bond referenda were defeated in many fiscal jurisdictions, and politicians advocating or supporting higher taxes lost public favor. Even the traditional view of public works as an antidote to mass unemployment lost public favor.

NOTES

This chapter is indebted to the research of Meredith Miller and Neil Fox.

1. For a fuller account, see chapter 4, part B.

2. Milton Derber, "Labor-Management Policy for Public Employees in Illinois: The Experience of the Governor's Commission, 1966–1967," *Industrial and Labor Relations Review* 21 (July 1968): 541.

3. *Report and Recommendations,* Governor's Advisory Commission on Labor-Management Policy for Public Employees, Springfield, Ill., March 1967, pp. 47–48.

4. *Proceedings* of 21st Annual Convention, Illinois State Federation of Labor and Congress of Industrial Organizations, Chicago, September 11–14, 1978, pp. 30–32.

5. *Industrial and Labor Relations Review,* July 1968, pp. 554–5.

6. Craig Sanders, "OSHA in Illinois: The Agony and the Ecstacy," *Illinois Issues* 2 (October 1976): 14–17.

7. Gilbert Y. Steiner and Samuel K. Gove, *Legislative Relations in Illinois* (Urbana: University of Illinois Press, 1960); Gilbert Y. Steiner, *Legislation by Collective Bargaining: The Agreed Bill in Illinois Unemployment Compensation Legislation* (Urbana: University of Illinois Institute of Labor and Industrial Relations, 1951), p. 57.

8. *Proceedings* of 18th Annual Convention, Illinois State Federation of Labor and Congress of Industrial Organizations, Springfield, September 22–25, 1975, p. 110.

9. *Proceedings* of 22nd Annual Convention, Illinois State Federation of Labor and Congress of Industrial Organizations, Springfield, September 24, 1979, p. 19 of the Executive Board Report.

10. *Proceedings* of 23rd Annual Convention, Illinois State Federation of Labor and Congress of Industrial Organizations, Rosemont, September 29–October 2, 1980, pp. 99–100.

11. Rubin Cohn, *To Judge with Justice: History and Politics of Illinois Judical Reform* (Urbana: University of Illinois Press, 1973).

12. Only 2 of the 116 delegates to the convention were affiliated with a union. In the primary only 23 of 575 candidates were unionists. See *Proceedings* of 12th Convention, Illinois State Federation of Labor and Congress of Industrial Organizations, Chicago, August 24–27, 1969, p. 158.

13. Ian D. Burman, *Lobbying at the Illinois Constitutional Convention* (Urbana: University of Illinois Press, 1973), pp. 4, 78, 38.

14. *Proceedings* of 15th Annual Convention, Illinois State Federation of Labor and Congress of Industrial Organizations, Chicago, September 25–28, 1972, pp. 112–13.

15. *Proceedings* of 18th Annual Convention, p. 119.

16. *Proceedings* of 21st Annual Convention, p. 102.

17. *Proceedings* of 22nd Annual Convention, pp. 15–16.

18. *Proceedings* of 23rd Annual Convention, pp. 96–97.

19. *Proceedings* of 12th Annual Convention, p. 159.

7

The Courts

The Illinois courts played a sizable part in determining the legal structure of industrial relations. The federal government, of course, preempted a major portion of labor law through its controls over interstate commerce. But as the preceding chapter has demonstrated, the segment left to state jurisdiction was not trivial. Of particular importance was the public sector—state and local government. However, Illinois courts also affected a number of other significant areas, including numerous small firms that were not within federal jurisdiction, statutory areas like workers' compensation and unemployment insurance, and portions of federal law that were expressly left to state responsibilities.

As illustrations of judicial impact, two topics will be discussed: the right of employees to organize and engage in collective bargaining, and the right to engage in collective action. Other important examples, like nondiscrimination in employment, will be treated in other chapters.

The Right to Organize and Bargain Collectively

In a 1955 article, Simon Stickgold noted that generally "labor organizations in Illinois have no statutory authority to organize."[1] Neither in 1955 nor at any time in the 1945–80 period was there any statute in Illinois like Section 7 of the NLRA, which gave employees "the right to self-organization, to form, join, or assist labor organizations, to bargain collectively through representatives of their own choosing, and to engage in other concerted activities for the purpose of collective bargaining or other mutual aid or protection. . . ."[2] In 1933, the state legislature did pass a law making yellow-dog contracts unenforceable,[3] but this provided only minimal protection.

However, in the private sector, employees not protected by Section 7 were for a long time before 1945 covered by firmly established case law that guaranteed that "labor has the right to organize as well as capital."[4] "Every man," the Illinois Supreme Court stated in 1923, "has a right, under the law, to full freedom in the disposal of his labor according to his own will, and the right of workmen to organize for the purpose of promoting their common welfare by lawful means is fully recognized and maintained by the courts."[5]

While the right of private-sector employees to organize has never been directly challenged in Illinois since 1945, in the public sector a rather different situation prevailed. Apart from some statutory exceptions that gave the right to organize and to bargain collectively to certain categories of public employees like Chicago Transit Authority employees,[6] there was no general statutory right of Illinois public employees to organize in labor unions. Unlike the private sector, there was no longstanding case law to fill in where the legislature left off. Indeed, the only Illinois Supreme Court case to rule directly on the issue was a 1917 decision, *People ex rel. Fursman v. City of Chicago*,[7] which upheld a Chicago Board of Education rule that prohibited teachers from joining unions and that provided for the discharge of any teacher who was a member of a union.

Fursman has never been explicitly overruled, but no appellate court during the 1945–80 period gave support to the case. How much *Fursman* was followed by both employees and employers to guide action and by trial courts in non-appealed cases is open to question. For example, the Corporation Counsel of Chicago relied on *Fursman* as authority for a longstanding 1944 order of the Chicago police commissioner that prohibited members of the police force from joining unions.[8]

Yet, it was apparent that despite *Fursman*, Illinois public employees did join labor unions during this period and were not fired. Indeed, Earl Strayhorn noted that even Chicago police force members formed their own unaligned labor organizations despite the prohibition by the department.[9] Moreover, by the early 1970s, despite *Fursman*, Illinois appellate courts uniformly recognized the right of public employees to organize.[10]

However, the basis of this position was a federal court decision grounded in the United States Constitution. In *McLaughlin v. Tilendis*,[11] two teachers employed by a Cook County school district sued for damages under 42 U.S.C. Section 1983 after being fired for union activities. The federal district court dismissed the complaint, holding that they had no First Amendment right either to join or form a labor union, and that the overriding community interest against the disruption of the functioning of governmental entities precluded judicial interference. On appeal, the United States Court of Appeals for the Seventh Circuit reversed and held that the union activities of teachers, so long as they did not involve illegal strikes or picketing, were protected by the First Amendment.[12]

Recognizing the rights of employees not covered by federal labor law to organize is one thing. It is quite another to allow employee organizations and employers to enter into collective bargaining agreements. In the private sector, of course, this was not a problem, because private parties were traditionally free to contract with whomever they pleased.

In the public sector, however, the authority of public employers to enter into collective bargaining agreements with employee organizations was in doubt for a large part of the 1945–80 period. Although there were no cases on this point from 1945 until 1966, the accepted attitude in the legal literature was that "most states, Illinois included, do not recognize or permit collective bargaining between public employee organizations and governmental officers."[13] Apart from the general argument that public-sector collective bargaining was against public policy, one major theory, derived from Dillon's Rule,[14] was that governmental bodies did not have the legal power to enter into such contracts. It was felt that governmental units had only derivative powers — that is, only that power and authority that was expressly granted to them by the legislature — and that these powers could not be delegated or shared with unions. The absence of express legislative authorization for collective bargaining was also relied on.

Despite such legal theories, the real state of labor-management relations moved in an opposing direction. As Barnet Hodes pointed out in 1960 after giving a survey of the law in Illinois:

> Notwithstanding that collective bargaining contracts with organized public employees may be of questionable binding force in the absence of statutory sanction, verbal agreements with respect to wages and other matters have in instances been made with organized public employees in the state service for over forty years. About twenty years ago agreements of this nature began to be written into "letters of understanding." Agreements reached in this way, although perhaps not legally enforcable, have been honored by the public employer.[15]

Given the growth in public-sector unionism in the 1960s, it was only a matter of time before the law caught up with reality. In Illinois, this occurred in Chicago in 1964.

In that year, reportedly at Mayor Richard Daley's urgings, the Chicago Board or Education recognized three unions — the Chicago Division of the Illinois Education Association (IEA), the Chicago Principal's Club, and the Chicago Teachers Union (CTU), affiliated with the American Federation of Teachers — as bargaining agents for their respective members. The following year the board adopted a plan to hold a representation election between the IEA and the CTU to see which union would be the exclusive representative for the teachers.[16]

The decision to recognize one union as the exclusive bargaining agent for all teachers provoked a lawsuit by the IEA and a taxpayer intervenor. The two plaintiffs raised the issues of public policy, non-delegability, and a lack of a statute empowering the board to bargain in their attempt to have the representation election declared void. The board and the CTU argued, in response, that no specific legislation was necessary for the board to bargain collectively, and that specific legislation was indeed needed to show that the board did not have the authority to enter into collective bargaining arrangements.

The trial court dismissed the complaint and decided that any exclusive bargaining arrangement that the board might enter into with a union would be legal and not an improper delegation of authority, so long as the union agreed not to strike and the board retained control of certain statutory duties (although these were not specified). Furthermore, the trial court ordered that "should negotiations fail to resolve differences, the decision of the Board of Education shall be final."[17]

On appeal, the First District Appellate Court upheld the lower court's decision in *Chicago Division of the Illinois Education Assoc. v. Bd. of Education of the City of Chicago*.[18] After a fairly lengthy coverage of the arguments on both sides, Justice Arthur Murphy concluded that "the Board of Education of the City of Chicago does not require legislative authority to enter into a collective bargaining agreement with a sole collective bargaining agency selected by its teachers, and we hold that such an agreement is not against public policy."[19] The Illinois Supreme Court declined to grant review of the case, and thereafter the authority of governmental units in Illinois to enter into collective bargaining relationships with employee organizations was generally recognized by the courts.

The fact that employees had the right to organize, and the fact that both private and public employers could voluntarily enter into collectively bargained contracts, did not resolve the issue of the employer who rejected collective bargaining. In 1955, Stickgold noted that there was no "Illinois law requir[ing] or compel[ling] an employer to recognize or to bargain collectively with a labor organization. . . . "[20] In the next twenty-five years, neither the legislature nor the courts would change this rule.

In the private sector, there was only one case not under NLRB jurisdiction taken to the appellate level that addressed the duty of employers to recognize and negotiate with employee organizations. This case, *Peters v. South Chicago Community Hospital*,[21] involved attempts to unionize the employees of two not-for-profit hospitals in Chicago. The employees were exempted from the coverage of the NLRA until 1974. The labor organization seeking recognition from the hospitals, the Hospital Employees Labor Program (HELP), sponsored by both the Teamsters' and the Service Employees' unions, brought suit against the hospitals, requesting injunctions restraining the hospitals from intimidating and coercing their employees with regard to union membership and "to compel the hospitals to meet with the union representatives for the purpose of negotiating and entering a collective bargaining agreement." The circuit court judge, Daniel A. Covelli, did not grant all the relief requested by the union. However, he did order the hospital to meet with the union: "for the purpose of selecting an impartial person or agency to supervise and conduct an election to determine whether a majority of the employees of [the hospitals] . . . desire[d] to be represented by [the union] for collective bargaining purposes and the parties shall participate in such an election . . . .[22]

On appeal, the First District Appellate Court reversed Judge Covelli's order. In an opinion written by Justice Arthur Sullivan, the court held that although employees generally have the right to organize, there is no statutory or common law duty on Illinois employers not covered by the NLRA to recognize or negotiate with organizations representing their employees. Therefore, there is no duty of employers to participate in negotiations about the desire of their employees to be represented by a union or a duty to participate in any elections. The court also severely reprimanded Judge Covelli:

> Courts may not formulate labor rules or policies when the legislature has failed to do so. The consequences of such action would be far reaching indeed and would convert our courts into labor boards sitting to settle any dispute that arose between the employees' representatives and the employer. . . .
>
> The court in the instant case took upon itself the burden of legislating rights and duties of the parties in the field of labor relations. . . . The court clearly exceeded the scope of judicial authority.[23]

Peters was to achieve some notoriety later on in its history on the issue of whether the Illinois Anti-Injunction Act applied in this case.[24] But, at this stage, the *Peters* case showed that the law as it stood in the 1950s would continue to be the law. Until the legislature acted, employers not covered by federal law were not required in the 1945–80 period to bargain with representatives of their employees.

Even though the rationale of *Peters* would seem to apply to the public sector as well as to the private sector, the *Peters* case did not seem to have any influence on the decisions of Cook County Circuit Court Judge Nathan M. Cohen, for example. In at least two cases that were appealed, Judge Cohen ordered the respective government units to bargain in good faith with the bargaining representatives of their employees.[25] In both cases, the appellate courts reversed and held that neither government unit had the duty to bargain with their employees or their representatives. Indeed, in one of the cases, *Harper College Faculty Senate v. Bd. of Trustees*, the appellate court held that even though the board had entered into a recognition agreement with the faculty senate, the board was not bound to negotiate with it because the board had a non-delegable statutory duty to set compensation for its employees. A recognition agreement could not alter that duty.[26]

The unwillingness of Illinois appellate courts to find a duty to bargain led them to hold that where employers did consent to bargain, all questions of unit determination were within the sole discretion of the employer. For instance, in *Chicago High School Assistant Principals Assoc. v. Bd. of Education of the City of Chicago*,[27] the plaintiff union presented to the board signatures of 164 of 220–25 high school assistant principals who desired to split off and to be represented separately from the large 25,000-member unit represented by the Chicago Teachers Union. Apart from the assistant principals, the unit included elementary and secondary teachers, truant officers, clerical employees, vision and hearing testers, and playground supervisors. The assistant principals brought suit seeking a temporary injunction compelling the board to recognize their association as their exclusive bargaining agent. They alleged that they were supervisory personnel, and, thus, it was inappropriate for them to be in the same unit as everyone else. The circuit court denied the requested relief, and the assistant principals appealed.

The First District Appellate Court upheld the lower court's ruling and held that although the assistant principals had the constitutional right of free association, the recognition of a collective bargaining representative by the board was purely voluntary. If the board chose to recognize one union to represent all employees because of efficiency in bargaining, it had the right to do so.[28] Thus, rather than a neutral party establishing the parameters of an "appropriate" unit, as under federal legislation, under Illinois law, the decision was solely the employers'.[29]

In the face of such reluctance by the courts to innovate, and because of legislative inaction, the only legal means for change available to some Illinois employees was executive action. As noted previously, in 1973, Governor Daniel Walker issued Executive Order No. 6–73, granting to some sixty thousand state workers, directly under the control of the executive branch, the right to organize and to bargain collectively and establishing the Office of Collective Bargaining (OCB) to determine units and to conduct elections.

The system set up by Executive Order No. 6–73 worked fairly well. Litigation concerning labor-management relations in the covered areas of public employment was kept to a minimum.[30] This lack of litigation was probably the result of the fact that the decisions of the OCB were not reviewable by the courts except in very rare cases, because the OCB was not covered by the Administrative Review Act.[31]

Shortly after the 1945–80 period ended, in 1983, two full-blown, federal-style bargaining laws were enacted—one for education, the other for most other categories of public employees—thus ending years of Illinois' isolation among northern industrial states for its failure to legislate in this area.[32]

Once the hurdles of getting an employer to enter into a collective bargaining relationship are over, the problem arises of determining the scope of bargaining—what subjects are to be negotiated? In the private sector, traditional principles of freedom of contract reigned, and the few appellate courts that dealt with the subject placed few, if any, restrictions on what could be negotiated.

In contrast, what was and was not legally permitted in a public-sector collective bargaining contract was a hotly litigated topic in Illinois courts. Although the only reported case in the early portion of the 1945–80 period (1953) appeared to adopt a hands-off attitude toward this matter,[33] as collective bargaining became more widespead, a long and confusing series of cases emerged dealing with the permissible scope of bargaining in the public sector. Invariably, these cases came before the courts because the public employer refused to follow certain terms of a collective bargaining agreement into which it entered previously.

An illustration of this occurrence involved the Chicago Board of Education and the Chicago Teachers Union (CTU) in the early seventies. Before 1971, all contracts between the board and the CTU were for one-year terms. To solve a bargaining impasse during negotiations for the 1971 contract, Mayor Daley, as mediator, got the parties to agree to a two-year contract that provided for a 7–8 percent pay increase for the second year, 1972. However, when it came time for the board to adopt its 1972 budget, it was faced with what it claimed was a shortage of funds. As a solution, the board decided to grant its employees only a 5.5 percent salary increase in violation of the previous year's contract.

The CTU took the case to arbitration. The board then filed a lawsuit attacking the authority of the arbitrator to decide the case on the grounds that a state statute, Section 34–49 of the School Code,[34] made contracts of the board void unless there was a prior appropriation, and that the 1972 provisions of the contract were adopted without the board first appropriating money for them.

Both the trial court and the First District Appellate Court accepted the board's arguments in *Board of Education of the City of Chicago v. Chicago Teachers Union, Local 1.*[35] The courts held that, despite the benefits of multiyear labor contracts, the statutory provision voiding contracts made without prior appropriation was "certain and unambiguous." Here a contract covering 1972 had been made without a prior appropriation. Thus, the contract was void for 1972.[36]

Because the board was required by statute to make up an annual budget, this decision meant that the board was effectively prevented from entering into multiyear contracts with the CTU that were legal and enforceable. This must have been of some concern to the Democratic machine because within months of the appellate court's decision, Chicago Democrats sponsored a bill in the legislature that amended Section 34–49 of the School Code to exempt from the ban on contracts without prior appropriations the making of "employment contracts with individuals or groups of individuals for any period not to exceed three years."[37]

In contrast to *Board of Education v. Chicago Teachers Union*, where there was no statute explicitly prohibiting contracts without prior appropriations, one appellate court held the public employer to the terms of its five-year contract. In *Libertyville Education Assoc. v. Bd. of Education of School Dist. No. 70, Lake Cty.*,[38] the board had insisted during bargaining that the teachers accept a five-year contract for salary provisions, subject to annual increases tied to the Consumer Price Index. After the third year, the board tried to give the teachers lower pay increases than the contact called for, and the teachers sought relief in court. On appeal, the appellate court held that absent a statute like Section 34–49 of the School Code, which applied only to Chicago schools, the board had the authority to enter into multiyear contracts, and accordingly, the board was bound by the contract. The court also rejected the board's argument that it was not bound by contracts that a prior group of board members had entered into.

The multiyear contract question illustrates the importance of existing statutory provisions to judicial treatment of public-sector collective bargaining agreements. Usually, statutes like the ban on multiyear contracts in Chicago were enacted without the possibility of public employee collective bargaining being taken into account. Once public-sector bargaining became widespread, the combination of these statutes with long-time common law rules governing the actions of governing units frequently became a source of conflict, as numerous public employers reached back into legal history to justify breaking one contract after another.

The result of these conflicts was well over twenty appellate court and Supreme Court decisions in the late 1960s and 1970s dealing with the permissible scope of collective bargaining in the public sector. Because the courts dealt with this subject matter on a case-by-case basis, little doctrinal regularity emerged. Two conflicting lines of cases emerged, each of which appeared to exist in isolation of the other.

One line of cases, the majority line, was distinctly hostile to public-sector collective bargaining. Courts following this approach concluded that many central features of standard collective bargaining contracts had no binding effect because the government unit had non-delegable powers that could not be shared with a union in the collective bargaining process. Certainly, according to this view, a public employer's legislatively granted powers could not be shared with an arbitrator.

Because school boards have the statutory duty to "appoint all teachers," school boards did not have to follow contractual provisions regarding promotions or transfers.[39] Similarly, the legislature gave school boards the non-delegable power to hire and dismiss nontenured teachers, with the goal of retaining only the most qualified teachers. Therefore, school districts did not have to follow contractual clauses that gave "due process" rights to nontenured teachers, clauses that guaranteed that nontenured teachers would have some procedural protections from the decision not to rehire them.[40] Some courts extended these doctrines to invalidate discharge and discipline procedures concerning even tenured teachers.[41] Another court invalidated a union shop agreement between a painters' union and a school district on the theory that because it was the union that determined if a painter was a member in good standing, the union had usurped the board's control over when an employee should be either retained or let go.[43] The hostility toward collective bargaining even let one court invalidate a salary agreement—"A school board," the court stated, "simply cannot bargain away its power to control its budget [and] its power to fix the salaries of its employees. . . ."[43]

In contrast to this hostile line of cases, a parallel line of appellate courts looked more favorably on collective bargaining in the public sector. These courts were of the view that a public employer does not delegate statutory authority if it voluntarily enters into a collective bargaining agreement. The employer is still exercising its statutory duties; it is just doing it in a different way with the collective bargaining process as one additional step. Moreover, it is only fair to hold a public employer to its contracts with its employees, just as it would be fair to require school districts and government units to adhere to their contracts with private businesses.

Thus, one court held a school board to its contractual obligation to follow certain procedures before transferring teachers. While the final decision to transfer was still in the hands of the employer, following the "due process" procedures can "only serve to maintain a high standard of efficiency and professionalism in the school system . . . [and] such a bargain is consonant with public policy and should by enforced."[44] One appellate court upheld an evaluation procedure and a grievance procedure that governed whether non-tenured teachers would be retained, although this case was ultimately reversed by the supreme court.[45] Another court rejected a school board's contention that it had a non-delegable power to establish and amend a budget and lay-off employees and upheld a "Memorandum of Understanding" to employ a unit of principals twelve months a year.[46] Still another court held that because there was no arbitration involved, a school board was bound to follow general procedures for the involuntary transfer and demotion of principals,[47] while another court held that a board of education was bound by its agreement to increase salaries over a five-year period according to changes in the Consumer Price Index. There was no delegation of power because there was no third party, that is, an arbitrator, who was determining the salaries of the teachers and, in the end, it was the board that was performing its duty to fix salaries by agreeing with the teachers what their salaries would be.[48] Finally, the Illinois Supreme Court in 1981 held that arbitration of grievances regarding a provision in a contract that the board pay full salary to teachers absent from work due to school related assaults did not constitute an impermissible delegation of the board's duty to set the compensation of teachers. Rather, Justice

Seymour Simon wrote, the "board set the salaries of its teachers. . . . The salaries were published in the appendix to the collective bargaining agreement." The arbitrator merely determined if the teacher affected was eligible to be paid her full salary under the terms of the contract and this was not a delegation.[49]

Thus, at the end of the 1945–80 period, it seemed as if there was substantial doctrinal confusion in Illinois appellate courts about the proper scope of bargaining. There were hopes by some commentators that changes in the Illinois Constitution of 1970 concerning home rule would provide the impetus to clarify the area.[50] These hopes, however, were not realized as the Illinois Supreme Court handed down a decision in 1981 that squarely favored the line of prior cases hostile to collective bargaining.

In *Bd. of Educ. of City of Chicago v. Chicago Teachers Union, Local 1*,[51] the court dealt with a board suit to enjoin the arbitration of grievances that arose when the board closed its schools one day early in the 1976–77 school year to save funds. The contract with the teachers prohibited this if the result was lower pay for the teachers. In a decision written by Justice Thomas Moran, the court firmly rejected arguments that contract provisions regarding the length of the school year were valid, or that an arbitrator had power to resolve grievances. Rather the court held that "the Board's powers here are discretionary unto itself and may not be delegated. . . . The Board's action in closing schools one day earlier was in compliance with its power granted by the Code. . . . In this case, any terms relating to the length of the school term in the collective bargaining agreement were subject to the Board's statutory power to close the schools early."[52] The contractual provisions guaranteeing salaries for a full school year were unenforceable.

Given this firm view by the supreme court, future legal battles over the scope of bargaining seemed bleak from the perspective of the employees. Luckily for them, the state legislature passed two public employment relations statutes in 1983 that made much of this entire area of the law obsolete.

Union Collective Action

Since the earliest years of this country's history, the courts have been, on the whole, hostile to strikes, picketing, boycotts, and other forms of union collective action. One of the more potent tools used to combat militant unionism has been the injunction. Even after the Norris–La Guardia Act of 1932 severely limited the power of federal courts to issue injunctions in cases growing out of labor disputes, state courts continued to have the power to enjoin union collective action.

In the 1940s, state court intervention in labor disputes began to be limited by the United States Supreme Court through the application of constitutional protections of freedom of speech.[53] In the 1950s, 1960s and 1970s, the emphasis turned to the doctrine of preemption as set out in *San Diego Building Trades Council v. Garmon*,[54] in which state courts were deprived of jurisdiction over labor disputes that were arguably protected or prohibited by federal labor law.

Yet both the constitutional and preemption doctrines did not completely deprive state courts of jurisdiction over labor disputes. A line of U.S. Supreme Court cases allowed for state regulation of union collective action if that regulation was in furtherance of certain legitimate state policies or matters of traditional local concern, such as the prevention of violence and libel.[55] State courts also continued to have exclusive jurisdiction over union collective action in occupations excluded from NLRA coverage, such as public employees, supervisors, and farm laborers.

Because the exact reaches of the constitutional and preemption limitations on state authority were never completely clear, state court attitudes toward labor disputes remained very important. Even if a strike or boycott were protected either by the First Amendment or by the NLRA, if a state court enjoined the activity, such an injunction could destroy whatever concerted activity the union was involved in and seriously alter the power of the parties to the labor dispute. A future reversal in an appellate court, years later, could not make up for the lost momentum when an erroneous injunction was issued. Because of the potential for such harm, many states adopted their own versions of the Norris–La Guardia Act, which curbed the common law and equitable powers of state courts.

In Illinois, the passage of a state Anti-Injunction Act in 1925 predated Norris–La Guardia.[56] This act prohibited Illinois judges from enjoining strikes and picketing arising out of disputes over the terms or conditions of employment. In 1934, the Illinois Supreme Court upheld the constitutionality of the Anti-Injunction Act in *Fenske Brothers v. Upholsterers International Union*.[57] The court also noted that the acts specified in the statute, which courts could no longer enjoin, had in effect been legalized by the legislature. However, the court did qualify its approval of the statute—not all union strikes and picketing were exempt from injunctions. For example, the Anti-Injunction Act would not apply to union activity that was violent, intimidating, and coercive. In addition, the court distinguished between proper and improper objects of union collective action and suggested that Illinois courts could continue to enjoin even peaceful strikes in furtherance of improper ends.[58]

The problem after *Fenske* was to decide just what were and what were not proper goals of union collective action. Given the sparseness of the Illinois Constitution and the lack of detailed Illinois labor legislation, the courts relied on prior cases and on judicially declared public policy to decide cases.

Between 1945 and 1980, there was no doubt that, whatever the ends, violence, property damage, and personal harassment were improper means to achieve union ends, and hence were enjoinable. For instance, in *General Electric v. Local 997, United Auto Workers*,[59] the court upheld the issuing of a temporary injunction against mass picketing during a strike at a G.E. plant in Danville when strikers damaged cars, harassed strikebreakers, and threw rocks at police. Likewise, the Fifth District Appellate Court in *Illinois Power v. Latham*[60] upheld the issuance of an injunction against the United Black Workers Federation and the Metro East Labor Council of East St. Louis when demonstrations to protest employment discrimination by the Illinois Power Company turned violent, with picketers allegedly beating up I.P. employees and destroying property with axe and pick handles.

The situation was not always so clear. In *Eads Coal Co. v. United Mine Workers*,[61] for instance, the court upheld the issuance of a temporary injunction against the UMW, whose members were picketing outside the Eads' mine in Mt. Vernon in an effort to recruit Eads' employees, members of the rival Progressive Mine Workers of America. Yet, compared to *Latham* or *General Electric*, there was very little violence in this case—a few telephone threats and abusive language on the picket line were the only substantiated excesses. In contrast, four years later, when the *Eads* case came up for review again on appeal of the lower court's order to make permanent the temporary injunction, the appellate court reversed the lower court's order. The appellate court relied on the prolonged period of industrial peace between the earlier situation and the present, and the lack of evidence that the prohibited activities would occur in the future to hold against the issuance of a permanent injunction.[62]

It should be stressed that in all of these cases the courts did not enjoin all picketing by the defendant labor organizations. In *General Electric* and *Eads*, for example, the courts enjoined the violent behavior and then restricted the number of picketers who could continue to picket peacefully to a certain limited number, such as two or ten. The constitutional problems with a total ban on picketing were too great.

With cases involving picket-line violence, the governing principles seemed relatively simple. In contrast, where a labor organization sought to obtain its goals through the use of a secondary boycott, the principles themselves remained confusing, and Illinois courts did not differ from federal courts in struggling to adopt a coherent view of the law.

A secondary boycott has been defined as "the application of economic pressure upon a person with whom the union has no dispute regarding its own terms of employment in order to induce that person to cease doing business with another employer with whom the union does have such a dispute."[63] Illinois courts viewed secondary boycotts as improper labor tactics because of their association with economic coercion. Secondary boycotts were considered therefore to violate a judicially determined public policy. Accordingly, neither the First Amendment nor the state Anti-Injunction Act prevented courts from enjoining them.

A classic secondary boycott case was *Collins v. Berry*,[64] a 1956 case. Here, in an effort to get partial owners and supervisory employees of two funeral homes to join the Building Service Employees Union, union members threatened suppliers of vaults, caskets, and flowers to the two funeral homes with strikes and other pressures, unless they withheld their services from the primary establishments. This was identified as a clear secondary boycott and, hence, illegal.

Distinguishing between permitted primary activity and prohibited secondary activity, however, often proved to be a difficult task. In an early postwar case, *Dinoffria v. Inter. Bros. of Teamsters, Local 179*,[65] the Teamsters were trying to get the owner/operators of two gas stations to join the union. When the owners refused, the drivers of oil delivery trucks, members of the union, refused to make any deliveries. There were also suggestions that the union put pressure on the employers of the delivery drivers as well. The owners sued the union and its officers, seeking an injunction to refrain from interfering with the deliveries, as well as $10,000 damages for business losses. Although a major factor leading to the appellate court holding for the owners was that the end of the Teamster's action—unionizing the owners—was improper, the court also decided that the union's means were improper. The court characterized the union's means as a prohibited secondary boycott that involved as much coercion as physical violence. Yet, many of the actions here, such as union members refusing to make deliveries, seem to fall more in the category of primary, rather than secondary, activity.

Another secondary boycott case that confused primary and secondary activity was *Twin City Barge and Towing v. Licensed Tugmen's and Pilots Protective Assoc.*[66] In this case, a new firm, Twin City, bought the tugboats of the firm that had previously employed members of the defendant union, but which had gone out of business. Twin City discharged all the old employees and brought in its own, who were members of another union. The defendant union began picketing not only sites where Twin City barges and tugs were docked, but also customers of Twin City. The union also threatened the latter with "labor troubles" if they did not cease business with Twin City. The appellate court upheld the issuing of a temporary injunction against all picketing of Twin City's customers and against threats and coercion directed toward persons and corporations doing business with Twin City. This was clearly secondary activity that was not protected by the First Amendment or the Anti-Injunction Act. On the other hand, the court also approved of enjoining the mobile pickets that followed Twin City's barges around—activity that is primary and should not have been lumped in with the illegal secondary activity.

In addition to illicit means, there were also some labor objectives that were considered illegal. Union action in furtherance of such ends was not entitled to the protections of the First Amendment or the Anti-Injunction Act, however peaceful or primary the activities were. One such illicit union end, as discussed previously in the 1947 *Dinoffria* case, was the coerced unionization of employers or the self-employed. The *Dinoffria* court viewed such an end as leading to monopolistic economic control by the union.[67]

More common was the situation in which a union picketed a business demanding recognition by the employer as the exclusive bargaining agent of its employees and demanding that the employer sign a collective bargaining agreement with a union shop clause. Such behavior raised concerns that a small employer might sign the agreement, despite the fact that the employees might not want to join the union.

This situation arose in *Bitzer Motor Co. v. Teamsters, Local 604*,[68] a 1953 case. Here, the Teamsters picketed the Bitzer car dealership in an effort to get the salesmen to join the union and for Bitzer to sign a collective bargaining agreement with the union. Bitzer's union mechanics honored the picket line and did not show up for work. Bitzer sought and received from the circuit court a temporary injunction against picketing.

On appeal, the union argued that the Anti-Injunction Act made the temporary injunction void, and that because the picketing was peaceful, the union's free speech had been violated. The appellate court rejected these arguments. The court held that despite the absence of state legislation on the subject, it would find there to be a valid public policy in ensuring that workers were only represented by unions of their own choosing. Any attempts to impose a union on employees via coercion were violative of this judicially created public policy, and hence enjoinable.

In 1954 and 1955, the same three judges that decided *Bitzer Motor* decided two more recognitional picketing cases—both times distinguishing *Bitzer Motor* and holding in the unions' favor. In *E. St. Louis Retail Druggists Assoc. v. Local 676–D, Retail Clerks Inter. Assoc.*,[69] the court reversed a temporary injunction against union recognitional picketing of stores in the employers' association. The court looked critically at the wording of the complaint and concluded that it did not properly charge that an illegal purpose was behind the picketing—that is, there was no charge that the union was seeking to impose a union on unwilling employees through coercion of the employer.

The following case, *Simmons v. Retail Clerks Inter. Assoc.*,[70] was more complex. Before setting up stranger pickets, the union sent a lengthy letter to the plaintiff's department store stating clearly that it intended to picket the store peacefully and orderly, solely to advertise to the public that the store was nonunion. The union hoped as well that the reduced patronage would persuade the employees "that Unionism is preferable and that it [the public] is desirous of dealing with Union store employees in making purchases."[71] The letter stated unequivocally that the union was not making demands on the employer for recognition, nor did it intend to coerce the employer to intimidate the employees to join the union.

The employer claimed that this letter was a sham and was merely a veil over implied coercion. The appellate court, however, relied on the conclusions of the trial court that the picketing was not carried out to force the employer into recognizing the union and was free of violence and coercion. The court reasoned that this case differed from *Bitzer Motor* and was not violative of public policy. Thus, the picketing could not be enjoined.[72]

Many of the cases described previously would seem to be covered by federal labor law. Yet, the existence of federal law did not influence the decisions of the Illinois courts in the early part of the 1945–80 period, except for an occasional infrequent reference. This began to change in the mid to late fifties, sixties, and seventies, as the United States Supreme Court began defining the preemption doctrine. Gradually, Illinois courts responded by excluding themselves from jurisdiction over certain types of labor cases.

One of the earliest examples of the growth of the preemption doctrine was the 1954 case *Precision Scientific Co. v. Inter. Union of Mine, Mill and Smelter Workers*.[73] In this case, the employer tried to obtain an injunction ordering the union from striking and from picketing. The union, Precision maintained, was communist-dominated and had called an illegal strike in order to overthrow the government by force. Moreover, Precision argued, the union was not in compliance with the anti-communist provisions of Taft–Hartley, and therefore was not a labor organization within the meaning of federal law. The union, however, had filed an unfair labor practice charge against Precision alleging that Precision was refusing to bargain with it. This charge was pending before the NLRB when the circuit court issued the temporary injunction that Precision had requested.

On appeal, the First District Appellate Court reversed the issuing of the injunction. The court first held that the Illinois Anti-Injunction Act precluded judicial interference in a peaceful labor dispute. It then cited the developing preemption doctrine and held that because the NLRB had assumed jurisdiction, state courts could no longer exercise jurisdiction through the medium of injunction proceedings. Any allegations that the union was communist-dominated and had filed a false noncommunist affidavit with the NLRB should not be dealt with by a state court, but only by the U.S. Justice Department.

In *Precision Scientific*, the union had already invoked the jurisdiction of the NLRB at the time the injunction was issued. However, as the preemption doctrine developed, Illinois courts began declining to exercise jurisdiction over cases in which the NLRB's jurisdiction had not already been invoked.

In *Jersey County Motor Co. v. Local 525, Inter. Bros. Teamsters*,[74] a 1959 case, the court was faced with a situation like the one in *Simmons* and *Bitzer Motors*, in which the union set up pickets outside the business and sent a letter to the employer very similar to the one approved by the court in *Simmons*. The employer charged "top-down organizing", that is, organizing by pressuring the employer and not persuading the employees, and argued that *Bitzer Motor*, not *Simmons*, controlled the outcome of the case. On appeal, the court held that whether the case was more like that in *Bitzer Motors* or *Simmons* did not matter, as the entire field of organizational picketing had been preempted by federal law. The court thus held that the circuit court had improperly enjoined the picketing.

Similarly, by the 1960s, Illinois appellate courts held the entire area of secondary boycotts to be preempted by federal law. In a series of cases, Illinois courts refused to uphold injunctions in cases involving such unlawful means of achieving union goals.[75]

One further extension of the preemption doctrine was made in 1975, this time by the Illinois Supreme Court. In *People v. Federal Tool & Plastics*,[76] there was an economic strike at Federal Tool. The company advertised for workers to replace the strikers, but failed to state in its advertisements that a strike was in progress—a violation of *Ill. Rev. Stat.*, ch. 48, par. 2c (enacted in 1941), punishable by a $300-a-day fine. A criminal complaint was filed, but the circuit court dismissed it on the grounds that the statute was preempted by federal labor law.

On appeal, the Illinois Supreme Court affirmed the dismissal, relying heavily on the U.S. Supreme Court case, *Teamsters Local No. 20 v. Morton*,[77] which expanded the preemption doctrine announced in *Garmon*. According to *Morton* not only were state courts preempted where the behavior was arguably protected or arguably prohibited by the NLRA, but there was also preemption concerning activities that Congress neither prohibited nor protected, but intentionally left free of government regulation. Such activities were meant to be unregulated, but nevertheless permitted.

Following this reasoning, in *Federal Tool & Plastics*, the Illinois Supreme Court noted that Congress specifically declined to adopt a federal law requiring employers to include in their advertisements for strikebreakers that a labor dispute was in progress, and also noted that Congress in fact specifically intended to allow struck employers to hire replacements for strikers. Accordingly, the court held that *Ill. Rev. Stat.*, ch. 48, par. 2c altered the balance of power set up by Congress. The court concluded that the interest in preemption overrode state concerns about avoiding violence on the picket line, and therefore the statute could not be enforced.

An alleged concern for violence, though, did not prevent the supreme court from finding no preemption in two cases involving union members' technical trespasses into employers' property. The first case, *People v. Goduto*,[78] was a 1961 trespass prosecution against two union organizers from the Retail Clerks Union. The two organizers came onto a parking lot leased by Sears, Roebuck, and Co. to leaflet and talk about the union to employees of a Sears store. When a manager asked them to leave, they refused and were arrested. A lower court found them guilty of criminal trespass.

On appeal to the Illinois Supreme Court, the two organizers argued that federal labor law divested Illinois of the power to intervene in a labor dispute by use of its criminal trespass laws—that the area of organizational activity had been preempted by federal law, and that organizational leafleting on an employer's property was arguably protected or arguably prohibited by the NLRA as explained by the United States Supreme Court in *NLRB v. Babcock & Wilcox Co.*[79]

The Court, however, approached the preemption question from a different angle. The state criminal trespass laws, the Court reasoned, originally "were not imposed primarily for the protection of property rights but were imposed for the protection of public safety." Without trespass laws, the right of self-help by the owner could lead to violence. Thus, the purpose of the trespass laws "is the prevention of violence or threats of violence."[80] In this case, of course, there was no violence, but this was only because the state had enforced the trespass laws, thereby preventing Sears from using violence to eject the two organizers. Because the prevention of violence was a legitimate area of state concern that survived the preemption doctrine, federal labor law did not prevent the state from convicting the two union organizers.

Significantly, the Court stressed that the union involved had made no effort to invoke the jurisdiction of the NLRB. Thus, there was no way for Sears to protect its property rights or for the state to prevent Sears from resorting to violence, save the invocation of the state trespass laws.

Fifteen years later, the Illinois Supreme Court extended *Goduto* in *May Dept. Store v. Teamsters, Local 743*.[81] Union organizers there had peacefully entered upon Venture Department Store property (Venture was owned by May) in Oak Lawn and talked with employees at the store's entrance before and after business hours. Apparently afraid that its employees would listen to the unionists, Venture went to court and obtained a preliminary injunction enjoining the union from soliciting the employees on Venture's property. However, before the order was issued, the union filed unfair labor practice charges against the employer with the NLRB. The First District Appellate

Court saw this fact as what distinguished this case from *Goduto* and held that the invocation of the jurisdiction of the NLRB preempted the state court from involvement.[82]

The Illinois Supreme Court reversed the appellate court and reinstated the injunction. The court first took judicial notice of the fact that the regional director of the NLRB had since refused to issue a complaint based on the union's unfair labor practice charge. But even if this had not been the case, even if the NLRB eventually decided the case in the union's favor, the supreme court believed that an injunction should issue against the trespass until the Labor Board's decision was made, and then the injunction could be vacated if need be. As in *Goduto*, the court again relied on the state's overriding concern in preventing employer violence in response to technical violations of property rights as a reason why the area was not preempted by federal law.

When attention is turned from the private to the public sector, the legal picture changes dramatically with regards to union collective action. Because public-sector labor disputes rarely involved secondary activity or attempts to get the self-employed to join unions, the Illinois cases dealing with those subjects were largely irrelevant in the public sector. So were those cases dealing with preemption, since state and local governments were explicitly exempted from coverage of the NLRA.

Instead, most legal disputes in the public sector relating to collective action dealt with the legality and enjoinability of primary strikes and picketing, and what could be done to avoid future labor disputes. Because Illinois did not have a comprehensive public labor relations statute (until 1983), and because Governor Walker's Executive Order No. 6–73 made no mention of strikes, collective action in the public sector was governed by judicially declared public policy, interpretations of the Illinois and federal constitutions, and interpretations of the Anti-Injunction Act.

The starting point for analysis in this area is *Board of Education v. Redding*,[83] a 1965 Illinois Supreme Court case. The custodial employees of a school district in Bond County joined the Teamsters' union and tried to get the board of education to enter into a collective bargaining agreement. The board refused, and the employees went on strike and picketed the school. At all times the picketing was conducted peacefully. However, the operation of the schools suffered. The strikers did not perform their jobs, some of the school buses did not run, various delivery and repair workers did not cross the picket line, and attendance by students dropped. The board went to court for an injunction, but the circuit court denied it on the grounds that the board failed to show irreparable injury, the picketing was peaceful and protected by the First Amendment, and the operation of the school had not been interfered with seriously.

On direct appeal, the Illinois Supreme Court reversed. In an opinion written by Justice Joseph Daily, the court noted that this was a case of first impression in Illinois. Even so:

It is, so far as we can ascertain, the universal view that there is no inherent right in municipal employees to strike against their governmental employer, whether Federal, State, or a political subdivision thereof, and that a strike of municipal employees for any purpose is illegal. . . . The underlying basis for the public policy against strikes by public employees is the sound and demanding notion that governmental functions may not be impeded or obstructed, as well as the concept that the profit motive, inherent in the principle of free enterprise, is absent in the governmental function.[84]

In addition to this judicially developed public policy ground, the court looked to a constitutional basis as well—the court held that the Illinois Constitution of 1870 gave to the legislature the duty

to "provide a thorough and efficient system of free schools," (const. of 1870, art. VIII, sec. I) and we believe it logically follows that those who, under the implementing statutes, become the agents to fulfill the will of the people in such respect are themselves charged with a duty to refrain from conduct which will render our schools less efficient and thorough. The drastic remedy of organized strikes against employing school boards is in direct contravention of such duty. . . . What is more, to be thorough and efficient, school operations cannot depend upon the choice or whim of its employees, or their union, or others, but must necessarily be controlled only by duly constituted and qualified school officials.[85]

The fact that the strikers in this particular case were not teachers, but were custodial employees, did not make any difference. The constitutional mandate was the same.

Thus, the *Redding* holding rested on two separate grounds. The first ground was a public policy ground that made all public employee strikes illegal. The second was a specific state constitutional provision that applied only to strikes by school employees.

Three years after *Redding*, in *City of Rockford v. Local 413, Intern. Assoc. of Firefighters*,[86] the Second District Appellate Court ignored the latter constitutional arguments against public employee strikes and relied entirely on the public policy aspects to uphold the issuing of an injunction against striking firefighters. In addition, the court held that even a partial (50 percent) work stoppage was no different from a full strike and was enjoinable.

In 1969, an appellate court extended the *Redding* decision even further and applied its public policy reasoning to a private-sector case. In *Peters v. South Chicago Community Hospital*,[87] the appellate court held that a strike by employees of a not-for-profit hospital to gain recognition by their union was enjoinable. The union argued that the Illinois Anti-Injunction Act prevented the court from enjoining a peaceful strike, but the court held that the Anti-Injunction Act did not apply where the purpose of the strike violated public policy. The court held the strike against the hospital in this case was as much against public policy as the strike against a school in *Redding*.

The Illinois Supreme Court reversed the appellate court's decision.[88] In its *per curiam* opinion, the court simply stated that its holding in *Redding* solely revolved around the constitutional expression of public policy to "provide a thorough and efficient system of free schools." Thus, "it was not this court that declared the public policy, as did the appellate court in this case, it was the constitution that declared the public policy."[89] Although not-for-profit hospitals were important, the court held that absent a clear constitutional mandate, as in *Redding*, the Anti-Injunction Act prevented courts from enjoining strikes.

The following year, the Illinois Supreme Court extended *Peters* outside the private sector to the noneducational public sector. In *County of Peoria v. Benedict*,[90] the court was faced with a situation very similar to that in *Peters*—a strike by nursing home employees. The only real difference was that the home was owned by Peoria County and was not a privately owned, not-for-profit organization. The circuit court had enjoined the strike, and the union members appealed.

The supreme court held in the union's favor. Without citing *Redding*, a public-sector case, the court relied on *Peters*, a private-sector case, and simply held that for the reasons set out in *Peters*, the Anti-Injunction Act prevented Illinois courts from enjoining the strike in this case.[91]

It was generally assumed that *Benedict* did not overrule *Redding*. Rather it was assumed that *Redding*'s constitutional arguments still prevailed to make strikes by educational employees illegal and enjoinable. However, it was unclear whether all other public-sector employees, who were not restrained by the constitutional mandate for "thorough and efficient" schools, could strike legally, or whether the Anti-Injunction Act just prohibited courts from enjoining noneducational public-sector strikes that were still nonetheless "illegal."[92]

The confusion ended in 1974 with *City of Pana v. Crowe*.[93] The water, sewer, street, and police employees of the small city of Pana went on strike in 1972, and the city received an injunction from the circuit court against any work stoppages. On appeal, the Fifth District Appellate Court reversed and held that the ruling in *Benedict* compelled a decision in the union's favor— the strike in this case was practically indistinguishable from the strike in *Benedict*.[94]

The Illinois Supreme Court disagreed and reinstated the injunction. In an opinion written by Justice Walter Schaefer, with no dissenters, the court held that the strike by Pana's employees could and should be enjoined. Without explicitly overruling *Benedict*, the *Pana* court announced the public policy of the state to be one opposed to all public-sector strikes, not just those in education: "The situation of the governing body, the public, and the employees differs sharply in a strike of governmental employees from that involved in a strike in private industry. Ordinarily the functions provided by government are not of such a nature that substitution of product or of service is possible, as it often is in the case of strikes in the private sector. Moreover, strikes of public employees are very apt to create immediate emergencies bearing sharply upon the health, safety and welfare of the public."[95] *Pana* thus settled the issue of strikes by public employees. For the rest of the 1970s, public-sector strikes in all areas of public employment were considered illegal and enjoinable.[96]

If public-sector strikes were illegal because of the disruption they caused, what about picketing by public-sector employees? In one early case (1963), *City of W. Frankfort v. United Assoc. of Journeyman*,[97] the court held that despite some disruptions in a city's provision of water services, informational picketing by plumbers at the scene of one of the city's plumbing projects could not be enjoined. The court analogized the city's water company to a private water utility and held that the city "was no more immune from peaceful picketing than a private corporation."[98]

City of West Frankfort, though, may not have survived the 1964 *Redding* decision.[99] In *Redding*, the supreme court held that picketing of a school in support of an illegal objective, such as a strike, could be enjoined no matter how peaceful it was if the effect was to "impede and obstruct a vital and important governmental function. . . ."[100] While there was also language in *Redding* that would support enjoining all strike-related picketing by public employees, even if it did not impede the provision of services,[101] later appellate cases only upheld injunctions against picketing where governmental services were actually interrupted.[102]

It should be noted that as in the private sector, if a lower court enjoined collective action, the union had to obey the injunction even if on appeal it turned out that it was issued improperly. Otherwise, the union, its officials, and its members were subject to contempt charges. Time and time again, the Illinois Supreme Court upheld contempt convictions for violations of injunctions, even in cases where the initial injunction was wrongfully issued.[103]

There were some special problems, however, in labor cases. Frequently these arose when the labor dispute was settled and the public employer did not want to continue the legal battle against the union. For example, in *Board of Junior Colleges, Dist. 508 Cook County v. Cook County Teachers Union, Local 1600*,[104] the board obtained a temporary injunction against a 1966 strike by its teachers. The board's attorney then tried to dissolve the temporary injunction, but Circuit Court Judge Daniel Covelli directed the board's attorney to prepare and file a petition for a rule on the union and its officers to show cause why they failed to comply with the temporary injunction. A settlement was reached shortly thereafter, and the board filed a petition withdrawing from the case, stating a conflict of interest existed. Judge Covelli attempted to get the Cook County state's attorney to assume the case, but he refused. Finally, Covelli found a private attorney to take the role of amicus curiae to pursue the contempt matter against the union. Judge Covelli eventually found the union and its president, Norman Swenson, guilty of contempt, fined the union $5,000, and sentenced Swenson to thirty days in jail, as well as fining him $1,000. On appeal, the court affirmed, stating that "as judges we must remind teachers and public employees that the interests of unionism do not justify standing in defiance of law."[105] Curiously, the next time Local 1600 went on strike, a similar situation arose, with the circuit court again ordering the board to file contempt charges against the union and Swenson. Again, the appellate court affirmed the contempt convictions, although by the time the court heard the case, Governor Walker had granted a pardon to Swenson.[106]

Once it became clear that public-sector strikes were illegal and picketing in support thereof was highly regulated, a good portion of court activity in the mid to late seventies turned to post-strike behavior. To begin with, because public-sector strikes were against public policy, a court could not enforce parts of subsequent collective bargaining contracts that sought to compensate strikers for money lost during the strike. In *Board of Trustees v. Cook County College Teachers Union, Local 1600*,[107] at issue was a contract clause regarding the assignment of extra summer jobs. A proper interpretation of the collective bargaining agreement, though, would have given preference for these jobs to teachers who had illegally gone on strike in 1975. Because the result was inconsistent with what the supreme court held to be public policy, in that strikers were rewarded, the supreme court refused to enforce an arbitration award in the union's favor.

A year later, the supreme court held in *Bond v. Bd. of Education of Mascoutah Comm. Unit Dist. 19*[108] that to avert future strikes it was entirely proper for a board of education to pay higher salaries to teachers who signed a pledge that they would refrain from any work stoppages, sit-ins, or strikes. In justifying the distinction in salaries, the court noted that the "public policy against strikes by public employees has been frequently and blatantly ignored."[109] In contrast, one court did not allow a school board to get a permanent injunction against all future employee strikes and picketing merely because of past strikes.[110]

Finally, there was a line of cases that allowed government employers to discharge striking employees.[111] Similarly, in two cases, the appellate courts upheld the selective discharge of union and other strike leaders. Such discrimination did not violate equal protection because the selective enforcement was rationally related to the twin legitimate purposes of deterring future strikes and not impairing government by firing all the strikers.[112]

Conclusions

In the thirty-five years after World War II, Illinois courts remained intricately involved in many facets of labor relations in Illinois. From the recognition of the legitimacy of collective bargaining in the public sector to the adoption of the preemption doctrine, Illinois labor law between 1945 and 1980 was an active and growing field.

While the Illinois judiciary followed many national trends, in no way can it be said that Illinois courts were innovators or national leaders in the development of the law. On the whole, Illinois courts tended to follow national trends, not set them. In certain key areas, such as developing the proper scope of public-sector collective bargaining or determining whether public employees had the right to strike, the performance of Illinois courts was at times grossly deficient.

The failure of the Illinois legislature to develop a unified statutory framework for state labor law in part contributed to the judiciary's reluctance to "legislate" in the field of industrial relations. Yet, it would be a mistake to see the judiciary's failure to devise solutions solely as a product of the reluctance of judges to interfere in the affairs of the legislative branch of government.

When it suited the appellate judges, cases were easily decided on the basis of what judges perceived to be "public policy." Thus, it was considered to be a proper exercise of judicial power to declare public-sector employee strikes to be illegal as a violation of public policy. Yet, the same courts reprimanded circuit court judges, like Judges Nathan Cohen or Daniel Covelli, who used what they perceived to be their judical power to order employers to bargain collectively with unions. Similarly, the Illinois Supreme Court had no problems determining that an employer's property rights were more deserving of protection than the union's right of leaflet outside the employer's store, and so upheld criminal convictions for trespass.

In this sense, Illinois courts were far from neutral arbiters of private disputes that used a value-free calculus to decide each case. Instead, the judiciary in Illinois is better seen as an active participant in the development of the shape of labor relations in Illinois, a participant no less partisan than the mayor of Chicago or the governor of the state.

NOTES

This chapter is a condensation and revision of a report written by Neil Fox.

1. Simon Stickgold, "Illinois Labor Law," *University of Illinois Law Forum* (1955): 256, 258.

2. 29 U.S.C. Section 157.

3. *Ill. Rev. Stat.*, ch. 48, par. 2b.

4. *Franklin Union No. 4 v. People*, 220 Ill. 355, 377 N.E. 176, 184 (1906).

5. *Anderson & Lind Mfg. Co. v. Carpenters Dist. Council*, 308 Ill. 488, 139 N.E. 887, 889 (1923).

6. *Ill. Rev. Stat.*, ch. 111 2/3, par. 328a (enacted 1945).

7. 278 Ill. 318 116 N.E. 158 (1917).

8. Barnet Hodes, *Illinois Labor Law* (Chicago: Commerce Clearing House, 1960), p. 83. Hodes was the corporation counsel.

9. Earl Strayhorn, "Municipal Employees and the Law," *University of Illinois Law Forum*, (1961): 377, 382.

10. See *Chicago High School Assistant Principals Assoc. v. Bd. of Chicago*, 5 Ill. App. 3d 672, 284 N.E.2d 14, 17 (1st Dist. 1972); *Classroom Teachers Assoc. v. Bd. of Education*, 15 Ill. App. 3d 224, 304 N.E.2d 516, 518 (3d Dist. 1973).

11. 398 F.2d 287 (7th Cir. 1968).

12. Id., at 288–90.

13. Strayhorn, "Municipal Employees," p. 384. Strayhorn notes that in 1945 the Illinois legislature passed a bill authorizing state and city officials to engage in collective bargaining, but the bill was vetoed by the governor.

14. F. Dillon, *A Treatise of the Law on Municipal Corporations* (Boston: Little, Brown, 1911), p. 460. "The principle is a plain one, that public powers . . . devolved by law or charter upon the . . . governing body, to be exercised by it when and in such manner as *it* shall judge best, *cannot be delegated to others*" (emphasis in original).

15. Hodes, *Illinois Labor Law*, p. 89, note 8.

16 For background on the winning of collective bargaining rights by teachers in Chicago, see Paul E. Peterson, *School Politics Chicago Style* (Chicago: University of Chicago Press, 1976), pp. 186–216.

17. See *Chicago Division of the Illinois Education Assoc. v. Bd. of Education in the City of Chicago*, 76 Ill. App. 2d 456 222 N.E.2d 243, 246 (1st Dist. 1966).

18. 76 Ill. App. 2d 456, 222 N.E. 2d 243 (1st Dist. 1966).

19. 222 N.E. 2d at 251.

20. Stickgold, "Illinois Labor Law," p. 258.

21. 92 Ill. App. 2d 37, 235 N.E. 2d 842 (1st Dist. 1968).

22. 235 N.E. 2d at 843.

23. 235 N.E. 2d at 846–47.

24. *Peters v. South Chicago Comm. Hospital*, 44 Ill. 2d 22, 253 N.E.2d 375 (1969).

25. *Cook County Police Assoc. v. City of Harvey*, 8 Ill. App. 3d 147, 289 N.E.2d 226 (1st Dist. 1972); *Harper College Faculty Senate v. Bd. of Trustees of Junior College Dist. No. 512*, 51 Ill. App. 3d 443, 366 N.E.2d 999, 9 Ill. Dec. 488 (1st Dist. 1977).

26. *Harper College Faculty Senate*, 366 N.E.2d at 1001.

27. 5 Ill. App. 3d 672, 284 N.E.2d 14 (1st Dist. 1972).

28. 284 N.E.2d at 16–17.

29. *Accord: Tobin v. Health and Hospitals Governing Commissions of Cook County*, 66 Ill. App. 3d 564, 384 N.E. 2d 77, 79, 23 Ill. Dec. 441 (1st Dist. 1978).

30. The only reported case on the subject is *Aldridge v. Boys*, 98 Ill. App. 3d 803, 424 N.E. 2d 886, 54 Ill. Dec. 136 (4th Dist. 1981), a case slightly outside the period under consideration. In this case, forty disgruntled union employees who were covered by the order unsuccessfully sued a government unit on the grounds that they were denied equal protection because they were paid less than comparable employees not covered by the order. In upholding the dismissal of the suit, the appellate court noted the positive stabilizing features of Executive Order No. 6–73.

31. For information on Executive Order 6–73, see Elliott H. Goldstein, "Current Trends in Public Employee Labor Law in Illinois: Alice-In-Wonderland Revisited?" *DePaul Law Review* 23 (1973): 382; Robert J. McIntyre, "Public Employee Collective Bargaining in Illinois Under Executive Order No. 6–73," *Illinois Bar Journal* 68 (1979): 276.

32. *Ill. Rev. Stat.*, ch. 48, par. 1601 *et seq.* and par. 1701 *et seq.*

33. See *Government and Civic Employees Organizing Committee, CIO, v. Cook County School of Nursing*, 350 Ill. App. 274, 112 N.E. 2d 736 (1953).

34. *Ill. Rev. Stat.*, ch. 122, par. 34–49 (1969).

35. 26 Ill. App. 3d 806, 326 N.E. 2d 158 (1st Dist. 1975).

36. 326 N.E. 2d at 161–63.

37. PA 79–748, Section 2, effective October 1, 1975. See also, *Chicago Patrolmen's Assoc. v. City of Chicago*, 56 Ill. 2d 503, 309 N.E. 2d 3 (1974).

38. 56 Ill. App. 3d 503, 371 N.E. 2d 676, 13 Ill. Dec. 741 (2d Dist. 1977).

39. See *Bd of Educ. Sch. Dist. 205 v. Rockford Ed. Assoc.*, 3 Ill. App. 3d 1090, 280 N.E. 2d 286 (2d Dist. 1972); *Bd. of Educ., South Stickney Sch. Dist. Ill v. Johnson*, 21 Ill. App. 3d 482, 315 N.E. 2d 634 (1st Dist. 1974); *Bd. of Trustees of Junior College Dist. No. 508 v. Cook County Teachers Union, Local 1600*, 87 Ill. App. 3d 246, 408 N.E. 2d 1026, 42 Ill. Dec. 317 (1st Dist. 1980).

40. See *Illinois Education Assoc. v. Bd. of Educ. Dist. 218, Cook County*, 62 Ill. 2d 127, 340 N.E. 2d 7 (1975); *Bd. of Trustees of Junior College Dist. No. 508 v. Cook County College Teachers Union, Local 1600*, 62 Ill. 2d 470, 343 N.E. 2d 473 (1976); *Lockport Special Ed. Cooperative v. Lockport Area Special Education Cooperative Assoc.*, 33 Ill. App. 3d 789, 338 N.E. 2d 463 (3d Dist. 1975); *Wesclin Ed. Assoc. v. Bd. of Education*, 30 Ill. App. 3d 67, 331 N.E. 2d 335 (5th Dist. 1975).

41. See, for example, *Lowe v. Bd. of Education of City of Chicago*, 76 Ill. App. 3d 348, 395 N.E. 2d 59, 62–63, 32 Ill. Dec. 112 (1st Dist. 1979).

42. *Bd. of Ed. of School Dist. No. 189 v. Cahokia Dist. Council No. 58*, 93 Ill. App. 3d 376, 417 N.E. 2d 151, 48 Ill. Dec. 749 (5th Dist. 1981).

43. *Weary v. Bd. of Educ. of Sch. Dist. No. 189, E. St. Louis*, 46 Ill. App. 3d 182, 360 N.E. 2d 1112, 1115, 4 Ill. Dec. 737 (5th Dist. 1977).

44. *Classroom Teachers Assoc. v. Bd. of Educ. of United Township High School, No. 30, E. Moline*, 15 Ill. App. 3d 224, 304 N.E. 2d 516, 519–20 (3d Dist. 1973).

45. *Ill. Educ. Assoc. v. Bd. of Ed. Dist. 218, Cook County*, 23 Ill. App. 3d 649, 320 N.E. 2d 240 (1st Dist. 1974), rev'd. 62 Ill. 2d 127, 340 N.E. 2d 7 (1975).

46. *Perlin v. Bd. of Educ. of City of Chicago*, 86 Ill. App. 3d 108, 407 N.E. 2d 792, 41 Ill. Dec. 294 (1st Dist. 1980).

47. *Chicago Principals Assoc. v. Bd. of Educ. of City of Chicago*, 84 Ill. App. 3d 1095, 406 N.E. 2d 82, 40 Ill. Dec. 381 (1st Dist. 1980).

48. *Libertyville Educ. Assoc. v. Bd. of Ed., Dist. 70, Lake Cty.*, 56 Ill. App. 3d 503, 371 N.E. 2d 676, 13 Ill. Dec. 741 (2d Dist. 1977).

49. *Bd. of Educ. of City of Chicago v. Chicago Teachers Union, Local No. 1*, 86 Ill. 2d 469, 427 N.E. 2d 1199, 1203, 56 Ill. Dec. 653 (1981).

50. See Comment, "Non-Salary Provisions in Negotiated Teacher Agreements: Delegation and the Illinois Constitution, Article VII, Section 10," *DePaul Law Review* 24 (1975): 731; Note, "Scope of Public School Collective Bargaining," *University of Illinois Law Forum* (1977): 443, 459–61.

51. 88 Ill. 2d 63, 430 N.E. 2d 111, 58 Ill. Dec. 1860 (1981).

52. 430 N.E. 2d at 1115–16. In a scathing dissent, Justice Simon noted that:

contract law was created to make legitimate expectations enforceable and thus encourage bargaining, which is the basis of our economic system. When a public agency is allowed to repudiate a contract, it loses some of the credibility it must have in order to continue its relationship to its employees. The ultimate loser is the public. Once the board of education signs an agreement and its obligations under the agreement come due, it is too late for it to raise "discretion" as an argument for nullifying the contract. In effect, the Board in now claiming the right to prefer some creditors over others, more or less as it pleases. I would not permit it.

430 N.E. 2d at 1120 (Simon, dissenting).

53. See *Thornhill v. Alabama*, 310 U.S. 88, 84 L.E. 1093, 60 S. Ct. 736 (1940).

54. 359 U.S. 236, 3 L.Ed.2d 775, 79 S. Ct. 773 (1959).

55. See generally, Robert A. Gorman, *Basic Text on Labor Law* (St. Paul: West Publishing, 1976), pp. 779–82.

56. *Ill. Rev. Stat.*, ch. 48, par. 2a.

57. 358 Ill. 239, 193 N.E. 112 (1934).

58. 193 N.E. at 115, 120.

59. 8 Ill. App. 2d 154, 130 N.E. 2d 758 (3rd Dist. 1955).

60. 15 Ill. App. 3d 156, 303 N.E.2d 448 (5th Dist. 1973).

61. 131 Ill. App. 2d 1082, 269 N.E.2d 359 (5th Dist. 1971).

62. *Eads Coal Co. v. United Mine Workers*, 27 Ill. App. 3d 692, 327 N.E.2d 115 (5th Dist. 1975).

63. Gorman, *Basic Text*, p. 240, note 56.

64. 11 Ill. App. 2d 119, 136 N.E.2d 597, 602 (1st Dist. 1956).

65. 331 Ill. App. 129, 72 N.E.2d 635 (2d Dist. 1947), writ of error dismissed, 399 Ill. 304, 77 N.E.2d 661, cert. den. 335 U.S. 815 (1948).

66. 48 Ill. App. 2d 1, 197 N.E.2d 749 (1st Dist. 1964).

67. Despite *Dinoffria*, in 1956, in *Collins v. Berry*, 11 Ill. App. 2d 119, 136 N.E.2d

597 (1st Dist. 1956), the court refused to find that it was an improper objective for a union to strike and picket in an effort to require part owners and managers of funeral establishments to join the union.

68. 349 Ill. App. 283, 110 N.E.2d 674 (4th Dist. 1953).

69. 3 Ill. App. 2d 325, 122 N.E.2d 66 (4th Dist. 1954).

70. 5 Ill. App. 2d 429, 125 N.E.2d 700 (4th Dist. 1955).

71. 125 N.E.2d at 702.

72. See also *Cielesz v. Local 189, Amalgamated Meatcutters*, 25 Ill. App. 2d 491, 167 N.E.2d 302 (2d Dist. 1960). (*Bitzer Moter* may no longer be good law.)

73. 2 Ill. App. 2d 531, 120 N.E.2d 356 (1st Dist. 1954).

74. 21 Ill. App. 2d 38, 156 N.E.2d 633 (3d Dist. 1959).

75. *Norman v. Local 4, IBEW*, 40 Ill. App. 2d 422, 189 N.E.2d 422, 189 N.E.2d 687 (4th Dist. 1963); *Larson & Sons, v. Radio & T.V. Broadcast Eng.*, 66 Ill. App. 2d 146, 213 N.E.2d 100 (2d Dist. 1965).

76. 62 Ill. 2d 549, 344 N.E.2d 1 (1975).

77. 377 U.S. 252, 12 L.Ed.2d 280, 84 S. Ct. 1253 (1964).

78. 21 Ill. 2d 605, 174 N.E.2d 385, cert. den. 368 U.S. 927 (1961).

79. 351 U.S. 105, 100 L.Ed. 975, 76 S. Ct. 679 (1956).

80. *Goduto*, 174 N.E.2d at 387.

81. 64 Ill. 2d 153, 355 N.E.2d 7 (1976).

82. *May Dept. Stores v. Teamsters Local 743*, 32 Ill. App. 3d 916, 337 N.E.2d 299 (1st Dist. 1975), rev'd. 64 Ill. 2d 153, 355 N.E.2d 7 (1976).

83. 32 Ill. 2d 567, 207 N.E.2d 427 (1965).

84. 207 N.E.2d at 430 (citations omitted).

85. 207 N.E.2d at 430–31.

86. 98 Ill. App. 2d 36, 240 N.E.2d 705 (2d Dist. 1968).

87. 107 Ill. App. 2d 460, 246 N.E.2d 840 (1st Dist.), rev'd. 44 Ill. 2d 22, 253 N.E.2d 375 (1969).

88. 44 Ill. 2d 22, 253 N.E.2d 375 (1969).

89. 253 N.E.2d at 378.

90. 47 Ill. 2d 166, 265 N.E.2d 141 (1970), cert. den. 402 U.S. 929 (1971).

91. 265 N.E.2d at 143. The court, however, upheld contempt convictions for strikers who violated the injunction.

92. See, for example, *Allen v. Maurer*, 6 Ill. App. 3d 633, 286 N.E.2d 135, 142 43 (4th Dist. 1972) (*Benedict* did not overrule *Redding* in cases of strikes by teachers); Goldstein, "Current Trends," p. 399, note 32 (arguing that nonschool public employee strikes continued to be illegal—they just could not be enjoined). Goldstein's view was adopted in 1972 in *Fletcher v. Civil Service Comm. of Waukegan* (6 Ill. App. 3d 593, 286 N.E.2d 130, 134 [2d Dist. 1972]), where the court suggested that, although a police strike could not be enjoined, still police officers who struck could be discharged.

93. 57 Ill. 2d 547, 316 N.E.2d 513 (1974).

94. *City of Pana v. Crowe*, 13 Ill. App. 3d 90, 299 N.E.2d 770 (1973), rev'd. 57 Ill. 2d 547, 316 N.E.2d 513 (1974).

95. 316 N.E.2d at 515–16.

96. Although *Pana* definitively established that striking by public employees was enjoinable, it was only enjoinable at the request of the governmental employer. In

Allen v. Maurer (6 Ill. App. 3d 633, 286 N.E.2d 135, 139–40 [4th Dist. 1972]), the court held that parents and taxpayers did not have standing to seek an injunction against striking teachers in Decatur. Paradoxically, at the same time the parents in this case were trying to get a court order to force the teachers back to work, the school board was trying to terminate the striking teachers' employment contracts.

97. 53 Ill. App. 2d 207, 202 N.E.2d 649 (5th Dist. 1964).

98. 202 N.E.2d at 651.

99. See notes 83–85 and accompanying text.

100. *Redding*, 207 N.E.2d at 432.

101. Id. Court noted that peaceful picketing for the purpose of "fostering and supporting an unlawful strike against a governmental employer . . . should have been enjoined for this reason alone."

102. *Bd. of Educ. of Danville v. Danville Educ. Assoc.*, 59 Ill. App. 3d 726, 376 N.E.2d 430, 17 Ill. Dec. 431 (4th Dist. 1978); *Bd. of Educ., Dist. 196, St. Clair County v. Parkhill*, 50 Ill. App. 3d 60, 365 N.E.2d 195, 7 Ill. Dec. 910 (5th Dist. 1977); *City of Rockford v. Local No. 413, Int'l. Ass'n. of Firefighters*, 98 Ill. App. 2d 36, 240 N.E.2d 705 (2d Dist. 1968).

103. *County of Peoria v. Benedict*, 265 N.E.2d at 143–44; *Bd. of Educ. v. Kankakee Fed. of Teachers*, 46 Ill. 2d 439, 264 N.E.2d 18 (1970). See also *UMW Hospital v. UMW*, 52 Ill. 2d 496, 288 N.E.2d 455 (1972) (private not-for-profit hospital).

104. 126 Ill. App. 2d 418, 262 N.E.2d 125 (1st Dist. 1970).

105. 262 N.E.2d at 130.

106. *Bd. of Trustees of Comm. College Dist. 508 v. Cook County Teachers Union, Local 1600*, 42 Ill. App. 3d 1056, 356 N.E.2d 1089, 1 Ill. Dec. 807 (1st Dist. 1976).

107. 74 Ill. 2d 412, 386 N.E.2d 47, 24 Ill. Dec. 843 (1979).

108. 81 Ill. 2d 242, 408 N.E.2d 714, 42 Ill. Dec. 136 (1980).

109. 408 N.E.2d at 717.

110. *Bd. of Educ., Peoria Sch. Dist. No. 150 v. Peoria Educ. Assoc.*, 29 Ill. App. 3d 411, 330 N.E.2d 235 (3d Dist. 1975).

111. *Fletcher v. Civil Service Comm. of Waukegan*, 6 Ill. App. 3d 593, 286 N.E.2d 130 (2d Dist. 1972).

112. *Battle v. Illinois Civil Service Comm.*, 78 Ill. App. 3d 828, 396 N.E.2d 1321, 33 Ill. Dec. 597 (1st Dist. 1979); *Strobeck v. Illinois Civil Service Comm.*, 70 Ill. App. 3d 772, 388 N.E.2d 912, 26 Ill. Dec. 911 (1st Dist. 1979).

PART IV

Labor in the Community

As Barbara Newell suggested in her insightful study of Chicago labor in the thirties, each city represents a distinctive environment or mould that helps shape its labor scene. This community environment is not all-inclusive—state, national, and international factors may also be powerful influences. However, the community has a filtering effect on outside forces as well as providing unique internal effects.

To illustrate the diverse roles of the community environment, brief studies of Chicago and five downstate communities were conducted. No attempt was made to achieve quantitative results for the state—an unlikely and high-cost prospect at best. However, the six cases were selected on the basis of several criteria, notably geographic spread, relatively large population size, economic and industrial significance, and relatively high degree of unionization, in order to capture a variety of important experiences. In each case the objective was to try to comprehend the central thrust or spirit of the community environment in relation to the structure and behavior of labor.

For example, the conservative cultural values of Rockford's substantial Swedish population and the struggles for status and political power of East St. Louis's black majority were found to be key elements in the histories of these two communities. In Peoria and the Quad Cities, the impact of a dominant industry like the manufacture of farm and road equipment was of paramount importance.

However, some community themes were more difficult to explain, and changes over time were often clouded in ambiguity and uncertainty. What was the key to Chicago Labor's relations with the Daley machine? How was this outwardly unprepossessing man able, for twenty-one years, to master the nation's third largest metropolis with one of the most diversified and complex Labor movements and a population of extraordinary ethnic variability? Why did such a strongly organized industrial city like Peoria fail to stimulate significant Labor political action? What accounts for the shift in Decatur from a generally harmonious industrial relations climate to a climate of substantial industrial turbulence?

Labor's community service role is much less understood or appreciated than its concerns with collective bargaining and political action. A study of this third dimension in chapter 14 reveals a diversified and important record. Community action—involvement in charitable enterprises like Community Chest or the United Way, aid to the poor and the handicapped, even support for music and other cultural projects—was strongly advocated by many unions in early post-World War II days. After the AFL–CIO merger it declined for a time and then was revived and expanded.

What conclusions are to be drawn from the six case studies and the discussions of Labor's community service and labor education? Clearly collective bargaining was of prime importance to Labor's status in the community because strong unions provided the basis for worker solidarity. However, strength in the work place did not automatically assure a strong communal role for Labor. To achieve the latter, Labor customarily turned to political action at the three levels of federal, state, and local government. But as the experience in Peoria and the Quad Cities indicates, many unions lacked either the motivation or the leadership to function effectively in politics.

More significantly, labor often encountered difficulty in uniting its ranks. This is reflected in the problems that the local AFL and CIO met in merging their central bodies. The AFL relations with the political organization of Chicago was fragmented in itself and even more so in terms of AFL–CIO relations. In Rockford, and the Quad Cities, the UAW dominance often reflected resistance from the Building Trades and the Teamsters. In Decatur, the Allied Industrial Workers represented one political force, while other unions reflected other interests. Furthermore, even a united labor movement was usually an insufficient power base in itself. As Chicago illustrated, Labor's political role was subordinate to the role of the machine politicians, and in other communities, like Rockford and Decatur, Labor's political success depended on the leaders' ability to build coalitions with other interest groups.

Ethnic and racial factors were also frequently key ingredients of labor's political success or failure. As noted previously, the black population of East St. Louis was a decisive force in that ailing community. In Peoria and the Quad Cities, the Hispanic minority was a source of grievance and division. In Chicago, the black pressure for affirmative action in construction seriously divided labor's ranks. On the other hand, in Rockford the Scandinavian work ethic was seen to have a major impact in limiting union organization and collective bargaining.

Finally, the community's economic and industrial environment often appeared to be a major determinant of Labor's communal status. The Quad Cities and Peoria were heavily dependent on both the internal and external fortunes of the farm and road equipment industry. In East St. Louis, a lengthy process of economic decline created serious unemployment levels and drove labor to seek political solutions that collective bargaining could not provide. In Decatur, the replacement of local industrial ownership by absentee interests appeared to have a powerful impact on the climate of relationships between labor and management in the community as a whole.

In addition to collective bargaining and political action, unions resorted to a variety of community service programs. These programs were of a dual nature. Perhaps the more important was the training of union counsellors to advise and assist union members who were adversely affected by strikes or layoffs and needed information and guidance as to sources of economic aid. Allied to this aspect of community service was help on workmen's compensation and health and safety. This type of activity was designed primarily to assist union members, although it was linked to community aid at large. Classes and workshops in labor education programs overlapped with this branch of community service.

The other type of community service was focused on labor involvement in programs benefitting the entire community. A prime example was Labor representation on the staffs of such agencies as the Community Chest or United Way. Other cases occurred in times of floods, fires, and civil defense.

Community service was primarily dependent on local union action. Although the state Industrial Union Council (CIO) gave considerable support to the concept in the early postwar years, the leaders of the State Federation were reluctant to divert their resources from political action. As a result, this third branch of Labor activity never gained the support or prominence attached to collective bargaining or politics. Nonetheless, it was an aspect of the labor movement that merited more attention than it received.

8

The Chicago Story

In her study of the labor movement in Chicago during the thirties, Barbara Newell identified two main union groups—the central core of "local market" (primarily service) unions consisting of the building trades, building service, and local trucking, together with their satellites such as the hotel and restaurant, retail and wholesale trade, bakery, and laundry unions; and the nationally oriented industrial (primarily manufacturing) unions like the garment, steel, farm equipment, and meatpacking unions. As at least partial explanation for the "environment or mould" of metropolitan unionism, Newell singled out "five important causal factors":[1] ethnicity, the social worker, the Catholic church, the ward boss and relations with the political system, and the historical heritage of the trade union movement and its effect upon the ideology and direction of trade union leadership.

The post-World War II experience suggested that most of these observations about Chicago unionism and the Chicago environment were still valid, although some factors became less important and additional factors wielded considerable weight. Chicago's reputation as an ethnic city continued to be justified, but the percent of ethnics both overall and in particular industries changed. Blacks, for example, grew from about 12 percent of the population in 1945 to 38 percent in 1973. While persons of foreign birth declined from 18.5 percent to 10.7 percent of the population, and those of foreign stock fell from 32 percent to 17 percent, the Spanish-surnamed and Asian communities grew significantly, and the proportion of earlier immigrant groups—Irish, Italian, Scandinavian, and Polish—fell.[2] In the clothing unions, the original heavy Jewish membership was largely supplanted by blacks, Hispanics, and Asian immigrant groups, although the top leadership was maintained by the original pioneers. In short, diverse ethnicity remained important but in a state of flux.

Female, middle-upper-class social workers of the Jane Addams–Hull House tradition were no longer a significant force in the labor movement despite the tremendous growth in public welfare programs. However, the rise of the women's movement, stimulated by both the World War II demand for female labor and the burgeoning civil rights movement of the sixties, played an analogous role. Chicago became a center for women's rights in general and women unionists in particular.

The role of the church is somewhat more difficult to assess. The majority of white ethnics was Catholic, and the Catholic hierarchy in Chicago, under the leadership of John Cardinal Cody, archbishop of the Chicago diocese, was among the most powerful in the nation. A significant symbol of continuing church influence was the annual Labor Mass sponsored by the Chicago–Cook County Building Trades Council, initiated and guided by its chaplain, the Reverend Joseph L. Donahue, since 1940, and involving such prominent labor leaders as Thomas Murray, Stephen Bailey, Stanley Johnson, William Lee, and Thomas Nayder.

In the case of the rapidly growing black community, religious leaders like the Reverend Jesse Jackson, a close associate of Martin Luther King, were in the forefront of the civil rights movement and played important roles in the struggle against employment and business discrimination. Most of the black ministers were from various Protestant denominations, although some were Catholics and some Muslims.

The major Jewish influence on the Chicago (and Illinois) labor movement was the Jewish Labor Committee, an offshoot of a national organization of the same name, formed in New York in 1934 to combat the rise of Hitlerism in Germany and race and religious discrimination in the United States. Because its organizational affiliates included important AFL and CIO unions like the ILGWU and the Amalgamated Clothing Workers, its leaders like Samuel Levin and Morris Bialis were prominent figures in the Chicago labor movement. The committee had the support of national union leaders like George Meany and Walter Reuther, and it was able to gain strong Labor backing during the post-World War II period both for Israel and for civil rights in the United States.

The fourth of Newell's environmental factors, municipal politics, had exceptional influence on Labor in Chicago during the period under study because of the intimate linkage between the Irish union leadership noted previously and the Democratic political machine that had been initiated in the early thirties by Anton Cermack, developed by Patrick Nash and his ally, Mayor Edward J. Kelly, and brought to its pinnacle during twenty-one-year administration of Mayor Richard J. Daley (1955–76). The political factor in Labor's development was to assume a different character under Daley's successors.

Labor history and ideology, Newell's final factors, also proved to be important in the postwar era, but their deep roots were entangled in somewhat different configurations than in the thirties. The business unionism of the mainstream AFL increased in scope, the long radical tradition epitomized by CFL president John Fitzpatrick and others to his left suffered major setbacks, and even the more moderate social unionism of the CIO lost ground. Gangster unionism became more sophisticated but less pervasive, and the civil rights movement came to fruition.

Two factors not included in Newell's list were of prime significance: technological change and shifting economic forces. New technology had a major impact on Labor and Labor relations in a number of important fields. In transportation, for example, passenger traffic on the railroads was supplanted by air, bus, and car travel; freight traffic was curtailed by truck competition and declining demand for Illinois' high-sulphur coal. The commercial publishing industry was radically affected by electronic printing equipment. And the meatpacking plants, long a central feature of Chicago industrial life, were wiped out by the rise of cheaper and more modern enterprises closer to the supplies of cattle and hogs in the plains states.

Domestic and foreign competition based to a considerable degree on cheaper labor and more efficient technology was another major negative influence on the welfare of important industries. One of the first sectors to be so victimized was the clothing (especially women's clothing) industry. Another was the radio and television industry. Later steel, farm equipment, autos, and their numerous satellite enterprises, confronted the same problem.

On the other hand, during most of the period Chicago shared in the general national prosperity. It was only during the mid-seventies that economic and industrial observers began to realize that Chicago was lagging behind the nation and that its economic strength was shifting from basic industry to finance, commerce, trade, and government. For local market unions, this shift had positive implications; for the nationally oriented industrial unions, it was a weakening force.

The thirty-five years between 1945 and 1980 may be divided into three political-economic periods: the "reform" administration of Mayor Martin Kennelly between 1947 and 1955; the golden age of machine politics in the Daley era between 1955 and late 1976; and the fractionation of the Democratic machine under Daley's successors, Mayors Michael Bilandic, 1977–78, and Jane Byrne, 1979–83.

The Kennelly period coincided with the rapid national postwar readjustment and the economically stimulating Korean War of 1950–53. After a short and shallow cyclical downturn in 1948–49, it was a time of general prosperity, and Labor prospered with it. As a report by the Business Executive Research Committee of Greater Chicago stated in 1955, "The Chicago metropolitan area is the fastest growing and most diversified industrial district in the United States. In the postwar period, 1945–54, the Chicago area $2 billion industrial expansion was the greatest of any metropolitan section in the country. . . . Although the rate of industrial expansion has been much greater in the suburban areas, Chicago experienced unprecedented industrial growth in the postwar period."[3]

However, Kennelly's reformism was limited and temporary. The historian Mary Watters noted that he was persuaded to run for the mayoralty by Jacob (Jack) M. Arvey, who had risen to leadership of the Chicago Democratic organization after the death of Pat Nash, the long-time chairman of the Cook County Democratic Committee, in 1943 and an aging Mayor Edward Kelly had become increasingly subject to criticism over "crime, wholesale illegal gambling, the Capone syndicate, and above all, political domination of the schools."[4] In Arvey's view, the machine needed to refurbish its public image with top candidates of unblemished public record and established integrity. Kelly agreed to step down. Thus, in 1947 and 1948, the Democratic party nominated Kennelly for mayor, Adlai Stevenson for governor, Paul Douglas for senator, and Judge Otto Kerner for state's attorney.

According to Watters, Kennelly was a fairly conservative businessman of rugged honesty and integrity but no zealot for social reforms. "As mayor, Kennelly emphasized economy, balanced budgets, reform of the school system, improvement of city services, a war on gambling. He functioned perhaps more in the manner of a city manager than a political boss: his nonpartisan administration provoked the comment that he was the best Republican mayor the Democrats had ever elected."[5]

Kennelly came from Bridgeport, the same neighborhood that produced Edward Kelly and Richard Daley, and he shared the same ethnic roots as the Irish–Catholic union leaders who dominated the Chicago Federation of Labor. Their support, however, was lukewarm because his role in the Democratic party was largely outside of or opposed to the party machine, and although he maintained the traditional hand-shake pay agreements for the trades employed by the city, he apparently extended no special favors to them. The CIO leaders were initially more enthusiastic, but they soon lost much of their enthusiasm when they discovered Kennelly's limited social vista and his virtual abdication of power to the city council.

Kennelly won renomination and reelection to a second four-year term in 1951 without serious internal party conflict and with weak Republican opposition, but by 1953 Daley was ready to make his bid for party leadership and secured the powerful post of Cook County Democratic chairman. Two years later he defeated Kennelly in the Democratic primary with party and CFL support and then defeated Republican Robert Merriam for what was to be the first of five and a half terms.

Despite the general weakness of the Kennelly administration, organized labor made impressive gains, principally in the private sector. The organizational process was not very different than it had been during the thirties and the war years. The experience described by Sidney Lens in his autobiographical work, *Unrepentant Radical,* was not representative, but it was reflective of the elements involved. Early in 1941, Lens, as a young radical, joined an organizing move by the CIO's Retail, Wholesale, and Department Store

Union (RWDSU) to oust Local 1248 of the AFL's Retail Clerks International Protective Association (RCIPA) at the Hillman's grocery chain, then under the control of a Max Caldwell who, according to Lens, "was an unsavory character, with known links to the Capone crime syndicate."[6] Caldwell, son-in-law of the advertising manager of the CFL's newspaper, had been able in the thirties to get a charter in the RCIPA although he had no employee members and signed sweetheart agreements at National Tea, Hillman's, and other grocery chains. After a number of employees complained about the behavior of Caldwell and his appointed agents and some physical violence ensued, Caldwell was expelled from the CFL but continued to receive strong employer support. The Lens group, however, succeeded in overthrowing him in 1941 and negotiated a new agreement and a new labor relations climate at Hillman's.

Getting no sympathy from the AFL, Lens's local became Local 329 of the CIO's RWDSU. But in the years that followed, Local 329 found itself in a hostile environment wherever it tried to extend organization. On the one hand, it encountered strong AFL competition often accompanied by back-door and sweetheart agreements, sometimes by corporate-racketeer collaboration. On the other hand, and more serious, according to Lens, "capital recognized that granting security to the labor officialdom in the form of the union shop, check-off of union dues, longer-term contracts was a sounder policy than permanent confrontation."[7]

A national factional fight within the RWDSU and continued union isolation convinced Lens and his associates that they must shift their affiliation. Returning to the RCIPA was impossible. The door to joining the Teamsters was closed. Despite strong ideological and moralistic differences, they were able in 1946 to strike a deal with the local head of the Building Service Employees International Union (BSEIU), William L. McFetridge, who had close ties with the Teamsters and other CFL and State Federation of Labor unions as well as strong political connections. The impact on relations with Hillman and with other firms was dramatic. The local grew from 600–700 members by a factor of four. Lens became a member of the seven-man executive board of the BSEIU Council (with 55,000 members) and served as its publicity and educational director for some years. Lens was to play a fairly independent radical role in Chicago, but he soon discovered that when he attempted organizing ventures or bargaining strikes that McFetridge was unenthusiastic about for political reasons or because of ties with Teamsters, Butchers, and other "business unionists," he rarely had successful results.

Lens's account was generally verified by John Cullerton, one of Chicago's most experienced labor relations experts.[8] Cullerton, member of a prominent family in Democratic politics, had started in the thirties on labor political action as an aide to Joseph Keenan, influential IBEW leader and secretary-treasurer of the CFL. After the war, he served as union organizer for AFSCME and the Retail Clerks, was executive director of the Chicago Joint Board of the Hotel and Restaurant Employees, became director of the Illinois Department of Labor under Governor Kerner, and then moved to private management, becoming in 1971 vice-president of employee relations for the Hilton Hotels Corporation.

Cullerton noted that organizing in Chicago in the thirties and forties was highly personalized. It was frequently organizing from the top. Getting a union charter was the goal. Once this was obtained, the charter was treated as personal title. Sometimes tradeoffs were made. Some of these organizers referred to their co-leaders as "partners." Individualized domains were achieved by radicals as well as conservatives or moderates, by gangsters as well as honest unionists. As an organizing or bargaining tactic, picket lines would be set up even if the local had few or no members. Many employers folded quickly. If the CIO was trying to organize a firm, that was a further aid to the AFL because employers preferred to deal with the latter. The NLRB was not an important factor in this process; it primarily affected the industrial unions in the large factory units.

This system finally changed, according to Cullerton, because of the Taft–Hartley Act and the courts. The Landrum–Griffin amendments as well as the widespread public and union concerns with incursions by organized crime also contributed. NLRB elections became more important. Unions and collective bargaining became institutionalized and legalized to an unprecedented degree.

The integration of Chicago politics and unionism, especially the building trades, Cullerton believed, went back to the 1920s and the regime of Republican Mayor William "Big Bill" Thompson. It was strengthened under Kelly, maintained by Kennelly, and carried to its peak by Daley. The keys were the mechanisms of prevailing wage rates, licensing, and patronage. Throughout the Daley regime, patronage jobs numbered in excess of thirty thousand, not only in the offices at City Hall, but also in many other units of government in both the city and in Cook County, including the Sanitary District, the Park District, nonteaching positions in the schools, and the offices of the county assessor and clerk of the circuit court.[9] Prominent unionists would be appointed to the sanitary, park, school, civil service, and other commissions and boards. Lesser unionists became precinct captains, or precinct captains became union leaders. Building and other safety inspectors were positioned to exert direct and indirect pressures on recalcitrant property owners and employers. There were no formal collective bargaining contracts. Agreements and grievances were all handled on a personal and informal basis—the handshake approach.

Daley had very close personal ties with top union leaders like McFetridge of the Building Service Employees, Stephen Bailey of the Plumbers, and William Lee, Teamsters' leader and longtime president of the Chicago Federation of Labor. He relied upon these men to maintain peace and stability in municipal labor relations and in closely related activities such as the great State Street department stores, the hotels and restaurants that fostered conventions and business travel, the commercial skyscrapers that dominated the Chicago skyline, and the hospitals that supplied essential health care.

Using the prevailing rates as a fulcrum, the Daley machine provided the unionists with some of the highest wage rates and fringe benefits in the nation and a domain of steady and secure jobs. Daley also conveyed prestige and status in the form of public appointments, invitations to meet with visiting celebrities, and open access to City Hall. In return, the unionists provided not only labor peace and stable employment relations, but also substantial funds for election and other political activities and a host of political foot soldiers who registered voters, got out the vote, and helped citizens in their wards with an infinite variety of day-to-day complaints and petitions.

Outside of the building and service trades, Daley was also the key determinant of employment relations in other important municipal areas—notably firefighter, police, education, and transit. With the first two categories, he reached informal understandings on pay and certain conditions but was adamantly opposed to formal collective bargaining contracts. In education, at both the school and community college levels, he left initial relations to the education board, which he appointed, and the teachers' organizations, but if they reached an impasse, he or one of his trusted union allies would step in as a mediator-arbitrator, often committing himself to help provide needed funds either through local tax increases or through deals with the governor and general assembly leaders in Springfield.

Daley's willingness to support a full-blown and generally open collective bargaining system in the Chicago public schools and colleges was unique for him (mass transit, the other main exception, was a carryover from private-sector ownership). But public education had long been one of the most critical areas for Chicago politicians.[10] School scandals had contributed to the termination of Mayor Kelly's lengthy tenure. Long a rich source of patronage politics, the schools had been converted during Kennelly's regime by Superintendents Herold Hunt and Benjamin Willis into a tight managerial-dominated system based on professional standards. However, Willis proved incapable of coping with the emerging school integration issue, and pressures brought by the black community combined with the disaffection of the politicians forced him to resign in 1966. Because a return to pure machine patronage was no longer possible, Daley decided to accede instead to the mounting teacher demand for collective bargaining, which he was confident he could control. According to William V. Grimshaw's analysis, he was successful in this belief for the next six years. Moderate union leadership and substantial teacher benefits enabled Daley to maintain control and relative stability. But in 1972, the conservative John Desmond was displaced by the more militant Robert M. Healy as Local 1 president, and the union, which expanded from 13,000 members in 1966 to 29,000 in 1975, became increasingly independent. In 1973 and 1975, strikes of two weeks and eleven days occurred over salary and governance matters. During the remaining years of the decade under Mayors Bilandic and Byrne the initiative remained with the union. In 1979, "record-setting pay scales" were negotiated in a new two-year contract between the union and superintendent Joseph P. Hannon—the first time in twelve years when the threat of a strike was not involved. However, at the very moment of the apparent collective bargaining triumph, declining enrollments and deteriorating economic conditions were endangering the job security of hundreds of teachers.[11]

The fourth major employment sector, mass transit, had been taken over by the public from the private sector in 1945, and the enabling state law had expressly authorized the continuation of the private collective bargaining system, including binding arbitration of disputes over new contracts as well as grievances. Hence the roughly twelve thousand transit employees were the first—and for two decades the only—public employees in Chicago to work under a collective bargaining system.

Beyond the unions of the inner circle and the second circle of important but less politically integrated employee organizations, other labor organizations got minimal assistance from City Hall and often were frustrated when their organizational efforts ran counter to the interests of the machine. This was one reason why AFSCME, for example, was unable to organize State Street or the city hospitals. It explains why Lens and his colleagues found it expedient to sever CIO ties and to affiliate with the ideologically hostile McFetridge organization. It also throws light on the tortuous seven-year process before the Lee-dominated CFL merged with the CIO Industrial Union Council led by the powerful Steelworkers and UAW.

A detailed picture of the inner circle operations is difficult to obtain because the key participants were extremely reticent. A few scholars and journalists, however, have obtained some insights that are enlightening. The University of Chicago political scientist J. David Greenstone, writing in the late sixties, noted that "the similarity of political styles and specific material goals (i.e., benefits and favors) helped produce close personal ties—even friendships— between the CFL and Democratic organization leaders." William Lee, for example, not only served as one of Daley's most trusted allies in civic affairs, but with the CFL "firmly opposed any proposal that might offend the party leadership." CFL endorsements "helped maintain the Democrats' popular image as the representative of lower-income groups."[12] The CFL also contributed financially, both by supporting party candidates and by backing fund-raising events. In addition, CFL leaders like McFetridge and Lee acted as the channel for the mayor in his dealings with other union leaders.

Greenstone also observed that the key political role played by CFL leaders had significant negative impact on other labor interest groups. The AFL's Labor League for Political Education (LLPE) was restrained to rather narrow lines of activity; the CIO Cook County Industrial Union Council's wider political objectives were often frustrated; and, after merger, the AFL–CIO Committee on Political Education (COPE) was subordinated to a degree not found elsewhere to the Chicago machine's local interests.

David Lewin of Columbia University, studying municipal labor relations in New York, Los Angeles, and Chicago in the late seventies, observed that "Chicago maintains an informal, undeveloped system of public sector labor relations, the characteristics of which include managerial autocracy, centralized negotiations, an absence of statutory guidelines, private-sector-oriented labor organizations, substantial patronage employment, and a close, even familial relationship between organized labor and the Democratic party."[13] Daley exercised control over labor relations, according to Lewin, "to a degree unmatched by a mayor of any other large American city."

On the prevailing rate system, Lewin noted that each fall Daley met with representatives of the Building and Construction Trades Council, the Teamsters, the Service Employees Union, and the Operating Engineers to work out pay agreements. The unions provided information about the highest, most recently bargained rates that they had negotiated in private industry, and these served as benchmarks for the prevailing rate system. "It was, in a sense, the 'price' Daley willingly paid to keep formal collective bargaining out of city government and yet preserve the political support of organized labor." Other municipal employee groups were not so favored. "Their requests for pay increases were purely advisory to the mayor."

Before the Kennelly regime, the patronage system had operated in a blatantly open fashion as it had in many other major cities controlled by machine politics. Kennelly tried to detach politics from municipal employment, he appointed technical experts regardless of party, and he stressed civil service principles. The ward politicians who performed the day-to-day work of the party resisted mightily. It was an important factor in Kennelly's overturn by Daley.

Under Daley, the Civil Service Commission functioned, as Thomas L. Beagley, an IBEW business agent on loan to AFSCME put it, as a "company union." Beagley stated in a labor education conference at the University of Illinois in December 1966:

> if a person seeks employment through the Civil Service Commission procedures in the City of Chicago, he finds that the Civil Service Commission . . . is ap-

pointed by the Mayor, who also appoints the department heads, one of which will be his boss. Since two of the three commissioners may be members of the same political party, the incumbent Mayor is reasonably sure of majority support on the Commission. Politics being what it is, it is difficult to believe that the Commission is not subject to pressure and/or suggestion from the person appointing it. This appointment also lends itself to the continued modified use of the spoils system since the Commission has the authority to renew temporary appointments, it is in an ideal position to foster patronage by simply not calling examinations or posting eligible lists in the various classifications under this jurisdiction.[14]

Milton Rakove, an academician who had achieved unusual entrée into the internal operations of the Daley organization, agreed that the temporary employee appointment was "at the heart of the patronage system in Chicago and Cook County."[15] Departmental administrators were allowed to hire temporary employees for 120 days. If at the end of this period a qualified replacement meeting requirements for permanent employment under the state civil service law could not be found, the temporary appointment could be renewed indefinitely. Yet Rakove was not entirely critical of the system. Many of the temporary people, he believed, were as competent as regular civil service personnel. Furthermore the power to change the system rested in the hands of the Illinois General Assembly, often controlled by the Republicans, but this power was not exercised because the pragmatic politicians from both parties preferred to reach compromises that respected each other's territories.

In 1975, Daley proposed, and the city council approved by a vote of 43–3, to modify the civil service system.[16] Promotions were no longer to be restricted to the "rule of three," that is to one of the three top candidates on the examination list. The procedure for discipline and discharge was streamlined. More flexibility was provided administrators with respect to the number of job classifications and the pay system. A new four-member Personnel Board, appointed by the mayor and unrestricted as to party, replaced the Civil Service Commission. Its function was confined to advising the mayor and the head of the Personnel Department. Exempted from the coverage of the personnel code were seasonal employees with not more than 180 days work in any calendar year and any additional persons in positions involving policy determination or implementation, confidentiality, or administrative necessity to affect a program.

Opponents of the patronage system on a number of occasions turned to the federal courts for help. In 1976, Daley's last year, a badly divided U.S. Supreme Court ruled in *Elrod v. Burns*[17] that non-civil service employees in the Cook County sheriff's office could not be discharged or threatened with discharge for the sole reason that they were not affiliated with or sponsored by the Democratic party. The plurality opinion (three justices) based its decision on violations of the First and Fourteenth Amendments of the U.S. constitution. Two other judges concurred in the result but not the constitutional argument, and three judges dissented on the ground that the patronage system was not unconstitutional per se. Court decisions in the eighties were to strengthen the attack on patronage, but the immediate effect of *Elrod* on Chicago appeared to be minor.

Daley's labor policies were largely if somewhat less skillfully maintained by his successor Michael A. Bilandic during his short two-year mayorality, which ended in April 1979 after a surprising defeat in the primary by Jane Byrne. According to Lewin, Bilandic was more willing than Daley to deal with the firemen, police, AFSCME, and other organizations not part of the inner circle, but he was less ready to intervene as mediator, counselor, or arbitrator in labor disputes.

Byrne, a former Daley protegeé but now a challenger of the machine, promised during the election campaign to give formal collective bargaining rights to municipal employees and to sign contracts with police and firefighter organizations. In June 1979, she appointed a thirteen-member Committee on Collective Bargaining headed by independent alderman Martin J. Oberman to study the problem and to draft a city ordinance that would give city employees bargaining rights. But she also indicated the belief that public employees should take impasses to arbitration rather than have the right to strike, a position that led in September to the resignation of two of the three union leaders on the Oberman Committee. The idea of a general city ordinance that might endanger the prevailing rate system was also opposed by the Building Trades and other craft unions of the inner circle. Thomas Nayder, president of the Chicago and Cook County Building Trades Council, asked: "Why disturb a good healthy relationship?"[18] William Lee strongly urged continuation of the old informal hand-shake approach. Aldermen and precinct committeemen were concerned that they might lose patronage. The Oberman Report was opposed by the CFL and rejected by the city council.

In the meantime, Mayor Byrne was confronted with an unprecedented series of Labor conflicts. In December 1979, some eleven thousand employees of the Chicago Transit Authority struck for four days over continuation of an escalator clause and other issues. In late January and early February 1980, some thirty thousand public school teachers struck for two weeks over late paychecks and teacher job cuts. Three days after this dispute was settled, some 4,300 Chicago firefighters (Local 2) went out on their first strike to secure a signed contract.

The firefighters strike, which lasted for twenty-three days, was particularly bitter, with charges of bad faith issued by both sides. The mayor attempted to continue the service by hiring more than seven hundred new employees. The new militant president of the union, Frank Muscare, was sentenced to five months in Cook County jail for criminal contempt, and stiff fines were levied against the local and its officers for refusing to end the strike. The Chicago Federation of Labor, which had earlier voiced opposition to a proposed strike, now resolved support for the strikers and urged members not to cross picket lines. In the end, an interim settlement was reached, including a provision for arbitration, and the strikers went back to their jobs, Muscare's sentence was commuted, and the fines against the local and its officers were substantially reduced. An interesting sidelight to the settlement was the mediatory role played by Jesse Jackson. One consequence of his role was the parties' acceptance of an affirmative action program to raise black employment from about 400 to at least 1,200 and Hispanic employment from 60 to 600. In addition, 45 percent of all new recruits were to be black or Hispanic, and the city agreed to publicize its recruitment in minority neighborhoods.[19]

Police posed a somewhat different problem. Daley had been particularly resistant to the idea of collective bargaining for police or even to approximate it indirectly. In 1971, when he rejected a request to establish a formal grievance procedure and a negotiating process similar to those allowed other city employees, the Confederation of Police, the largest of several police organizations claiming some six thousand members among the approximately ten thousand patrolmen, went to court alleging a violation of the First and Fourteenth Amendments. In 1974, the Northern Illinois District Court dismissed the complaint, holding that police had no constitutional right to grievance procedure or collective bargaining.[20] In 1975, however, another suit challenged the constitutionality of the Department of Police rule 54A denying Chicago police the right to join any union that was not limited to full-time law-enforcement officers. The court, in 1979 shortly before Byrne's election, held that this rule violated the First Amendment's freedom of assembly rights. In April 1979, the movement expanded to get the promised collective bargaining rights from the new mayor. In addition to the Confederation of Police, which had recently received a charter from the AFL–CIO, the Fraternal Order of Police (FOP), an unaffiliated organization, and the Afro-American Police League, which claimed to represent some two thousand minority police, Teamsters Joint Council 25 set up a Teamster Law Enforcement Organizing Committee, and Chicago Police Officers Local 1975 of the United Paperworkers was formed. An election for representation rights was held in October, with "no union" receiving 2,471 votes (26.4 percent of the 10,300 eligible), and the FOP receiving 2,050 (22 perecent). The following month, the FOP defeated "no union" by a vote of 7,050–1,578 in a run-off. Arrangements were made for the start of negotiations, and in July 1981 the Chicago police agreement finally was signed.

Public employment relations were a major direct concern of the mayors and their administrations. However, the latter were also concerned with the private sector's labor relations whenever the city's general welfare or the administration's political relationships appeared to be threatened. In such situations the mayor sometimes intervened directly by calling in the parties and trying to work out a settlement or, more often, by unpublicized measures such as personal telephone calls or steps by aides to achieve a desired outcome. Unionists like McFetridge and Lee served as channels of communication to union leaders in the CFL or the national heads of AFL unions involved in conflict situations. If a CIO union was affected, a prominent local official like Joseph Germano of the Steelworkers or Robert Johnston of the Auto Workers would be contacted.

But it was not only a matter of collective bargaining disputes, important as they were. Blacks had tasted the first fruits of their potential political and social power in a number of industries during the war years and were not content to forego further gains, let alone lose the initial advances (chapters 4B and 17). Women, who had experienced unprecedented employment opportunities during the war but who had largely returned to their traditional roles of housewife and mother, began to express renewed interest in the labor market, thereby opening up new issues and problems for local communities. On the negative side of the labor relations scene were the abuse of power and, at the extremity, the incursion of organized crime.

The first postwar decade covered the reconversion years from war to peace under Mayor Kelly and the rapid growth years of Kennelly's two terms. Nationwide, the reconversion years (1945–47) were dominated by two developments—the rapid demobilization of the huge armed forces and an unprecedented series of major industrial strikes in the steel, auto, rubber, meatpacking, telephone, and other key industries.[21] As a great industrial center, Chicago was directly affected. Among the major strikes involving the Chicago area were those in basic steel (January 21–February 15, 1946), meatpacking (January 16–26, 1946), the railways (May 23–25, 1946), and at International Harvester (January 21–April 16, 1946), Western Electric (January 9–16, 1946), American Telephone and Telegraph (April 7–May 20, 1947), and Inland Steel (May 1–8, 1947). Only New York City exceeded the 141 stoppages involving 93,500 workers and 2,530,000 mandays idle in 1946 and the 126 stoppages involving 42,700 workers and 655,000 mandays idle in 1947.[22] Fortunately, the violence that had accompanied many of the strikes of the thirties was not repeated. But the scope and duration of the stoppages had severe, if temporary, economic consequences.

These major strikes were national in character. They essentially involved union efforts to increase pay in order to offset earnings loss from a reduction in wartime hours and company determination to increase prices notwithstanding federal wage and price control programs. The settlements entailed federal, not state or local, intervention. The meatpacking stoppage, the first national strike in that industry, was illustrative.[23] Because of the low national supply of meat at the time, and the fear of spoilage of the stock on hand, the U.S.

secretary of labor appointed a fact-finding board the day after the strike began to make recommendations for settlement; the following week, contrary to the advice of the fact-finding board, the president ordered federal seizure of the plants and their operation under the authority of the secretary of agriculture. The workers went back to work, and the recommendations of the fact-finding board were accepted by the secretary of agriculture. However, the companies refused to acquiesce for some two months until they were allowed by the Office of Price Administration to put their total requested price increase into effect.

Although the great national strikes captured national attention, local disputes also concerned the municipal authorities. Printing was a particularly challenging problem in the immediate postwar period. In the fall of 1945, for example, the Typographical Union (ITU) struck for three weeks to establish a 36 and ¼-hour work week in commercial printing plants in Chicago, thereby achieving parity with newspaper plants. The action set a pattern for New York and other cities. However, it was not until 1947, shortly after the Taft–Hartley law was enacted, that a more critical conflict occurred. According to Robert K. Burns of the University of Chicago, the ITU under the leadership of Woodruff Randolph, who became president in 1944, adopted a militant policy in defiance of the new statute, a policy that attempted to mandate prohibited employment conditions such as the closed shop upon resisting employers.[24] The result was a strike of Local 16's 1,500 typographers against the Chicago Newspaper Publishers Association that started November 24, 1947 and ended twenty-two months later on September 18, 1949. Although the union had the nominal sympathy of all sectors of the Chicago labor movement in their assault on the hated Taft–Hartley law, newspaper publication by all five Chicago papers involved was not interrupted. The publishers were able to bypass the composing room by substituting varitype machines and a photoengraving process, hiring some 350 varitypists and 100 proofreaders. They also went to federal district court to enjoin the strike and later to obtain a contempt citation against the striking union. Although the newspapers resorted to the use of considerable dated filler material, sales fell only slightly overall, and advertising revenues went up. The union effort to discourage sales by producing their own paper was not successful. The end of the strike, with a new two-year contract and the rehiring of the strikers, was clearly a union defeat. Although the varitype process was discontinued and the varitypists dismissed (with severance pay and some bonuses), the publishers got a provision in the contract that allowed the future use of a new more efficient electronic teletypesetter on six month's notice, as well as contract terms fully compatible with the Taft–Hartley law.

By 1948, Chicago strikes recorded by the Bureau of Labor Statistics had fallen from 126 to 66 and, except for the Korean War years of 1952 and 1953, they were an insignificant part of the Chicago scene throughout the Kennelly and the first half of the Daley mayoralties. The collective bargaining system was widely accepted and functioned smoothly. Business was good, jobs were plentiful, and most veterans had been absorbed either in their original places of employment or in new enterprises. Unemployment in the Chicago metropolitan area in October 1946 was estimated at only 3 percent of the civilian labor force, compared with 15 percent in 1940. Manufacturing employment increased from 943,000 in 1946 to 1,067,100 in 1953 but then fell back to 997,700 in 1955; nonmanufacturing employment, in contrast, grew from 1,245,000 in 1946 to 1,501,000 in 1953 and to 1,537,300 in 1955.[25] Contract construction employment had one of the sharpest growth rates, going from 60,000 in 1946 to 116,000 in 1955.

Two developments marred this generally favorable picture. One was the resurgence of organized crime in the labor field, attracted by the growing and prosperous Labor movement and by the affluent pension and welfare funds of the labor-management system. Reports from the Chicago Crime Commission, the 1950 hearings of the U.S. Senate's Kefauver Committee, and the 1954 Ives–Douglas inquiry brought this ugly development to the public eye and set the stage for an aroused countermove by the Labor movement itself as well as by the subsequent U.S. Senate McClellan Committee.

Kennelly himself proved an inept although well-intentioned reformer in the crime control area. The Kefauver inquiry revealed "massive police corruption and ties with organized crime."[26] His relations with the stirring black community and the influential black political leader U.S. Congressman William L. Dawson were also poor. Although the size of the black community was steadily mounting, its job opportunities were receding. The drift of whites to the suburbs and the shift of industry from the central city made it much more difficult for blacks to obtain and hold jobs. Relatively few of them could afford the cost of daily travel to plants outside of the inner city. Racial prejudice in the suburbs was also high.

Blacks were disproportionately hurt by the end of war production, and discrimination mounted. While the federal Fair Employment Practices Commission (FEPC) wound down, they pressed for local anti-discrimination legislation. Chicago was the first of the major cities to respond. In 1943, Mayor Kelly appointed a Human Relations Committee (later Commission) to promote racial harmony and to open job opportunities for blacks and other minorities. On August 21, 1945, the city council adopted an FEP ordinance and funded the Human Relations Commission despite attacks on its constitutionality by the Illinois Manufacturers' Association and the defeat of similar legislation in the General Assembly (chapter 17). The new ordinance had more symbolic than practical results, however. It was not until the sixties when state (1961) and federal (1964) FEP legislation was enacted and black organizations adopted more intensive pressure tactics (marches, boycotts, picketing) that minority discrimination barriers were broken down in appreciable ways.

The two decades of Daley's regime witnessed the high point of Labor's achievements as well as signs of serious cracks in the edifice of "Big Labor" and mature labor-management relations. The welfare of the construction industry was of critical importance. Kennelly had set the stage for a massive public and private building program, including enlargement of the mass transit system, creation of a network of major expressways, construction of O'Hare Airport, slum clearance and public housing projects, and encouragement of huge private structures like the Prudential building.[27] Daley, upon election, immediately began to implement and enlarge this program, much to the pleasure of Labor and business. Employment in contract construction increased from 116,000 in 1955 to 138,300 in June 1956.[28] Between 1966 and 1971, Chicago led all major cities including Los Angeles and New York in millions of dollars of new construction and value and numbers of new housing units constructed.[29] The Association of Commerce and Industry labeled it the nation's "Construction City." The building unions and the contractors rapidly became integrated into Daley's political and industrial system. So too did the hotel and restaurant industry, the transport industries, the department stores and smaller retail establishments, and the entertainment fields—all of which benefitted from Chicago's importance as a major commercial center. The opening of the great McCormick convention complex in 1960 and its rapid replacement after the fire of 1967 were perhaps symbolic of the importance attached to commerce, building, and service.

The industrial sector provided a different picture. The stockyards, for example, once the world's largest center of meatpacking and processing, began to decline with the shutdown of Wilson (3,200 employees) in November 1955. Armour, which shut five small plants in other locations between 1956 and 1959, closed its large Chicago operation and five other plants in July 1959. About the same time, Swift reduced its Chicago production to a minimum. By 1970, the meatpacking center, once the employer of thirty thousand workers, was completely out of business. The closing was commemorated by the Illinois Labor History Society on February 1, 1971, at a dinner at the Stockyards Inn.

One of the notable features of this otherwise dismal development for Chicago labor was the establishment in August 1959 of the Armour Automation Fund by negotiations between the Armour Company, the industry's collective bargaining pacesetter as well as the nation's second largest packer, and the two principal unions, the United Packinghouse, Food and Allied Workers and the Amalgamated Meat Cutters and Butcher Workmen.[30] The purpose of the fund (initially $500,000), which was administered by a tripartite committee of company and union representatives with a neutral chairman, was to study the problems of displacement and relocation of workers from obsolete, high-cost urban plants to new, mechanized plants in rural communities closer to the cattle- and hog-raising areas. Although the Automation Fund program received widespread acclaim during its roughly eight years of operation, the impact of the shutdowns on thousands of displaced workers was severe.

During its prime period, the Packinghouse Workers Union (UPWA) affected the Chicago scene in two important ways. More than any other labor organization in the area, it provided leadership opportunities for black workers. Among the notable figures who rose to public prominence was Charles Hayes, international vice-president, who in 1983 was to be elected a U.S. congressman succeeding Harold Washington after the latter won the mayoralty of Chicago. For many in the vast black community in Chicago, the UPWA came to symbolize the path to economic as well as personal achievement by organized collective action.

The second important UPWA impact on Chicago was its collective bargaining record. It was not always a peaceful record, partly because the union set high goals, but also because it dealt with hard-bargaining corporations in a difficult economic and technological environment. Major strikes involving one or more of the major packers occurred in 1946, 1948, 1959, and 1960. However, out of the militancy came unprecedented terms and conditions of employment for an industry that had an unenviable history in these respects. Unfortunately, external forces were too great to cope with.

Garments manufacture, another major reservoir of industrial unionism in the thirties and forties, also suffered the effects of outside forces. Competition from low-wage plants in small towns, especially in the South, and from low-wage foreign countries had a devastating impact. Ladies' garments were particularly hard hit, and the membership of the ILGWU in Chicago plummeted from about 11,000 in 1947 to 1,285 in 1980. Men's clothing was not quite as rapidly or as adversely affected thanks to the continuing (although reduced) operations of Hart, Schaffner and Marx, the nation's leading manufacturer of quality suits. The import problem did not emerge until about 1970. Hart's chief rival, B. Kuppenheimer, ceased production in Chicago in 1972. Membership of the Amalgamated Clothing Workers Union in men's suits shop declined from more than eight thousand in 1948 to between three and four thousand in the late seventies.

In contrast to meatpacking and garments, the leading centers of industrial unionism in the Chicago area—Steelworkers District 31 under Joseph Germano and UAW Region 4 under Duane "Pat" Greathouse and Robert Johnston—maintained a relatively high level of employment until the late seventies, when foreign competition began to take its toll on steel, autos, and farm equipment. During most of the postwar period until about 1977, District 31 membership, which included huge steel mills and metal products plants in northwestern Indiana as well as Chicago, fluctuated between 100,000 and 125,000. Region 4 of the UAW covered Illinois and Iowa. The major plants in this region produced farm and construction equipment; auto assembly was limited to one large Chrysler plant at Belvedere, some seventy miles west of Chicago, and a sizable Ford plant in South Chicago. Both unions were industry and nationally oriented and had relatively limited concern with and impact on Chicago politics.

In addition to such adverse economic developments as occurred in packing and garments, Labor's standing in the community was negatively affected by several social factors. One, as noted earlier, was the renewed incursion of organized crime, a second involved the issue of affirmative action. The recurring congressional investigations into organized crime in Chicago, capped by the McClellan Committee hearings in the late fifties and the passage of the Landrum–Griffin Act, left a general image of labor corruption that the unions found difficult to counter even though only a small minority of unions were involved (chapter 16).

The civil rights movement appeared to be making strong headway during World War II and immediately thereafter but then it floundered for a decade or more on the job front, in the public housing field, and in the fruitless effort to persuade Superintendent of Schools Benjamin Willis to integrate the schools. The black community was badly divided despite Albert Raby's Coordinating Council of Community Organizations (comprised of forty-three groups, both black and white).[31] Kennelly antagonized the black leadership in his public housing program by yielding to the white neighborhood and real estate interests. Daley co-opted many of the leaders and bought off the poor. As Barbara Reynolds put it, "As long as indigent blacks vote for the Democratic candidates the Mayor slates, as chairman of the Cook County Democratic Central Committee, they are entitled to their poor man's credit card. Their cooperation supposedly protects them from losing their public housing, welfare, a green card to hospital care or a menial job. It also brings a bonus on election day. . . . While the rewards may seem paltry, they are real."[32]

The turning point occurred in February 1966, when Dr. Martin Luther King, Jr., came to Chicago at the urging of Raby and others to enlist the support of some three hundred black ministers at Jubilee CME Temple to publicize the Operation Breadbasket program.[33] Within a year, King's close aide, Jesse Jackson, emerged as the Chicago leader of the Breadbasket program, which later evolved into his national Operation Push. Both Operation Breadbasket and Operation Push were designed to pressure corporate America to open up job and business opportunities for blacks. They were compatible in these objectives with the affirmative action programs developed by the federal Equal Employment Opportunities Commission under the civil rights laws of 1964 and 1972. Success, however, was spotty and erratic.

In Chicago, the major affirmative action test took place in the contract construction industry during the seventies (chapters 4B and 17), but the agreed-on plan for Chicago was implemented on a very small scale in part because of a decline in construction work and in part because of resistance from the craft unions. When in 1973 the Labor Department imposed a "Philadelphia Plan" with specified targets and quotas, the plan unfortunately coincided with the severe recession of 1974–75. During the remainder of the decade, limited progress was achieved but black hopes and expectations continued to be frustrated.

The rise of black militancy, which in the second half of the sixties took the form of protest marches and demonstrations as well as several cases of firesetting in impoverished black neighborhoods, shifted into the sphere of independent black political action in the seventies. As long as Congressman William Dawson prevailed, the Daley machine maintained political control. During his final years (he died in 1970), Dawson's domination of black politics had been challenged, and in 1967 two black independents had been elected to the city council, but this was only a minor setback for Daley. More serious was the defection of Dawson's influential successor, Congressman Ralph Metcalfe, concerned over the issue of police brutality toward blacks. Jesse Jackson was another leading activist who tried to get local black officials opposed to the machine elected. Jackson's efforts proved fruitless as far as Daley's reelection in 1971 and 1975 was concerned, but the independence movement gained steam during Daley's last years and that of his successors, Mayors Bilandic and Byrne (who was backed by Jackson), culminating in the election of Harold Washington as mayor in 1983.

Radicalism provided another important facet of the Chicago scene. During the cold war years and the McCarthy period of the late forties and early fifties, radical workers, especially communists, were subjected to considerable harassment and pressure, especially in firms with government contracts. The question of loyalty oaths became an issue in private industry under the Taft-Hartly law and in public employment. Only a few insignificant pockets of radicalism were evidenced within the ranks of the AFL. In the CIO, however, the communists were more outspoken and more of an issue. Joseph Germano, leader of the Steelworkers and president of the State Industrial Union Council, followed the policy of his international union president, Philip Murray, in vigorously and aggressively attacking communists. In the CIO state conventions of 1947 and 1949, the issue of communists membership on the Executive Council was hotly debated, and the alleged communists were squeezed out. In the important farm equipment industry, the communist leadership of the

Farm Equipment Workers was attacked and then absorbed by the Reuther forces of the UAW. In a few unions like the Packinghouse Workers and the United Electrical and Radio Workers, communist elements persisted, even as in the case of the UE, after the international had been expelled from the CIO and a rival union had been established to supplant it. By the late fifties, however, the issue of communists within the Chicago labor movement had largely subsided.

The most dramatic radical event of the next decade was the debacle at the 1968 national Democratic Convention, during which a large anti-Vietnam War demonstration was broken up with undisciplined violence by the Chicago police. The Daley administration was subjected to widespread national criticism for its failure to deal effectively with the demonstration. The subsequent federal court trial of the seven leaders of the anti-war movement, the "Chicago Seven," with the repeated hijinks of the defendants and their lawyers and the frustrated reactions of the judge, gave Chicago added notoriety. Workers and union leaders were conspicuously absent from the entire episode and, with a relatively few exceptions, played little part in the anti-war movement. By the early seventies, both the communists of the forties and the student radicals of the sixties were almost wholly silenced.

The second half of the seventies witnessed the gradual disintegration of the once-powerful Daley political machine, a slowdown of the Chicago industrial economy, and the foreshadowing of the emergence of black and Hispanic political power. Organized labor in the public and service sectors grew in strength, but the construction trades were at least temporarily weakened by recession in building and an upsurge of open-shop construction; the teamsters were set back by deregulation of over-the-road trucking; and the major manufacturing industries were declining from the forces of domestic and foreign competition. The "city that worked"—a proud Daley boast—revealed discomforting cracks.

NOTES

1. Barbara Newell, *Chicago and the Labor Movement: Metropolitan Unionism in the 1930's* (Urbana: University of Illinois Press, 1961), chaps. 10 and 11.

2. These statistics are taken from Wesley G. Skogan, *Chicago since 1940: A Time Series Data Handbook* (Urbana: University of Illinois Institute of Government and Public Affairs, 1976).

3. *Chicago's Metropolitan Growth* (Evanston: Northwestern University Press, 1954–55), Factual Synopsis, p. 17.

4. This discussion and the quote are from Mary Watters, *Illinois in the Second World War*, Vol. 2 (Springfield: Illinois State Historical Library, 1951–52), pp. 508–13.

5. Watters, *Illinois in the Second World War*, p. 513.

6. Sidney Lens, *Unrepentant Radical* (Boston: Beacon Press, 1980), pp. 96, 99.

7. Lens, *Unrepentant Radical*, pp. 105–7.

8. Interview with John Cullerton, October 1, 1981.

9. Anthony M. Halmos "Public Sector Collective Bargaining Legislation in Illinois," tutorial paper, University of Illinois Institute of Labor and Industrial Relations, March 1979, p. 24.

10. This discussion is based primarily on Paul E. Peterson, *School Politics Chicago Style* (Chicago: University of Chicago Press, 1976); and William J. Grimshaw, *Union Rule in the Schools* (Lexington, Mass.: D. C. Heath, 1979).

11. The Bureau of National Affairs, *Government Employee Relations Report*, 833:22 October 22, 1979.

12. J. David Greenstone, *Labor in American Politics* (New York: Vintage Books, 1969), pp. 94–96.

13. David Lewin, "Mayoral Power and Municipal Labor Relations: A Three-City Study," *The Employee Relations Law Journal* 6 (Spring 1981): 651.

14. Halmos, "Public Sector Collective Bargaining Legislation in Illinois," p. 26. It is interesting to note that shortly after Daley's 1955 election, he appointed William Lee president of the Civil Service Commission.

15. Milton Rakove, *Don't Make No Waves, Don't Back No Losers* (Bloomington: Indiana University Press, 1957), p. 205.

16. The discussion in this and the following paragraph is derived from Halmos, "Public Sector Collective Bargaining Legislation in Illinois," pp. 27–29.

17. 427 U.S. 347 (June 28, 1976).

18. *Business Week*, October 8, 1970, p. 98.

19. *Government Employee Relations Report*, 853:27–29, March 17, 1980.

20. *Confederation of Police v. City of Chicago*, No. 71C 3005, October 7, 1974, 87 LRRM 2573.

21. See Joel Seidman, *American Labor From Defense To Reconversion* (Chicago: University of Chicago Press, 1953).

22. U.S. Bureau of Labor Statistics, *Work Stoppages Caused by Labor-Management Disputes in 1946 and 1947*, Bulletins No. 918 and 935 (Washington: Government Printing Office, 1947 and 1948).

23. Edwin E. Witte, "Industrial Relations in Meat Packing," in *Labor in Postwar America* ed. Colston E. Warne et al. (Brooklyn: Remsen Press, 1949).

24. Robert K. Burns, "Industrial Relations in Printing," in Warne, *Labor in Postwar America*. See also *Chicago Tribune*, September 15, 1949, p. 1 and September 19, 1949, p. 1; *New York Times*, September 15, 1949, p. 18 and September 19, 1949, p. 14.

25. *Illinois Labor Bulletin*, March 1947, p. 3; July–August 1956, p. 15.

26. Percy R. Duis and Glen E. Holt, "The Real Legacy of 'Poor Martin' Kennelly," *Chicago* (July 1978): 165.

27. Duis and Holt, "The Real Legacy," pp. 164–65.

28. *Illinois Labor Bulletin*, July–August 1956, p. 15.

29. Brian J. L. Berry et al., *Chicago: Transformations of an Urban System* (Cambridge: Ballinger Publishing, 1976), p. 11.

30. For detailed accounts see George P. Shultz and Arnold R. Weber, *Strategies for the Displaced Workers* (New York: Harper and Row, 1966); James J. Healy, ed., *Creative Collective Bargaining* (Englewood Cliffs, N.J.: Prentice-Hall, 1965); and

Harold E. Brooks, "The Armour Automation Committee Experience," in *Proceedings of the 21st Annual Winter Meeting, Industrial Relations Research Association,* December 1968, pp. 137–43.

31. Barbara A. Reynolds, *Jesse Jackson: The Man, The Movement, the Myth* (Chicago: Nelson-Hall, 1975), pp. 48–49.

32. Reynolds, *Jesse Jackson,* p. 50.

33. Ibid., p. 108.

9

Rockford

Rockford, an industrial city in Winnebago County, is located in the extreme north central part of the state approximately twenty miles south of the Wisconsin state border and ninety miles northwest of downtown Chicago. In 1980, it was the second largest city in the state, with a population of approximately 150,000. Rockford's population grew slowly during the depression and World War II, increasing from 85,864 in 1930 to 92,927 in 1950. The impact of the postwar baby boom was felt between 1950 and 1960, and the population grew to 126,706.[1] By 1970, Rockford's population surpassed 147,000.[2] After 1970, however, growth in population slowed significantly and appeared to be stagnating. Indeed, in the ten years between 1970 and 1980, Rockford experienced an out-migration of seventeen thousand.[3]

The Rockford community was distinguished by its strong ethnic loyalties. The most significant group were people of Swedish descent; many of Rockford's major companies were founded by Swedish immigrants. More significant than the mere presence of the Swedes, however, was their philosophical orientation. Rockford's Swedish community was essentially conservative, placing a high value on individual rights, quality work, and adherence to the work ethic.[4]

Persons of Italian, German, Polish, and Lithuanian descent also made major contributions to the growth of the city.[5] The Italian community was particularly important in small business, education, and local politics. The Germans contributed to some important earlier industries, notably furniture, and later small business.

Rockford also experienced growth in its black population after the war. From a very small black community before World War II and in the immediate postwar period, Rockford experienced a relatively rapid increase of blacks during the fifties. By 1960, the black population was 4.3 percent of the city's total and grew slowly but steadily thereafter.[6]

Another small but increasingly important part of Rockford's population was made up of Spanish-speaking people, primarily from Mexico and Cuba. They were attracted to the area by the opportunities for migrant agricultural labor, particularly with Green Giant Corporation in nearby Belvidere.[7]

As a result, Rockford had a varied culture, albeit one somewhat dominated by its Swedish segment. This domination was perhaps responsible for the transfer of essentially conservative, individualistic attitudes to other national groups. Perhaps this is why Rockford long had the reputation as a city with a highly productive work force that produced superior products.

Although there was often one industry that was more important than the others, Rockford was never dominated by a single industry in the manner of Detroit, Gary, or Peoria.[8] Major products included machine tools, hardware, farm implements, appliances, automotive accessories, aircraft parts, furniture, fasteners, paint, and containers. Many of Rockford's industries can be traced back to the middle or late 1800s.

Rockford had a sizable number of clothing and textile companies, but during the forties and fifties, most of these firms either closed or moved to other locations. Only a few small knitting companies remained. In the furniture industry, Rockford had as many as thirty-eight plants in 1926.[9] During the depression, several companies closed, and by the end of the forties, the once proud furniture industry had all but disappeared.

Most of the original machine tool companies survived, although some of them diversified. Most important were Sundstrand Corporation, which had several different divisions; W. F. and John Barnes, purchased by Babcock and Wilcox in 1963; three companies related to the early work of John Barnes— Barnes Drill Company, John S. Barnes, and Metal Cutting Tools Co.; Ingersoll Milling Machine Company; Greenlee Brothers Company; and Barber-Colman Corporation.[10] Most of these companies remained locally owned or controlled.

Two major Rockford companies were important in the hardware industry. National Lock Company, founded in Rockford, was purchased in 1938 by Keystone Steel and Wire Company of Peoria. National Lock operated two plants in the Rockford area. Amerock Corporation, locally owned, was also a major manufacturer of cabinet hardware and was among the largest employers in Rockford.[11]

The largest fastener company in Rockford was Rockford Products Corporation, owned since the early seventies by Rexnord. Started by Swedish immigrant Swan Hillman in the thirties as Rockford Screw Products, Rockford Products developed several plants and employed well over one thousand people.[12] Most companies in this industry were quite different from Rockford Products, however, in that they were small, employing fewer than one hundred people. Many small shops employed as few as six to ten people.

In the aircraft parts industry, Lundstrand, Atwood, Barber–Colman, Woodward Governor, Mechanics Universal, and Rockford Clutch were prime contractors. Companies important in the automotive parts industry included Atwood Vacuum, Mechanics Universal Joint, and Rockford Clutch.[13] Both

Mechanics and Rockford Clutch were owned by Borg-Warner Corporation, purchased in 1928 and 1929, respectively. Other major employers included Woodward-Governor Corporation; the international concern Yates-American Machine Company; and Ispen Industries, a manufacturer of heat treating equipment owned by Alco Standard Corporation of Philadelphia since 1966. Finally, Chrysler Corporation operated a large assembly plant in Belvidere, Illinois, twelve miles east of Rockford.

Although these are by no mean all of Rockford's employers, it is clear that Rockford is indeed a city of diverse industries. This diversity helped insulate the city from extreme volatility in economic fluctuations. However, because of the importance of the machine tool, fastener, and hardware industries, the economic slump of the late seventies had a marked impact on the city. Unemployment was among the highest in the state, and overall economic activity was slow.

Some of Rockford's major employers were owned by corporations based outside the city and with no local interest, a trend that appeared to be accelerating slowly in later years. According to some observers, this factor seemed to make a difference in labor relations; outside owners often took a harder stand on Labor issues.[14]

The percentage of the work force unionized in Rockford was estimated in 1980 to be comparable to the total national level, about 20–25 percent. No exact figure was available. Part of the reason for the relatively low level of unionization can be attributed to the fact noted earlier that most of Rockford's Swedish-origin residents were basically conservative and apparently valued individual rights more than collective security.[15]

Another reason for the seemingly conservative attitude of Rockford's labor force was the impact of migration from the South during the twenties and thirties. According to Lawrence Schmidt, retired personnel director at Greenlee Brothers, many of the people who came to Rockford looking for work rejected the concept of unions. Like the area's Swedes, their backgrounds were also based on socialization patterns that emphasized hard work and individual pride.

A third reason for limited union penetration was the preponderance of small shops in the city. While the previous summary of business in the city highlighted the major employers, the majority of Rockford's work force was employed in small businesses in which there was relatively close contact with their employers and, hence, a lower probability of conditions leading to demands for a union.

Finally, it has been suggested that a major reason that some of the largest employers were not unionized was that they were good employers.[16] In companies such as Woodward Governor, which had an innovative employee stock option plan, there apparently was no reason for employees to either form or join a union.

All of this should not be taken to mean that unions were not important in Rockford. Many of the city's largest employers were unionized, including National Lock, Sundstrand, Rockford Clutch, Mechanics Universal Joint, Twin Disc, Mattison Machine Works and Foundry, Greenlee Brothers, and Essex Wire. Major nonunion employers, however, included Atwood, Woodward Governor, Ingersoll, Amerock, Rockford Products, Warner Lambert, and the city's largest employer, Barber-Colman.

Two unions were dominant in Rockford manufacturing: the United Auto Workers and the International Association of Machinists. The UAW was organized with a separate local at each plant or company. The IAM had one local that covered several employers. Both the IAM and UAW, however, bargained with each employer individually.

Other unions that were important at some stage included the United Steelworkers, United Furniture Workers, United Electrical Workers, Sheet Metal Workers, Retail Clerks, Teamsters, and the various building trades. The oldest union, Local 213 of the International Typographical Union, dated from July 1, 1889.[17] One particularly successful pre-World War II union was the United Furniture Workers (UFW), which was founded in Rockford. As noted previously, at one time there were nearly forty furniture factories in Rockford, and the UFW had most of these plants organized. At its peak of power, the United Furniture Workers had more than seven thousand members.[18] With the decline of the industry in the forties, however, union power diminished, and the union disappeared from Rockford.

Despite these examples, Rockford was noted as an "open-shop" city for most of the period before the end of the war. Following the war, large-scale organizational drives began in many industries. The successes in this period established Labor as a fixture in the Rockford area.

Growth continued into the fifties, but during that decade stagnation set in. Throughout the later fifties and most of the sixties, unions turned their attention away from organizing and more toward community involvement.[19] Both local politics and community social work agencies became more important to Labor.

In the middle sixties, a significant challenge to the then existing status quo developed: public-sector unions began to appear. Rockford experienced its first public-sector strike in 1965,[20] and by 1971 had recognized its first public-sector union.[21]

From late 1945 to 1950, the United Auto Workers organized many plants in the Rockford area. The 1949 Rockford CIO Handbook included the names of twelve thousand members.[22] Organizing temporarily came to a halt during the Korean War years, but it resumed at the war's end. According to Emmet "Bud" Poyer, longtime UAW leader, 1953–55 represented the end of industrial union expansion in the Rockford area. By late 1955, in his view, the companies at which employees desired to unionize had been organized; the remaining plants were bastions of "scabs," persons not interested in union protection.

One of the most important organizational successes was the UAW organization of National Lock Company. In June 1945, the employees chose the UAW, then a CIO affiliate, to represent them in negotiations with management. By late October 1945, the first contract had been signed.[23] Major provisions of the agreement included pay increases, a grievance procedure with binding arbitration, plantwide seniority both for job security and job promotions, time and a half for Saturday, double time for work on Sunday and holidays, paid vacations, and maintenance of union membership and union checkoff.

There were some significant strikes as well. On April 28, 1944, the UAW companywide contract with J. I. Case expired, including the plant in Rockford. Until December 27, 1945, the company and the union attempted fruitlessly to negotiate a new contract. The UAW was seeking an extra week of paid vacation, back pay for certain workers, maintenance of membership and dues check-off, permission to have a chief steward, procedures for final and binding arbitration, a 35-cent-per-hour pay increase for toolmakers, and other general wage increases. The company was resisting the nonmonetary provisions of the proposals, and offered wage increases of 20 cents per hour to toolmakers and 1 to 20 cents for pieceworkers.[24]

A major breakthrough did not materialize until November 6, 1946, when the parties agreed on an arbitration procedure.[25] The arbitrator was designated as the Winnebago County Circuit Court judge, or someone appointed by the judge if he would not serve. The arbitrator's decision was to be final and binding. In early December 1946, the UAW negotiators presented to the local membership a tentative agreement, which was accepted by a 196–48 vote; workers returned to work December 9, 1946, almost one year after the strike began. The strike, one of the longest in Rockford history, reputedly cost the company some $8–10 million in sales, and the employees almost $2.25 million in wages.[26]

The intensity of this early J. I. Case strike reflected a management attitude that could be described as at best grudging acceptance of the union. Interviews with knowledgeable observers indicated that management in general had no use for unions. Emmet Poyer said that local management never came to accept the union's presence; bargaining was always tough.

Following the years of growth immediately after the Korean War, a period began during which union growth virtually ceased. This period has been labelled "union stagnation," but that designation should not be taken to imply that there was no union activity of consequence. Indeed, some of the most important events in the labor history of Rockford took place during this period.

Probably the most significant event was the merger of the American Federation of Labor and Congress of Industrial Organizations into a single body. In accordance with the national goal, local labor organizations also merged. Serious talks regarding the AFL and the CIO merger began in Rockford during early 1956. The task was left to Rockford AFL President Raymond Froehlich of the Teachers Union and CIO Council President Emmet Poyer, aided by several special committees comprised of members of both federations.

Talks went slowly during the latter half of 1956, and it was not until June 15, 1957, that merger of the two federations into Rockford United Labor (RUL) was approved by the respective central bodies of the two organizations.[27] The merger became official on July 28, 1957, and the new organization was reported to represent about twenty thousand workers.[28] Emmet Poyer was the first president; former CIO persons were dominant in RUL in part because many of the building trades refused to participate.

The immediate goals of the new labor organization included organization of unorganized workers and increased involvement in community politics and betterment.[29] According to Poyer, the UAW became involved in politics simply because union leaders realized that their members could also be influenced by events and problems outside the workplace. If a union truly desired to represent its members, that union must become involved in all forums that may have impact on membership.

Poyer cited several ways in which political decisions may have an impact on union members, for example, a simple zoning decision might ultimately cost union members thousands of dollars in lost wages, real estate reevaluations, or other changes. Which roadways were paved could influence the quality of life in a particular neighborhood. Representation on the local school board might have a major impact on the quality of education, and, hence, the future of union members' children. Still another critical issue was the assessed valuation of property, which union leaders long thought to be unfair. In particular, Poyer noted that gains for members from collective bargaining could be taken away by legislators, and that legislators could often block legislation considered desirable by union leaders.[30] It was this latter situation that led to a substantial role in politics for the UAW in Illinois, starting in 1949.

According to Fay Calkins, who did a study in depth of the UAW–Rockford involvement in politics, the idea of trying to influence the Democratic party from within was initiated by UAW representative Willard Allen, who had been servicing UAW locals in the area for several years.[31] Allen's aim was to try to capture as many of Winnebago County's precincts as possible and to run Russell Goldman, a labor lawyer, for Congress. In addition, in 1950, State Representative Ted Hunter, the local Democratic party chairman who had long been considered a friend of labor, voted against civil rights legislation by organized labor. UAW leaders decided that they could no longer support Hunter for reelection. In the Democratic primary electrion, labor supported William Pierce, then president of the National Lock local. Pierce beat Hunter and local real estate developer Joe Barbagallo in that primary and was successful in the general election when labor formed a coalition with the Fifth Ward All-American Democratic Club, an Italian group. This was a significant labor victory because labor elected its preferred candidate, and because the coalition with the Democratic Club was to endure.[32] The campaign for Goldman was less successful. He won the Democratic primary, but lost by a large margin to a Republican candidate.

Pierce served through the fifties and early sixties and retired shortly before his death. He was replaced by E. K. "Zeke" Giorgi, who was still serving in the state legislature in 1980. Giorgi was the type of person Labor liked to back. As Poyer put it, "Zeke isn't a labor guy, he's a community guy." Giorgi originally was a member of Poyer's local at Roper Stove and later a representative of the Retail Clerks union.

Poyer asserted that Rockford Labor got involved in local politics because of a newspaper strike, assisted by the UAW. The then publisher of the Rockford newspapers, E. Kenneth Todd, allegedly attempted to dominate local politics. Faced with a coalition among the CIO, the Fifth Ward All-American Democratic Club, and the long-established Progressive party, Todd supported a hand-picked candidate, City Engineer William Day, under the Republican party banner, thus injecting national parties into the local political scene. The CIO picked the candidate for city clerk, the Progressives picked the candidate for mayor, and the Democratic Club picked the candidate for city treasurer. The Coalition party elected its candidates for mayor and city clerk, and narrowly lost the city treasurer position.[33]

Poyer felt that this change in local politics presented an instructive lesson. Local politics, he felt, was best left to choosing qualified candidates regardless of party affiliations. This was consistent with the old adage of the AFL, "reward your friends, punish your enemies."

Poyer's assessment of local politics was very different from the assessment provided by former Rockford Mayor Benjamin Schleicher. Schleicher asserted that before 1957, when he was elected to the first of four terms, local politics was dominated by the CIO. He felt that Labor did not actually run candidates, but that a person seeking office ran either with the support of the CIO or as an independent. Schleicher felt that this situation was bad, that local politics should be free of such ties wherever possible.[34]

The power of Rockford Labor was evaluated in mid-1955 by Joseph Ator, a reporter for the *Chicago Tribune*.[35] Ator noted, first, the unique character of Rockford among major industrial cities in Illinois: it was essentially an open-shop city. But Ator also noted the power of the Democratic-labor political alliance. At the time, Labor had one-half of all seats on the city council, despite its minority status among employees.

Ator attributed this dual situation to two influential men in the city. Francis Spence, secretary of the Chamber of Commerce, was a dynamic and vocal advocate of the business point of view. The other power figure was Emmet Poyer, who had proven to be a tough competitor, an able organizer, and a successful politician. He was considered largely responsible for the increased power of the Democratic party in Rockford and Winnebago County.[36]

The mayoral election in 1957 provided another interesting example of local as contrasted with party politics. A major issue that year was the insistence of local unionists that pickets be permitted to block shipment of finished goods from a struck plant.[37] The business community felt this issue was of such importance that it altered its previous election policy in which a national party label had been used unsuccessfully. In place of a Republican candidate, the business community ran Benjamin Schleicher as a nonpartisan candidate for mayor on an All-Rockford ticket. This tactic proved successful, and Schleicher was elected. Schleicher had never worked in a union shop, having been employed by Woodward Governor Corporation before his entry into politics.[38]

Ator's conclusion was that Rockford politics were not what one would expect in a sizable midwestern industrial city.[39] His characterization of Rockford in 1958 closely resembled Rockford in 1980. Little changed over the years except the actors.

The ten-year period 1955–65 was not all politics, of course. There were strikes at several major employers, although none exhibited the intensity or duration of the Case strike in 1945–46, nor was the volume of strikes equal to 1946. Rockford Crescent Manufacturing Company, however, won a decertification election in 1961 against the IAM after fifteen years as a union plant.

As the period drew to a close, two particularly significant events took place. In 1962, Poyer was indicted on charges of embezzlement of funds from the UAW building fund. Poyer pleaded *nolo contendere* to these charges,[40] which led to his disappearance from the Rockford labor scene for five years, beginning in 1963. Undoubtedly the loss of Poyer's vigorous presence had a negative impact on the local union scene.

A second major event, which also took place during 1963, concerned Rockford's largest employer, Barber-Colman Company.[41] Significantly, Barber-Colman had never lost a union election and was known as an antiunion employer. In April 1951, the UAW had gained enough signatures to force an NLRB election. The vote was 1,344 against the union, 515 for it. In 1956, the UAW again petitioned for an election. In a vote held February 16, 1956, the union was unsuccessful by a 1,358–849 margin. The UAW attempted a third organizational drive in 1960 and 1961. In an election held March 15,

1961, the UAW was yet again unsuccessful. The margin of victory for the company remained large, with 1,720 employees voting against the union, and 1,007 voting for the union.[42]

All of this changed, however, during 1963. In a representation election held February 6, 1963, the Sheet Metal Workers International Association won by a vote of 1,261–1,140. For the first time Barber-Colman employees had voted to unionize, and the company's 2,700 production workers were represented by a union. As might be expected, negotiations went slowly. After eight months of negotiations, union members voted on September 25, by a 670–62 margin, to strike "at any time the union deems it necessary."[43] The threat appears to have worked, for on October 9, 1963, a first contract was approved by seven hundred members.[44]

Barber-Colman management did not take this turn of events lightly; they felt that the union victory was a fluke. This perception may have been fairly accurate, especially since it appeared that the Sheet Metal Workers were not taking the victory particularly seriously. Most affairs were apparently run from the union's Washington, D.C., headquarters; local people had little input. This led the company to seek a decertification election, which was held May 13, 1964.[45] The decertification effort failed, although the margin was close; 1,222 to retain the union, 1,111 to remove the union, with 12 votes voided and 49 challenged.

The first contract at Barber-Colman expired May 31, 1964, being of short duration. On May 28, the employees voted to extend the contract to June 4, but also voted to strike June 5 if no new contract had been negotiated.[46] Negotiations broke down, and a strike began as scheduled. The strike proved to be fairly violent, with several arrests of union leaders and pickets.[47] Still, the outcome was something of a surprise.

On October 20, 1964, the strike ended when the company signed a new three-year contract.[48] The union workers had successfully endured a bitter twenty-week strike and were victorious, although the new contract was reportedly not as strong as UAW or IAM contracts in the area. It appeared, however, that Barber-Colman would remain a union employer. As the period ended, things looked promising for Labor in Rockford; there had been few losses over the past ten years, and Barber-Colman had to be considered a major Labor victory, at least psychologically.

How accurate was this interpretation of the importance of the Barber-Colman unionization? Apparently not as important as it seemed. Emmet Poyer felt that the entire situation surrounding the unionization of Barber-Colman was tainted; he suggested that there may have been some sweetheart contracts signed and under-the-table dealings. He also felt that the union at Barber-Colman was never strong, and that it was ill-prepared to strike.[49]

Lawrence Schmidt added some other interesting information that helps to shed light on the Barber-Colman situation. Schmidt noted that there were outside pressures put on Barber-Colman management to accept the union. Apparently, Sheet Metal Workers in a variety of locations throughout the United States refused to work on Barber-Colman products. This boycott was having an impact on the company, so Barber-Colman accepted the presence of the union until they could find a method to defeat the Sheet Metal Workers. Schmidt also noted that the union was run by a person from Washington, D.C., and this hurt the union. The Sheet Metal Workers did not seem to be in step with local conditions; priorities were apparently set from outside the city by persons with their own conceptions of vital issues.[50]

Lewis Moore, former Rockford IAM official and since 1972 a federal mediator, felt that Barber-Colman's unionization was important at least in the sense that the union victory shook up complacent employers all over the city.[51] It is important to remember that many large employers in Rockford were not unionized; when Barber-Colman succumbed, Moore asserted, many employers probably began to reevaluate their policies and practices. They wanted to avoid the same fate. In this sense, then, the unionization was important.

Moore, like the others, agreed that the union did not do a very good job for its members. The Sheet Metal Workers struck early in the relationship, probably before their position was consolidated. Moore believed that such poor tactics led to the early demise of the union at Barber-Colman.[52]

The next period may be called the "public-sector period" because the years from 1965 reflected the growth of public-sector unionism in and around Rockford. The first rumblings of public-sector unions came in January 1965. In January 1965, the *Rockford Register-Republic* reported that some of Rockford's municipal blue-collar workers, represented by Local 296, Building Service Employees International Union, voted by a 4–1 margin to strike the city if they did not receive a 12 percent pay raise.[53] The local represented about 175 workers in the sewer, water, street, and forestry departments and also included meter maids.

The battle lines were drawn early. Mayor Ben Schleicher proposed to the city council a 5 percent pay increase, which the council supported. Amedeo Georgi, president of Local 296, made it clear that a 5 percent raise would not suffice. City attorney Lawrence Ferolie warned the union, still unrecognized, that any strike could result in termination for the strikers.[54] On the morning of February 15, 1965, Rockford residents awoke to find Local 296 on strike.[55]

Milton Murray of the Building Service Employees International Union reiterated the union demands: a dues check-off system, three weeks' vacation after ten years of service and four weeks after twenty years, a plan of payment for on-the-job injuries, and job wage reclassifications. The city rejected these demands.[56]

On the third day of the strike, striking city workers were notified that they would be suspended if they did not report to work Thursday.[57] That night the strikers voted to accept a new city offer and return to work the next day. The agreement gave workers three weeks' vacation after thirteen years and four weeks after twenty years; a 5 percent pay increase; a job classification and evaluation survey; and an agreement to negotiate issues still unresolved.[58] The union did not receive the dues check-off.

In retrospect, this first strike by Rockford public employees was an extremely significant event despite the fact that the union was not formally recognized by the city. It was the first step toward permanently altering the basis of labor relations between the city and its employees. Commenting on this strike, Schleicher noted that it awoke the politicians and the public to the fact that all was not well.[59] Schleicher particularly noted the apparent dissatisfaction among city employees with communications and salaries. Rockford was using at the time a loose civil service system that had no adequate provision for airing grievances or expressing real concerns. This strike was ultimately to change that situation.

Throughout the balance of 1965, there was little in the way of major local Labor events in either the private or public sectors. An article in the April 21, 1966, *Rockford Morning Star* noted that Rockford United Labor had recently gained more than four thousand new members, and the total number of union members in Rockford surpassed twenty thousand. This included 15,000 in the UAW, 1,800 Teamsters, 2,200 Machinists, 970 Letter Carriers, 4,000 building tradespeople, 2,100 Sheet Metal Workers, 900 Retail Clerks, and 1,500 members in various other small unions.[60]

Other news reports during 1966 focussed on the extreme labor shortage in the Rockford area. In mid-August 1966, Mayor Schleicher sought to pool job applicant information in the private and public sectors to find a supply of labor for the city.[61] Near the end of October 1966, it was reported that there was a critical labor shortage in Winnebago and neighboring Boone counties.[62] Only 2,200 persons from a work force of 119,950 were unemployed, or 1.8 percent. That rate of unemployment was officially the lowest since 1962, and probably the lowest since the Korean War.

A major event, or more accurately the conclusion of an event, took place in 1967. The union contract between Barber–Colman and the Sheet Metal Workers International Association expired, and the parties were unable to reach a new agreement. On May 18, 1967, Local 573, Sheet Metal Workers struck, idling most production workers at Rockford's largest employer.[63] Main issues, in addition to economics, were a union shop and the scope of arbitration. The parties settled in for a long strike. A break did not come until October 18, 1967, when the National Labor Relations Board conducted a decertification election. The results were 1,536 votes against retaining the union, 927 to retain the union, 326 votes challenged, and 11 ballots voided.[64] The union was decertified to its leaders' dismay and to the delight of Barber-Colman officials.

The reasons for the union defeat appeared to hinge on the general failure or unwillingness of the union to consolidate their victory before asking for too much. As noted previously, several persons interviewed stressed the fact that the union was never really run locally; most decisions were made in Washington, D.C., and, as such, did not appreciate local conditions or needs. The union victory margin was never large, and the fact that some 25 percent of all workers in the bargaining unit continued to work during the strike should have been taken as an indication that union support was not solid. These problems, coupled with an employer willing to try to unseat the union, spelled disaster for unionization at Barber-Colman.

Major attention was once again focussed on the public sector in 1968. On March 26, Rockford firemen walked off the job after they were denied wages equal to police wages.[65] Pickets were seen at all firehouses, and only skeleton crews were on duty. Major businesses and hospitals went on special alert in the event fires erupted.[66]

It did not take the city long to make clear its position. Immediately after the strike began, Rockford Corporation Counsel William Collins sought an injunction in Winnebago County circuit court. The injunction was granted on the second morning of the strike, March 27, 1968.[67] Chief Circuit Judge Albert S. O'Sullivan ruled the strike illegal and ordered the firefighters back to work. They returned at 1:00 p.m. that day.

The firefighters' strike again showed that public employees felt strongly that wages and conditions should be improved. The major issue was money; the 5 percent increase in wages passed by the city council was not adequate for most strikers. They sought at least another 5 percent, which firefighters claimed was necessary to keep pace with inflation.[68]

The public sector returned to the news in two years. AFSCME Local 1058 was organized in November 1970 and was accepted by members in the public works and water department by a vote of 105–11 as the bargaining agent for those employees.[69] Alderman Richard Baer, chairman of a special labor relations committee, recommended to the city council that the city recognize AFSCME as bargaining agent for city employees.

The fact that several aldermen and Mayor Schleicher would even consider a unionized city work force indicates how far they had come since the first public employee strike in 1965. In an interview, Schleicher asserted that there was still some lingering skepticism among the city council and the public, but that the apparent benefits outweighed the potential problems. In particular, Schleicher said, unions made it easier for the city to discuss grievances; formal channels were better than individual handling of problems.[70] On July 6, 1971, AFSCME was accepted as the bargaining agent for employees in the public works and water departments.[71] On August 2, the city council also recognized bargaining agents for firefighters and police officers.[72]

The victory of AFSCME can be seen as a victory for both the union and the city. Schleicher indicated that the city was much better off with the union. This might not have been the case in his view, however, if the Teamsters had been successful in organizing city employees. Schleicher indicated that the city could not have accepted the Teamsters as the union for city employees.[73]

A very different sort of problem came to the Rockford area during 1969. The United States Department of Labor expressed concern over the number of minorities in the construction trades in the Rockford area, feeling that minorities were vastly underrepresented. To resolve this problem, the Northern Illinois Construction Affirmative Action Program (NICAAP), a voluntary "hometown plan," was established with private funds to bring more minorities into the building trades.[74]

Minority hiring in the building trades, however became an issue once again in late 1973. An article in the November 2, 1973, *Rockford Register-Republic* reported that the Office of Federal Contract Compliance (OFCC) threatened to enforce minority hiring quotas for the building trade unions. Neither the unions nor the contractors felt this would happen, though. Allen Baily, program director for NICAAP believed that the plan adopted in the Rockford area would become the pattern for other areas of the country. He felt that good progress had been made in Rockford, noting that quotas had been exceeded by most unions.[75]

On January 17, 1974, Mayor Robert McGaw went to Chicago to meet with Housing and Urban Development representatives regarding minority hiring on the new Central National Bank building being constructed in Rockford.[76] According to the news report, McGaw expressed concern that HUD and Labor Department pressures would result in a strongly negative response from labor unions. HUD officials were pressing for project-by-project compliance with minority guidelines, and the Labor Department wanted compliance with general goals. The "hometown plan" being pursued in Rockford sought to fill general quotas to bring minorities into building trades on a more comprehensive basis. The *Rockford Morning Star,* on January 19, reported that HUD and OFCC (Labor Department) officials had agreed to let OFCC guidelines prevail on the Central National Bank project and all future projects.[77]

The battle over minority hiring was not settled, however, in the eyes of the editors of the Rockford newspapers. An editorial published on January 19, attacked the minority hiring compliance program.[78] The editorial noted that unions had done their part in bringing more minorities into construction industry positions. Little more could be expected. At the same time, however, HUD, OFCC, and the federal Fair Employment Practices Commission all claimed jurisdiction over the area of minority hiring. The editors felt that competing federal pressures and the proposed solutions of these agencies represented little more than tokenism in minority hiring. The plans advocated by these agencies, the editors wrote, would not result in meaningful, long-range commitment to recruitment, training, and permanent jobs for minority workers. The editors suggested that the union's approach, emphasizing permanent positions, was superior; in the absence of such a positive goal, all plans should be abandoned.

An abrupt change in the seemingly resolved issue occurred on January 21. The *Rockford Morning Star* reported that the unions were threatening to abandon minority hiring efforts.[79] The threat came in the wake of renewed efforts by federal officials to impose project-by-project compliance. George Chabucos, president of the Rockford Building and Construction Trades Council, said the problem was that project-by-project compliance would require unions to admit more workers but not to keep them on the job long enough to teach them the skills of the trade.[80] Labor leaders were willing to suffer the loss of federal building projects to support their position.

The labor warning was reiterated on January 26, 1974.[81] Labor leaders said that if their proposals were not recognized within thirty days by the federal government, Rockford labor would abandon efforts to bring minorities into the building trades.

The dispute was never really resolved, and Rockford labor unions and contractors technically ceased to meet specific quotas for minority hiring. Still, labor leaders promised to continue to admit minority workers. They recognized the OFCC would make head counts of minority workers, and the unions desired to show progress. NICAAP, however, ceased to exist as a functioning organization, in part because of the decline in construction work.

Other major events in the seventies all centered on strikes and unemployment. In 1974, for example, local and regional construction was at a standstill for more than six weeks, as all major building trades unions in a multicraft bargaining coalition asked for an increase in wages.[82] This experiment, the first attempt at multicraft bargaining in Rockford, proved to be a failure for two reasons. First, contractors were extremely reluctant to grant across-the-board wage hikes because the cost of supplies was also rapidly increasing; the resultant pressure on overall prices was too great for many employers. Second, and perhaps more important, the unions involved failed to maintain a united front in bargaining. As negotiations dragged on, union solidarity weakened; some unions indicated a willingness to settle for less than the $1.10

per hour increase, while other unions upped their demands. The best the employers could attain were one-year contracts in many cases.

Strikes in construction were again in the news during the summer of 1975. Several major unions, including the Iron Workers and the Teamsters who drove ready-mix concrete trucks, struck at various times.[83] When the Teamsters could not reach agreement with ready-mix concrete contractors, Mayor McGaw and his staff became involved in negotiations.[84] The strikes all ended by late July 1975.

Rising unemployment hampered progress on affirmative action. George Chubacos, president of the Rockford Building and Construction Trades Council said that the quotas were impossible goals.[85] Unemployment in construction trades averaged between 28–30 percent and was as high as 40 percent in some cases. Representatives for the Bricklayers, Electricians, Iron Workers, Plasterers and Cement Finishers, Plumbers and Pipe Fitters, Sheet Metal Workers, and Operating Engineers expressed doubt that any meaningful minority representation could be achieved. Even goals could not be set easily. So continued the dilemma of minority hiring.

With respect to Labor's overall role in the community, most people interviewed felt that by 1980 it remained small and insignificant. Lawrence Schmidt, for example, said that Labor's role in the community was on the periphery of activities that tie together the whole community. He said that there was a good reason for this. When Labor failed to cooperate with the United Way Program for a time in the late sixties and set up its own counterpart, much of the community was alienated. This dispute had long-term impacts. As a result, acceptance of Labor in local affairs of any type was less than it could have been.

John Swanson felt that Labor's failure to gain general legitimacy had been transferred into its poor role in community affairs. As long as Labor was not accepted, little would change. Of course, Labor did undertake programs that it saw as worthwhile for the community. The initial efforts to promote John B. Anderson for U.S. Representative was one example of such activity. In terms of more specific city projects, however, Rockford Labor had little input.

Lewis Moore was slightly more optimistic. He argued that unions were definitely showing more concern toward community affairs, particularly in politics and Labor's United Way efforts. Still, Rockford Labor's influence on local politics—an area on which it could have a great impact—had been much less than in other cities where there were stronger and larger labor movements.

Emmet Poyer, though, was highly positive toward Labor's contribution to local affairs. He cited participation in United Way, various community-betterment projects, and politics as the major contributions. Poyer admitted that Labor could do more on the political front by coordinating the voting of its members and relying less on friends in the city council, but he expected that situation to change.

The central conclusion to be drawn from the Rockford experience is that Labor cannot maintain an effective community role for long unless the unions are able to establish a firm base in private and public enterprise. Enduring, as contrasted to temporary, success in politics and other community affairs requires an underlying foundation of solidarity in the critical job territories. The UAW provided one important building block, but other labor organizations often went their own way.

NOTES

This section is a condensation and revision of a report researched and written by Kraig Kircher.

1. William Snyder, "Birth of a City," in *Sinnissippi Sage,* ed. C. Hal Nelson (Rockford, Il: Winnebago County Illinois Sesquicentennial Committee, 1968), pp. 67, 71.

2. Bureau of the Census, *1970 Census* (Washington, D.C.: Government Printing Office, 1971).

3. Interview with Charles Sinclair, statistical analyst, Illinois Employment Service, Rockford, Illinois.

4. Herman Nelson, "From Many Far Places," in *Sinnissippi Sage,* ed. Nelson, pp. 10–13.

5. Ibid., p. 11.

6. Ibid., p. 11

7. Interview with Emmet Poyer, retired UAW Subregional Director.

8. Robert Monahan, "Business and Industry," *Sinnissippi Sage,* ed. Nelson, p. 136.

9. Ibid., pp. 143–145.

10. Ibid., pp. 145ff.

11. Ibid., p. 150, pp. 152–53.

12. Ibid., p. 153.

13. Ibid., pp. 153–54, 150–51.

14. Interviews with Lewis Moore, FMCS mediator; Lawrence Scmidt, retired personnel director for Greenlee Brothers and Chamber of Commerce member; and John Swanson, retired head of the Rockford National Association of Letter Carriers.

15. This opinion was supported by interviews with John Swanson; Lawrence Schmidt; and Harold Grahn, long-time head of the Rockford Credit Bureau and Chamber of Commerce member; and Emmet Poyer, long-time UAW leader.

16. This opinion was reflected in the comments of former Rockford Mayor Benjamin Schleicher and Harold Grahn.

17. James Brady, "Growth of Organized Labor," in *Sinnissippi Sage,* ed. Nelson, p. 344; "Celebrate Day with Banquet," *Rockford Register-Republic,* June 24, 1939.

18. Interview with Emmet Poyer.

19. Ibid.

20. "Vital Services Hit By City Walkout," *Rockford Register-Republic,* February 15, 1965.

21. "City Decides to Recognize Municipal Employees' Union," *Rockford Morning Star,* July 7, 1971.

22. "CIO Locals Claim 12,000 Members in New Directory," *Rockford Morning Star*, September 11, 1949.

23. "1,900 Covered by CIO National Lock Contract," *Rockford Register-Republic*, October 20, 1945.

24. "Employees of 4 Case Company Plant Strikes," *Rockford Morning Star*, December 26, 1945.

25. "Arbitration Agreed on in Future Case Disputes," *Rockford Morning Star*, November 7, 1946.

26. "500 Return to Work in Farm Machine Plant," *Rockford Register-Republic*, December 9, 1946.

27. "A.F.L., C.I.O. Here Approve Union Merger," *Rockford Morning Star*, June 15, 1957.

28. "Merger Rockford AFL, CIO Groups," *Rockford Register-Republic*, July 29, 1957.

29. Ibid.

30. Interview with Emmet Poyer.

31. Fay Calkins, *The CIO and the Democratic Party* (Chicago: University of Chicago Press, 1952), pp. 88ff.

32. This account was derived from both Calkins and Poyer.

33. Ibid.

34. Interview with Benjamin Schleicher.

35. Joseph Ator, "Unions Fail on Rockford's Labor Front but Score Well in Politics," *Chicago Tribune*, June 30, 1958.

36. Ibid.

37. Ibid.

38. Interview with Benjamin Schleicher.

39. Ator, "Unions Fail."

40. "Poyer Found Guilty of Embezzlement," *Rockford Morning Star*, February 20, 1963.

41. Monahan, "Business and Industry," p. 152.

42. "B–C Union Votes Began 13 Years Ago," *Rockford Register-Republic*, October 21, 1964.

43. Ibid., see also "Union Wins NLRB Vote at Colman," *Rockford Register-Republic*, February 7, 1963.

44. "Workers OK Pact at Barber-Colman," *Rockford Register-Republic*, October 10, 1963.

45. "B–C Union Votes."

46. Ibid.

47. "Barber-Colman Set for Monday Work; Four Arrests Made," *Rockford Morning Star*, June 6, 1964; "Official of Union Is Arrested Here," *Rockford Morning Star*, June 19, 1964.

48. "Barber-Colman Union Members Accept New Contract; Strike Ends," *Rockford Morning Star*, October 21, 1964.

49. Interview with Emmet Poyer.

50. Interview with Lawrence Schmidt.

51. Interview with Lewis Moore.

52. Ibid.

53. "City Workers Vote Strike in Pay Issue," *Rockford Register-Republic,* January 29, 1965.

54. "Strike Could Cost Workers City Jobs," *Rockford Morning Star,* January 30, 1965.

55. "Vital Services Hit By City Walkout," *Rockford Register-Republic,* February 15, 1965.

56. "City Stands Pat on Budget; Strike Enters Second Day," *Rockford Morning Star,* February 16, 1965.

57. "Union Tells City Workers, 'Ignore Suspension Notes'," *Rockford Morning Star,* February 17, 1965.

58. "End Strike Against City; Workers Back on Job Today," *Rockford Morning Star,* February 18, 1965.

59. Interview with Benjamin Schleicher.

60. "Unions Here Claim 20,000 Members," *Rockford Morning Star,* April 21, 1966.

61. "Mayor Asks Help in Labor Shortage," *Rockford Morning Star,* August 19, 1966.

62. "Labor Shortage Here Called Critical," *Rockford Morning Star,* October 27, 1966.

63. "Union Strike at Barber-Colman," *Rockford Register-Republic,* May 18, 1967.

64. "Union Loses Vote at Barber-Colman," *Rockford Morning Star,* October 19, 1967.

65. "Firemen on Strike," *Rockford Register-Republic,* March 26, 1968.

66. "Skeleton Crews Guard Community," *Rockford Register-Republic,* March 26, 1968; "Hospitals, Factories Go on Fire Alert," *Rockford-Register-Republic,* March 26, 1968.

67. "Court Rules Firemen Must End Walkout," *Rockford Register-Republic,* March 27, 1968.

68. "Firemen Tire of 'Empty Promises'," *Rockford Register-Republic,* March 26, 1968.

69. "City Must Face Employee Union: Baer," *Rockford Morning Star,* June 25, 1971.

70. Interview with Benjamin Schleicher.

71. "City Decides to Recognize Municipal Employees' Union," *Rockford Morning Star,* July 7, 1971.

72. "City Council Recognizes Police, Fireman Groups," *Rockford Register Republic,* August 3, 1971.

73. Interview with Benjamin Schleicher.

74. "Trade Unions Open Doors to Minorities," *Rockford Register-Republic,* March 27, 1969.

75. "Minority Hiring in City Defended," *Rockford Register-Republic,* November 2, 1973.

76. "McGaw gets Minority Guidelines," *Rockford Register-Republic,* January 17, 1974.

77. "Current Minority Hiring Practices Declared OK," *Rockford Morning Star,* January 19, 1974.

78. "Why Support a Phantom?", *Rockford Register-Republic,* January 19, 1974.

79. "Minority Job Setup Threatened," *Rockford Morning Star,* January 2, 1974.

80. Ibid.

81. "2nd Warning Given on Minority Hiring," *Rockford Register-Republic,* January 26, 1974.

82. "New Building Trades Bargaining Scheme Failing," *Rockford Register-Republic,* May 15, 1974.

83. "Iron Workers Post Pickets at 3 Projects, Resume Talks," *Rockford Register-Republic,* June 3, 1975; "Second Strike to Shut Down Projects," *Rockford Morning Star,* June 17, 1975.

84. "McGaw Intervened as Strike Hurt City," *Rockford Register-Republic,* July 23, 1975; Ira Teinowitz, "Mayor's Office Helps Settle Cement Strike," *Rockford Morning Star,* July 23, 1975.

85. Dean Todd, "Minority Job Quotas Called 'Impossible'," *Rockford Register-Republic,* August 6, 1975.

10

The Quad Cities

The Quad Cities is the name given to the metropolitan area comprised of twelve cities straddling the Mississippi River at the junction of the Mississippi and Rock Rivers. The area covers portions of northwestern Illinois and east-central Iowa. Eight cities are located in Illinois. In order of population, from largest to smallest, they are Rock Island, Moline, East Moline, Milan, Silvis, Coal Valley, Carbon Cliff, and Hampton. Four cities are located in Iowa: Davenport, Bettendorf, Eldridge, and Riverdale. The 1978 population was estimated at 376,900, which made the Quad Cities larger than Peoria or Rockford in Illinois, and Des Moines in Iowa.[1]

Although the area is identified as one unit, to view the Quad Cities as a consistent and contiguous whole can be quite misleading. In reality, the region suffers from what might be termed gross fragmentation. As a result, understanding the Quad Cities is made much more difficult than understanding the history of a single city such as Rockford or Peoria.

Although the focus of this study is on the Illinois side of the river, one cannot ignore the fact that nearly one-half of the metropolitan area is physically located in Iowa and has some distinctive features. For example, Iowa is a "right-to-work" state; Illinois never enacted such a law. As a result, employers operating in the area with locations in both states are confronted with different laws governing the workplace even though the attitudes of employees with respect to union membership tend to be similar.

Although the area as a whole is sizable, none of the individual cities qualify as large. Only Davenport had a population in 1980 exceeding 100,000.[2] Rock Island and Moline reported 47,000 and 46,000 respectively.[3] Both had been losing population at a slow rate for the previous fifteen to twenty years.

Rock Island is the oldest of the Quad Cities, having been established in 1835 as Stephenson. The name was changed to Rock Island in 1841.[4] It was settled by people of Swedish and Belgian stock who tended to be conservative and hard-working.[5] The Swedes ran many of the local businesses, whereas the Belgians more often worked in shops and factories. The major exception to this division of occupation was in the local dairy industry, which was predominately run by the Belgians. Over the years, settlers arrived from

Greece, Germany, Denmark, Norway, Lithuania, Poland, Mexico, Canada, Scotland, The Netherlands, Russia, Austria, and Hungary.[6]

There was a clear division of labor in the sense that the English-speaking immigrants tended to rise to positions of authority mach faster than immigrants whose native language was not English. The major exception to this was the Swedes, who, because of their early arrival in the area, had managed to establish many of the important local businesses.

The future of Rock Island and surrounding territories appears to have been decided early. A major government employer, the Rock Island Arsenal, was established in 1861.[7] By 1870, industry was flourishing in Rock Island, notably lumber and farm implements.[8] The largest companies were Weyerhauser and Denkmann Lumber Mill, Keater Lumber, and Rock Island Plow Works. Weyerhauser remained in Rock Island until the seventies, when it finally closed its last operation there. Rock Island Plow Works eventually became the Rock Island plant for J. I. Case Company.

Armaments, lumber, and farm implements were by no means the only industries in the area. Other industries included rubber-soled canvas footwear, men's clothing, sashs and doors, millwork products, hardware specialties, plumbing supplies, electrical household appliances, auto safety equipment, extracts and beverages, food products, paints, steel barrels, regalia and lodge supplies, corrugated boxes, and refined oil.[9]

Moline was founded in 1843 (incorporated in 1872), and its major claim to fame was determined early. In 1848, John Deere opened his first factory in Moline, and soon workers from Sweden, Germany, Belgium, and France had come to Moline to work in Deere's factories. Growth was more or less continuous, and Deere products came to be recognized as among the best farm implements in the world.

Moline became the third largest Belgian center in the United States. In the mid-seventies, there were some eighteen thousand Belgians among the city's forty-six thousand population. Still, Swedes outnumbered Belgians in the community, and perhaps accounted for many of the conservative tendencies exhibited by city officials.[10] For example, of the three major cities on the Illinois side, Moline had the most restrictive ordinances governing bars and had managed to completely exclude adult theaters and bookstores, although they still operated in both East Moline and Rock Island. Moline also had a small but distinctive Hispanic community. John Deere was so large and important in the local economy that diversity of industry was significantly less than in Rock Island and Davenport. In addition to agricultural implements, major products in Moline included elevators, escalators, machine tools, heavy machinery, foundry equipment, and metal products.[11]

East Moline was more of a bedroom community, although it did have several major agricultural implement plants. Founded just after the turn of the century, the city served as home for blue-collar workers employed in the local factories, particularly in the farm implement industry.[12] Both John Deere and International Harvester had major operations in East Moline.

East Moline was one of the centers of radical activity during the forties. International Harvester's East Moline works was the scene of many battles between the United Auto Workers (UAW) and United Farm Equipment Workers (UFE), and the site of a tremendous amount of wildcat strike activity. Both John Deere Harvester Works and John Deere Foundry experienced similar situations. Later, East Moline became the local political stronghold for the Democratic party.

The entry and decline of lumber, steel, and automobile/carriage production over the years meant rapid changes in employment opportunities, and often in the ethnic and national makeup of the communities. The shift toward warehousing and distribution operations and away from near total reliance on manufacturing meant that the local economy had been strong even in poor times.[13] it was only within the last few years of the period under study that unemployment remained at high levels for extended periods.

In the early years of the Quad Cities communities, most industry was locally owned. Over time, however, many of these companies relocated elsewhere or sold their operations to companies headquartered outside the Quad Cities. J. I. Case, International Harvester, and the Aluminum Corporation of America (ALCOA), were prime examples of companies headquartered elsewhere. The only notable exception was John Deere and Company. The significance of this point is that often labor-management relations tend to be troubled where there is absentee ownership. Most of the poor relationships in the Quad Cities were in the agricultural implement industry, and particularly at J. I. Case and International Harvester.

Unions achieved a relatively high degree of penetration in the Quad Cities. Although no accurate figures are available, clearly the total was above the national average, and probably significantly so. Nearly 90 percent of employees were unionized at companies included on the list of Quad Cities' manufacturers employing a hundred or more; add to this the construction trades and services that had unionized work forces, and the Quad Cities' union ratio was undoubtedly well over 30 percent.[14]

According to Hal Parmalee of the Associated Employers of the Quad Cities, this situation was changing in later years. Part of a trend away from unions was attributed to better personnel and labor relations policies at the newer companies. This was especially true in the warehousing and distribution services. Carl Adrian, vice-president of the Quad City Development Group, noted that a Honda of America Distribution Center was not organized even though it shared a common wall with an organized company. He felt that there was no desire to organize there and added that this was probably a reflection of a growing employee sentiment in the Quad Cities.

Within the Quad Cities area, one union was clearly much larger than all others: the United Auto Workers. The UAW accounted for approximately one-half of all union membership, all in the agricultural implement industry. This was not always the case, however. For many years the UAW was in competition with the United Farm Equipment and Machine Workers of America for control of bargaining in that industry.

Other significant unions included the International Association of Machinists, the Aluminum Workers International Union, and the Teamsters. The IAM had organized many of the employees at the Rock Island Arsenal, as well as at several other companies on the list of larger Quad Cities employers. The Aluminum Workers represented most of the employees at ALCOA. The Teamsters organized a wide variety of local firms, including many small construction firms. Most of the traditional craft unions were also represented. The Carpenters Union Local 166, which was founded March 27, 1886, was the oldest union in the Quad Cities area.[15]

During the late thirties and World War II, the UFE was quite successful in organizing most of the agricultural implement industry, particularly John Deere and International Harvester. The UAW attempted to organize J. I. Case Company, but because of extreme employer resistance it was not recognized as the bargaining agent until after the end of World War II.[16] Most local shops related to the agricultural implement industry were organized by the UFE, UAW, or United Electrical, Radio and Machine Workers of America (UE). All of these were at the time CIO unions.

In the early postwar period, most of the activity on the local scene reflected national trends. That is, there were many strikes for higher wages, better benefits, and, in some cases, reduced working hours.

J. I. Case employees struck December 26, 1945, for a first contract after several years of unsuccessful efforts to gain corporate acceptance. This strike was very bitter and violent, lasting into March 1946 in the Quad Cities—and even longer in other locations.[17] International Harvester was hit with an equally bitter strike that began in January 1946 and lasted until late April. Other strike activity affected the city of Moline (garbagemen), various job shops in the pattern-making industry, a major foundry, the construction industry, commercial bakeries, part of the local steel industry, and various small businesses. The only major employer that escaped without a major strike was John Deere and Company.

Business was expanding, though. ALCOA announced plans for a new $30,000,000 plant near Bettendorf, Iowa, which would create 2,000 new jobs. J. I. Case announced an expansion of its Rock Island facility valued at $1,500,000, and which created 250 new jobs. Case also purchased some International Harvester war product facilities in Iowa for future development. International Harvester expanded its East Moline facility.

In 1947, the internecine struggle surfaced between the UFE and UE on one hand and the UAW on the other. Hardest hit was International Harvester Corporation, which had two major plants in the area, one in East Moline and the Farmall plant in Rock Island. Together they employed nearly eight thousand people. The UFE was determined to use militant tactics to gain significant wage and benefit concessions from IH. Wildcat strikes became common at the two Harvester plants during 1947. International Harvester officials regularly called the wildcat strikes illegal, and most often refused to bargain as long as the strikers remained off their jobs.

UAW leaders recognized that a single union in the agricultural implement industry could wield greater bargaining power than any of the three major unions (UAW, UFE, UE). However, the active role of communists within the UFE and UE posed a serious challenge to the forces of UAW president Walter Reuther; if the rival CIO unions in the agricultural implement industry were merged, the radicals might gain control of the new organization.[18]

At a Milwaukee conference in May 1947, some UAW locals in the agricultural implement industry called for a merger with other CIO unions in the industry, that is, UFE and UE.[19] Ruether forces prevailed, however, and the proposal was voted down. To complicate issues the UAW as well as the AFL Auto Workers launched drives in UFE-organized plants.[20]

In mid-January 1947, a major wildcat strike idled some 1,700 employees at Harvester's East Moline plant.[21] The ostensible issue on which the UFE members struck was the company's refusal to follow an arbitration ruling from the previous December, It was thirteen days before the wildcat ended, and the UFE threatened to strike again in five days if adoption of the disputed ruling was not forthcoming. The company held firm, and a second strike ended February 9.

The UFE activities at East Moline did not go unnoticed elsewhere. The controversy regarding radical influences at International Harvester's East Moline plant had been raised in a congressional hearing in Washington, D.C.[22] Grant Oakes, national president of the UFE, objected to the hearing; he claimed that the union had no opportunity to testify before the congressional committee and stressed IH's poor labor relations reputation. IH officials allegedly informed the press that they would not negotiate a new agreement with the UFE, citing as their reason the crippling number of wildcat strikes under the previous agreement.[23] This threat was not backed by action, however, and Harvester began to negotiate with the UFE for a new contract at both the East Moline and Farmall plants.

Before a settlement was reached, a split developed within the Quad Cities CIO-Industrial Union Council (IUC) that led to the immediate withdrawal of the United Auto Workers, United Steel Workers, United Paper Workers, and

Amalgamated Clothing Workers Union. Ironically, the United Electrical Workers also joined the breakaway group over charges that the UFE was un-American. That left the UFE as the dominant union within the original CIO–IUC; its membership then totalled about ten thousand.[24] The splinter unions tentatively formed a rival CIO–IUC, the Mississippi Valley CIO–IUC.

One week after the revolt, two more CIO unions indicated their intentions to move to the new group—the United Rubber Workers and the United Brewery Workers.[25] The following day, the strike at IH, East Moline, changed course as the strikers voted to strike "to a successful conclusion" in a reclassification and pay dispute.[26]

This strike grew during the last days of July, and by the end of the month all production workers were off the job.[27] The company charged that the union leaders were "irresponsible radicals and published a full-page advertisement concerning the cost of 202 wildcat strikes during the past two years at Harvester facilities in the Quad Cities.[28]

As the strike continued, the tension between the rival CIO–IUC bodies grew. The UAW group reported "tacit" approval from national CIO officials.[29] It was also reported that the CIO–IUC in Iowa split on a right-wing/left-wing basis as the Quad Cities CIO–IUC had a few weeks earlier.

The UFE strike at East Moline came to a climax on September 17, 1948. East Moline and Illinois State Police joined forces as thirty-one police officers confronted the picketers after last-ditch efforts to settle the strike failed. The resulting clash led to five arrests and several people being sent to hospitals.[30] Three days later, the strikers were back at work with both sides set to resume negotiations, which ultimately led to an agreement.

During the last three months of 1948, the UFE was under attack from two sides. The UAW successfully challenged the UFE at the new J. I. Case plant in Bettendorf, winning a bargaining unit of nearly two thousand.[31] The UFE was also challenged at a more fundamental level by the national CIO Executive Board, which voted to order the UFE to disband and join the UAW; all UFE locals were to become UAW locals.[32] On November 30, 1948, UFE leaders in the Quad Cities vowed not to join the UAW, and on December 2, Local 109 leaders at IH Farmall sent to Philip Murray a telegram condemning the order to merge the UAW and UFE.[33] By now the largest stronghold of UFE members was in the Quad Cities. On January 11, 1949, the CIO regional director charged that the Quad Cities CIO–IUC was run by communists.[34] Nevertheless, the CIO did not revoke the charter of that organization. The rival Mississippi Valley CIO–IUC was not chartered despite the fact that the CIO leadership had lost all faith in the Quad Cities CIO–IUC. What the CIO leaders apparently had in mind was to let the UAW challenge the UFE directly for control of the agricultural implement industry.[35]

During February 1949, the battle between the UAW and UFE seemed to reach a climax. On February 9, distribution of UAW handbills led to violence at the East Moline plant of International Harvester. A Moline *Daily Dispatch* reporter on the scene noted that UAW members distributed handbills taunting UFE members as they left the plant. This taunting was countered by violence from UFE members, leading to a riot involving about three hundred people.[36] UAW leaders asked the following day for the arrest of UFE leaders. The UFE called for an election to determine which union agricultural implement workers in the Quad Cities preferred.

Handbill distribution began again on February 21 at International Harvester's East Moline plant; some seventy local and state police were there. Although there was no violence, the UAW suffered a temporary setback. While the handbills were being passed out, UAW leaders were arrested in another part of the city after a UFE leader pressed charges of disorderly conduct, rioting, and conspiracy to riot.[37]

During March it became clear that the UFE was losing ground. Some of John Deere's local operations had become UAW shops, and pressure was building for all UFE members to switch loyalties. On March 4, UAW Local 79 at John Deere Harvester Works in East Moline passed a resolution calling on all John Deere employees not in the UAW to join that union.[38] On March 7, Local 104, UFE, at International Harvester in East Moline attacked the UAW and started a new wage drive.[39]

On March 23, John Deere Company began to negotiate a new contract with the UAW.[40] It was no longer clear who was the bargaining agent at Deere. Six days later, the UFE district president suspended several UFE leaders at John Deere Plow Works, charging them with supporting the UAW.[41] On March 30, it was reported that the UFE charged John Deere Plow Works officials with refusal to bargain with them while bargaining with the UAW.[42]

During April, International Harvester Farmall Works was hit by a major wildcat strike that idled 4,200 people for five days. At John Deere Plow Works in Moline, an NLRB-supervised election requested by the UAW was held. The UFE won by a large 922–224 vote over the UAW.

John Deere Spreader Works and International Harvester, both in East Moline, were hit by wildcat strikes early in May, and late in the month John Deere Harvester Works Foundry in East Moline also experienced a wildcat strike.[43] During June 1949, the UAW began to make serious inroads into once-UFE-held shops owned by John Deere Company by reaching an agreement for seven plants.[44] At the end of July, John Deere Plow Works and UFE negotiators had reached a new contract for the Moline plant.

No major confrontations between UAW and UFE members occurred during August or September. The only major events during those months were a narrow UAW victory over "no union" in an NLRB representation election at J. I. Case's Bettendorf plant,[45] a UFE vote to strike IH's Farmall and East Moline Plants if necessary,[46] and, as September ended, a decision by the Mississippi Valley CIO–IUC to seek official recognition from the CIO Executive Board at a national convention in October in Cleveland.[47]

October 11 brought the unexpected announcement that the UFE would merge with the UE.[48] UFE officials at International Harvester's East Moline plant urged their members to vote for the merger, and the announcement came eight days later that 83 percent of the voters approved.[49] UFE locals were given UE charters November 1, 1949.

On November 2, it was announced that UE had been expelled from the national CIO because of domination by communist leaders.[50] Although many UE and UFE members apparently expected this action, the expulsion may have made some members reconsider. It was reported on November 8 by the Moline *Daily Dispatch* that there was a major split within UE; some 107,000 members nationwide were allegedly considering rejoining the CIO and the International Union of Electrical Workers (IUE), including some Quad Cities locals.[51] By November 11, the defections were apparent as UE Local 814 at the Minneapolis–Moline Company, a major agricultural implement company in the Quad Cities area, voted to leave UE and rejoin the CIO through the IUE.[52]

As the year ended, the UAW–UFE conflict was joined in the courts. Leaders of the old UE Local 814 at Minneapolis–Moline Company obtained an injunction prohibiting IUE Local 814 from destroying or disposing of any records, cash, bonds, or other property that once belonged to the UE local.[53] One week later, two IUE officials sued the local UE officers for defamation and malicious remarks.[54] Finally, the NLRB was asked to resolve a dispute concerning the bargaining representative at Minneapolis–Moline Company.[55]

The conflict did not end in the forties, even though its ultimate fate may have been determined. The UFE–UE attempted to maintain influence in the face of adverse public opinion, growing employer resistance, and the attraction of a proven track record at UAW plants. By late 1953, virtually all remnants of UFE power had been destroyed. In some cases, employees became part of UAW shops, and a few joined the IAM. In other cases, disaffiliation was followed by a period of no union membership, and only later by UAW, IUE, or IAM membership.

The next period (1955–68) in the history of Quad Cities labor marked a change to stability. With the exclusion of UFE and UE unionists and their more militant activities, labor relations began to focus more upon bargaining and formal grievance procedures than on wildcat strikes to settle major differences. Although the wildcats did not disappear, their frequency diminished substantially.

In 1955, the major labor events were a strike at International Harvester Farmall plant during August and September, and the signing without a strike of a new three-year agreement between International Harvester, East Moline, and the UAW.[56]

The following two years proved to be economically favorable for most of the community. Building construction begun during 1956 reached an all-time high.[57] International Harvester Farmall completed the year with no major work stoppages by any of the three unions in the plant. The two major negative events were a four and one-half month strike at John Deere and the failure of voters to approve a bond issue for the Moline public school. No significant labor interruptions were reported at John Deere, International Harvester, or J. I. Case during 1957. Employment and production at both IH plants were at their highest levels in recent years.[58]

Perhaps more important than any other event was the merger of the AFL and CIO in the Quad Cities, following the national merger. William Keith, publisher of the *Tri-City Labor Review*, the Quad Cities' labor-owned paper, gave two reasons: One was psychological—the feeling that united labor could have a significant impact on local politics and controversial issues. More important, a united Labor movement could coordinate its activities and consolidate its goals so that is could work with the greatest possible degree of power.[59]

Some labor people opposed the merger, though. Rosa DeYoung, the wife of the late John DeYoung, who at the time was editor of the *Labor Review* and prominent in the Quad Cities Federation of Labor (AFL), commented that her husband did not favor the merger. DeYoung apparently felt that the differences between AFL and CIO unions were so great that a merger would prove more of a hindrance than benefit.[60] Some AFL unionists felt they would be outnumbered by the CIO membership.

The labor relations scene continued to be generally quiet during the next three years. John Deere Company and the UAW signed a new three-year contract on November 6, 1958, after nearly five months of bargaining. The agreement continued provisions that the union said were better than the most recent contract in the automobile industry.[61]

Despite the fact that production and employment remained high during 1963 (unemployment dropped below 3 percent), one of the more violent labor conflicts took place that year.[62] At National Gould Battery, a division of American Container Corporation, Rock Island, negotiations broke down on May 14 between the company and Local 1570, International Brotherhood of Electrical Workers.[63] About 175 employees went on strike. The walkout was peaceful and without incident until August 16, when police were called in to remove a picket line so that several box cars of products could be moved in and out of the plant.[64] The use of police in an apparent strike-breaking role angered the strikers. On August 18, an explosion hit the plant and caused significant damage; the same day, a charge of mob action was filed against nonunion supervisory personnel.[65] A second bombing on August 26 caused even more damage than the first.[66] Then on September 6, the peace was again shattered. Battery charges were filed against seven persons in the aftermath of picket-line scuffles. That night a rocket was fired at the plant.[67] This last incident brought the matter to a head; something had to be done before more serious injuries and property damage resulted. American Container closed the Gould facility and left the area.

Growth continued into 1965, and affected virtually all Quad Cities' industries. Growth and prosperity, however, brought a flurry of strikes. A total of 111,000 man-days were lost to strikes during 1965 because of several wildcat strikes at John Deere and International Harvester plants, a long strike by Local 36 of the Bakery and Confectionery Workers against the National Licorice Company in Moline, and short strikes in East Moline by the IAM against AMETEK, Inc., Williams White Company, and several other smaller employers.[68]

Relative labor peace returned in 1966, as only 68,100 man-days were lost to strikes. Numerous wildcats and short strikes were reported, but no major stoppages occurred. The UAW and J. I. Case reached a new three-year agreement as the year ended.[69] For the fifth consecutive year, industrial employment increased.

Volatility returned in 1967 and 1968 as major contracts expired in the agricultural implement and heavy machinery industries. UAW Local 215 struck a Caterpillar Tractor Company division October 1 as part of a companywide three-week strike. Another nationwide strike by the UAW against John Deere Company lasted until January 4, 1968.[70] Wildcat strikes at several other companies raised total man-days lost to 238,000 for 1967.

In 1968, a fifty-day strike by the IAM against AMETEK, Inc., East Moline, ended in a new agreement. Other lengthy strikes were conducted by the IBEW at ALCOA in Davenport,[71] by the UAW at Quad-City Die Casting, Moline, and by IAM Local 388 at Bendix Instrument and Life Support Division, Davenport. A total of 205,500 man-days were lost to strikes in 1968.

Perhaps more important than strike activity, however, was the national split between the AFL–CIO and UAW in mid-1968. In the Quad Cities, the UAW withdrew from the Quad City Federation of Labor and set up its own group. The split left the federation with about thirteen thousand members and the UAW with some seventeen thousand. The IAM, with some five thousand members, became the largest union in the Federation of Labor. Total union membership in the Quad Cities was put at fifty thousand in 1968.[72] No parties reported much change in local labor-related matters after the split. The UAW reportedly continued to work with its old allies on projects of mutual interest.[73]

The third period (1969–80) in Quad Cities union history may be called the retrenchment period. It reflected the apparent greater willingness of employers to oppose unions in bargaining and through utilization of the legal system. In a sense, employers (with some notable exceptions) took the offensive. As a result strikes seemed to be longer and relations more bitter in comparison with the years from 1955 through 1968.

The first year of this period, 1969, was marred by several lengthy strikes, although they did not affect any of the very large employers. Building construction, in particular, was disrupted during much of the summer. On June 19, East Moline was hit by a sixteen-hour epidemic of "blue flu" as policemen attempted to make their case for a new agreement with the city. A more positive and enduring development occurred when the Moline city council adopted a proposal to institute equal employment opportunity procedures in city hiring.[74]

During 1970, a split appeared within the United Auto Workers. Local 1356 President David De Barres charged Region 4 Director Robert Johnston with failure to serve local unions properly, as well as with corruption.[75] However, no visible consequences resulted from these accusations.

UAW contracts with John Deere Company and International Harvester expired near the end of 1970, but were extended into 1971. Harvester was hit by a nine-day strike in January. No strike resulted at John Deere, and a new pact was finally reached March 1, which gave the employees major new benefits. During August, the International Brotherhood of Electrical Workers struck Iowa-Illinois Electric and Gas Company and tied up some operations there for most of the remainder of 1971.[76]

A major stoppage at Montgomery Elevator by the IAM began April 6, 1972; the union called it a lockout.[77] Although an agreement was negotiated in late May, the employees were not called back until July 28 because the company's business had been badly hurt. The only other major disruption that year began July 7, when a wildcat strike was called concerning discipline of a union official at Bear Manufacturing.[78] Two additional events occurred during 1972, which again demonstrated an apparent employer determination to challenge unions. The NLRB was asked to investigate unfair labor practice charges against Lenox Photo, Inc., Moline, filed by Local 257 of the Lithographer and Photoengravers International Union. Two weeks later, the NLRB ordered Midland Tractor and Equipment Company in rural Moline to cease and desist interrogating employees about Teamster Union activity.[79]

It appeared in the fall of 1973 that John Deere would have a strike by the UAW as their contract was being renegotiated.[80] Instead, a new agreement was reached, although Deere factories in the Quad Cities were closed for several days as UAW members honored IAM picket lines. Negotiations were not so successful at International Harvester, however, and a strike began October 18. Violence between picketers and police erupted on October 30 and 31, as police escorted nonstriking office employees through the picket lines.[81] The strike was settled November 5.

Legal maneuvering appeared once again during 1974. Teamsters Local 371 struck Eagle Discount Supermarkets and picketed the company's Milan warehouse. U.S. District Judge Robert Morgan issued an injunction to halt the picketing. The controversy ended with twenty-five employees fired and arbitration pending. Once more building construction was interrupted during parts of May and June as Iron Workers and Teamsters struck.[82] On July 8, Teamsters Local 371 struck Borden Company Milk Depot, Rock Island, over wages and benefits. One week later the company responded by closing the depot.[83] While the company would not say directly that the strike was the reason for closing the depot, Borden officials intimated that the strike was in fact the reason.

The major conflict during 1975 was another construction industry strike, which ran from May 1 to early July. Frank Foundries was hit by a twenty-three day strike by the UAW during July. A major wildcat at International Harvester Farmall idled some 2,500 workers for six days. Employees walked off the job after a female employee charged that a supervisor made advances.[84]

In 1976 a 54 week strike by Local 433 of the Motion Picture Projectionists against the Dubinsky Theater Chain was ended with agreement on a new three-year contract.[85] This was reportedly one of the longest strikes in the history of the Quad Cities, although its general impact was slight. The major event of the year was a strike by the UAW against John Deere, which began October 1. The major issues were subcontracting and early retirement in addition to wages. After thirty-nine days, an agreement was reached that the UAW hailed as the best ever in the agricultural implement industry.[86]

Several lengthy strikes also made news during 1977. A one-and-one-half-month strike by the Teamsters against F. W. Means, East Moline, ended with acceptance of a previously rejected proposal after the company announced that it planned to permanently replace the strikers. This strike was marred by violence and several arrests. Three Montgomery Elevator plants were struck in April 1977 by the IAM in a strike that lasted until June 16. Several offers were rejected before an agreement was reached.[87] Finally, a lingering issue for most of 1977 was the use of nonunion labor to build a motel in Moline. The Laborers Union continually picketed the site, and violence and at least one bombing were reported.[88]

Other than a number of short wildcat strikes in the agricultural implement industry and a strike by the Amalgamated Meatcutters and Butcher Workmen in January,[89] there was only one major strike during 1978. Frank Foundries was hit by a ten-week strike by the UAW that ended on September 14.[90] The first eight months of 1979 were also quiet. On October 1, however, the UAW struck John Deere, idling some ten thousand Quad Cities employees for three weeks. Another 1,400 Deere employees honored the IAM picket lines at the Plow and Planter Works in Moline. At the same time, two thousand UAW members were on strike against Caterpillar in Bettendorf and Mount Joy, Iowa. On November 1, the UAW struck International Harvester in a nationwide strike; almost 6,400 employees in the Quad Cities were idled.[91]

The major event during 1980 was resolution of the International Harvester strike on April 23.[92] The Rock Island local at the Farmall plant was the last local to ratify the agreement. The strike lasted 173 days, the longest in UAW–IH history. It was described in the *Wall Street Journal* as "bitter"; major issues concerned job security, mandatory overtime, and job transfer limits.[93] The length and intensity of the strike were renewed evidence of employer resistance—in this case both in and outside the Quad Cities. By comparison, all other labor problems during 1980 were insignificant.

However, the period of conflict was about to be supplemented by a major new problem—mass unemployment. The agricultural implement industry was beginning to experience a substantial business decline, in great part because of general recession and record high interest rates. Layoff was about to become a way of life in the area. Ironically, this shift occurred at a time when the UAW had more than twenty-five thousand members in the Quad Cities, other unions were in a strong position, and union leaders felt the future looked bright.[94]

As noted earlier, the largest public employer in the Quad Cities was the Rock Island Arsenal. The original purpose of the Arsenal, which was established in 1861, was "for the deposit and repair of arms and other munitions of war." In each subsequent war period, the same up-and-down employment pattern occurred. During World War II, employment increased from 2,735 in 1939 to a high of 18,675 in 1974, then decreased to 2,469 by July 1, 1947.[95] Employment increased slightly and then remained steady in the fifties as new technology was added to the products under research and development as well as manufacture. Employment increased once again during American involvement in Vietnam, and remained high in the years after that involvement (in 1980 it stood at 7,525) as the defense industry retained its place of high priority in the United States budget.[96]

Despite its prominence as an employer and as a source of economic income for the area, in contrast to the agricultural implement employers, the Arsenal enjoyed a quiet background role in the Quad Cities industrial relations scene. As William P. Grogan, long-time labor relations officer at the Arsenal, reported, unions were of little significance before 1962. Following President Kennedy's Executive Order of January 1962, employee organizations became more active, and a number of bargaining units were recognized. The units of the International Association of Machinists (1,650 craft employees), the National Federation of Federal Employees (3,500 employees), and the Na-

tional Associations of Government Employees (800 nonprofessional employees, 300 professional employees) were the most important.

Relations, according to Grogan, were generally peaceful, and the overall
plant environment was cooperative. Between 1945 and 1980, the works was
strike-free. This did not mean that friction was totally absent. The growth of
unionism had driven "somewhat of a wedge between supervisors and employees." Arsenal employees were not always happy when they witnessed the
greater economic gains achieved by the UAW and other industrial unions. On
the other hand, in times of industrial unemployment, they appreciated the
benefits of greater job security. Moreover, the Department of the Army left
considerable discretion to local Arsenal management, and gradually over the
years bargaining with the unions came to encompass more issues and there
was less management emphasis on "management rights."

This picture was generally confirmed by Albert Halx, IAM local president
from 1969 to 1981. Halx saw the 1962 Executive Order as throwing a "crumb"
to the unions, but nevertheless it was a start. Although management retained
a more favorable position, the unions did make bargaining progress. Halx
attributed much of the success of the relationship to Grogan's savvy and
expertise. The IAM was the union leader in negotiations. For a short time in
1973–74, a joint council of unions existed, but IAM dropped out, claiming
it put in more than it got back. Nevertheless, relations with the other unions
in the Arsenal were satisfactory.

The relationship between the Arsenal and the Quad Cities area in industrial
relations terms was slight. According to Grogan, the main external impact of
the Arsenal was on the smaller industrial firms for whom the Arsenal's wages
set patterns. The only time that he could recall when the Arsenal influenced
relations in the large enterprises like Case, Caterpillar, Deere, and Harvester
was with regard to safety shoes. The Arsenal paid for the cost of the shoes,
whereas the private firms had previously insisted that the employees bear the
cost. Halx generally agreed with Grogan's perception. He noted that the
Arsenal regularly conducted a locality wage survey; typically it lagged about
10–15 percent behind the agricultural implement levels. Although it was able
to attract journeymen from the smaller industrial enterprises, it lost employees
to the bigger companies.

Halx felt that the Arsenal unions were "in a different world." A similar
conclusion was suggested by Jack Smith, a long-time Quad Cities' social
activist. Smith recalled an incident in the late sixties when he and others were
demonstrating in Omaha against the Vietnam War. Someone in the demonstration asked if there was not a large arsenal in Rock Island. Smith replied
that there was, but somehow it had been overlooked.

Another facet of the Quad Cities' labor experience was the status of
minorities. In 1970, minorities (blacks and Hispanics) in Rock Island County
totalled only 8,002, or 4.8 percent. By 1980, however, Rock Island County

had a total of 14,522 minority residents, or 8.8 percent of the population on the Illinois side of the metropolitan area. The split between Hispanics and blacks was about even. Rock Island had the largest minority population (17.5 percent), East Moline ranked second (13.4 percent), and Moline had the lowest percentage of minorities among its population (4.4 percent).[97]

Historically, minorities in the Quad Cities' area had not been treated well. Davenport once was the home of a Nazi party, and all indications are that minorities long felt uncomfortable in the region.[98] The position of minorities, and particularly the plight of blacks, became an issue after enactment of the Civil Rights Act of 1964. A series of articles written by black residents of the Cities appeared in the Moline *Daily Dispatch* in late 1965 to highlight the situation.

The Rev. William Grimes attacked segregation in all its forms: economically, sociologically, psychologically, and physically. Grimes noted that blacks simply wanted to become part of mainstream America, to be accepted as human beings, and to be able to live without constant fear of having someone discriminate because skin color was different.[99]

Ralph Beal, then vice-chairman of the Davenport City Human Relations Commission, wrote that the black experience in the Quad Cities "is rather empty, dull, and insignificant." Beal attributed this fact to the lack of any significant number of professional, business, and skilled persons among blacks in the Quad Cities. Most blacks, according to Beal, left the Quad Cities once their training had been obtained. He felt that the Quad Cities area was guilty of talking equality and practicing inequality.[100]

An article by Mel Pettis who was in a managerial position at John Deere corporate headquarters, highlighted the plight of a black seeking good housing. He recounted the resistance he met from local real estate agents when they learned he was black. Most often agents would not show the Pettis family homes in areas they considered desirable. Some home owners refused to sell to Pettis. When the family finally purchased a house through a white friend, they found neighbors quite hostile. Problems were ultimately resolved, but only after all parties sat down together.[101]

The racial controversy in the Quad Cities seemed to center on housing as symbolic of all forms of discrimination. Major cities on both sides of the Mississippi set up Human Relations Commissions and focused on the housing situation. The Rock Island Human Relations Commission on February 6, 1967, presented a report to the city council that acknowledged the problems of a segregated community and called on Rock Island residents to change their attitudes. The commission, like the city council, was reluctant, however, to propose a nondiscrimination ordinance.[102]

The Moline Human Relations Commission and the Moline–East Moline Board of Realtors addressed the problem of open housing in April 1967. The Human Relations Commission desired an open housing commitment from the realtors, and they received it. As in Rock Island, though, there was opposition to a city ordinance requiring that home owners not discriminate when selling. The realtors said that such an ordinance would be useless because sellers would simply bypass real estate agents.[103]

Despite the opposition to fair housing laws, all three major Illinois cities passed such laws during 1967. Public housing became an issue during 1968. Moline *Daily Dispatch* staff writer Vince Thomas explored the reasons for the lag in low- and moderate-income housing. He found that the city was in immediate need of 105 two- and three-bedroom housing units in the $100 to $135 gross monthly rental range. At the same time, Moline officials were working to rid the city of some 1,800 substandard houses.[104] Thomas found that one major element accounted for this poor situation: fear of low-income people. Despite the obvious need, aldermen were concerned that the availability of low-income housing would automatically attract low-income persons and families to the city. Faced with the potential loss of federal funds, local officials began to investigate the possibility of scattered housing.

Over the next several years the controversy appeared to take a better course. Acceptance of blacks increased somewhat, and the perceived need for fair housing laws diminished. All the ordinances were permitted to expire. Greater black acceptance did not end all discrimination issues, however, as the plight of Hispanics in the area came into sharper focus.

In March 1971, Mexican-American representatives of the G.I. Forum of Moline asked the Moline city council for financial assistance.[105] The Mexican–Americans cited education and language problems they faced, but stated that they wanted to stay off welfare. Financial assistance, they asserted, would help with education and jobs. The same issue arose the following summer. This time, the G.I. Forum threatened to sue the city over the city's refusal to continue educational and job programs. Forum members were particularly concerned that youth employment would become much worse without continued city assistance. Again, the city helped, but only in a minimal way.[106]

During July 1973, some 96 persons petitioned Moline's mayor and city council for a permit to open a recreation hall in the Mexican–American neighborhood in Moline. The city refused to act on the proposal. The mayor cited opposition from fifty-two residents who said that the recreation hall would be a billiards center. Opponents claimed that such a center would attract undesirable elements.[107]

The plight of Mexican–Americans in local industry was highlighted in November 1975, when Mexican–Americans picketed International Harvester Farmall to protest employment and promotion policies. They were protesting what they saw as better programs for blacks and women than for Mexican-Americans. Picketing closed the first shift at the plant.[108]

Although public attention to the Hispanic community declined, their problems did not subside. In informal discussions with several people at the West End Resource Center, a Hispanic-supported organization, it became clear that Hispanics felt that little had changed; they generally were stuck in low-paying and dirty jobs in the major industries. Further, they felt discrimination continued to be a way of life for them.

Overall, there had clearly been some changes by 1980. The position of blacks was improved; they were more likely to be accepted in employment and housing opportunities. For Hispanics, on the other hand, little had changed. Discrimination in both employment and housing was still a way of life for Quad Cities' Mexican-Americans.

With respect to the relationship between Labor and community politics, the Democratic party was the "natural" majority party given the overwhelmingly blue-collar nature of the area. The reality, however, was that although the Democratic party received relatively heavy financial and public support from the Labor movement, and particularly from the United Auto Workers, it did not dominate the political scene. Instead, both Republicans and Democrats were regularly elected to local, state, and even federal offices. In short, politics in most of the area was competitive. The only exception to this was East Moline, where, according to Hal Parmalee, the Auto Workers largely ran local politics.[109]

An article in the October 19, 1976, Moline *Daily Dispatch* reported political contributions to date for the 1976 elections. The John Deere-sponsored Illinois Fund gave candidates $15,200 over the ninety days ending October 3. These contributions went to a variety of candidates, primarily Republicans. The United Auto Workers, on the other hand, had raised and distributed over the same time period only $9,500 to the Rock Island County Democratic Central Committee, and $1,000 to other candidates.

Reviewing the strength of the Quad Cities' unions, an article in the September 4, 1977, *Daily Dispatch* noted that there were about forty-six thousand union members in the Quad Cities. Some twenty thousand were UAW members, six thousand were in the Teamsters, and about twenty thousand were in unions affiliated with the Quad Cities Federation of Labor. The article concluded that the Auto Workers were the major political force in the area because of the activities of its Community Action Program.

The apparent clout of the UAW was again reported in the September 8, 1978, *Daily Dispatch*. According to the article, candidates for Rock Island County and County Board officers were to meet soon to explain their positions on issues to representatives of the UAW. After hearing the candidates the UAW would pick the candidates they felt were best. This UAW endorsement was considered by some as a help to one's candidacy.

On September 13, 1978, the *Daily Dispatch* compared the local relationship between organized Labor and the Democratic party with the same relationship nationally. A split had developed at the national level and threatened Democratic candidates in many areas. This was not the case in Rock Island County. Organized Labor, and especially the UAW, helped register voters, raise funds, and endorse candidates. Traditional ties were not threatened.

The strength of Labor-Democratic links was again highlighted in an article in the October 24, 1978, *Daily Dispatch*. According to the article, the UAW, since July 1, had funneled $13,500 into the Democratic treasury. This represented approximately 45 percent of all contributions to the Democratic party in Rock Island county.

Not all of the Quad Cities' unions were as politically involved as the UAW. Wilbert Exline, secretary and business manager of Local 431, Meatcutters in Davenport explained: "We have always been a conservative organization. You can't afford to get too involved in the Federation [i.e., Quad Cities Labor Federation] and in politics and so forth, because you have your own job to take care of . . . we have taken an active part but not to the point where we had to suffer losses on our own. . . . We have used our office, put in banks of telephones and things like this from time to time. But other than that not too involved."[110]

And Rosa DeYoung, one of the most active of the women in the local Labor movement and wife of John DeYoung, editor of the *Labor Review* and a prominent unionist until his retirement in 1955, noted: "John's position was that basically he was a Democrat but he supported some Republicans. . . . Local people. He voted for a Republican Mayor in Rock Island. . . . Because he thought he was the right guy . . . and if it's local and he's a Republican, okay."[111] During the course of this interview, the interviewer stated: "Now, there was this group in the Tri-Cities Federation of Labor [i.e., AFL Central Body] that took the position that labor had no business in politics. . . . But the Teamsters were an exception to that. The Teamsters apparently . . . in the late forties were among the most active political unions here in the Quad Cities."

Historically, what had happened in the Quad Cities reflected changes in many other communities in which the UAW was strong. Once the Union found in the mid-fifties that organization membership had apparently peaked, it began to look to community involvement and politics. This was developed through the UAW Community Action Program (CAP), sometimes independently run and sometimes very close to the Democratic party. It appeared that in the Quad Cities the importance of the UAW had led to a symbiotic relationship between the UAW and Democrats. Both organizations helped each other. Over the years in the Quad Cities, this linkage had developed into a strong, if not always successful, organization.

The labor experience of the Quad Cities between 1945 and 1980 contained a relatively high degree of conflict, initially within the ranks of organized labor between the radical UFE and the more moderate UAW, concurrently and later between organized labor and many employers (John Deere and the Rock Island Arsenal were notable exceptions), and throughout most of the period between black and Hispanic minorities and the communities at large. Although the labor movement was split in a variety of ways—over the mechanics of the AFL–CIO merger and the expulsion of the Teamsters by the national AFL–CIO, the local unions appear to have worked out a reasonably positive accommodation over community service programs and political action. On the political level the UAW was in the forefront of the drive to establish a liaison with the Democratic party. As in Rockford, political action expanded as union organization reached a plateau.

NOTES

This section is a condensation and revision of a report researched and written by Kraig Kircher; material on the Rock Island Arsenal is based on interviews conducted by Victor Kisch.

1. Quad City Development Group, *A Directory of Manufactures* (Quad Cities: no date), p. 2.
2. This figure is based on preliminary 1980 census figures.
3. *Moline Daily Dispatch*, March 27, 1981.
4. "Rock Island, Illinois," in Julie Jensen McDonald, *Pathways to the Present in 50 Iowa and Illinois Communities* (Davenport: Boyor Booles; 1977), p. 251.
5. McDonald, *Pathways to the Present*, pp. 252–53; See also Winifred Stiegel and Harold Cottingham, *A Community Survey of Moline, Illinois* (Moline: Moline Public Schools, 1945), and B. Karl Zorbist, "The Influence and Contribution of the Immigrants to the City of Moline, Illinois from 1865–1890," unpublished paper.
6. Stiegel and Cottingham, *A Community Survey.*
7. U.S. Army, *Rock Island Arsenal, 1862–1966* (Rock Island: U.S. Army, 1967).
8. McDonald, *Pathways to the Present.*
9. Ibid.
10. "Moline, Illinois," in McDonald, *Pathways to the Present*, pp. 191, 193.
11. Ibid, p. 194.
12. "East Moline, Illinois," in McDonald, *Pathways to the Present.*
13. Discussion with Hal Parmalee, Associated Employers of the Quad Cities, and Carl Adrian, vice-president of the Quad Cities Development corporation.
14. With a workforce of approximately 180,000 people. This figure of 30 percent was derived by totalling all the known union members and adding to this total several percent to account for indefinite figures, for example, building trades.
15. Pamphlet issued on the 90th anniversary of Carpenters Local Union 166, 1976.
16. Gary A. Cameron, "Labor Relations at J. I. Case," unpublished paper, Graduate School of Business, University of Chicago, 1965, pp. 6–7.
17. Cameron, "Labor Relations," pp. 7–8.
18. *Moline Daily Dispatch*, July 16, 1947.
19. Ibid., May 16, 1947.

20. Ibid., March 19, 1947.
21. Ibid., January 24, 1947.
22. Ibid., February 17, 1947.
23. Ibid., April 6, 1948.
24. Ibid., July 17, 1948.
25. Ibid., July 23, 1948.
26. Ibid., July 24, 1948.
27. Ibid., July 31, 1948.
28. Ibid., August 4, 1948.
29. Ibid., August 9, 1948.
30. Ibid., September 17, 1948.
31. Ibid., October 5, 1948.
32. Ibid., November 30, 1948.
33. Ibid., December 2, 1948.
34. Ibid., January 11, 1949.
35. Ibid., January 27, 1949.
36. Ibid., February 10, 1949.
37. Ibid., February 21, 1949.
38. Ibid., March 4, 1949.
39. Ibid., March 7, 1949.
40. Ibid., March 23, 1949.
41. Ibid., March 29, 1949.
42. Ibid., March 30, 1949.
43. Ibid., May 4, 1949; May 5, 1949; May 19, 1949.
44. Ibid., June 2, 1949.
45. Ibid., August 9, 1949.
46. Ibid., August 13, 1949.
47. Ibid., September 30, 1949.
48. Ibid., October 11, 1949.
49. Ibid., October 28, 1949.
50. Ibid., November 2, 1949.
51. Ibid., November 8, 1949.
52. Ibid., November 11, 1949.
53. Ibid., December 1, 1949.
54. Ibid., December 8, 1949.
55. Ibid., December 29, 1949.
56. Ibid., December 31, 1955.
57. Ibid., December 31, 1956.
58. Ibid., December 31, 1957.
59. Interview with William Keith.
60. Interview with Rosa DeYoung.
61. *Moline Daily Dispatch*, November 6, 1958.
62. Ibid., December 31, 1963.
63. Ibid., May 14, 1963.
64. Ibid., August 14, 1963.
65. Ibid., August 19, 1963.

66. Ibid., August 26, 1963.

67. Ibid., September 6, 1963.

68. Data compiled and supplied by Associated Employers of the Quad Cities; *Moline Daily Dispatch*, February 2, 1965; April 1965; April 12, 1965; June 2, 1965; June 19, 1965.

69. Ibid., December 30, 1966.

70. Ibid., October 1, 1967; November 18, 1967; December 21, 1967.

71. Ibid., May 20, 1968; June 1, 1968; August 12, 1968.

72. Ibid., December 31, 1968

73. Discussions with Hal Parmalee and Willam Keith.

74. *Moline Daily Dispatch*, May 1, 1969; June 2, 1969; June 11, 1969; June 16, 1969; June 19, 1969; June 28, 1969, August 18, 1969.

75. Ibid., April 10, 1970.

76. Ibid., January 13, 1971; August 14, 1971; August 28, 1971.

77. Ibid., April 6, 1972.

78. Ibid., July 7, 1972; July 11, 1972; July 12, 1972; July 14, 1972; July 18, 1972; July 21, 1972; July 27, 1972; August 1, 1972; August 4, 1972; August 18, 1972; November 21, 1972; January 20, 1973.

79. Ibid., July 11, 1972; July 24, 1972.

80. Ibid., September 17, 1973.

81. Ibid., October 18, 1973; October 30, 1973; October 31, 1973.

82. Ibid., May 1, 1974; May 2, 1974; May 7, 1974; May 13, 1974; June 3, 1974.

83. Ibid., July 9, 1974; July 11, 1974; July 16, 1974.

84. Ibid., July 1, 1975; July 23, 1975; July 24, 1975; July 26, 1975; July 30, 1975.

85. Ibid., September 12, 1976.

86. Ibid., October 1, 1976; October 3, 1976; November 6, 1976; November 7, 1976; November 8, 1976.

87. Ibid., March 7, 1977; March 15, 1977; March 24, 1977 April 4, 1977; April 15, 1977; April 22, 1977; June 1, 1977

88. Ibid., November 3, 1977.

89. Ibid., January 11, 1978; January 11, 1978; January 12, 1978; February 4, 1978 February 13, 1978; February 19, 1978.

90. Ibid., September 14, 1978.

91. Ibid., October 1, 1979; October 2, 1979; October 29, 1979; November 1, 1979.

92. Ibid., April 23, 1980.

93. *Wall Street Journal*, April 23, 1980.

94. *Moline Daily Dispatch*, February 3, 1981.

95. U.S. Army, *Short History of the Island of Rock Island, 1816–1966* (Rock Island: Rock Island Arsenal, 1967).

96. *Moline Daily Dispatch*, December 31, 1962.

97. Ibid., March 27, 1981, p. 1.

98. Interview with Jack Smith.

99. V. Murphy, "Quad City Negroes Struggle to Become 'Individuals'," *Moline Daily Dispatch*, December 7, 1965; Rev. William Grimes, "The Big Lie . . . The Deep Hurt," Ibid., December 9, 1965.

100. Ralph Beal, "A Dull State of Affairs," Ibid., January 6, 1966.

101. Mel Pettis, "A Right to a Home," Ibid., February 17, 1966.

102. Ibid., February 7, 1967, p. 7.

103. Ibid., April 21, 1967, p. 3.

104. Vince Thomas, "Public Housing Lag: One Reason Is Fear of Low Income Family Influx," Ibid., September 10, 1968.

105. Ibid., March 17, 1971.

106. Ibid., July 6, 1972.

107. Ibid., July 18, 1973.

108. Ibid., November 3, 1975.

109. Interview with Hal Parmalee.

110. Interview with Wilbert Exline, Iowa Labor History Oral Project, May 29, 1980, pp. 29–30.

111. Interview with Rosa DeYoung, Iowa Labor History Oral Project, Labor Center, University of Iowa, July 16, 1980, p. 25.

11

Peoria

Peoria is the center of a three-county standard metropolitan statistical area (SMSA) composed of Peoria, Tazewell, and Woodford counties. The city is located in the east-central region of the state and sprawls along the western shores of the Illinois River. It was incorporated in 1839[1] and almost at once became a leading trade center for the entire midwestern United States. It also became an early leader in industrial manufacturing and agricultural processing. Peoria grew in population to be the state's "second city" behind Chicago and only relinquished that position in the seventies, when it fell to third place behind the city of Rockford.

Peoria and its three-county area was a product of cross-cultural merger traced by Daniel Elazar in *Cities of the Prairie*. "Except in a few cases where individual entrepreneurs promoted townsites, the towns first settled by people from the South either 'just growed' where farmers came to drink, play, or market their goods or were virtually forced into existence by the territorial and, later, state legislatures which had to create seats of government for newly formed counties. Belleville, Springfield, Decatur, Urbana, Peoria, and Rock Island were founded in this manner."[2]

These southern settlers brought with them "an extremely individualistic attitude toward society." Their sense of responsibility did not extend further than the family circle, and this was reinforced through intermarriage between family groups. Most of their churches were Baptist, but there were also Methodist and Presbyterian congregations that functioned primarily as transmitters of the traditional values. On politics, Elazar observed: "Their politics began with efforts to imitate the traditional gentry-dominated politics of the states from whence they came with its system of interlocking family alliances struggling for political control primarily as a means of wealth and social position."[3] The attempt to establish a political power based on a type of aristocracy was not possible without the slavery system, which did not typically make the move west. For this and other reasons, the southern heritage for the cities of the prairie came to be one of rugged individualism.[4]

In the early- to mid-nineteenth century, southern migrant culture was blended first with the people of the Middle Atlantic states (Delaware, Pennsylvania, and Maryland,) and then with Yankees from New England, who began settling in earnest after the opening of the Erie Canal. To southern ideals of kinship and individualism, the middle-staters brought ideas of commerce and community organization needed to stabilize commercial development. This governmental organization was supported by a Calvinist form of religion and a political conservatism that became an enduring blend of liberal and traditional Republicanism.

The Europeans most influential in their migration to the Peoria area were the Germans, who began to enter the greater West in substantial numbers after 1830.[5] The Germans were what Elazar called "the first true urbanites" to settle in the American west. They were divided between Catholic and Protestant groups. As craftsmen, small industrialists, and small businessmen they served the agricultural economy but were committed to building an urban way of life.

By the end of World War I, a diversity of European migrants had reached the Peoria area. The black population from 1900 to 1940 was constant at approximately 2.5 percent–3 percent. From 1940 to 1950, however, that number nearly doubled to approximately 5.3 percent.[6] By 1950, the European immigrants had been totally absorbed into the fabric of local life. Kalman Goldberg of the Bradley University Economics Department has identified several significant ethnic residential boundaries in Peoria. The far south end of the city was primarily white and blue collar. The near south side was the traditional black ghetto until the expansion of opportunities increased migration to the "better" neighborhoods in the sixties and seventies. The "North Side" stretched along the river north of downtown and was inhabited largely by Appalachian whites. This area was termed "the Valley" section of the city. The area extending further west and north that overlooked the river valley was commonly referred to as "the Bluffs." It has here that the middle and upper classes lived. These people began, in the prosperous fifties, a migration to suburban areas such as Richwoods Township. Most residents of the Valley were sympathetic to Democratic candidates, whereas the Bluffs' constituency, many of whom were professionals and businessmen, consistently supported the Republican party.

The Caterpillar Tractor Company, which had become a nationally recognized producer of heavy machinery and construction equipment, was the most significant employer in Peoria and its adjacent towns. Peoria also was a major distilling center; the Hiram Walker Distillery was then the world's largest. For more than two decades, the labor history of Peoria, following the end of World War II, was a story of economic growth and prosperity.

The population of the city grew 6.45 percent between 1940 and 1950, from 105,087 to 111,856 persons.[7] The 1949 median income was a comparatively high $2,281, and area joblessness totals for December in 1946 and 1948 were only 2,300 and 2,100 persons, respectively.[8] Peoria's industrial diversity enabled it to serve as a major wartime production area. The Federal War Manpower Commission consistently classified the Peoria area as a Group 1 or Group 2 "labor shortage area."[9]

Caterpillar Tractor Company, as an important contributor to the war effort, found its labor-management relations influenced heavily by federal government agencies. The National War Labor Board set the tone and content of collective bargaining at Caterpillar. When Local 105 of the United Farm Equipment and Metal Workers of America (CIO) was officially certified by the NLRB as the East Peoria plant's bargaining representative in 1942, a pattern of bargaining between the company and the union took place. Contracts were one or two years in duration. In these early years of bargaining, the NWLB, usually through directive orders in dispute cases, specified the broad contract terms over which negotiations would proceed.[10] Under this process the union won provisions covering grievance arbitration, maintenance of membership, preferential seniority for union officials, and dues check-off. In addition, the issue of wage increases was often settled by NWLB order after the company balked at a mediator's suggested wage increase. The result was that under government action to prevent stoppages of war production because of labor disputes, the union was able to gain many rights and benefits that the company might otherwise have been unwilling to relinquish.

At its peak, the wartime labor force at Caterpillar totaled 26,000 employees at the firm's plant in East Peoria.[11] To meet its manpower needs, the company had begun to recruit workers from among the white and black southern agrarian population. At first only white workers were sought, but continuing high labor demand forced the company to seek black workers also. It was during the war years that local blacks as well as the new southern migrants began to be integrated into local industries in large numbers. Labor shortages also forced an expansion in female employment. Growth of these two segments of the labor force paralleled each other in the plants.

Industrial relations between Caterpillar and the UFE developed although negotiations remained strike-prone. A strike over a new contract in 1946 lasted for twenty-eight days. An eighteen-day strike in 1948 was precipitated by a continuing struggle for representation among the UFE and a number of union challengers, notably the UAW–AFL, the UAW–CIO, the IAM, and the Boilermakers union.

Local 105 successfully withstood the other local organizations for several years. However, the passage of the Taft–Hartley amendments to the National Labor Relations Act in 1947 provided the opportunity for renewed efforts by its rivals. The act mandated that all union officials sign sworn statements to the effect that they were not communists, nor had they ever been involved with communist organizations. The union's leadership decided not to sign such affidavits and, under the provisions of the act, lost the legal protection of the NLRB. With other unions requesting representation, Caterpillar decided it would not bargain with the UFE, and the resulting impasse quickly became a struggle for union survival. The leadership of Local 105 did not address the communist issue directly; its position simply was that the act's requirement was illegal. The union argued that the company was refusing to bargain with an elected bargaining unit representative. As the representation struggle intensified, other unions attempted to discredit the UFE as an organization sympathetic to communists.

The 1948 strike raised tensions throughout the community. There soon arose differences over the validity of the strike vote, as well as differing positions of rival union factions both opposed to and supportive of the strike effort. Community and religious leaders tried to intervene; on at least one occasion, a black churchman was threatened by members of the pro-strike faction. The UFE came to be perceived as an obstacle to ending the strike.

A representation election was held on May 12, 1948. The UFE was excluded because of the leadership's failure to comply with the Taft–Hartley provision. The election results necessitated a run-off election on May 20, 1948, between the two UAW unions to determine which one would become the plant's bargaining representative. On May 13, the UFE terminated the strike, and workers began returning to their jobs the next day. The UAW–CIO won the run-off election and was officially certified by the NLRB as the bargaining agent on June 10, 1948.

The years following the end of World War II were thus characterized by the replacement of the radical UFE by a more moderate UAW Local 974 as the official bargaining representative for Caterpillar workers. During this time, the basic conservatism of the community led to a concern primarily with jobs and income retainment and embraced labor movement activities only as long as these did not restrict the postwar "return to normalcy." The self-interests of residents and businessmen alike in postwar prosperity were not tolerant of labor disputes founded on what could arguably be termed communist sympathies. However, it is significant that the public apparently accepted the right of industrial workers to seek collective representation. There seemed to be no quarrel with labor organization actions to exact wage and benefit increases justifiably predicated on employers' ability to pay. As the local economy prospered throughout the fifties, labor disputes were based on issues of wage and benefit increases, and public tolerance of collective actions to gain such increases went no further than that. It is noteworthy that UAW strikes declined in number and duration from the fifties until the eighty-day stoppage of 1979.

In the fifties, unions were aggressive in their efforts to raise wages and benefits. Employers were enjoying steady growth and improvement of their businesses and were less reluctant to accede to union demands. As a consequence, employees in Peoria gained increasing compensation levels. The construction industry experienced heavy growth largely because of an increase in demand for new housing, primarily in suburban areas, although new factory construction and renovation also increased. In 1950, families' median income was just over $3,000 in Peoria and $3,127 in Peoria County, and the percentage of unemployed among the civilian labor force was estimated at 4.8.[12] By 1960, the median income of families in Peoria had risen to $6,387, and the percentage of males unemployed in the work force was estimated at 4.2.[13] The median value of owner-occupied single family homes rose from $8,617 in 1950 to $11,500 in 1960.[14]

Manufacturing, both of durable and nondurable goods, was the primary source of jobs in Peoria. The 1952 industrial directory of the Peoria Association of Commerce listed 165 firms engaged in some segment of manufacturing.[15] Of these 165 firms, six employed more than one thousand workers, and seven employed from five hundred to one thousand workers. One hundred and twenty-nine firms employed fewer than a hundred workers. It was estimated that Caterpillar had approximately thirty thousand workers in 1952.

Peoria's major products during this period were tractors, earth-moving equipment, motor graders, diesel engines, washing and ironing machines, paper bags, air conditioners, whiskey and spirits, beer, malleable castings, marine hardware, wire and steel, and industrial lift trucks.[16] In 1950, 34,481 employees were engaged in manufacturing according to U.S. census data; this was 40 percent of all those who were employed in Peoria. Wholesale and retail trade was the second largest employer in the city, with a total of 20,122 employees. Professional and related services were third highest, with 7,701 employees. This group was followed by transportation, communication, and other public utilities, which employed 7,228 workers. The diversity of industry served to give Peoria a strong economic base.

In contrast to later decades, few plant closures took place in the 1950s. The closure of the Gipps Brewery in the early fifties and the shutdown of Altorfer Brothers (ABC Washing Machines) in 1958 were two of the most significant during the decade. It was reported that Gipps was simply unable to compete successfully with the other local brewers (primarily the Pabst Company). The loss of jobs totaled approximately two hundred; some of the unemployed later found employment with Caterpillar. The shutdown of ABC's operations involved nearly eight hundred jobs and was felt much more by the community. The Altorfer Brothers Company was an old Peoria family firm. Its operations were purchased by the Kelvinator Division of American Motors Company several years before the Peoria closing. When the parent company decided to consolidate the Peoria operations into the Grand Rapids, Michigan, Kelvinator plant, the union at the plant, Local 1144 of the United

Electrical Workers, tried to convince management to keep the plant open. The union sought the help of local businessmen in the effort but finally had to settle for a negotiated severance agreement that came only after a two-week strike at the plant.[17]

Job losses were cushioned by new opportunities elsewhere in the area. Westinghouse and the R. G. LeTourneau concern, another old Peoria employer, built a new million-dollar complex on the riverfront in 1957–58.[18] Caterpillar hired 150 workers who lost their ABC jobs. The Pabst Company bought out a competitor and expanded operations at its Peoria Heights plant.

An article reprinted from *Business Week* magazine in the *Peoria Journal Star* had this comment on Peoria's labor history: "Formerly Peoria was thought of as a high wage town with a poor labor history, but the days of capricious labor behavior passed in the late 1940's when the Farm Equipment Workers of American was ousted from the old CIO—and from Peoria.[19]

The area had seen its share of labor strife, not all of which was based on issues of wages and working conditions. Of particular note was the bitter struggle of the president of the Toledo, Peoria, and Western railroad, George P. McNear, with the organization of trainmen. Their dispute predated World War II and was renewed with full force in 1945, when the government returned the carrier to McNear's private ownership. A violent strike ensued when McNear attempted to override bargaining and union status rights won by the unions during the war. At one point McNear attempted to operate a train headed by an armed gondola, and two union pickets were killed. Later, in March 1947, with the strike still going strong, McNear was killed in an as-yet unsolved murder. It was only then that the unions, bargaining with new management appointed by McNear's heirs, reached an agreement providing for standard wages and working conditions.[20]

The Peoria area had long been a stronghold of the construction trades and craft unions. The Sheetmetal Workers (Local 1), the Iron Workers (Local 112), and the Building Laborers (Local 165) were a few of the strong craft unions in the construction industry. The Teamsters Local 627 and the Operating Engineers were other strong unions. The postwar years also saw rapid organizations in the public sector. The city's Public Works Department manual laborers became represented by the Laborers. The Teamsters represented truckers and heavy equipment operators in that city department, as well as some garage mechanics. Carpenters Local 183 represented "facility maintenance" workers, while IBEW Local 34 bargained for employees in the city's traffic engineering department. All painting of city signs and buildings was done by members of the International Brotherhood of Painters Local 157 who were city employees. Also during the late forties and early fifties, Peoria's fire and police departments were organized by the International Association of Fire

Fighters Local 574 and the Policemen's Benevolent Association. Unions in other important economic sectors included the Distillery Workers Union, the Boilermakers, and the Hotel and Restaurant Employees union.

Peoria's government, until 1953, was of the mayor-aldermanic form, a system that exhibited all of the spoilage and corruption of machine politics. Allegiances in the city's voting wards were solidified by favors and favoritism. By the start of World War II, Peoria's reputation as a center for vice and corruption was known far and wide. As Herbert Gamburg observed: "In World War II, many young Peorians in their journeys throughout the country learned with some pique and humiliation of the ribald image of their town. Upon returning, a group of these veterans resolved to make over their community."[21]

This group of veterans, loosely organized under the Junior Chamber of Commerce, faced the problem of reforming city government that was semifeudal in form. Commenting on the dichotomy between the Bluffs and Valley sections of the city, Gamburg stated: "It is characteristic of cleavages of this type in American cities that the poorer strata, having the larger population and the most to gain from politics, have been politically organized in a fairly efficient way, while the wealthier classes have been busy striving for or stabilizing opulence. Thus, while decrying the lack of good leadership, the elite of Peoria had done little in an enduring way to stem the tide of municipal corruption."[22] While the business elite was often successful in electing candidates for mayor, the power of the system was too pervasive to succumb to a reform mayor's good intentions.

The returning veterans and reformers organized themselves into a movement called "Peorians for Council-Manager," (PCM). Their goal was to establish a city-manager form of government. Changing the traditional system of ward elections to an at-large system, taking parties out of local politics, and separating the legislative from the administrative branch of the government seemed to constitute a remedy to government corruption. The PCM launched a referendum drive and were successful in getting the issue placed before the voters. On a 1952 election day highlighted by an ice storm, the referendum carried by a vote of 15,000–7,000. The largely war-veteran PCM was able to benefit from liaisons with politically active corporate executives (primarily from Caterpillar and the Commercial Bank) in pressing their case for a more efficient system of city government.

However eight years later, in 1960, a referendum passed that was proposed by the old guard to reinstate the ward system. According to Gamburg, "Peoria is . . . in the throes of a rather incongruous political situation—ward elections combined with a city manager." Gamburg further described the political situation as "a body of activities paralleling the economic marketplace in goals and in consequences."[23] While unions in Peoria were generally perceived to favor Democrats, successful candidates, no matter what their party affiliation, were conservatives.

Looking back to the fifties, it appears that the economic expansion and the overall prosperity of the era permitted many Peorians to attain an improvement in individual status and success. Increasingly, Peorians appreciated the importance of the Caterpillar Tractor Company to the economic health of the community. Goldberg termed the situation as a "classic case of a one-industry town." A traditional coalition of liberals, unionists, and civil rights activists was conspicuously absent from the community.

Despite the high degree of unionization in Peoria, little attention was given to social issues. Labor movement coalitions were pragmatic, usually focused on a particular election or legislative issue, and usually were short-term in duration. The building trades, through the vehicle of the West Central Illinois Building Trades Council and UAW Local 974, generally carried the clout behind interunion activities. In the 1949 mayoral election, the Democratic challenger Joseph Malone, a member of Local 29 of the Typographical Union, defeated the Republican incumbent Carl Friebel by a margin of 575 votes. The victory margin was in the working-class Valley wards.[24] Malone was perceived as the man who could give back control of the city government to the people. He was endorsed by the Peoria Trades and Labor Assembly. In later elections, particularly after the PCM reform, however, the unions appear to have been content with being powerbrokers for candidates judged to be acceptable to them. There remained an attitude among residents that the city's business interests were quietly directing events.

In addition to the PCM program, significant political events in 1953 were the election of Myrlia J. Harms as the first woman council member, and Peoria's first selection as a *Look* magazine "All-American City." The *Look* award apparently was based on PCM activity and the move to clean up vice in the city. In 1959, the city elected its first black councilman. There was no indication of official labor movement activity in any of these three developments.

Peoria emerged from the World War II years poised to enjoy nearly twenty years of uninterrupted growth and prosperity. Although Peoria's economy "oscillated with larger national economic trends,"[25] it seemed that the business of Peoria was business. In 1956, the Caterpillar Company reported sales of $339 million and profits of $28 million in the last six months of the year, while employing twenty-seven thousand persons at the end of the year. The company began construction of a new general office building in 1963. In 1964, it announced its plan to build the Mapleton Foundry. From the old single plant in East Peoria during World War II, the company had, by 1979, expanded to seven area facilities representing about 40 percent of its worldwide employment of eighty-eight thousand. Thus, employment at Caterpillar grew almost uninterrupted to 37,312 by February, 1979.[26]

The *Peoria Journal Star,* in a November 1957 article, chronicled a building boom in the area. In 1962, the newspaper reported an employment expansion of 2,900 for 1961. In two articles in March 1962, the paper's headlines read: "Most Peoria Building Trades Wage Scales Higher than National Average" and "Peoria too Well Off to Qualify for President's Jobless Aid Plan."[27] In 1967, the Pabst Company announced plans to expand its Peoria Heights Brewery, and Keystone Steel and Wire began building new steel-making furnaces at its Bartonville, Illinois, complex.[28] In 1969, the Operating Engineers Local ratified a new contract reportedly providing a $9 per hour wage by 1974.[29] Illinois State Employment Service labor force annual averages of unemployment for the decade showed a bright picture (Table 9).

Table 9. Averages of Unemployment in Peoria, 1960–70

Year	Unemployment (%)
1960	4.6
1961	5.8
1962	4.8
1963	4.4
1964	3.4
1965	2.2
1966	2.9
1967	3.0
1968	3.2
1969	3.3
1970	3.1

Source: Illinois Department of Employment Security

Prosperity, however, was accompanied by a number of major strikes, including IBEW against television station WMBD in 1962; a 23–day strike by UAW Local 974 at Caterpillar in 1964, and an 89–day strike by the Independent Steel Workers Alliance against the Keystone Steel and Wire Company in 1966.[30]

The Keystone strike was the longest in the company's history. The firm, established in 1889, reported annual sales in 1980 of $200 million.[31] The ISWA, previously a company union, had been the bargaining agent at the plant since 1942. A main issue in the strike was seniority. Before the strike, labor-management relations had been characterized by the company's "Golden Rule" policy wherein executives were inclined to concede to union demands as long as they were not "unreasonable." The goal was to keep operations going. The firm looked on uninterrupted production as a market advantage and looked askance at organization attempts by the United Steelworkers. The union's policy was to give all grievances their day in court. However, as higher costs, restrictive work rules, and old equipment impeded productivity, the company felt a need to seek relief. Another factor may have been the lack of an outside union official to intervene with a broader perspective in labor-management disputes. Until 1966, there had never been a strike. As late as 1980, the company was still feeling the effects of the 1966 strike as it tried to recoup its loss of market.

All was not satisfactory in Peoria on the civil rights front, either. Blacks, as the last "immigrants" to arrive, were clearly relegated to low-status positions in terms of jobs and sociopolitical power. Elazar wrote that politically, "the Negroes were quiescent subjects within the civil community until the civil rights revolution."[32] Their numbers and lack of status generally did not enable Peoria's blacks to agitate effectively until the sixties. By 1960, the black population had increased to 9.5 percent of Peoria's population, the highest ratio among all minority groups.[33]

In the forties, it could be argued that wartime labor demand overrode overt racism in industrial employment, and that the numbers of blacks in Peoria were not large enough to constitute a threat to white employment. However, interviews indicated that the building trades generally excluded blacks and, initially, blacks found employment only in the dirtiest industrial jobs and in food service and other low-paying services. The industrial situation changed appreciably in the fifties largely because of the policy of many of the unions to treat all industrial workers equally. The construction trades were another matter, however. In Peoria, typically, a young man was recommended for apprenticeship by a father, uncle, or brother who was himself a tradesman. Given that blacks were initially excluded from the unions, there would be no familial tie to open the door for a black who aspired to be a carpenter or electrician.

The earliest seeds of black agitation began to sprout in the war years when southern blacks were recruited for industrial work. Long-time black residents of Peoria had some difficulty in getting better jobs and felt that they should have been recruited first. Moreover, the newly arrived blacks found life in Peoria more than acceptable than the conditions they left in the rural South. Thus, they were less disposed to "rock the boat" than the more established black citizenry. However, a small number of blacks did become doctors and lawyers and tradesmen such as barbers and drycleaners and provided leadership in the local NAACP, the Tri-County Urban League, and other self-help organizations. Peoria did not employ black schoolteachers until the fifties, however, and did not elect a black city councilman until 1959. A black member of the Boilermakers union observed that although the black vote was concentrated in the Valley wards, divisiveness and the co-optation of black leaders prevented the election of black candidates.

According to John Gwynn, executive director of the Peoria NAACP, stratification in the black community between the new arrivals and long-time residents made concerted action against prejudice difficult until the 1960s. He also noted that employment in city agencies, the utilities, and in managerial positions was largely closed to blacks until the 1960s. Census materials indicate that of 1,644 blacks employed in the Peoria SMSA, in 1950, 691 were employed in manufacturing. The largest number of these (326) were employed in nonelectrical machinery manufacturing. The other large manufacturing segment (128) was employed in meat products processing. In professional employment, out of 53 persons, 27 were found in welfare, religious, and membership organizations. Another 20 were listed in medical and allied services.[34] The median income in 1950 for the Peoria SMSA was $2,385; for blacks, the median income was $1,648. In 1960, among a total of 3,235 enumerated as employed, 772 (approximately 24 percent) were employed in professional (512, or 15.8 percent) as in personal service jobs (519, or 16 percent). Median income for all Peoria families in 1960 was $6,387, compared to the black family median income of $3,751 in 1959.[35] These figures indicate that most blacks were dependent on the industrial jobs. Blacks in professions or services generally served the black community; the income figures also show that blacks could not hope to make very large incomes from services rendered.

Equal employment opportunity was the overwhelming focus of civil rights activities in Peoria's black community in the sixties, which also meant agitation for opening up the construction and skilled trades to blacks. There was not much urban violence during this time, however. Most actions took the form of mass picketing and sit-ins.[36] Marches on the school board were staged to push for increased hiring of black teachers. Around 1963–64, a bus boycott of ten days' duration was organized to push for integration of the city's bus drivers. During this time, picketing and sit-ins also took place at the electric utility, Central Illinois Light Company, to protest the lack of black employment. A "Quality Education Committee" was formed to advocate school integration, its actions coinciding with the annexation of the Richwoods School District and a resulting busing controversy. Participants on this committee included the NAACP, the Urban League, and several executives from the Commercial Bank and the Caterpillar Company. The committee was still in existence as late as 1980, but performed primarily a citizens' oversight function on education quality.

By the late sixties, pressure was building for anti-discrimination programs in the craft unions. In December of 1964, the *Journal Star* reported on the extent of discrimination in the building trades under a headline, "Skilled Craft

Unions virtually Devoid of Negroes Here." The article disclosed survey results of 22 trade unions having an estimated total membership of 6,078,
including 34 to 39 blacks. The paper reported further that "of 341 trainees in
apprentice programs of the unions which have them, eight are Negroes."[37]
The response of union officials interviewed was that few blacks sought to be
considered for apprenticeships, and that those who did were unqualified.
None of those interviewed attributed the lack of black representation to
discrimination.

In 1968, it was announced that the Peoria Building Trades Council was
considering the recruitment of more blacks following an agreement between
the AFL–CIO and Secretary of Labor Willard Wirtz on anti-discrimination
and minority recruitment. As part of that agreement, the unions pledged "to
work with responsible civil rights groups to carry out the program"; specifics
were not provided.[38] After local civil rights groups, the Peoria Human Relations Commission, and union representatives engaged in extensive consulta-
tions, an agreement was reached in September 1969. The agreement was to
provide seventy-five jobs for blacks in the building trades within sixty days
and the establishment of a tripartite committee to administer the plan.[39] The
group, the "Construction Action Committee," was able to announce in March
1970 that thirty-five men had completed the first phase of the program. However, by 1971, disputes over what was a reasonable affirmative action goal
and what the goal should be based on led to the resignation of the union
representatives. Debate centered on squaring goals of 14 percent minority
participation (based on estimated area minority population) with requests for
a more modest goal of 4–5 percent, pushed by area contractors and the unions
and based on projected construction employment. The unions were particularly unhappy over what they perceived to be publicity negative to them. They
claimed to be willing to hire more blacks, but that the level of construction
work available was too low to justify a 14 percent figure. By 1972, the Federal
Office of Contract Compliance became involved, and all parties agreed to a
5 percent goal for minority hiring.

The black population percentage rose to 11.5 percent, a 51.8 percent change
between 1960 and 1970. In 1969, Peoria's median family income was
$10,665, whereas the figure for blacks was $7,039. Also in 1969, 7.7 percent
of Peoria's families were estimated to be below the poverty level, whereas
the figure was 23.5 percent for all black families.[40]

In 1966, the Armour Company announced plans to halt slaughtering and
processing operations in Peoria.[41] This closing was one of the first to highlight
the ensuing problem of job loss because of technological obsolescence. Peoria
was about to become familiar with the plight of low-skilled, chronically
unemployed workers. Local business, led by Caterpillar, began hard-core
training programs. It seemed that, economically, Peoria had discovered an

economic underclass with severe employment problems despite the general prosperity.

During the decade before 1980, Peoria's economy in general began to reflect problems, although outwardly the decade was a period of substantial prosperity for the community as a whole. The real estate and construction industries became overheated, home prices soared, and there was a shortage of skilled workers. Caterpillar added new facilities: in August 1977, its Peoria work force was 32,932; by February 1979, it stood at 37,312. At the same time, wage spirals and lowered productivity were reducing competitive ability and tipping the scales in favor of plant closing and consolidating operations elsewhere. By late 1979 and 1980, the labor market tightened as contraction hit even the giant Caterpillar enterprise. The construction industry also contracted sharply relative to the earlier boom.

Table 10. Unemployment in Peoria, 1970–80

Year	Unemployment Rate
1970	3.9
1971	4.0
1972	4.7
1973	3.4
1974	3.5
1975	4.2
1976	4.5
1977	5.3
1978	5.0
1979	5.4
1980	8.1

Source: Illinois Department of Employment Security

The contrast between the late seventies and the earlier decades was revealed in some basic unemployment statistics (Table 10). Not only did unemployment gradually rise, but the median income rise also marked a sharp rise in inflation that translated into slower living standards increases.

Labor relations had now matured over a thirty-year period. The president of the Teamsters in Peoria, Robert Barker, cited union success in maintaining union pay scales and the evolution of cooperative labor management relations. In the economic expansion period, he believed that the UAW had doubled its membership while the Teamsters' membership tripled. However, as Kalman Goldberg observed, the unions were no longer able to instill much sympathy for the Labor movement in the community. Indeed, several union officials cited the difficulties in getting strong support from the rank-and-file membership in progressive community and political activities. The president of the UAW local noted that union activism may be cyclical; that in times of prosperity the members take their gains for granted. Dale McNary, a former business agent for the Boilermakers, stated that below-average unemployment levels dissipated much of the force generated over social problems when there was high unemployment.

As interest rates and inflation rose, local firms found themselves saddled with high wage costs that could no longer be passed on in an economy with slackening product demand. As they looked for relief from restrictive work rules and for productivity improvement, they clashed with organized workers resistant to making concessions. Robert Schmitt of the Illinois State Employment Service believed that a two-tiered wage structure existed in Peoria: the high pay scale at Caterpillar and the wages paid by other concerns.

In the end, several severe shocks hit the community. In 1976, a local firm, Chipper Cartage, closed, allegedly because of refusing to give in to the wage demands of the Teamsters in contract negotiations.[42] The Hyster Company, also in 1976, closed its Peoria plant, with a loss of five hundred jobs. In the opinion of Lou Hesse, executive director of the Central Illinois Industrial Association, the company could no longer operate under a system in which the three independent unions at the three Central Illinois facilities bargained separately. Agreements with one bargaining unit would be a source of whipsawing by other units because there was no coordination of bargaining. The unions at Hyster were independent; without an international to intervene in disputes, there was no leverage for the firm. In 1977, there was an uproar over layoffs at Keystone Steel and Wire. The firm began moving some operations to the South in an effort, it said, to retain profitability.

In 1979, UAW Local 974 struck Caterpillar for three months, from October to December. The eighty-day strike was the longest to that date in Caterpillar's history. (It was to be surpassed by an even longer 205–day strike in 1982–83). Interview sources consulted agreed that the strike was ill-advised. The dispute seemed to arise from the feelings of maverick union officials with strongly held animosities toward company management. The impact on local business from the loss of payroll was dramatic, and Peoria became more divided as the strike progressed. In addition, Local 974's action was not sanctioned by the international, which provided no strike benefits. In 1980, the union was still setting its finances in order. Also, in 1980, the company, citing severe reductions in demand, announced layoffs of more than three thousand. The layoffs were termed "the most in a non-strike year since 1960." In August of 1980, the company began offering bonuses to managers who retired early.

Finally, beginning in 1979, Hiram Walker started a process leading to the shutdown of its Peoria operations. The final job loss totaled approximately 1,900 and destroyed the local Distillery Workers Union.[43] The company cited plant obsolescence and poor profitability, but as a former employee observed, "the company was merely running from the labor unions."

In summary, Peoria of 1945–80 can be characterized as a diverse industrial area blessed with increases in the standard of living and employment levels. If Peoria developed a reputation as a "bad labor town" in later years, it did not stem so much from militancy on labor's part, but rather appeared to be related to the economic reality of a "highly unionized, high priced" area—notably construction and manufacturing. For most of this period, Peoria indeed appeared to be recession-proof. Labor relations, generally speaking, exhibited a mature character, with the parties firmly in control of their respective roles in the relationship. Political conservatism and self-interest were prominent sociopolitical factors. Labor's limited concern with community programs contrasted significantly with the size and strength as their numbers increased and as civil rights issues became prominent for a time. It appears that the negative economic events of the late seventies, and particularly from 1980 onward took Peoria as a whole by surprise.

NOTES

This section is a revision of a report prepared by Curtis A. Scott.

1. Daniel M. Johnson and Rebecca Veach, *The Middle-Size Cities of Illinois* (Springfield: Sangamon State University, 1980), p. 22.

2. Daniel Elazar, *Cities of the Prairie: The Metropolitan Frontier and American Politics* (New York: Basic Books, 1970), p. 157.

3. Elazar, *Cities of the Prairie*, pp. 157–58.

4. Ibid., p. 158.

5. Ibid., p. 172.

6. Johnson and Veach, *The Middle-Size Cities*.

7. Ibid., p. 235.

8. State of Illinois Department of Labor, *Labor Market Trends* (Peoria), December 1946 and December 1948.

9. *Peoria Journal*, March 21, 1945.

10. David Stevens, *History of Labor Relations at Caterpillar*, unpub. manuscript, Peoria, p. 4.

11. Frank Campbell, "An Analysis of the Techniques of Racial Integration in Three Manufacturing Firms," master's thesis, University of Illinois Institute of Labor and Industrial Relations, 1954, p. 30.

12. U.S. Bureau of Census, *U.S. Census of Population, 1950* (Washington: Government Printing Office).

13. U.S. Bureau of the Census, 1960.

14. Taken from Table 30, "Economic, Demographic and Governmental Characteristics," Johnson and Veach, *The Middle-Size Cities*, p. 235.

15. Campbell, An Analysis of the Techniques," p. 21.

16. Ibid., pp. 22–23.

17. *Peoria Journal Star,* October 19, 1958.

18. The founder and president of Le Tourneau was a religious man who regularly began employees' shifts with prayers. When the company was challenged with a NLRB unfair labor practice charge, Le Tourneau denied personal responsibility and said his decisions came from God.

19. George W. May, *Student's History of Peoria County, Illinois* (Peoria: Peoria Historical Society, 1968).

20. Colston E. Warne, ed., *Labor in Postwar American* (Brooklyn: Remser Press, 1949), p. 453.

21. Herbert Gamburg, *The Escape from Politics: Power in Middle-Sized Cities,* preface.

22. Gamburg, *The Escape from Politics.*

23. Ibid., p. 21.

24. *Labor Temple News,* vol. 14, no. 12, February 8, 1949.

25. May, *Student's History,* p. 225.

26. *Peoria Journal Star,* April 1, 1979.

27. Ibid., March 17, 1962; March 28, 1962.

28. Ibid., January 11, 1967; January 30, 1967.

29. Ibid., May 22, 1969.

30. Ibid., February 15, 1962; February 1964; May 4, 1966.

31. Elmer Crager "Employee-Employer Relations, Keystone Group, Bartonville, Illinois," research paper, Institute of Labor and Industrial Relations, University of Illinois, 1980.

32. Elazar, *Cities of the Prairie,* p. 184.

33. U.S. Census of Population, 1960.

34. U.S. Census of Population, 1950.

35. U.S. Census of Population, 1960.

36. Interview with John Gwynn.

37. *Peoria Journal Star,* December 20, 1964.

38. Ibid., February 19, 1968.

39. Ibid., September 25, 1969.

40. U.S. Bureau of the Census, *Statistical Abstract,* (Washington: Government Printing Office, 1977).

41. *Peoria Journal Star,* December 9, 1966.

42. Ibid., July 17, 1976.

43. Ibid., April 13, 1979.

12

Decatur

In the early 1820s, most of the population in Central Illinois was concentrated around the rivers. By the late 1820s, however, there were enough people in the rural areas to warrant breaking the large rural counties into smaller administrative units; for example in 1829, Macon County was formed out of Shelby County. In that same year, Decatur became the Macon County seat.[1]

Decatur remained a rural town until 1854, when the Wabash Railroad came through. In 1857, Hieronymus Mueller opened a gun repair and machine shop, thus establishing the city's first industrial enterprise.[2] Decatur's central location also made it ideal as a marketing center for agricultural products going out of the area and retail products coming in. By 1860, Decatur's population was four thousand; it exceeded seven thousand by 1870.[3]

O. T. Banton, local historian, described Decatur's first industrial boom in 1870, when the Decatur Rolling Mill moved in from Cleveland, Ohio, and provided four hundred jobs. This event also created a real estate boom. Banton lists other industries that developed in Decatur. "There were brickyards, coal mines, breweries, cigar factories, textile and garment plants, farm equipment makers and grain processors. Many of these once stable businesses have disappeared."[4]

The first union established in Decatur was the Brotherhood of Locomotive Firemen and Engineers, Local No. 44, in 1880. Typographical Union Local No. 215, organized in 1883, and the Finishers and Plasterers Union Local 103, chartered in 1886, were the two next unions to be established.[5] During the 1930s, the International Ladies Garment Workers Union organized a number of small garment plants on an industrial union basis, but these plants closed shop in the post–World War II period. The first enduring industrial unions were organized in 1942 by the United Auto Workers, AFL. In the next years, Wagner Castings Company, Chambers-Bearing-Quinlan Company, A. W. Cash Company, and Houdaille-Hershey Corporation were organized by the UAW. The Mueller Company was organized in 1943, and the A. E. Staley Manufacturing Company in 1944. These and other UAW–AFL organized plants became part of the Allied Industrial Workers of America (AIW) when the AFL and CIO merged in 1955.[6]

By 1980, there were approximately 120 union locals in Macon County: in addition to the building trades, seventeen were AIW affiliates, and nine were comprised of railroad workers. In addition, there were the Rubber Workers, the UAW, and IBEW, and the Communication Workers as well as several public employee organizations—teachers, police, firefighters, and miscellaneous municipal workers.

The Trades and Labor Assembly (TLA) was formed in Decatur in 1895. After a temporary setback in 1898, it was reactivated and claimed to represent some 2,500 unionists in 1900. Long dominated by the AFL craft unions, the Assembly included a number of industrial unions as well in the post-World War II period. Most of the AIW locals remained aloof, although a number affiliated and the AIW periodically cooperated with the Assembly on political and social issues. In 1980, the TLA had about thirty-five affiliates representing between twenty-five and thirty thousand workers.

The immediate post-World War II period was one of rapid industrial growth for Decatur. The expansion Decatur experienced came about "largely through the opening of plants by international firms."[7] Daniel Elazar commented that a large number of nationally known companies opened branches in Decatur in order to exploit its good location and reportedly good labor market.[8] These companies included General Electric (1947), Marvel-Schebler Division of Borg-Warner (1948), and Caterpillar (1954).

A major influence on the industrialization of Decatur after World War II was the city's excellent industrial performance during the war. Houdaille-Hershey made a "top-secret" war product that turned out to be a barrier (shell) for an atomic bomb; Mueller's made shell casings (for which it received an honorary army and navy E flag for meritorious performance); A. W. Cash Valve made air regulators; and numerous other companies such as A. W. Cash, Chambers-Bearing-Quinlan, Decatur Pump, and Wagner Castings contributed to the war effort.[9]

Decatur was able to gear up quickly for war production partly because Henry Bowles and John Wagner of the Association (later Chamber) of Commerce "developed a complete inventory of machines, manpower, tools, skills, and training [of the people] of the city of Decatur and presented it to the War Board in Washington in order to best use the facilities Decatur had."[10] The War Production Board used this inventory to direct federal contracts to Decatur businesses, and after the war prospective business owners made plant-locating decisions with it. Edwin Huntley, Bowles's successor at the chamber, believed that this inventory was a major attraction to business.[11]

Before the postwar companies moved into the city, labor-management relations were "fraternal." According to a variety of knowledgeable observers, the employers and employees could "talk to each other" and "work out their problems."[12] A paternalistic atmosphere was clearly evidenced at the "local" companies such as Staley's, Mueller's, and Wagner Castings. This situation changed, however, when Caterpillar, Archer-Daniels-Midland, GE, and later Firestone came to Decatur. Ray Maulden, a prominent unionist, commented that "GE brought into this area what is known as Boulwarism. It is something labor absolutely refuses to deal with."[13]

Vern Talbott, formerly personnel director at Borg-Warner, felt that because many of these new companies had plants across the nation or abroad, they were used to dealing with Labor on a large scale. This attitude was less personal than Decatur labor was used to, and many viewed it antagonistically. Also, the new companies had no stake in the community. Mueller's, on the other hand, had grown from Decatur's first shop into one of its larger employers. The company was instrumental in forming the Decatur Chamber of Commerce in 1903.[14] Staley's was long the community's largest employer, and the company had encouraged the building of Lake Decatur in 1920–22. The company's president had wanted to stay in the city, so he put pressure on the Chamber of Commerce and the city government to dam the Sangamon River.[15] Edwin Huntley commented on the Staley dam: "Because we built the lake, we were able to keep Staley's and we attracted other heavy industry here. If we didn't have the lake, we would be another Mattoon or Shelbyville [referring to size and concentration of industry]."[16]

These two companies and others such as Wagner's and A. W. Cash Valve were heavily involved in the community and their owners/executives were active, visible members of the community. Donald Wray commented on these family-company leaders: "They developed a feeling of social and civic responsibility and a willingness to meet new situations in a problem-solving manner."[17] The managements of ADM, GE, Borg-Warner, Caterpillar, and other new companies were initially not so involved. These companies were attracted to Decatur because of its labor market and the desire of the people of Decatur for new businesses. However, with the companies came new, powerful people who were to change the status quo.

Shortly before these new companies entered Decatur, another event occurred that also changed labor-management relations. Joseph O'Dell, a building trades official, believed that "WW II helped union [organizing] activity because government and industry didn't have time to take issue with the union. They had to mobilize, so they allowed unions to come in and be the bargaining agents for the war plants (and in the construction industry I suppose it was the same way). They were too preoccupied with winning the war to notice whether the workers were union or nonunion."[18]

The large family-owned businesses were organized during the war, which was an opportune time for the unions because these companies could not oppose them. Most of the union organizing activity was led by Earl Heaton, then regional director of the UAW–AFL. Heaton, a vigorous and able man, was reportedly particularly disliked at Staley's: "When Staley's was approached by a union, the president of the company [A. E. Staley, Jr.] said they would close their doors rather than have a union."[19] Merrill Lindsay, newspaper publisher and former president of the Chamber of Commerce, commented: "A lot of businessmen didn't like it [the unions' organizing activity], and they thought those Joes didn't have any business coming into town and organizing the workers here."[20]

Furthermore, Heaton was not a Decaturite. This was important because he gave the impression that he "didn't care about Decatur, only about the unions."[21] For companies that placed pride on personal atmosphere and familiarity between employer and employees, the problems associated with bringing in a union, especially one initiated by an outsider, were magnified.

A third event that shaped the labor relations in Decatur was the death of A. E. Staley in 1940 and the retirement of Adolph Mueller in 1939. These men were old-line businessmen who strongly opposed industrial unionism. They were two of the most active and outspoken business leaders in the community, and their deaths created changes in the management structures and outlooks of their respective companies. These changes "facilitated the adjustment process and minimized conflict between the old and the new orders."[22]

All available information indicates that except for understandable initial difficulties with the unions (such as in negotiating first contracts), the employer-employee relations were exceptionally good during the late fifties. Such a relationship existed at Mueller's, as is evidenced in the following excerpt from *Plant Union-Management Relations: From Practice to Theory*, a case study done on Mueller's between 1955 and 1959:

> We found a relationship in which the union had a relatively high level of participation in decision-making about employment conditions, both sides were satisfied with the union role, the parties were extremely successful in settling their differences without the aid of conciliators or arbitrators, pressure was generally absent, the emotional tone of contract negotiations and grievance settlement was usually calm, and the attitudes of the two sides were favorable to each other. Although there had been two changes in plant managers and one of these managers had been criticized by the unions as too production-minded and not enough human-relations-minded, these changes appear not to have affected the relation significantly . . .[23]

The labor-management relations that Mueller's enjoyed seemed to be a fairly accurate barometer of the relations in the whole community. Decatur enjoyed a reputation as a town free of labor troubles, and small businesses trickled in throughout the fifties.[24] Jack Hartley of the AIW, however, believed that the employers had only a "grudging acceptance" of the unions, although the negotiations were not as bitter as they were to become later.

Throughout the fifties, Decatur and Macon County continued to grow in population and in commercial enterprise. Many of those people who were attracted to Decatur in the forties settled there as residents, as the increase in home ownership from 7,838 in 1940 to 17,685 in 1960 indicates. The city also dominated the surrounding area in terms of retail trade. The population serviced by Decatur retail business numbered 277,000, and 40 percent of the work force was engaged in services and commercial activity.[25] Industry was diversified as well. It included manufacturing of iron and gas products, chemical and pharmaceutical compounds, meat, corn and soy products, plastics, garments, and other miscellaneous items.[26] The unions (both industrial and craft) were reported in 1955 to have the busiest work year since 1946. Workers in locals from surrounding counties were called in to do construction work.[27]

The garment industry was one exception to the general trend during the fifties. Production and employment in the industry reached a peak between 1930 and 1940, then declined sharply. During the fifties, five garment firms closed, and employment fell from two thousand in 1930 to three hundred in 1958.[28] Merrill Lindsay explained this decline: "The garment workers had a nasty strike here right after WW II and those ladies had a terrible time getting their wages. Afterwards there was only one garment factory left in town. The employers said they could not pay union wages and sell their product at competitive prices."[29]

During the fifties, the Decatur Chamber of Commerce (the association revived its original name in 1967) was particularly active in promoting the city's good reputation. Edwin Huntley commented: "Although you need the cooperation on the job for high production, you [also] need good schools, churches, and roads and parks, and this is what the chamber is all about—bringing all these things together." Huntley went on to say that the Decatur Chamber of Commerce was also one of the most progressive chambers in the area. It was one of the first to develop a city plan (in the twenties), have a church advancement committee, and have a safety committee to "look into safety" at industrial plants.[30] Wray commented that the chamber "attempted to define itself as the major integrating structure of the city. It [had] achieved this goal insofar as the business class was concerned; it had attempted to establish collaboration with organized labor by incorporating union leaders in its activities."[31] Several labor leaders were members of the construction and other committees of the chamber. Their initial involvement aroused resentment among some employers; however, they were accepted more easily in the later war years. By this time, the large manufacturers had "recognized organized labor as a social, economic and political force which had to be incorporated in any attempt to plan and control city development."[32] During the postwar housing shortage, the chamber construction committee (with union representatives) was instrumental in maintaining a working relationship between business and labor.[33]

Despite these friendly overtures to labor leaders, the chamber was distinctly a businessmen's organization. Business leaders emphasized constantly the need for getting the "right type" of union representative before any cooperation was possible. In defining the "right type," they specified ability to recognize common needs that could be jointly achieved, ability to conduct group meetings and make public appearances, and such personal qualities as good speech, proper manners, and acceptable personal appearance. These considerations for cooperative action were rather clearly distinguished from the business class appraisal of the union leaders in representing the interests of the rank and file.[34] Charles "Bud" Riley of the AIW in 1981 explained it this way: "I think the chamber's policies and problems are completely different [from the unions']. I think we both have common interests like bringing new business to Decatur, and that we have good schools . . . but outside of that, when it comes to the basic philosophy of the union, about whether there ought to be unions or not, I don't think you'll find us in agreement."[35]

The Chamber of Commerce was also involved in the city government. Edwin Huntley commented that he didn't know how two groups "could have worked together better," and that even though "a little arm-twisting went on," a good working relationship existed. The chamber and the leading newspaper (*Decatur Herald and Review*) were instrumental in the city's adoption of the council-manager form of government in 1958. In the early fifties, Decatur won the "All-American City Award" given by the U.S. Chamber of Commerce. Decatur received the award "not because of the material goods Decatur has, rather for the atmosphere of good working conditions and the cooperation of the people."[36]

The relationship between organized labor and city government was a good one as well. Edwin Huntley said: "There has been someone from labor on the city council for years and years." In 1957, Mayor Clarence Sablotny sent a letter to the Allied Industrial Workers praising contributions by locals and union leaders toward civic endeavors. The union was "highly instrumental in the growth of this city in a climate truly beneficial to the best interests of the general public."[37]

However, there was no one power base (i.e., union, political organization, company, or the Chamber of Commerce) that dominated in Decatur. The diversity of industry and commercial business "forced the expression of more general goals through the mechanism of community-based organizations, rather than through the direct action of individual managements or union locals."[38]

Another factor that apparently contributed to the general stability was the diversity of ethnic and religious groups in the community and the absence of any dominant one. The black population was small—about 3,400, although it grew rapidly after 1950, reaching a figure of about 13,000 in 1980, or 10.2 percent of the 127,000 population. Black-white relations in the workplace as well as in the community at large were not perceived as significantly diverse. As Bud Riley stated, "race and ethic factors are not important around here."

Unfortunately, the era of harmony was not to endure. On January 1, 1966, in the midst of a lengthy UAW Caterpillar strike, the Association of Commerce issued the following statement:

The Association of Commerce believes the current situation at Caterpillar Tractor Co. is one to be resolved between company management and union officials. However, the Association regrets the unfortunate reputation Decatur is acquiring as a "poor labor town." The evidence indicates that the labor climate and the rash of strikes during the past year led to the refusal of the Graf-Apsco Co. to locate in Decatur. The company manufactures optical and other scientific instruments. Mr. J. M. Graf cancelled an appointment with Association officials after arriving in Decatur and reading about local strikes. He said that his firm had enough trouble without coming to Decatur to look for it.

Decatur has in the past enjoyed a reputation as a good labor town. Until several lengthy strikes occurred at major manufacturing plants in the community last year, it was rare for a labor dispute to last more than a few days at a time. We were proud that differences could usually be settled at the negotiating table rather than through long drawn-out work stoppages in which frequently nobody is the winner. We all lose—the worker, the company, and the community. It will take years to reestablish our earlier image.

It has been stated that the current strike is costing Caterpillar employees nearly $100,000 a day. The loss becomes even more staggering when it is considered that, on the average, a dollar changes hands from five to seven times before it leaves the community.

We urgently hope that an early agreement will be reached that is fair to all parties.[39]

The strike at Caterpillar lasted seventy-one days and affected three thousand workers. This strike and the chamber statement seem to indicate that the good labor relations in Decatur had eroded in this period. In the early sixties, not only were there few strikes, but they were also short—generally two or three days. By the mid-sixties, strikes were more numerous and longer; in 1967–68, there were thirteen strikes in Decatur. One strike lasted three days, one lasted ten days, one lasted eleven days, and the rest ranged from 14 to 91 days. Nonetheless, a 1969 Chamber statement on work stoppages reported: "Only 3 unions have had more than 2 stoppages and account for 37 of the total number [49] of stoppages [in the past 12 years]. There has been no labor strife and when community improvement or education was involved unions were in most cases responsible for the passage of a referendum which would increase taxes."[40]

This optimistic chamber position of the sixties was generally supported by the interviewees of the 1980s, although they also agreed that there were some problems. Chamber president Richard Lutovsky commented: "Our problems have been with the building trades—common laborers, carpenters, teamsters—in the relations with the contractors. We have projects that are bidding 20 percent high in Decatur, because of the low productivity. That is part of the problem with the reputation we have."[41]

Some of the problems in the industrial sector were also allegedly caused by new managers at some of the older firms. Bud Riley of the AIW commented that Mueller's, which had a two-week strike in 1968, and Staley's, which was struck for more than eighty days in 1970, got so large that "other people came in to run the business[es] and that [fraternal] relationship is no longer there. Once someone says, 'Well this is the way we used to do it', the company takes the position that, 'well, those people aren't here anymore,' and they in effect say that [they] can't be bothered or assumed to take responsibility for their liabilities." So it seems that for a second time, the fraternal feeling in labor relations had been disrupted. Riley gave another example of how this "new management" changed the status quo in Decatur:

> Over at Mississippi Valley we had a strike in 1977. Prior to that time it was pretty much owned by local people. Then a fellow named Hall from St. Louis, and following Hall some people from Bristol, VA, and Bristol Steel Co. bought it. We had a strike, it was quite a lengthy strike; we had had strikes there before. And this time they immediately began hiring strike-breakers. They put an ad in the paper, set up a hiring hall, and hired about 150 workers. That was very rare for the town of Decatur, because in the past employers had not done that. And once that happened and other strikes came along, we had a strike at Borg-Warner, and they hired strike replacements. That is something that has gotten started in this town. It was also very rare for employees to cross the picket line, but times were kind of bad and people were looking for jobs.[42]

Riley's comment on times being bad was illustrative of the dependence the Decatur economy of the seventies had on the national economy. A substantial percent of the work force was involved in heavy manufacturing, and 50 percent of the city's income was generated from industrial firms according to Lutovsky. As a result Decatur began to suffer more from swings in the national economy than did less-industrialized towns. Unemployment grew from a low of 2.8 percent in 1973 to 9.6 percent in 1975 and, after a moderate recovery, to 11.9 percent in 1980. This problem did not enhance the relationship between labor and management.

Ironically, one of the most bitter and highly publicized strikes in Decatur history occurred not in construction or manufacturing industry, but in the public schools.[43] It began after a bitter controversy over school integration and busing in the late sixties led to the election of a highly conservative school board, which also opposed unionism. The contract with the Decatur Education Association, an affiliate of the IEA, was to expire August 15, 1971, and the new board majority refused to budge from its opening position that included removing limits on class size, reinstituting unlimited transfer policy, and eliminating binding grievance arbitration. Also, the teachers were to lose the salary index they had struck for and won in 1966. An impasse in negotiations was declared in June, and in August, a fact-finder from the University of Chicago, Joel Seidman, was called in. He presented a report to the school board on August 24, the day before school was open. His report challenged the soundness of the board's position. The teachers were ordered into the classrooms by the board the following day. The teachers refused, and 763 of them struck. Only three of the thirty-eight schools in Decatur opened, including one staffed by twenty members of the rival Illinois Federation of Teachers.

The strike caused tremendous upheaval in the community, although much sentiment seemed to favor the teachers. The two local newspapers also took pro-teacher stances and urged renewed negotiations. Despite these attitudes, the board fired fourteen of a hundred nontenured teachers in the DEA, an act that became a major issue in the strike.

During the second week of the strike, Michael Bakalis, Illinois State Superintendent of Public Instruction, directed his staff to undertake mediation, which went on for five days without success. He then attempted to impose a settlement that the teachers voted to accept, but the board rejected. The Bakalis proposal called for the school board to rehire the fourteen fired teachers, but the board refused on the grounds that the superintendent exceeded his legal authority. After fourteen days, the teachers were ordered back to work by a court edict and the Bakalis settlement proposal was set aside. Although the school board achieved most of its objectives, the weakened association survived, and a few years later a newly elected board replaced the hard-liners. Although collective bargaining was resumed, the strike had a traumatic and enduring effect on the association.

Ray Mauden, of the Rubber Workers and a labor liaison to United Way, thought that many people in the community did not agree with the good relations idea: "I think the uneducated people [about union-management relations] in the community view the unions as trying to get too much power. It's a majority of the people, but I think we are whittling away at that majority, especially in the past year. It includes some uneducated union members. It's been the attitude for a long time."[44]

Bud Riley agreed: "But overall I think, the labor relations in Decatur are exceptionally good. There are certain people that don't feel that way in the labor movement. If Rick Lutovsky has a problem he calls me if I can help, and vice versa. On the other hand, there is bitter hatred between the National Chamber of commerce and the AFL-CIO. But if we can help each other, we do it. People who don't think they're good just don't get involved to find out what's happening and what the problems are."

When asked how their union members felt about their unions, interviewees gave quite different answers. Jack Hartley, from the AIW, said: "People don't care about their unions. If you ask a guy on the street what International he belongs to, he probably couldn't tell you. The days of the old crusades are over. The only thing the members ask is 'what have you [the unions] done for me today?' There are no union people to organize the white-collar people. People in the union only view it as 'they take money out of their paychecks every week'—no active involvement, no caring."[45]

Ray Maulden saw it the same way, except he felt that members are "taking a second look at what the unions can do for them. It's not 100 percent but the problems in the past have been getting to younger union members. They have not realized what it was like when we fought for dignity, equity, and justice. They have had it too good for too long."[46]

Bud Riley agreed that union members were changing their attitudes about union: "Now that times are beginning to get tough again, and people are getting laid off, they are getting together. They realize how important it is to have a contract to protect their jobs if they have seniority and to have insurance, unemployment benefits. I think the unions are more important to the people again. I think the feelings about the union are linked to the economy."[47]

Joe O'Dell of the building trades thought that craft workers were more active in their unions:

> They probably have more enthusiasm about their union than, say, an industrial union, because they've had to work so darn hard to get in the apprenticeship program. And besides this being a source of their employment, whereas factory workers envision theirselves belonging more to Caterpillar's or Mueller's than to AIW, whereas the casual nature of employment in the construction industry makes these people of ours come through the hiring hall fairly often. So they see this as their source of employment rather than a specific company. So they take a very special interest. Of course, you're always going to have nominal members, but I would say that that's a very small percentage. We've got a group that is really proud of their organization, really proud of their trade, and it works for a real good attitude for the membership.
>
> We have a pretty good turnout for union meetings. Not everyone shows up every night, you've always got some hardcore zealots, and a group that is not that committed, but like when there's a contract. I would characterize our union as a strong union. They all have a lot of respect—they realize everyone out there is a skilled tradesman.[48]

Were the craft union members' strong loyalties to their unions linked to the problems in the building trades that Richard Lutovsky cited? The answer was unclear, but what was interesting was that members of the Building Trades Council, the governing body of the crafts unions, did not think there was a problem.

Despite the earlier evidence to the contrary, both Jerry Koehler and Bud Riley felt that there was no history of bad feelings between union and nonunion workers in Decatur. Koehler said that there were only two nonunion contractors in the Decatur area, and "we get into picket situations with them sometimes, but we still speak to each other when we see them on the street." Koehler cited a problem with nonunion labor during the construction of a local restaurant: "The contractor hired nonunion labor, which was a sore spot because the unemployment in trades in town was high. We were picketing, but it was peaceful. We also figured that the contractor would have to go union with cement, however, because all the cement companies in town were unionized. However, when he was ready for cement, he had bought his own cement company! The restaurant got built, but it closed a short time after it opened."[49]

Overall the craft union representatives gave the impression that the relations with the contractors and in the community in general were good. Koehler noted, however, that if it had not been for the Illinois Power Company's atomic energy project in nearby Clinton, unemployment levels could have risen to 20 percent during the late seventies.

Ray Maulden, like the other interviewees, felt that Decatur considered itself a "union town," but that some problems existed with the images the union had. Maulden spoke of the 1976 Firestone strike when he was president of the United Rubber Workers local: "You should have read some of my 'Fan Mail.' The general population believed that I was responsible by myself; that I could by myself have all those people back up to work. What they don't realize [is] that it takes a vote from the rank and file to call a strike."

Joe O'Dell also said that the building trades "had some pretty rough times . . . , and our image has suffered because of it." What O'Dell was referring to in particular was a huge demonstration in 1980 by the buildings trades at Archer-Daniels-Midland. The company had subcontracted out work on a new grain alcohol building and the subcontractors brought in out-of-state, nonunion workers for the job. A large body of a thousand Decatur-area building tradesmen gathered to protest the use of nonunion labor on the ADM grounds, and some force was used to break up the demonstration. Several cars were overturned, and windows and fences were broken.[50]

In the aftermath of the demonstration, the building trades leaders realized that the negative community reaction, as well as the reputation Decatur had acquired as a poor labor town, was hurting their industry, as well as the community as a whole. In a way, the ADM demonstration was a last straw for labor—management relations in Decatur, and leaders on both sides realized that a change was imperative. This realization resulted in the formation in 1981 of the Decatur Area Labor-Management Committee, which had representatives from Labor, the Chamber of Commerce, Millikin University, and the Council of Community Services. The goals of the committee were to broaden the community's knowledge about issues affecting labor and management; to provide an open forum for discussions; and to promote the benefits of the Decatur area to prospective and established businesses and industries in order to move toward fuller employment of the work force.

In the governmental area, Ray Maulden indicated that there was some labor discontent with the council-manager government: "He [the city manager] is viewed as having too much power, and he has too much say so as to who has a job. He is hired and gets fired by the city council, and I think there is dissatisfaction with a person who has too much power without being elected."[51] Richard Lutovsky, in contrast, commented that the Chamber of Commerce and the population in general were satisfied with the present form of government, and that it was a minority that "makes a lot of noise."[52]

Was the dissatisfaction that Ray Maulden perceived caused by an inadequacy of labor representation of the city council? But Riley did not think so: "We have two people on the city council that are union people. I don't think it would be beneficial to have more union influence in the city council. I think that if an issue comes up that really affects you, you're certainly going to rally around or get a petition to let the city council know that it is an important issue, or that they should take one course of action or another."[53]

Jerry Koehler felt that the local politicians made an effort to include labor in the city council: "They [the local politicians] ask us to serve on committees and they seek union representation on just about everything that goes on communitywide. We don't have enough people in the city government, but most of it is related to apathy. People just don't care. It's not until it hits you that you get involved."[54]

Decatur moved, during the first two postwar decades, from a climate of business paternalism to a state of mature and harmonious collective bargaining coupled with extensive labor involvement in community life. In the seventies, however, the economy of the community deteriorated, and industrial relationships hardened, particularly as outside ownership interest came to the fore. That the earlier forces of accommodation were still influential, however, was reflected in the formation of the Decatur Area Labor-Management Committee in 1981.

NOTES

This section is a revision of a report prepared by Janet Snow-Godfrey.

1. Daniel M. Johnson and Barbara Veach, *Middle-Size Cities of Illinois* (Springfield: Sangamon State University, 1980), p. 70.

2. Oliver T. Banton, *History of Macon County* (Decatur: Macon County Historical Society, 1976), p. 216.

3. Johnson and Veach, *Middle-Size Cities of Illinois*, p. 780.

4. Banton, *History of Macon County*, p. 220.

5. Ibid., pp. 269–71.

6. Ibid., p. 268.

7. Ibid., p. 232.

8. Daniel Elazar, *Cities of the Prairie: The Metropolitan Frontier and American Politics* (New York: Basic Books, 1970), pp. 82–83.

9. Elazar, *Cities of the Prairie*, pp. 398–400.

10. Interview with Edwin Huntley, former secretary, Decatur Chamber of Commerce.

11. Ibid.

12. Interview with Merrill Lindsay, former publisher, *Decatur Herald and Review*.

13. Interview with Ray Maulden, labor liaison, Council of Community Services.

14. Interview with Edwin Huntley.

15. Banton, *History of Macon County*, p. 250.

16. Interview with Edwin Huntley.

17. Donald Wray, in Milton Derber et al., *Labor-Management Relations in Illini City* (Urbana: University of Illinois Institute of Labor and Industrial Relations, 1953), p. 60.

18. Interview with Joseph O'Dell, business agent, Plumbers and Pipefitters, and president of Decatur Building and Construction Trades Council.

19. Interview with Edwin Huntley.

20. Interview with Merrill Lindsay.

21. Interview with Jack Hartley, regional representative, AIW.

22. Wray, *Labor-Management Relations*, p. 61.

23. Milton Derber et al., *Plant Union-Management Relations: From Practice to Theory* (Urbana: University of Illinois Institute of Labor and Industrial Relations, 1965), pp. 82–83.

24. See the Chamber of Commerce's list of manufacturers.

25. Wray, *Labor Management Relations*, pp. 40–41.

26. Ibid., p. 41.

27. *Decatur Herald and Review*, January 1, 1956, p. 3.

28. Banton, *History of Macon County*, p. 222.

29. Interview with Merrill Lindsay.

30. Interview with Edwin Huntley.

31. Wray, *Labor-Management Relations*, p. 14.

32. Ibid., p. 91.

33. Ibid., p. 92.

34. Ibid., p. 97.

35. Charles "Bud" Riley, regional representative, AIW.

36. Interview with Edwin Huntley.

37. *Allied Industrial Worker*, February 1958, p. 6.

38. Wray, *Labor-Management Relations*, p. 41.

39. Statement provided by the Association of Commerce.

40. Ibid.

41. Interview with Richard Lutovsky.

42. Interview with Bud Riley.

43. Most of the following discussion on the school strike is based on materials compiled by Vernon Talbott, associate professor, University of Illinois Institute of Labor and Industrial Relations.

44. Interview with Ray Maulden.

45. Interview with Jack Hartley.

46. Interview with Ray Maulden.

47. Interview with Bud Riley.

48. Interview with Joe O'Dell.

49. Interview with Jerry Koehler.

50. Interview with Joe O'Dell.

51. Interview with Ray Maulden.

52. Interview with Richard Lutovsky.

53. Interview with Bud Riley.

54. Interview with Jerry Koehler.

13

East St. Louis

East St. Louis was incorporated in 1865. The large tracts of open land on the east side of the Mississippi River were attractive to heavy industries supplying goods to St. Louis and other midwestern cities. Stockyards were opened in 1873, just outside the city limits, and soon the area became one of the largest pork-producing centers in the world. "Activity in other industrial enclaves surrounding East St. Louis made for numerous employment opportunities in the first two decades of the 20th century."[1] Before 1917, goods shipped by rail as far as East St. Louis had to be ferried across the river; in that year the Municipal Bridge was opened, allowing railroad transport to flourish. From that time, railroads and warehousing occupied extensive land areas along the East St. Louis riverfront. Meatpacking and nondurable goods manufacturing became the major employing industries, along with the railroads. As recently as 1973, East St. Louis ranked second only to Chicago in the amount of acreage devoted to rail use.[2] From 1900 to 1950, the city's population increased steadily, reflecting the attraction of its labor-intensive industries for largely unskilled workers. The population was 29,655 in 1900, 66,767 in 1920, 75,609 in 1940, and 82,295 in 1950.

As in the case of Peoria, the earliest settlers of the Madison-St. Clair County area (in which East St. Louis is located) were from the South: "The civil communities of those two counties, located as they are on the upper edge of the greater South, have remained quite Southern in culture and orientation."[3] Among foreign immigrant settlers, the Germans were prominent in neighboring Belleville, and the French influence was also significant in St. Clair County: "As an identifiable group, however, the French element has disappeared. The French who remain in St. Clair County are concentrated in their village of Cahokia and have had little impact as a group beyond their local parish, where they maintain a very distinctive subculture."[4]

After World War I, the pattern of economic development resulted in the recruitment of a more homogeneous but bimodal population consisting of ethnic white and southern black immigrants. The large numbers of unskilled workers coming to the city reflected the growth of a highly dependent population. These dependents were often manipulated by business and political interests: "Racial antagonisms were inflamed by politicians running racist campaigns and companies threatening union organizers and strikers with replacement by black workers. Deep fear and suspicion of blacks by whites combined with widespread lawlessness and corruption in East St. Louis, culminated in the bloody race riot of July 2, 1917, which took 46 lives, 39 of them black."[5]

Such lawlessness and corruption were important features of life in East St. Louis for most of its history. Most of the major firms in town incorporated the areas contiguous to their operations into "tax towns." National City, for example, was incorporated in 1907 by several meatpackers and sat just upriver from the city's northernmost border. The downriver community of Sauget was for years little more than the Monsanto Company's own satellite city. These tax towns "were characterized by absentee ownership, unfair labor practices, no municipal services or levies, and under-assessment for school taxation purposes."[6] In the period 1945–80, the city would come to feel the full impact of such problems as insufficient tax revenues, irresponsible company policies, and old, obsolete factories.

With the end of World War II came the beginning of the city's steady economic decline. According to statistics from the Illinois Department of Labor's *Labor Market Trends* for December 1946, total unemployment in Madison–St. Clair Counties was 3,850, compared to 2,300 in the Peoria–Pekin area. By December 1948, the figure for Peoria–Pekin was reduced to 2,100, whereas unemployment in Madison–St. Clair Counties had spiraled to 5,750. This occurred at a time when East St. Louis's population was approaching 82,000, and Peoria's was 111,000. The reason for the city's loss of jobs in the postwar period lay in the technological obsolescence of many of its largest factories. According to most of those interviewed in East St. Louis, this was the single most significant development and a factor that distinguished the city from other sizable nearby communities such as Alton and Granite City. Many of the plants were in need of extensive capital investment, but with the high percentage of absentee ownership, there was little inclination to make the needed investments. Perhaps because few company officials lived in the city they had no appreciation of the damage being done there. Charles Mohr, president of the Machinists Local in Alton, said simply that the companies "bled" the plants.

The Institute of Labor and Industrial Relations at the University of Illinois did a study of the area in 1955–56. Among its findings was that "of the 18 largest manufacturing establishments, all but two originated prior to 1930."[7] It further found that one-third of all workers were employed in the manufacturing concerns. The impact of declining employment due to plant closures was already serious: "Since 1950 . . . , East St. Louis consistently had a higher percentage of claimants for unemployment compensation to covered workers or insured unemployed to covered workers (the system of reporting changed in 1954) than the state as a whole."[8]

The railroads, which had employed large numbers of people, were unable to compete with the evolving air and trucking carriers, and between 1960 and 1975, there were an estimated two thousand fewer railroad jobs. Where in 1920 the area accounted for 30 percent of the meat processing in the industry, by 1968, it accounted for only 10 percent of that production. Johnson and Veach estimated that total manufacturing employment in East St. Louis declined by 50 percent between 1950 and 1970.[9]

As employment dropped, the city grew poorer relative to the surrounding area and the state as a whole (Table 11).

Table 11. East St. Louis Median Income in Dollars and as a Percent of Other Areas

Area	1950	1960	1970
East St. Louis	$2,557	$3,967	$4,686
St. Clair County	2,631 (97%)	5,219 (76%)	8,030 (58%)
St. Louis SMSA	2,966 (86%)	5,489 (72%)	8,831 (53%)
State of Illinois	3,163 (81%)	5,589 (71%)	8,914 (53%)

Source: Johnson and Veach, Middle-Size Cities of Illinois, p. 110.

In the sixties, when other areas of the country were prosperous, East St. Louis was still experiencing plant closures. By that time, blacks comprised nearly 45 percent of the population and appeared to be most adversely affected by the loss of manufacturing jobs. In 1959, the Amour meatpacking plant was shut down. Obsolescence of the plant as well as changes in market conditions and shipping requirements led to the closure, a process similar to that which occurred in the Chicago meatpacking industry.[10]

The Amour closing was a big shock to East St. Louis. The labor intensity of the plant coupled with the low-skill requirements and a strong union had meant relatively high wages for workers who had few transferable skills. Many of the employees were older men with meager educations. Because the city had been losing jobs generally and was having difficulty attracting new industry, the possibility of obtaining new jobs was low. In July 1959, the month the Armour plant closed, unemployment in East St. Louis stood at 4.6 percent. It was 4.6 percent again in September and did not go below 5 percent during 1959, but it rose to 6.8 percent in March 1960. By contrast, in Peoria in September 1959, the jobless rate was a low 1.6 percent; by January 1980, it had risen only to 3.8 percent. There also was some evidence to suggests that the many blacks who had worked at Armour encountered some discrimination in getting new jobs.[11]

The American Steel Company closed its East St. Louis plant in 1960. The company had another plant in Granite City that it kept running. Both plants had been supplying the railroads' steel demands, and although that market was cyclical by nature, it was not so much market economics as it was the age of the East St. Louis facility that forced its closure. Approximately 500–600 jobs were lost, although a few former East St. Louis employees found jobs at the Granite City plant. The Aluminum Company of America (ALCOA), which averaged about 1,500 employees in the mid-fifties, ceased operation in October 1963. Swift and Company shut down in 1967–68, with a loss of 600 jobs. Also in the sixties, the American Zinc Company closed its Fairmont City operation, and 200 jobs were lost. Another 100 jobs disappeared when the Darling Fertilizer Company closed in 1967. Other closures included Norfolk and Western Railroad (365 jobs lost as a result of a warehouse fire), Obear-Nestor Glassworks (1979, 725 jobs), and finally Hunter Packing Company (1980, 700 jobs).[12]

East St. Louis's 1950 population total of 82,295 was to be its highest. The 1960 Census showed a small decline in population of 582 down to 81,712. During the decade, however the white population fell by some 26,000 and by the time of the 1970 Census, the population stood at 69,996. The black population, enumerated at 48,368, represented 69.1 percent of the total. By 1975, the population had declined another 17.4 percent to 57,929, with blacks comprising 68.9 percent of the residents.[13]

Clearly those who could afford to leave the city—primarily the middle class—were leaving it. The exodus came in stages: whites in the fifties and sixties, blacks in the seventies.[14] Jane Altes, a researcher from Southern Illinois University-Edwardsville, characterized the exodus and its impact: "Employers and employees moved from the central city to the suburbs, taking with them their tax monies, their purchasing power and all the other attributes of the urban middle class. They left behind a population increasingly unable to pay for the necessities of life. Welfare rolls grew while public revenues declined. School needs rose while the capacity to pay for such needs fell. Housing deteriorated. Retail establishments closed as the public ceased to patronize them. Crime rates increased. Racial composition changed as the more affluent whites, choosing their residences without encountering discrimination, left the central city."[15]

The percentage, in 1969, of the total of all families with income below the poverty level was 28.5; the percentage of black families below the poverty level was 37.8.[16] In 1964, according to Jane Altes, 21 percent of the total labor force, and 33 percent of nonwhites, was unemployed. In 1969, she found the numbers of unemployed looking for work to be close to 10 percent. She observed that conditions had not really improved because "the kind of person who, in 1964, was 'looking for work' has now dropped out of the labor force entirely."[17]

The foregoing numbers paint a rather bleak picture of life in East St. Louis, and the question must be asked, How did things deteriorate? Much of the blame must go to corrupt politicians who for so many years enjoyed limitless power, in collusion with some business interests and at times with certain labor unions. Newly arriving white ethnics and southern blacks alike were powerless to challenge, or even understand initially, the ways of the established power elites. The middle-class population no longer lived in the city or, if they did, they were likely to be businessmen profiting from devices such as licensing fees or construction contract kickbacks. Elements of rugged individualism and kinship were seized upon early and forged into a system of family-controlled voting precincts or other patronage-providing vehicles. Political power was centralized in a machine early in this century. "The pervasiveness of the machine gave it a virtual monopoly over most avenues to financial and political success and even survival."[18] Power centralization was given official sanction when the commission form of government was adopted in 1919; "Five commissioners chosen at large in a nonpartisan election were to operate as legislators, executives and administrators. While the commission form of government was conceived as reformist, capable of quick action in an emergency, in East St. Louis it proved to be an effective device for accumulating power and dispensing jobs and favors."[19]

An Irish-American "dynasty" controlled politics in East St. Louis for fifty years after World War I.[20] Alvin Fields, the last king of the dynasty, and mayor from 1951 to 1971 became one of the best-known machine politicians in the state. He was a shrewd and skilled negotiator and conciliator who controlled Democrats and Republicans alike.

Although the old political machine had benefitted from the city's earlier tenuous economic prosperity, grievously declining city revenues in the postwar period made it more difficult to maintain political power through patronage jobs and favoritism in letting city contracts. As businesses left the city, the traditional partners in corruption either disappeared or suffered setbacks. Beginning in the fifties, the machine was challenged by some of the remaining businessmen and middle-class residents through calls for reform, redevelopment, and better city government. In 1959, Community Progress, Inc. (CPI), a group of neighborhood organizations (primarily white), pushed through a proposal for an urban renewal project adjacent to the central business district. One year later, in 1960, CPI requested that the mayor initiate several reforms in city government, use tax monies more efficiently, and revitalize the business district. "Faced with a deficit budget and a continually declining tax base, Mayor Fields could not afford to ignore these requests from the neighborhood groups and the downtown bankers and merchants who had given long-time support to the machine."[21]

According to Elazar, Southern Illinois University was responsible for organizing CPI in 1957 through its Department of Community Development. In assessing the university's activities, he observed that, "the intervention of that institution has become the most important single factor in raising the level of government and public services in the two counties. . . . "[22] The group's promotion of city redevelopment activities and what Elazar termed its "unusual record of successes" in a difficult political environment led to national recognition in the form of the *Look Magazine*–National Municipal League All-American City Award in 1960.[23]

The SIU professionals were just the first of a stream of outside academicians, professional administrators, and federal government officials who arrived during the sixties to improve the quality of life in East St. Louis. An SIU-commissioned study of city administration problems recommended numerous improvements, including hiring of an administrative assistant to the mayor responsible for city planning and administration. In 1963, George Washnis came from a successful career in Evanston to fill the position. He was responsible for overseeing the development of many new programs and initially guided the city toward its selection as a first-round Model Cities area in 1967. This period, the time of Lyndon Johnson's Great Society, was characterized by extensive federal reform programs. The "outsiders" who came to run these programs were sympathetic to the rising call for black grass-roots participation. The Model Cities program was the most significant lever with which grass-roots civil rights activists were able to push their demands for power:

> Model Cities became a rallying point for emergent black leaders. Joining with federal officials whose main concern was administrative reform in East St. Louis, the two groups advocated hiring practices other than loyalty to the political machine. In December 1968, Mayor Fields clashed with Model Cities leaders over the appointment of six resident assistants in an urban renewal program. Though precinct committeemen fought for the jobs, the Model Cities group won, and an agreement was reached to establish quasi-civil service procedures for all federal programs. After this loss black politicians seemed less and less willing to accede to Fields' leadership.[24]

The political machine was fast losing its power. In the 1967 mayoral election, the Fields slate was challenged for the first time by an all-black opposition slate. Fields managed to prevail, but 25 percent of the vote went to the black opposition slate. Some of the black vote for Fields was clearly related to patronage and favors, but there was also widespread suspicion of voting fraud.

By 1971, Fields was being pressured not only by opponents preaching reform (and black power), but also by restive members of the black political group who now felt strong enough to challenge him. This group was composed of most of the black precinct committeemen whom Fields had appointed over the years, as well as the building commissioner, Virgil Calvert. The committeemen had been forged into a strong organization, the Paramount Club; they practiced patronage hiring and vote-brokering and generally copied the tactics of machine politics so long established in the city. As blacks struggled for control and conditions in the city worsened, the power struggles became meaner. However, despite the large reservoir of social unrest, the city did not experience the urban violence that marked many communities in this period.

This combination of factors led to Fields' decision not to seek another term in the 1971 primary elections for mayor. The race was left to Calvert; Charles Merritts, Sr., the black school board president; a white law-and-order candidate; and James E. Williams, executive director of the St. Clair County Legal Aid Society and a classic reform candidate. Williams advocated extension of civil service to all city hall jobs and other reform measures. Calvert was labelled the machine candidate. Williams's opposition to Merritts centered on an alleged lack of leadership in school affairs. When the primary returns came in on February 9, 1971, Williams had beaten Merritts for second place by 75 votes. Calvert and Williams, the two run-off candidates for the April election, received 5,193 and 3,898 votes respectively. "In a rare East St. Louis election, precinct committeemen and election judges appointed by the election commissioners were closely watched at the polling places by non-machine poll watchers."[25] Included in this group were the Belleville League of Women Voters, the East St. Louis United Front, and the Citizens for an Aldermanic Government.

In his mayoral race, Williams sought to run as "unbought and unbossed." He declined acceptance of support from Merritts, who expressed his own desire to "block the Calverts." Although Williams was thought to be too idealistic to win the election, he gained Republican party support—the first mayoral Republican activity in nearly forty years. He was endorsed by the East St. Louis Republican City Central Committee, which also wanted the machine out. A traditionally Republican newspaper in St. Louis endorsed Williams, and Illinois Republican Governor Richard Ogilvie held out a promise through one of his appointees to build a state office building in East St. Louis if Williams were elected.

On April 6, 1971, James Williams became the first black mayor of East St. Louis by defeating Virgil Calvert by a vote of 10,813 to 8,202.[26] It was indeed a turning point for the city, although East St. Louis's problems would not be solved by a change in the racial and ideological complexion of the mayor. Williams lasted for one stormy term. However, the transition from white to black control was not fully achieved until 1979, when Carl Officer, Jr., son of a prominent black mortician with strong state Democratic ties, was elected the third black mayor. His coming to power was reported widely, because he represented a newer type of young, articulate, and "well-connected" politician thought needed to channel state and federal aid to East St. Louis. Whether he could overcome the severe problems of his city in the midst of national economic stagflation remained to be seen.

By the end of World War II, East St. Louis had gained a reputation as a "difficult environment for industrial management."[27] This poor labor history was no doubt earned in an earlier era when business interests, with the aid of the political machine, manipulated and fanned racial antagonisms among both white and black workers. There is evidence, for example, to suggest the use of black strike-breakers early in the century to curb organization attempts in the meatpacking and aluminum industries contributed to the violence of 1917.[28]

Union organization began in the late nineteenth century, and organizational strength was particularly significant among the railroad and building construction workers. Local 169 of the Carpenters Union was chartered in 1886. By 1940, it was estimated that the AFL, CIO, and Railway unions had about twenty thousand members out of a civilian labor force of nearly thirty-one thousand.[29] Others among the organized were barbers, musicians, restaurant workers, public utilities workers, store clerks, salespeople, and many city employees, including firemen, policemen, and sanitation workers. "Collective bargaining in its variegated forms is thus the prevailing pattern for the determination of conditions of employment in the community. This pattern did not emerge without strife."[30]

A comparison of the number of work stoppages in the first postwar decade between East St. Louis and Peoria revealed fairly similar experience. Both communities gained a reputation for labor-management conflict (Table 12).

Table 12. Number of Work Stoppages, East St. Louis and Peoria

	1946	1949	1950	1952	1953	1954	1955
East St. Louis	21	11	13	16	13	5	14
Peoria	11	below 10	11	11	10	12	14

Source: Milton Derber, *Union-Management Relations in East St. Louis* (Urbana: University of Illinois Institute of Labor and Industrial Relations, 1957), Table 2, p. 8.

However, the negative perception of labor relations in East St. Louis was gradually replaced in later observations. Interviews in 1980 agreed with the 1957 observations of the Institute of Labor and Industrial Relations: "A factor in this recent community development has been a somewhat greater recognition by union leaders that the power which they have achieved in the industrial life of the community requires a corresponding measure of responsibility not only in their industries but in the community at large. . . ."[31]

In 1963, news columnist Victor Reisel wrote a column about the recent trial of Edgar F. Smith, second vice-president of the Hod Carriers and Building Laborers International Union, who had been accused of shaking down contractors. Reisel suggested that the Southern Illinois labor movement was dominated by criminals. The column prompted a strong response from John R. Hundley, Jr., director of industrial relations and personnel of Granite City Steel.[32]

Hundley's letter noted that "labor conditions as described in that column may well have existed in the past. However, the fact is that they do not exist today and have not existed for some years." Hundley then recounted how in 1956 his company in cooperation with Monsanto Chemical and Dow Chemical conducted an extensive survey of construction costs in Southern Illinois compared with the rest of the United States. They found that indeed national contractors customarily added "an East Side factor" of 15–75 percent to their estimates of labor costs when bidding on jobs in the area. But labor was not the sole culprit. The contractors and the industries for which they worked were also responsible for "some of the most costly working restrictions." In 1957, Hundley's group approached the local unions and contractors and urged an agreement that would eliminate or reduce featherbedding and make-work practices and would prevent jurisdictional disputes. By mid-1959, the officers of the contractors and nine local unions agreed to a "statement of policy." In 1959, Arthur D. Little, Inc., which conducted a study of industrial site potential in the St. Louis area, reported a drop of as much as 20 percent in construction labor costs in the Granite City area, and Secretary of Labor James P. Mitchell called the program "a lesson to the rest of the nation."

The Hundley development was only one aspect of the attempts to improve labor-management conditions. The University of Illinois Institute of Labor and Industrial Relations staff found greater union participation in 1956 in cooperative labor-management activities and an increase in union-sponsored charitable activities. Several sources emphasized the extensive union participation in United Way activities as one important example. However, perhaps the major factor was the recognition by both labor and management of the need to combat the loss of jobs and profitability during the period under study. One example was the "Spirit of St. Louis" Labor-Management Committee. In 1976, this group established an education program designed to educate the parties to issues affecting the industries on both sides of the river, such as foreign competition, mergers and shutdowns, and legislative issues such as workers' compensation.

East St. Louis is an example of an industrial city in a state of continuous economic decline. Adding to the complexity of the economic situation are the factors of a long history of political corruption, a high degree of unionization, and a majority black population struggling for political power and social status. The black power struggle came to a successful conclusion as a result of sheer numbers. Reform eliminated much of the corruption. Black social status inevitably advanced into all phases of communal life. But overcoming economic decline was another story because the industrial decision making largely emanated from outside of the community. By 1980, there was little evidence of reversing the trend.

NOTES

This section is a revision of a report prepared by Curtis A. Scott.

1. Daniel M. Johnson and Rebecca Veach, *The Middle-Size Cities of Illinois* (Springfield: Sangamon State University, 1980), pp. 222, 90.

2. Dennis R. Judd and Robert E. Mendelson, *The Politics of Urban Planning: The East St. Louis Experience* (Urbana: University of Illinois Press, 1973), p. 4.

3. Daniel J. Elazar, *Cities of the Prairie: The Metropolitan Frontier and American Politics* (London: Basic Books, 1970), p. 156.

4. Elazar, *Cities of the Prairies*, p. 171.

5. Dennis R. Judd, "Social Reform in Model Cities: The East St. Louis Case," Ph.D. diss., University of Illinois, 1972, p. 120.

6. Judd, "Social Reform," p. 119.

7. Milton Derber, *Union-Management Relations in East St. Louis* (Urbana: Institute of Labor and Industrial Relations, University of Illinois, 1957), p. 4.

8. Derber, *Union-Management Relations*, p. 3.

9. Johnson and Veach, *Middle-Size Cities of Illinois*, p. 10.

10. Clark Kerr, *Progress Report: Armour Automation Committee*, June 1961, p. 4.

11. Richard C. Wilcock and Walter H. Franke, *Unwanted Workers* (Glencoe: Free Press Collier-MacMillan, 1963), p. 41.

12. Judd and Mendelson, *The Politics of Urban Planning*, pp. 18–19.

13. 1977 Statistical Abstract, *City and County Data Book* (Washington: Government Printing Office, 1977).

14. Johnson and Veach, *Middle-Size Cities of Illinois*, p. 103.

15. Jane Altes, *East St. Louis—The End of a Decade*. RUD Report no. 3 (Edwardsville: Regional and Urban Development Studies and Services, Southern Illinois University, January 1970).

16. *Data Book*, 1977.

17. Altes, *East St. Louis*, p. 35.

18. Judd, "Social Reform," p. 130.

19. Johnson and Veach, *Middle Size Cities of Illinois*, p. 92.

20. Ibid., p. 102.

21. Judd, "Social Reform," p. 143.

22. Elazar, *Cities of the Prairie*, p. 397.

23. Ibid., p. 398.

24. Judd, "Social Reform," p. 147.

25. Ibid., pp. 159, 160, 161.

26. Ibid., pp. 163, 117.

27. Johnson and Veach, *Middle-Size Cities of Illinois*, p. 101.

28. Elliott M. Rudwick, *Race Riot at East St. Louis, July 2, 1917* (Carbondale: Southern Illinois University Press, 1964), p. 16.

29. Derber, *Union-Management Relations*, p. 5.

30. Ibid.

31. Ibid., p. 6.

32. The following discussion is based on an article in the *Southern Illinois Labor Tribune*, February 14, 1973, which reproduces most of Hundley's letter.

14

Community Service and Labor Education

The foregoing sections on Labor in the community indicate that Labor was often concerned with matters other than collective bargaining and politics, although these were of prime importance. This chapter deals with a variety of activities that many Labor groups describe as community services (CS). One category relates primarily to advising members about off-the-job services or benefits that they might get from government or voluntary social welfare agencies. Another deals with encouraging unionists to contribute money and/ or service to the voluntary organizations. And a third is devoted to getting public recognition for Labor's contributions and having agencies pay more attention to the specific needs of workers.

Community Service

The community service programs of Illinois labor unions had an uneven history between 1945 and 1980. Although the national CS program had its beginnings in war relief committees during World War II and CIO unions in Chicago had begun CS programs during the war, it was not until 1950 that the Illinois Industrial Union Council (CIO) held a statewide CS conference at the UAW Conference Center in Ottawa and thus began its efforts to expand the CS program statewide. From 1950 until the state AFL–CIO merger in 1958, the Illinois CIO energetically offered organized CS programs to unions in about twenty downstate communities, both large and small, principally through local union counselor training courses. There is some evidence to support the claims by top-ranking leaders of the Illinois CIO that their CS program was among the most active in the United States during these years.

Following the AFL–CIO merger in Illinois, however, the CS program received little active support from the leadership of the merged State Federation. During this post-merger period, the reports by the state Community Services Committee (CSC) to the federation's annual conventions were chiefly rhetorical exercises, varying little from year to year, affirming in the most general terms the leadership's satisfaction that Illinois unions had achieved an active and acknowledged role in community affairs. The only extended debate about the state CS program that occurred at the federation conventions during these twenty years arose over repeated resolutions calling for the appointment of a full-time, paid CS director for the federation. The former CIO CS director, Robert Gibson, did become a member of the State Fed staff, but other duties prevented his spending much time on CS. The delegates introducing CS resolutions were told by Federation President Reuben Soderstrom or his successor Stanley Johnson that the organization could not afford to fund a CS position and that the first priority of the federation must always remain legislative lobbying in Springfield. This debate reached a rather heated climax on the floor of the 1975 convention, only three years before a change in the federation's top leadership (when Gibson became secretary-treasurer) led to the convening of the first statewide CS conference in thirteen years.

The lack of supportive leadership on a statewide level did not mean that CS activities came to a halt in Illinois after the mid-fifties. Annual union counselor training courses, the backbone of the CS program, continued in many of the larger cities, and Labor participation in Community Chest or United Way campaigns was widespread. Nonetheless, during most of the postwar period, Illinois labor leaders generally seemed unwilling or unable to launch major initiatives in response to the problems that were increasingly besetting their communities during the sixties and seventies.

In 1966, the leaders of the United Packinghouse Workers reported that "we are losing the place in the forefront of creative social leadership which was at one time the acknowledged role of the labor movement—an ominous development."[1] Within Illinois this development was probably most evident in Chicago, where top-ranking labor leaders remained largely aloof from such critical urban problems as racial tensions, inadequate housing, or deteriorating public services. The record of Chicago Federation of Labor leaders in this regard stood in marked contrast to that of many leaders of the city's large Catholic community, who furthered a noteworthy tradition of community activism by the Church, or of Saul Alinsky's protégés, who turned Chicago into a national center for working-class community organizations outside the orbit of trade unionism. But by the late seventies an increasing number of unionists both in Chicago and downstate were beginning to break out of this isolation from community affairs and, through such organizations as the Illinois Public Action Council, to align themselves with community and consumer groups in coalition work revolving around health-care reform, escalating energy prices, and other pressing concerns.

An illustration on the front page of the August 1953 issue of *Illinois Labor,* the monthly state CIO newspaper, suggested the multipurpose nature of a state CS program. Entitled "Pillars of CS," the drawing depicted four such purposes: union counseling, agency representation, workmen's compensation, and health and safety.[2] An article inside the same issue noted that this concept of CS differed from that of national CIO CS representatives, who believed that CS was a "two-legged" program consisting of union counseling and agency representation. The article further stated that involvement in CS programs led inevitably to a concern for better legislation, and thus political action should be considered another "pillar" of a comprehensive CS program.[3] Because the main vehicle for promoting these aspects of CS was an ambitious statewide schedule of CS classes for union members, CS and labor education often overlapped.

The expansion of this multifaceted CS program throughout the state occurred in the fifties, during the tenure of Pat Greathouse, UAW Regional Director, as state CIO CS chairman. As he stated at the 1950 state CIO convention, the necessity for a statewide program was first discussed at the previous year's convention, where it was noted that, unlike Chicago, no downstate areas had a functioning CS program.[4] In contrast, the CIO in Chicago had been sponsoring CS activities since 1943 or 1944,[5] and since 1947 had been publishing, with the Community Fund and the Council of Social Agencies of Chicago, a monthly CS paper, *Labor in Our Community*. The first steps toward a statewide program were setting up the CS under Greathouse and convening a statewide conference in August 1950. Greathouse observed that "we did not have the participation we should have had throughout the state" at this initial conference; however, it did result in the establishment of the first two downstate CS programs, in Joliet and Rockford.[6]

Following the second CS conference in 1951, the Executive Board of the state CIO hired Samuel Guzzardo from Rockford as a full-time CS director. Guzzardo, a former school teacher in Rockford and a member of UAW Local 39 (Roper Stove Company), served the CIO as CS director until 1957, when he became education director for UAW Region Four and was succeeded as CS director by Robert Gibson, a USWA official from Granite City and future secretary-treasurer and president of the state AFL–CIO.[7] Guzzardo's main responsibilities were expanding the CS program in downstate areas and ghostwriting the "CIO–CSC Statewide" column that appeared under Greathouse's name in the monthly CIO paper, *Illinois Labor,* from October 1951 until at least May 1956. These columns, plus numerous feature articles on CS activities in *Illinois Labor,* represented the only regular coverage of unions' CS activities in Illinois during the postwar period; neither the State Federation's *Weekly Newsletter* nor the Chicago Federation of Labor's *Federation News* provided regular coverage of CS programs, even following these organizations' mergers with their CIO counterparts. After the UAW withdrew from the AFL–CIO, it developed its own Community Action Program (CAP), which emphasized political action.

Throughout these early years of the CIO's CS program, indeed throughout its entire postwar development in Illinois, the union counselor training courses were the first priority. They typically ran for eight weeks, with one class meeting per week. Resource persons from such public and private agencies as the local Community Fund or Red Cross, the Public Aid Commission, or the state Unemployment Compensation Division, along with nurses, workers' compensation lawyers, township supervisors, and others served as speakers in the training courses. Both Guzzardo and Ellsworth Smith, who became secretary of the state CSC, personally taught in many of the course sessions throughout the state. Between 1951 and 1955, some communities offered counselor training courses to CIO members.[8] Overall, the two largest CIO unions in the state, the UAW and the USWA, provided by far the most participants for these courses (and other CS activities), both in Chicago and downstate. The UAW was active in Rockford, Peoria, the Quad Cities, and Danville; the Steelworkers were predominant in Alton and Granite City, Joliet, LaSalle–Peru, and Sterling. The Amalgamated Clothing Workers participated in CS programs in Kewanee and Jacksonville and some Glassworkers' locals in the Ottawa area. Another union that was not nearly as large as the UAW or the USWA, but that was very supportive of CS activities in Chicago and many of the downstate towns, was the Communication Workers of America, whose international president Joseph Beirne was chairman of the national CIO CS for many years. Participation in the CIO counseling courses by AFL unionists was reported in two locations, Danville and Galesburg.[9] According to CS reports to the CIO conventions, some 325–450 counselors were enrolled in these courses downstate each year during the mid-fifties, while some 100–400 participated in Cook County annually.[10]

The emphasis in the counseling courses was on teaching local union leaders how to secure for their members the services and benefits to which they were entitled in times of need, particularly during strikes. Union counselors were undoubtedly busiest during such times of strife, helping to administer various types of strike relief to their fellow workers. For example, in 1954, the CS in Kewanee reported that during a lengthy strike by steelworkers at Walworth Products, "400 families have been placed on the Veterans' and Township assistance, and 60 people are receiving Social Security. Arrangements have been made with virtually all business and loan companies to defer payments until after the strike is settled."[11]

Union counselors also devoted effort to securing unemployment and workers' compensation benefits for their members. Much of this work was of a routine nature; however, when the agricultural implement industry in the Quad Cities plunged into a deep recession in late 1953 and more than ten thousand industry workers were laid off, Sam Guzzardo held an emergency unemployment counseling conference for six UAW and FE–UAW counselors, who then staffed three emergency offices to assist unemployed workers with their financial and health problems.

Sessions on workers' compensation were prominent features of the regular CS courses and the annual CS summer institutes in Ottawa. Instructors such as Harold Katz, an influential Chicago labor lawyer, and Nicholas Di Pietro, an AFL Typographical Union official and member of the Illinois Industrial Commission, led sessions on ways in which workers' compensation claims could be competently handled by a union counselor and what type should be referred to a workers' compensation lawyer.[12]

Although the focus of CS efforts was on alleviating the problems of union members "outside the plant gates," involvement in workers' compensation claims was coupled with concern for in-plant health and safety. Union counselors were taught how to detect health and safety hazards at their workplaces, to work for stricter enforcement of state safety codes, and for a greater commitment of resources to workplace health and safety by the state government.

In contrast to the preceding services, the aim of "agency representation," which attempted to increase the number of union members serving on the boards of the Community Fund or Community Chest, the Red Cross, and other public or private agencies, was oriented more toward the Labor movement's role in the larger community. The chief rationale for promoting union representation on local agency boards was the belief that unions should have some voice in the management of philanthropic organizations that received a significant percentage of their funds from the contributions of union members. Furthermore, union officials felt compelled to seek greater representation on service agencies whenever they encountered a lack of cooperation from such groups. Concern over management domination of these agencies was often expressed.[13]

Not all the CSCs in Illinois, however, had difficult relationships with the directors of the Community Chest or other civic groups. In Chicago, for example, after World War II the Community Fund and the Welfare Council of Metropolitan Chicago each had one CIO representative and one AFL representative on staff, and later two others were added. By the time of the last state CIO convention in 1956, a number of downstate communities were able to report two CIO members sitting on their Community Chest boards, including at least one, Kewanee, where the CIO's board seats were reportedly guaranteed in the constitution of the local Community Chest.[14]

The vast majority of CIO–CSC activities in the fifties revolved around the programs discussed previously. However, CSCs in sections of Illinois undertook, from time to time, miscellaneous projects in response to needs of their communities. For example, union counselors in both Rockford and Moline participated in emergency relief programs when those towns were hard hit by floods in 1952.[15] In 1955, following a fire at the Carr-Consolidated Biscuit Company plant in Chicago that left two people dead and five hundred employees out of work, the Chicago CIO–CSC and the AFL Bakery and Confectionery Workers Local 15 organized a "visiting team" to meet the injured workers in hospitals and advise all employees of their unemployment compensation rights; an employment committee was also established to help search for similar work.[16] Counselors in Chicago and Rockford also participated in civil defense programs, both during the Korean War period and afterward.[17] For many years, different CIO locals in Chicago would take turns hosting monthly breakfasts for servicemen at the Chicago U.S.O. Club.[18]

In September 1952, in order to "round out the CIO attack on basic community problems," the Chicago IUC established a new Committee on Civic Government headed by Pat Greathouse, which was "to build a CIO program aimed at better municipal services for CIO members through making recommendations in the field of municipal government organization, taxation, elimination of corruption, and similar issues." There is no evidence in subsequent issues of *Illinois Labor* or *Labor-Welfare in Our Community*, however, that the Civic Government Committee remained an active group.

One area of reform in which the Chicago IUC was quite active in the early postwar years was housing issues, particularly rent control. For example, in 1947 the Chicago CSC pressed for the passage of a city bond issue to finance slum-clearance housing projects,[19] and successfully fought, with other labor and civic organizations, against a 15 percent blanket rent increase recommended by the Chicago Area Advisory Board.[20] After a new rent control law went into effect in Chicago on April 1, 1948, CSC counselors were instructed on the statute's provisions so that they could advise tenants of their rights. When the city council was debating a new building code in 1948, Michael Mann, IUC secretary, regional CIO director, and member of the Chicago Area Rent Control Board, testified in favor of the proposed code despite the opposition of the building trades and the CFL.[21] When the city council finally passed the new code on December 30, 1949, Dorothy Rubel, the director of the Metropolitan Housing and Planning Council, stated that "the CIO Council could justly claim a large part of that three-year-delayed victory."[22]

The Illinois CIO, both in Chicago and downstate, together with other union groups, became most involved in preserving rent controls during 1952. Overall, the efforts to extend controls were successful in Chicago (despite a 7 percent increase in rents), Springfield, Ottawa, and LaSalle, but unsuccessful in Waukegan–North Chicago, Danville, and Galesburg.[23] All federally mandated rent controls, however, expired in Illinois on July 31, 1953.[24]

It appears clear that the CS program was for some time a high priority among leaders of the Illinois CIO, who were able in the fifties to build upon a strong, preexisting Chicago program and extend community service training to many downstate cities with sizable numbers of CIO members. On the other hand, there are some indications that the progress of the CSC program in Illinois was not one of unbroken successes. For example, in 1953, for the second consecutive year, a special workshop on community services for union representatives at the annual Ottawa CSC Institute was cancelled for lack of attendance. Furthermore, the Illinois IUC Executive Board voted to drop the entire Ottawa institute in 1954 "due to the press of other business by most of the international unions,"[25] although the institute was revived in 1955, for the last time under sole CIO sponsorship.[26]

The CS program entered a period of uncertain goals and reduced activities following the merger of the state AFL and CIO in 1958. Although the merger agreement provided for the continuation of a CSC as one of only four advisory committees to the new federation's Executive Board, there was no report at all on CS activities at the federation's first unified convention in 1958. However, at the 1959 convention a report was received from a Committee on Community Services and Civil Rights, chaired by federation vice-president George Bynum of Barbers Local 139 in Chicago, with Robert Gibson, the CS director for the state CIO in 1957 and 1958, and Laurence Yeast, a Machinist from Bloomington, as co-secretaries. Bynum's report affirmed the goals of active community involvement by unions and full civil rights for all citizens; he also strongly supported WCFL, a powerful radio station owned and operated by the Chicago Federation of Labor since 1926 (the only such union-owned and union-operated radio station in the U.S.) which, Bynum claimed, "fully explains labor's position within the community and also labor's dedicated task from the farms to legislative halls. . . ."[27] Although he applauded the Jewish Labor Committee for its civil rights work, Bynum also urged the creation of a Civil Rights Committee, separate from community services, by the state AFL–CIO. A separate Civil Rights Committee was set up by the time of the next convention in 1960. At that convention the state AFL–CIO CSC was beginning to assume the identity it would maintain for the next two decades. The new chairman of the CSC was Thomas Burke, president of Building Service Employees' Local 25 in Chicago, who was to serve as chairman until 1974; the two co-secretaries of the CSC were Gibson and Lee Allaman from UAW Local 1357 at the International Harvester plant in Canton, Illinois.

Because neither the old state "Fed" nor the CFL had had CSCs before their mergers (although the CFL had two full-time staffers on the Chicago Welfare Council Staff), Burke, who as first vice-president of the Service Employees' International Union and a close ally of William McFetridge, was a powerful figure in both Chicago and national union affairs, had held no formal CS responsibilities before becoming state CSC chairman in 1960. He had, however, been largely responsible for two of the most significant CS-type projects undertaken by any union—AFL or CIO—in Illinois, the Olivia Bautsch Health Center and the Union Eye Center. The health center opened in downtown Chicago in 1955 and was named after the secretary-treasurer of Local

25, who had pioneered the idea of group health centers in Chicago before her death in 1952. According to Burke, Olivia Bautsch, State Senator William J. Connors (D-Chicago), and Governor Adlai E. Stevenson had been instrumental in the passage of the Voluntary Health Services Plan Act of 1951, which allowed employer-financed union health and welfare funds to be used to finance group health centers. In 1965, Local 25 opened a new $1.5 million medical facility at Chicago's sprawling West Side Medical Center, also financed through its health and welfare funds and leased to both the Union Health Services and the Union Eye Center. Burke's local had established the eye center in 1951, even before it opened the Bautsch Health Center, as a Labor-owned medical cooperative offering complete eye care to union members and their families for nominal fees. The Union Eye Center was owned by individual union locals, which would invest in cooperative certificates according to the locals' size. Some seventy AFL and CIO locals, with more than eighty thousand members, had joined by the time the Chicago CIO endorsed the center in 1953, and by the time the center moved into the new West Side facility in 1965, some one hundred locals were members.[28]

Despite Burke's laudable involvement in pioneering union-sponsored health centers during his long term as chair of the state AFL–CIO CSC, he appeared not to have been a functional leader in statewide CS activities during the sixties or seventies. It was State Fed staff member Robert Gibson who remained the most important state figure in CS. However, as the Executive Board reported in the 1960 proceedings, "Due to circumstances, Staff Representative Gibson does not devote full time just to work in connection with social services. However, items such as civil defense, the White House Conference on Children, the older and aged worker, civil rights, education, and safety certainly cannot be overlooked in our definition of Community Services. All of these have been the assigned duties of the Staff Representative."[29]

The Executive Board also reported on two favorite projects of Executive Vice-President (later President) Stanley Johnson: the Rehabilitation Institute of the Northwestern University Medical School, which had been founded in 1951 with private donations by Dr. Paul Magnuson, an orthopedic surgeon and chairman of President Truman's Commission on the Health Needs of the Nation, and the Chicago Committee on Alcoholism, which had opened in 1949 as Portal House under the guidance of University of Chicago physiologist Dr. Anton Carlson and which operated a pilot clinic and outpatient service for alcoholics. The Executive Board's reports on these two institutions were to be regular features of the convention proceedings for most of the next two decades, but there was no indication that the federation's support of them involved either the CSC or the membership in any significant way.[30]

The Executive Board's report on CS at the 1960 convention was not well received by the Committee on CS, which recommended nonconcurrence, noting disagreement with the officers' concept of CS and urging that the state AFL–CIO institute a full-time CS training program, including a revived annual CS institute. The recommendation of nonconcurrence was defeated, however, after Federation President Reuben Soderstrom explained that the organization did not have the money to support it.

The heated debate on the convention floor and subsequent discussions led the federation officers to offer, in the following year's proceedings, a defense of convictions about the role of CS in the federation's affairs:

> What must be remembered first and foremost is that your State Organization is fully aware that some of our people place their interest in Community Services. Others place their interest in safety, education, civil rights, apprenticeship, organization, publicity, legislation, political action, or some pet charity or local project. All of this proves that folks in the Labor Movement have just as many ideas and interests that all other groups in our Country have. What it does point up, however, is that your State Organization could be running all over the State on a dozen or more ventures, trying to stir up the interest and enthusiasm of the balance of the membership on all of these items at once. Human nature being what it is, we doubt that local unions and their membership would respond to all of these important ideas at the same time. Bluntly, even if we had twice the per capita tax, your officers would not recommend wasting the money and energy on a dozen projects. If anyone thinks that the officers and members of local unions are going to embrace a dozen programs all at once, and keep them all going with enthusiasm, such person is just indulging in wishful thinking.[31]

Despite the Executive Board's assurance that Robert Gibson was devoting the bulk of his time to community service activities, the biggest bone of contention for convention delegates committed to a strong CS program continued to be the federation officers' failure to appoint a full-time CS director. The controversy was to last until 1975, when it finally died away.

Despite the keen disappointment obviously felt by some delegates at their eventual defeat in this fifteen-year controversy within the federation, it should be remembered that only a small number of state federations ever had CS directors. On the other hand, Soderstrom's and Johnson's frequent pleas that the Illinois AFL–CIO could not afford to hire a CS director were credible largely because they felt it was necessary to keep the organization's per capita dues at a very low level. Before the federation voted at its 1971 convention to double the per capita dues from 4 cents a month to 8 cents, the old rate had been the lowest in the United States, and even the new rate ranked in the lowest third among all the state federations. In addition, comments made by Stanley Johnson and other officers at the time of this dues increase made clear that the increased revenues would be earmarked largely for the traditional first priority of the State Federation—legislative activity—rather than CS or any other secondary pursuits.[32]

Furthermore, the growing number of full-time Labor staff members on the payrolls of local Community Chest/Community Funds (later known as United Way) in Illinois may have reduced the importance of having a CS director employed by the State Federation, regardless of the continuing symbolic importance of this issue to a number of union representatives. The appointment of such paid Labor staff persons at a local level had been a goal of organized Labor in Illinois even before the state AFL–CIO merger.

In 1962 the Executive Board reported that they had "assisted in negotiations of new Labor Staff persons in Illinois in the cities of Springfield, Granite City, and East St. Louis. We met with United Fund executives in at least four other communities to explore the possibility of their employing a full-time Labor Staff member on their Funds."[33] In a 1966 report, typical of a number of other years, the board simply stated that "the State Organization is continuing its efforts in cooperation with the National AFL–CIO CS Department in securing labor staff in a number of downstate communities, and will do so in the future."[34]

In 1975, the Executive Board could report that "we are indeed fortunate to have eleven people [i.e., labor staff] in eight cities of our state."[35] Four of these eleven would have been the two AFL and the two CIO staff members who had served on the Metropolitan Welfare Council and Community Fund of Chicago since the earliest postwar period. Peoria, Decatur, the Quad Cities, and Rockford joined the list between 1968 and 1973. The last CS report to mention the expansion of Labor staff was the 1978 one, which noted that "this ongoing program of establishing a full-time Labor staff in the communities around our State was very active this past year, and we welcome the Alton–Wood River Area to that list of cities enjoying this liaison between organized labor and the United Way agencies at the local community level."[36] The growth in full-time CS Labor staff in Illinois during the sixties and seventies, from four staff representatives in one city to twelve in nine cities, was apparently broadly representative of national trends encouraged by the national AFL–CIO's CS Department.[37]

The leadership of the Illinois AFL–CIO appeared to appreciate the importance of having full-time labor staff on local United Ways in order to maintain ongoing CS programs. The federation officers urged that union counseling "be made an integral priority program of every local union in our State."

The State Federation apparently did not attempt to keep records of functioning volunteer CSCs sponsored by either central labor bodies or local unions. However, judging from the comments of current United Way labor representatives in the early eighties, active CSCs in local unions were the exception rather than the rule, and the active sponsorship of CSCs by central labor bodies was also often a very uncertain proposition.

If professional CS staff persons paid by the United Way did indeed come to supplant the volunteer efforts of local and state CSCs, at least two advantages to Illinois labor leaders from this new arrangement can be posited. First, a CS professional could assure at least a minimal level of liaison work between union members and social welfare agencies on a local level without any expense by central labor bodies or the State Federation. These professionals were paid out of United Way funds, although according to various estimates, approximately one-third to one-half of all United Way funds were donated by union members.[38] Second, having most CS responsibilities assumed on a local level by one paid professional rather than one or more active CSCs would remove for local union leaders the possibility of any rival leadership coalescing around the CSCs. CS professionals who worked out of the local United Way office were strictly discouraged from any sort of union political involvement by the national AFL–CIO CS Department under the leadership of Leo Perlis, who resigned in 1980.

It is particularly noteworthy that the United Way labor staff was responsible for achieving a long-time goal of Illinois unionists who were dissatisfied with the state AFL–CIO's leadership in the CS area, the revival of the annual statewide CS conference. In December 1977, the State Federation appointed a committee comprised of the full-time CS representatives to organize such a conference, which was held at Edwardsville in June 1978—the first such conference since 1963—and attended by approximately 110 delegates, more than half of whom were reportedly receiving their first introduction to CS programs. It is perhaps significant that a resolution concerning this conference introduced at the 1978 convention stated that it had been carried out "with the full cooperation and assistance of the Officers of the Illinois State AFL–CIO."[39]

The attendance at the 1979 CS conference held in Peoria increased significantly, to 140 delegates. The theme of that conference was "To Your Good Health"; national health insurance and health maintenance organizations were discussed, and all delegates were given Red Cross C.P.R. training.[40] The theme of the 1980 conference in Galesburg was "Services to the Unemployed," and attendance jumped 38 percent. The Executive Board reported that following this conference the full-time labor staff and conference delegates held counseling courses through their local unions and central labor bodies to make their members aware of what services were available to them during extended periods of unemployment.[41]

Mainly through interview research, we have some idea of a variety of CS initiatives in the larger Illinois communities. In Rockford, for example, after a period of CS dormancy during the sixties, George Andrew, the CSC chairman of UAW Local 1268 at the Chrysler Belvidere plant, initiated considerable labor involvement with criminal rehabilitation programs during the early seventies. With varying degrees of success, Andrew, who was appointed to the advisory board of the State Department of Corrections in 1972, and other members of Local 1268 pushed for the local implementation of a work-release program authorized by state legislation, which would allow prisoners convicted of minor offenses to hold a job during the day and return to jail at night; served as Volunteers-in-Probation counselors with parolees and probationers; and helped in the founding of Youth Homes, Inc., a residential program for juvenile offenders in Rockford.[42]

Andrew also initiated a joint labor-management committee concerned with alcohol and drug abuse at the Chrysler plant in 1973 and was able to extend such efforts to other large Rockford employers such as Borg-Warner and National Lock. Much of this work was done in cooperation with the Anderson Alcoholism Rehabilitation Center in Janesville, Wisconsin, which would send staff members to Rockford-area plants to train both supervisors and union stewards on alcoholism detection and treatment. Andrew noted, however, that the recessionary economic climate in Rockford during the late seventies caused this program to be "placed on the back burner."

According to Leonard Davis, president of the Quad Cities Federation of Labor and the United Way Labor representative during the seventies, the federation there began a program of substance abuse education in the mid-seventies, and some of the area's larger employers, such as John Deere Company and J. I. Case, did establish early intervention and labor-management employee assistance programs for workers with such problems. Sandy Mendenhall, who became the United Way Labor representative in Peoria in 1975, also pointed to a labor-management alcoholism program at the huge Caterpillar UAW local there, but both she and Davis seemed agreed that in the late seventies and early eighties these problems were increasingly addressed through contract provisions calling for individual counseling.[43]

Another area of CS activities in almost all these communities could be termed "services to the unemployed." The rising toll of unemployed workers in Illinois during the recessionary climate of the mid and late seventies was clearly a major impetus behind a renewed interest in community services on both a local and statewide basis. Although the revival of CS state conferences did not center on the problems of the unemployed until 1980, Robert Gibson claimed that rising concern with unemployment and its attendant problems was an important factor in the resumption of these conferences in 1978. George Andrew in Rockford was particularly proud of the "one stops" he organized in the mid and late seventies, which were large and well-publicized meetings at various community centers at which unemployed workers and their families could meet with representatives of the Illinois Job Service, the food stamp program, and all other relevant assistance programs in one stop. Andrew also did counseling work with unemployed workers having trouble making their FHA mortgage payments.[44]

Much the same story was told by Sandy Mendenhall in Peoria and Leonard Davis in the Quad Cities. Harold Wright, from the Letter Carriers Union and the United Way Labor representative in Belleville since 1978, cited little initial CS activity in the greater East St. Louis area, with the exception of a few blood banks sponsored by local unions and the participation of Laborers Local 100 of East St. Louis in the annual Salvation Army's Christmas bell-ringing program to raise funds for needy families. In 1979, however, union counselor classes were offered for the first time in years, and the closing of the Obear-Nestee Bottling Company in East St. Louis led to a major CS effort to assist the 500–700 laid-off, heavily minority workers.[45]

Another problem that the professional CS staff and volunteers were encouraged to address during the seventies was rapidly escalating health-care costs. Unfortunately, they appeared to score few victories against this seemingly intractable problem. Neither Robert Gibson nor CS officials could point to any specific labor involvement in the establishment of HMOs in downstate Illinois, although a number of CS people, including Harold Wright in the East St. Louis area and Ray Maulden, chairman of the CSC in Decatur in the seventies, did attempt to initiate local efforts at establishing HMOs.[46] Labor people were involved in the establishment of HMOs in the Chicago area.

During the late seventies a number of delegates at the State Federation conventions, particularly Sol Brandzel of the ACTWU Chicago Joint Board, introduced resolutions supporting the goals of the National Health Planning and Resources Development Act, which established state and local health planning agencies with "majority consumer participation" throughout the United States. The resolutions specifically called on Governor James Thompson "to ensure that Labor's representation of seven members on the Statewide Health Coordinating Council be continued without any reduction," and on the local health system agencies to consult with local Central Bodies to ensure labor representatives did sit on these "HSAs" in a number of Illinois communities. The consensus was that these agencies were quite ineffectual.

When the Chicago Federation of Labor and the Cook County Industrial Union Council finally merged in January 1962, William Lee, president of the CFL, spoke of a distinguished past and a promising future for community involvement by organized labor in Chicago.[48] Lee referred, among other activities, to two of Labor's most ambitious efforts to further the economic development of Chicago: the twin sixty-story towers of Marina City, a unique downtown development project then under construction that was conceived by William McFetridge and financed in considerable part by Service Employees' health and welfare funds, and the recently completed Lake Calumet project, for which Labor lobbied extensively and which, together with the St. Lawrence Seaway and the Calumet-Sag Channel, was designed to make Chicago a world port.

Chicago indeed soon became the busiest Great Lakes port and the fifth busiest port in the United States, even if the volume of traffic on the St. Lawrence Seaway did not fully meet early expectations, and the steel industry that centered on the Calumet region continued to widen its lead over Pennsylvania as the premier steel-producing region of the United States during the sixties and seventies, following the completion of these important waterway projects.

However, the history of Marina City and two of the three other major building projects sponsored by Chicago unions during the postwar period revealed more dubious results. What began as a pioneering labor project to be emulated by the Building Service Employees International in other large cities around the United States, ended as a strictly business venture, funded mainly by banks.

Three other union-sponsored housing projects were built in Chicago during the sixties and seventies with the more conventional goal of housing unions members and other middle-income individuals, but only one (the Amalgamated Clothing Workers' Kenwood Square project) achieved any success, and it was not meant to house exclusively ACWA members or retirees, but as subsidized housing for middle-income tenants at a lakeside setting normally reserved for affluent residents of Chicago.

Despite the problems encountered in building or managing Marina City, the Teachers' Fewkes Tower, and the Steelworkers' Germano-Millgate Apartments, it is doubtful that any other large American city matched Chicago's record of four major union-sponsored residential projects built since World War II. Excepting Fewkes Tower, these undertakings were intended to revitalize the areas in which they were built. However, such urban renewal efforts were exceptions to the general rule that urban unions, both in Chicago and other large U.S. cities, did not pursue broad social goals on the local level.

On the other hand, important union leaders in Chicago were successful in receiving appointments to public boards concerned with a wide variety of urban problems. For example, the first major appointment made by Mayor Richard J. Daley after taking office in 1955 was to name CFL President William Lee to head the city's Civil Service Commission—a post he held, however, for only two years before resigning to run for international president of the Teamsters in 1957.[49] Lee also served on the board of the Chicago Park District from 1969, when Mayor Daley appointed him to replace the deceased William McFetridge, who had been the vice-president of the board from 1946 to 1967.[50] According to the co-authors of *Who Runs Chicago?* (1979), "As head of the CFL, Lee found himself serving on every kind of civic committee and commission imaginable as Daley developed his theory of bringing labor and business neatly together to agree on what he deemed important for Chicago. Lee has probably served on more committees than any [other] living Chicagoan, and his clipped, high-pitched, and always brief remarks have blessed every idea conceived in City Hall in the past thirty years."[51]

Chicago labor leaders also took particular pride in the fact that two seats on the board of education were reserved for union officials; one of these labor representatives, John D. Carey from the Steelworkers, served as the board's president for ten years before resigning in 1979 and was succeeded first as member and then as president by the retired head of the ACTWU Joint Board head, Sol Brandzel.[52] One seat was also reserved for the unions on the Chicago Housing Authority Commission, and two officials from the BSEIU served as CHA chairman—Martin Dwyer, president of Elevator Operators Local 66, and Henry Kruse, the vice-president of Flat Janitors Local 1, who also served as vice-president of the Chicago Metropolitan Area District Council.[53] During the seventies, James Kemp, president of SEIU Local 189 and a black McFetridge protégé, served on the board of the Regional Transit Authority, while Edward Brabic, the business agent of Plumbers Local 130, served on the Chicago Transit Authority's board.[54] Dozens of more examples of Chicago union leaders serving on important public boards could be cited.

There is, however, little in the record of these Labor representatives that would refute the 1953 observations by the sociologist James McKee that such representatives "have not brought to the decision-making process a new set of interests, a new program, a new ideology. They do not have a specific labor program."[55]

Both national and state spokesmen for Labor consistently promoted union representation on community boards as a means of raising "the voice of Labor" in community affairs, but Chicago was a particularly unlikely city for such a Labor voice to emerge as a strong, coherent perspective on urban issues, distinct from the "voices" of leading political and business figures who served alongside Labor representatives on the various public boards in Chicago. As J. David Greenstone noted in *Labor in American Politics*, such public service by union leaders was probably most significant as a means of cementing the close political alliance between the Chicago Federation of Labor and the local Democratic party—an alliance in which the union leaders were, according to Greenstone, clearly subordinate to Mayor Daley and other party leaders.[56]

Besides securing the local union-party alliance, such Labor representatives in Chicago served another important purpose that Thomas Burke touched upon in a report given at the 1960 BSEIU convention on the civic involvement of Chicago union officials. Burke said, "there isn't a better way to create the proper climate for the organizing of public employees than to have labor representation on public agencies."[57]

Union leaders in Chicago were apparently less successful in establishing union bargaining rights or wage scales in certain social service agencies that received funding from the Crusade of Mercy (as the annual United Way fund-raising drive was known there). As various unions became more involved in trying to organize the employees of such agencies during the seventies, the resistance to unionization allegedly shown by some of them was to become a national issue addressed by the national AFL–CIO Community Services Department.

The Illinois State AFL–CIO in 1974 passed a CSC-endorsed resolution introduced by SEIU officers from Chicago opposing "the allocation of any Community Fund [i.e., United Way] monies to any agency which fails to affirm its willingness to recognize a duly-chosen collective bargaining representative of its employees."[58] In both 1978 and 1979, Eugene Moats, head of the SEIU Joint Council in Chicago, and some officers from SEIU locals in the city introduced resolutions deploring the alleged use of United Way funds by certain agencies to hire "union-busting" consultants and lawyers and stating that the SEIU would "re-examine its practice of wholehearted cooperation in United Way fundraising activities" if Chicago agencies did not comply with the 1976 national memorandum of understanding between the AFL–CIO and the United Way, recognizing the right of agency employees to collective bargaining representation. According to Hazen Griffin, president of SEIU Local 372, the impetus for these resolutions came from the resistance encountered at the Lutheran Welfare Services of Illinois, the Christopher House of the United Christian Community Services, Chase House, and other nonprofit Chicago organizations, where, Griffin claimed, his local had won representation elections held among day-care and other service employees in 1975 but had never been able to sign a contract. In 1978, the state AFL–CIO's CSC concurred with the "intent" of the SEIU resolution opposing such behavior, but merely referred it to the Executive Board "for further study." In 1979, there was reportedly strong opposition to the repeat SEIU resolution within the State Federation, and the CSC had rewritten it to tone down its language, but the full convention restored the language after pleas to do so by SEIU leaders.[59]

One last problem arose in Chicago during the late seventies which, like the problems surrounding the unionization of charitable agencies' employees, did not appear to be a factor in the smaller, downstate communities. After United Way Labor representatives began introducing union counselor training to combat alcoholism among union members in Chicago-area plants in 1975, many firms, especially larger firms with relatively sophisticated personnel policies, began hiring social workers and developing their own employee assistance programs to deal with their workers' alcohol and drug abuse problems, along with any other personal problems. According to the labor representatives, the companies adopted these measures "very quietly," much to the dismay of community services supporters in the unions, who felt that management was expropriating the original union initiative along these lines. They also contrasted the companies' eagerness to take over what have been a community services program with the continuing reluctance of many Chicago local unions to sponsor an active CS program. Labor representatives also believed that "union avoidance" or a weakening to union loyalties was the primary motivation for management's willingness to supplant union counselors' traditional role of social workers to their fellow members.

Labor and Education

Labor's interest in public education in the United States can be traced back to the early part of the nineteenth century, in terms of both general education and the acquisition of vocational skills. Education designed for the advancement of union leadership goes back to the beginning of the twentieth century, with earlier roots in England. By the forties, many national unions in the United States had developed extensive education programs of their own. Several of them had full-time education staff members at regional or district levels. In Illinois, the Steelworkers, UAW, Packinghouse Workers and Meatcutters, Men's and Women's Clothing Workers, Machinists, Chemical Workers, Rubber Workers, Communication Workers, IBEW, AFSCME, Allied Industrial Workers, and Postal Workers, among others, carried on programs at regional and state levels, including leadership training, collective bargaining, steward training, and political action. A distinctive feature of the post-World War II period was the development of assistance from universities.

Labor or workers' education programs, including independent union classes and workshops as well as joint cooperative ventures with public and private universities, had been pioneered long before the war.[60] The Rand School of Social Science, the University of Wisconsin School for Workers, Bryn Mawr, Barnard, Brookwood, the Pacific Coast School for Workers, and the Highlander Folk School were only some of the more prominent examples. Mainstream, radical, and Catholic interests were all contributors. The AFL's program of labor institutes, which were held on university campuses, was organized at Rutgers in 1931. But the chief momentum for university involvement in labor education came in the early forties when the state legislatures of New York, New Jersey, and California (among others) authorized and financed the establishment of labor education programs at their major universities and a strong, although unsuccessful, effort was made over a three-year period culminating in the spring of 1948 to set up a national labor extension service in the Department of Labor comparable to the extension service that had so long and successfully served farmers.

In Illinois, the leadership in university labor education was taken by the University of Chicago, Roosevelt University, and the University of Illinois.

The first two institutions concentrated on the Chicago metropolitan area; the third was statewide in scope and included Chicago. A few community colleges in Chicago and downstate also introduced programs with varying success.

The origin of the University of Illinois program may be attributed to a resolution proposed by representatives of the Chicago Milk Drivers Local 753 and adopted at the 1942 annual convention of the State Federation of Labor.[61] After this resolution, State Federation President Reuben Soderstrom and Secretary-Treasurer Victor Olander contacted both university and legislative leaders about the establishment of a labor college that would serve Labor as the College of Commerce served business and the College of Agriculture served farmers. The proposal quickly aroused fears in the business community that a labor college would become a center of pro-unionism and radicalism. Prolonged study by a university committee and extensive negotiations between the university's administration and labor, management, and legislative representatives led to a compromise. Instead of a Labor College or even an Institute of Labor Relations, the new unit was to be called the Institute of Labor and Industrial Relations—neutral among the parties and with three functions—on-campus graduate instruction, research, and extension work with both labor unions and management groups. In June 1945, the state legislature voted to authorize the establishment of the program and added the sum of $150,000 to the University budget to finance it. The university's board of trustees approved the institute on March 9, 1946, and it began operations in September of that year on the Champaign-Urbana campus. Its first director, Phillips Bradley, was a well-known political scientist recruited from the New York State School of Industrial and Labor Relations at Cornell University, where he was head of the extension division.

During its initial half dozen or more years the institute's labor education activities were a source of public controversy. The major business organizations in the state had accepted the compromise "with apprehension."[62] Representatives of the Manufacturers' Association in several parts of the state (Granite City, Peoria, Rockford) insisted on sitting in on union classes to observe and participate in the proceedings. For a time, officials of the Manufacturers' Association argued that separate classes for labor should be banned and only joint labor-management classes and conferences should be held, but they were ultimately persuaded that the educational interests of neither labor nor management would be served by such a requirement.

Perhaps the high point of the controversy came in the spring of 1949, when a group of legislators, including the university's normally staunch Republican supporters from Champaign-Urbana, Representatives Ora Dillavou and Charles Clabaugh, publicly attacked the institute for being pro-labor and socialistic and called for a severe cut in university appropriations. At a time when McCarthyism and cold war emotions were reaching a high pitch and the legislature had recently enacted a loyalty oath law for state employees (the Broyles bill), the institute director was accused of once being a member of the Society for Cultural Relations with Russia, and a faculty member was attacked for having allegedly stated to the campus Socialist Club that there was "more incentive for workers under socialism than under capitalism." Lobbyists of the Manufacturers' Association were reported to "have been active in Springfield in stirring up opposition to the Institute."[63] University president George Stoddard strongly defended the institute and its director, and a series of conciliatory discussions were held to assuage the critics. In the end, the university budget escaped intact, and the institute continued to function, but with the cautionary note to avoid controversial statements. In the years that followed, criticisms from business and industrial organizations gradually dissipated, and the labor education program as well as other institute activities developed without further serious incidents.

Throughout the years Labor's interest in the institute was largely focussed on the labor education program rather than on the resident instruction (M.A. and later Ph.D. programs) or research programs. In the late fifties, both the William Green and Philip Murray Funds as well as affiliates of the state AFL–CIO made substantial financial contributions (totalling more than $135,000), which served as the foundation for much larger state appropriations ($350,000) to provide a building to house the institute. In 1965, the institute established a permanent office with a small full-time staff to conduct its Chicago Labor Education Program.

From its beginning, with a few experimental exceptions (including international affairs), the labor education program dealt primarily with bread-and-butter rather than liberal arts subjects. The objective was to satisfy the expressed desires of the labor unions, and these invariably related to union and job-oriented functions. Throughout the state, eight- and sixteen-week classes were conducted for a wide variety of local union groups on how the economy worked, labor legislation, collective bargaining, grievance handling, leadership psychology and communications, parliamentary procedure, steward training, labor history, and health and safety. In addition, one- or two-day conferences on current economic, political, or social topics were held annually or ad hoc with particular organizations like the state AFL–CIO, the Machinists Union, the IBEW, and the Postal Workers, or groups like local central labor bodies and full-time labor editors. During the summer, week-long resident programs were developed in conjunction with the Steelworkers Union and a number of other national or state organizations. An intensive one-week program on arbitration techniques for union staff persons was presented annually on the University of Illinois campus and drew participants from around the country. In Chicago, a series of six- or twelve-week classes, operating from the university's campus there, was set up in the late sixties to provide "union leadership with a better understanding of the pressing problems faced by labor in our urban society."[64] Successful completion of a set of courses resulted in a special certificate. In the seventies, a Latino labor leader was added to the staff, and classes for Spanish-speaking unionists were set up. Work with groups of women unionists was also undertaken, as well as several programs in occupational health and safety.

The labor education programs of the University of Chicago and of Roosevelt University were similar to those of the University of Illinois. The University of Chicago, the first of the three to set up a program as part of its Industrial Relations Center, in the late forties developed "a nine-month long (one hundred hours of classroom instruction) non-residential program" in a large number of subjects for local union and staff officers in the Chicago area.[65] It also developed a few home study courses for local leaders on union administration and grievance handling and prepared materials for the use of unions in their own training activities. The program was discontinued in the early sixties, when available funds ran out and administrative backing declined.

Roosevelt University was established in 1944 with strong union financial and organizational support. From the outset it had a Labor Education Division headed by a director with the status of a dean that engaged in conferences and co-sponsored short courses. In 1963, it organized a four-year classroom program for local union officers and activists, but its union contacts and enrollments were much wider than the University of Chicago's. Graduates of the union leadership program received a special certificate. In the seventies, Roosevelt also set up a related set of courses with a broader social science content that enabled a few more academically minded unionists to receive a bachelor's degree from the university. Like the University of Illinois, the Roosevelt Labor Education Division offered ad hoc courses as well as nonresident conferences and institutes for particular unions. It also became active, as did the Illinois ILIR, in providing training programs for foreign trade union leaders. In contrast to the University of Chicago, both Roosevelt University and the University of Illinois maintained their labor education activities throughout the entire period of this study. Thousands of local unionists were exposed to enlarged visions of industrial society; scores of them were aided in moving up to significant leadership positions in unions, and a few in government.

NOTES

The section of this chapter that deals with community service is based on a report researched and written by David Nicolai.

1. "1964–1966 Report of Officers, United Packinghouse, Food, and Allied Workers," *Packinghouse workers*, May 1966, p. 7.

2. *Illinois Labor*, August 1953, p. 1.

3. Ibid., p. 4.

4. *Proceedings* of the 8th Annual Convention, Illinois Industrial Union Council, December 1950, p. 121.

5. Mel Wyrick, chairman of the Chicago CIO–CSC, wrote in the March-April 1955 edition of the *National Newsletter* of the Labor Participation Department of the Community Chests and Councils of America that the Chicago CSC program had been instituted "twelve years ago." The January 1953 CIO convention proceedings reported that the Chicago CSC "Has been in operation some nine years" (p. 73).

6. *Proceedings* of the 8th Annual Convention, p. 122.

7. "CIO–CSC Statewide," *Illinois Labor*, October 1951, p. 2; *Labor-Welfare in Our Community*, March 1957, p. 1; and biographical information provided by Samuel Guzzardo.

8. Various "CIO–CSC Statewide" columns in *Illinois Labor*, 1951–54; CSC reports to state CIO conventions, 1951–54.

9. *Illinois Labor*, October 1951, p. 2 and July 1952, p. 1. In fact, the first CS counseling courses offered in Danville in October 1951 were sponsored not by the CIO, but by the "United Labor Committee," with the participation of CIO, AFL, and independent unions.

10. *Proceedings* of the 10th Annual Convention, Illinois Industrial Union Council, January 1953, pp. 72 and 73; *Proceedings* of the 11th Annual Convention, Illinois Industrial Union Council, December 1953, pp. 93 and 105; *Proceedings* of the 12th Annual Convention, Illinois Industrial Union Council, January 1955, p. 163; and *Proceedings* of the 13th Annual Convention, Illinois Industrial Union Council, January 1956, pp. 199 and 208.

11. "CIO–CSC Statewide," *Illinois Labor*, November 1954, p. 2.

12. *Illinois Labor*, August 1952; August 1953, p. 4.

13. *Proceedings* of the 13th Annual Convention, p. 209.

14. *Proceedings* of the 11th Annual Convention, p. 104; *Proceedings* of the 13th Annual Convention, pp. 200, 202, 203, 206, 207.

15. *Illinois Labor*, August 1952, p. 2; *Proceedings* of the 10th Annual Convention, p. 175.

16. *Labor Welfare in Our Community*, September 1955, p. 2.

17. *Proceedings* of the 11th Annual Convention, p. 102 (Rockford); *Labor-Welfare in Our Community*, October 1956, p. 1 (Chicago).

18. *Illinois Labor*, December 1953, p. 3; February 1954, p. 11.

19. *Labor in Our Community*, November 1947, p. 1

20. Ibid., December 1974, p. 1.

21. Ibid., November 1948, p. 1.

22. *Labor Welfare in Our Community*, January 1950, p. 1.

23. "CIO–CSC Statewide," *Illinois Labor*, October 1952, p. 2; February 1953, p. 5.

24. *Illinois Labor* July 1953, p. 2.

25. Ibid., August 1954, p. 1.

26. *Proceedings* of the 13th Annual Convention, pp. 208–9.

27. *Proceedings* of the 12th Annual Convention, p. 266.

28. Robert M. Levin, "Union Medical Center Planned for West Side," *Chicago Daily News*, November 9, 1962; D. J. R. Bruckner, "Union to Open Major Group

Health Center on Monday," *Chicago Sun-Times*, August 15, 1965, p. 24; see also two articles on Union Eye Center in *Labor Welfare in Our Community*, January 1954, p. 2 and October 1954, p. 1.

29. *Proceedings* of the 3rd Annual Convention, Illinois Industrial Union Council, 1960, p. 119.

30. Ibid, pp. 119–20.

31. *Proceedings* of the 4th Annual Convention, Illinois Industrial Union Council, 1961, pp. 130–31.

32. James Strong, "State AFL–CIO Doubles Its Dues," *Chicago Tribune*, October 7, 1971; William C. Harsh, Jr., "State AFL–CIO Votès per Capita Tax Hike," *Chicago Sun-Times*, October 7, 1971.

33. *Proceedings* of the 5th Annual Convention, Illinois State Federation of Labor and Congress of Industrial Organizations, 1962, p. 137.

34. *Proceedings* of the 9th Annual Convention, Illinois State Federation of Labor and Congress of Industrial Organizations, 1966, p. 149.

35. *Proceedings* of the 18th Annual Convention, Illinois State Federation of Labor and Congress of Industrial Organizations, 1975, p. 149.

36. *Proceedings* of the 21st Annual Convention, Illinois State Federation of Labor and Congress of Industrial Organizations, 1978, p. 128.

37. *Proceedings* of the National AFL–CIO Convention, 1961, p. 272; 1979, p. 234.

38. In 1964, the State Federation's Executive Board noted that "on the national level, nearly 35 cents of every dollar donated to these voluntary campaigns comes from the pocket of trade unionists. We have reason to believe that it is that good or better in our State" (*Proceedings*, 1964, p. 141). Austin Perlow, however, states that the United Way has more recently estimated that union members contribute closer to half of all United Way funds (Austin Perlow, *What Have You Done for Me Lately?*, [New York: Rutledge Books, 1979, p. 140]).

39. *Proceedings* of the 21st Annual Convention, p. 301.

40. *Proceedings* of 22nd Annual Convention, Illinois State Federation of Labor and Congress of Industrial Organizations, 1979, pp. 60–61.

41. *Proceedings* of the 23rd Annual Convention, Illinois State Federation of Labor and Congress of Industrial Organizations, 1980, p. 136.

42. Interview with George Andrew, October 25, 1983, Rockford, Ill,; clippings and vita provided by Andrew.

43. Interviews with George Andrew, Leonard David, and Sandy Mendenhall, October 27, 1983, Peoria, Ill.

44. Interview with George Andrew.

45. Interview with Leonard David and Harold Wright, December 7, 1983, Belleville, Ill.

46. Interviews with Robert Gibson and Harold Wright, December 7, 1983, St. Louis; interview with Ray Maulden, November 29, 1983, Decatur, Ill.

47. *Proceedings* of the 20th Annual Convention, Illinois State Federation of Labor and Congress of Industrial Organizations, 1977, p. 292; *Proceedings* of the 21st Annual Convention, Illinois State Federation of Labor and Congress of Industrial Organizations, 1978, p. 298.

48. *Federation News*, January 13, 1962, p. 3.

49. *Chicago Tribune*, April 24, 1957, p. 8.

50. McFetridge obituary in *Chicago Daily News*, March 17, 1961, p. 9; Lee ousted by Byrne, *Chicago Sun-Times*, April 9, 1980 and *Chicago Tribune*, April 2, 1980, p. 17.

51. F. Richard Ciccone, Connie Fletcher, and Michael Killian, *Who Runs Chicago?* (New York: St. Martin's Press, 1979), p. 242.

52. *Chicago Tribune*, October 12, 1976, sec. 3, p. 1 and October 18, 1976, sec. 4, p. 11.

53. Martin Dwyer obituary in *Federation News*, April 1974, p. 3; Henry Kruse, *Proceeds* of the 12th BSEIU General Convention, New York, 1960, p. 330.

54. *Federation News*, May 1974, p. 1 and November 1975, p. 8.

55. James McKee, "Status and Power in the Industrial Community: A Comment on Orucker's Thesis," *American Journal of Sociology*, January 1953, p. 369.

56. David Greenstone, *Labor in American Politics* (New York: Vintage Books, 1969), p. 95.

57. *Proceedings* of the 12th BSEIU General Convention, p. 164.

58. *Proceedings* of the 17th Annual Convention, Illinois State Federation of Labor and Congress of Industrial Organizations, 1974, p. 247.

59. *Proceedings* of the 21st Annual Convention, Illinois State Federation of Labor and Congress of Industrial Organizations, 1978, pp. 299–330; Michael Flannery, "Some Crusade Units Anti-Union, State AFL–CIO Says, *Chicago Sun-Times*, September 26, 1979, p. 12.

60. Three background sources that were helpful were: J. B. S. Hardman and Maurice F. Neufeld, eds., *The House of Labor* (New York: Prentice-Hall, 1951); Jack Barbash, *Universities and Unions in Workers Education* (New York: Harper and Brothers, 1955); and Ronald J. Peters, "Factors Affecting Labor Extension Legislation 1945–1950," Ph.D. diss., Michigan State University, 1976.

61. This brief account of the University of Illinois labor education program is derived from the files of the Institute of Labor and Industrial Relations, discussions with Phillips L. Garman, Ronald Peters, and other members of the Institute's labor education faculty, and the writer's personal observations.

62. Notes by H. M. Gray, associate dean of the Graduate School, of a conference held by representatives of the University with representatives of labor, industry and management at the University Club, Chicago, February 21, 1946.

63. *Champaign-Urbana News Gazette*, June 5, 8, and 14, 1949.

64. *Report of Activities*, Chicago Labor Education Program September 1965–August 1967, p. 3.

65. Peters, "Factors Affecting Labor Extension," pp. 132–33. The brief discussions of both the University of Chicago and Roosevelt University programs are derived primarily from this source and from personal discussions with Peters, who worked at Roosevelt University before coming to the University of Illinois as head of the labor education unit there.

PART V

Social Forces

Although organized Labor experienced advances and some setbacks, several profound social forces emerged and crystallized which, in varying degrees, reshaped the ideas and the status of individual workers and work groups as well as the structure and functions of unions.

One of these social forces involved the ideology of the labor force. With the growth of the affluent society, radical ideologies to overhaul the economic system lost appeal. Although the idea of the welfare state, particularly stressing full employment, safety, and health protection and retirement benefits, appeared to have wide support, socialist thoughts about nationalized industry exercised very limited attraction. During the late sixties and early seventies, radical thinking in the nation shifted to civil rights, antinuclear, and antiwar movements, but these movements were dominated by student and middle-class groups, and only a small segment of organized labor participated. If anything, the great majority of the working people were opposed to the new radicalism.

A second social force that had serious implications for the labor movement was the increased involvement of organized crime in the financial affairs of a number of trade unions. Although only a small minority of unions were victimized by the spreading tentacles of organized crime, the widespread media attention devoted to a few of them, notably the huge Teamsters Union, cast a shadow over the entire labor movement. In Illinois, the spotlight was focussed particularly on the city of Chicago because of a series of congressional inquiries and Justice Department investigations. The AFL–CIO, under the leadership of George Meany, formulated a set of codes of ethical practices and expelled the Teamsters and several smaller unions for corrupt practices. Congress enacted the Landrum–Griffin law and other anti-crime regulatory acts while the Justice and Labor Departments stepped up their programs to eliminate union corruption. After two decades of national attention and remedial action in which Illinois was prominently featured, a more balanced perspective on the corruption problem was finally achieved.

Another major social force of the period was the attack on discrimination in employment of blacks, Hispanics, and women. Illinois, with its large and rapidly expanding minority population, was a leader in the civil rights movement although it was also strongly influenced by national developments. Success in the movement for more rights for working women followed shortly after the initial black civil rights campaigns. However, by 1980 proponents of these movements could only report that the initial barriers of discrimination had been scaled and that much work was required to achieve their goals. One of the significant features of the civil rights movement was the gradual change in the position of organized Labor from uncertainty and (in some branches) active opposition to general acceptance if not always energetic support.

In some respects the struggle for improved quality of working life paralleled the antidiscrimination force. Illinois was not distinctive in this respect although some unions like the clothing, meatpacking, and coal mining workers were in the forefront of the national movement. Work hours were reduced, compulsory overtime was modified, paid leisure time was increased, health and safety conditions were improved. But joint labor-management programs were relatively few.

15

The Decline of Labor Radicalism

At the conclusion of World War II in 1945, unions headed by left-wing leaders (i.e., radicals advocating the replacement of capitalism by a socialist economy and ranging from right-wing socialists to communists of many shadings) were a strong presence in the Illinois labor movement, both in Chicago and in a number of downstate communities. The rapid economic growth and high employment levels of most of the state's industries during the war years, combined with favorable rulings by the NLRB and War Labor Board, had allowed left-wing leaders of such unions as the Farm Equipment Workers, United Electrical Workers, and Mine, Mill, and Smelter Workers, to organize thousands of Illinois workers and establish themselves as influential figures in the state CIO during the war years. Among the major firms organized by these unions were International Harvester and Caterpillar Tractor in the farm and heavy construction equipment industry; Armour, Swift, and Wilson in meatpacking; Stewart-Warner and Sunbeam in the electrical and radio industries; the Campbell Soup Company, and Florsheim Shoe Company.

Other left-wing-dominated unions represented in the Illinois labor movement by 1945 included a number of midwestern "outposts" of international unions generally associated with other regions of the country and with the specific radical traditions of those regions. Examples of these relatively isolated locals were the two Illinois locals of the International Longshoremen and Warehousemen Union (ILWU), an international led by Harry Bridges and composed overwhelmingly of West Coast port workers; Chicago's Local 236 of the Transport Workers Union, a union dominated for years by the Irish-American workers on the New York City transit systems and their fiery leader Michael Quill; and the Chicago locals of the International Fur and Leather Workers (IFLWU), which drew heavily upon the radical traditions of its Jewish members and leaders in New York City, the national center of the industry. The International Union of Mine, Mill, and Smelter Workers, although descended from the Western Federation of Miners and steeped in the class-conscious unionism of the western miners, established more than twenty locals in Illinois during the thirties and forties at a time when its national membership was gradually expanding eastward. In fact, delegates to the 1944

"Mine-Mill" convention voted to move their international headquarters from Denver to Chicago at the recommendation of Mine-Mill President Reid Robinson.[1] Mine-Mill headquarters remained in Chicago from January 1945 to January 1951, when it returned to Denver after the 1950 convention had voted, at a time of mounting membership losses, deteriorating finances, internal ideological strife, and government prosecution of the union in Illinois and elsewhere, to move the headquarters back to the center of its traditional jurisdiction.[2]

Unlike the ILWU, which was not active in Illinois until 1940 and which enjoyed few successes in its basic warehouse jurisdiction, the International Fur and Leather Workers' Union had a lengthy prewar history of organizing in its basic jurisdiction, the fur industry in Chicago. And unlike ILWU Local 208, an isolated unit of the international that never really penetrated its San Francisco-based leadership, the leaders of the Chicago Fur Workers, particularly Abe Feinglass, were prominent figures in the international's history both before and after World War II and were experienced veterans of the same sort of intense Left-Right ideological strife and inroads by gangster elements that characterized the dominant New York City locals.

Besides the UE, Mine-Mill, ILWU, and IFLWU, some smaller and lesser-known unions that were also expelled from the CIO in 1949 and 1950 for alleged communist domination were active in Illinois. One such union was the United Cannery, Agricultural, Packing, and Allied Workers of America (UCAPAWA), whose efforts to organize groups of agricultural workers in all regions of the United States during the late thirties bore many more defeats than successes.

UCAPAWA, which reorganized itself in 1946 as the Food, Tobacco, Agricultural, and Allied Workers Union of America (FTA), could claim a number of relatively small Illinois locals organized outside of Chicago, during the war years, including Local 11 at the Northern Illinois Cereal Company in Lockport, near Joliet; Locals 17 and 18 at California Packing Company (Del Monte) plants in Rochelle and DeKalb, respectively, in north central Illinois, and Local 52 at a Libby, McNeill, and Libby plant in Morrison, forty miles northeast of the Quad Cities.[3] In addition, in 1946 the FTA joined forces with the FE and Mine, Mill, and Smelter Workers in a joint organizing campaign at a Stokley Foods plant and a number of can manufacturing plants in Hoopeston, a small town near the Indiana border, about thirty miles north of Danville.

The majority of FTA members in Illinois, however, worked in Chicago, a great center of agricultural processing industries. Since 1937, FTA Local 47 represented approximately five hundred workers at the Libby, McNeill, and Libby plant in south suburban Blue Island,[4] while Local 194, one of the largest locals in the international, represented some 2,500 workers in six Chicago firms by the end of the war.

Fully 2,200 of these 2,500 workers were employed at just one firm, the Campbell Soup Company, often described by the FTA as the largest cannery in the world. With the assistance of the Packinghouse Workers' Organizing Committee, UCAPAWA won bargaining rights at the large Campbell plant, which was located near the stockyards and which employed 3,000 workers in season and 2,000 out of season, by a 1139–459 NLRB vote in October 1940.[5]

Two left-wing, white-collar CIO unions that organized a number of locals in the state were the United Office and Professional Workers of American (UOPWA) and the United Public Workers of America (UPWA). The UOPWA was a small union (43,000 members in 1944) that was short-lived (1937–50) and heavily concentrated in New York. It listed locals in all the major downstate Illinois cities in convention proceedings during the forties, but the very small size of these locals, their general failure to send delegates to the conventions, and their absence from the pages of extant issues of the union paper strongly indicate that none of the downstate locals were ever fully functioning units of the international. Thus, the UOPWA presence in Illinois was effectively confined to three Chicago locals—14, 39, and 78—all of which were represented at the international's first convention in 1938. A 1947 article in *Work*, the paper of the Catholic Labor Alliance and a quite reliable source of information on left-wing unions in Chicago, stated in 1947 that "the three UOPWA locals in Chicago claim a total membership of 2500 among insurance agents, social workers, and general clerical and technical employees." This article also confirmed the opinion of many other observers that the UOPWA was "one of the most completely Communist-dominated unions in the CIO."[6]

It is difficult to reconstruct the UOPWA's exact accomplishments in organizing white-collar workers and securing contracts for them in Chicago, but it is clear that Social Service Employees Local 39 was confined to nonprofit organizations in the city. A promotional pamphlet put out by Local 39 in the late forties claimed membership (but not contracts) in nineteen different agencies.[7] Articles from extant issues of the union paper, *Office and Professional News*, indicate that Local 39, the majority of whose membership and leadership were women, had stable bargaining relationships or written contracts with very few, if any, of these agencies. In this context, two of the locals' most concrete accomplishments came rather late in its brief history. In December 1947, shortly before the local leaders' unstinting loyalty to the communist leadership of the international brought upon it even further instability, Local 39 secured a "full contract instead of the previous personnel practices code"—a contract that reportedly included maintenance of membership and dues checkoff for approximately two hundred social workers employed by the four major Jewish social welfare agencies in Chicago. At the same time, Local 39 secured a written contract for approximately fifteen social workers employed by United Charities, often described by the union as the second largest nonsectarian agency in the United States, although it was apparently a very weak contract.[8]

The United Public Workers of America (UPW) was, like the UOPWA, a small (1946 membership approximately sixty thousand, down to fourteen thousand by 1949) and short-lived (1946–50) union created from the 1946 merger of two left-wing, public-sector CIO affiliates founded in 1937, the United Federal Workers and the State, County, and Municipal Workers of America.[9] Even less is known about the early activities of the Federal Workers of the State, County, and Municipal Workers in Illinois than about the UOPWA. At the first convention of the Illinois Industrial Union Council (the state CIO body), held in September 1941, the Federal Workers' four Illinois locals sent five delegates who were entitled to seven votes, indicating a maximum statewide membership of approximately seven hundred,[10] while the State, County, and Municipal Workers' three locals sent three delegates with four votes, for a maximum membership of around four hundred public workers.[11] At the 1943 IUC convention, the Federal Workers were down to two locals entitled to three votes, but the State, County, and Municipal Workers had expanded to six locals entitled to thirteen votes.[12] In his *Chicago Journal of Commerce* series, Andrew Avery, who described the Public Workers as "the most dangerous union in the country," stated, without further details, that "In Chicago . . . it has organized chapters in the public library, the municipal [actually, Cook County] welfare department, the housing authority, the juvenile court, and other offices."[13]

Chicago's UPW Local 2, which had members in the Welfare Department, the State Department of Labor, and the new Chicago campus of the University of Illinois, claimed to represent almost 1,500 workers in 1949.[14] This local, which was organized in 1937 as Local 88 of the State, County, and Municipal Workers (CIO), also claimed in 1949 that its successful legislative campaign in Springfield resulted in salary increases of 20–14 percent for some seven hundred professional and clerical employees of the Chicago Public Library—a remarkable claim, if true, for a union that probably had as little effective bargaining power with public agencies in Chicago as the UOPWA had with the nonprofit agencies where it had members.[15] UPW Local 568 had some sort of bargaining relationship with the University of Chicago for six years, 1943–49, and bits and pieces of correspondence from the files of Myers, Myers, and Rothstein, a law firm that then represented most of the left-wing unions in Chicago, indicate that the State, County, and Municipal Workers were active in 1943 organizing janitors and grounds workers at Northwestern University and in the city of Evanston, and that in the late forties the UPW had Local 248 at the Chicago Post Office and at least some membership at the Argonne National Laboratory in suburban Chicago.[16]

All of the Illinois unions discussed, with the important exception of Packinghouse Workers District 1, were affiliated with international unions expelled from the CIO in 1949 and 1950 for alleged communist domination. To complete this examination of the rise of the more radical CIO unions in the state, we must finally note three Chicago unions affiliated with CIO internationals that narrowly averted expulsion from the CIO by last-minute shifts in their leadership's policies after bitter internal Left-Right struggles. All three of these Chicago unions—Transit Workers Local 236, Furniture Workers Local 18-B, and Shoe Workers Joint Council #25—were active participants in the ideological skirmishes that absorbed their internationals during the mid and late forties. Also, coincidentally, all three were born, like IFLWU Luggage Workers Local 415, out of revolts against allegedly corrupt AFL locals.

Labor radicalism was by no means confined to the unions expelled from the CIO. The CIO's principal affiliates—the Steelworkers, UAW, Amalgamated Clothing Workers, and Packinghouse Workers—included communist activists as well as advocates of socialist or social democratic ideologies. Although the AFL was less accessible and less attractive to active radicals, a number of AFL unions, such as the Ladies Garment Workers, Machinists, Meat Cutters, Painters, Printers, and Building Service Employees also had radical members and leaders. How numerous the respective categories of radicals were cannot be determined from available data.

In some cases, such as the UAW and the ILGWU, the most effective opponents of the communists were moderate socialists. The farm equipment industry provides an example where a communist-led union, the FE, was defeated and absorbed by socialist or Social Democratic UAW rivals led by Walter Reuther. In other cases, like District 31 of the Steelworkers and the Illinois Industrial Union Council, the forces led by Catholic anticommunist Joseph Germano succeeded in pushing communists or communist sympathizers out of important union offices. In still other unions, like the Packinghouse Workers, radicals of various ideologies worked together more or less harmoniously to challenge powerful management forces. At one point, in 1946, when the differences between the communists and socialists and other activists became intense, a compromise agreement was reached to elevate the union's general counsel, Ralph Helstein, to the presidency. He served until he retired in 1972. When the Fur Workers sought refuge from the anticommunist provision of the Taft–Hartley law and other governmental pressures, twenty-nine communist leaders, including president Ben Gold, were forced to resign before the merger was carried through with the AFL Amalgamated Meatcutters and Butcher Workmen. Gold's successor, Abe Feinglass, was a noncommunist, but he held views that were clearly left of center.[17]

A unique Chicago labor organization, the Catholic Labor Alliance, provided a different kind of voice for radical trade unionism from its founding in 1943 until its gradual disengagement from labor issues and eventual demise in the mid-sixties. Its origins can be traced back in part to the mid-thirties when two Catholic Workers Houses of Hospitality were established under the influence of Dr. Arthur Falls, a black Chicago physician, and Dorothy Day, a Chicago native who had become a national leader of the Catholic Worker movement in New York. The St. Joseph's House was opened in 1937 by Ed Marciniak and Alex Resner, who became, together with other "talented and highly articulate" young workers such as John Cogley, leaders of the Catholic workers movement in Chicago.[18] Another strand of influence on the Chicago Catholic Labor Alliance was the Association of Catholic Trade Unionism that was started in New York in 1937 by John Cort and had an active Chicago chapter for a few years. Social reform as well as support for labor unions were also lent encouragement by Cardinal George Mundelein and Auxiliary Bishop Bernard Sheil while moderating Catholic radicalism.

Drawing its inspiration from an authoritative but little-known body of Catholic doctrine on trade unionism in industrial societies, the Catholic Labor Alliance, which at peak included about 250 trade union activists and a few outside intellectuals, combined adherence to the Church's anticommunist teachings with strong opposition to the "primitive" anticommunism that pervaded much of American life, including organized labor, during the postwar period. Catholic Labor Alliance leaders, particularly through their widely read journal *Work*, continually condemned the shortcomings of "business unionism" in Chicago and elsewhere and promoted a humanistic vision of American unionism as a potential movement for transforming the very nature of capitalist economic life in the United States.

The Catholic Labor Alliance, as well as a variety of socially oriented unions, strongly emphasized the rights of blacks, women, and others particularly susceptible to labor market exploitation. For example, a conference on migrant agricultural workers sponsored by the Alliance in 1959 was instrumental in focusing nationwide attention on these workers. Women's conferences sponsored by UPWA District 1 and UE District 11 in Chicago in the early fifties were among the first such conferences in the country, and a number of Chicago unions provided substantial support during the fifties and sixties to both the fledgling civil rights movement in the South and to breaking through the "iron curtain of Jim Crow" in Chicago itself.

When the Reverend Martin Luther King launched his Chicago Freedom Movement in 1966, his efforts were supported by a number of local unions, notably from the UAW and Packinghouse Workers, which cooperated with King's staff in a pioneering effort to organize residents of the West Side black ghetto into tenants' unions to engage in collective bargaining with landlords over housing conditions. With such long-standing efforts by progressive unions in the area to promote the rights of minority workers, it is not surprising that in 1972 Chicago was the site of the founding conventions of two new national groups, the Coalition of Black Trade Unionists and the Coalition of Labor Union Women, whose leadership drew heavily from local veterans of the earlier struggles for minority union members' rights.

During the sixties and seventies in Illinois there were other important attempts, many led by younger workers, to both give new meaning to the ideal of social unionism and to strengthen the voices of dissident union members. In 1966 and 1967, the young leaders of a new union representing some four thousand welfare caseworkers employed by Cook County demanded not only union recognition, higher wages, and better working conditions, but also the caseworkers' right to join forces with their clients in an effort to overhaul the welfare system (Chapter 4, part G). In 1971, two veterans of the welfare caseworkers' strikes, who were then employed at the federal Office of Economic Opportunity in Chicago, led a similar nationwide but ineffective attempt by American Federation of Government Employees (AFGE) activists to form alliances between certain federal employees and their disadvantaged clients and to grant such employees extensive control over the managerial policies of their agencies.

The AFGE activists in Chicago formed, in the words of sympathetic social historian Staughton Lynd, a "national rank-and-file caucus dedicated to aggressive, socially concerned industrial unionism."[19] Chicago became, in fact, the nation center for what its supporters called rank-and-file unionism during the seventies. National attention focused on the activities of the rank-and-file caucus of Steelworkers' District 31 in Chicago and northern Indiana when the young radical District Director Edward Sadlowski began to promote a more active role in union affairs by black, Hispanic, and younger workers. But Sadlowski's challenge to the national leadership proved futile, and his term in office was short. Another Chicago-based group, Trade Union Action and Democracy, which combined a more traditional Marxist perspective on union affairs with the newer concerns of the rank-and-filers, garnered relatively little influence or attention. During the late seventies, union support of the Illinois Public Action Councils' efforts promoting utilities and health-care reform through grass-roots citizen involvement helped to bridge some of the distance between the old and new Left in the state. Activists from such groups as the New American Movement and the Democratic Socialist Organizing Committee had slight impact on the Illinois labor movement.

Within a few years of the end of World War II, the high tide of radical labor began to recede rapidly and, except for a few minor exceptions to be noted later, the activities and influence of radicals on organized labor were of little consequence for the remainder of the study period. The explanation for this development lies in at least five different factors:

1. the anti-radical steps taken by the mainstream leadership of the CIO and the AFL;
2. the shift in the national climate of opinion from a view of the Soviet

Union as a major wartime ally to the Cold War perception of its role as major ideological and political foe;

3. the enactment of anticommunist legislation;

4. the economic prosperity and the emergent welfare state that made traditional Marxist and competing ideologies increasingly unattractive or irrelevant; and

5. the rise of New Left ideologies dominated by students and intellectuals.

Three major developments occurred within the labor movement to sharply diminish the influence of left-wing unionists. At the individual union level, it took the form of active raiding of vulnerable Left-dominated locals by the two leading CIO unions in Illinois—the Steelworkers and the UAW—and by a number of AFL unions, notably the Machinists and the IBEW. Perhaps the major case was that of the UAW–FE competition that ended in 1954 in the total absorption of the remaining FE membership by the UAW in the important farm equipment industry (chapter 10). A second key development took place in 1946 and 1947 within both Chicago Industrial Union Council and the state CIO (chapter 4, part C).

Finally, in 1949 and 1950, the national CIO leadership launched a determined anticommunist drive that resulted in the expulsion of ten affiliates, most notably the FE and the UE, on grounds of alleged communist domination and established several new organizations to supplant them. This action also set the stage for the ensuing AFL–CIO merger that materialized nationally in 1955 and in Illinois between 1955 and 1962.

Although a small number of communist-led locals in Illinois survived these assaults, for example, the UE local at Stewart–Warner in Chicago, most succumbed to mainstream organizations either through absorption (as in the case of the FE) or merger (as in the case of the Fur Workers) or replacement by other unions, or simply disappeared. Leftists continued to be active within a number of mainstream locals such as Local 6 of the UAW (chapter 4, part D) and Local 65 of the Steelworkers (chapter 4, part C). By and large, however, the extreme Left was obliged to either moderate or conceal its basic views.

The internal union attacks on leftist activists were abetted by a variety of government actions during the cold war period of the late forties and early fifties, even though the mainstream unionists often themselves opposed the form of governmental intervention. From 1939 to 1959, the U.S. House of Representatives' Un-American Activities Committee (HUAC) conducted periodic hearings on the political and union activities of left-wing unionists around the country, including those in Illinois. Although none of these unionists was ever legally prosecuted on the basis of their testimony before HUAC, the conduct of such inquiries in Chicago during farm equipment and packinghouse strikes in the fifties led to vehement protests by union leaders in these industries that HUAC, major Illinois firms, and rival unions were conspiring to break the strikes and to oust leftists from their major positions of strength in the state.

Another type of anti-radical government action was that of the Chicago Police Department's so-called "Red Squad," officially titled Security Section of the Intelligence Division, which had been formed in the twenties as the Industrial Unit to keep an eye on and harass labor union radicals. It remained active until 1975, when legal action forced its abolition. During its tenure, the unit compiled some four hundred thousand pages of documentation on about 1,300 organizations and more than one hundred thousand individuals.

Throughout the first half of the fifties, Illinois labor radicals were also subject to the discomforting atmosphere of McCarthyism as Senator Joseph McCarthy of Wisconsin traversed the country hurling his mostly baseless accusations of communism at government and defense industry personnel and conducting intimidating hearings.

Legislative enactment also affected left-wing unionists as well as others. The Taft–Hartley Act of 1947, for example, required officers of unions appearing before the NLRB to file affidavits certifying that they did not advocate the forceful overthrow of the United States government. Many unionists, including noncommunists like the leaders of the United Mine Workers, refused to sign such affidavits as an invasion of their privacy and constitutional rights, and the provision was eliminated in 1959. Nonetheless, the provision had an important impact on such events as the violent Mine-Mill strike against the American Zinc Company in East St. Louis in 1948 and the defeat of the UE at the large Stewart-Warner plant in Chicago in the same year. A small number of unionists, like Packinghouse Workers Union District 1 Director Herbert March, admitted their Communist party affiliation and resigned their posts rather than comply with Taft-Hartley. However, overall, the Taft-Hartley provision proved to be more a nuisance than an effective instrument for attacking labor radicalism. The great majority of left-wing labor leaders in Illinois eventually decided to sign affidavits certifying that they were not communists; those who were, either found means of evading the act or were sufficiently entrenched so that the act had little impact on them.

The Broyles Act, which imposed a loyalty oath on all state employees, proved even more futile. It aroused the strong opposition of both the CIO and AFL as well as academic associations like the American Association of University Professors, and it was vetoed by two Illinois governors before passage in 1956. However, the McCarthy period was drawing to a close and concerns over the loosely worded act soon disappeared.

Radical political action was also affected by the courts. When in 1948 the newly formed Progressive party, with active left-wing union support and with Henry Wallace as its presidential nominee, attempted to get on the Illinois ballot, the state courts ruled that Illinois's restrictive rules governing third-party candidacies precluded it. This path for independent radical political action was not to be cleared of barriers until a decisive ruling by the U.S. Supreme Court in 1979.

A fourth and very different factor leading to the decline of labor radicalism in Illinois was the sustained economic prosperity of the times (at least until the mid-seventies) and the expansion of the welfare state. The relatively favorable economic conditions that prevailed in Illinois and nationally throughout most of the fifties and sixties are discussed in Chapter 2. As wage-earners in basic industries like steel, autos, construction, and trucking secured wages and benefits that compared favorably with and often surpassed white-collar conditions, the incentive of union labor to turn to radical programs appears to have practically vanished. Indeed, something of a reversal occurred as white-collar employees, like teachers and nurses, especially in the public sector, adopted militant union structures and tactics to improve their economic conditions and to offset what many perceived as a widening gap between their pay and benefit levels and those of the unionized blue-collar wage-earners. During the severe recession of 1974 and 1975, the deepest since the Great Depression, there appears to have been some revival of radical sentiments, but little evidence is available of significant growth.

Finally, and perhaps most important, the concept of radicalism itself underwent a profound change from traditional nineteenth-century Marxism to the New Left concerns in the sixties and seventies with civil rights; the advancement of blacks, Latinos, and women in the workplace; antiwar (especially anti-Vietnam) and antinuclear policies, and environmental pollution. Apart from black civil rights, the New Left movement was essentially the product of university students and academic intellectuals. Neither trade union leaders (except for a few secondary figures like Sid Lens or Abe Feinglass) nor rank-and-file workers played a role in its development. When New Left activists attempted to woo trade unionists, they made little progress, not only among mainstreamers but also among labor radicals who, by and large, adhered to neo-Marxist or social democratic views. One widely publicized exception in Illinois was the Sadlowski-Balanoff rebellion against the successors of Joe Germano in District 31 of the Steelworkers (chapter 4, part C). But this success was short-lived. Other efforts to infuse their ideology into trade unionism were generally futile.

The prime reason for this lack of success was that most of the issues of concern to the New Left had little direct relation to the workplace, and those that did impact seriously, as in the case of employment discrimination and certain aspects of environmental pollution, often appeared to threaten the job security of some workers.

The New Left approach to organizations and decision making also proved to be an ineffective basis for appeal to workers. By relying on informal organizational structure and on consensual decision making, the New Left devoted inordinate amounts of time to discussion and was unable to mount any consistent organizational campaigns. As a consequence, it experienced frequent shifts in leadership and fragmentation of its membership. For its labor appeals, the model was the hopelessly obsolete IWW. It is therefore not surprising that the New Left movement rapidly lost its momentum in the early seventies with the winding down of the Vietnam War and split into a number of diverse and largely isolated fractions—separate black and Hispanic civil rights, women's liberation, antinuclear and disarmament, and environmental protection. As for its role within the ranks of labor, it can be said as a loose generalization that New Left ideology had only limited and isolated impact on younger workers.

During the period before World War II, labor radicalism had not only played an important role in the trade union movement but had also engaged in a variety of forms of political action ranging from Independent Labor party or Socialist and Communist party organizations to efforts to influence the major Democrat and Republican parties. Except for the brief Henry Wallace episode in 1948, radical electoral politics in Illinois, as nationally, practically vanished. Tiny radical parties from time to time appeared in the ballot, but their support was negligible, and they received virtually no public attention.

NOTES

This chapter is based on a lengthy report by David Nicolai.

1. *Mine-Mill Union*, September 11, 1944, p. 13.

2. Ibid., January 15, 1951, p. 1.

3. *FTA News*, February 15, 1946, p. 6; April 15, 1946, p. 5; May 1, 1946, p. 5.

4. *FTA News*, January 1949, p. 4.

5. *CIO News*, October 14, 1940, p. 1; *Proceedings* of 3rd UCAPAWA Convention, Chicago 1940, p. 5.

6. *Work*, June, 1947, p. 3.

7. UOPWA Local 39 pamphlet from the papers of Irving Myers, Ben Myers, and David Rothstein, Chicago Historical Society.

8. *Office and Professional News*, January 1948, p. 3.

9. The latter union should not be confused with its AFL rival, AFSCME.

10. The IUC stipulated that each local would have one delegate with one vote for each 100 members or majority fraction thereof.

11. *Proceedings* of 1st Constitutional Convention of Illinois Industrial Union Council, Springfield 1941, pp. 21 and 22.

12. *Proceedings* of 3rd Constitutional Convention of Illinois Industrial Union Council, Chicago 1943, pp. 107 and 109.

13. *Chicago Journal of Commerce*, January 29, 1947, pp. 1 and 4.

14. *Flash* [Local 2 newspaper], February 25, 1949, p. 1 (from Myers, Myers, and Rothstein papers).

15. *Illinois Labor*, August 1949, p. 10.

16. Local 568 ILWU *Dispatcher*, July 22, 1949, p. 4; other information from Myers, Myers, and Rothstein papers.

17. Harvey A. Levenstein, *Communism, Anticommunism, and the CIO* (Westport, Conn: Greenwood Press, 1981), p. 324.

18. A principal source of information on the Chicago Catholic Worker Movement is Mel Piehl, *Breaking Bread: The Catholic Worker and the Origins of Catholic Radicalism in America* (Philadelphia: Temple University Press, 1982).

19. Staughton Lynd, "New Concept of Unionism," *The Nation*, January 24, 1972, p. 111.

16

Corruption and Organized Crime

While radical ideologies, which had flourished in the labor movements of the thirties and World War II, declined rapidly in importance in the postwar decades, the forces of corruption and organized crime reached new levels of penetration and evoked widespread public concern and condemnation. At the conclusion of what is probably the most comprehensive and best balanced study of corruption in the American labor movement, John Hutchinson wrote in 1970:

> What should be the verdict? Like Israel, as John L. Lewis once said, labor has many sorrows. The labor movement in America, like other social and economic movements, has suffered the privations of an unfriendly environment and the arrows of armies of critics; like many such movements, it has struggled for years with the problems of growth and influence in a time when prosperity, technological change and the skill of the opposition present the prospect of decline; its problems are universal. But corruption has been a special sorrow. Alone among its peers, the American labor movement has been accused of corruption in intolerable degree. The charges, and various versions of the facts, have become a currency of international conversation, and have left a mark at home.
>
> The need is perspective. Corruption there was, prominent and irrefutable; but it was never as widespread as the public seemed, or was often urged, to believe; in terms of undoubted culprits, it was very small in scale. Tolerance there was, a disparity between language and action which persisted for over half a century; but the labor movement was not an agency of the law—itself most imperfect— and finally demonstrated a capacity for self-expurgation probably without parallel in the world of free trade unions. Culpable the labor movement was, but so was the nation; such corruption as existed sprang as much from the sicknesses of American society as from the imperfections of the labor movement. . . .[1]

Chicago was inevitably the center of labor corruption activities in Illinois and the focal point of measures to cope with them. The record was long, bitter, often shameful, and sometimes heroic. As Hutchinson details, it goes back to the nineteenth century. For much of the early decades corruption was practiced by "amateurs" —trade unionists, often in league with employer representatives, who exploited the union rank and file as well as the small employers, who quickly succumbed to coercive threats and pressures.

In the twenties and thirties—the Capone era—in large part because of Prohibition, organized crime emerged on a sizable and more centralized scale, and labor racketeering joined gambling, prostitution, and illegal liquor as major sources of underworld income. The economic stakes grew much bigger, and so did the ties between organized crime and corrupt politics. As Senator Estes Kefauver stated in 1950, "There was no doubt in the minds of any of us, after the sort of testimony we heard in Chicago, that organized crime and political corruption go hand in hand, and that in fact there could be no big-time organized crime without a firm and profitable alliance between those who run the rackets and those in political control."[2]

The problem took a substantial jump in a new direction in the post-World War II period because of the rapid increase in union members and the wide-spread negotiation of health and welfare fringe benefits, with the consequent potential for misuse of vast amounts of insurance and retirement monies. At the outset, government regulation of these welfare funds was limited, and enforcement against violations was weak. It was only gradually that the labor movement itself as well as the public at large realized how much abuse of fiscal responsibilities was occuring and how extensive was its scale.

The multiple forms—new and old—that corruption took were brought out in great detail in a series of investigations conducted by the Chicago Crime Commission, the Illinois Institute of Technology Research Institute, and a succession of congressional committees between 1950 and 1978, including the Kefauver Committee of 1950, the 1954 Ives–Douglas investigation into welfare funds, the McClellan Committee of 1957–59, and the Senate labor racketeering committee of 1977 and 1978. Numerous cases of corruption were uncovered, but coping with them was often difficult.

One example was that of Joey Glimco, strong-arm boss of Local 777 of the Taxicab Drivers Union, an affiliate of the Teamsters Union. Virgil W. Peterson, executive director of the Chicago Crime Commission and a former FBI man, relates that in 1959 Glimco and four associates were tried in a criminal case for allegedly having "induced poultry merchants [in the Fulton Street poultry market] to comply with their demands for money and other property by promising in return smooth and pleasant labor relations. . . ."[3] All five defendants were found innocent when the men who had paid the money to the defendants changed their original testimony to the grand jury and denied in court that they had been threatened. Subsequently, the Internal Revenue Service successfully brought a suit against Glimco for the payment of income taxes on $120,780 paid by Local 777 to defend Glimco in the poultry market racketeering case. The McClellan Committee in 1958 heard extensive testimony that Glimco was a close associate of gangsters known to be part of the Chicago crime syndicate, that he had muscled his way into control of Local 777 and other businesses, and that he had extracted union funds for personal reasons. His chief opponent, Dominick Abata, leader of the Democratic Union Organizing Committee (DUOC), was the object of a car-bombing attack in 1966 that severely injured two of Abata's associates, but the perpetrators could not be identified.[4]

The McClellan Committee pursued another case involving the restaurant industry. After two weeks of hearings, Senator McClellan issued a concluding statement: "The hearings clearly established that a number of local unions in the Chicago area are and were controlled by gangsters and hoodlums and individuals whose primary interest is not in the welfare of the members but in the use of the union as a source of income."[5] He specifically cited locals of the Hotel and Restaurant Workers Union. He also castigated the Chicago Restaurant Association for using "men with extensive underworld connections" and for paying union representatives large sums to avoid picketing or unionization. Among the actions recounted by restaurant owners was the payment of dues for an arbitrarily selected number of union members who were not even aware of being in the union and who received no collective bargaining benefits. The signing of so-called "sweetheart agreements"—with below-standard employment provisions in return for a payoff to the union negotiators—was another manifestation of this type of deal.

In addition to cases of locals being taken over by force and intimidation and then being milked for the personal benefits of the controllers, or of being used to pressure or make deals with employers to pay tribute to "keep the peace," the major form of criminal abuse in the first two decades after World War II was the manipulation by trustees of pension and welfare funds for private advantage rather than for the benefit of the covered workers. The most notorious case was that of the Teamsters' Central States Pension and Welfare funds from which millions of dollars were siphoned off through the payment of huge insurance commissions and the making of loans and investments to criminal elements, frequently accompanied by kickbacks. As of 1980, the federal government was still struggling with the problem of achieving permanent reform.

The line between the activities of organized crime and malpractices by legitimate trade unionists was not always clear. For instance, some union leaders achieved exceptionally high incomes by accepting multiple salaries (as local president, international union representative, or trustee) or by blowing up their expense allowances to extreme proportions. Typically this was rationalized as justified by the importance of the functions, or by comparison with the salaries of employers, or simply by the statement that "The membership wants me to have it."

More serious was the tampering with election returns in hotly contested elections for key positions. Even a union with a reputation as generally free of corruption as the Steelworkers experienced this abuse. A case in point was the 1973 race between Ed Sadlowski and Sam Evett for director of District 31, which led to a challenge by the former of the initial ballot count and of a wide reversal of the outcome in a re-run supervised by the U.S. Department of Labor in 1974.

Although Chicago was the site of most of the publicized cases of corruption and the involvement of organized crime in labor affairs, downstate Illinois was not entirely immune. A 1971 study by the IIT Research Institute alleged that "a high degree of labor racketeering exists in the East St. Louis area and was reported to be significant in Peoria. In both communities the racketeers were described as having held membership in the Shelton or Frank (Buster) Wortman gangs." The report on Peoria was limited to the statement that former members of the Shelton gang had positions of responsibility in a number of union locals.[6]

The statement on East St. Louis was somewhat more extensive. It noted first that organized crime in East St. Louis operated (in 1970) as a satellite of the St. Louis crime organization or "outfit" although before the death of Buster Wortman in 1968, "the influence of Chicago mobsters was significant." Labor racketeering was now the mob's primary activity. "Four union locals were described as being controlled by figures affiliated with organized crime and as having some officials who are relatives of outfit members. These locals were reported to engage in coercive featherbedding and kickbacks from (construction) contractors." Outfit control was allegedly begun by Wortman "sometime after 1951" as a "classical hoodlum take-over." The IIT interviewees noted "the absence of 'hard evidence' of labor racketeering in East St. Louis," attributing this to the "amazingly tight" operation of the locals involved. It was added that after several union officials had been convicted, "more sophisticated and concealed means of extortion" were adopted.

The report concluded that "most reputable contractors refuse even to bid on work to be performed . . . and that labor leaders regard the community as their personal bailiwick, in which they dictate contractor costs and manpower needs to bidders. Their status in this regard is allegedly maintained by union musclemen."[7] Given the absence of hard evidence, these conclusions must be treated as tentative, but they reflected a widely held popular view of the time.

As in previous decades, the incursions of organized crime and other corrupt elements into the labor-management field after World War II were resisted strongly by private community reformers, primarily those from business and the professions; by some governmental authorities, especially at the federal level; and by important segments of the labor movement itself. The persistent seriousness of the problem was reflected in the number and recurring nature of the public investigations that were made, the legislation that was adopted, and the cases that necessitated varying forms of governmental intervention.

The Chicago Crime Commission, which was initially formed in 1919, regularly published annual reports until the early seventies on crime in Chicago, publicized anti-crime developments, and frequently pressed local and federal government law enforcement agencies to inquire into racketeering situations that had come to their attention. It also developed a legislative program for action by the Illinois General Assembly. The commission kept a close watch on syndicate gangsters and the individuals who associated with them and attempted to alert state's attorneys, police, and other law enforcers of suspicious relationships and events. For example, in August 1964, the commission wrote State's Attorney Daniel P. Ward about a wave of bombings and other violence affecting the restaurant industry and urged a special grand jury inquiry:

> The starting point should be the printed testimony of the McClellan Rackets Committee which thoroughly investigated the restaurant situation in the Chicago area in 1958 . . . there is strong reason to believe that some of the individuals who figured prominently in the McClellan Committee hearings in 1958 are still active in restaurant rackets today. . . . This is true, for example, of John Lardino, a dominant figure in Local 593, Hotel and Apartment Employees and Miscellaneous Workers Union. Lardino was supposedly forced out of this union as a result of the McClellan Committee disclosures. We have received information indicating that Lardino is again active in the affairs of the Restaurant Workers Union. . . . Particular attention [also] should be given to the relationship of restaurant owners with the bartenders union. It will be recalled that Local 278, Chicago Bartenders and Beverage Dispensers Union was once under the domination of Capone gangsters and the original charter for Local 450, Bartenders, Waiters, Waitresses, and Miscellaneous Workers Union . . . in Cicero was obtained by the infamous Joseph Aiuppa.[8]

References to corruption in the labor field declined during the sixties and early seventies in the commission reports, but it is not clear whether this was an indication of a decline in activities, or a change in underworld tactics, or increased attention by the commission to other aspects of crime.

During the fifties, labor corruption made national front-page news thanks especially to the two and a half years of hearings and investigations of Senator John L. McClellan's Select Committee on Improper Activities in the Labor or Management Field.[9] The reports of the McClellan Committee (some 58 volumes and 20,432 pages) received so much attention in print from scholars and journalists that another detailed discussion appears unnecessary. As far as Illinois was concerned, the committee concentrated its searchlight primarily on the Chicago restaurant industry and on selected elements of the Teamsters Union. In particular, the testimony applied 1) to the intimate relationship between Teamsters president Dave Beck and Chicago labor relations consultant Nathan W. Shefferman, who achieved labor peace by working out deals between the Teamsters and client firms (including Sears, Roebuck); 2) to organized crime associate Joey Glimco, who dominated and exploited taxi-cab, poultry, and other local businesses; 3) to certain Teamster officials who received exceptionally high salaries, often by holding a number of Teamster positions concurrently; and 4) to the financial abuses engineered by Jimmy Hoffa and his alleged underworld friends, such as the Dorfmans, in the administration of the Central States Pension and Welfare Funds. The Chicago investigations also directed lesser attention to criminal domination of the juke-box industry through Local 134 of the International Brotherhood of Electrical Workers; to serious misuse of union funds by top officials of the Bakery Workers Union and the Operating Engineers Union; and to the takeover of Teamsters Local 46 in north central Illinois.[10]

The principal objective of the committee was to trace alleged connections between syndicate and other criminals and union officials in the administration of pension and welfare funds and in the operation of unions. It is significant that the construction trades, which had been a prime target of corrupt and gangster elements from the earliest years of Chicago union-management relations through the thirties, were hardly mentioned, suggesting that the struggle of legitimate union leaders to eradicate the criminal element had been largely successful. It is also noteworthy that the huge mass-production industries seemed to be largely immune from the poisonous tactics of organized crime. Industries comprised of small employers and dispersed union members appeared to be most vulnerable.

The hearings of the McClellan Committee had a number of significant consequences. One was greatly increased public awareness of the insidious growth of organized crime. A second was the support provided the leadership of the labor movement to clean house. Finally, the enactment of the federal Landrum–Griffin Act of 1959 introduced and tightened legal safeguards relating to the democratic government of trade unions, the imposition of trusteeships, and fiscal accountability.

Despite these and other anti-corruption measures such as the revived enforcement of the Hobbs Act of 1945, the anti-crime provisions of the Taft–Hartley law (1947), and the Employee Retirement Income Security Act (1974), the battle was seemingly endless. In 1977, the Permanent Subcommittee on Investigations of the U.S. Senate's Committee on Governmental Affairs was empowered "to investigate organized crime and the extent to which criminal activities have been engaged in the labor-management field." Of particular concern was the degree of effectiveness of the Department of Labor's enforcement of the Landrum–Griffin Act and the "adequacy of the support given by the Department of Labor to the Department of Justice organized crime program in labor racketeering cases."[11]

In his testimony, Benjamin Civiletti, acting deputy U.S. attorney general, noted that the attorney general had publicly identified labor-management racketeering ("An employer who saves money by paying off a union official is as guilty of a crime as the union official") as a very serious national problem. He added: "There are roughly, I understand, 75,000 local unions in the country. We believe that only about 300 of them are severely influenced by racketeers, which is a percentage of less them one-half of 1 percent, but in absolute numbers, 300 is an awful lot of racketeering influence in local unions. . . . Most of these locals are concentrated in a handful of national or international labor organizations. Equally serious is the problem of corrupt businessmen who conspire with corrupt union officials to deprive workers of the wages they might have earned had there been no illegalities."[12]

Unfortunately, as Peter F. Vaira, attorney in charge of the Chicago Strike Force of the U.S. Department of Justice, pointed out, the degree of corruption in the Chicago labor movement was "among the worst in the country." Vaira stated that nearly every major local union of three international unions (unidentified) was controlled by the Chicago Crime Syndicate, that is, that officers of these unions answered directly to, or were actual lieutenants in, the syndicate.[13] "The most frightening aspect of this control is that the corrupt union leaders are accepted by many as legitimate members of the business community, and wield enormous political power."

Vaira was critical of the work done by the Department of Labor compliance officers: the lack of an information base (e.g., in 1975 the information supplied by the DOL to the Justice Department was at least ten years old); the investigations were often badly performed; the compliance officers were given restrictive operating instructions; and the number of compliance officers assigned to the Chicago Strike Force was totally inadequate. He was complimentary, however, of the FBI, which had made a "substantial effort to move into the labor racketeering field in Chicago" with significant results. Later testimony by Secretary of Labor Ray Marshall indicated that the Departments of Labor and Justice often differed in their perceptions of the nature of the problem and how to go about resolving it (i,e., the relative significance of civil and criminal enforcement) although Marshall did not dispute Vaira's basic factual statements.

The response of the labor movement to postwar corruption took a variety of forms. Article VIII, Section 7 of the Constitution of the newly merged national AFL–CIO in 1955 strongly condemned corrupt or unethical practices that endangered the good name of the trade union movement. The first constitutional convention established an Ethical Practices Committee, which was empowered to formulate a series of ethical practices codes for approval by the Executive Council and the general convention. The six codes formulated in 1956 and 1957 covered such topics as the issuance of local union charters (to prevent the misuse of charters by corrupt individuals through the establishment of "paper locals"); the administration of health and welfare funds; the prohibition against office-holding in the federation or any affiliate by any person convicted of any crime "involving moral turpitude offensive to trade union morality" or who was "commonly known to be a crook or racketeer preying on the labor movement and its good name for corrupt purposes; investments and business interests of union officials to prevent any conflict of interest with union duties; appropriate standards guiding financial practices and proprietary activities of unions; and ethical practices with respect to union democratic processes."[14]

Under the blunt and decisive leadership of President George Meany, the federation modified its historic policy of nonintervention in the affairs of its affiliate internationals not only in words, but also in actions. It removed Teamsters' president Dave Beck as a vice-president of the AFL–CIO and as a member of the Executive Council on grounds of gross misuse of union funds. It endorsed and supported congressional committee investigations such as the 1954 Douglas subcommittee of the Senate Labor Committee, which exposed cases of corruption by labor officials and others in the handling of health and welfare funds and laid the basis for disclosure and ethical practice legislation. It enunciated the policy that if a union official decided to invoke the Fifth Amendment for his or her personal protection to avoid proper legislative scrutiny, that official should not continue to hold a union position. It expelled corrupt officials of several small federal locals. And it applied its ultimate power by expelling or suspending a number of unions from the federation, most notably the giant Teamsters Union, as well as forcing or assisting others to clean house under threat of expulsion. Some critics of the labor movement claimed that these AFL–CIO measures did not go far enough, but the ability of the Teamsters and the East Coast Longshoremen (among others) to flourish outside the federation exposed the limitations of federation action and explained the great caution that it exercised in coping with allegations of corruption.

There was another side to the picture as a speech by AFL–CIO secretary-treasurer William F. Schnitzler to the eighth annual convention of the Illinois state AFL–CIO in 1965 revealed. Organized labor believed that the mass media had greatly exaggerated the significance of labor corruption and had unfairly singled out labor in contrast to other groups in society. It asserted that the great majority of its affiliates were honestly and cleanly run and that the notoriety attached to labor corruption far exceeded that attributed to banking, business, and industry. Schnitzler noted, for example, that the strict bonding requirements initially contained in the Landrum–Griffin Act had imposed an unnecessary and discriminatory burden on the unions and that the experience during the first few years had persuaded Congress to repeal "the faithful discharge feature of the fidelity bonding" and to place the unions on the same basis as other institutions.[15] He added that the Surety Association, which was comprised of all fidelity bonding insurance companies, indicated "there is not a single national institution in America that has as good an honesty record as the American trade union movement."

The first convention of the Illinois merged AFL–CIO took place in October 1958, shortly after the national body had adopted its codes of ethical practices and just before the enactment of Landrum–Griffin. One of its most important actions was to approve the new constitution that endorsed and subscribed to the codes. As the final report of the state AF of L's executive board stated: "Where crookedness, collusion between employer and labor representatives and other abuses exist, it is the duty of the AFL–CIO Ethical Practices Committee to give pitiless publicity to such acts and to the persons involved. Proof of guilt means expulsion from membership in the AFL–CIO."[16] The report also emphasized a column written for the Catholic press by Monsignor George G. Higgins, director of the Social Action Department of the National Catholic Welfare Conference, which pointed out that although the labor movement may have "been too slow to put its own house in order," no other comparable business organization had ever done as much to enforce a code of ethical practices upon its affiliates.[17]

Many unionists had a sense of unease over the AFL–CIO's expulsion policy. As a resolution introduced by a group of Painters' representatives indicated, they were not opposed to the anti-corruption and anti-racketeering program as such, but the remedy of expulsion of entire international unions penalized the rank and file and impaired the entire labor movement as well.[18] The consequences, the resolution proclaimed, threatened to become even more destructive as applied at the local level, especially in Illinois. "Whereas, the hard-won gains of organized labor rest on the principle of solidarity of the entire labor movement, and in particular the support of the largest single international in the Nation, the Teamsters' Union, whose relationships are bound up with the workers of all industries," the remedy must be found "inside the family of labor and not through expulsions."

As former Senator Paul H. Douglas stated in his memoirs regarding two national unions accused of corruption, the Chicago Brotherhood of Painters "were managing a pension-and-welfare fund with conspicuous integrity." And the Decatur, Illinois, local of the Allied Industrial Workers had not been involved in any of the skulduggery of its national officials or in that of the Chicago local"; Douglas made a special trip to Decatur at that time to "make it plain to the local citizens and the press."[19] In short, according to the critics of the expulsion policy, corruption tended to be localized. Most cases involved one or more local unions or, occasionally, a joint council. A few international unions (at various times—the Teamsters, Operating Engineers, Bakery Workers, East Coast Longshoremen, Laborers) fell under the control of criminal elements and, when they did, the corrupt activities extended only to segments of the organization. Most affiliates were not affected except insofar as their contributions to national or regional funds were misused.

In Chicago and elsewhere around the state, although the Teamsters were required to withdraw from the local central bodies, they continued for the most part to maintain cooperative relations with the AFL–CIO unions, particularly with the Building Trades. Bill Lee, president of the Chicago Federation of Labor since 1946, a long-time Teamsters' official, president of Bakery Drivers Local 734, international vice president, and a strong opponent of Jimmy Hoffa, was obliged to assume membership in the Flat Janitors Local 1 of the Service Employees International Union in order to retain his federation presidency. However, in his address to the 1958 convention of the State Federation, he stated: "As long as I can, I will continue as I have in the past and particularly in recent months to bring these two great organizations (e.g. the AFL–CIO and the Teamsters) together again. . . . On behalf of the Teamsters, particularly of Chicago and I know I speak for the Teamsters of the State of Illinois, may I say we still consider ourselves part of the labor movement, and we never want to be considered anything else. . . . "[20]

Available data do not afford a precise measurement of how much corrupt practices affected post-World War II labor-management relations in Illinois compared to the pre-war decades. Nor is there much reliable information on the actions taken by courageous and honest local unionists to combat corrupt practices in their organizations, but certain conclusions are possible.

First, the stakes in the postwar era were much higher than in the days of the Great Depression or in the prosperous twenties. Union treasuries were greatly enlarged by rising memberships. Businesses were more affluent. Pension and welfare funds were huge and growing. The temptations and incentives for corruption were strongly intensified.

Second, organized crime, as developed and refined by the heirs of Al Capone, was far better equipped to exploit the situation. Not only were the forces for violence more centralized and sophisticated, but they also had superior legal and accounting resources at their beck and call.

Third, the ties between corrupt labor-management practitioners and corrupt politicians were less conspicuous in the postwar period. Chicago politicians were increasingly sensitive to the reputation that the city had acquired as a center of crime and violence. The Kennelly administration (1947–54) was viewed as a reform government, but it actually had limited effect on the crime scene. The twenty-one years of Richard J. Daley's regime (1955–76)—the high period of machine politics—were tainted by numerous cases of petty corruption and a toleration of gang-land crime as long as they did not infringe on the everyday lives of the citizenry. As Milton Rakove noted, "the citizens tolerate a high degree of crime and corruption;" however, "the contemporary record (1975) is pallid pink in comparison with Chicago's scarlet past."[21] Daley was particularly proud of his labor relations record and his closest associates included such prominent labor leaders as William L. McFetridge of the Building Service Employees Union, William Lee of the Chicago Federation of Labor, and Stephen Bailey of the Plumbers.

Fourth, the glare of congressional committee publicity, focussed on labor-management corruption in the fifties and early sixties combined with the enactment or strengthening of regulatory and punitive legislation, had a strong deterrent effect. Some of the worst abuses were eliminated, or at least curtailed. A number of criminals were sent to prison. Others were forced out of their union positions. Several were assassinated in gang-land style. Legitimate union leaders were assisted in the clean-up process. Several of the most seriously infested industries of the thirties, such as the building trades, the theatrical field, and building service were hardly mentioned by the investigating committees—a good sign that most of the serious corruption had been eliminated. Others, like hotels and restaurants, were improved after the investigations.

Fifth, as the U.S. Justice Department indicated, despite significant improvements, corruption persisted in certain branches of Chicago business. It was not until the early eighties that the abuses of insurance companies and the Teamsters' Central States Pension and Welfare Funds were finally controlled. Organized labor, however, had concluded by the seventies that corruption was no longer a crisis issue.

NOTES

1. John Hutchinson, *The Imperfect Union: A History of Corruption in American Trade Unions* (New York: Dutton, 1970), pp. 389–90.

2. Estes Kefauver, *Crime in America* (Garden City, N.Y.: Doubleday, 1951), p. 88.

3. See Virgil W. Peterson, *A Report on Chicago Crime for 1968* (Chicago: Chicago Crime Commission, August 27, 1969), p. 99. See also McClellan Committee *Hearings*, March 11, 1959, pp. 17731ff.

4. Chicago Crime Commission, *A Report on Chicago Crime for 1966*, August 11, 1967, p. 104.

5. *Hearings*, pp. 13108–9.

6. IIT Research Institute and the Chicago Crime Commission, *A Study of Organized Crime in Illinois* (Chicago: Illinois Institute of Technology, 1971), pp. 85, 218.

7. IIT Research Institute, *A Study of Organized Crime*, pp. 220–21.

8. Chicago Crime Commission, *A Report on Chicago Crime for 1965*, August 5, 1966, pp. 48–49.

9. The McClellan Committee had been preceded by a number of congressional committee investigations into labor racketeering, but they had netted slight returns.

10. A detailed personalized account of the major activities of the McClellan Committee was provided by chief counsel Robert F. Kennedy in his book, *The Enemy Within* (New York: Harper and Brothers, 1960). Good journalistic accounts of the Teamsters experience are Steven Brill, *The Teamsters* (New York: Simon and Schuster, 1978); Walter Sheridan, *The Fall and Rise of Jimmy Hoffa* (New York: Saturday Review, 1972); and Clark R. Mollendoff, *Tentacles of Power: The Story of Jimmy Hoffa* (Cleveland: World Publishing, 1965). Sheridan was chief aide to Robert Kennedy during the McClellan Committee investigations.

11. Opening statements by Senator Henry Jackson and Senator Sam Nunn, *Hearings*, April 24, 1978, pp. 1–2.

12. *Hearings*, p. 9.

13. Statement to subcommittee, p. 82. In a later hearing in September 1983, Jeffrey Kent, chief of the special prosecution bureau in the Cook County State's Attorney's Office, stated that Chicago organized crime exerted considerable influence over the International Brotherhood of Teamsters, the Laborers Union, the Hotel and Restaurant Employees (especially Local 450), the Projectionists Union, the Union of Dolls, Toys, Playthings, Novelties, and Allied Products, and Local 707 of the National Production Workers Union. Bureau of National Affairs, *Daily Labor Report*, no. 189, September 28, 1983.

14. *AFL–CIO Executive Council Statements and Reports*, 1956–75, vol. 1, pp. 43, 97–104.

15. *Proceedings* of the 8th Annual Convention, Illinois State Federation of Labor and Congress of Industrial Organizations, 1965, pp. 290–91.

16. *Proceedings* of the 76th Annual Convention, Illinois State Federation of Labor, 1958, p. 80.

17. Ibid.

18. *Proceedings* of the 1st Annual Convention, Illinois State Federation of Labor and Congress of Industrial Organizations, 1958, pp. 170–71.

19. *In the Fullness of Time: The Memoirs of Paul H. Douglas* (New York: Harcourt Press, 1971), pp. 384–85.

20. *Proceedings* of the 76th Annual Convention, pp. 72–73.

21. Milton Rakove, *Don't Make No Waves, Don't Back No Losers* (Bloomington: Indiana University Press, 1975), pp. 23–35.

17

Blacks, Hispanics, and Fair Employment

Perhaps the major social theme of the postwar era affecting labor-management relations was discrimination in employment because of race, religion, sex, or other reasons. Illinois was the last large industrial northern state to enact a Fair Employment Practices Act. Several early attempts were made to pass such legislation. However, in 1943, not only a number of trade and industrial associations, but also the State Federation of Labor spoke out against a proposed bill. In 1945, the bill was again opposed by employer groups, although it was now supported by all state labor groups. The apparent disinterest of Governor Dwight Green served to strengthen legislators' opposition to fair employment (FEP) legislation.[1]

Instead of legislation, a state Interracial Commission was set up in 1943 by executive order of Governor Green. The General Assembly established the Illinois Interracial commission (later named the Illinois commission on Human Relations) as a permanent body with no conciliation, mediation, or enforcement powers. Its principal function was an educational one of improving interfaith and interracial relations in the hope of decreasing employment discrimination.[2]

In July 1943, Chicago Mayor Edward J. Kelly created the Mayor's Committee on Race Relations, but it operated without specific charter or authority. In 1945, the city council passed an ordinance prohibiting discrimination in employment and providing public funds for the committee despite questions of constitutionality raised by private employers. On December 12, 1947, the city council replaced the committee with the Commission on Human Relations as an official department of the city government .[3] Both the Chicago Commission on Human Relations and the Chicago Conference on Home Front Unity grew out of the Mayor's Committee on Race Relations. The Chicago Conference held its first session in May and June of 1945, and established a subcommittee on housing, recreation, and employment. The subcommittee studied the situation of blacks and other minority workers in Chicago and noted that during the war many minority groups entered into occupations and trade unions that had previously been closed to them. However, there were still sections of the labor movement in Chicago that discriminated by limiting equal employment opportunities for minorities.[4]

Both the Committee of Race Relations and its successor, the Commission on Human Relations, worked to secure voluntary compliance by private employers. These efforts quickly revealed the limited amount of cooperation that could be achieved through a voluntary approach. The experience led to the conclusion that a state fair employment law was essential.[5]

The drive for FEP legislation nearly succeeded in 1949, but consistently failed in the conservative rural-dominated Republican Senate, even when a Republican governor supported it. From 1949 until 1961, the bill passed by a wide margin in the House and failed in the Senate. The voting was split primarily along geographical and party lines; both Cook County Democrats and Republicans supported the bill, while some of the downstate Democrats and most of the downstate Republicans were in opposition.

In 1949 and again in 1951, the State Chamber of Commerce led the attack on the bill. The State chamber maintained that education not legislation was the key to nondiscrimination. It believed that the real problem was not opening up jobs for minority group members, but finding qualified people to fill the job openings that already were available.[6]

In the 68th General Assembly (1953), despite the support of Republican Governor William Stratton, State Chamber witnesses, as in past years, testified in opposition to the proposed legislation. The bill passed the House by a vote of 81–31, but was rejected by the Senate Industrial Affairs Committee by a vote of 11–4.[7] It was not until July 21, 1961, after five unsuccessful attempts in the legislature, that a strong push by Democratic Governor Otto Kerner, abetted by a number of liberal Republicans, notably Charles H. Percy, then chairman of Bell and Howell and later U.S. senator, helped the bill pass. Five Republican state senators joined the Democrats to pass the bill by two votes.[8]

Apart from ethical values, the Democrats had consistently supported the legislation for political reasons, and certain Republican liberals were interested in the black vote and wanted to have a pro-civil rights record. The Chicago Association of Commerce and Industry was pressured into supporting the bill by two of its black board members, who threatened publicly to resign if the bill was not supported by the association. In addition, William G. Caples, vice-president of Inland Steel Company and a frequent chamber spokesman, now publicly stated that the voluntary merit employment program that the chamber had always supported had failed. Charles Percy's testimony before the Senate was believed to be a key factor in the FEP act's passage.[9]

In order to get the FEP legislation enacted, however, a watered-down bill had to be accepted by the civil rights supporters. The new law had more limited coverage than in other industrial states, applying initially to firms with a hundred or more employees, extending jurisdiction only to the private sector, and relating only to race, color, religion, and national origin or ancestry. In 1965, coverage was extended to employers of fifty or more employees.[10]

The business community agreed to the bill largely because of an implicit three-point understanding that they assumed the new Fair Employment Relations Commission (FEPC) would follow: 1) the commission would not possess or utilize any initiatory power; 2) once a charge went to the public hearing stage or the conciliation stage, the complainant and the respondent would be treated as adversaries before the commission, with the commission's interests limited to an adjudicative role; and, 3) the commission would not be active or aggressive in the enforcement area, allowing business association groups to conduct an educational campaign in order to obtain voluntary compliance and acceptance.[11]

Business qualms were reflected in the Senate's rejection of two of Governor Kerner's first five nominees to the commission on the grounds that they would apply the law in a biased (i.e., excessively affirmative) way. In September 1961, Governor Kerner nominated Charles W. Gray, industrial relations director of Bell and Howell, for the unpaid chairmanship of the commission. In November, the Senate approved Gray and two of the other commissioners, Robert Myers and Mrs. Orville Foreman, but challenged the nominations of Ralph Helstein, president of the Packinghouse Workers Union and Earl B. Dickerson, a prominent black lawyer from Chicago.

Dickerson was questioned for several hours by the Senate Executive Committee about his past association with various "subversive" organizations. Senator Paul W. Broyles, for example, produced documents pertaining to Dickerson's past connections with the National Council of American-Soviet Friendship, the Emergency Civil Liberties Commission, the National Lawyers Guild, and more than a dozen others. Dickerson responded by stating that "during the period in question in the late 1930's and early 1940's, the situation of the Negro people was very bad. I was active in politics and was ready to aid groups and individuals who appeared to be fighting for the betterment of the impoverished Negro living in our slums. When I helped them or joined them, I had no knowledge that the organizations were in any way un-American. All that was evident to me was that they were aiding in the battle to improve the Negroes' lot. I defy anyone on this committee to say that I am un-American or that you are any more American than I. I fought on the battlefront in the last war and was wounded. I organized the first Negro legion post in Illinois."[12] With voting along party lines, the Republicans on the Senate Executive Committee rejected Dickerson's appointment 11–8.

Ralph Helstein was questioned concerning his practice of allowing officers to remain on the payroll of his union after they had been identified as communist sympathizers by the same committee. Helstein stated that he had followed the codes of the AFL-CIO ethical practices committee, but November 9, 1961, the Senate voted 30–24, along party lines, to reject Helstein's appointment.

Thus the FEPC did not start off on good footing, and the situation worsened. This worsening occurred, in part, because the commission allegedly did not conform to the terms of the legislative compromise in administering the enforcement provisions of the act. The Commission believed that its chief purpose was to administer the enforcement provisions of the law and to do so fully. It saw the black community, rather than the business community, as its chief clientele. Its philosophy was that it should not limit its own powers; rather, that the courts could restrict them if they felt it necessary. This conflict in philosophy between the business community's expectations and the commission's beliefs and practices came to a head with the *Motorola* case in 1963.[13]

The Illinois FEPC's ruling in *Myart v. Motorola* led to widespread public controversy. Leon Myart filed a charge on July 29, 1963 with the FEPC, stating that

> I charge on my own behalf to have been personally aggrieved by an unfair employment practice committed by Motorola, Inc., on the 15th day of July, 1963 at Chicago, Illinois because of my race. The facts of the alleged unfair employment practice are: I applied for the position of Analyzer and Phaser. I am well qualified for this position. I worked for four years in the U.S. Army. I have completed a 19-month course of study—combination General Electrical and Radio-Television Technician Course and another Electronics Shop Course of 423 hours. I applied for employment on the above date, took and passed the Company test. They hired whites during this period. I believe the reason I was not hired was because of racial discrimination. The company is widely known for racially discriminatory hiring practices.[14]

Motorola claimed that Myart failed a screening test, but the company did not produce Myart's test. The commission proceeded to give Myart the Motorola screening test, which he passed. The investigation also showed that Motorola employed no blacks in production jobs. Thus, the commission found substantial evidence to support Myart's charge and ordered a conciliation conference.[15] Motorola refused to attend the conciliation conference because, according to the FEPC's rules, a court reporter could not be present during such a conference. Subsequently, according to the law, the commission issued a complaint, and a public hearing was held in Chicago on January 28 and 29, 1964, before Examiner Robert E. Bryant. On February 26, Bryant concluded that the evidence indicated that Myart had passed the test and was denied the job because of his race.[16]

The commission decided on November 18, 1964, that based on all the evidence, Leon Myart had indeed passed the preemployment test, but his test score was recorded by Motorola on his application form as a failing grade of 4. The commission concluded that Myart was not offered employment by Motorola because of his race and awarded him a $1,000 settlement.[17] Motorola and the press generally attacked the decision as punitive and exceeding the commission's authority. In addition, the Illinois attorney general, who, by law, represented the commission in court, stated that he would not defend the commission's decision and believed it was an error.[18]

During 1964, Motorola and its supporters continued their attack on the commission and denounced several commissioners.[18] In the spring of 1956, the Illinois State Senate, voting on party lines, rejected Governor Kerner's reappointment of Gray as Chairman of the FEPC. Senate Majority Leader B. Russell Arrington (R-Evanston) said that "Gray has lost the confidence of the business community."[19]

Opponents of the FEP act felt that the commission was wrong to use money as a redress for racial discrimination; they were also angered by the commission's practice of providing lawyers to complainants. They felt that the commission was not acting as a judicial body. When the Motorola decision was appealed to the courts, the commission's finding of discrimination was upheld, but the monetary award was set aside.[20]

The role of the Illinois FEPC was soon outshadowed by the enactment in 1964 of the Federal Civil Rights Act, with its Title VII relating to nondiscrimination in employment. Nonetheless, despite the furor over the Motorola decision and the controversies over the composition of the commission, the Illinois law, like the local human relations committees, played a small but significant role in promoting the nondiscrimination movement. Furthermore, the federal legislation encouraged and reinforced the role of the state law, especially in the late sixties and seventies.

On July 10, 1963, Governor Kerner issued an executive order containing a code of fair practices for state government agencies based partly on recommendations from the commission. The order also provided that all contracts for work or services of any kind for the state must contain a nondiscrimination clause and forbade discrimination in any vocational training, guidance, counseling, or apprenticeship programs supported by the state. It required the Illinois State Employment Service to fill jobs on a nondiscriminatory basis and provided that discriminatory job orders be rejected and the identity of employers seeking to place such orders be forwarded to the FEPC.[21]

In 1963, the commission supported two bills dealing with fair employment. The first, which was passed by the General Assembly and signed by the governor on August 13, 1963, extended the jurisdiction of the FEP act to public-sector employment and strengthened certain enforcement provisions relating to conciliation agreements. The second, which proposed to extend coverage from employers with fifty or more employees to employers with ten or more employees, was passed by the House but defeated in the Senate. It was not until 1972 that the coverage provision was changed from fifty to fifteen, and jurisdiction was enlarged to include sex and physical or mental handicap.

During 1962, picketing and other forms of demonstrations by blacks began to occur in different parts of the state. Cairo made history as the first Illinois community to be challenged directly. In June 1962, the Cairo Nonviolent Freedom Committee staged demonstrations in order to desegregate the community. The Illinois Commission on Human Relations attempted to ease the racial tension in Cairo with educational and consultative programs.[23]

There were also demonstrations in Alton, Chicago, East St. Louis, and Peoria aimed at bringing about changes in local employment practices. In the summer of 1963, there were twelve demonstrations in East St. Louis alone. On August 2, 1963, the FEPC publicly urged employers in Illinois to take positive direct action to achieve merit employment and equality of economic opportunity throughout the state. The commission also urged black citizens in Illinois to file charges with the commission whenever they believed they had been discriminated against in employment.

During the summer of 1963, the city councils in East St. Louis and Alton adopted fair employment practices ordinances modeled after the 1945 Chicago ordinance. They prohibited employment discrimination on the part of the municipalities, provided for a nondiscrimination clause in city contracts and contained a general prohibition against employment discrimination.[24]

With the passage of the Civil Rights Act in 1964, state fair employment laws assumed new significance. The federal commission at first was guided, in part, by the experiences of already existent state commissions. The Civil Rights Act directed the federal commission to defer to the states for a reasonable time when a discrimination charge occurred "in a state or political subdivision of a state, which has state or local laws prohibiting the practice alleged and establishing or authorizing a state or local authority to grant or seek relief from such practice or to institute criminal proceedings with respect thereto upon receiving notice thereof."[25]

The federal Equal Employment Opportunity Commission (EEOC) was authorized to enter into agreements with similar state bodies, giving jurisdiction to the latter in those areas of employment discrimination covered by both Title VII and the state law. It could also reimburse state commissions for investigating charges filed with it. On July 22, 1966 the Illinois FEPC entered into a memorandum of understanding with the EEOC. This memorandum provided for the exchange of information between the two agencies, under the Illinois and federal laws, and set up a procedure for investigation and handling aimed at avoiding duplication of efforts on the part of the respective agencies.[26] In 1974, the Illinois commission entered into contracts with EEOC to receive federal funds in exchange for processing a specified number of cases.

In a 1963 speech to the Illinois Baptist General State Convention Governor Kerner stated:

At the last session of our Illinois General Assembly [1961] we passed a milestone in legislation. A fair employment practices law. While this legislation has placed us well along on the road to equal employment opportunity for all, there is much more to be done. The time had come for us to take a closer look at fair employment practices legislation and to face up to some hard facts. While FEP legislation is important and is necessary to bring about the elimination of artificial barriers of employment, it should in no way or under any circumstances be looked on as the one and only answer to obtaining the good life for our citizens. Simply removing the artificial barriers to employment by passing a law doesn't mean that those people who have been discriminated against automatically will be caught up in the mainstream of a productive life. Many of the men and women who have been discriminated against lack the education, training and experience to qualify for the jobs that are now open in today's labor market. A great task now before us lies in the area of education and training.[27]

These words were still valid twenty years later, despite substantial progress in removing discrimination barriers to minority employment.

Blacks and Politics

As a group, blacks were long without political and community powers proportionate to their numbers. Major decisions affecting black employment, education, and residence were usually made by white decisionmakers. In Chicago, power was usually controlled by the large businesses and political institutions. Very few blacks held positions of authority within industry, government, or unions, and there were few large black-owned companies. A survey in the late fifties of major public and private institutions in Chicago found that of 10,997 policymaking positions in both private and public sectors, only 285, or 2.65 percent, were occupied by blacks.[28]

Black political leaders in Chicago were not able to create and sustain an active, influential political life despite the fact that blacks comprised the largest single ethnic bloc in the city. Black politicians served mainly as a part of the white Democratic organization controlled by Mayor Daley from 1955 to 1976. It was extremely difficult to form an influential black organization outside of the machine.[29]

Congressman William Dawson was the largely undisputed black political leader from 1942 to 1970. Before Dawson became part of the machine, he was a "raceman," that is, he was outspoken in his support for racial causes. However, once he was co-opted into the Democratic organization, he no longer fought overtly for racial causes. Dawson secured a position as committeeman of the 2nd Ward and also created a network of obligations and loyalties that gave him control of the 2nd, 3rd, 4th, 6th, and 20th Wards. These five wards comprised the largest part of the South Side's black community, which included 420,687 people in 1950. Traditionally, these wards produced party voting, with little ticket-splitting.[30]

The Dawson machine's purpose was to elect men to office. Six of Chicago's fifty councilmen were black, and seven delegates from the Dawson organization sat in the state legislature, one senator and six representatives. By the mid-sixties, at least five of the six black wards in Chicago and the seven black Democrats in the Illinois state legislature were part of the machine and remained unchallenged.[31] The black caucus tended to vote with the Chicago Democratic party in policy areas.[32]

The black machine did not deal with the civic issues that were important to the black community, such as open-occupancy, fair employment practices, and medical integration. The reason the machine was so successful in the black wards was because of the tangible incentives it offered to members, for example low-paying jobs, political favors, and material assistance.[33] When Dawson first started, very few black businessmen or professionals were engaged in politics, but the machine changed this. Young professionals began to seek office, eager to gain the influence and prestige of these positions.[34]

Dissatisfaction with the machine's lack of attention to racial issues did exist. With Mayor Daley, black politicians found that they could not influence the appointment of blacks to important or prestigious jobs on public boards or agencies. Particularly on the issue of judicial reform, the black machine felt that its interests were being subverted by the mayor. Officers of black associations began to go directly to Daley to discuss racial issues and bypassed the black machine, which was losing influence. Following Dawson's death in 1970, Congressman Ralph Metcalfe replaced him. This started a major change in how race issues were treated by the black machine, because Metcalfe was outspoken on these issues.[35] The majority of the voluntary associations initially involved in race relations were operated by whites (e.g., the American Civil Liberties Union, the Commission on Human Relations, and the Anti-Defamation League) The strongest single source of white liberal civic leadership in Chicago lay in the Jewish organizations.[36]

From 1943 to 1957, efforts to secure Fair Employment Practices legislation progressed in spite of limited black support. In 1959 and again in 1961, when the law was finally enacted, the black contributions were much more substantial, largely due to the strengthened and more stable positions of the Urban League and the National Association for the Advancement of Colored People (NAACP), which started in Chicago as a white-led organization. After World War II, however, blacks increasingly began to dominate its policymaking committee, until whites became a small minority. By the fifties, there were only one or two white officers in the association and the Chicago membership increased dramatically—from 4,000 members in 1953 to 18,500 in 1958.[37]

The Urban League was founded and financially supported by white businessmen in industries such as meat packing, steel, telephone and merchandising that had a stake in the black community, that is, a need for black labor; a desire to upgrade their laborers' quality and skills; improvement in the relations between blacks and white workers; and the need to protect investments in plants in black areas.[38]

Sidney Williams, the executive secretary of the league from 1947 to 1955, was personally active in the campaign for fair employment legislation. At the start though, the Urban League as a group held the view that the fair employment legislation was outside the league's field of operation. They believed the league should deal only with social issues and not get involved in legislative action.[39] In March 1949, the executive committee finally decided that the board of directors should make a statement of policy in favor of fair employment legislation. The decision was apparently made not because of the merits of the legislation, but because of the fear that failure of the league to take a stand on fair employment might hurt its image in the black community.[40]

Between 1947 and 1955, the league was in turmoil because of a lack of agreement among members of the board of directors over the proper functions and methods of the league in dealing with the critical race relations situation in Chicago, which led to confusion in policy and procedures. The league reorganized in 1955–59, and when the fair employment practices legislative proposal came before the executive committee again, the committee resubmitted a weak resolution stating the League's position "that the elimination of discrimination in employment was of primary concern to the League and that the agency had pertinent information to the question, which it was willing to share with members of the legislature. From this information and data it appears that voluntary efforts to reduce discrimination in job opportunity have not substantially reduced the problem. Therefore, we now *reluctantly* have come to feel that this is a matter for legislative concern and action. The form of the specific bill is beyond the competence of the Urban League."[41]

Because of its tax-exempt status, the league could not actively lobby for fair employment legislation, but it did cooperate and work with lobbying groups in the 1961 campaign. Thirty votes were needed in the Senate in order to pass the legislation. Twenty-five to twenty-six Democratic votes were expected; thus the fate of the bill was dependent on the Republican votes. In 1959, only one Republican had voted for the Fair Employment Practices Act. Members of the league's board exerted influence on the Republican senators. In mid-April 1961, the Chicago Association of Commerce and Industry was also induced to endorse the fair employment legislation.[42]

In addition to legislative matters, the league was also active in promoting fair employment through training programs. In Chicago, the league's pilot placement project after 1947 helped more than five hundred firms integrate blacks into white-collar jobs. Approximately three thousand other firms hired blacks in a wide range of jobs that had formerly been closed to them.[43]

Black Economic Pressure

In 1966, the Reverend Martin Luther King decided that his organization, the Southern Christian Leadership Conference, should start a movement in northern cities. Chicago was chosen as the pilot city because of its large black population, and because it was considered to be the most segregated northern city. King named the Reverend Jesse Jackson to head the newly formed Chicago chapter of the Southern Christian Leadership Conference's Operation Breadbasket.[44] The aim of the chapter was to win jobs for blacks in white-owned businesses in the black community through moral persuasion, and, if necessary, picketing and boycotts. Breadbasket leaders believed that it was immoral for white manufacturers and merchants to fail to utilize the resources of the black community in providing goods and services, and then to profit from that same community.[45] Breadbasket got support from ministers, religious groups, and black pastors in the ghetto. The ministers rallied community support and helped to supply volunteers necessary to run the programs. The three main objectives of Breadbasket were: 1) to increase the employment and occupational status of blacks in white-owned establishments; 2) to induce white-owned business to rely on goods and services of black entrepreneurs; and 3) to channel money into black-owned financial institutions in the ghetto.[46]

In early 1966, Breadbasket began with the dairies and went on to win an agreement from about twenty companies, including A&P, National Tea, and Walgreen's. Hi-Low Foods, which operated fifteen supermarkets in the black area, was selected as the first grocery chainstore target of Breadbasket. Hi-Low was approached on October 25, 1966, and agreement was reached on November 19 that provided for hiring or promoting 183 black employees, giving display space and competitive markups to black-made products, and placing some funds from at least thirteen stores into black-controlled banks. On December 1966, National Tea signed an agreement, and Jewel followed in early 1967.[47]

In May 1967, A&P signed an agreement with Breadbasket that promised the hiring and upgrading of 770 blacks within one year. In 1968, there was a sixteen-week boycott of A&P's four hundred ghetto stores; the boycott won an agreement to hire 268 more blacks in the following year; to promote twenty to managerial and executive positions in these stores; to use minority-owned garbage collection firms, exterminators, and janitorial services in the stores; to hire black public relations firms; to advertise in black media; and to bank in black institutions. Breadbasket also obtained a number of private business and government building contracts for black building contractors.[48]

By April 1969, A&P had promoted eighteen blacks to management positions, and hired 130 new black employees. Forty of the stores in Chicago were marketing products of twenty-five black manufacturers and using the trucking, garbage collection, and extermination services of another twenty-five.[49]

In 1967, Breadbasket ran Black Expo, a trade fair that resulted in millions of dollars of new business for the city's black business community. Reverend Jackson reported that in total Breadbasket had obtained approximately five thousand jobs for blacks, with an annual payroll of nearly $50 million.[50]

Operation Breadbasket acquired considerable economic power through boycotts. Although it appeared to represent the most influential black pressure group in Chicago, however, Operation Breadbasket failed to gain any power within the political sphere.[51] Despite his stature in the Chicago black community, Jesse Jackson failed to shake the political hold of Daley's Democratic machine over the city's black voters.[52]

In the mid-seventies, blacks began to defect from the Democratic organization. This defection was already under way before Daley's death, but it was intensified under Mayors Michael Bilandic and Jane Byrne. The decline in black voter support for machine candidates began with the 1975 primary and general elections and continued through 1979, when Byrne was elected over Bilandic by a 3–1 margin. Blacks voted against the machine and gave Byrne 63 percent of their votes. There was great disillusionment with Byrne's administration though, and in the 1980 Illinois primary, black voters defeated almost all of Byrne's candidates for political office.[53] In 1982, Byrne herself was defeated in the Democratic primary by black congressman Harold Washington, who became mayor in 1983.

Blacks in the late seventies comprised 33 percent of the Chicago population, yet only three blacks held major appointive city positions—the director of the Model Cities Program and the Chicago Committee on Urban Opportunity, the director of human resources, and the head of the Public Vehicle Commission. In addition, there were a few blacks at the deputy level. However, blacks fared better with elective jobs. Joseph Bertrand, the city's first black treasurer, had the highest elective job.[54] As of 1979, there were also fourteen blacks among the fifty aldermen in the Chicago City Council. Of this group, nine were Democratic party committeemen. Chicago, reportedly, had more black elected officials than any other American city, but the black machine politicians were still accountable to the machine's position rather than their black constituency.[55] Change, however, was close at hand.

Even though many businesses opposed a fair compulsary employment statute, a number of them made an effort to increase black employment on their own volition. Certain industries, such as meatpacking, farm equipment, and construction machinery, made significant use of black employees. During World War II, International Harvester hired blacks in unprecedented numbers.

President Fowler McCormick, from 1941 on, insisted on fair employment practices throughout the company. In general, from 1945 through 1960, blacks in farm equipment production maintained their wartime gains in employment, increasing them in some firms and decreasing them in others.[56] In 1945, 11.6 percent of Harvester's workers were black; by 1952, the percentage rose to 13.8. By 1951, 75.6 percent of the workers at the McCormick Twine plant in Chicago were black. In 1952, however, this particular plant was closed for economic reasons, reducing the ratio of blacks at Harvester to 9.8 percent. In 1960, the proportion of black workers employed by Harvester was 9.3 percent, the lowest in twenty years. In addition, the McCormick Works in Chicago, which was 37.1 percent black in 1959, was closed in 1961.[57]

Caterpillar Tractor also engaged in a variety of affirmative action programs during the early sixties, in Peoria and elsewhere. Programs were aimed at expanding the number of black craftsmen, recruiting blacks, employing and training hardcore unemployed, and upgrading blacks already employed. Between February 1, 1963, and February 1, 1965, Caterpillar doubled its minority employee workforce from 637 to 1,278.[58] In addition to fair employment practices within Caterpillar plants, many officers and managers of Caterpillar in Peoria worked to increase citizen awareness of racial discrimination in the city. Bus tours to blighted areas of the city were conducted for Peoria civic leaders and citizens. Results, at least in part, of these tours were changed policies by some of the real estate companies, a city council request to the State of Illinois for a state equal housing law, a local ordinance on equal housing, and movement of a few blacks from the ghetto to white neighborhoods.[59]

Blacks experienced substantial occupational gains in the early fifties in the Chicago Swift and other packing plants. However, decentralization of the meatpacking industry occurred in Chicago, which caused major losses in employment. In the early fifties, Armour began a process of modernization that drastically reduced its labor requirements. Swift began to close some of its plants in Chicago, along with other firms. Black employment in the Chicago, Kansas City, and St. Louis meatpacking centers fell by almost seven thousand; more than 80 percent of these job losses were in Chicago.[60]

After the closing of its major plants, Chicago was left without any processing plants in meatpacking, although the three largest firms, Swift, Armour, and Wilson, retained their headquarters in downtown Chicago. Although black workers then constituted 14 percent of employed persons in the Chicago metropolitan area, few blacks worked in meatpacking company offices. In January 1965, these three firms had only twenty-two black workers among the 3,300 white-collar employees in their general offices. By 1968, these firms increased their white-collar employment of blacks to 62 or 1.8 percent. This contrasted poorly with black employment in white-collar jobs in all Chicago firms, which was 4.7 percent in 1966.[61]

The telephone company began to hire operators on the basis of merit in 1947, and all the major public utility companies in Chicago broadened their fair employment practices between 1947 and 1950. During 1948, nonwhite workers in banks and insurance companies were hired for the first time in white-collar positions. A major electrical company was the first in its industry in Chicago to hire black office workers in 1949, and a major chemical company followed a year later.[62]

After 1947 there was also a growing demand for black sales persons and distribution and promotional representatives. Typical of the progress in sales and services was the employment of bakery driver salesmen. No major bakery company employed black driver salesmen in 1946. Following negotiations by the Commission on Human Relations and other agencies, the removal of barriers to black employment began. By 1951, all of Chicago's major bakery companies hired qualified blacks as driver salesmen. Major gains were also made in large taxicab companies and some petroleum and manufacturing firms.[63]

Blacks and Organized Labor

The relation of organized labor to the struggles of the black community was complex. Some unions tended to exclude blacks altogether (as in certain building trades and railroad unions), other attempted to relegate them to all black locals (as in some AFL craft unions), and still others encouraged blacks to play an active role in the union affairs (as in packinghouse, steel, and autos). Thus, there was no unified Labor position for dealing with the racial issue in Chicago.[64]

The greatest degree of black representation was found in the CIO industrial unions; only one-fourth of those unions in the Chicago area did not have blacks in some leadership positions. In approximately one-half of the Chicago CIO locals, 15 percent of the leaders were blacks. The building trades, on the other hand, tended to bar or discourage blacks from membership. Overall, the AFL unions (excluding the building trades) had a higher rate of exclusion of blacks than those of the CIO. Two-fifths of the AFL unions had no blacks at all in policymaking posts. However, in one-third of this group, 15 percent or more of the leadership positions were filled by blacks. In general, the number of policymaking posts in Chicago held by blacks tended to be related inversely to the powers vested in these positions. The more powerful the posts, the fewer the black policymakers.[65]

The United Packinghouse Workers of America (UPWA) was widely known for its active pursuit of equal rights. Many of the UPWA's locals were dominated by blacks, and one of the Swift locals moved its business office into a black neighborhood, which substantially reduced the participation of white members. One of the most important UPWA efforts on behalf of minority groups was the filing of grievances alleging discrimination at one of Swift's Chicago plants in 1950. The grievance action was aimed at enforcement of a provision of the collective agreement that prohibited discrimination in hiring. The union won the award that included reinstatement of thirteen black women, back pay, and retroactive seniority.[66]

A majority of Labor representatives from around the state, however, opposed the passage of a fair employment statute in 1945 in Springfield.[67] Representatives from the AFL and CIO reflected the different approaches of these organizations toward the black employment question. Within the AFL, there were trade and local differences on the race issue. Therefore, the AFL felt that the best solution was through the slow process of education. The CIO was impatient with a policy of "gradualism" that tolerated discrimination, and demanded legislation to change local practices.[68]

AFL policy changed gradually between 1947 and 1951; at least two AFL unions in Chicago whose constitutions contained discriminatory provisions altered these regulations. In both AFL and CIO locals, an increasing number of contracts with employers included nondiscrimination clauses applicable to both union and employer.[69] In 1951, the Illinois State Federation of Labor, consistent with the AFL's national policy, supported the establishment of nondiscrimination policy in housing, educational opportunity, and employment. President Soderstom of the Illinois State Federation of Labor worked actively for the passage of the Fair Employment Practices Bill in 1951.[70]

Because organized Labor had supported the implementation of fair employment practices legislation since the fifties, when a bill was finally passed in Illinois in 1961 Governor Kerner appointed James Kemp as one of the five members of the Fair Employment Practices Commission. Kemp, a black, was a business representative of Building Services Employees' Local No. 189, Chicago, a member of the Executive Committee of the Chicago Federation of Labor since 1959, and a member of the executive board of the Chicago branch of NAACP since 1949. His wife, Maida Springer Kemp, was equally active as a consultant to the African Labor History Center, general organizer and international representative for the ILGWU, and vice-president of the National Council of Negro Women.[71]

In the sixties, a number of unions became major targets of civil rights groups because of segregatory or discriminatory practices. Official policy of unions on equal employment opportunity often differed from actual practice. Officially, unions supported fair employment legislation, and the AFL–CIO pushed for the addition of equal employment opportunity requirements in the federal civil rights bill. However, in practice many locals discriminated.[72]

Traditionally, blacks in Chicago had been denied entry into most crafts. Discrimination by unions included exclusion from union membership by constitutional provision or by ritual; segregation of minority group members in separate union "auxiliaries"; the use of work permits for minorities instead of union membership; and denying minorities full participation in union activities and equal employment opportunity.[73] The Washburne Trade School, the major Chicago school training plumbers, electricians, carpenters, and other building trades workers for many years, had a policy of admitting only apprentices named by the unions, which rarely selected blacks as apprentices.[74] In 1961, approximately 1 percent of the enrollees at the Washburne were black (26 out of 2,682). Out of twelve trades, only five had any black apprentices. In 1965, only 97 out of 2,834 apprentices enrolled at Washburne were black. Among the building trades in 1965, there were fifty black apprentices; by September 1966, the number had risen to 147.[75]

Hymer believed that the factors that limited the entry of black youngsters into apprenticeships were 1) that information about apprenticeship openings was not distributed on a mass basis to counselors in black high schools; 2) that most unions still practiced tokenism, admitting only a few blacks in order to satisfy watchdog agencies and committees; 3) that few crafts practiced affirmative action, by actively seeking out young blacks for apprenticeships; and 4) that unions did not publicize their method of selection and placement of applicants from waiting lists. Therefore, no safeguards prevented these unions from discriminating against blacks in hiring or placement.[76]

With the passage of the Civil Rights Act in 1964 and the urban ghetto riots of 1964–68, the union-civil rights alliance weakened. Many union members saw blacks as a threat. These members had acquired higher income and status in the sixties and appeared to be less interested in social reform. At the same time, the civil rights movement moved from a legal-legislative orientation to a search for economic improvement.[77]

In the fall of 1965, the Chicago Freedom Movement (CFM) was formed. The movement had a meeting in February of 1966 sponsored by District 1 of the UPWA, and attended by 78 Chicago labor leaders and Dr. Martin Luther King. This meeting resulted in pledges of moral and financial support for CFM and the establishment of a steering committee of trade unionists to work with CFM.[78]

On July 15, 1966, a march to City Hall was held. Some of the marchers were members of the UPWA, UAW, AFSCME, USW, Meatcutters, and the Industrial Union Department of the AFL–CIO. In another action, AFL–CIO unions sent organizers into city slums to form tenant associations and bargain with landlords. Before the drive was over, nearly ten thousand ghetto tenants had reportedly been unionized.[79]

Black members of Local 241, Amalgamated Transit Union, AFL–CIO, began early in 1968 to organize a caucus that they called the Concerned

Transit Workers (CTW), with the aim of ending the all-white union leadership of a local that was 60 percent black. Wildcat strikes of black Chicago bus drivers gave publicity to the backward working conditions to which black union members were subjected because of their exclusion from leadership positions.[80]

In a separate movement, in the summer of 1969, the Chicago Coalition for United Community Action, a group of about sixty minority organizations, halted work for several days on construction jobs valued at $100 million. The coalition demanded ten thousand jobs and the easing of qualification requirements for minorities. The Chicago and Cook County Building Trades Council, in a plan endorsed by George Meany, promised to obtain employment for a thousand qualified journeymen to be supplied by the coalition, to accept workers of uncertain skills for thirty-day probationary periods, and to expand information, recruiting, and training programs.[81]

Unfortunately, fewer than a hundred black workers were actually hired, and many of these were only employed on a part-time basis. By the early seventies, the exclusion of blacks from better building trade jobs became the major economic and symbolic issue in the efforts of blacks to attain a fair deal from organized labor.[82]

A policy statement of the AFL–CIO in 1958 had supported equal rights for all in the shop and community. When a survey was conducted on how this policy was being carried out at the local level, it was found that only about half of the locals had incorporated written nondiscrimination clauses in official documents. However, many of the unions that lacked a written clause claimed that they had well-developed human relations programs. More than half of the local officials reported that the most common form of discrimination was hiring. They felt that their antidiscrimination policies and human relations programs had been successful in the aiding in the hiring of large numbers of minority group members and the representation of these members in top-rated jobs under union jurisdiction.[83]

Minorities were estimated in 1974 to comprise 35 percent of organized labor in Chicago. However, the number of minorities in policymaking positions did not reflect minority membership. When minority membership percentages were obtained by the *Chicago Reporter* for twenty-five Chicago-area unions, it was found that more than 50 percent of twelve unions' memberships were minorities. Many black labor members, however, expressed discontent with minority status in their unions. Some said that progress toward ending discrimination was too slow, while others said minority members did not aggressively demand recognition and equality within their unions.[84] The Chicago Federation of Labor had two blacks, James Kemp and James A. Pate, on its executive board. Two black males sat on the nineteen-member executive board of the Illinois state AFL–CIO.

Changing Economic Status of the Black Worker

In 1950, the census reported 8,046,058 whites and 666,118 nonwhites in Illinois. By 1960, whites had increased to 9,010,252, or 10.1 percent, and nonwhites increased to 1,070,906 or 60.8 percent. The majority of nonwhites lived in Cook County—888,852, or 83 percent of the state total.[85] Between 1950 and 1960, the nonwhite population in Chicago increased by 64 percent. According to the 1960 census, 39,061, or 47.5 percent, of all suburban non-whites were concentrated in the seven suburbs of North Chicago, Waukegan, Joliet, Evanston, Maywood, Chicago Heights, and Robbins.[86]

Black males had a lower rate of labor market participation than whites; 82 percent of white men over 14 in Chicago were in the labor force compared to only 77 percent of black men over fourteen. Baron and Hymer estimated that more than 5.5 percent of the nonwhite male population in 1960 in Chicago were discouraged workers, without jobs and out of the labor force. During the prosperous sixties, they found that the population of discouraged black workers grew in the Chicago labor market.[87]

Black unemployment in 1959–61 was three times that of white unemployment. In the early sixties, white unemployment was 4 percent, whereas black unemployment rates were between 10 and 15 percent. Even in 1965, when the Chicago labor market was tight, white unemployment was 2 percent and nonwhite unemployment was 6 to 7 percent. At every educational and occupational level blacks experienced a considerably higher rate of unemployment than whites.[88]

Between 1957 and 1966, the city of Chicago lost 48,000 jobs. At the same time, suburban areas gained 276,000 jobs, with the biggest increase in the north and west where few blacks lived. Housing segregation confined the black labor force to certain geographical areas of the labor market. Proximity to the job was often used as a criterion for hiring, even when the worker was willing to travel long distances.[89]

The residential remoteness of blacks from new jobs in growing industries reinforced the pattern of hiring them in declining industries. Because of auto-mation and other technological innovations, the unskilled and semiskilled occupations were gradually becoming smaller. Because a large part of the black labor force was concentrated in these occupations, many of the jobs available to blacks were in the process of decline because of automation. In addition, racial segregation in Chicago schools increased the skills and train-ing differential between whites and blacks.[90]

Blacks were concentrated at the bottom of the occupational hierarchy throughout the Chicago labor market. In 1960, three-quarters of black males were in lower-paying unskilled and semiskilled occupations compared to one-third of the white males. Only one out of twenty black males was employed in higher-paying professional and managerial jobs, whereas almost one out of every four white males was in these jobs. As for women, in 1960, 71 percent of black women in Chicago and 35 percent of white women were in lower-paying unskilled and semiskilled occupations. Eight percent of the black female labor force and 15 percent of the white female labor force were in higher-paying professional and managerial jobs.[91]

The Chicago Urban League contended that there were two labor markets in Chicago, one black and one white. The black market represented a surplus pool of workers to be drawn on when the white market was tight. Each market had its own separate mechanisms for the recruitment, training, and allocation of jobs and workers. Employers were believed to be aware of the dual labor market, and only tapped the sector from which they were interested in hiring workers. Over time there was a transfer of jobs from the white sector to the black sector as the economy developed and as the black labor force expanded.[92]

There was also racial concentration by industry. Twenty percent of employed black males worked for federal, state, or local government, compared to only 6 percent of employed white males. Six percent of black males were in the primary metal industry, compared to 3 percent of white males; 1.5 percent of white males were in the banking and finance industry, compared to 0.2 percent of black males.[93]

The Urban League reported that employment conditions for blacks began to improve significantly in 1965 and reached relatively high levels of demand in late 1967. However, nonwhite unemployment rates remained at two-and-a-half to three-and-a-half times that of white rates, and the relative position of blacks in both jobs and income had not improved.[94]

By 1970, 33 percent of Chicago's population was black; the unemployment rate for blacks was 5.4 percent and 3.3 percent for whites. Sixteen percent of the jobs in the metropolitan area were held by blacks. Blacks held 16 percent or more of the jobs in retail general merchandise, medical and other health services, primary metals, and food and kindred products. They held fewer than 10 percent of the jobs in trucking and machinery, except the electrical industries.[95]

Between 1966 and 1970, there was some improvement in the percentage of jobs held by blacks. However, the occupational distribution continued to show a high degree of concentration in low-level, white-collar, blue-collar, and service jobs. White-collar workers (excluding office and clerical) constituted about 33 percent of the total work force of the fifteen major industries in the area. However, white-collar workers who were black only accounted for 4.7 percent of the total. Even in the four industries in which black participation was highest, white-collar participation among blacks ranged from only 2.1 percent to 9.6 percent. Blacks occupied 21.7 percent of all blue-collar jobs in the fifteen major industries and were usually classified as operatives and laborers. Almost 90 percent of the blue-collar labor force that was black and 57 percent of the total black work force were classified as operatives and laborers.

The recessions of the mid and late seventies trimmed back the gains made by blacks in the sixties. By 1980, blacks comprised 39.8 percent of the Chicago population. Black unemployment, however, stood at 15.9 percent compared to the whites' unemployment rate of 6.1 percent. The median household income of blacks in 1979 was $12,609, compared to $22,501 for whites. The percentage of black families with income below the poverty level was 26.6 percent, compared with 4.1 percent for whites. The struggle for racial equity clearly had a long way to go.

Hispanics in Illinois

Another minority that was growing rapidly throughout the United States and Illinois was comprised of Hispanics. Chicago was the only major northern city in the United States with a substantial percentage of all the major ethnic groups constituting the nation's Spanish-speaking population. According to the 1970 U.S. census, the Spanish-speaking population of the city of Chicago was 247,343. This represented 7.3 percent of the city's total population. It is estimated that there was a 125 percent increase in Chicago's Hispanic population between 1960 and 1970.[97] By 1980, the U.S. census reported that 14 percent of the city's population was of Spanish origin.

The two largest Hispanic groups in Illinois were persons of Mexican and Puerto Rican descent. A typical pattern among Mexicans who came to the United States was to work as migrant workers in Texas and then slowly travel to Chicago by way of St. Louis. Many Mexicans worked on the railroads; once in Chicago, many settled in South Chicago.[98] The vast majority of the hundred thousand Mexicans in the mid-seventies was employed in the steel mills, automobile plants, or on the railroads.

Puerto Ricans were relatively recent arrivals to Illinois. They were estimated in the 1960s at from 45,000 to 65,000 in the Chicago area, and approximately 5,000 downstate. Many of these new residents came to Illinois under the auspices of the Midwest office of the Commonwealth of Puerto Rico Labor Department, which helped them find housing and employment.[99] By 1973, the Puerto Rican population probably surpassed the first- and second-generation Mexican Americans in total population.[100]

The resettlement program for Cuban émigrées from the Castro regime helped in the growth of Chicago's Cuban population, which had a higher labor force participation rate in Chicago than in New York or Miami.[101] The Cuban community was not very close knit or active in politics, probably because the majority of Cubans were professionals and did not live or identify with any particular community or organization.[102] Between 1960 and 1970, the Cuban population increased from two thousand to about fifteen thousand.

Chicago's Spanish-speaking families had a median income of $8,369 in 1969, compared to $10,394 for the non-Spanish-speaking. The proportion of Spanish-speaking families with incomes under $10,000 (63 percent) was considerably higher than that for non-Spanish-speaking (47 percent). In the highest income range ($15,000 and over), there were only 12 percent of the Spanish-speaking families, compared to 24 percent of the non-Spanish-speaking.[103]

Hispanics were underrepresented in every industry in Chicago except in manufacturing, where 56 percent of all Hispanics were employed compared to 30 percent of all non-Spanish-speaking workers. Eight percent of Hispanics in the city of Chicago and 11 percent in the suburbs were in professional occupations.[104] Chicago ranked highest among six cities studies in the proportion of Spanish-speaking workers employed in the durable manufacturing sector, second in transportation, and third in nondurable manufacturing. Chicago ranked second to last among the six cities in government work and construction, and last in communications and utilities, wholesale and retail trade, financial service, and professional occupations.[105]

The socioeconomic status of Spanish-surnamed Americans (SSA) in Chicago improved at a slow but steady pace. During the period of 1966–73, the employment of SSAs in private industry more than doubled. SSAs increased in several large industries that were reducing their total employment. However, SSAs remained underemployed in white-collar jobs that generally demand good verbal communications and/or specialized training. More than two-thirds of the SSAs in 1973 were working at semi- or unskilled blue-collar jobs, often dead-end jobs that offered low pay and few opportunities for advancement.[106]

In 1969, SSA males sixteen years and older with earnings had a median annual income of $6,418, compared to $8,987 for all men. SSA women earned a median annual income of $3,345, compared to $4,509 for all females. The median family incomes of SSAs in the Chicago SMSA in 1969 was $9,016, or 75 percent of the median income for all families. Only 16 percent of all SSA families earned yearly incomes of $15,000 or more, compared to 32 percent of all families. Approximately 13 percent of all SSA families earned incomes below poverty level, compared to 7 percent of all families. SSA males earned a median income of 75 percent as great as those of all men. Women of Spanish origin earned about 60 percent as much overall as SSA males.[107]

Between 1966 and 1973, SSAs doubled their participation rate in the Chicago labor market, from 2.6 percent to 6.3 percent. The proportion of white-collar SSAs rose from 10 percent to 15 percent. However, the participation rate of SSAs in operative and laborer jobs jumped from 7 percent to 12 percent and from 9 percent to 18 percent, respectively. Seventy-seven percent of SSAs remained in blue-collar jobs.[108]

For approximately five hundred thousand residents (mostly Spanish-speaking) of Illinois in 1970, English was a second language. In order to improve this situation, the 76th Illinois General Assembly created the Spanish-Speaking Peoples Study Commission to interview people in Spanish communities and to make recommendations for new laws. Between 1970 and 1971, the commission held seventeen public hearings on six major areas of interest: employment, housing, education, political representation, justice and police, and health. As a result of these hearings, Representative Arthur Telcser (R-Chicago) successfully sponsored a series of bills, fifteen of which were signed into law by Governor Richard B. Oglivie in September 1971. In addition, the governor instituted numerous programs in education—recruitment of Spanish teachers, intercultural exchange programs, high level appointments of Spanish-speaking persons, and the expansion of bilingual education programs.[109]

One bill that the governor signed into law to improve employment conditions provided for state agencies with a direct contact with a substantial number of non-English-speaking citizens to employ persons with bilingual ability to administer services. In addition, Oglivie appointed several Spanish-speaking persons into high-level positions. These included the first Latino to serve on the Pardon and Parole Board, and director of a Spanish-speaking division in the governor's Office of Human Resources, and advisor to the governor on Spanish affairs, an assistant director in the Department of Registration and Education, manpower coordinators in the Office of Manpower Development, and a member of the executive staff of the Illinois Commerce Commission. The Fair Employment Practices Commission opened an office for the Spanish in Chicago, staffed with Spanish-speaking persons, and the Office of Human Resources opened a branch office in Moline-Rock Island. In addition, positions were opened for the Spanish-speaking in the Illinois Bureau of Investigation and the Illinois State Police.[110]

Spanish-speaking people had to deal with cultural differences, lack of skills, and a language barrier. The Roman Catholic Archdiocesan Latin American Committee of Chicago established a program, known as "Spanish Manpower," which attempted to resolve these problems through bilingual vocational education under the Manpower Development Training Act (MDTA), personalized supportive services, and a program of community participation. The Cardinal's Committee also acted as a liaison between the Illinois State Employment Service and the Spanish community.

According to Hispanic labor leader, Jesse Rios, the Spanish-speaking community was slow to organize:

In general, in Chicago, there was nothing going on in the Hispanic community in the sixties. The Hispanic movement was born in the late sixties, flamed by the civil rights movement of blacks. Between 1969 and 71, there was a great deal of problems with the CTA. On the westside there were almost riots because of the poor bus service, and the lack of Latino bus drivers. Also around this time, Hispanics blockaded the streets of Pilsen with garbage, to protest poor sanitation service. These demonstrations of activism worked and received a positive response, improved service and more Latinos were hired by the CTA.

Currently, Hispanics can be seen to be moving into the hotel and restaurant industry. Service industries especially are big, including employment in and ownership of taverns. Typically, Hispanics use the same type of network for employment that blacks in Chicago use, word of mouth advertising. Usually Hispanics are employed in industrial manual labor jobs, so they do not usually use employment agencies. A major problem in the Mexican community is the continual flow of illegal Mexican immigrants who are illiterate. They keep Hispanics as a group back, and slow their movement into white collar professional occupations. The total Hispanic educational level will never have a baseline, because of this immigration of illiterates and the high Hispanic dropout rate [70 percent] from school. Therefore, it will be very difficult for Hispanics to improve as a group educationally and occupationally, in the near future.[112]

It is estimated that in the early seventies from 5 percent to 7 percent of all Chicago union members were Latino. Not only did Latinos face the same employment problems as other minorities, but these were also compounded by the group's lack of education and the language barrier. In order to alleviate some of these problems, the Hispanic American Labor Council (HALC) was organized in October 1973. HALC had a membership of about fifty Chicago Hispanic labor leaders, and their goals were to increase Hispanic participation in unions, lesson job discrimination, promote bilingual education in unions, and increase Hispanic political participation.
According to Jessie Rios:

> HALC is not affiliated with the AFL–CIO but they do work with them. Our purpose is to get Hispanic representation and participation in our own unions. I am now president of HALC and am the Compliance Officer for the American Federation of Government Employees, Local No. 648. Currently, there are only three Hispanic officers in the Government Employees Union. Since HALC started, many union members have benefitted by becoming officers, organizers or business agents. HALC tries to get people to participate and develop. . . .

> In 1975, HALC, in cooperation with the University of Illinois, developed a Labor Education Program for Spanish Speaking People at Chicago Circle. HALC helped develop the idea of bilingual labor education, supported it and went to the Governor and his representatives to push for it. Most factories have a fairly large Hispanic population; through the Labor Education Program, HALC gives small scholarships to Latino union members in order to learn about collective bargaining, organizing, etc.[113]

August Sallas, the first chairman of the council and delegate to the International and Illinois State AFL–CIO conventions for the Chicago Typographical Union, Local 16, felt that the organization had much to accomplish and its formation was overdue.[114]

When Sallas ran for office in the Typographical Union in the late sixties, he was told he would never win because there were few Hispanic members to support him. However, he did get elected as alternate delegate and then as delegate to the international convention, and was elected for three terms to the position of recording secretary and organizer of Local 16. Sallas was the first Mexican to hold office in the union in Chicago. By 1980, there was a Mexican-American shop chairman at the *Tribune*, a Mexican-American delegate to the Lake County central body, and a Cuban on the Typographical Union's executive board. Sallas was also a delegate to the Chicago Federation of Labor and State AFL–CIO, secretary-treasurer of the Chicago Allied Printing Trades Council, and secretary-treasurer of HALC.[115]

In 1973, the national AFL–CIO, approved and granted a charter to the Latin Council for Latin-American Advancement (LCLAA). The Illinois chapter was located in Chicago. The purpose of LCLAA was to bring about more participation of the Latino members in the AFL–CIO and to assist in the organizing of various international unions among Latin Americans.[116]

In the seventies, the Mexican-American community began to realize the necessity of achieving political power. They formed various political groups, for example, the Mexican-American Democratic Organization, Amigos for Daley, and the Spanish-Speaking Democratic Organization.[117] By the mid-seventies they had gained three elected officials: Irene Hernandez, Cook County commissioner; David Cerda, circuit court judge; and Arthur Velasquez, Jr., University of Illinois trustee. There were also a number of appointed officials in city government, such as Miriam Cruz, administrative assistant for Spanish-speaking affairs to Mayor Daley; Guillermo O. Perez, director of finance for the Chicago Board of Elections Commissioners; and Carmen Velasquez, member of the Chicago Board of Education. At the state level, Jose "Tito" Pacheco was administrative assistant to Governor Dan Walker and Manuel Toledo was administrative assistant to Lieutenant Governor Neil Hartigan.[118]

In terms of political life, however, Hispanics in Illinois were the most limited of ethnic-racial minorities. Part of the reason for this lack of political involvement can be explained by their low economic level. Another reason was the political structure of Chicago. By 1977, it was estimated that there were 225,000 adult Spanish-speaking persons in Chicago; only about 73,000 were registered to vote. Chicago was divided into fifty wards, but only two, the 1st and 31st, had a large proportion of precincts with a majority of Spanish-speaking persons. Both of these wards covered Mexican communities, yet these wards did not show a majority of Latinos on the rolls of registered voters. Many Mexicans, because of the high number of illegal aliens in the community, were apparently afraid to vote, or afraid not to vote for the incumbent. Most Latino voters in Chicago were Democrats, but subordinated to the machine. In 1975, four Latino candidates attempted to win the position of ward alderman for the 22nd, 26th, 31st, and 46th wards. Each candidate ran as an independent Democrat. They all lost.[119]

In the 1979 mayoral campaign, Mayor Michael Bilandic secured 55.3 percent of the vote in the Latino wards. Latinos made headlines when they staged sit-ins and harassed his opponent Jane Byrne because she failed to appear at a meeting with Latino community people. When Byrne won the mayoralty, she tried to appoint Mary Gonzales, Latino, to her transition team of advisors. However, Gonzales refused the sppointment, charging that she had only been invited to join the team after Byrne used her name to indicate Latino support. After the election was won, Byrne dismissed her Latino campaign organizer, Elna Martinez, rather than rewarding her with a high-paying job.[120]

Mayor Byrne removed all of the Bilandic-appointed Latino officials and did not replace them. Her first Latino appointment was Dr. Hugo H. Muriel, an old family friend, as head of the Chicago Public Health Commission. This appointment was criticized by both the Latino community and the medical profession. Typically, the majority of those considered for appointments were educated Cubans and Puerto Ricans living in the city's upper-income neighborhoods; they had little contact with the daily workings of government.[121]

More than two hundred Latino organizations operated in the community, but typically, these organizations were isolated from the Democratic organization. Latino leaders rose from the comunity organizations, but they lacked legitimate power. Because the economic level of Hispanics in Chicago was fairly low, the majority of Hispanic activities were oriented to local community issues and to deal with immediate issues bearing on the people of the community, rather than citywide reform. It was not until the early eighties that changes in this approach became visible.[122]

Minority employment made its greatest gains in the state government during the seventies. As of September 1973, Governor Dan Walker had appointed more blacks and Hispanics to high positions than any other governor in Illinois history. By the end of the summer of 1973, thirty-three blacks and eleven Hispanics had been appointed to posts ranging from the directorship of the Department of General Services to a variety of seats on advisory boards and commissions. Blacks constituted 11 percent of all appointments, and Hispanics some 3.3 percent. These percentages were closely aligned to the state's minority population in 1970—12.8 percent black and 3.3 percent with a Spanish-surname.[123]

Illinois was second only to Ohio among the seven largest states in employing blacks and Latinos in the state's government service in proportion to their numbers. As of June 30, 1974, the 66,099 state employees included 19.3 percent who were black and Latino, compared to the state's black and Latino population of 16.1 percent. Although the proportion of black state personnel exceeded the black population percentage, the state government's Latino employees were below the Latino proportion of the state's population. However, blacks and Latinos were, for the most part, low-paid paraprofessionals. Of 2,270 officials and managers in state government, 9.6 percent were blacks and 9.7 percent Latino.[124]

The biggest push for hiring Latinos came in the Department of Public Aid after a suit was filed by Latino community groups charging that the department discriminated in hiring and did not provide bilingual services. Within eight months after this, the Chicago offices of the department increased the number of Latino employees from 89 to 145.[125]

Black and Latino employees were 28.1 percent of the Chicago City Hall work force in 1976, an increase of 3.8 percent over 1974. Of 2,816 new employees hired by the city during fiscal year 1974, 41 percent were either black or Latino. During fiscal year 1976, 37 percent of 3,443 new hires were minority.[126]

Minority city employees generally earned less and were in lower level positions than their white counterparts. The wage gap, furthermore, was not shrinking. Almost two out of every three white city employees earned more than $16,000 annually, compared to nearly one of every three black city employees and one out of every four Latino city workers. Of the city's total white employees in 1976, 92.9 percent earned $10,000 or more annually, compared to 71.9 percent of the city's black employees and 63.2 percent of the Latino employees. Of 28,637 white full-time employees, 2,033 (7.1 percent) earned less than $10,000 annually in 1976. Of 9,736 black full-time employees in 1976, 2,735 (28.15 percent) earned less than $10,000 annually. Of the 965 Latino full-time employees in 1976, 355 (36.8 percent) earned less than $10,000.[127]

The heaviest concentrations of minorities continued to be in the paraprofessional, office and clerical, service, and maintenance job categories and in the hospitals and health departments. Of 1,941 officials and administrators in 1974, 78.2 percent were white, 20.1 percent were black, and 1.8 percent were Latino. Of 1,406 employees in the top job category in 1976, 78.8 percent were white, 18.8 percent black, and 1.8 percent Latino.[128]

As the foregoing evidence indicates, Hispanics were latecomers in the Illinois labor force, lagging behind blacks as well as the general white population in terms of occupational level, extent of employment, and average income. Nonetheless, in the seventies, despite the language barrier and internal cultural differences, they began to make visible progress in all three respects through labor union involvement and political action.

NOTES

This chapter is largely based on two reports by Christina E. Shalley.

1. Committee on Education, Training and Research in Race Relations of the University of Chicago, *The Dynamics of State Campaigns for Fair Employment Practices Legislation*, April 1950.

2. Illinois Legislative Council, *State Educational Fair Employment Practice Laws*, Bulletin 3–701, Springfield, February 1960.

3. Mary Watters, *Illinois in the Second World War*, vol. 2, chap. 3 (Springfield: Illinois State Historical Library, 1951).

4. *Human Relations in Chicago*, (Chicago: Chicago Conference on Home Front Unity, October 30, November 6, 1945).

5. *Race Relations in Chicago*, (Chicago: Mayor's Commission on Human Relations, 1945 and 1946).

6. *State Educational Fair Employment Practice Laws*.

7. *What Happened in Springfield*, Illinois State Chamber of Commerce, July 1953.

8. *Illinois State AFL–CIO News*, Chicago, 1961.

9. Joseph Minsky, "FEPC in Illinois: Four Stormy Years," *Notre Dame Lawyer* 41 (December 1965): 152–81.

10. Minsky, "FEPC in Illinois."

11. Ibid.

12. *Chicago Sun-Times*, November 1, 1961.

13. Minsky, "FEPC in Illinois."

14. Charge filed by Leon Myart with FEPC, July 29, 1963 in *Myart v. Motorola*.

15. Minsky, "FEPC in Illinois."

16. Ibid.

17. FEPC, State of Illinois, *A Summary Report of the Case of Myart v. Motorola*, Chicago, January 18, 1965.

18. *Chicago Tribune*, November 25, 1964.

19. Ibid., April 22, 1965.

20. Minsky, "FEPC in Illinois."

21. Illinois FEPC, *Annual Report*, 1963.

22. J. E. Champagne and R. Gillooly, *Equal Employment Opportunity under Federal and State Laws*, 3rd. ed. (Houston: Center for Human Resources, 1976).

23. Illinois Commission on Human Relations, *Tenth Biennial Report*, May 1963.

24. Illinois FEPC, *Annual Report*, 1963.

25. Bureau of National Affairs, *The Civil Rights Act of 1964* (Washington: BNA, 1964).

26. Illinois FEPC, *Annual Reports*, 1962–66, Chicago and Springfield.

27. Speech, June 16, 1963, Springfield, Illinois.

28. Bennett Hymer, *"Racial Dualism in the Chicago Labor Market"*, Ph.D. diss., Northwestern University, Evanston, Ill., 1968.

29. James O. Wilson, *Negro Politics: The Search for Leadership* (Glencoe: Free Press, 1960).

30. Wilson, *Negro Politics*.

31. Ibid.

32. Lee Augustus McGriggs, *Black Legislative Politics in Illinois* (Washington: University Press of America, 1977).

33. Wilson, *Negro Politics*.

34. Ibid.

35. Norman Bonney, "Race and Politics in Chicago," *Race* 15 (January 1974): 329–50.

36. Wilson, *Negro Politics*.

37. Ibid.

38. Ibid.

39. A. H. Strickland, *History of the Chicago Urban League* (Urbana; University of Illinois Press, 1966).

40. Strickland, *History*.

41. Ibid.

42. Ibid.

43. Chicago Commission on Human Relations, *The People of Chicago: Five Year Report*, 1947–1951.

44. *Wall Street Journal*, March 16, 1972.

45. Gordon F. Bloom, *The Negro in the Supermarket Industry* (Philadelphia: University of Pennsylvania, The Wharton School, 1970).

46. Bloom, *The Negro in the Supermarket Industry*.

47. Ibid.

48. *Wall Street Journal*, March 16, 1972.

49. Bloom, *The Negro in the Supermarket Industry*.

50. *Wall Street Journal*, March 16, 1972.

51. Norman Bonney, "Race and Politics."

52. *Wall Street Journal*, March 16, 1972.

53. Michael B. Preston, "Black Politics in the Post-Daley Era," in *After Daley: Chicago Politics in Transition*, ed. Samuel K. Gove and Louis H. Masatti (Urbana: University of Illinois Press, 1982).

54. *Chicago Reporter*, June 1978.

55. Preston, "Black Politics."

56. Robert Ozanne, *The Negro in the Farm and Construction Machinery Industry* (Philadelphia: University of Pennsylvania, The Warton School, 1972).

57. Ozanne, *The Negro in the Farm and Construction Machinery Industry*.

58. Ibid.

59. Ibid.

60. Walter A. Fogel, *The Negro in the Meat Industry* (Philadelphia: University of Pennsylvania, The Wharton School, 1970).

61. Ibid.

62. Chicago Commission on Human Relations, *The People of Chicago*.

63. Ibid.

64. Wilson, *Negro Politics*.

65. Harold M. Baron, "Black Powerlessness in Chicago", *Transaction*, vol. 6, no. 10 (1968): pp. 27–33.

66. Fogel, *The Negro in the Meat Industry*.

67. Chicago Conference on Home Front Unity, *Human Relations in Chicago*, October 30, November 6, 1945.

68. Watters, *Illinois in the Second World War.*

69. Chicago Commission on Human Relations, *The People of Chicago.*

70. *Proceedings* of 69th State AFL Convention (1951).

71. *The Ebony Success Library,* vol. 1 (Chicago: Johnson Publishing, 1975).

72. Hymer, "Racial Dualism"; see chapter 4, part B for experience in Chicago Building and Construction industry.

73. Chicago Conference on Home Front Unity, *Human Relations in Chicago.*

74. Ibid. For the later years, see Joy G. Carew and Michael B. Preston, *The Washburne Report: The Exclusion of Blacks and Other Minorities from the Construction Trades in Chicago, 1977–1984* (Chicago: Illinois Senate Committee on Higher Education, January 20, 1985).

75. Hymer, "Racial Dualism."

76. Ibid.

77. Harry A. Ploski and W. Marr, ed., *The Negro Almanac* (New York: Ballwether, 1975).

78. Philip S. Foner, *Organized Labor and the Black Worker, 1619–1973* (New York: Praeger Publishers, 1974).

79. Foner, *Organized Labor.*

80. Ibid.

81. Ploski and Marr, *The Negro Almanac*; see chapter 4, part B for more details.

82. Ibid.

83. Illinois Commission on Human Relations, *A Study of Labor Unions and Minority Groups in Metropolitan Chicago,* State of Illinois, Chicago, January 1958.

84. *Chicago Reporter,* November 1974.

85. Illinois Commission on Human Relations, *Nonwhite Population in Illinois, 1950–60,* State of Illinois, Chicago.

86. Illinois Commission on Human Relations, *Nonwhite Population in Changes in Chicago Suburbs,* State of Illinois, Chicago, January 1962.

87. Harold M. Baron and Bennett Hymer, "The Negro Worker in the Chicago Labor Market," in *The Negro and the American Labor Movement,* ed. Julius Jacobson (New York: Doubleday, 1968).

88. Baron and Hymer. "The Negro Worker."

89. Ibid.

90. Ibid.

91. Ibid.

92. Ibid.

93. Ibid.

94. Frank H. Cassell, "Chicago 1960–70: One Small Step Forward," *Industrial Relations* 9 (May 1970): 277–93.

95. EEOC, *Employment Profiles of Minorities and Women in the SMSA's of 17 Large Cities* (Washington: Government Printing Office, 1971).

96. Ibid.

97. City of Chicago, Department of Development and Planning, *Chicago's Spanish-Speaking Population: Selected Statistics,* September 1973.

98. Interview with August Sallas, first chairman of the Chicago Hispanic American Labor Council.

99. Illinois Commission on Human Relations, *Ninth Biennial Report*, State of Illinois, Chicago, 1961.

100. City of Chicago, Department of Development and Planning, *Chicago's Spanish-Speaking Population*.

101. George L. Wilber and Robert J. Hagen, *Metropolitan and Regional Inequalities Among Minorities in the Labor Market*, vol. 3 (Washington: Department of Labor, 1975).

102. Interview with Jesse Rios, organizer and recording secretary of American Federation of Government Employees, Local 648, and president of HALC.

103. City of Chicago, Department of Development and Planning, *Chicago's Spanish-Speaking Population*.

104. Ibid.

105. Ibid.

106. U.S. Department of Labor, *The Employment Status of Spanish Surnamed Americans in Chicago SMSA, 1966–1973*, Research Report no. 48. (Washington: Government Printing Office).

107. Ibid.

108. Ibid.

109. *Illinois News*, November 1, 1972.

110. Ibid.

111. Delia Villegas, *"Partnership for Training,"* testimony presented at the Cabinet Committee Hearings on Mexican-American Affairs, El Paso, Texas, October 28, 1967.

112. Interview with Jesse Rios.

113. Ibid.

114. *Chicago Reporter*, November 1974.

115. Interview with August Sallas.

116. *Proceedings*, 19th Annual Convention, State AFL–CIO, 1976.

117. *Chicago Reporter*, July 1975.

118. Ibid.

119. Joanne Belenchia, "Latinos in Chicago Politics," in Gove and Masotti, *After Daley*.

120. Ibid.

121. Ibid.

122. Ibid.

123. *Chicago Reporter*, September 1973.

124. Ibid., January 1975.

125. Ibid.

126. *Chicago Reporter*, June–July 1977.

127. Ibid.

128. Ibid.

18

More Voice for Working Women

Women were an important part of the Illinois labor force (as they were nationally) long before World War II, but they suffered from numerous disabilities and were often treated in industry and employment legislation more as children or wards than as adults. A general scenario that applied to Illinois, as to the United States as a whole, may be depicted briefly as follows:[1] Men were expected to work to support themselves and their families and lost social standing without jobs unless they were part of the small wealthy leisure class. Women's "place" was in the home as wife and mother; many women were believed to work for "pin money" rather than economic need or, if they came from the upper income class, as social benefactors. The great bulk of women worked in a limited group of occupations—as domestic help, subordinate office employees, food services, teachers, nurses, librarians, retail trade, and factory workers in light industry (notably textiles, clothing, and electrical assembly). Women's pay was significantly below men's wages and salaries. In some occupations like education, women were often refused employment or forced to resign if their husbands or fathers were employed in the same institution. And employment legislation such as minimum wage and maximum hours was often designed to treat women workers in more protective fashion than men.

The seeds of rebellion against this Victorian heritage were sown in the nineteenth century, but the decisive turning point came during World War II, when critical labor shortages emerged. As Mary Watters illustrated in brilliant detail: "A survey of more than 100 plants showed only one, a machine tool manufacturer, which did not use women for production jobs. They worked in the fluorspar mines in Rosiclare, the oil refineries of Wood River, [in the] Danville foundries, in the South Chicago steel mills, at the Seneca shipyards, and on the railroads. . . . They did precision grinding, foundry core making. They excelled as precision inspectors. . . . In Chicago, they took jobs as taxi drivers, street car conductors, park traffic police, life guards, meter readers, even as garbage collectors."[2] Between 1940 and 1944, the employment of women in Illinois increased about two-thirds and in manufacturing by nearly 120 percent.

The war experience demonstrated, in the words of Esther Saperstein, the prominent unionist and legislator, that women could do the same work as men if they were given proper training and opportunity. However, it was widely assumed that at war's end the returning veterans would reclaim their earlier occupations, and this indeed happened. Many women remained in clerical occupations because fewer men sought these jobs. But most women left their production jobs and assumed the role of housewife; marriage and birth rates soared.

The postwar low point in women's participation in the work force was reached in 1947, but within two years they began returning to the workplace. The rising cost of living and family need for additional income forced many women back into the labor market. In addition, increased employment opportunities encouraged women to seek employment outside of the home.[3] By 1950, 31 percent of the women in Illinois, comprising 29 percent of the total labor force, were employed, and married women were in the majority.[4] During the next three decades, women became increasingly important as members of the labor force, (Table 13).

Table 13. Participation of Women Workers in the Illinois Labor Force

	Labor Force Participation Rates		Percent of Total Labor Force		Number of Women in the Labor Force
	Women	Men	Women	Men	
1940	27%	79%	25%	75%	854,000
1950	31	81	29	71	1,067,000
1960	36	78	33	67	1,338,000
1970	43	77	38	62	1,755,000
1975	48	80	40	60	2,012,000
1980	53	79	42	58	2,283,000

Sources: Women in Labor Force Reports, Bureau of Employment Security; U.S. Department of Labor; U.S. Census Reports

In addition to increased participation in the labor force, women entered a greater variety of nontraditional occupations, including highly skilled professional and technical positions. This mobility was facilitated by the fact that the economic system as a whole was shifting from blue-collar to white-collar work. Table 14 presents census data on the changing occupational distribution of Illinois women between 1940 and 1960 and Illinois sources for 1970 through 1980. During the first two decades, despite a 71.7 percent overall increase in female employment, the occupational distribution, with two exceptions, remained relatively stable. Private household workers declined in relative number, from 12 percent to 4.4 percent, whereas only one occupation, clericals, grew appreciably, from 28.4 percent to 34.5 percent.

In the next two decades, however, the women's movement became more

Table 14. Percent Distribution of Employed Women Workers in Illinois by Selected
Occupations

Occupations	1940*	1950*	1960*	1970	1975	1980
Total percent	100%	100%	100%	100%	100%	100%
Professional and						
Technical	12.5	11.2	11.9	14.8	16.3	17.5
Nonfarm mgrs.						
and adm.	3.3	4.0	3.1	3.0	4.8	6.4**
Sales	8.1	8.1	7.4	7.3	7.0	7.1
Clerical	28.4	33.4	34.5	39.4	38.1	35.3
Crafts and kindred	1.4	1.9	1.4	1.8	1.5	1.8
Operative,						
nontransport	n.a.	n.a.	16.2	14.3	11.2	10.4
Transport						
operatives	n.a.	n.a.	n.a.	0.4	0.6	0.6
Laborers	1.4	1.1	0.6	1.2	1.1	1.2
Service workers	n.a.	n.a.	17.1	19.5	18.8	18.9
Private household						
workers	12.0	5.0	4.4	n.a.	n.a.	n.a.

Sources: U.S. Census for 1940 and 1950; Illinois Bureau of Employment Security, *Women and
the Labor Force*, 1978 and 1981. Comparisons over time are rough approximations
because of changing concepts and definitions.
    * Includes fourteen-and-fifteen-year-olds. Other years are sixteen and over.
    ** Includes farm as well as nonfarm managers.

pronounced. The civil rights movement in general took hold in the sixties,
the surging militancy of the blacks influenced similar pressure activities by
women's organizations, and both federal and state antidiscrimination laws
lent support to women's efforts to improve their occupational status.

The principal change was a fairly sizable increase in the professional and
technical category from 11.9 percent in 1960 to 17 percent in 1979, although
the figures are slightly biased by the inclusion of the fourteen- and fifteen-
year-olds in the 1960 enumeration. Service workers also grew in relative
importance, from 17.1 percent to 19.7 percent. On the other hand, non-
transport operatives declined from 16.2 percent to 10.1 percent. The largest
single occupational class—clerical workers—grew during the sixties but lost
part of that gain in the seventies.

Despite advances into higher level professional, technical, and administrative positions and limited but path-breaking gains in the skilled crafts, most
women remained in traditional women's jobs and industries.[5] Nevertheless,
the massive attention paid to the women's movement in newspapers,
magazines, radio, and television was not illusory. For one thing, the number
of young women enrolled in colleges and universities grew rapidly—50 per-

cent between 1970 and 1978 alone[6]—so that by 1980, they slightly outnumbered male students. The doors opened (in varying degrees) to virtually every occupation with high educational prerequisities. Of equal importance, the demands of society during the postwar era shifted dramatically from blue-collar to white-collar occupations in which women were already ensconced. Occupational expectations provided strong incentives to women to either move into, or to prepare for, new or newly expanding segments of the labor force such as computers, telecommunications, banking and insurance and real estate services, and health care.

Numerous women's organizations, both federal and local, played significant roles in the activities and gains of the Illinois women's movement, but center stage was occupied by the Commission on the Status of Women. Modeled after the President's Commission on the Status of Women created by President John F. Kennedy in December 1961, the Illinois Commission was set up initially by the legislature, with the strong support of Governor Otto Kerner, in August 1963; its eighteen members were appointed in January 1964. Spearheading the drive were three women in the General Assembly: Esther Saperstein, a Chicago Democrat who was a longtime leader of the Chicago Teachers Union, a House member from 1957–66, a Senate member from 1966–75, and chairwoman for the commission from its inception until 1973; Lilliam Piotrowski, also a Chicago Democrat, who was elected to seven terms in the House (1951–64); and Frances L. Dawson, a Republican from Evanston and a House member from 1957–70.

Passage was by no means easy because many male legislators were initially unsympathetic. In 1978, Saperstein, in describing the early history of the commission, said that "the men in the legislature did not take the Commission seriously and made many jokes about it . . . in 1967 [then] Senator Saperstein requested a $10,000 appropriation (i.e., the same amount as the first two commissions received). Several male senators tried to reduce the appropriation, but Saperstein, refusing to give in, asked Senate President Shapiro to help her filibuster, and he agreed. Senator Saperstein then asked that every bill be read in full. Finally, the opponents conceded and the Commission received its $10,000 appropriation."[7]

The commission was authorized to "study the status of women in this state and make recommendations for constructive action in the following areas:

a. Employment policies and practices;

b. Illinois labor laws;

c. Legal rights;

d. The family and the employed woman;

e. Expanded programs to help women as wives; mothers; and workers;

f. Women as citizen volunteers;

g. Education."

It was to submit a report with recommendations to the governor and the general assembly not later than March 1, 1965.

The assignment was taken seriously. The eighteen (later sixteen) members consisted of four representatives from the House, four senators from the Senate, and ten public members appointed by the governor (eight of whom were women carefully selected to represent a wide variety of interests). The commission members in turn selected some sixty-eight community leaders who served on five subcommittees as consultants and resource aids. In their report, the commission presented a variety of salient facts as well as a large number of recommendations based on public hearings and documentary evidence. Most important, it concluded that its activities represented only a start, and it urged the continuation of the commission's inquiries with an adequate staff and appropriations.

Governor Kerner was strongly supportive of the commission's role. In 1965 he appointed a second two-year commission by executive order, again under the leadership of Esther Saperstein, and subsequently recommended the establishment of a permanent commission to the General Assembly. In September 1967, now-Senator Saperstein led a strong and successful drive to set up a Commission on the Status of Women on a permanent basis. The new statute was almost identical to the 1963 temporary law but provided for the commission to submit an annual report to the governor and general assembly, including recommendation for legislative consideration.[8]

In 1969, the commission noted that despite its predecessor's recommendations in 1965 and 1967, "Illinois still had no minimum wage law, no comprehensive, enforceable law providing equal pay, no law against employment discrimination on the basis of sex. But no one can doubt that, because the Commission exists, progress toward the goal of equal opportunity and equal protection for all citizens of Illinois has been accelerated."[9] Public hearings and conferences were believed to contribute significantly to this progress.

More concrete testimony to the commission's impact gradually appeared on the legislative front. In 1971, for example, the state's Fair Employment Practices Act was amended to include sex among the antidiscrimination criteria. In 1973, the Public Works Contract Act was also amended to prohibit discrimination in employment based on sex; a similar change was applied to the State University Civil Service System. Another law recommended by the commission allowed the director of the Department of Personnel for the state to authorize 10 percent of all positions for which the department determined hours of work as "flexible hours positions." Subsequently, the flexible hours concept was extended to all state departments and agencies under the Personnel Code.

Perhaps the most divisive issue affecting female employment (as well as other women's issues) was the Equal Rights Amendment to the U.S. Constitution. The new 1970 Illinois constitution, thanks to the efforts of many energetic women lobbyists, had incorporated the equal rights principle. But the anti-ERA forces, led adroitly by Phyllis Schlafly, who was a public member of the commission, developed sufficient political support to frustrate passage of the resolution endorsing the federal provision by the necessary three-fifths majority in both houses. A sizable majority of the commission advocated passage, but to no avail.

The division between the pro-ERA and anti-ERA forces inside the commission was not confined to this issue, as a series of strong minority reports made clear. These differences were stated emphatically in the February 1982 *Report and Recommendations*. Five of the sixteen members of the commission signed a minority statement that concluded:

> The underlying fallacy of the Majority Report of the Illinois Commission on the Status of Women is that it pretends to speak for "women", when, in fact, it speaks only for the aggressive feminists for whom the Equal Rights Amendment is the Centerpiece of their ideology and their legislative activism. One thing we have learned from the nine-year battle over the Equal Rights Amendment is that those who are pro-ERA do not believe in equal rights for those who are anti-ERA. The pro-ERA majority on the Commission has elected all pro-ERA Commission officers, appointed all pro-ERA chairmen and members of all committees, appointed all pro-ERA staff, set a totally pro-ERA agenda for all meetings, and invited speakers who would serve those goals, and generally pretended that no contrary point of view exists in the State of Illinois.[10]

A comparison of the commission's recommendations affecting employment for women in its first report (1965) with its recommendations in the 1981 report (covering the year 1980) may suggest the progress that had been made and the challenges that lay ahead.

The 1965 report included the following recommendations:

1. Establish statewide counseling and information centers for women who wish to return to education or the workplace.
2. Include in labor statistics more data concerning women in the labor force.
3. Urge industry to provide training programs for women employees.
4. Expand day care services.
5. Request appropriations to provide adequate day care facilities.
6. Enact a minimum wage law.
7. Enact equal pay for women by legislative action.
8. Publicize the facilities of the Illinois State Employment Service and other nonprofit agencies.
9. Make a survey of absenteeism and turnover among workers.
10. Maintain a roster of women qualified for (high-level) appointive positions.

11. Develop a program of part time employment.
12. Amend the Illinois Fair Employment Practices Act of 1961 to include women.[11]

The report for 1980 reflected a continuing concern over some of these issues but also emphasized important new issues:

1. Ratify the proposed Equal Rights Amendment to the U.S. Constitution.
2. Make available apprenticeship programs and nontraditional job training to women incarcerated in the Dwight Correctional Center.
3. Provide minimum wage protection for private household workers in the state.
4. Define sexual harassment in the workplace as an unlawful employment practice and establish appropriate redress of employment complaints.
5. Have the state government encourage and support programs to recruit and train women for non-traditional careers.
6. Have a comparable worth study (equal pay for jobs of comparable worth) of all state job classifications be performed.
7. Build "career ladders" into lower-level positions in state employment.[12]

In addition to its public hearings, conferences, and study projects, the commission was authorized to "survey activity in the area of status of women carried on by any commission, agency or department of the federal government or any State or any private organization or association and may cooperate with any such body in conducting investigations and studies." In accordance with this provision, it maintained close ties to a wide variety of organizations such as the federal Commission on the Status of Women, it was affiliated with the National Association of Commissions for Women, it was represented in international women's conferences, and it cooperated with the federal EEOC. It requested and received reports from the Illinois Fair Employment Practices Commission and served as a support and prod to that committee. In 1977, for example, it expressed deep concern about the EEOC's "alleged destruction of case records in the Chicago regional office" and recommended "that the EEOC funding of the Illinois Fair Employment Practices Commission not be reduced."[13]

Because of its bipartisan composition (e.g., Republican Frances Dawson served as co-sponsor of the original commission law with Democrat Esther Saperstein, and when the latter retired as commission chairperson in 1973, she was succeeded by Republican Susan Catania) and because its membership included prominent female and male legislators as well as a wide array of women leaders in the state, the commission exercised significant political influence. It coalesced the growing number of women members of the General Assembly (twenty-seven in the House and four in the Senate in 1980) on women's issues. It also maintained close lines of communication with the governor's staff, the state bureaucracy, and the state's congressional delegates.

The relationship of organized Labor to the women's movement was of special significance. According to Esther Saperstein,

> The idea for the Illinois Commission on the Status of Women came out of the trade union movement, the women's division. The regional office of the Women's Bureau contacted her and together they conceived of the idea of the Commission which would study the needs of women in eight different areas. . . . At this time, the problems that women encountered in employment were just beginning to emerge. The director of the Department of Labor, Mr. Cullerton, was sympathetic to those problems. There was no minimum wage and there was disagreement about whether the eight-hour work day law (prohibiting more than eight hours work per day for women) should be repealed so that women could receive overtime pay.[14]

For many years, however, the attitude of organized Labor toward the women's movement (including that of many women unionists themselves) was extremely ambiguous, and more militant women unionists had a difficult time persuading the male leadership to accept their goals. For example in 1948 and again in 1949, the State Industrial Union Council adopted a resolution that read in part:

> Whereas: CIO has always fought discrimination against women whether on or off the job. We have advocated, through collective bargaining and legislation, measures to provide for women's special needs as workers and mothers, but at the same time we have supported equal pay for equal work to protect the wage standards of men and women alike; Therefore Be It Resolved that:
> 1. We renew our efforts to obtain equal pay for equal work through our collective bargaining power and through state and federal laws;
> 2. We continue to oppose the so-called Equal Rights Amendment which would outlaw essential [protective] labor legislation for women, and support the Women's Status bill which would maintain such legislation and at the same time help to end discrimination against women;
> 3. We support all measures that permit women to earn a living without unduly jeopardizing the welfare of their families or their own health, including community projects such as school lunch and child care programs, expansion of opportunities for part-time employment, and amendment of federal income tax laws to permit tax exemption for money spent by working mothers for child care. . . .[15]

And as late as March 22, 1967, Reuben G. Soderstrom, president of the Illinois State Federation of Labor and Congress of Industrial Organizations, strongly opposed repeal of the Women's Eight-Hour Day law because, like a legislative fire department "it will stop a blaze of exploitation if unhappily our women workers are again victimized."[16] It was not until 1973 that the national AFL–CIO endorsed the ERA and modified its paternalistic although long-popular attitude toward women labor. The State Fed followed soon after.

Women became involved on a large scale in the trade union movement during the first decade of the twentieth century. However, as Helen Marot, executive secretary of the Women's Trade Union League of New York, 1905–13, wrote:

> Where women are eager to organize they usually find it possible to secure the cooperation of the union representing their trade. . . . The discrimination against women is within rather than without the membership. Women are discouraged from taking an active part in the executive affairs of organization. There are no women among the national officers or the national executive of the American Federation. In the 111 national unions there is but one woman president. It would be rare to find women presiding over a city or state organization. . . . Labor union men are like other men: they are not eager to trust office-holding to women. . . . The real problem of the organization of women in labor unions is not discrimination, but the position of women in their domestic relations and industry. This is complicated by a special attitude assumed toward women, of which their attitude toward themselves is a part.[17]

Many of these factors were still dominant in the fifties; long and slow in development, the women's movement in its contemporary sense did not burgeon until the sixties and seventies. Organizationally in the Labor field the National Women's Trade Union League played a key role in supporting trade unionism and strikes among women workers and in fighting for protective legislation as well as in sponsoring social, recreational, cultural, and educational activities.[18] But the league, which was formed in 1903, was more heavily dependent upon the support of upper-income women such as Jane Addams, Florence Kelly, Margaret Dreier Robins, and Eleanor Roosevelt than upon the AFL. It lost ground in the twenties and was gradually supplanted by the new unionism of the thirties, finally being dissolved in 1951.[19]

The post-World War II period witnessed a substantial increase in women unionists in Illinois, initially in older organized industries like the garment trades, later in the meatpacking industry, communications (mainly the Bell Telephone system), hospitals and health care, public school education, building service, and state and local government. Reference to a few prominent women unionists in Illinois may reflect some of the gains.[18] For example, Joyce Miller came from the Amalgamated Clothing Workers, first as education and social services director and member of the Chicago Joint Board, later international vice-president, and as of 1980 the first woman member of the AFL–CIO's Executive Council. She was also one of the founders and the second president of the National Coalition of Labor Union Women (CLUW) formed in 1974 in Chicago. Miller, a graduate of the University of Chicago, came into the Labor movement from the staff side.

In contrast to Miller, Alice Peurala came up through the ranks. For twenty-six years a metallurgical process control observer and a mechanical equipment tester at the South Works of the U.S. Steel Company, she won, at the age of fifty-one, by a narrow margin (1,205 votes to 1,077 and 1,168 respectively for two male rivals) to become the first woman president of a major Local (65) in the basic steel industry. Peurala represented the class of "angry" women who had turned to militancy out of frustration over what they perceived as persistent discrimination against women workers in steel. She not only became one of the local's most aggressive "grievers" against management over such issues as promotions, health and safety, compulsory overtime, and washrooms, but also won a reputation as critic and dissenter of the international union's policies. She supported Edward Sadlowski in his anti-administration campaigns at the district and national levels and led an unsuccessful campaign at the union's 1980 convention to set up a department of women's affairs. At the end of her three-year term she was defeated for reelection, but in 1985, she was voted in again as Local 65 president.

Lillian Herstein provides a leading example of the trade union women pioneers whose Labor career started before World War I, when as a public school teacher she helped found the Federation of Women's High School Teachers, which later became part of the Chicago Teachers Union and continued well into the post-World War II era until her retirement in 1956. In addition to her trade union activity, which included longtime membership on the executive board of the Chicago Federation of Labor, she taught trade union education classes at the Bryn Mawr Summer School for Women Workers, the School for Workers at the University of Chicago, and for the Chicago Women's Trade Union League.

A final example is Addie Wyatt of the Amalgamated Meat Cutters, who rose from packinghouse production employee to a leading role in her union as director of women's affairs and then became a founder of CLUW, serving as the keynote speaker at the first convention and being chosen as vice-president of that organization. Wyatt was one of a number of black women who rose to prominence in their unions and represented the dual interests of both the black and the women members who joined the Labor movement. She was the first unionist to be appointed a public member of the Illinois Commission on the Status of Women.

In its special series on women in the Chicago Labor movement, the *Federation News*, organ of the Chicago Federation of Labor and Industrial Union Council, listed many other outstanding Illinois women trade unionists. For example, Mollie Levitas, who served as secretary to the heads of the Chicago Federation from 1926–1957, was a founder of the Office and Professional Employees International Union. Other women were most active in the post-

World War II period; for example; Jerre McPartlin, financial secretary of the Hotel and Restaurant Employees Local 126 and a member of the Executive Board of the CFL–IUC; Jacqueline Vaughn, vice-president (later president) of the Chicago Teachers Union and member of the executive board of the state AFL–CIO; Anne Rimington, business representative of the Hotel and Restaurant Employees Union in Peoria and a vice-president of the State Federation during the fifties; Gwendolyn Martin, assistant to the regional vice-president, Communications Workers of America and a vice-president of the State Fed; and Johnnie Jackson, longtime staff member of the ILGWU and president of Chicago's CLUW. Also notable was Manny Tuteur, the first president of the Chicago CLUW and director of the day care center run by the ACTWU.

Although their growth in numbers was substantial (reliable overall figures are not available) and some unions had a majority of female members, many women trade unionists continued to face some of the same frustrating problems that were encountered in earlier decades. Certain problems were linked to their domestic situations. As Harry Kurshenbaum, a veteran official of Hospital Employees Labor Program (HELP), stated about his predominately female membership: "Many of HELP's women members are 'bread winners,' raising families, often divorced, and often too tired to take a stand on women's rights. . . . Further, many others are young females who view themselves as only temporary workers and so they feel that they don't have much to gain from active participation in union activities" (see chapter 4, part F).

A second obstacle was the attitude of the male leadership. Among the powerful Teamsters, for example, only one local was an exception: Local 743 of the Teamsters, one of the two unions involved in HELP, with some seventeen thousand women members out of a total of thirty thousand, most of them working either for large enterprises like Montgomery Ward in mail order and warehouse operations, or in miscellaneous small manufacturing jobs. In part because of the number of these members, Local 743 was also almost unique among the Teamsters locals in Chicago in placing women into full-time paid union positions. In 1977, of ninety-one organizers, business representatives, and business agents employed by all the locals, only eight were women and seven of these were employed by Local 743. One of the most notable of these women officials was Clara Day, a member of Local 743's executive board, of the Chicago Commission on Human Relations, and vice-president of the Illinois Commission on the Status of Women, succeeding Addie Wyatt. Day, who was also black, took an active part in the establishment of CLUW and was elected Midwest regional vice-president. Another outstanding Local 743 woman organizer was Regina Polk, a University of Chicago graduate who helped unionize women workers at the University of Chicago and other universities. She was tragically killed in an airplane accident in 1983.

A third set of problems for women workers emanated from management or management-union policies. In 1977, for example, declining business in the steel industry led to sizable layoffs entailing a disproportionate number of women workers with low seniority. A caucus of some fifty women workers from District 31 of the Steelworkers' union organized to protest; they claimed further that women were often harassed and discriminated against by foremen and supervisors. But James Balanoff, then the district director and a staunch supporter of women's rights and activities in the district, defended the seniority system, and Frank Stanley, personnel supervisor at U.S. Steel's South Works, denied that harassment was worse than in other industrial areas.[21] Later attempts by the caucus to get the international union to set up a department for women's affairs were turned down.

These and other problems inspired more than three thousand women trade unionists from some fifty unions around the country to meet in Chicago in 1974 to form CLUW.[22] The new organization was in a sense the spiritual successor to the old National Woman's Trade Union League, but it differed in important respects. First, it did not depend upon philanthropic or reform-oriented women of wealth; membership and leadership were confined to trade unionists although not limited to AFL–CIO unions. Second, union membership among women was far more advanced than in 1903, and a principal objective was to unionize white-collar women as well as blue-collar employees through existing and emerging union structures. Third, a central concern was with the implementation of affirmative actions programs and policies in the workplace, both in terms of racial discrimination and sex discrimination. CLUW also shared with NWTUL a determination to advance the role of women within unions at all levels and to eliminate wage inequities betweeen men and women workers. The idea of comparable pay for work of comparable worth, going far beyond the long-advocated idea of equal pay for equal work, was to emerge gradually during the decade fo the seventies.

CLUW was designed to concentrate on trade union-related issues within and affecting unionism and collective bargaining. However, its leaders recognized its relationship to the general women's movement, and it strongly advocated Labor support for the ERA. At its outset, George Meany and other AFL–CIO officials displayed a lukewarm attitude toward CLUW and rejected its pleas for ERA support, but in 1977, Meany personally addressed a CLUW legislative conference in Washington, and his assistant Tom Donahue brought greetings from Meany at the CLUW's 1979 convention. More important, the status of women became a major subject of discussion in the AFL–CIO, and support finally emerged in the second half of the decade in behalf of both ERA and the idea of appointing women to AFL–CIO and international union executive and other committees. Joyce Miller, who became CLUW president in 1977 and was the first woman elected to the AFL–CIO Executive Council in 1980, stated in a newspaper interview at the time that "When we organized CLUW in 1974, there wasn't one woman on any committee of the AFL–CIO. . . . Today you will see women on every AFL–CIO Committee."[23]

The detailed story of CLUW is outside the purview of this study. The foregoing discussion, like the discussion of the Women's Trade Union League, is intended to demonstrate the important part that Illinois women (Miller, Wyatt, Day and others) played in its formation and to reflect the integral relation between the Illinois experience and national institutions and trends.

How successful were women workers during the three and a half decades after World War II in achieving more equity and voice in the work place? In many respects the progress was dramatic. The percentage of women in the Illinois labor force rose from 29 in 1950 to 42 in 1980. Women's participation rate rose from 31 percent to 53 percent, while that of the men fell from 81 percent to 79 percent. The number of women in the labor force rose from slightly over 1 million to nearly 2.3 million. All of these figures were expected to rise because of changing social attitudes, the rising educational levels of women (especially the numbers graduating from college), and because the white-collar sector in which women were heavily concentrated was the expanding sector of the economy.

By 1980, women could be found in virtually every branch of employment, from professional engineering to bus driving, from electronics to basic steel. But many nontraditional occupations were still difficult to attain. Of the 2,706 apprentices registered in 1982–83 in Washburne Trade School, the top Chicago post-high school training center for eight construction trades, only 76, or 2.8 percent, were female.[24] According to the Midwest Women's Center, an information and referral center in Chicago for women interested in the skilled trades and unions, the number of Illinois apprenticeships held by women rose from 45 (.3 percent) in 1974 to 166 (1.3 percent) in 1978 to 637 (4.8 percent) in 1980.[25]

In colleges and universities, a 1979 survey of the Illinois Board of Higher Education found that although women comprised 50.8 percent of the total employees, women were 27.2 percent of the executives, 26.6 percent of the faculty, and 91.8 percent of the secretaries. Only 47 percent of the women faculty were tenured, compared to 66 percent of the men; 10.4 percent of the full professors, and 19.4 percent of the associate professors were women.[26]

The difficulty of climbing various promotional ladders was also evidenced in data on state government employment. A House committee report of December 1974 indicated that although women were 53 percent of the 56,802 employees under the Illinois Personnel Code, only 18.4 percent were officials or managers. On the other hand, 44.2 percent were classified as professionals, and 66.8 percent as technicians.[27]

Not all of these statistics were attributable exclusively to discrimination. Women frequently lacked the skills or the motivation to enter new fields.

Older women often found it easier to follow conventional pathways than to break new ground. Younger women needed more time and support to fulfill their aspirations. But a hard core of discrimination prevailed beyond any doubt.

To break down the barriers of discrimination, new institutions and support organizations were essential, and the decades of the sixties and seventies were notable for their emergence and development. A wide variety of women's organizations, from the League of Women Voters and the Business and Professional Women's Club to the National Organization for Women and the Coalition of Labor Union Women, either directly or indirectly, affected the employment of women. In Illinois, the Commission on the Status of Women played a central role by compiling and disseminating information, by holding public hearings and sponsoring or co-sponsoring conferences throughout the state, by overseeing and prodding the FEP and other governmental units, and by pressing for legislation. The CLUW arrived relatively late on the scene but within individual unions such as those in meatprocessing, autos, steel, electrical products, communications, and public services, activist women had ground breaking success in gaining more voice and better conditions for women. Smaller and more limited womens' groups, like the Midwest Women's Center and Women Employed, as well as more general organizations like the Urban League and the Hispanic League in Chicago, provided information, counseled, helped find jobs, and fought for affirmative action.

A variety of educational programs also contributed to the rise of women union leaders. In 1980, for example, the Chicago Labor Education Program of the University of Illinois began special programs for women in union leadership. Since 1976, the University Institute of Labor and Industrial Relations had cooperated with other university labor education programs to operate a Midwest school for women workers.

The Illinois FEPC, which did not cover women in Illinois until 1971, also helped influence women's conditions. Between 1971 and 1977, the annual number of charges of sex discrimination filed with the commission ranged from 359 to 1,049 and represented from 20 percent to 45.6 percent of all charges filed. The national EEOC was even more important because it was responsible for major national proceedings that led to important affirmative action agreements affecting women as well as minorities in basic steel, Bell Telephone, and other key industries.

Although ERA was defeated in Illinois, its basic principal was embodied in the state constitution of 1970, and a number of laws were enacted that improved minimum wage standards, eliminated bans on overtime work, and prohibited discrimination in both private and public employment.

Despite all of these advances, the end of the study period found a large unfinished agenda for women workers in Illinois. The most troublesome issue was the persisting earnings gap between men and women employees. The major problem was not so much the failure of employers to provide equal pay for work in the same occupations, although there continued to be serious inequity cases of that kind notwithstanding the equal pay and nondiscrimination laws. Instead, as the Illinois Bureau of Employment Security wrote: "The lower median income for women results partly from the fact that although women are represented to some degree at every income level, the proportion of women in higher paying jobs is much lower than the proportion of men in those same jobs."[28] Or as the Commission on the Status of Women reported after a 1980 hearing, "The theme emphasized throughout the hearing was that jobs traditionally held by women rate lower salaries than jobs traditionally held by men, regardless of skills."[29] The educational gap was related to the income gap, but, as noted above, this was changing rapidly. The difference in job concentration was much more difficult to overcome. Given the rapid rise in educational levels, however, the expectation was that the entry of women into higher-level positions would accelerate sharply in the next few decades. In the meantime, the principle of comparable worth was raised in legal proceedings and collective bargaining as a more immediate remedy. As for the serious problem of women at the bottom, particularly black and immigrant groups employed in domestic service and in factory sweatshops, the hope was expressed that their lot could be improved through raising statutory minimum wage levels, extending coverage, and enforcing the laws more effectively.

Pay discrimination was only one of several employment issues that Illinois womens' groups continued to stress as the decade of the seventies came to an end. Another was sexual harassment on the job. As Roosevelt University Professor Elizabeth Balanoff stated, "Particularly in the craft industries, like construction, a woman is often the only female on the worksite and is not accepted. They often have to do twice the work to prove that they can do the work. Many of these women are victims of sexual harassment."[30] The Illinois Task Force on Sexual Harassment in the Workplace and Sangamon State University, with the assistance of the Commission on the Status of Women, conducted a survey in 1979 of female state government employees about "unwanted sexual attention."[31] Fifty-nine percent of the respondents reported experiencing one or more incidents of unwanted sexual attention, 52 percent had been subject to sexual remarks and teasing; 41 percent had received suggestive looks or gestures; 25 percent had been physically touched or grabbed; 20 percent had been sexually propositioned; 2 percent had experienced some form of coercive sex; and 9 percent reported other miscellaneous forms of unwanted sexual attention. In May 1980, the General Assembly enacted a law that prohibited employers and businesses from taking retaliatory action against an employee because she (or he) declined sexual advances.

Day care continued to be a serious problem for many working women throughout the post-World War II period. During the war, a national network of day-care centers was established by the federal government and private industry. Most of them vanished after the war. For women who continued to work, a variety of day-care homes emerged, but they were not adequate. The Merrill-Palmer Directory reported 227 nursing and child-care centers in Illinois in 1950, of which 151 were private commercial agencies, 40 were maintained by communities, 17 were church-sponsored, 8 were cooperatives, and a few were child research centers or miscellaneous agencies.[32] A survey in the early fifties revealed that more day-care centers were needed. Many women who would have liked to work could not because of the lack of adequate child-care facilities; there were long waiting lists for day nurseries. As the Korean War increased the number of employed women, the issue of day care intensified.

While the day-care movement grew, laws were enacted to require licensing and inspection of day-care facilities by the Department of Children and Family Services. The Illinois Department of Public Aid began to operate day-care centers in the sixties, as did the University of Illinois, housing authorities in the larger cities, the Postal Workers Union, and the federally supported Head Start program. The Amalgamated Clothing Workers negotiated employer-paid child-care for its members. Nonetheless, in 1968, the Department of Children and Family Services estimated that at least 174,000 children needed day-care services but the 1,397 licensed centers in existence could only provide for a maximum of 42,543 children.

The sixties and seventies witnessed an extraordinary acceleration of womens' participation in the labor force, including large numbers of married and divorced women with preschool children. According to the 1970 census, about 20 percent of all working women in Illinois had children under six years. Fulltime day-care costs were high and, unlike some other states, Illinois did not allow tax deductions or credits for child-care expenses. The Commission on the Status of Women estimated after a hearing on the subject in September 1971 that nearly a million children were in need of some type of child-care, but fewer than a hundred thousand spaces were available for these children. By the decade's end, despite continuing progress, the problem of day-care facilities and related financing problems were still matters of concern. As the commission stated in its February 1982 report, "There is seldom a hearing held or survey conducted that does not reveal the need for low-cost, quality child care."

In 1980, Day Piercy, director of Women Employed, summed up the status of working women: "Clearly the seventies did provide access to jobs that women never had before. And that is just absolutely a remarkable result of the decade. But at the same time, women's overall economic status did not improve. Millions of women did not achieve anything close to equality. The problems are still the traditional ones including violations of the Equal Pay and Civil Rights Acts."[33]

NOTES

This chapter is largely based on a report by Christina E. Shalley.

1. For a scholarly perception of the mid-thirties, see John R. Commons and John B. Andrews, *Principles of Labor Legislation*, 4th ed. (New York: Harper, 1936). For a much more recent feminist perspective, see Francine D. Blau, "Women in the Labor Force: An Overview" in *Women: A Feminist Perspective*, 3d ed., ed. Jo Freeman (Palo Alto: Mayfield Publishing, 1984).

2. Mary Watters, *Illinois in the Second World War*, vol. 2 (Springfield: Illinois State Historical Library), pp. 252–53.

3. Interview with Esther Saperstein, April 1982.

4. A. M. Wheeler and M. S. Wortman, *The Roads They Made: Women in Illinois History* (Chicago: Kerr Publishing, 1977). The labor force participation trends for Illinois were similar to the national trends. See Blau, "Women in the Labor Force," pp. 303–4 for relevant national data.

5. For a good discussion based primarily on national data, see *Women and the Labor Force, Illinois*, Bureau of Employment Security, Springfield, September 1979, pp. 10–13.

6. See *Women and the Labor Force, Illinois*, September 1980, p. 4.

7. *Minutes of Meeting*, Commission on the Status of Women, 1978, p. 5.

8. Annual reports were apparently not submitted in 1968, 1970, 1972, 1976, and 1978.

9. Commission on the Status of Women, *Report and Recommendations, Illinois*, Macomb, 1969, p. 11.

10. Commission on the Status of Women, *Report and Recommendations*, Springfield and Macomb, February 1982, p. 77.

11. Commission of the Status of Women, *Report and Recommendations*, 1965.

12. Commission on the Status of Women, *Report and Recommendations*, 1980.

13. Commission on the Status of Women, *Report and Recommendations*, 1977.

14. Interview with Esther Saperstein.

15. *Proceedings* of the 7th Constitutional Convention, Illinois State Industrial Union Council, CIO, Chicago, 1948, pp. 55–56.

16. *Proceedings* of the 10th Annual Convention, Illinois State American Federation of Labor and Congress of Industrial Organizations, 1967, p. 123.

17. Helen Marot, *American Labor Unions: By a Member* (New York: Henry Holt, 1914), pp. 67–68.

18. See Joyce L. Kornbluh and Mary Frederickson, eds., *Sisterhood and Solidarity: Workers' Education for Women, 1914–1984* (Philadelphia: Temple University Press, 1984), chap. 1.

19. Barbara Mayer Wertheimer, *We Were There: The Story of Working Women in America* (New York: Pantheon, 1977), pp. 267–92.

20. Except for the cases of Alice Peurala and Addie Wyatt, most of the discussion on women trade union leaders is derived from a two-part series of articles appearing in the February and March 1982 issue of the *Federation News*, published by the Chicago Federation of Labor and Industrial Union Council. The Peurala illustration comes from articles in the *Chicago Tribune*, April 26 and 27, 1979, and May 13, 1979, and the *Sun-Times*, November 15, 1979, and August 6, 1980. A brief sketch of Joyce Miller also appeared in the *Tribune* on March 18, 1981.

21. *Chicago Tribune*, August 15, 1977.

22. A detailed account of the steps leading to the establishment of CLUW and its organizing convention is provided in Philip S. Foner, *Women and the American Labor Movement: From World War I to the Present* (New York: The Free Press, 1980), chap. 25 and 26.

23. *Chicago Tribune*, March 18, 1981.

24. *Chicago Reporter*, May 1983.

25. Interview with Kathy Johnson, April 1982.

26. Commission on the Status of Women, *Report and Recommendations*, February 1982, p. 15.

27. House Committee on Employment of Women and Minorities in State Government, State of Illinois *Report*, December 1974, p. 5.

28. *Women and the Labor Force, Illinois*, 1978, p. 13.

29. Commission on the Status of Women, *Report and Recommendations*, February 1981, p. 42.

30. Interview with Elizabeth Balanoff.

31. Illinois Commission on the Status of Women, *Report and Recommendations*, February 1981, p. 40.

32. *Employed Mothers and Childcare* Bulletin of the Women's Bureau, no. 246 (Washington: Department of Labor).

33. *Chicago Tribune*, 1980.

19

The Quality of Working Life

The quality of work life attracted national attention during the postwar period; although it was focussed on the work place, the concept was discussed so widely in the mass media that it assumed the stature of a social phenomenon.

Labor's concern with the quality of working life, in fact, goes back to the earliest days of hired work. That it should become a major phenomenon in the post-World War II period is therefore not a reason for surprise. Nonetheless, the latter period contained several ingredients that gave the subject some new and distinctive features. Chronologically, two overlapping stages can be identified. The first stage was characterized by the development, through collective bargaining and then unilateral employer decision, of a wide array of health and welfare benefits that—together with retirement plans, expanded paid holidays and vacations, "paid sabbatical leaves," supplemental unemployment benefits, and many other supplemental payments—came to be called "fringe benefits." This stage ran in expanding form from the end of the war to the recessions of the middle and late seventies. The second stage began in the late fifties and continued on through the seventies. Its focus was on the concept of enhancing work and workplace life by involving workers and their organizations in many types of decision making previously believed to be the exclusive prerogative of management. The span of participative decisions ranged from safety and occupational health to equal employment opportunity, from how to reduce absenteeism and turnover to redesign of work or work groups.

Although these stages were part of national movements, Illinois failed to make major innovations, with the possible exception of some pioneering efforts going back to the second decade of the century in Chicago by the Amalgamated Clothing Workers and of the Armour Automation Plan in the meatpacking industry in the fifties. Nevertheless, the concept of improving the quality of work life profoundly affected life in and out of the workplace for Illinois workers and employers and therefore merits attention; a few Illinois developments even warranted special attention.

Both stages had their roots in World War II. During the war, the National War Labor Board maintained a fairly tight lid on pay increases in order to contain inflation. In response to union and employer pressures, it chose to increase fringe benefits, but the increases were generally confined to ceilings that already prevailed for particular benefits throughout industry. For example, a standard for paid vacations was set at one week after one year's service and two weeks after five years' service. If an industry or area lagged behind this standard, the board readily permitted or, when requested, ordered advances up to the standard. Paid vacation plans in excess of the standard, however, would not be approved unless there was a "clear and well defined practice in the appropriate area or industry" or where a strong case for equity could be made.[1]

Once the wage stabilization policy was terminated following the war's end, governmental barriers to pay increases vanished. They were reimposed in varying forms for short periods during the Korean War, the early years of the Kennedy presidency, and in the early seventies under President Nixon. Generally speaking, however, free collective bargaining as well as unilateral employer decisions in nonunion enterprises prevailed. Fringe benefits proved to be a favored topic for expansion.

The results are found in national labor statistics and in industry-union case studies of the types presented in chapter 4. To illustrate the developments in Illinois, which did not differ much from the nation at large, brief reference may be made to a few selected collective bargaining agreements in the late seventies contrasted to the World War II standards. The agreements cited were benefit leaders, but by no means exceptional.

For example, the December 1976 agreement between the Caterpillar Tractor Company, headquartered in Peoria, and the UAW provided that each employee with fewer than ten years' service would be eligible for three weeks' vacation; after ten years' service, a fourth week of vacation would be paid, and after twenty years', a fifth week. This advance from the wartime standard of one-for-one and two-for-five was matched by comparable increases in the number of paid holidays (ten compared to the wartime standard of six) and the rate of pay for holidays worked (double time instead of time-and-a-half). The agreement also included a paid twenty-minute lunch period, whereas the NWLB confined its orders to limited industry and area practice. The issue of compulsory overtime work, a longtime industrial practice, was extensively modified in the agreement. At least one day's notice of such work was required. Employees not desiring overtime work could be excused if another employee competent to do the work was available or if there was compelling personal reasons, such as family illness, or if the employee had worked six days a week for two or more consecutive weeks. Nor would any regularly scheduled employee be required to work more than ten hours in any day.

Perhaps the greatest change came in the area of health and welfare. By the time of the war, this area was just beginning to be developed for production workers. For example, the NWLB issued instructions to its regional boards in 1943 that it would approve "any reasonable sick leave plan," but it was rarely willing to order the adoption of a plan in any dispute. Most plans covering blue-collar employees were modest—for example, two weeks' sick leave at half wages at the Swift and Company packinghouses. The disparity between office and production employees was substantial. By 1976, however, paid sick leave at companies like Caterpillar had been tied into elaborate group health insurance plans (typically noncontributory by employees), and the blue-collar, white-collar distinctions had largely disappeared. The same development occurred with respect to pension and retirement plans.

Beyond these basic conditions the Caterpillar agreement contained provisions that were unknown or rare in prewar years: bereavement pay, attendance bonus days, pay during temporary military service or for jury duty and witness service, and paid absence allowances. Following the pattern set in the auto industry, the Caterpillar agreement also provided for a supplemental unemployment benefit (SUB) plan that maintained the near-normal pay of laid-off employees for lengthy periods (up to a year or more depending on the size of the SUB fund and the volume of layoffs).

Farm equipment, like autos and basic steel, was a national fringe benefit leader, but many other industries moved in similar directions. The 1974 agreement between A.E. Staley Manufacturing Company (a major soybean and corn processing firm) and the Allied Industrial Workers Union in Decatur provided paid vacations that ranged from seven days with forty hours' pay for one year of service to thirty-five days with two hundred hours' pay for twenty years of service. Both paid and unpaid leaves were substantially liberalized in case of family illness, to settle a lawsuit or an estate, because of death or marriage in the family, for union business, jury duty, and funeral leave. The number of paid holidays was increased to ten, and the rate for work on those holidays was two ad a half times the regular rate. The assignment of overtime work was subject to extensive safeguards in the interest of equity for workers desiring such work while easing the traditional requirements of mandatory overtime for those who were disinclined. Perhaps most important was the development and elaboration of group insurance plans covering employees and their dependents with respect to hospitalization and medical benefits, life insurance, and retirement.

A third type of agreement may be illustrated by that between the Southern Division of the Central Illinois Public Service Company and Local 702 of the International Brotherhood of Electrical Workers (July 1, 1977–June 30, 1980). Here paid vacations varied from five working days for one year's service to thirty working days for thirty years' service. The number of paid holidays was eleven, and the rate of pay for work on such holidays was double time. Overtime was to be divided as "equally and impartially" among all employees doing the same class of work "as is practicable." Overtime work was required but could not exceed sixteen hours without the employee's consent. Reflecting the special character of the work was a provision that employees should have their lodging, transportation, and meal expenses paid by the company when working away from headquarters. Regular employees were also allowed sick leave, with pay for periods ranging from 120 to 240 working hours in any one year. For longer periods, half-time pay was provided. Other paid leave periods related to serious illness of family members, death in the family, and funeral service for another deceased employee or retired employee. Group insurance plans covered retirement (noncontributory after July 1, 1979), life insurance (noncontributory), medical benefits (noncontributory for employees, 45 percent of the cost of dependent coverage by the employee), and long-term disability (equal sharing).

Not all unionized employees (especially in secondary industries) nor numerous nonunion employees in small enterprises enjoyed fringe benefits like the above, but it is clear that the national and state standards of the seventies had moved appreciably above the standards prevailing in 1945. Implicit in the new standards was a new conception of one aspect of the quality of working life that became a target for achievement throughout the work force. Equally important, the traditional differences that had long existed between white-collar and blue-collar employees, and which had served as a principal symbol of status differentation (more so than basic pay) disappeared. Where pronounced differences in fringe benefits now prevailed, they were usually a sign of depressed enterprise, illegal immigration, or low social status. By 1980, the new standard (with variations) had been adopted in the pattern-setting and pattern-following industries and firms of the private sector (both union and non-union) and were widely accepted throughout the public—local, state, and federal—and quasi-public or publicly regulated sectors.

One significant consequence of the elaboration of fringe benefits, in addition to its impact on the quality of working life, was its introduction of many highly technical and professional issues into the workplace. This was particularly true of the various insurance programs that called for the expertise of accountants, lawyers, and insurance and financial specialists. Management and union representatives were unable to cope without the aid of the specialists. Collective bargaining and personnel management were professionalized to an unprecedented degree, thereby incorporating a new dimension into the life of the workers and opening the door to abuses such as those described in chapter 16.

This professionalization was to overlap with a countermovement that called for increased worker participation in the decision-making process of the workplace as a basis for enhancing the quality of working life. Joint labor-management committees had enjoyed a remarkable renaissance during World War II, when some five thousand productivity programs were established under the stimulus of the War Production Board. However, at the conclusion of the war, most of these programs ceased to function as management asserted its managerial rights and unions became absorbed in maintaining and expanding their wartime economic gains.[2]

Interest in developing Labor's participation in decision making beyond the traditional scope of collective bargaining was restored and enlarged by three very different sets of forces: (1) the public interest in and pressure for a reduction in labor disputes; (2) mounting concerns over technological unemployment and shifting product markets; and (3) a widening belief that worker dissatisfaction with work and work relations could be reversed by establishing a more democratic climate in the workplace.

One illustration of a highly successful effort to reduce conflict was the Chicago Labor Peace Formula established by unions ad contractors in the construction industry to resolve jurisdictional disputes.[3] Although not unique to Chicago, the Labor Peace program produced an outstanding record in one of the construction industry's thorniest phases. Study of the program suggested that its success, at a time when jurisdictional strikes accounted for a fifth of all strikes in the industry nationwide, was attributable not only to the formal decisions of the Chicago Joint Board of union and contractor representatives (twelve from each side), but also to the informal cooperation between business representatives at the job site as well as among union officials in the Building Trades Council. These settlements appear to have had a carry-over effect on industrial peace in general. It was estimated that only about thirty work stoppages in Chicago construction occurred between 1945 and 1980 over the terms of new contracts—a considerable achievement in so complex and diversified an industry.

Another case of effective joint labor-management action to promote industrial peace occurred in the then leading farm implement company, International Harvester.[4] Harvester had experienced a stormy history in the early postwar years, exacerbated by the rivalry between the radical UFE and the more pragmatic UAW. By the mid-fifties, when the UFE-UAW struggle had been won by the latter, accumulated grievances numbered in the thousands, often prolonging contract strikes. In 1952, the company appointed a new, highly skilled vice-president for industrial relations, William J. Reilly; in 1955, the UAW restructured its organization with a new Harvester department head, Seymour Kahan. From the new leadership, assisted by arbitrator David Cole, came a series of steps to expedite grievance settlements before they went to arbitration. By 1960, the "new look" in grievance handling consisted of an emphasis on speedy oral discussion and settlement at the shop level closest to the origin of the grievance. The result was a phenomenal reduction in the grievance load, particularly in the controversial area of production standards. This new climate was to persist into the late seventies, even after Reilly's retirement. It deteriorated when the company began to experience serious competitive forces from both domestic and foreign sources and a new top company executive began to apply strong pressure to cut costs, often disregarding internal sensitive union concerns and resulting in bitter union reactions.

The second important stimulus for greater worker/union involvement in joint decision making emanated from a concern over job security. One source of this concern was technological innovation as it affected the changing demand for labor and for job skills. Another source was the dynamism of product competition, both domestic and foreign. These sources often interacted as new technology reduced costs and enabled other firms to become more competitive. But intensified competition was also influenced by geographic and transport advantages, foreign exchange rates, governmental supports, comparative wage levels, and union status. Two examples may be illustrative.

Before the fifties, Chicago had for decades been the national center of the meatpacking industry. In the late thirties and during the forties, two unions, the CIO Packinghouse Workers and the AFL Amalgamated Meat Cutters (later to be merged) had gained considerable power and status. But the Chicago plants failed to keep up with changing technological developments, and labor costs rose far above those of plants newly established and close to the supply of cattle and hogs. During the second half of the fifties, the major companies begun to shut down their Chicago plants and to erect more efficient and cost effective plants elsewhere.

To facilitate the relocation and to minimize the impact on the Chicago (and other comparable) labor force(s), the Armour Company and the two unions negotiated an Armour Automation Fund and set up a top-level joint management-labor committee, with a prominent neutral chairman and staff.[5] The program was designed to help Armour's displaced employees get new jobs—either in the new plants or with other companies—and to provide both financial and retraining assistance. Special studies were sponsored to obtain sound factual data on which to base relocation policies.

National publicity was given to the Armour program and its cooperative spirit during the eight years of its operation. About the same time, a number of other labor-management cooperation efforts with varying objectives were undertaken—the Mechanization and Modernization Agreement of the West Coast Longshore Industry and the Basic Steel Human Relations Committee, among others.

The men's clothing industry in Chicago, led by Hart, Schaffner, and Marx and the Amalgamated Clothing Workers Union, had a long and distinguished record of labor-management collaboration to secure industrial peace and to stabilize the competitive forces of this highly volatile industry.[6] The opening of new clothing centers throughout the country as well as new technology, however, seriously undercut Chicago employment from a peak of thirty to forty thousand during World War I to fifteen thousand at the end of World War II. This process continued after World War II, as companies shifted from the Frost Belt to the Sunbelt and serious competition emerged from abroad.

A vital factor in the relationship between the Amalgamated and the employers was the former's concern with the welfare of the industry as a whole. The Amalgamated recognized that how the industry fared had a powerful impact on the economic and social status of its members, and it therefore spread its resources and expertise over virtually every aspect of the industry. This included campaigns to promote industry sales, technical and sometimes financial assistance to employers in competitive difficulty, and demonstrations against cheap labor from foreign competitors. Some of these activities were conducted unilaterally by the union or in collaboration with other unions like the ILGWU. Other activities, such as lobbying in Washington or in state capitals, were carried on through intimate labor-management cooperation. Despite this climate of harmony and mutual understanding, the relentless pressures of cost competition gradually ground down the strength and status of the Amalgamated.

During the sixties and early seventies, a third major stimulus for greater worker/union participation in decision making within industry emerged—a belief, strongly promoted by the mass media, that workers were becoming increasingly dissatisfied with their work and desired a more democratic climate in the workplace. Popularly written best-sellers like Studs Terkel's *Working* and the U.S. Department of Health, Education, and Welfare's widely discussed report, *Work in America*, as well as highly publicized events like the 1972 General Motors strike at Lordstown, Ohio, added fuel to this belief. It was reinforced by President Nixon's appointment in July 1970 of a National Commission on Productivity, which was reorganized and elaborated by Congress in 1974 and 1975 under the successive names of the National Commission on Productivity and Work Quality and the National Center for Productivity and Quality of Working Life. From academe and journalism in this country and Europe came a flood of publications on worker alienation, job enrichment and enlargement, autonomous work groups, co-determination, and humanization or democratization of the work place.[7]

A central process for the achievement of higher job satisfaction within a new democratic framework was the joint labor-management committee. As noted earlier, joint committees had flourished during World War II, mainly for the attainment of great productivity. But these committees had generally evaporated at the war's end. Thereafter, new committees had cropped up on a limited scale in the form of Scanlon Committees or other innovative ideas to increase efficiency and make firms more competitive as well as to reduce industrial conflict or to cope with technological or market-induced unemployment. The new wave of joint committees in the sixties and seventies gave a fresh impetus to the quality of work life concept.

Again, Illinois was neither leader nor follower but part of the national stream. In 1979, the Institute of Labor and Industrial Relations of the University of Illinois made a survey of joint labor-management cooperation committees in the private sector, and in 1980 a comparable study was made of the public sector in the state. About the same time, two graduate students made studies of a coal-mining communication committee in Southern Illinois and a more general survey in the city of Rockford. These were virtually the only studies of this subject in Illinois apart from the writings noted above and a Ph.D. dissertation in the late sixties from the University of Wisconsin that included a sample of committees in northern Illinois, mainly concerned with technological change.

The statewide private-sector project uncovered more than one hundred enterprises employing a hundred or more workers, with joint union-management committees, eighty-four in manufacturing, thirteen in construction, and the others in a miscellany of other industries.[8] However, this was clearly only a partial sample because the Rockford study indicated at least twenty-one joint cooperation committees in that one city.[9] In addition, the public-sector survey reported 259 units (mainly schools and municipalities) with joint committees.[10] Beyond these cases, an unknown number of nonunionized enterprises had some form of labor-management cooperation program. The total remained only a tiny proportion of the thousands of companies in the state; nevertheless, the absolute numbers appeared significant. In comparison with the 201 manufacturing companies reported by Ernest Dale in a national survey in 1948, and 303 cases in Wisconsin reported to Arie Shirom in 1967, an upward trend seemed to be in process following the sharp turndown immediately after the war.[11]

The subjects dealt with by the joint committees indicate the wide range of items that had been perceived by different groups of workers as affecting the quality of their working life. The Derber-Flanigan study, for example, found that the largest percentage of committees (85 percent) dealt with safety and occupational health, followed by apprenticeship and training (50 percent), employee welfare (44 percent), employee benefits (39 percent), absenteeism and turnover (32 percent), production problems and technological change (29 percent), work incentives (28.6 percent), and work hours (25.2 percent). A miscellaneous group of other subjects from work redesign to sales promotion was found in few enterprises. Most of these subjects had been targeted by worker groups for a very long time.

The experience of these committees also ranged widely—from very successful to early demise. A more detailed analysis of twenty-six cases concluded that in eight the effect on employee morale was positive, in ten mixed, in four there was no effect, and in four the impact of the committee was uncertain. The picture with respect to effects on harmony or conflict was more favorable: it was positive in seventeen cases, mixed in three, nil in four, and uncertain in two. On the other hand, insofar as productivity was concerned, the committee impact was positive in nine cases, mixed in six, nil in nine, and uncertain in two.[12]

Vernon Bozarth's detailed case study of a Mine Communications Committee in Inland Steel Coal Company Mine No. 1 in Southern Illinois sheds further light on the difficulties of implementing the joint participation idea.[13] This committee was established following the negotiation in 1974 of a new national agreement between the Bituminous Coal Operator's Association and the United Mine Workers. The agreement came during a time of frequent wildcat strikes, both of local and outside origin, that were having a destabilizing effect. The committee was designed to reduce strife, not to promote the quality of working life. The study, which was concluded in 1979, found that during the committee's existence grievances processed through the grievance procedure increased while work stoppages of local origin declined and were settled faster. Arbitrations also declined because more grievances were settled at a lower stage. On the other hand, stoppages originating from outside forces increased until after the bitter 111-day strike of 1977–78. Bozarth, a personnel officer at the mine, concluded that the direct effects of the committee were unclear, but interviews with management and labor leaders indicated an improvement in the overall labor-management climate, better mutual understanding and trust, and more effective handling of grievances. However, there was no evidence as yet that productivity had improved.

The survey of the Illinois public service at the local level revealed that by 1980 numerous joint labor-management cooperation committees had been established.[14] More than 60 percent of the units responding to the surveyors reported one or more such committees. The subjects covered were similar to those in the private-sector study, although the proportions differed. For example, the top ten list included employee benefit plans (62.2 percent), work hours (35.1 percent), work incentives (30.1 percent), safety and health (22.4 percent), job security (22.4 percent), charitable contributions (17 percent), equal employment opportunity (15.4 percent), citizen and community relations (10.4 percent), absenteeism and employee turnover (9.3 percent), and apprenticeship or other training programs (9.3 percent).

More detailed case studies were conducted in fifteen of the public units. Among the more interesting findings were that two-thirds of the committees in 1980 had been in existence only one to three years, the oldest for twelve years. This suggested either that committees of earlier years had failed to survive or that the joint cooperation idea was of very recent origin. Of some twenty-eight purposes or objectives of these committees, the great majority (twenty-one) were related to better communications, the resolution of conflicts, and the avoidance of grievances. Obtaining employee input per se was a secondary objective. With only one exception, all of the committee members interviewed perceived the committees in positive and constructive terms. In more than half of the cases, the number of formal grievances decreased. The maintenance of continued interest in the committees was perceived to be a serious problem in a majority of the cases. All in all, the reports of public-sector experience with labor management cooperation were more favorable than in the private sector, although the limited evidence on employee reactions (in contrast to that of the leaders) prevented definitive conclusions.

The principal impression derived from the foregoing data is that the general quality of working life during the 1945–80 period improved in physical terms—such as supplementary wage payments, safer and healthier working conditions, reduced work schedules, and more frequent leaves. There were, of course, many exceptions, especially among lower-level, nonunion employees. New problems emerged as a result of the increased use of carcinogenic materials and other forms of environmental pollution, but in general, advances in scientific understanding and curative techniques counteracted them. The overall status of the individual in the workplace also appeared to advance for a variety of reasons—the shifting trend from blue-collar to white-collar work, the new legal protections for minorities and women, and a moderation of adversarial labor-management relations, which included greater worker and union participation in decision making.

NOTES

1. *Termination Report of the N.W.L.B.* vol. 1 (Washington: U.S. Department of Labor, no date), pp. 338–41.

2. See, for example, Milton Derber, "Collective Bargaining: The American Approach to Industrial Democracy," in *Industrial Democracy in International Perspective: The Annals*, ed. John P. Windmuller (Philadelphia: The American Academy of Political and Social Sciences, May 1977).

3. See chapter 4, part B.

4. See chapter 4, part D.

5. See chapter 9.

6. See chapter 4, part A; see also Milton Derber, "Employer Associations in the United States," in John P. Windmuller and Alan Gladstone, *Employers Associations and Industrial Relations: A Comparative Study* (New York: Oxford University Press, 1984).

7. This development is detailed in Derber, "Collective Bargaining," pp. 86–91.

8. Milton Derber and Kevin Flanigan, "A Survey of Joint Labor-Management Cooperation Committees in Unionized Private Enterprises in the State of Illinois, 1979" (mimeographed, 1980).

9. Kenneth H. McDonald, "Quality of Working Life and Labor-Management Cooperation: An Initial Perspective on Rockford, Illinois" (mimeographed, undated).

10. Vernon Talbott et al., "Survey of Joint Labor-Management Initiatives in Illinois Local Governments" (Urbana: Institute of Labor and Industrial Relations, University of Illinois, 1980).

11. Ernest Dale, *Greater Productivity Through Labor-Management Cooperation* Research Report no. 14, 1949 (New York: American Management Association, 1949); Arie Shirom, "Industrial Cooperation and Adjustment to Technological Change: A Study of Joint Management Union Committees," Ph.D. thesis, University of Wisconsin, Madison 1968.

12. Derber and Flanigan, *A Survey*, p. 24.

13. Vernon L. Bozarth, "An Analysis and Evaluation of a Communication Committee" (Urbana: Institute of Labor and Industrial Relations, University of Illinois, mimeographed, undated).

14. Talbott et al., "Survey of Joint Labor-Management."

Conclusions

What conclusions are to be drawn from this survey of Illinois labor during the thirty-five years following World War II? It was obviously a period of great change. The national economy boomed in unprecedented fashion, fueled by the world war, the Korean conflict, and the Vietnam disaster. Growth was also accelerated by more than a decade of high birth rates; by spectacular technological innovations such as television, jet air flight, and chemical synthetics; and by an exceptional expansion in international trade. At the same time, economic advance was accompanied by a series of progressively serious recessions—each relatively short in duration but raising anxious questions about future technological unemployment, the effectiveness of income policy, and the dangers of stagflation. The oil crisis of the mid- and late-seventies added to the turbulent economic scene.

The jaggedly upward economic trend had dual consequences for the rapidly growing labor force. On the one hand, the standard of life for most workers improved substantially, and even the poor, abetted by expanding welfare programs, were beneficiaries. On the other hand, discontent heightened because expectations for the good life remained considerably ahead of achievement. Furthermore, the dynamics of economic change seriously upset the hard-won gains of workers in industries like meatpacking and clothing while benefitting other industrial sectors like construction, autos, and retail trade. Even more significantly, the seeds were being sown (although most people were unaware of it) for the deep recession of the early eighties and longer-run structural changes—notably, the declining ability of basic industries like steel, autos, and clothing, to compete in domestic and international markets and the shift of mass employment from high-skill, high-pay occupations to less skilled and lower paid. This duality applied to unionized jobs as well as to unorganized ones. Although the nation of the seventies was not anticipating the Reaganomics of the eighties, and the Japanese challenge was only dimly appreciated, the Carter administration had already set the stage for a more competitive enterprise system.

Farreaching economic and demographic changes were not only affecting the size and composition of the labor force, but were also influencing work values—the attitudes of employees toward work, the work place, and relations with management and unions. National and scattered Illinois studies suggested a growing deterioration of the so-called Protestant Ethic, especially among younger people. The duty to work hard and to accept traditional industrial discipline underwent challenge, especially in the late fifties and throughout the sixties. Drives for shorter work schedules and longer paid holiday and vacation periods as well as campaigns against compulsory over-time work were reflective. Resistance against discharge and layoff mounted, although not to the extend prevailing in many other nations. The position of the lower-level supervisor became more tenuous and vulnerable. Not until the severe recession of 1974–75 and, especially, the very deep recession of the early eighties did this attitudinal rebellion start to recede. The fear of job loss undermined the confidence engendered by a high-employment economy.

Throughout the postwar period, organized labor in Illinois maintained its national position as a stronghold of unionism. A few unions such as the meatpacking, clothing, and electrical workers suffered major blows from domestic or foreign competition as early as the late fifties, and others were adversely affected by technological developments in transportation, coal min-ing, and steel production. But these losses and setbacks were largely offset during the sixties and seventies by the spectacular growth of public unionism, notably among state employees, the public schools, hospitals, and police and firefighters. The conversion of professional associations (e.g., the Illinois Education Association and the Illinois Nurses Association) to unionlike be-havior contributed to this organizational development. As a result, the national tendency, which Illinois shared to an above-average degree, for white-collar and service employment to exceed blue-collar employment had only a limited negative impact on the status of organized labor. In absolute numbers, union and association membership encompassed a minority of the labor force, but organizational strength and influence seemed to be unim-paired. Not until the serious recession of the eighties and the hostility of the Reagan administration did the situation appear to change. And even then the state's Republican administration of Governor James Thompson maintained a generally positive posture toward Illinois employee organization as reflected in the enactment in 1983 of public employee bargaining legislation.

The institution of collective bargaining flourished during most of the period studied. Perhaps its most innovative features were the development and elab-oration of fringe benefits, especially health and welfare plans, and the im-provements adopted in grievance processing, especially grievance arbitration. A few examples of union-management cooperation, such as the Armour Au-tomation Commission and the shop-floor grievance settlement plan at Interna-tional Harvester, attracted national approval, but they proved to be short-lived and had no apparent spill-over effects. Although there were pockets of persisting conflict (e.g., in basic steel in Chicago, farm and construction equipment in Northern Illinois, Decatur and Peoria, and coal mining downstate) and a relatively high record of illegal strikes in public schools, the general strike picture compared favorably with past experience, and violent encounters were conspicuously infrequent. Most of the serious strikes originated outside of Illinois in industry bargaining systems. It was only in the late seventies and early eighties that two collective bargaining consequences attracted widespread attention: that unions in major branches of manufacturing, construction, and other industries had pushed labor costs to noncompetitive levels in comparison with both nonunion domestic and foreign competition, and that management in numerous important corporations had ignored the advantages of dramatic technological and managerial advances and were no longer able to pass increased costs on to consumers.

The greatest blot on organized labor at this time came from the enlarged inroads of organized crime, which had been attracted by the possibilities of draining away large sums of money from expanding union treasuries, employer payoffs to buy labor peace, and misuse of health and welfare funds. As evidence of these incursions came to light, a series of congressional investigations got underway, focussing in Illinois, particularly on the city of Chicago. These inquiries culminated in the McClellan Committee hearings and the subsequent passage of the Landrum–Griffin Act of 1959. The widespread publicity emanating from the hearings and reports appears to have dampened the criminal activities and encouraged a vigorous anticorruption movement by the AFL–CIO. Corruption was not entirely eliminated, but in the seventies it receded from the headlines with occasional exceptions. Criminal exploitation of labor organization and labor-management relations has had a long history in the United States and has generally been found in industries and areas where other brands of criminality have taken root. The affluent labor movement of the post-World War II era was inevitably a tempting morsel.

Organized labor has been deeply involved in Illinois state and local politics since the latter decades of the nineteenth century. As the labor movement grew in importance and influence, its political activities intensified. Three aspects characterized these activities in the postwar period. One was their relatively modest objectives—to help elect labor's friends and defeat its enemies, to enact improved legislation in areas of direct labor concern, such as unemployment compensation, workmen's compensation, occupational health and safety, and public-sector bargaining; and to resist the passage of restrictive labor laws. These were traditional goals and were generally achieved despite considerable friction within the labor movement itself—for example, in the early pre-merger days between the AFL and CIO unions, and in the sixties and seventies between rival public employee organizations such as AFSCME and the craft unions. Perhaps the major disappointments were the failure of the state OSHA program and the lengthy breakdown in the agreed bill process affecting unemployment compensation, workmen's compensation, and occupational health and safety.

The striking feature of the state legislative process was the balance of power between the labor movement and its business lobby rivals. With few exceptions, neither side could assert or long maintain the power to enact or to retain laws that the other side most strongly opposed. The result was that little significant labor legislation found its way to the legislative books other than the so-called agreed bills. Apart from an early anti-injunction act adopted in 1925, private-sector labor relations laws were conspicuously absent. Comprehensive public-sector bargaining legislation was not to be enacted until 1983 after a nearly forty-year struggle.

In the course of this period organized labor shifted its state electoral loyalties from an essentially nonpartisan to a strong pro-Democrat party position. With a few notable exceptions from the mid-fifties on, it supported Democratic state and federal candidates. This ideological switch, however, had limited impact on labor law. Indeed some of labor's most successful years in the state legislature came during Republican administrations.

Labor's political role at the municipal level differed markedly from that at the state level. In Chicago, which for the core twenty-one years of 1955–76 was dominated by Mayor Richard Daley, the crafts were an integral part of the Daley machine and relied heavily on the mayor's personal policies and judgments. The old federally oriented CIO unions and other "outside" groups acquiesced in a subordinate role. The only significant challenge to the machine came from the rapidly ascending black community, and its impact was not serious until after Daley's death. In downstate communities, labor's political activity and influence ranged from nil to the East St. Louis replica of the Chicago model. In some industrial areas like Moline, Rockford, and Granite City and in some mining communities of Southern Illinois, there were periods of considerable Labor influence, either through independent or coailition organizations. In most parts of the state labor's political role was minimal.

A survey of state appellate and supreme court decisions in labor-related cases suggests a generally traditionalist, noninterventionist approach. Few important issues involved the private sector since federal legislation preempted most of the field. In the public sector, absent comprehensive legislation, the high courts authorized voluntary collective bargaining but declared strikes to be illegal and curtailed the role of grievance arbitration, especially in the schools. At the trial-court level, the picture was mixed—a few district judges actively intervened to promote strike settlements while others vigorously upheld the strike ban by issuing injunctions, ordering strikers to return to work, and in some cases fining the union and/or sentencing recalcitrant strike leaders to short jail terms. Many judges equivocated, apparently reluctant to antagonize important segments of their electorate, whether taxpayers or teachers and municipal employees. The absence of statutory law governing public employee relations was one of the most glaring deficiencies of the period, encouraging uncertainty and ambiguity.

One of the most interesting features of Illinois labor history is its diversity on a community and area basis. Barbara Newell has suggested, in her detailed study of labor in Chicago in the thirties, that each metropolitan area develops a distinctive mold out of the composition and size of its population and other environmental factors. Our study supports this thesis. Sometimes change is dramatic, at other times it is moderate, depending on the degree of dynamism of such elements as the death or decline of powerful organizational leaders, the shutdown or outflow of key industries, and the expansion or contraction of militant ethnic groups.

Chicago, as the only metropolis in Illinois, was of course in a class by itself. Its uniqueness was reinforced by its extraordinary political machine under Mayor Daley, by its ethnic complexity, by the strength of its labor movement, and by its changing industrial character from traditional manufacturing industry to predominantly service and trade. Daley, the master politician, was facing strong new challenges before the end of his long regime; after his death, the walls of his political edifice began to crumble although significant change did not occur until the eighties. Meanwhile throughout the post-World War II period under study, organized labor was centrally involved in the life of the city and participated actively in almost every branch of community affairs from welfare and charity to culture, from health to crime control, from public communications to recreational facilities. Labor helped welcome distinguished national and overseas visitors and extended aid to unions in foreign lands.

In the smaller cities and towns the involvement of labor in the community was relatively modest and varied with multiple factors. Rockford, for example, appears to have developed a conservative culture formed by the values of its substantial Scandinavian population, stressing individualism, cooperation, and gradual social change. Apart from electoral politics, labor's role was small. In southwest Illinois, East St. Louis shared some of the characteristics of Chicago on a miniature scale. For many years labor (especially the construction trades) was linked to the Irish-American dynasty of white mayor Alvin Fields. Finally, in the seventies, a growing black majority obtained control of the community, both politically and socially. Unlike Chicago the economy of East St. Louis was in a state of decline throughout the period, severely handicapping the possibilities of community reform despite cooperative efforts by both labor and management with the city's administrations.

As in Chicago, the tentacles of organized crime were wrapped around a few labor organizations but were gradually removed.

In central Illinois, including the industrial cities of Decatur and Peoria, the story of labor's involvement in community life was influenced in considerable measure by the attitudes of local management. In Decatur, the Association of Commerce had a policy of encouragement and cooperation with the local union leadership. As a result, labor representatives gained the opportunity to participate in numerous community programs, although rarely in a dominant way. In contrast, Peoria employers, most importantly the long-dominant Caterpillar Company, as well as the political leadership appear to have been less inclined to promote labor's communal role, and organized Labor made no major effort to assume an important role on its own initiative.

Mt. Vernon, in the south, offers another interesting set of variations. In the early postwar years, this thriving small community in the heart of Illinois' coal-mining region could properly be labeled a labor town and the unions were an influential, if not dominant, force in numerous aspects of communal life. The shutdown of a major company and the decline of coal mining in the surrounding area greatly reduced labor's strength. While it continued to exercise considerable political influence, its social role declined.

Finally in the northwestern industrial sector of the Quad Cities, with its dominant farm implement industry, the community labor mold seems to have paralleled the situation in Peoria—essentially limited labor involvement in an environment of relatively little labor-management-government cooperation and considerable industrial conflict.

For the most part, labor's community service programs dealt with participation in United Way or Community Chest campaigns and with counseling of union members who had financial, family, or personal problems stemming from alcoholism or drugs. Aid and advice to strikers were often provided. In the first postwar decade, the CIO State Industrial Union Council actively pursued a policy of promoting community service and training local counselors. The State Federation of Labor, on the other hand, left the initiative almost entirely to local central labor bodies. After the merger, centralized activities were minimal.

One of the longest and most deeply engrained traditions of organized labor was advocacy and support of public education. This tradition continued in the postwar era, as an increasing number of blue-collar families were enabled to send their children to the state's colleges and universities by the enactment of G.I. loans and the extraordinary expansion of the community college system. Another important development was the establishment of labor education programs on a joint labor-university extension basis for local union officers and activists. The aim of such programs was to train union leaders to perform their roles more efficiently in collective bargaining, grievance handling, internal union government, and political action. Thousands of unionists around the state benefitted from the programs, particularly those of the University of Illinois, Roosevelt University, and the University of Chicago.

Nationally this was a period of profound social change, and Illinois was both a leader and a follower in several major areas. With economic affluence came a retreat in political radicalism. Socialists as well as communists were largely silenced or converted to an acceptance of the evolving welfare capitalist system. Even after the demise of McCarthyism, traditional political radicalism was unable to make a serious comeback. The new radicalism of the sixties revolved around civil rights, anti-nuclear protest, the Vietnam War, the women's movement, and the quality of the environment—and was dominated by students and middle-class intellectuals. From labor's ranks only a small group of leaders emerged to challenge the majority position of the trade union movement on these issues. In contrast to the old radicalism, the new radicalism did not seek to overhaul the entire economic and political system, but instead focussed on specific issues that were not necessarily interrelated with each other. A variety of interest groups emerged that sometimes coalesced but often went their separate ways and occasionally clashed. When, as in the case of the Vietnam War, the crisis issue disappeared, the interest group rapidly faded away. In the case of civil rights, following the passage of the 1964 Civil Rights Act, blacks replaced sympathetic whites in most of the movement's leadership positions and followed several different paths in their pursuit of various economic, social, and political objectives. The counter culture movement that flourished from the late fifties to the early seventies left an enduring mark on popular music, the movies and television, sexual relations, and the use of drugs, but then slowly declined from the public scene. Organized labor largely adhered to the conservative mainstream and was generally satisfied with what the welfare state had to offer. New ideas were conspicuously absent. To the extent labor activists were attached to a new radical movements, they were marginal actors.

In Illinois, as in the country as a whole, the civil rights movement and particularly the movement to eliminate discrimination in employment was a principal social theme. The state adopted relevant legislation even before the Congress. Engraving nondiscrimination principles in the statute books and on the court records, however, was not enough. Many years of conflicting attitudes and practices were not to be eliminated overnight. There was no denying that historic progress had been achieved in breaking down the barriers of prejudice between 1945 and 1980. But the unemployment rate for blacks remained twice as high as for whites, and black youth unemployment remained appallingly high, even in time of general prosperity. In periods of recession, the latter skyrocketed to 40 percent and more.

The industrial union branch of organized labor strongly supported the civil rights movement from the beginning, although blacks had to exert considerable pressure before the gates of high union office and staff positions were opened. In some cases the barriers remained entrenched in 1980. The craft unions, especially in the building and construction trades, were the most resistant to change, but they too began to give way in the seventies. Throughout the period, Chicago, with its enormous and expanding black population, was the center of civil rights action. A similar process occurred with respect to Hispanics, but on a much smaller scale and at a somewhat later time.

The movement for greater voice and more equitable treatment of working women accompanied the black civil rights movement, and several black women unionists played important roles in both in Illinois. It is significant, however, that the Illinois Commission on the Status of Women was not established until two years after the federal commission was created; that the Illinois Fair Employment Practices Act did not apply to women until 1971, a decade after the law was initially enacted and seven years after the federal Civil Rights Act was passed; that the state of Illinois was one of the last of the industrial states to adopt an effective minimum wage law; and that the Equal Rights Amendment proposal failed to receive legislative approval although the new state constitution of 1970 incorporated a similar provision. This lagging record must be attributed in considerable part to the complexities of the Illinois legislative process, to internal splits within the ranks of prominent women in the state, and to the lack of interest of many old-line male union leaders.

On the other hand, Illinois women were in the forefront of the new national movement to expand their role in the trade union movement. The new movement differed from the old in that reliance on sympathetic women of wealth was largely eliminated, and trade union women assumed the leadership as well as the followers' roles. Joyce Miller of the Amalgamated Clothing Workers and Addie Wyatt of the Amalgamated Meat Cutters were two of several prominent Illinois figures in the founding and government of the national Coalition of Labor Union Women. Other women rose to positions of influence in their international and district unions. Still, as in the case of the minorities, by 1980 the agenda of working women for nondiscrimination in employment remained far from resolved.

Advances in the society at large were paralleled by a national movement to improve the quality of life in the workplace. It could be said that the entire history of the labor movement had been devoted to this end. The struggles for higher wages, shorter hours, safer and more pleasant working conditions, job security, resistance to work speedup, and due process—all of these traditional labor goals and many more reflected a strong desire to further the quality of work life and to enhance the dignity of working people.

Two new phases of this movement were discernible in the postwar period under study. First came the vast enlargement of the scope of collective bargaining (and in nonunionized establishments as well) in respect to health and welfare benefits, retirement programs, paid holidays and vacations, and a wide array of other fringe benefits. This phase began to develop immediately after the expiration of the National War Labor Board, which had considerably extended existing benefit provisions to the highest prevailing standards, but had deliberately refrained from breaking new ground for fear of increasing inflationary pressures. It lasted until the severe recession of the mid-seventies.

The second phase was more a phenomenon of the sixties and seventies, reflecting a variety of stimulating factors—the fear of technological and other forms of unemployment, the rapid development of codetermination ideas in West Europe, and responses by unionized and unorganized employers to the mounting expressions of employee discontent with work and work relations. Worker and union participation in decision making was the key theme.

Despite the memorable prewar achievements of labor and management cooperation in the Chicago men's clothing industry, Illinois could not be said to have been a national leader in the quality of work life movement. There were indeed some notable examples of cooperative efforts such as the procedure to settle jurisdictional disputes in the Chicago construction industry, the Armour Automation plan to facilitate the restructuring and relocation of major establishments in meat packing, the short-lived but remarkably effective grievance settlement program at International Harvester, and the development of new personnel channels at Bell Telephone. In 1979, a survey of joint labor-management cooperation committees in unionized private industries revealed more than a hundred mostly unpublicized cases of company programs to advance the quality of work life. In the nonunion sector, which had not received much serious study, there were also apparently numerous similar activities. A survey of the public sector permitted a similar conclusion in the seventies.

On the whole, however, the quality of work life movement either through increased union or worker participation in decision making was limited. The traditional adversarial system continued to dominate the collective bargaining scene. In both the organized and unorganized sectors the leading cases involved health and safety (the new aspect was on the control of cancer-inducing elements in the enterprise environment) and nondiscrimination in employment (generated by civil rights legislation).

In summary, how well did Illinois labor fare during the 1945–80 period? To what extent did it achieve the historic goals of American industrial democracy: equality of opportunity, democratic and just procedures in the workplace, a living wage, satisfying work, adequate leisure, equal pay for equal work, human dignity in the workplace, industrial peace, and a more just distribution of wealth?

By and large, substantial progress was achieved. Job opportunities for women, blacks, and other minorities were extended. Public employees organized on an unprecedented scale, and collective bargaining systems were developed comparable to those in the private sector. Due process and other democratic procedures were widely established at the level of the workplace to resolve grievances and other disputes. Real wages improved, and supplementary wage payments were either introduced or advanced on a wide array of subjects. The principle of equal pay for equal work gained substantial support, and some discussion of the comparable worth idea occurred. Paid vacations and holidays as well as opposition to mandatory overtime work reflected a growing interest in more leisure time. The human dignity of workers was enhanced.

However, there were also serious flaws in the picture. Unemployment and lack of promotional opportunity were persisting problems for many workers, especially minorities and women; work for many of the employed was an increasing source of dissatisfaction; the work environment in many establishments continued to be subject to health and safety hazards; income and wealth varied widely; some labor organizations remained subject to exploitation by organized crime despite the efforts of union leaders and governmental agencies; and recognition of human dignity lagged in many small enterprises, including some unionized ones.

What did the foregoing developments signify in the light of the longer Illinois labor history, and what do they portend for the future of Illinois workers?[1] Were the thirty-five years following World War II a "natural progression of a trend line going back to the origins of labor organization in the nineteenth century and crystallized in the dramatic events of the Great Depression and World War II? Or were they an aberration derived from a quite different trend line characterized by the management-dominated decade of the 1920s and the Reagan period of the eighties.

An alternative way of formulating the key questions is to assume the existence of competitive trend lines that are limited in time and are subject to replacement by one another (as the mainstream) in more or less irregular fashion. On this assumption, did the thirty-five years reflect a half-century or more of continued progress for labor, or were they the end of one era and the start of a new one?

The natural progression thesis is supported by an abundance of data in this volume. Illinois labor was strongly organized throughout the period, achieved considerable advances in economic terms, fringe benefits, and work rules, and gained political respect and influence in both political parties, especially at the state levels and in the city of Chicago. Although legislation giving public employees the right to bargain collectively did not materialize in the broadest sense until 1983, public-sector employees were able to make substantial organizational and bargaining gains at the state and local levels, thereby offsetting at least partially the membership losses suffered by a number of private-sector unions. Nonunionized employees and welfare beneficiaries—two other major segments of the population—also gained both from the spill-over effects of the front runners and from the enlargement of individual rights through antidiscrimination legislation, NLRB and court decisions on the duty of fair representation, and progressive corporate personnel policies.

The record of progress has been amply documented in the literature, despite the varying standards adopted for comparative purposes and the various time periods on which the comparisons are based.[2] A listing of standards for comparison has been suggested in the preceding summary. When these standards are contrasted between the 1945–80 period and other distinctive periods of American labor expansion such as the turn of the century, World War I, or the New Deal years, there can be little doubt of a continued upward trend in labor's fortunes.

On the other hand, as noted in the summary statement above, there were disquieting signs of change generally or partially unfavorable to the working population and to the union sector in particular. The incursion of gangsterism and corruption in a number of unions, including the Teamsters, was an extreme example. The growth in union size leading to increased centralization of power in the hands of a few top leaders and a subservient bureaucracy was another.

However, from the standpoint of the labor movement the most serious threats to its status and influence were derived from technological advances and the spread of competitive markets. Technological change has been, of course, a continuing phenomenon in American economic life and its long-run impact has been in most cases favorable to worker living standards and worker voice. But its immediate impact on employment and long-held job skills, as in the newspaper printing and railroad industries (two important Illinois enterprise areas) was psychologically and economically painful—even where protective rules were negotiated to fashion a gradual transition.

Still more threatening to organized labor was the economic impact of spreading and shifting product markets. One of the earliest major victims was the Packinghouse Workers Union, which had achieved unprecedented benefit levels after a decade of intense struggle only to see the bulk of Illinois production shifted to newer and more competitive plants in areas close to major cattle and hog raising areas. The ladies and men's clothing unions underwent a similar experience with the transfer of production to the lower-cost and mostly nonunion southern states and to nearby offshore countries in the Caribbean and Latin America. The clothing sector and later the so-called "smokestack" industries (notably steel and fabricated metals) as well as electronics, automobiles, farm equipment and other manufacturing enterprise also witnessed the spread of market competition internationally. Some Illinois producers like clothing and steel faced lower-cost competition on both the domestic and international levels. In the case of a technologically lagging industry, Illinois steel was confronted with specialized "minimills" at home and with European, Japanese, Korean, and Brazilian competition from abroad.

From organized labor's viewpoint of enhancing job security and safeguarding pay and working conditions, the situation was aggravated by the decision of some firms to transfer their production facilities to low-cost foreign plants or to subcontract processes to foreign producers in Mexico, Hong Kong, Singapore, and Taiwan. The result was that a sizeable number of manufacturing jobs were lost to Illinois workers. Severe recessions in the mid and late seventies, in addition, brought unemployment to the highest levels since the Great Depression. But as late as 1980, unionists and nonunionists alike expected cyclical recovery to restore employment as it had on numerous other occasions in the past. What few anticipated was that most of the new jobs would not be a restoration of the old but would emerge in lower-paid, lower-skilled, and poorly organized service industries. The full impact of the new situation did not dawn on most unionists until the bitter recession of the early eighties and the determination of the Reagan administration to rely upon the forces of unregulated market competition. Concession bargaining took over on a limited scale in the seventies and on a comprehensive scale in the eighties.

As of 1980, most observers of the Illinois labor scene as well as most participants were still thinking in terms of the old trend line—the traditional evolution of adversarial collective bargaining. The guiding spirit of the labor movement was seen to be expressed in pragmatic collective bargaining. This job-conscious economic unionism, celebrated in the writings of Selig Perlman, was extended by a number of important unions led by the United Auto Workers and the United Steel Workers into what came to be known as social unionism—concern with public issues beyond the narrow confines of the workplace. During the high employment periods of the fifties and sixties, many workers became less fearful of losing their jobs because most of them could quickly find new positions; they therefore either developed interests in societal matters or retreated into a personal world of consumerism. In time of recession, however, particularly in the seventies, job location and security regained their priority positions. Thus organized labor had two approaches, either of which predominated depending on economic circumstances. Both approaches, however, were strongly linked to the rapidly evolving welfare state, which tended to serve as a substitute for the traditional self-help philosophy.

The views of the younger workers particularly disturbed many veterans of the labor movement. Many baby-boom members were ignorant of the heroic struggles that underlay the labor movement and were content to judge the union role by the economic return on their dues dollars. Others appeared to attach little importance to the collectivity and were absorbed in achieving their individual goals. Subjects like discrimination, privacy, sexual harassment, fair representation, and use of drugs and alcohol on and off the job came to the fore. The older union leaders were often puzzled by and had little empathy with the "new breed," a feeling that was reciprocated by the younger members.

From the perspective of adversarial collective bargaining or of social unionism, the decade of the 1920s represented a temporary deviation from the longtime trend. Other decades in the present century had witnessed labor gains on a wide front, and even the twenties had produced significant economic and other benefits for many workers despite the decline of unionism.

If the evidence is clear that the years from 1945 to the late seventies reflected a continuation of progress for unionists and nonunion workers alike, the question remains whether the decade of the seventies with its two recessions and its rampant inflation and the Reagan period that followed portended the start of a different trend or was simply a temporary break in the old trend to be followed by recovery as in the past.[3] Here speculation becomes a prime factor. The historian records what has occurred, and projections into the future are problematic at best. Some factors may be projected with confidence, others are subject to considerable uncertainty, some fall in the realm of guesswork.

A few things are apparent from the experience of the seventies in Illinois as well as the impact on Illinois of the Reagan administration's national labor and economic policies in the first half of the eighties. One is the growth in the internationalization of product and labor markets, especially in manufacturing. As John R. Commons argued around the turn of the century, the spread of market competition strongly affected labor organization and labor-management relations.[4] Commons's analysis extended through the national stage of industrial evolution. Now we are faced with a further stage, global market competition. This internationalization of product markets had implications for important segments of the service economy as well as for manufactured goods.

Of equal if not greater significance is the rapidly developing science of low-cost microelectronics and computers, robots, chemicals, biotechnology, and most recently, superconductivity. Illinois labor, historically, has accepted technological change in a cooperative way but has insisted on safeguards for the affected employees. The failure to work out such safeguards amicably has led to some exceptionally bitter disputes. More often new technology has been adopted with little or no conflict.

The spread of markets and the new technology indicates continuing changes in the environment for labor and labor relations and calls for new responses by organized labor as well as management. The labor force will increasingly be devoted to services rather than production. New occupations and industries will emerge. The nature of work in many instances will be radically transformed. Enterprise units will be smaller and more decentralized than in the past. Women and minorities will play increasingly important roles in economic life. Product competition will lead to greater protectionist pressure against foreign products that encourage more foreign involvement in domestic markets. All of these developments have already partially occurred. More exotic and more problematic changes, such as the restructuring of enterprise ownership and the redefinition of management, including much greater employee involvement, may be expected in the long run.

A great deal depends on how imaginatively and creatively the major interest groups respond to the economic-technological changes and to their interrelationship. On the other hand, unexpected catastrophes, such as war, economic collapse, the emergence of new leaders with different ideologies, values, or strategies than the old ones, changes in the political arena resulting in new legislation and administrative agencies—these and other developments can occur to alter labor's status, orientation, and effectiveness.

Despite more than a decade of setback, Illinois labor remains in a relatively strong position, both economically and politically to cope with the future. The state possesses an abundance of skilled and semiskilled workers, exceptionally rich natural resources, and a highly advanced institutional structure of education, vocational training, technical know-how, financial systems, and managerial expertise. It has a tradition of resiliency, having gone through numerous cyclical and secular changes, and it has demonstrated the ability to adapt its structures and resources to new challenges. Likewise, organized labor has played a vital role in the protection and enhancement of worker interests for more than a century and has revealed reservoirs of talent, experience, and pragmatic flexibility to adjust to changing environments.

NOTES

1. I am indebted to two anonymous reviewers for some of the ideas discussed below.

2. See for example, my volume, *The American Idea of Industrial Democracy, 1865–1965* (Urbana: University of Illinois Press, 1970). In addition to standard histories like those of Rayback and Dulles, see Harry A. Millis, ed., *How Collective Bargaining Works* (New York: The Twentieth Century Fund, 1942) and Gerald G. Somers, ed., *Collective Bargaining: Contemporary American Experience* (Madison: Industrial Relations Research Association, 1980).

3. See my comment in *The Shrinking Perimeter* ed. Hervey A. Juris and Myron Roomkin (Lexington, Mass: D.C. Heath, 1980), pp. 55–58.

4. John R. Commons, "American Shoemakers, 1648–1895" in *Labor and Administration* (New York: Macmillan, 1913), pp. 219–66.

APPENDIX

Principal Interviewees

Carl Adrian, Quad City Development Group
John Alesia, labor lobbyist, Springfield and Chicago
George Andrew, CSC chair, UAW, Rockford
Lester Asher, labor lawyer, Chicago
Elizabeth Balanoff, director, Oral History project, Roosevelt University, Chicago
James Balanoff, former director, District 31, United Steelworkers, Chicago
Robert Barker, Teamsters, Peoria
Michael Bugel, business agent, Amalgamated Clothing Workers, Chicago
William Caples, former industrial relations executive with Inland Steel, Chicago
Frank Cassell, former industrial relations officer with Inland Steel, Chicago
John Cullerton, vice president, Hilton Hotels Corporation, former Illinois Director of Labor, Chicago
Leonard Davis, Quad Cities Federation of Labor
John Desmond, president, Teachers Union, Chicago
Rosa DeYoung, wife of former labor editor, Quad Cities
Attilio DiNello, business agent, Amalgamated Clothing Workers, Chicago
William Dodds, Local 6, United Automobile Workers, Chicago
Stanley Eisenstein, labor lawyer, Chicago
Herman Erickson, labor educator, University of Illinois, Champaign-Urbana
Samuel Evett, assistant district director, District 31, United Steelworkers
Jeffrey Fisher, organizer, HELP, Chicago
Robert Gibson, president, Illinois AFL–CIO, Chicago
Kalman Goldberg, Professor of Economics, Bradley University, Peoria
Harold Grahn, Rockford Credit Bureau
William P. Grogan, labor relations officer, Rock Island Arsenal
Arthur Gundersheim, staff member, Amalgamated Clothing & Textile Workers Union, Chicago
John Gwynn, executive director, NAACP, Peoria
Albert Halx, International Association of Machinists, Rock Island Arsenal
Jack Hartley, regional representative, Allied Industrial Workers, Decatur
George W. Howard, attorney, Mount Vernon

Edwin Huntley, Decatur Chamber of Commerce
Kathy Johnson, Midwest Women's Center, Chicago
Sherdie C. Jones, retired labor leader, Urbana-Champaign
Larry Keller, education director, District 31, United Steelworkers, Chicago
Jerry Koehler, building trades, Decatur
Harry Kurshenbaum, business agent, HELP, Chicago
Merrill Lindsay, publisher, Decatur Herald and Review
Richard Lutovsky, Chamber of Commerce, Decatur
Ray Maulden, labor liaison, Council of Community Service, Decatur
Sandy Mendenhall, United Way Labor Representative, Peoria
Lewis Moore, Federal Mediation and Conciliation Service, Rockford
Thomas Nayder, president, Chicago Building Trades Council
Joseph O'Dell, building trades, Decatur
Hal Parmalee, Associated Employers of the Quad Cities
Emmet Poyer, United Automobile Workers, Rockford
Harl Ray, secretary-treasurer, Illinois AFL–CIO, Urbana-Champaign
Charles "Bud" Riley, regional representative, Allied Industrial Workers, Decatur
Jesse Rios, Hispanic leader, Chicago
Frank Rosen, district director, United Electrical Workers, Chicago
Sherman Rosen, corporate vice president, Hart, Schaffner, and Marx, Chicago
Norman Roth, Local 6, United Automobile Workers, Chicago
David Ryan, Local 6, United Automobile Workers, Chicago
August Sallas, Hispanic leader, Chicago
Esther Saperstein, labor leader and state legislator, Chicago
Raymond Scannell, director of employment services, Chicago Commission on Human Relations, later staff member of Construction Employers Association, Chicago
David Schacter, Jewish Labor Committee, Chicago
Benjamin Schleicher, former Mayor, Rockford
Lawrence Schmidt, former personnel director and Chamber of Commerce activist, Rockford
Robert Schmitt, Illinois State Employment Service, Peoria
Loren Scott, president, Central Trades Assembly, Mount Vernon
Carl Shier, international representative, United Automobile Workers, Chicago
Jack Smith, social activist, Quad Cities
Jack Spiegel, United Shoe Workers, Chicago
Robert Stack, Local 6, United Automobile Workers, Chicago
John Swanson, Rockford National Association of Letter Carriers
Harold Wright, Letter Carriers Union, Belleville
Glenn Zipp, regional director, NLRB, Peoria

Index

AFL-CIO Ethical Practice Committee, 377, 379
Agreed bill, 190–91
Alesia, John, 94, 97, 178
Amalgamated Clothing and Textile Workers Union, 40–55, 337, 346, 347, 420, 435–36
American Federation of State, County, and Municipal Employees (AFSCME), 34, 143–45, 159–70, 181, 186, 187, 263
Annunzio, Frank, 94, 97, 176
Asher, Lester, 61, 71
Askin, Steve, 137, 138, 139
Auto Workers, 31, 38–39, 97–98, 108–26, 246, 255, 256, 257, 259, 262, 273–83, 287–89, 296, 301, 306, 315, 336–37, 344–45, 363, 366, 431, 434

Baby Boom, 10, 427, 452, 453
Bailey, Stephen, 70, 71, 235
Balanoff, Elizabeth, 426
Balanoff, James, 90, 102, 103, 104, 105, 423
Bilandic, Mayor Michael, 232, 237, 240, 248, 406
Blacks, 1, 10, 16, 18, 19, 21, 25, 38, 43, 53, 59, 60, 73–81, 100, 101, 111, 112, 118, 137, 138, 140, 145, 147, 150, 156, 167, 241, 246–48, 264–65, 284–86, 295, 300, 302–4, 314–15, 326–30, 383–401, 421
Brandzel, Sol, 41, 48, 52–54
Byrne, Mayor Jane, 186, 240, 248, 393, 406

Caples, William, 92–93, 95, 384
Cassell, Frank, 92–93, 94, 95
Caterpillar Tractor, 294, 295, 296, 297, 299, 300, 301, 303, 304, 305, 306, 394, 431
Catholic Labor Alliance, 363, 364
Central Illinois Public Service Company, 432
Chicago Board of Education, 96, 181–82, 236–37, 348

Chicago Building Trades Council, 58–81
Chicago Commission on Human Relations, 383
Chicago Crime Commission, 372, 375
Chicago Federation of Labor, 33, 237
Chicago Teachers Union, 236–37
Coalition of Labor Union Women (CLUW), 420, 421, 423, 424, 425
Cohen, Judge Nathan, 149, 150, 202, 220
Coleman, John, 142, 143, 144, 145, 149, 152
Collective bargaining, 43–45, 48–49, 59, 61–68, 105–6, 108–16, 118–19, 123, 125, 137, 153–55, 160–61, 165–67, 169–70, 235
Communists, 89–91, 94 113, 359–69
Community politics, 231–41, 257–59, 327–29
Community services, 334–50
Constitutional convention of 1970, 192–93.
Corruption, 131–35, 371–81
Courts and labor law, 198–220
Covelli, Judge Daniel A., 147, 150, 201–2, 219, 220
Cullerton, John, 234–35, 419

Daley, Mayor Richard, 58, 69, 70, 74, 75, 78, 86, 159, 161, 167, 177, 180, 181, 182, 231, 233, 235–37, 238, 239, 240, 241, 245, 248, 249
Dawson, Frances L., 415, 418
Dawson, William L., 389, 390
Day–care, 51, 427
Day, Clara, 137, 422
Education and unionism, 20, 21, 22, 199, 200, 201, 202, 203, 207, 215–19, 236, 237, 316–17, 350–53
Electoral politics, 174–83, 232–42
Employment, 1–3, 9–12, 13–18, 41–44, 53–55, 67–68, 72, 80, 81, 85, 88, 100, 105, 142–43, 159–60, 232, 239, 244, 245,

246–47, 252, 262, 279, 280, 283, 294–98,
  300–5, 306, 312–15, 316, 324–26, 412–15
Equal rights amendment, 194–95, 417, 419,
  423, 425
Ethnic factors, 11, 22, 42–43, 59, 60, 71, 71,
  94, 118, 230, 231, 246, 252, 253, 254, 271,
  272, 284, 285, 286–87, 294, 303, 304,
  314,–15, 326, 327, 329, 383–407
Evett, Samuel, 101–3

Feinglass, Abe, 360, 363, 368
Finley, Murray, 41, 46, 49, 51, 52, 53
Foreign competition, 41, 52–55, 232, 245,
  246, 247, 441, 443, 451, 452, 454

Germano, Joseph, 86–101, 246–48
Gibson, Robert, 189, 194, 335, 336, 340,
  341, 342, 346
Greathouse, Duane (Pat), 97, 124, 246
Green, Governor Dwight, 71, 175, 176, 185,
  382
Greenstone, J. David, 70, 72, 97, 98, 99,
  180, 237, 238, 348
Grievances, 44–45, 109, 113
Grimshaw, William V., 72
Gunness, Robert C., 64

Hart, Schaffner, and Marx, 435–36
Health and safety, 119–22, 188–89
Helstein, Ralph, 363, 385, 386
Herstein, Lillian, 421
Hispanics, 286–87, 400–7
Hospital employees, 142–56
Housing, 18, 19, 51, 285, 286, 339, 347, 399

Illinois Commission on the Status of Women,
  415–19
Illinois Federation of Labor–Congress of In-
  dustrial Organizations, 31–36, 175–79
Incomes, 14–16
Injunction, 207–11
Institute of Labor and Industrial Relations
  (University of Illinois), 324, 330, 437, 438
International Harvester, 108–36, 393
Irish and labor, 70, 71

Jackson, Reverend Jesse, 392, 393
Jews and labor, 42, 93, 231, 390
Johnson, Stanley, 71, 193, 341
Johnston, Robert, 98, 242, 246
Jurisdictional disputes, 62

Karsh, Bernard, 90, 91, 109
Kelly, Mayor Edward, 59, 383
Kemp, James, 193, 396, 398
Kennelly, Mayor Martin, 180, 232–33, 238,
  244
Kerner, Governor Otto, 97, 98, 99, 161–63,
  384, 385, 387, 389, 415, 416
King, Dr. Martin Luther, Jr., 364, 392
Kornblum, William, 22, 99, 100
Kurshenbaum, Harry, 151–53, 422

Labor in the community, 334–50
Labor legislation, 184–96
Lee, William A., 181, 240, 347, 348, 380
Leisure, 22–24
Lens, Sidney, 70, 233–34, 368
Levin, Samuel, 40, 48
Lewin, David, 238
Living standards, 14–25

Management strategy, 154–56
Marciniak, Edward, 74, 76
McCabe, William, 63
McClellan Committee, 372, 373, 375, 376
McFetridge, William L. 181, 234
McMahon, Earl, 71
Meatpacking, 245, 246, 394, 395
Merger of AFL and CIO, 256, 257, 279, 280
Mid–American Regional Bargaining Associa-
  tion (MARBA), 64, 65, 66, 67
Miller, Joyce, 41, 50, 420, 423
Murray, Thomas, 59, 73
Myart v. Motorola, 386

National Association for the Advancement of
  Colored People (NAACP), 390
Nayder, Thomas, 61, 67, 71
Newell, Barbara, 230–32
New left, 366, 368, 369

Ogilvie, Governor Richard, 71, 99, 195, 403
Organized labor, 31–36, 46–48, 287–88, 310
Ozanne, Robert, 119

Percy, Senator Charles, 173, 176
Peters, Donald, 128–40, 143–56
Peterson, Paul E., 181–82
Peurala, Alice, 421
Politics and labor, 257, 258, 259
Politics at the state level, 175–83
Poverty, 10, 17, 18, 326

Preemption, 212–15
Prevailing wages, 59, 67, 68, 69, 185, 187
Public employees, 185–188

Quality of work life, 430–39

Radicalism, 359–69
Rakove, Milton, 58, 177–78, 239, 381
Ray, Harl, 193
Reilly, William J., 116, 434
Rios, Jesse, 403, 404
Rock Island Arsenal, 283–84
Rosen, Sherman, 54–55

Sadlowski, Edward, 101, 102, 103, 104
Sallas, August, 405
Saperstein, Esther, 415, 416
Scannell, Raymond, 75
Schlafly, Phyllis, 417
Shier, Carl, 111, 116
Social unionism, 43, 48–52
Soderstrom, Reuben, 175, 178, 342, 351, 396, 419
Stack, Robert, 121–23
Stagflation, 15

Staley, A. E. Manufacturing Co., 432
Stevenson, Governor Adlai, 233
Stratton, Governor William, 71, 384

Tax policy, 195
Teamsters Local 743, 128–40
Thompson, Governor James, 165, 191

Unemployment, 15, 301
United Steelworkers of America, (USWA)
    District 31, 85–105
Urban League, 391, 400

Vital statistics, 24–25

Wages, 43, 44, 62, 153–54
Walker, Governor Daniel, 163, 165, 406
Washburne Trade School, 73, 397, 424
Watters, Mary, 233, 412
Weber, Arnold, 167
Work stoppages, 63, 66, 148–51, 242–44,
    246, 260, 261, 316, 330
Working women, 412–28
Wyatt, Addie, 421

About the Author

Milton Derber has been exploring modern American labor history since his doctorial dissertation on the unionism of the New Deal period. During and after World War II, he observed the wartime, as well as the early postwar experience, from vantage points of positions on the National Labor Relations Board, the National War Labor Board, and the U.S. Bureau of Labor Statistics. In subsequent decades, he has focussed research, teaching, and public service on contemporary and recent labor relations history. *Labor in Illinois* is coextensive with the forty years since Professor Derber joined the faculty of the Institute of Labor and Industrial Relations at the University of Illinois at Urbana-Champaign.